THE COLLECTED WRITINGS OF
JOHN MAYNARD KEYNES

Managing Editors:
Professor Austin Robinson and Professor Donald Moggridge

John Maynard Keynes (1883–1946) was without doubt one of the most influential thinkers of the twentieth century. His work revolutionised the theory and practice of modern economics. It has had a profound impact on the way economics is taught and written, and on economic policy, around the world. *The Collected Writings of John Maynard Keynes*, published in full in electronic and paperback format for the first time, makes available in thirty volumes all of Keynes's published books and articles. This includes writings from his time in the India Office and Treasury, correspondence in which he developed his ideas in discussion with fellow economists and correspondence relating to public affairs. Arguments about Keynes's work have continued long beyond his lifetime, but his ideas remain central to any understanding of modern economics, and a point of departure from which each new generation of economists draws inspiration.

In this volume, the third of three concerned with Keynes's involvement in the problems of financing Britain's war effort after 1939, the concentration is on the final stages of Lend Lease and the negotiations with the United States for the transition to peacetime conditions and the 1945 loan to Britain.

Keynes with Frank Lee at the International Monetary Conference, Savannah, 1946.
(From Dr Milo Keynes's collection)

THE COLLECTED WRITINGS OF
JOHN MAYNARD KEYNES

VOLUME XXIV

ACTIVITIES 1944–1946

THE TRANSITION TO PEACE

EDITED BY
DONALD MOGGRIDGE

CAMBRIDGE UNIVERSITY PRESS

FOR THE

ROYAL ECONOMIC SOCIETY

Published for the Royal Economic Society
throughout the world by

CAMBRIDGE UNIVERSITY PRESS
Cambridge, New York, Melbourne, Madrid, Cape Town,
Singapore, São Paulo, Delhi, Mexico City

Cambridge University Press
The Edinburgh Building, Cambridge CB2 8RU, UK

Published in the United States of America by
Cambridge University Press, New York

www.cambridge.org
Information on this title: www.cambridge.org/9781107681156

This edition published 2013

Printed and bound in the United Kingdom
by the MPG Books Group

A catalogue record for this publication is available from the British Library

ISBN 978-1-107-68115-6 Paperback
30-volume set ISBN 978-1-107-67772-2

$29.69

CONTENTS

GENERAL INTRODUCTION

This new standard edition of *The Collected Writings of John Maynard Keynes* forms the memorial to him of the Royal Economic Society. He devoted a very large share of his busy life to the Society. In 1911, at the age of twenty-eight, he became editor of the *Economic Journal* in succession to Edgeworth; two years later he was made secretary as well. He held these offices without intermittence until almost the end of his life. Edgeworth, it is true, returned to help him with the editorship from 1919 to 1925; Macgregor took Edgeworth's place until 1934, when Austin Robinson succeeded him and continued to assist Keynes down to 1945. But through all these years Keynes himself carried the major responsibility and made the principal decisions about the articles that were to appear in the *Economic Journal*, without any break save for one or two issues when he was seriously ill in 1937. It was only a few months before his death at Easter 1946 that he was elected president and handed over his editorship to Roy Harrod and the secretaryship to Austin Robinson.

In his dual capacity of editor and secretary Keynes played a major part in framing the policies of the Royal Economic Society. It was very largely due to him that some of the major publishing activities of the Society—Sraffa's edition of Ricardo, Stark's edition of the economic writings of Bentham, and Guillebaud's edition of Marshall, as well as a number of earlier publications in the 1930s—were initiated.

When Keynes died in 1946 it was natural that the Royal Economic Society should wish to commemorate him. It was perhaps equally natural that the Society chose to commemorate him by producing an edition of his collected works. Keynes himself had always taken a joy in fine printing, and the Society, with the help of Messrs Macmillan as publishers and the Cambridge University Press as printers, has been anxious to give Keynes's writings a permanent form that is wholly worthy of him.

The present edition will publish as much as is possible of his work in the field of economics. It will not include any private and personal correspondence or publish many letters in the possession of his family. The edition is concerned, that is to say, with Keynes as an economist.

Keynes's writings fall into five broad categories. First there are the books which he wrote and published as books. Second there are collections of articles and pamphlets which he himself made during his lifetime (*Essays in Persuasion* and *Essays in Biography*). Third, there is a very considerable volume of published but uncollected writings—articles written for newspapers, letters to newspapers, articles in journals that have not been included in his two volumes of collections, and various pamphlets. Fourth, there are a few hitherto unpublished writings. Fifth, there is correspondence with economists and concerned with economics or public affairs. It is the intention to publish almost completely the whole of the first four categories listed above. The only exceptions are a few syndicated articles where Keynes wrote almost the same material for publication in different newspapers or in different countries, with minor and unimportant variations. In these cases, this series will publish one only of the variations, choosing the most interesting.

The publication of Keynes's economic correspondence must inevitably be selective. In the day of the typewriter and the filing cabinet and particularly in the case of so active and busy a man, to publish every scrap of paper that he may have dictated about some unimportant or ephemeral matter is impossible. We are aiming to collect and publish as much as possible, however, of the correspondence in which Keynes developed his own ideas in argument with his fellow economists, as well as the more significant correspondence at times when Keynes was in the middle of public affairs.

Apart from his published books, the main sources available to those preparing this series have been two. First, Keynes in his will made Richard Kahn his executor and responsible for his economic papers. They have been placed in the Marshall Library of the University of Cambridge and have been available for this edition. Until 1914 Keynes did not have a secretary and his earliest papers are in the main limited to drafts of important letters that he made in his own handwriting and retained. At that stage most of the correspondence that we possess is represented by what he received rather than by what he wrote. During the war years of 1914–18 Keynes was serving in the Treasury. With the opening in 1968 of the records under the thirty-year rule, many of the papers that he wrote then and later have become available. From 1919 onwards, throughout the rest of his life, Keynes had the help of a secretary—for many years Mrs Stephens. Thus for the last twenty-five years of his working life we have in most cases the carbon copies of his own letters as well as the originals of the letters that he received.

There were, of course, occasions during this period on which Keynes wrote himself in his own handwriting. In some of these cases, with the help of his correspondents, we have been able to collect the whole of both sides of some important interchange and we have been anxious, in justice to both correspondents, to see that both sides of the correspondence are published in full.

The second main source of information has been a group of scrapbooks kept over a very long period of years by Keynes's mother, Florence Keynes, wife of Neville Keynes. From 1919 onwards these scrapbooks contain almost the whole of Maynard Keynes's more ephemeral writing, his letters to newspapers and a great deal of material which enables one to see not only what he wrote but the reaction of others to his writing. Without these very carefully kept scrapbooks the task of any editor or biographer of Keynes would have been immensely more difficult.

The plan of the edition, as at present intended, is this. It will total thirty volumes. Of these the first eight are Keynes's published books from *Indian Currency and Finance*, in 1913, to the *General Theory* in 1936, with the addition of his *Treatise on Probability*. There next follow, as vols. IX and X, *Essays in Persuasion* and *Essays in Biography*, representing Keynes's own collections of articles. *Essays in Persuasion* differs from the original printing in two respects: it contains the full texts of the articles or pamphlets included in it and not (as in the original printing) abbreviated versions of these articles, and it also contains one or two later articles which are of exactly the same character as those included by Keynes in his original collection. In *Essays in Biography* there have been added a number of biographical studies that Keynes wrote both before and after 1933.

There will follow two volumes, XI–XII, of economic articles and correspondence and a further two volumes, already published, XIII–XIV, covering the development of his thinking as he moved towards the *General Theory*. There are included in these volumes such part of Keynes's economic correspondence as is closely associated with the articles that are printed in them. A supplement to these volumes, XXIX, will print some further material relating to the same issues, which has since been discovered.

The following thirteen volumes deal with Keynes's *Activities* during the years from the beginning of his public life in 1905 until his death. In each of the periods into which we divide this material, the volume concerned publishes his more ephemeral writings, all of it hitherto uncollected, his correspondence relating to these activities, and such other material and correspondence as is necessary to the understanding of Keynes's activities. These volumes are edited by Elizabeth Johnson and Donald Moggridge, and it has been their task to trace and interpret Keynes's activities sufficiently to make the material fully intelligible to a later generation.

Elizabeth Johnson has been responsible for vols. xv–xviii, covering Keynes's earlier years and his activities down to the end of World War I reparations and reconstruction. Donald Moggridge is responsible for all the remaining volumes recording Keynes's other activities from 1923 until his death in 1946.

The present plan of publication is to complete the record of Keynes's activities during World War II with the group of two volumes of which this forms one, and with a further three volumes that will follow. These five volumes will cover not only the problems of war finance, internal and external, but also his contributions both in the Treasury and at Bretton Woods and elsewhere to the shaping of the post-war world. The new material relating to the evolution of the *Treatise* and the *General Theory* will be published separately before the last of these World War II volumes. It will then remain to fill the gap between 1923 and 1939, to print certain of his published articles and the correspondence relating to them which have not appeared elsewhere in this edition, and to publish a volume of his social, political and literary writings.

Those responsible for this edition have been: Lord Kahn, both as Lord Keynes's executor and as a long and intimate friend of Lord Keynes, able to help in the interpreting of much that would be otherwise misunderstood; the late Sir Roy Harrod as the author of his biography; Austin Robinson as Keynes's co-editor on the Economic Journal and successor as Secretary of the Royal Economic Society. Austin Robinson has acted throughout as Managing Editor; Donald Moggridge is now associated with him as Joint Managing Editor.

In the early stages of the work Elizabeth Johnson was assisted by Jane Thistlethwaite and by Mrs McDonald, who was originally responsible for the systematic ordering of the files of the Keynes papers. Judith Masterman for many years worked with Mrs Johnson on the papers. More recently Susan

Wilsher, Margaret Butler and Leonora Woollam have continued the secretarial work. Barbara Lowe has been responsible for the indexing. Susan Howson undertook much of the important final editorial work on the present group of volumes. Judith Allen has been responsible for seeing the present group of volumes through the Press.

EDITORIAL NOTE

In this volume, the third of three concerned with Keynes's involvement in the problems of financing Britain's war effort after 1939, the concentration is on the final stages of Lend Lease and the negotiations with the United States for the transition to peacetime conditions. A further three volumes will be devoted to Keynes's efforts to shape the post-war world.

The main sources for this volume are Keynes's surviving papers, materials available in the Public Record Office, and the papers of colleagues and friends, most notably Sir Frederick Harmer, Professor J. E. Meade and Lord Robbins. Where the material used has come from the Public Record Office, the call numbers for the relevant files appear in the List of Documents Reproduced following page 641.

In this and the other wartime volumes, to aid the reader in keeping track of the various personalities who pass through the pages that follow, we have included brief biographical notes on the first occasion on which they appear. These notes are designed to be cumulative over the whole run of wartime volumes.

In this, as in all the similar volumes, in general all of Keynes's own writings are printed in larger type. All introductory matter and all writings by others than Keynes are printed in small type. The only exception to this general rule is that occasional short quotations from a letter from Keynes to his parents or to a friend, used in introductory passages to clarify a situation, are treated as introductory matter and are printed in the smaller type. Throughout, Keynes's footnotes are indicated by symbols, while editorial footnotes are indicated by numbers.

Most of Keynes's letters included in this and other volumes are reprinted from the carbon copies that remain among his papers. In most cases he has added his initials to the carbon in the familiar fashion in which he signed to all his friends. We have no certain means of knowing whether the top copy, sent to the recipient of the letter, carried a more formal signature.

Chapter 1

PREPARING FOR STAGE II

With 1944 the problems of overseas war finance became even more closely intertwined with those of the post-war, transitional period. Keynes's activities from the very beginning of the year bring this interdependence out most clearly, for the turn of the year saw him preparing a memorandum on the transition. He passed an early draft to Sir Richard Hopkins on 7 January and, after discussing it with Hopkins on 9 January, he revised it slightly before circulating it to the Treasury and the Bank on 11 January.

NOTES ON EXTERNAL FINANCE IN THE POST-JAPANESE-ARMISTICE TRANSITIONAL PERIOD

I. *The Magnitude of the U.K. Deficit*

Some months ago the Economic Section estimated the aggregate external deficit of the U.K. in the first *two post*-war years at £575 million. This needs revision in the light of later facts, but such a revision (if the basic assumptions remain unchanged) may not involve more than (say)±£100 million.

It is based in some respects on optimistic, in other respects on pessimistic, assumptions. In particular:-

(i) It assumes, especially in the second year, a significant relaxation of war-time restrictions on consumption. An alternative estimate on the basis of *minimum* civilian consumption reduces the two-year deficit to £75 million. The programme which the Ministry of Food is contemplating would tend to produce, I think, the higher, rather than the lower, figure of deficit. The proposal to furnish full civilian outfits free of charge to all demobilised men also tends in the same direction (by reducing our capacity to export). Indeed the present general trend of ministerial policy would have to be drastically reversed if anything approaching the lower figure is to be realised.

(ii) The residue of abnormal government expenditure abroad still to be paid for is put very low—£150 million in the first year and £50 million in the second. Unless there is a long post-German Japanese phase allowing a good deal to be cleared up before the final end of the war, accrued accounts settled late and prolonged demobilisation and compensation expenses might easily make the total £100 million greater or even more.

(iii) On the other hand, we might, if necessary, live on stocks more largely than seems to be assumed.

(iv) Prices of exports are assumed to rise no more than the prices of imports (namely 50 per cent compared with pre-war). The absolute figure of increased price for exports is more likely to be nearer 100 per cent above 1939 and, in this early period, to exceed the corresponding increase for imports. Currently our export prices are 93 per cent, and our import prices 78 per cent above pre-war. If we were to assume that prices of post-war exports rise by 100 per cent and of imports by 75 per cent compared with pre-war, this does not help so much as one might think (compared with the assumed rise of 50 per cent for both alike) owing to our volume of imports in this period being so much greater than that of our exports, but, nevertheless, the gain over the two years might be something more than £100 million. It is indeed essential that we should, in the early years of strong demand, obtain a significantly higher price for our exports than we pay for our imports.

(v) Nothing is allowed for European or other relief or for rehabilitation in Burma and Malaya.

(vi) Nothing is allowed for the renewal of credit lines and the time-lag in the payment for exports compared with imports.

(vii) Nothing is allowed for the use of their existing sterling balances by purchasers of our exports to pay for some part of such purchases.

(viii) Nothing is allowed for the possible cost of acquiring lend lease goods, e.g. ships, having an end-value.

(ix) Nothing is allowed after the second post-war year, yet it will be a miracle if we balance our account so soon as that.

Taking all the above into account (except that (vii) is dealt with separately below so far as it relates to the sterling area), it would seem rash to assume a cash deficit of less than £500–£700 million during the interim period as a whole before we achieve a balance, though with good and careful management we might, perhaps, be entitled to hope for an outcome nearer to the lower than to the higher figure.

II. *The 'Sterling Area' Solution for the Interim Period*

This amounts to a continuation, extension and adaptation of the methods which have served us so well during the war, namely:-

(1) the continuance, and in some respects the tightening up and consolidation, of the sterling area arrangements;

(2) bilateral arrangements with certain European central banks providing for mutual lines of credit;

(3) payments agreements, on the model now used with neutral countries, with special accounts attached to them;

(4) a line of credit with the Federal Reserve Bank of New York or the U.S. Treasury.

Let us consider the probable adequacy of such arrangements in the early post-war period, on the assumption that the other parties concerned would accept them. First of all, however, it may be useful to set out clearly what is meant by the 'sterling area arrangements'.

III. *The 'Sterling Area' System as it now exists*

There are two widely prevailing misunderstandings about the nature of this system. It is often supposed that the members of the area are not free to use the sterling balances, accruing to them in London, to make purchases outside the sterling area; so that, by this means, we can freely make purchases within the area without incurring a dollar, or other outside currency, liability. And as a corollary of this, it is supposed that the system puts some pressure or inducement on other members of the area, who find their sterling balances on the increase, to expend these balances in the U.K., not being free to expend them outside the area.

Unfortunately both these suppositions are incorrect. They apply in the case of payments agreements such as we have with several neutral countries, the Argentine for example, but not to the sterling area system, which is an arrangement by which London, through the agency of the Bank of England, acts as external banker for the members of the area, receiving from them the outside currencies which they earn, but being under a corresponding liability to furnish them against the sterling balances they hold with all the outside currencies they require.

The only limitations to their freedom of action, which they have observed with varying degrees of strictness (indeed their agreement to them is only informal), are–

(1) that they do not, without our permission, use their balances to acquire gold from outside or to build up balances of foreign currencies beyond a working balance for immediate needs;

(2) that, by means of exchange control, they prevent capital transactions outward from the area;

(3) that, by means of a system of import licensing, they restrict their imports of goods to their genuine needs.

The first limitation has been loyally observed, except that

S. Africa has not agreed to turn into the pool more than a limited proportion of the excess of her newly mined gold over her immediate exchange requirements for goods and war expenses and the repatriation of her securities. It is obvious, however, that in time of peace, members of the area can be expected to observe this condition only to the extent of their confidence in our willingness (and ability) to turn their sterling balances at any time into a required foreign currency. This confidence is necessarily impaired by their having already accumulated sterling balances greatly in excess of the reserves we hold wherewith to implement our obligations.

The second limitation has also been observed, except that the controls are not all equally effective. In Australia the prohibition against the export of capital also extends, I believe, to other parts of the sterling area itself. It must be doubtful how far we ourselves will be in a position after the war to allow unimpeded movement of our own capital to other parts of the sterling area. At present there is no impediment apart from the indirect and partial control of the New Issues Committee. If we have to restrict outward capital movements to other parts of the sterling area, that will involve a large extension of the existing exchange control which at present, broadly speaking, excludes all sterling area transactions from its operations. Apart from that, it will be dangerous to rely on the effectiveness of peace-time capital control in certain parts of the area, e.g. on Egypt's effectively preventing its residents from acquiring assets in U.S.A.

The third limitation was operating very imperfectly in the early days of the war, when some parts of the area had no effective import restriction. Shortly before the beginning of the lend lease phase it was becoming stiffened up. More recently shipping and supply limitation and Joint Planning Boards have, for practical purposes, taken the place of import restriction as the effective control. Obviously it will be rather much to expect those parts of the area which have ample

5

sterling funds strictly to limit their imports in peace-time conditions below what shipping and supply limitations would otherwise allow, so long as these sterling funds are freely available to them. Much embarrassment might arise from this, if we were to attempt to continue the sterling area system after the war in its present form, which in any case is likely to be beyond our power. For it would not help much for us to limit our own imports, if the resources thus husbanded can be drained away by other parts of the area pursuing a less austere policy. We have been impoverished by the war, they have been enriched, on international account. It will be difficult to drive in harness animals in such different condition.

IV. *The Sterling Area in the Transition*

The main point which emerges from the above is that the sterling area system is in the nature of a banking arrangement. We act as bankers, taking deposits from the other members when they are in funds, and accepting a corresponding liability to pay out on demand when they need the money. The extent to which it helps us depends, therefore, on whether the other parties have a favourable or unfavourable balance with the rest of the world. During the war the rest of the sterling area has had a large favourable balance, which in virtue of the sterling area system they have made available to us. We have benefited from this up to the tune of more than £2,000 million. We took about £600 million from this source in 1943. Indeed, together with lend lease and Canadian aid, it has been the backbone of our wartime finance. It has proved, in combination with the special accounts for neutrals, a brilliant conception for wartime use.

Whether we gain by the continuance of such an arrangement depends on whether the other members of the area go on accumulating a favourable balance. If they do not, the existing sterling area system places on us the liability to find the external finance required to cover their deficit (to the extent, which is large, that their accumulated London balances permit); and *their* adverse balance has to be added to our own to give the measure of what we shall have to find in the foreign exchange of the creditor countries of the world (whichever these may turn out to be).

Now most of the other members of the area have been suffering from an accumulated shortage of imports and expect after the war, when shipping and supplies are again available, to run for a period an adverse balance. The maintenance of the sterling area system would put us under a continuing contract to make the accumulated London balances of the rest of the area available to meet this deficit. (It will be important at the Dominion talks to ask the Dominion and Indian representatives, and also the Colonial Office, whether they have made any estimates of their probable balance of payments in the two or three years after the war. We also need these figures for the Middle East.)

We must, therefore, expect that the maintenance of the sterling area system during this period on its present basis will be more likely to add to our liabilities (perhaps substantially) than to provide us with means of meeting them. Provisionally (and pending considered estimates) it would be rash to put the possible burden thus arising during the three years or so of the interim period after the war at a lower aggregate than (say) £200–300 million.

It must again be emphasised that the sterling area system as at present conceived does not put any pressure whatever on the rest of the area to make their purchases in U.K. rather than in (e.g.) U.S. or anywhere else. We undertake a liability to finance their purchases wherever they may choose to make them.

It does not follow from this that it would not be desirable, in so far as we see our way to shoulder the liability, to propose to the rest of the sterling area the continuance of some version of the present arrangements during the transitional period; though we shall have to find ways of modifying the present basis which will limit the extent of our liability. For one thing, it would be extremely difficult to pull out of present arrangements in advance of the re-establishment of more or less normal conditions. But chiefly we owe it to our future credit and to the advantages we have been taking from the system hitherto, to the extent that it is in our power to do so, to continue it for a time. Having set up a pooling system when it suited us and having taken more than £2,000 million out of the pool, we cannot suddenly and forthwith freeze it when the current turns the other way. We have persuaded the other countries concerned to entrust us with virtually the whole of their accruing external reserves, and we cannot refuse to make at least part of these available in so far as they are required for immediate needs; though in due course we must, of course, find some suitable means of spreading over a sufficient period repayment of what we cannot hope to meet currently. The continuance during the interim period of a modified sterling area system, revised to suit the new circumstances, would be very much the easiest and most honourable and least disturbing way of meeting an inescapable obligation.

But the conclusion not to be overlooked (and it has been, perhaps, in danger of not being fully appreciated) is that the maintenance of the sterling area system during the transitional period is *not* a means of solving our financial problem during that period. On the contrary, it will probably add to our liabilities on a substantial scale; it will certainly put us at greater risk and add to the sum of liabilities which we must prepare ourselves to meet if necessary.

V. *Agreements with European Central Banks*

Some of the above considerations also apply to the suggested bilateral central bank arrangements, though here there is not the same reason for taking on the additional risk. Take, for example, the Anglo-French Agreement. If the French Colonies have a favourable balance with the sterling area, it will help us. If they have an unfavourable balance, it will add to our burdens. Is not the latter more likely than the former? Assuredly, if we were to make similar agreements with Belgium or Holland or continental France or Russia, we should be taking on additional burdens. For it is most unlikely that these countries will develop a favourable balance with the sterling area in the early post-war period.

Indeed, such arrangements would cut us off from what might otherwise prove a most useful source of liquid resources. The Western European powers agreed at Atlantic City that they would use a substantial part of their large gold and dollar resources (which are considerably larger than ours, having been, fortunately for them, frozen early in the war) to pay for their relief and rehabilitation needs. It seems probable that Russia also has the intention of dipping into her huge stocks of gold. Sweden, Switzerland and Portugal are in the same position. Sterling area sales to these countries against spot gold are our best hope of replenishing our resources out of which to meet the claim of those countries which will be in the creditor position in the post-war period. If, on the other hand, we were to enter into central bank arrangements with these countries based on opening up mutual lines of credit, they would be able to meet their adverse balance with the sterling area, or some part of it, by means of these credits, and use their gold to satisfy less accommodating creditors or to be held in reserve against more distant needs.

To these countries we have no obligations arising out of the war similar to those we owe to the rest of the sterling area; the obligation, if any, is the other way. It would therefore, be most imprudent to open up mutual lines of credit with any of the European countries.

Indeed, it should not need much argument to demonstrate that to enter into pooling arrangements with other debtors is not a helpful means of meeting one's creditors. In our case, such arrangements, if carried out on the lines indicated above, would run the risk of consolidating on our backs the adverse balance, not only of ourselves, but of all the other chief debtor countries. We might find ourselves, once more, acting as the conduit pipe of American credit to the rest of the world. Nothing would suit America better. Yet there is nothing that we ought to be more careful to avoid; though our obligation to the rest of the sterling area means that we cannot avoid a substantial measure of it. To set up as the banker of Europe and the sterling area might mean that we should become liable to America for the greater part of America's favourable balance with the rest of the world. Nor, in the long run, will it prove to the advantage of our credit or our prestige to assume liabilities far beyond any resources we have in sight with which to support them.

VI. *The Creditor Countries*

If we are right to expect that Europe and the sterling area will be running adverse balances on current account in the early post-war period, it follows that certain other countries will be running favourable balances of the same amount. Which will these countries be? Nothing is more difficult than to forecast either the direction or the amount of the favourable balances,—great surprises will not be surprising. I cannot improve at present on what seems the obvious conclusion, namely that the favourable balances will mainly accrue to the countries of the North and South American continents, particularly the U.S., Canada, Argentina and (perhaps) Brazil.

It follows that it is with these countries that we have to arrange our deficit financing.

What is the magnitude probably or possibly involved? The extremely precarious estimates we have used hitherto are as follows:-

	£ million
Adverse balance of the U.K. with the rest of the world in the transition period	500–700
Adverse balance of the other members of the sterling area with the rest of the world	200–300

Let us add to these figures a further guess that during the same period the sterling area will have (apart from their own contributions to UNRRA) a favourable balance of (say) £200 million per annum with Europe and Russia, to be paid for (largely one hopes) in gold or out of UNRRA free exchange. This has to be added to (not subtracted from) the above to give the sterling area's adverse balance with the Americas, as distinct from the world as a whole.

It follows that the sterling area adverse balance with the Americas might be of the order of £900 to £1,200 million, against which (say) £200 million might have been earned in gold and dollars from Russia and Europe, if we manage our affairs well.

Here let me interject a very rash, personal, opinion that I am inclined to prefer the lower of these figures to the higher. My instinct is that it is easy to make these figures too high. The world's trade may have a greater self-equilibrating power than can be expected on the basis of known facts before the event. Looking at the figures the other way round, I am not convinced that the U.S. will run such a large favourable balance (in addition to her contribution to UNRRA etc.) immediately after the war (whatever may happen later on) as some people expect. Over this whole field of forecast there is, as I have said, room for great surprises. Nevertheless, if we assume full liability for the sterling area, we ought in prudence to be prepared for as much as a gross deficit with the Americas of £1,200 million (before allowing for the gold and dollars we and the rest of the area earn from Europe), whilst hoping for a figure not exceeding £1,000 million.

However this may be, we are brought back to the fact that we cannot hope to avoid a major financial operation with the U.S. I would emphasise that this is inescapable – unless we fall back on the altogether different type of solution outlined in XI below.

VII. *Arrangements with N. and S. America*

The means of meeting the ultimate deficit with the Americas are the following:-

(1) Currently accruing gold and dollars earned by the sterling area from Europe and elsewhere, estimated above (perhaps optimistically) at £200 million.

(2) Depletion of the gold and dollar reserves with which we shall end the war.

(3) A credit from the U.S.

(4) A credit from Canada.

(5) Payments agreements with the S. American countries by which they are induced to hold still more sterling or to re-purchase from us further sterling securities.

We may hope to end the war with gold and dollar reserves of £300–£500 million according to the firmness and success of our financial diplomacy in Washington. We ought on no account to bring our reserves below £200 to £300 million during the interim period. Thus we may have from £100 to £200 million to spare with which to bridge the gap.

It will make an enormous difference to our financial freedom and diplomatic independence at the end of the war whether it is the lower or the higher figure of reserves that we have at our disposal. I credit Dr Harry White, equally with ourselves, with being aware of that fact. But I doubt if such considerations play much part as yet in the minds of the State Department. Perhaps that is why we find them easier to deal with.

Sources (4) and (5) together, i.e. credits from Canada and South America might bring in £150–200 million.

Taking one thing with another and allowing for all the other resources indicated above, it would appear that for reasonable freedom of action we may need interim financial assistance from U.S.A. to the extent of (say) two billion dollars (£500 million). It is by no means inconceivable that we might do with less, say 1½ billion dollars. But it will probably be as easy to get accommodation up to the higher figure as the lower; and the less we have to draw on our liquid reserves, the stronger our future position. With the higher figure our resources for the interim period would then be:-

	£ million
Gold and dollars earned by sterling area from	
Europe	200
Depletion of reserves	100–200
Canada and South America	150–200
U.S.A.	500
Total	950–1100

This completes our preliminary diagnosis. It scarcely needs to be mentioned that the specific figures used are highly precarious, and should be regarded, pending further study, as being not much more than illustrative of the orders of magnitude perhaps involved.

VIII. *The Interim Arrangements to be Offered to the Sterling Area Countries*

Should we not begin by agreeing amongst ourselves that it is impracticable to assume an unlimited liability to transfer into outside currencies the sterling balances accumulated by the rest of the sterling area during the war? The extent to which we can allow such transfers in practice will largely depend on the size of our post-war reserves and on the arrangements we can make with the Americas; but the exact answer can only be given as we go along. We must do our best. But we must not enter into commitments beyond what we can see our way to carry out. If this is agreed, we might make proposals to the other members of the area on the following lines:-

(1) Members of the sterling area will pool their receipts of gold and hard currencies in London as heretofore.

(2) Members' sterling balances shall be freely transferable by them within the area. Their requirements of currencies outside the area will be met by the London exchange control to the best of its ability, but the control will retain the discretion to ration any particular currency, provided that any member shall always be entitled to take out of the pool in terms of any hard currency the equivalent of the gold and hard currencies which it has put into the pool after zero-hour (i.e. after the interim phase has begun).

This means that no member of the area can lose currently accruing resources of hard currencies by remaining a member, but the extent to which they are free to convert into hard currencies old accumulations of sterling, accrued to their account during the war, must remain within the discretion of the control.

(3) Members shall maintain exchange and import controls with a view to keeping hard currency requirements within their ration, and if at the end of an annual period it is found

that they have exceeded this ration, they shall make good the excess out of their own gold reserves or by borrowing hard currencies or during the next ration period.

(4) The above arrangements shall be reconsidered at the end of three years, or sooner by mutual agreement.

(5) After three years, unless it is agreed otherwise, any 'abnormal' sterling balances shall become subject to special arrangements for gradual release.

Prima facie it would be to the advantage of members of the sterling area to remain members on these terms. All their current hard currency earnings are free cash; and a ration of their 'abnormal' sterling balances is released to them. If they withdraw from membership, their existing and accruing sterling balances would *only* be available within what remained of the sterling area, and they would not be entitled (as they would be by remaining members) to use any part of them to acquire outside currencies.

These arrangements would lend themselves to gradual evolution towards a freer system. They would be compatible with membership of the International Monetary Union under the transitional clause of the latter.

They would provide an inducement to a member of the area to make his purchases within the area rather than outside, but only to the extent that he was developing an adverse balance which could not be met out of his ration of freely convertible pre-zero-hour sterling balances in London. No objection to this can be reasonably taken by the Americans; and if they will provide us with sufficient credit on terms we can accept, any severe rationing of hard currencies can be avoided from the outset.

IX. *The Proposals to be made to the Americans*

Unless the above estimates are very erroneous, or unless we accept the austere alternative mentioned below, special post-war financial assistance from U.S. on a major scale seems inescapable. At any rate, it is certain that we could not undertake the liabilities of the sterling area on terms which the other members are likely to accept, without such assistance. This need not amount to the five billion dollars suggested by Mr Leon Fraser, but as we have seen above, we might well require aid of the order of two billion (£500 million) during the interim period as a whole.

Whatever the technique in detail, this clearly has to be an inter-governmental arrangement and exceeds what could be arranged as a line of credit with the New York Federal Reserve Bank. Moreover we should resist, I suggest, a market operation, whether or not subject to guarantee as tentatively suggested by Dr White. Such a credit should be regarded as a part of war finance. It should not carry interest and should be repayable by instalments over a period of (say) fifty years.

This should be within our capacity (£10 million a year) even allowing for our other liabilities and for the fact that we cannot, if our commerce is to progress, employ the whole of our net external earnings for many years to come to discharge dead-weight debt. But should we not resolutely refuse to undertake a materially greater liability than the above, for the reason that this time we intend to run no risks of being unable to meet our engagements? For example, if we were offered a market loan of 3 billion carrying 3½ per cent per annum liability for interest and sinking fund (£26,250,000 per annum), it would not be prudent to accept.

The best way of getting a no-interest credit would be, I suggest, to put up the proposal in the form of a loan of gold repayable by instalments. We might ask the U.S. Government to give us a call on gold up to two billion, any gold taken under this arrangement to be replaced by instalments. A proposal put in this way might well be acceptable.

We must expect that the U.S. would attach to this the conditions that, during the transitional period, we should not ration the members of the sterling area in so far as they required dollars to meet current purchases, and that we ourselves would apply no discriminatory import control against American exports. These conditions would be reasonable.

X. *The Allocation of the Available Resources*

The gravest objection to the above arrangements is that they are too free-and-easy for the initial period. We shall never attain equilibrium except under severe pressure. The danger of the above proposals is that, by relieving the pressure, they would lead to our reaching the end of the three year period without having attained equilibrium and without having further exceptional resources to fall back on. Meanwhile we should have formed post-war habits and have relaxed controls.

It might be a partial safeguard against this if the Treasury were to set a target in the shape of a gradually diminishing maximum of overseas disinvestment to be allowed in each post-war year. For example, allocations of external exchange might be limited to figures which would prevent overseas disinvestment for U.K. purposes from exceeding £250 million in the first year, £150 million in the second year, £100 million in the third year and £50 million in the fourth year; whilst allocations to the rest of the sterling area, in addition to their own earnings, might be restricted to £100 million in the first year, and £50 million in each of the second and third years.

XI. *The Austere Alternative*

Suppose, however, that we are unable to obtain American assistance on terms which we think it prudent and advisable to accept, is there an alternative open to us?

None that I can see, except a determination to live within our current resources, eked out partly by drawing on physical stocks and by using our monetary reserves, and partly by some further accumulations of blocked sterling belonging to other members of the area and under payments agreements. There is much to be said for a closer approximation to this state of affairs than seems likely to be compatible with the present trend of policy.

Nevertheless, under such a system, however salutary from some points of view, we should not be able to cut much of a figure in the world. Moreover the social and political difficulties involved in the consequential domestic decisions might be overwhelming. I conclude, therefore, that our right course is to work out an international economic policy on more expansive lines in close harmony with the Dominions and the United States, even though this means taking some risks and accepting some commitments which we might have preferred to avoid.

KEYNES

11 January 1944

The Bank of England commented on the memorandum on 9 February. It suggested that Keynes's sterling area proposals had overlooked the diversity of the sterling area, that his statistical estimates were suspect, as the exact outcome would depend on future policy decisions, and that the formality of his sterling area proposals would break up the area. The Bank suggested that no attempt to obtain American assistance was necessary for the present and that an extension of the existing sterling area system would prove satisfactory over the transition.

After some informal discussions within the Treasury and with the Bank, the matter was deferred, although parts of it continued to appear in the concurrent controversy concerning the I.M.F.[1] During these discussions Keynes commented on the Bank's reactions to his paper.

NOTES ON THE BANK OF ENGLAND'S PROPOSALS
FOR THE STERLING AREA

1. Unless I misunderstand the top of the second page of the covering letter, the Bank's proposal is that we should now ask the Dominions if they are prepared to continue exchange controls against the non-sterling area, only payments for current imports being allowed through the control. It would be easier to understand just what this amounts to and exactly how it differs from my own proposals if we had the answers to the following questions:-

(a) Is it proposed that British residents should be free to export capital anywhere within the sterling area? Is this compatible with the control of the domestic market? If so, has not some addition to be made to our adverse balance of payments in respect of such capital exports which, with the great abundance of funds in the hands of some firms, are exceedingly likely to take place?

(b) Would members of the sterling area be expected to exercise pressure on their residents to effect purchases within, rather than without, the area, i.e. would foreign exchange only be allocated by their exchange controls after the possibility of buying within the area instead had been fully explored? Or would, in fact, the pre-armistice balances be free without limit for expenditure outside the sterling area, provided they are to pay for imports? It is stated in the Bank's memorandum that 'it is not our normal practice to seek to influence members of the area on the amount of their current expenditure outside the area, although in some circumstances

[1] On this see *JMK*, vol. xxv.

we might wish to make representations'. This sentence deserves further elucidation.

(c) It is said that 'we can presumably issue instructions to the Crown Colonies in the matter of their import policy, exchange control, etc.' Does this mean that the Crown Colonies would be prevented from importing, though they had the money and though the goods were available? Does it mean that they would be instructed to buy only within the sterling area when, left to themselves, they would buy outside it?

(d) Is it believed that exchange controls against capital movements will be effective in peace-time conditions in, e.g., Ireland, Egypt and South Africa?

(e) Would South Africa and other gold producers within the sterling area be allowed to sell their gold, e.g., to India?

(f) Would silver be a 'current import' for India?

(g) It is stated that we must reckon on the necessity of making special arrangements with India and Egypt. What sort of special arrangements are here intended?

(h) Is it right to infer that the inducement to members of the sterling area to remain within the area will be a threat that otherwise their pre-armistice balances would be blocked for all purposes? There is a passage in the middle paragraph of page 5 which implies this.

Only after such questions have been answered will it be possible to estimate what the full freedom to use pre-armistice balances is likely to cost us, compared with my proposal to ration the quantity so used in accordance with our resources. Whatever the quantitative answer, this arrangement is open to the obvious objection that it means taking on a liability, the amount of which is not easily calculated, before we know whether we have the means to meet it.

2. My statistical estimate of the probable deficit is admittedly very precarious, and I was hoping that the Bank would provide data for a better figure. Instead of that there are a

number of general points in which they seek to take comfort. All these grounds for comfort are, I fear, illusory.

(i) I have not, I think, made the logical or arithmetical mistake imputed on the top of page 4. I first estimated the adverse balance of the U.K. with the rest of the world, including the rest of the sterling area. I then estimated the unfavourable balance of the rest of the sterling area with the rest of the world, including U.K. To add these two figures together is the correct way of arriving at the deficit of the whole of the sterling area with the rest of the world.

(ii) It is quite true that an important part of the sterling balances represent legal reserves of currency systems. But, so far from this being a ground of comfort, it is exactly the opposite. The inhabitants of the Crown Colonies, India and the rest are full of unexpended cash, largely represented by notes. When they are able to spend this money on imports the note issue will contract and the equivalent will have to be released from the sterling reserves, to pay for the imports.

(iii) It is quite true that a fairly large proportion of the sterling balances can be regarded as stable. I did not suggest the contrary. By the end of June next the sterling balances of the sterling area will exceed £2,000 million, and by the date we are thinking of they will probably be of the order of £2,500 million. I suggested that, in the course of 3 or 4 years, we ought to try to find means to liquidate about £200 million, i.e. 8 per cent of the total, or (say) 2½ per cent per annum. Unless there is a rationing system, I believe that the sterling area will draw on their balances at a rate greater than 2½ per cent per annum. I should be hopeful, indeed, that considerably more than a half of the sterling balances could either be regarded as stable, or capable of being funded, or unlikely to be drawn upon in the early future. It is only the unstable margin, not exceeding perhaps more than a quarter to a third of the whole, from which the danger comes.

(iv) In paragraph 10, page 7, the Bank 'disagree with the

view that by maintaining and developing existing arrangements we shall add to our difficulties'. This implies that the sterling area are likely during the early post-war years to add to their sterling balances rather than diminish them, or, at any rate, will not diminish them to any serious extent. I suggest that it would be useful to ask the Dominion representatives whether they have made any estimate of the probable movement of their sterling balances in the first 3 or 4 years after the war, on the assumption that they are freely available to meet current payments.

(v) The Bank say quite truly that the size of our prospective deficit will depend on policy. So far from disagreeing with this, I pointed out that the figures with which I started might be materially reduced if the Cabinet were to enforce a policy of strict austerity. Is there, however, a reasonable chance of this? Unfortunately, such evidence as I have seen lately is extremely depressing. The programmes in view seem likely to require imports on a greater, rather than a smaller, scale than these assume, whilst it is becoming increasingly difficult to see in what industries the increase of exports, on which we are relying, is going to be developed.

3. The essence of the situation is that our own deficit is exceedingly likely to exceed the whole of our gold and dollar reserves. Yet, clearly, we cannot let our reserves fall to nothing in the first three years. Apart from this we shall have a liability of £2,500 million to the rest of the sterling area and perhaps another £500 million to the rest of the world. Is it not rash, in such circumstances, to try to conduct a banking business on the basis that we are prepared to cash freely the balances we already hold, provided they are to pay for current imports? Is not such rashness likely to end in extreme catastrophe?

KEYNES

15 February 1944

Meanwhile, the lend lease cuts under discussion at the end of 1943[2] continued their way through the pipeline. On 8 January when Lord Halifax, Ben Smith[3] and Sir David Waley met Hull, Morgenthau, Crowley and some of their officials to discuss the situation, Morgenthau emphasised that the changes under discussion were not designed to reduce U.K. dollar balances in any other way beyond removing 'politically difficult' items. Crowley re-affirmed this in a discussion on 20 January, saying that once the cuts had gone through he would be the first to cooperate in finding ways of replacing the amounts involved.

However, these discussions did not prove to have conclusively settled the balances issue. At a cabinet meeting in Washington on 18 February, Crowley again raised Britain's reserve position and lend lease cuts. Roosevelt asked for a memorandum on the problem. Stettinius provided one, which he had not cleared with either Crowley or Morgenthau, for transmission to Churchill. The last paragraph asked for a reduction in the reserves to $1 billion. Churchill received the paper on 23 February. It led to a stiff reply on 9 March with the result that Roosevelt suggested on 24 March that discussions continue between the two Treasuries. Eventually, in the absence of renewed questioning from the American side, the British decided to defer the discussions until the negotiations connected with Stage II, the period between the end of the war in Europe and the defeat of Japan. However, during the rest of the year, the British authorities accepted further small cuts in lend lease as the reserves rose and as they attempted to gain further freedom to export.

An examination of Britain's balance of payments prospects during the rest of the war heightened the Treasury's concern with these issues during this period. After seeing the Bank of England's forecasts for 1944, Keynes minuted

To SIR RICHARD HOPKINS *and others, 13 March 1944*

The full version of the Bank's dossier, giving the particulars of overseas finance for 1943 and the forecast for 1944, has just arrived. The revision now made in the forecast of what our

[2] On these see *JMK*, vol. XXIII, p. 307.

[3] Ben Smith (1879–1969) K.B.E. 1945; Labour M.P. for Rotherhithe, 1923–46; Parliamentary Secretary, Ministry of Aircraft Production, 1942; Minister-Resident for Supply in Washington, 1943–5; Minister for Food, 1945–6; Chairman, West Midlands Divisional Coal Board, 1946–50.

balances will become is so important that it should, I think, be urgently in front of those who are currently concerned with this question.

The Bank's statistics imply that the various measures which the lend lease authorities have been enforcing on us, in conjunction with the present rate of gold sales in the East, are sufficient, given time, to give Mr Morgenthau the trick which we have been trying to defend from him. According to the Bank, our net gold and dollar reserves will reach their peak next June and will thereafter decline sharply. If this is even approximately correct, our hopes of reaching net reserves of £500 million will be quite certainly disappointed. We shall be more likely to end 1945 with something not greatly in excess of Mr Morgenthau's ceiling of £250 million.

The figures given below involve a small amount of estimation on my part, since the Bank do not attempt an exact forecast of the gold liabilities which have to be deducted to arrive at the net results. Since, however, they do give this estimate for Portugal, which is the major item, my figures below are not likely to be very much out.

Net gold and dollar reserves £ million

End of December 1943	352
End of March 1944	370
End of June 1944	412
End of December 1944	360

This drastic revision in our expectations is due to four factors, which are admittedly conjectural and where the Bank could do no more than put in the best figures they could extract from the Departments. These four factors are:-

(a) *The recent removal of certain supplies from the ambit of lend lease.* These are put at £100 million per annum. To a considerable extent, the financial effect of these removals will only operate after June.

(b) *Additional reciprocal aid in the shape of raw materials and food.* This should operate fully throughout 1944 and is put at £50 million. It should be understood that this figure relates only to the addition to the reciprocal aid, which we are giving under other headings, as the result of our conceding raw materials and food purchased in the sterling area by the U.S. Government.

(c) *Gold sales in the Middle East and India.* The estimate of the cost of this for the calendar year, measured at the par value of gold, is £88 million.

(d) *A large reduction in receipts from the American troops after next June.* Such receipts by the U.K. in the second half of 1944 are estimated at not much more than half the receipts in the first half of the year. The movements in this item are worth setting out in detail.

	1942	1st half 1943	2nd half 1943	1st half 1944	2nd half 1944
			(£ million)		
Direct U.K. Receipts from U.S. Forces	12·6	11·3	36·5	89·0	47·0
Rest of sterling area receipts from U.S. forces	48·6	41·6	49·7	56·0	56·0
	61·2	52·9	86·2	145·0	103·0

Partial allowance had, of course, been made previously for all these factors, but I do not think we had fully realised their cumulative effect. At least, I had not. I am still of the opinion that the Bank may prove to be unduly pessimistic. But there is no disputing, I think, that their figures are the best available on the present evidence. I fancy that we shall not pay out cash during 1944 in respect of the items now excluded from lend lease on so great a scale as £100 million, owing to time lags and a possible decline of needs. I shall also be surprised if the receipts from the U.S. troops fall off so seriously. So long as U.K. remains a base, one would expect larger figures than those estimated for the second half of the year. Moreover, if there is a shift to the Pacific war, there might be some off-set not allowed for in the receipts of the rest of the sterling area in respect of troops. For these reasons, we need not be surprised if the estimate proves a bit too low. Nevertheless, we should assuredly take it seriously.

I draw two conclusions. We have allowed the Americans, in their recent depredations on lend lease and extension of reciprocal aid, to trade too extensively on our large current and immediately prospective receipts from American troops without allowing sufficiently for the fact that this is anything but a permanent source of income. We have, it seems to me, a stronger case than we thought we had. We should, therefore, remain exceedingly firm and even try to regain a little lost ground. The second conclusion is that we cannot afford to continue much longer the present scale of gold sales in the East. Our present commitments, I believe, extend to the end of June. I suggest that from then on they should be halved which, if the sales on American account remain the same, means rather less than halved from the point of view of the Governments concerned. We ought, in common prudence, to aim at ending 1944 with reserves of £400 million as a minimum. If a sagging tendency to the tune of £50 million per half-year has already set in during the second half of 1944, we shall clearly be in danger of ending the war with something totally inadequate for even a semblance of financial independence. I may mention that the Bank of England estimate of our gross overseas liabilities at the end of 1944 (i.e. before deducting the gold etc. we hold against them) is of the order of £3,000 million.

Further reflection has led me to draw certain other conclusions about how we should arrange our external financial policy from now onwards, with particular relation to what is to happen after the war. I find the prospects somewhat gloomy and do not feel that we are yet tackling them with sufficient vigour and realism. That is too long a story for this paper.

KEYNES

13.3.44

Further revisions of the raw data by Mr Grant and Mr Jones[4] raised the December 1944 estimate somewhat but did not alter the trend. As Keynes put it on 2 April

It looks as if the time may come when we shall be wishing that the proposal we had put to President Roosevelt was not that our reserves should be allowed to exceed a billion dollars, but rather that we should have asked him to guarantee that they should never fall below this figure!

In April, Mr Stettinius, who had now become Assistant Secretary of State, visited Britain. Around the same time, his book on lend lease appeared in the book shops.[5] In an 'indiscreet letter which I thought it discreet to send' Keynes commented on the book.

To E. R. STETTINIUS, *18 April 1944*

My dear Stettinius,

I have been reading your book at breakfast whilst consuming an enormous pat of your delicious butter. So I owe you a double thanks. And if the one form of food is more lasting than the other, that is not your fault.

I should have written to thank you long before now for the book on lend lease if I had not wanted to finish reading it before writing to you. I did not get the freedom to do that until a short time ago I got for a space into the doctor's hands, which gave me the opportunity.

It really is a most splendid effort. I cannot imagine a book better written from the point of view of the right presentation

[4] Edgar Jones (b. 1911), Consultant to I.M.F. since 1977; Assistant Lecturer, University College, Swansea, 1939–41; Economic Assistant to Sir Dennis Robertson and Keynes at the Treasury, concerned with balance of payments statistics, 1941–6; Financial Counsellor, British Embassy, Washington, and alternate Executive Director, World Bank, 1946–50; Assistant Secretary, Treasury, 1950–3; I.M.F. 1953–9; Financial Adviser, Government of Chile, 1959–61; I.M.F. 1965–76.

[5] *Lend Lease: Weapon for Victory* (New York and London, 1944).

of the facts to your public. But, quite apart from any useful purpose it may serve, I have found it a fascinating piece of writing in itself. A catalogue of material facts and figures like this very easily turns itself into most indigestible matter. Not so this book of yours. I particularly enjoyed much of the early part. For it is extraordinary how quickly even matters with which one has been concerned oneself pass out of mind in all their detail. It was extraordinarily interesting to be reminded of the early phases and to see them, as one could not at the time, in their proper perspective. I think the treatment in your early chapters—the first nine, let us say—is from the historical point of view the most important and interesting of all. That does not mean that the rest is not, from a different point of view, just as interesting, and, as I have said, I am sure the information furnished in this digestible form will do a vast amount of good in both countries.

There remains one point, perhaps worth mentioning, which has particularly struck me, namely, an aspect which you have almost omitted or, at any rate, from which you have scarcely drawn the veil. I do not criticise this omission, but I find it extraordinarily interesting that, when you came to write the book, this seemed the right course to pursue. The point I have in mind is this.

As you will well remember, the greatest source of anxiety to us, and I think one can fairly add the greatest cause of friction over a very long period, was the problem of what we used to call the old commitments, arising out of the fact that lend lease did not come into anything like full operation for some nine months or more after it had come legally into force. The whole episode of the Viscose transaction, the Jesse Jones loan, the process of what we called scraping the barrel, you leave in complete obscurity. You do not emphasise the point that the U.S. Administration was very careful to take every possible precaution to see that the British were as near as possible bankrupt before any assistance was given. Nor do you recur at the end of the volume to the recent recrudescence of these same standards, according to which lend lease ought to be appropriately abated whenever there seems the slightest prospect that leaving things as they are might possibly result in leaving the British at the end of the war otherwise than hopelessly insolvent.

Now what particularly interests me is this. Hardly any of the Americans with whom we have been dealing frankly in these matters have appeared to be in favour of them on their merits or have supported them to us on that ground. They have always argued that this was an inevitable concession to public opinion and to Congress and that the whole splendid project would be put in jeopardy if we did not acquiesce in this course of policy. They were not, they have always told us, and I believe quite truthfully, doing these things because they themselves thought them right and necessary, but as an unavoidable concession to public opinion.

But now I find that you when you come to address public opinion and want to present the picture to them in the most convincing way, instead of putting all this prominently in the window, keep it under a veil. Evidently, when you approached the practical task of commending all that had happened to the American public, you instinctively felt that the right way to put it was on the basis of the generosity of the plan, of the spirit of pooling and co-operation which entered into it and the gradual tendency towards mutuality as reverse lend lease came into play. You did not instinctively feel that all this would be a bit dangerous and that what really would be necessary to make the American public feel that the whole thing had been worth while would be to play up the other aspect.

And surely your instinctive treatment of all this was dead right. It not infrequently happens that things are done to appease a totally non-existent public opinion.

I venture to say all this quite frankly, since I know to whom

I am writing. I expect I personally can scarcely be expected to see all this objectively. But when I try to do so, I still remain with a very firm conviction that the policy of ensuring that the United Kingdom shall emerge from this struggle having made external financial sacrifices vastly in excess of anyone else and with reserves wholly inadequate to meet their liabilities will prove, at long last, a considerable embarrassment to everyone. There will be all sorts of occasions when in every respect it is right and proper that we should enter into post-war problems as equal partners, without undue regard to financial considerations. It will be far more difficult to remedy all this when the present emergency is over. I think problems for the future are being laid up which very few people are foreseeing in their full seriousness.

I wonder if there is any chance of seeing you before you go back. I am not sure how much longer you are staying. For the last three or four weeks I have been in the doctor's hands and away from Whitehall. So it has been useless to try to get into touch with you. I am now, however, escaping from him and will be spending two or three days at the Treasury this week. Next week I hope to be properly back to work again. I know that you will be hopelessly full of engagements, but, if there is any free moment, let me know. Since evening engagements, in present conditions in London, are not quite so common as they used to be, possibly you might be able one evening to come and have supper with us in our kitchen at 46 Gordon Square. Winant has often joined us there, and it would be very nice to have you there too. At any hour which suited you.

Sincerely yours,
KEYNES

Keynes also provided the Chancellor with a note on the reserve problem. The Chancellor passed this on to Stettinius on 19 April. Along with the letter and other discussions, it may have contributed to his more helpful attitude to Britain after his return to Washington.

NOTE HANDED BY THE CHANCELLOR OF THE EXCHEQUER
TO MR STETTINIUS 19/4/44

(1) In spite of the huge volume of lend lease, there is no very marked diminution in the deterioration of the U.K. overseas financial position. In the last four calendar years the deterioration has been as follows:-

	$ million
1940	3024
1941	3188
1942	2540
1943	2620

The estimate for 1944 is $m2800.

(2) Including the more modest deterioration in 1939 and the estimate for 1944, the aggregate loss of overseas assets or increase of overseas liability by the end of this year will exceed $15 billion. Part of this has been met by the outright sale of assets, but, even after allowing for this, it seems likely that our external liabilities at the end of 1944 will be of the order of $12 billion. (We have parted outright with more than $[4] billion, but we started the war with certain external liabilities, against which our reserves at that time were held).

(3) On the other side of the account, after being almost cleaned out by the middle of 1941, we had been gradually building up a modest reserve. Our net gold and dollar balances at the end of 1943 amount to $1·3 billion. It is estimated that by the end of this year they will have risen to $1·6 billion, or about one-seventh of our probable liabilities at that date.

(4) These balances represent our only quick assets against our liabilities and are in fact the central reserves of the whole sterling area. The sterling area turn over to us their net receipts of dollars, which are substantial, in return for sterling, and against this we are under certain obligations to provide them with dollars when they require them.

(5) The improvement during 1944 is wholly due to the very large receipts estimated to be received during this year from the United States troops. We expect to receive from U.S. troops in the U.K. $585 million and from U.S. troops in the rest of the sterling area $475 million, being a total of over $1 billion in the year.

(6) Thus, in effect, the recent reductions in lend lease assistance and increase in mutual aid on our part mean that we are in fact indirectly having to find a considerable part of the pay of the U.S. troops outside America, namely the difference between the $1 billion received from the troops and 0·3 growth of balances.

(7) The most dangerous part of this from our point of view is, however, the obvious fact that, particularly so far as the U.S. troops in the U.K. are concerned, this source of income is highly temporary. The above figures suggest that as soon as the German war is at an end the maintenance of the existing scale of lend lease will put us on the wrong side of the account and mean a fairly rapid reduction of our balances during the rest of the war.

(8) We have been warned that after the end of the German war the scale of lend lease is likely to be further diminished rather than increased. In particular the new proposals, by which we have to pay for all raw materials which enter into exports will cost us very much more during the subsequent period.

(9) Thus there is every prospect of our balances going down hill during the period of the Japanese war, whilst our external liabilities will continue to grow.

(10) Looking so far ahead, it is impossible to make a reliable estimate, but it is not unlikely that by the end of 1945 or shortly afterwards we shall find our reserves reduced to $1 billion and our liabilities increased to $15 billions, which will mean that the ratio will have fallen from one-seventh to one-fifteenth.

In the course of his discussions in London, Stettinius had raised the possibility of a large interest-free loan from the United States to meet Britain's overseas financial needs in the period after the defeat of Japan. In response to this stimulus, plus the approach of Stage II, Keynes returned to the subject of transitional arrangements in a memorandum, dated 16 May, entitled *Our Financial Problems in the Transition*. Keynes circulated this memorandum within the Treasury as well as sending copies to Sir Otto Niemeyer,[6] Mr Cobbold, Mr Bolton and Mr Catterns[7] in the Bank and Professor Robbins in the Cabinet Office. This draft, which Sir Wilfrid Eady called 'one of the most readable 10,000 official words of recent times' was then discussed at two meetings in the Treasury on 24 and 25 May. Keynes then prepared a less technical and slightly shorter version for other departments and ministers, dated 6 June, entitled *The Problem of Our External Finance in the Transition*. This draft, and the next revision of 12 June, contained stronger passages in opposition to a sterling area solution to the problems of the transition and, as a result of Keynes's talks with R. H. Brand, then in London, took much more account of contemporary American opinion on the problems.[8]

Two meetings of ministers on 14 and 21 June, the first of which Keynes attended, considered the draft before circulating it to the War Cabinet on 1 July with a covering memorandum from the Chancellor outlining the action already taken and recommending further discussion amongst the departments concerned with a view to future action.[9] The War Cabinet discussed the memorandum on 20 July and agreed that there should be early negotiations on Stage II which should take full account of the post-war position in discussions of the British effort against Japan and Britain's Stage II needs and that steps should be taken to begin preparations for the export drive.

The Cabinet version of Keynes's memorandum appears below.

[6] Sir Otto Niemeyer (1883–1972); Controller of Finance and Supply Services, Treasury, 1922–7; joined Bank of England, 1927; Director, Bank of England, 1938–52; Bank for International Settlements, 1931–65, Chairman, 1937–40, Vice-Chairman, 1941–64.

[7] Basil Gage Catterns (1886–1969); Director, Bank of England, 1934–6, 1945–8; Deputy Governor, 1936–45.

[8] The later drafts also brought the statistics up to date. Otherwise the drift of the memorandum had not changed from that of the first draft.

[9] In the short period, the most important decisions made by the Chancellor were:
  (1) that during the Stage II negotiations, preparations for which were in hand, the U.K. negotiators should set out Britain's post-war position along Keynes's lines,
  (2) that abnormal sterling balances should be funded,
  (3) that serious steps should begin to get the post-war export drive ready for the appropriate moment.

THE PROBLEM OF OUR EXTERNAL FINANCE
IN THE TRANSITION

1. It is generally recognised that the problem of our external finance after the war will be greatly aggravated compared with 1919, because (1) the absolute amount of our overseas indebtedness is much greater, (2) the loss of our foreign investments available as a reserve is more complete, and (3) the current adverse balance of overseas trade which we shall have to meet by an increase of our exports is much larger.

2. It is not so generally recognised that, in addition, two considerable mitigations which were present last time will be absent. The policy of restraining the rise of prices has many advantages, but it will greatly increase the real burden of indebtedness as fixed in terms of money. The other outstanding difference is that last time we borrowed *money* from the United States which we used to meet our requirements in all parts of the world, so that we ended the war without abnormal indebtedness to any other country; whereas this time the United States has only aided us with goods she could herself supply and has not furnished us with cash to buy goods from elsewhere. Thus, nearly the whole of our 1914–18 external debt was canalised into the American debt—and that we shuffled out of. On the assumption that this time we intend to pay, the fact that we owe money all over the place has, as we shall see, some important offsetting advantages to our export trade. But it means that the effort required to emerge without loss of honour, dignity and credit will be immensely greater.

3. The Government's post-war domestic policy is based on the assumption that we shall be able to import all the raw materials and foodstuffs necessary to provide full employment and maintain (or improve) the standard of life. This assumption is, at present, an act of blind faith. No means of making it good has yet been found. There has never been

34

a more distinguished example of 'It will all come right on the day'. This memorandum is an attempt to persuade those concerned to support faith with works. Otherwise, great disappointments and disillusions lie ahead.

The Dimensions of the Problem

4. So long as lend lease and Canadian mutual aid continue, the ultimate difficulty of our position is masked. The following is an approximate balance sheet of our overseas position in 1943:–

	£ million		£ million
Imports (excluding munitions and ships)	1,150	Exports (excluding munitions)	300
Munitions and ships on lend lease and mutual aid	1,150	Munitions, services, etc., supplied by United Kingdom (on mutual aid terms)	500
Other war expenditure abroad (mainly munitions and United Kingdom Forces abroad)	750	Earnings from American forces in United Kingdom (and Dominion contributions to W.O.)	400
Other 'invisible' payments	250	Other 'invisible' income	360
		United States lend lease and Canadian mutual aid (1,590) less mutual aid and loans provided by United Kingdom (500)	1,090
		Overseas disinvestment	650
	3,300		3,300

5. This table shows that we are, at present, meeting less than a quarter of our external expenditure out of our exports together with the mutual aid we ourselves are affording. If, however, all war expenditure, lend lease and mutual aid were to come to an end tomorrow, our imports would be still running at *four times* our exports. For if all military expenditure were to cease, the imports of food and raw materials which we should require, whilst to some extent changed in

35

character, would not be reduced in amount, since there will be more, not fewer, men in the country to consume food and to be employed in working up raw materials. Provisional estimates which have been made indicate that the current figure of £1,150 million for our imports would also be about right for our import requirements in the first post-war year. Indeed, it is clear that there will be no time-lag in our import needs, except to the limited extent to which we can live on stock-piles, surplus stores and salvage. Perhaps the aggregate amount of the once-for-all relief from this source might be guessed at £300 to £400 millions, but our stocks are so ill balanced that the enjoyment of this relief would have to be spread over a period. Better statistics bearing on this from the Ministries of Supply and Food would be helpful. On the other hand, there will be a considerable time-lag in the development of exports to fill the gap and a still longer lag in the date of payment for them. Even if the export deficit can be made to taper off over a fairly short period of years, the accumulated excess of imports over exports, before equilibrium is reached, will be very large. Would anyone guess the cumulative deficiency in the first three post-war years at less than £750 to £1,000 million? A reasoned guess could only be made by preparing a practicable target for exports in each successive post-war year, carefully itemised between different classes of goods and agreed with those in touch with the facts of industry. No one, so far as is known, is attempting to collect such material. Should not the Board of Trade be invited to make such an estimate? The figures disclosed might be extremely disquieting. It is generally believed that we require an increase over pre-war of 50 per cent in the *volume* of our exports, which at present price levels means an increase to nearly *three times* in their *value*. If, as is probable, this has now become an underestimate, the Government's post-war plans for full employment are assuming an increase of at least three times the pre-war figure in the value of our exports.

Yet there is not the foggiest hope of achieving this, unless far more vigorous measures are taken than are (to the best of one's knowledge) at present contemplated. Ministers seem, at present, to be more concerned with the airy pinnacle than with preparing the foundations.

6. So far we have been dealing with 'visible' trade. Shall we have any net 'invisible' earnings from shipping, merchant and banking business and investments to help bridge this gap? In the long run we should have something substantial from this source, say £200 to £300 million. But in the early period after the war transactions on 'invisible' account are more likely to increase, than to decrease, the net deficiency. The scale on which they may do so will partly depend on our own policy (to which we shall return below). The abnormal outgoings likely to cause the deficiency include expenses arising out of the demobilisation of forces overseas and the clearing up of outstanding accounts and claims for damage and the like. Our cash expenditures abroad, which now amount to some £800 millions a year, will not suddenly sink to zero when the war comes to an end. We can make no reasoned guess as to the amount of such expenditure after the war or of the period over which it will continue. Can the Service Departments? Unless we alter our present policy considerably, relief and reconstruction abroad will be another large source of expense. To begin with, there is our contribution of £80 million to UNRRA. This does not (at present) include our share of the cost of relief to enemy countries. It includes nothing for the restoration of Burma or Malaya. It appears that various departments are contemplating loans on credits to Russia (whose reserves are several times greater than ours), China, Czechoslovakia, Poland and other European countries, amounting altogether to £100 million or more. Lady Bountiful is likely, to the best of one's observation, to continue her gracious activities until she feels the bailiff's clutch on her shoulder, unless something is done

about it. Finally, it is strongly argued in many quarters (and with considerable force) that there are important markets in which we shall not get a footing for our exports unless in the early years we are prepared to furnish a considerable volume of goods on credit. It is pointed out that the United States will offer medium and long-term credit and that we cannot compete unless we do the like. What the cumulative total of all this is likely to be in the early period, it is very difficult to guess. Would anyone care to put it at less than £250 to £500 millions net in the first three years after the war, unless there is a considerable change in the present trend of policies?

7. We have not yet made any provision for the burden of overseas war indebtedness largely in the shape of demand-balances accumulated in London, which at present can be drawn upon with varying degrees of freedom. Finally, therefore, there is the question of the lowest rate at which we must allow these balances to be repaid and drawn upon, if we are to maintain our honour and credit. The largest elements in our total indebtedness, as for example, to India, are not, in this connection, so dangerous in proportion to their amount as the smaller sums which we owe to a great variety of smaller creditors. Once we owe (say) £500 million to India, which is far greater than we can possibly discharge in the early period, a further increase to £1,000 million does not really affect the dimensions of the early-period problem. Thus we have to regard the composition of the debt as well as its aggregate. In particular there are certain claims against us to which we must surely accord a high priority. The Crown Colonies have lent to us the whole of their currency reserves. The populations of these countries are full of money and starved of goods. Can we, by blocking the reserves held against the money, compel them to remain in this position for an indefinite period? We also hold the greater part, or the whole, of the currency reserves of Ireland, India, Egypt and Palestine.

8. Apart from the larger creditors and from certain less liquid liabilities, the following smaller and more dependent or necessitous countries held sterling resources in London at the end of March 1944 as follows:–

	£ million	
West African Colonies	76	
East African Colonies	72	
Other British Africa		
(excluding South Africa)	34	
Ceylon	39	
Malaya	95	
Hong Kong	32	
British West Indies	54	
Palestine	93	
Other Colonies and Mandates	79	
	—	574
Iraq	64	
Netherlands and Colonies	53	
Belgium and Colonies	17	
Free France and Colonies and		
French blocked balances	64	
Norway	43	
Greece	59	
Iceland	9	
China	21	
Persia	15	
	—	345
		919

9. There are, in addition, the following liabilities of more varying degrees of urgency:–

(*a*) the balances in the major sterling area countries whose currency reserves we hold—

	£ million
India	797
Egypt	297
Eire	93

(b) the balances of the sterling Dominions—

	£ million
Australia	77
New Zealand	22
South Africa	24

(c) the secured loans, etc., from the United States and Canada—

	£ million
United States	79
Canada	162

and (d) the special account balances owing to South America and neutral Europe—

	£ million
Argentina	52
Brazil	23
Other South and Central America	12
Portugal (a gold liability)	62
Other neutral Europe	16

10. The grand aggregate, as at the end of March 1944, stood at £2,670 million. By the end of 1944 the figure will exceed £3,000 million. Admittedly a considerable proportion of this, say, a half or even two-thirds, can be funded, or perhaps, if we are tough (which we are not) written off, or represents normal working balances and currency reserves which will be maintained and therefore, constitute no immediate danger. (Nevertheless even this half will add considerably to our future burden if any significant amount of interest is payable on it.) It is the remaining one-third to one-half, i.e., £1,000 to £1,500 million as at the end of 1944, which is dangerous, because it represents entirely abnormal accumulations which the countries concerned will certainly seek to withdraw at the earliest opportunity. Unless, there-

fore, steps are taken to the contrary, it would be prudent to assume that during the transitional period as a whole attempts will be made to utilise at least £500 to £750 million, either in the shape of British exports or by demanding foreign currency in exchange.

11. As matters now stand and before reckoning any relief from the application of the measures recommended below, we are left, therefore, with the following prospective deficit during the transitional period of (say) the first three years after the war, to be found in the shape of new loans or equivalent aid:–

	£ million
Excess of imports over exports	750–1,000
Excess of other overseas cash expenditure over income (i.e., liquidation of war expenses and demobilisation in overseas theatres, relief, reconstruction loans, export credits, etc., *less* shipping earnings, net interest earnings, etc.)	250– 500
Repayment of abnormal sterling balances	500– 750
Total deficit	1,500–2,250

Nor is there any certainty that we shall have reached equilibrium at the end of the three years.

The Means of Solution
I. *The Sterling Area*

12. The easiest way to effect a large change for the better in the above estimate of the total deficit is to restrict, during the transitional period, the repayment of the abnormal sterling balances. If the measures recommended below are adopted, there will be a reasonable hope of greatly reducing, or even eliminating, this item. For, in this case, whilst certain balances would have to be reduced, other balances might increase, with the result that there might be no large net change. This will

require, however, a material change in the present sterling area arrangements, about the practice of which there is a widespread and most dangerous misunderstanding.

13. With certain foreign countries, of which Argentina and Brazil are the most important, we have established what are called *special accounts*, which are blocked within the sterling area (except to the extent that we agree otherwise) and can only be utilised to discharge sterling loans or to buy exports from the United Kingdom or other members of the area. Thus the use of the balances in these accounts may exhaust a part of our export capacity without adding to our current resources, or may increase the burden of the balances owing by United Kingdom to the other members of the sterling area. But they cannot cause a direct drain on our reserves of gold and dollars. Now it is commonly believed that the sterling balances of the members of the sterling area are in the same position as the special account balances, that is to say, that they can only be drawn upon for payments in this country or for making transfers to other members of the area or to special accounts and are, therefore, effectively blocked within it. Unfortunately, this is very far from being the case. The arrangements, made at the beginning of the war and still in force, are briefly as follows. (The sterling area covers the British Commonwealth, excluding Canada, and also Egypt, Palestine and Iraq.)

14. The members of the sterling area turn over to us the proceeds of any gold they may sell and the non-sterling currencies they earn from their exports, from United States troops or in any other way. They also undertake to set up local exchange controls to prevent movements of capital outside the sterling area and to limit their requirements of exchange to pay for imports coming from outside the area to what they themselves consider essential. We, on our side, provide their exchange controls with whatever non-sterling currencies they may, at their own discretion, require. This is not a contractual

undertaking, and, strictly speaking, no sterling can be remitted outside the sterling area without the specific approval of our Treasury in each case. But the arrangement as described above is the present understanding. The other exchange controls in the sterling area are autonomous and, so long as the present practice continues, we have no means of influencing their policies, apart from remonstrance. In the early years of the war, these exchange controls were of varying efficacy. Shortly before the lend lease phase, we were engaged, with some success, in tightening them up. With the lend lease phase, and more particularly with the evolution of the Combined Boards and allocation of goods and shipping, the exchange controls ceased to be the effective safeguard. Broadly speaking, most goods which could be allocated would be lent leased, so that no question of dollar requirements would arise. As soon, however, as dollar goods become available outside lend lease, then the other members of the area could call upon us to turn their sterling balances into dollars to the full extent determined by the policy of their own local exchange controls in granting licences for the importation of such goods. With the recent chiselling of lend lease such demands are already beginning to arise, especially in the Middle East. But it is, probably, only after the end of lend lease and with the increasing availability of shipping, that these demands for dollars will be serious. After that, our only protection under the present practice will be the measure of austerity voluntarily enforced for our good (and to their own disadvantage) by such countries as, for example, India and Egypt. It will be seen, therefore, that, unlike the special accounts, the sterling area system is not a blocking arrangement. It is, essentially, a *pooling* arrangement.

15. During the war all the members of the sterling area, apart from ourselves, have had a favourable balance of payments with the rest of the world. They have also had a

favourable balance in terms of United States and Canadian dollars. In such circumstances, a pooling arrangement has been, of course, wholly to our advantage. The sterling balances, approaching £2,000 millions, which the other members of the area have accumulated in London are an exact measure of the favourable balance of each of them with the rest of the world (including ourselves), which they have placed at our disposal. It is this system which, in conjunction with lend lease from the United States and mutual aid from Canada, has solved so successfully the problem of our war-time finance.

16. But if, after the war, the tide turns the other way and these countries seek to use these balances for reconstruction, for deferred consumption and to replenish their stocks, so that they have an adverse balance of payments, the advantage of a full pooling arrangement is precisely reversed. Our practice (at present) is to let them draw on their sterling balances to meet the deficiency. Now before the war most of these countries were borrowing countries for capital development purposes, i.e., they had an adverse balance on current account. Apart from this, they will emerge from the war starved of goods, with abundant purchasing power in the pockets of their consumers and in the bank balances of their developing industries, and with almost unlimited sterling reserves upon which to draw. In so far as we can provide them with the kinds of goods they require to the full extent of their requirements, it would be reasonable to expect them to give us priority. But in the early days this will be beyond our capacity, whereas supplies which are both desirable and necessary may be available from the United States. There is no reason to expect that their exchange controls will voluntarily refuse licences for all imports from outside the sterling area for a period which may run into years, if the goods are plainly required and if they are available.

17. The notion that the sterling area, as at present con-

stituted, is something which we can live upon, is one of the most dangerous of the delusions with which we are at present infected. Some people suppose that we can acquire any produce we need from the sterling area and also the area's earnings from the outside world, in return for blocked sterling which can be used in the last resort for no purpose except to purchase such volume of our exports as we find ourselves able to supply. It is not generally understood that the pre-war availability of sterling area balances for expenditure outside the area has not, in practice, been suspended, except to the extent that the local exchange controls of the other members of the sterling area choose to refrain from exercising it. At the present time we are protected by the non-availability both of shipping and of goods beyond what is released, with our approval, by the Combined Boards. As soon as shipping and goods from the United States and elsewhere outside the sterling area are again available, full pooling arrangements with the sterling area cease to be an asset and become an overwhelming liability. It becomes our responsibility to find dollars not only for ourselves, but for all the other members of the area.

18. It is, therefore, an indispensable condition of our remaining master of our own situation that we should in practice convert the sterling area into the closed system which some people believe it to be already. This is possible by a simple change which will allow us to preserve the full virtue and value of the rest of the sterling area arrangements substantially unchanged in all other respects. Whilst there can be no hope of persuading the rest of the sterling area to continue indefinitely on these conditions, we can reasonably press that they accept them for the transitional period, as the best and indeed the only means of safeguarding the balances which they already hold with us, and to prepare a gradual evolution away from the war-time system. Moreover, the proposal below lends itself to a further simple change, to be introduced

at the end of the transitional period when we feel strong enough for it, which would allow a permanent retention of a closely knit sterling area on principles compatible with the long-term requirements of the proposed International Monetary Fund.

19. The proposed change is that we should limit our liability to find dollars for the local exchange controls of the rest of the sterling area to the amount of their own current dollar earnings from exports or borrowing, supplemented by such additional ration of dollars, if any, as we may be able, at our discretion, to provide for them from time to time out of our own resources. It would then be for them to decide without interference or remonstrance from us how best to spend the dollars thus at their disposal. For this purpose we can probably treat the Colonial Empire, as, in principle, forming a single pool with the United Kingdom.

20. This has three signal—indeed, indispensable—advantages. It limits our liability to find dollars out of our own resources to what we ourselves think we can afford, and gets rid of an indefinite liability which depends in the last resort on the decisions of others. Secondly, it makes explicit a principle of our post-war financial policy which we must proclaim as indefeasible, namely, that we cannot undertake any legal liability to discharge our overseas debt except in the shape of our own exports (though we shall try to arrange *transfers* of indebtedness to the mutual convenience of all concerned). The formal adoption of this principle will, of course, give an immense advantage to British exports, since sterling will be the opposite of a scarce currency and must necessarily in the end find its outlet in British exports. Thirdly it enables us to escape from the invidious position of having to criticise or remonstrate against, the *particular* requirements of the local exchange controls for foreign currencies. For us to have to argue, without much knowledge of the facts, that India or Egypt is importing too large a volume of American

goods would put us in an impossible position both towards the applicant exchange control and towards America. The proposed change could be brought about with the smallest amount of trouble and publicity, because it would merely establish in practice a state of affairs which almost everyone, including the Americans, believes to exist already. It would not run counter to any formal commitment to the sterling area and could be put forward (as would indeed be the reality) as an interpretation of the *de facto* position.

21. This would be the first stage in the evolution of the sterling area system. But we could not hope to hold the area together permanently on this basis. We should, therefore, have to prepare for the second stage when we should feel strong enough to allow members of the area an unqualified right to spend outside it the *whole* of their net current earnings, and not merely what they earned outside the area. This would be tantamount (together with the liquidation of the special accounts) to the acceptance of general convertibility in the terms of the International Monetary Fund. We could gradually feel our way to this by increasing the latitude allowed to the local exchange controls, until we felt strong enough to go the whole way.

22. To prepare for this it would be necessary during the first stage to fund the abnormal balances in the sense of tying them up in the shape of inter-governmental credits which could only be drawn upon at a stipulated rate and subject to agreed safeguards. There are two foundation principles of policy in handling the abnormal overseas sterling balances which will keep us safe if we hold fast to them. The first has just been stated, namely, that we cannot repay our war indebtedness in any form except our own exports. This means that we do not accept a liability to find gold or any foreign currency. The second principle is that this indebtedness should carry no significant rate of interest pending its discharge.

47

23. This principle is just. To commercialise a war debt between Allies which leaves no productive asset behind, as though it were yielding an annual income, would be unreasonable and wrong. Interest, where there is not and in the nature of things could not have been any current income yielded by the loan has been stigmatised in most ages of history, except when the false analogies of trade were wholly dominant, as an intolerable and immoral imposition. To repay capital instalments is bad enough when no asset corresponds to the loan. But it is honourable, having received assistance in kind, to return the equivalent as time and opportunity permit.

24. An appeal to this principle is also inevitable. By the end of the transitional period, our overseas indebtedness may reach as much as £4,500 million. To pay (say) 3 per cent, interest and amortisation on this might be within our power some years hence, in spite of the fact that our own offsetting income from foreign investments is greatly reduced. But for the time being it is clearly impossible, and probably for some time to come. Last time we humbugged to the end—though the end came almost immediately—on the basis of accepting the commercial analogy. We did this in the name of our honour and dignity. And thereby we lost our honour and dignity, as well as our good word and any reputation we may have possessed for common sense and good management.

25. If we are wise enough this time to refuse the commercial analogy, it should not be beyond our power to discharge the whole of the capital sum in the shape of our own exports by gradually rising instalments over a period of (say) forty years; for example, with annual instalments beginning at £50,000,000 and rising by £3,000,000 a year, with some right to anticipate and to delay according to our capacity to furnish, and the willingness of our creditors to accept, a surplus of our exports. This should not mean that all our creditors are paid at the same rate, since a creditor more willing than

others to accept capital goods exports, which we are in a position to furnish additional to normal exports, would be paid off more rapidly. This system should prove a most servicable aid to the policy of full employment, since we could offer to expedite the repayment of our debt by special exports at times when normal demand was falling away. To declare what we hope to perform and to perform it will be a better course than to try once again a financier's confidence trick of accepting in name liabilities greater than we can meet, and then hope by deft management to keep so many of the chickens in the air that they never all come home to roost.

26. The practical application of this principle will involve many difficulties into which it would be premature to enter in this paper. It will be necessary to determine what liabilities are abnormal and due to the war, and by what date (which may be some time after the end of the war) accumulating balances are no longer 'abnormal and due to the war'. It will require a distinction between 'official' and 'unofficial' balances. It may be advisable to allow Treasury bill rate, at least on those balances which represent currency reserves; though even if Treasury bill rate is reduced to ½ per cent., it would cost £22½ million a year to pay this on the whole amount, which would add nearly 50 per cent to the burden of the suggested initial rate for the discharge of the capital obligation.

27. In order to freeze the situation pending the completion of funding agreements on the above lines, it would be highly advisable to prohibit the investment of non-resident money in Stock Exchange securities, except on special grounds with official approval. This would prevent the earning of interest by (for example) our overseas creditors' purchasing gilt-edged securities, and also (which is of the first importance) a growing foreign ownership of British equities on what might become a substantial scale. Without this provision, which would not be intended to prevent foreign ownership of stocks

49

of commodities or permanent direct investments, a time will surely come when Americans will begin to buy us out of house and home and acquire from us our fundamental overseas equities and enterprises. The early introduction of this prohibition is important.

28. If India or any other participant is prepared, in the light of the completed story, to make a free contribution to our costs of the war out of their accumulated sterling balances, well and good. But such gestures, however welcome, cannot go far towards solving the problem or provide the basis of our general policy. The right course is for us to declare that we will repay in full out of our own exports the capital sums advanced as and when we can, but without interest; and then make it our business to fulfil this promise to the letter. There is dignity and honour in this. Less clear-cut solutions will leave us permanently with one leg in the bog, out of which we shall eventually decide to shuffle somehow, covered with mud.

II. *The Strengthening and Subsequent use of our Gold and Dollar Reserves*

29. A year before the outbreak of war our reserves were very substantial and stood at £1,043 million. The expectation of war led to a large-scale withdrawal of foreign balances, and at the outbreak of war we were reduced to £620 million. At the commencement of lend lease (April 1941) we were practically cleaned out, having gold and dollar reserves of £66 million with £63 million gold liabilities against them, so that our net reserves were down to £3 million. Thereafter came the Jesse Jones loan; the old (pre-lend lease) commitments had been substantially met; almost all our current requirements from United States were for a time lent leased; and the sterling area was beginning to gain substantial earnings from the United States troops; with the result that our reserves began to rise quite steadily. They are likely to reach a

peak somewhat in excess of £400 million before the end of
1944. Unfortunately, awareness by the United States Administration of this recovery in our reserves has led to a large-scale
curtailment of lend lease facilities, with the result that we are
now dependent on our precarious earnings from the United
States troops to prevent our reserves from falling. When the
war in Europe is over, we shall be on the wrong side, perhaps
by as much as £100 million a year, even if lend lease continues
as at present; whereas Mr Stettinius has recently warned us
that after the end of the German war we must expect food
and raw materials to be cut off lend lease which would be
restricted henceforward to munitions only. Thus, as matters
now stand, we shall be lucky if we emerge from the Japanese
war with reserves of as much as £300 million, instead of with
the £500 million for which, at one time, we were hoping. Since
reserves of about £250 million probably represent somewhere
near the bed-rock figure below which we should not allow our
reserves to fall except for the gravest cause and in extreme
urgency, it follows that, unless we bestir ourselves, the relief
we can obtain by drawing on our reserves in the transitional
period is so small in relation to our possible requirements
that it is hardly worth bringing into the picture.

30. A major improvement in our reserve position can only
be achieved if we can persuade the Americans that it is as
much in their interest as in ours to facilitate the growth of
our reserves up to a level more commensurate with our
responsibilities. As we approach the war settlement, it will not
be convenient to either party that we should always have to
plead *in forma pauperis* to be excused from full participation.
Mr Stettinius has told Lord Halifax that he agrees with this,
although his actual suggestions for helping us are miscon-
ceived. It may prove politically difficult for the United States
Administration to furnish us at a later stage with cash dollars,
as distinct from assistance in kind, even though they may wish
to do so; yet for many purposes it will be cash that we shall

51

need. It will be a cause of general embarrassment if one of the three Great Powers responsible for settling the world has no free cash at all. The seriousness of this prospect is not as yet fully realised by those who will be most hampered by it if it arises. On the assumption that we end the Japanese war with net gold and dollar reserves not much above £250 millions, not only would the amount be negligible which we could regard as available; but our free resources would be entirely out of proportion to those of our associates. The United States would have sixteen times as much; Russia about three times; France more than double; Belgium, Holland, Switzerland with comparable absolute amounts and much greater free amounts; and so on. Our position would be ludicrously out of proportion to our responsibilities. We should, therefore, aim at an end-war figure of at least £500 million net and refuse to undertake any post-war liability to Europe or to anyone else until it was assured to us. Have we enough guts, here and now, to make the harsh, difficult decisions which are necessary to save ourselves from grave, subsequent embarrassment?

31. If the United States Administration could be persuaded that this is fair and reasonable and in the general interest, they could help on the desired result in various ways. No further chiselling at lend lease either currently or after the end of the German war. A generous, instead of a pernicketty, interpretation of the present arrangements. Above all, the assumption by the United States of the entire liability to find gold for the Middle East and India, the proceeds being turned over to meet common war needs in those areas. The last-named measure has been recently proposed by the Governor of the Bank of England. Is it not indispensable that we should now take the initiative to this end? The truth is that we have fallen into a rut in our financial relations with the United States, and we must jolt them and ourselves out of it. In fact, we are bearing a wholly disproportionate share of the financial

burden of the war. In practice we have allowed critics in the United States to establish the position that we are a lot of parasites and outsmarters who are milking the poor Americans for our own enrichment. It is clearly beyond our power after five years to finance the Japanese war on anything like the present basis. It seems, if this may be said, in parenthesis, that the time and energy and thought which we are all giving to the Brave New World is wildly disproportionate to what is being given to the Cruel Real World, towards which our present policy is neither brave nor new.

32. To make a concrete suggestion. The aggregate war expenditure incurred in India, including the pay of the forces but excluding the cost of munitions and other war supplies despatched to that theatre of operations, should be divided into (say) five parts, of which India should bear two, the United Kingdom one, and the United States two. These proportions are, at this stage, only for the purpose of illustration and would need careful working out. They considerably overstate the real share of India, since they would cover her total war expenditure, whereas in the case of the United Kingdom and United States the large amount of munitions and stores shipped to India and also naval expenditure would be additional. Thus, a two-fifths share for India, given above for purposes of illustration, is not too high. The proposed relation between the United Kingdom and United States shares would be justified by the greatly disproportionate share which the United Kingdom has borne hitherto, and the unmanageable proportions of our already existing indebtedness to India. The United States would be asked to meet their share in the first instance by taking over the full responsibility for sales of gold in India and, if possible, of silver also, and for the balance by obtaining rupees from the Government of India in exchange for dollar balances which would be earmarked for post-war use by India. This arrangement would be of advantage both to India and to the United

States, by providing the former with surplus funds wherewith to purchase American exports after the war, instead of her being (apart from her current dollar earnings) wholly dependent on imports from the sterling area.

33. By disposing of the United Kingdom's present liability to find gold for sale in India, this arrangement would relieve our reserves of an important cause of depletion. But there is also another source of seepage which should be stopped up. This flows from the nature of the financial arrangements which we found ourselves compelled to make with certain neutral countries in the hour of our weakness. The 'special accounts' for Argentina, Brazil and other South American countries, described above, are entirely satisfactory and mean, in effect, that these countries have advanced credits to us which cannot be spent outside the sterling area. But Sweden and Switzerland have succeeded, so far, in insisting that we should meet all our requirements from them in gold; so that they have very greatly augmented their gold reserves and have accorded us no financial facilities whatever; while to Persia we have to pay in gold for 60 per cent of the Persian currency we require. Portugal is in an intermediate position; we do not pay her gold currently, but we have agreed to let her remove her balances in gold five years after the end of the war, if she so wishes, and she already holds £62 million subject to this undertaking. These various liabilities to find gold are currently costing our *net* reserves about £45 million a year. Is there any sufficient justification for continuing these agreements a day longer than is required by the length of notice to determine them? It will be essential, in any case, to replace them by special accounts on the Argentine model after the war. Has not the time and the necessity for appeasing these countries come to an end? The arguments for continuing financial appeasement which are always readily forthcoming, are not always equally impressive.

34. These measures, if taken promptly, should go a long

way towards achieving the desired result of raising our *net* end-war reserves towards £500 million. But each month's delay in putting them into force means some £10 to £15 million off our final aggregate of reserves. The indispensable preliminary to a solution is to persuade the Americans that the above goal is a desirable one for us to reach in the interests of both countries. Until recently they were bending all their efforts to reduce our reserves to £250 million, and have been far too successful in this direction. At the moment there is a moratorium on further chiselling and we are being left (comparatively) at peace. But sniping still goes on and an outbreak of more active measures may recommence at any time. It is essential, therefore, frankly to put our whole case, set out in this memorandum, before the American Administration and invoke their aid on the lines indicated.

III. *A stiffer attitude towards new obligations*

35. The next question is whether a stiffer policy is not called for from all Departments of Government so as to reduce the prospective burden on our post-war balance of payments. Our present attitude towards our Allies and Associates is the result of several ingredients. In the financial field we have never escaped from the consequences of the Dunkirk atmosphere, when we felt alone: that this is *our* war; that if anyone helps it is very nice of them, but we cannot, of course, expect that it should be otherwise than on their own terms; that so far as we, but not they, are concerned, the future must be entirely sacrificed to the overwhelming needs of the present; and that if anyone wants a *douceur* he must, in the interests of getting on with the war, have it. This is the ingredient of appeasement, right and inevitable once, not so clearly necessary now. Next there is our position as a Great Power, equal in authority and responsibility and therefore equal in the assumption of burdens. This is the ingredient of pride and

prestige—easily understandable, but nevetheless short-sighted if pride and prestige are, in fact, to be preserved. And, finally, the most sympathetic and natural of all the ingredients, what we have called the gracious activities of Lady Bountiful, all-oblivious of the bailiff's clutch, the universal and unthinking benevolence of a family which has always felt rich and for whom charity has become not so much a sacrifice as a convention. How promptly and handsomely we should all subscribe to the Lord Mayor, if there were to be an earthquake in New York! It never occurs to Lady Bountiful that it may be her own dinner that she is giving away. If she did, the gift would be worth a great deal more; but would she, in this case, give it?

36. One feels more critical of our own approach after one has noted the more realistic and entirely successful methods of the Russians. For one then understands how little appeasement and gentleness contribute to pride and prestige. But, on the other hand, one feels less critical when one compares how the Europeans and the South Americans and the Neutrals and the Dominions feel about us and how they feel about the Americans. Much to be said for our following the dictates of our own nature. Our Foreign Office could justly claim that it has achieved immeasurably more than the State Department and can count with pride the number of our genuine friends, even though we have not yet found the answer to the Russian technique. Less critical again, when one meets the European Allies face to face and appreciates the extremity of their need and how immensely they can, if they are succoured, contribute to the excellence of the world. Therefore the criticism of the previous paragraph, though it is expressed with deliberate harshness, should be applied with much circumspection and moderation.

37. Nevertheless, certain concrete suggestions can survive this scrutiny. The Western Europeans hold large quantities of gold, with an important portion of which they intend to part

to pay for relief and reconstruction. It is right and reasonable that they should do so; for they have escaped hitherto that part of the costs of the war which would have drained off their overseas resources. It will be in the interests of general equilibrium that as much as possible of the gold they part with should come our way in the first instance. It follows that we should strictly avoid granting them credits or any special reliefs, and that our just needs for payment from them should be frankly expounded to them. Nor is it right that France should entirely escape the external costs of the war. At present it is we who have discharged out of our exiguous gold reserves, far less ample than hers, the cost of French munitions ordered in the United States and delivered after the collapse. It is expected that by the time we have recovered Metropolitan France, we shall, as a result, owe the French Government, for whom we have recovered it, a very substantial sum. Are Ministers fully deliberate and purposeful in all this? Or is it just happening?

38. In regard to Russia in particular we have got into a false position. No one knows accurately the extent of her gold holdings. They may well, by the end of the war, be nearer to £1,000 million than to £500 million. It is clearly their policy to borrow all they can on easy terms, and to reserve their gold for eventualities. It is common form today to say that Russian credit is the best in the world. Don't believe it! They will do whatever suits them best as circumstances change. (Those who claim her credit is good simultaneously argue that we should risk losing our money if we try to press the agreed terms of repayment for what she owes us already.) No one's credit for an overseas loan is worth much. However that may be, granting even that her credit is good, we are in no position to lend, whereas she is in a position to pay. Moreover, any little thing we could do for her she would regard as chicken-feed and laugh in our face. Let our financial policy to Russia, therefore, be realistic and firm to the fullest extent.

In particular, she should pay cash in full for all supplies reaching her from the sterling area after the German war is over—even though she decides to think again about her relations with Japan. Here is surely a case where weakness can serve no good or sufficient purpose. This is not one of the good cases for running our exports by credits. Russia is as capable of paying us cash now as she will be in five or ten years' time. And it will be easier to persuade her to pay for goods she wants before she gets them, than it will be after she has got them.

IV. *The Export Drive*

39. One final remedy remains, and by no means the least important, before we turn to the residual problem of post-war financial aid from the United States. This is the overcoming, so far as possible, of the time-lag in the recovery and expansion of our exports.

40. The present prospect seems to be that, after the German war is ended, the American economy will be promptly demobilised on a scale sufficient not only to allow a return to normal civilian standards, but to provide a considerable surplus for export. Our degree of demobilisation, on the other hand, although we have been fighting two years longer, will be greatly less and will not allow any considerable margin for exports. This will have a double disadvantage to our post-war finance, both currently in increasing the time-lag and because, when we start seriously to recover markets, we shall start behind in the race. Should not the War Cabinet ask the Chiefs of Staff to think again about the rate of demobilisation appropriate to our comparative situation, and the conditions of achieving it?

41. This bad prospect is, of course, aggravated by the fact that, whilst exports are a luxury to the United States, they are a matter of life and death to us. A frontal attack is needed

on the American attitude to our exporting programme. Mr Stettinius has recently given it as a reason why food and raw materials must be taken off lend lease as soon as the German war ends, that the continuation of lend lease (apart from munitions) is incompatible with our being allowed to lift a finger to improve our export prospects. We should impress it on the American Administration that during the Japanese phase it is indispensable for us to make a serious beginning at the recovery of export trade entirely freed from White Paper conditions, whilst at the same time suffering no abatement in lend lease aid. A frank show-down with the Americans on this and all the associated issues will conduce, whatever the result, to better relations between us than an indefinite acceptance on our part of what we all of us believe to be both intolerable and unfair. It is time for us, too, to take thought not merely of how to survive, but of how, surviving, we shall live.

42. It also seems to one, who is admittedly not fully cognisant of what is going on, that the early problems of each individual export industry are not receiving the urgent, intensive and realistic study, in collaboration with the industries themselves, which is necessary to reduce to a minimum the inevitable time-lag of recovery. No one Department is responsible for covering the export field as a whole or for setting a target and seeing that it is reached. One cannot say that nothing is being done. But no serious attempt is being made to bring our actions into clear conformity with our needs.

43. It is all the more reason for vigour in prosecuting the export drive that the prospects of success are by no means poor. Our competitive position after the war is likely to be better than it has been for years. Of our chief competitors, Germany and Japan will be temporarily out of the picture; and the rest of Europe under great handicaps. The hourly wage in this country is now, on the average, a little less than

2s, but the hourly wage in the United States is about 5s ($1); it would be unnecessarily defeatist of British industrialists to assume it to be inevitable that their own methods are so relatively inefficient, that they cannot compete in straight manufacture with Americans who are paying two and a half times their wages. It is true that the members of our own Commonwealth will be rapidly developing their own industries, but for some time at least this will create a demand for capital goods which we are well qualified to supply, and in the longer run new needs and the demand for higher standards of quality may maintain demand. Finally our best customers are in command of as much sterling as we feel able to release to them, solely available (if the above recommendations are accepted) for purchases in our market—an entirely novel situation. Sufficient vigour applied to these initial advantages may produce results far in excess of the present general expectation. These results will not just happen, any more than the creation and equipment of a great army just happens. But the application of the same energy and the same single-mindedness of purpose will work the same miracle, and work it quickly. This will require at the start not merely the means and the incentive to produce, but also the same severe stinting of the home consumer, although, having already put up with it for so long, he could reasonably have expected relief. The country must learn to believe that these are the conditions of our economic health and financial independence, and the only means by which we can consolidate the position which we shall have won in other fields.

The Residual Problem of Aid from the United States

44. The adoption of the above recommendations would very greatly reduce the size of the uncovered balance. But inevitably there will remain a substantial sum for which we must look to the United States. There is no sufficient reason to

doubt that the Americans will, on terms, give us all the accommodation we may require. That is what both the present Administration and the New York bankers are contemplating. Indeed, they are likely to offer us considerably more than it will be wise for us to accept. It is not the *quantity* of the accommodation about which we need worry. It is the *terms* and the consequences of losing our financial independence which should deeply concern us. There are three reasons why we must reduce our requirements for American aid to the least possible—say, to $2 to $3 billion (£500–£750 million); and even be prepared, if the worst befalls, to do without it altogether.

45. In the first place, we shall never reach financial equilibrium with the outside world except under heavy pressure. If money is too easy to come by in the early stages, we shall acquire habits which it will be beyond our capacity to maintain, and which must lead to an eventual general default to our overseas creditors, with all the loss of prestige and authority which that will involve.

46. We must not engage ourselves beyond our reasonable capacity to pay, conservatively estimated. From this point of view $2 to $3 billion may be fully high, even if the terms of repayment are as easy as those suggested below.

47. Any accommodation we accept from the United States must be on our terms, not theirs. Recent discussion in the United States and evidence given before Congress make it quite clear that there are quarters in the United States intending to use the grant of post-war credits to us as an opportunity for imposing (entirely, of course, for our good) the American conception of the international economic system. It is not as generally recognised in Whitehall as it should be, that the Article VII conversations, if carried to a successful conclusion with all the safeguards on which we should insist, may become our sheet-anchor of safety. In recent evidence before Congress, the views were expressed

(and sympathetically received) that the conditions of financial assistance to Great Britain should include the abolition of Imperial Preference, the linking of sterling to the dollar (thus, as it was said in the hearing, defeating Lord Keynes's efforts to prevent by a monetary plan any effective return to gold), and the abolition of exchange controls preventing purchase of American exports. Not all of this need be taken too seriously. But three conditions are, undoubtedly, in view and would probably commend themselves to Congress and to American opinion generally as being just and reasonable. The first is the linking of sterling to the dollar, which every American banker puts in the forefront. The second is the freeing of some part at least of the sterling area balances in London for the purchase of American exports, thus canalising debts, which we now owe to our normal customers and which are only payable in terms of our exports, into a debt payable in gold to a country which does not buy our goods on any scale. The third, which is vaguer, might relate to the form of the assistance, which would not be in the shape of free cash but would, though repayable in cash, be on the model of lend lease and require us to take American produce on a scale and at prices which would not suit us.

48. The Americans also probably contemplate, at present, an interest rate of 2 to 2½ per cent as well as the repayment of the capital sum by annual instalments. A substantial loan (say, $5 or 6 billion) on such terms would involve us in a liability greater than we can, with any confidence, expect to discharge. It may be, however, that even a serious doubt about our capacity to pay would not trouble the Americans unduly. They want to get their stuff out somehow, and our obligation is better than most. They would not be unduly reluctant to accept the risk of our falling into the humilating position of bankruptcy and having to come back to them for mercy later on.

49. In the negotiations with the United States we must,

therefore, regard one principle as absolute. We will not borrow dollars on our own credit in order to allow sterling area countries (other than the Crown Colonies) to buy United States exports out of their sterling balances. Any accommodation which is found for them must be on their own credit. This principle is of first-class importance because, as we have seen, there will be great pressure on us to abandon it. The United States Treasury will be very jealous of the benefit to British exports if it is British exports, and British exports alone, which can be purchased out of the sterling balances. They will be quite happy to canalise a proportion of our present debt to the sterling area into a debt to themselves. We can predict with some confidence that their offer will in fact be along these lines. For example, they may offer us $5 billion on easy terms, provided we devote (say) $2 to 3 billion of this to turning abnormal sterling area balances into dollars. Sometimes it appears to us (perhaps unjustly) that the United States Treasury would prefer us to end the war with exiguous gold and dollar reserves so that they will be in a position to force this solution on us. Moreover, this plan would obviously suit other members of the area, who would be organised to put pressure on us to accept it.

50. In view of all this, what form and measure of assistance should we aim at? Clearly we should seek to obtain as much as possible on lend lease terms—in other words, as a contribution to the costs of the war. This would have to be under new legislation. But if the United States Administration *wished* to help us (and others) on these lines, all sorts of formulae of justification could be worked out. The ideal arrangement would be (say) $1 or 2 billion in goods on lend lease terms and $1 or 2 billion in cash repayable. But whether the cash accommodation is $1 or 3 billion, it must be without interest, at any rate until we can see our way clearly to repay. For example, assistance might take the form of an advance without interest fixed for ten years, at the end of which term

the conditions of repayment would be considered, and mutually agreed in the light of our capacity at that time to discharge it out of our exports.

51. Rather than accept terms we think unsuitable or beyond our power to satisfy, we should decline assistance altogether. This is hard doctrine. It might mean a postponement of much that the public is being led to expect. But if we take thought for our ultimate strength and independence, it will be greatly worthwhile. Moreover, if we are genuinely prepared to take this course, we shall, in all probability, get what we want. For one thing, when the world knows the whole story, our case is just. There is no reason why we alone should emerge with vast war debts to our Allies. We must declare unequivocally that the limits within which we will accept this position are narrowly defined and will be defined by ourselves. For another thing the Americans, rightly approached and frankly handled are a generous people. Above all, perhaps, the advantage is not all on our side. If we refuse to accept financial assistance from the United States, it will cause nearly as much embarrassment to them as to us.

Conclusion

52. Our own habits are the greatest obstacle in the way of carrying out almost every one of the above recommendations. All our reflex actions are those of a rich man, so that we promise others too much. Our longings for relaxation from the war are so intense that we promise ourselves too much. As a proud and great Power, we disdain to chaffer with others smaller and more exorbitant than ourselves. Having been so recently in dire extremity, our financial diplomacy is rooted in appeasement. Above all, the financial problems of the war have been surmounted so easily and so silently that the average man sees no reason to suppose that the financial problems of the peace will be any more difficult. The Supply

Departments have demanded of the Treasury that money should be no object. And the Treasury has so contrived that it has been no object. This success is the greatest obstacle of all to getting the problems of this memorandum taken seriously. And when we come to exports, no one ever seems to suppose that we need expect to be paid cash for them in full—exports for relief purposes, exports on credit, exports for prestige and propaganda, exports below world price so as to gain satisfied customers five years hence; never exports so that we can live.

53. Our final conclusion concerning the scale of residual assistance required from the United States is, unfortunately, based on the assumption that the preceding recommendations have been substantially (and successfully) acted upon. If they are largely rejected, the best alternative (and one which it is ill-omened to mention, since it is so likely to be adopted) is to borrow all we can from the United States on any terms available, and in due course shuffle out. The Americans, as we have mentioned above, may positively tempt us to this course. No comfort, therefore, unless it be from the following story. In 1755 Lord Chesterfield, under the influence of gout, wrote from Bath to Mr Dowdeswell, the Chancellor of the Exchequer in that time of war, that Lord Orford (Sir Robert Walpole) 'who was as sanguine as anybody, used always to say that whenever the National Debt should amount to 100 millions, the whole would be over and the game up. And this will certainly be the case should this war last four years longer'; to whom the Chancellor replied that he knew no answer to His Lordship's argument, but that he had great faith in the *dictum* of Voltaire that 'the probable very seldom occurs'.

12 June 1944

In the course of the period of discussion of Keynes's memorandum, the Bank of England on 7 July put forward its proposals for the handling of sterling balances during the transitional period. Under these proposals, members of the sterling area would agree not to reduce their total sterling balances below the level existing at the time of their making the agreement by more than an annually determined sum. On this basis, sterling area countries could use current foreign exchange earnings, plus the annual amount of past balances released, for expenditure anywhere in the world. This arrangement would be accompanied by anti-inflationary policies in the countries concerned, a high degree of U.K. import and exchange control and the freezing of the asset distribution of sterling balances. On reading these proposals, after Bretton Woods, Keynes minuted.

To SIR DAVID WALEY *and* SIR RICHARD HOPKINS, *13 August 1944*

I have only now found time to study the Bank of England note entitled 'Sterling Balances and Transitional Arrangements' dated 7 July, which Waley sent to Eady some time ago with a copy of his, Waley's, covering note to Sir R. Hopkins.

In substance the Bank's proposal is the same as that which they produced about six months ago and was fully discussed in Sir R. Hopkins' room with the Deputy Governor and Mr Cobbold. We then produced arguments which we thought had shaken them. They now come back, however, without any reference to those arguments, or any attempt to meet them. Alas, one might as well speak to stone walls.

The banking advantage of the proposals is obvious, and one might therefore sympathise with it if there were any chance of our resources running to it, though even if they did, it would, I think, have to be in a different form, which would need still more resources to implement. This banking advantage flows from the proposal making it a matter of indifference to other members of the sterling area whether they earn sterling or whether they earn dollars.

The balancing objection to this is, of course, that correspondingly it makes no difference to them whether they spend sterling or spend dollars, which is precisely the opposite of what we wish to enforce. Having carefully provided that it makes no difference to them which they spend, the Bank would then fall back on a gentleman's agreement with them that they should not act accordingly. Even if one could rely on this, would it not from their standpoint largely undo the advantage aimed at?

There is, however, a much more fundamental objection namely, that the proposal sacrifices both the country's solvency and the country's trade to the supposed interests and the prestige of sterling, which in fact can, of course, only be served by preserving solvency and expanding trade.

It would sacrifice solvency because it would mean that we almost necessarily owe the whole of our total adverse balance of payments to the dollar countries instead of this being much more widely distributed; and indeed more than the whole of it if, as is proposed, we were to allow an annual ration of free exchange.

It would sacrifice trade for the reason already mentioned, namely, that there would no longer be any inducement, as S.D.W[aley] points out, to buy sterling goods.

There is, however, a still more fundamental objection to the present version of this scheme to which no allusion is made in the memorandum. If the text is read literally, sterling area countries will not be allowed to use their sterling balances even to make payments in the sterling area if this would have the effect of reducing their balances below their zero hour figure minus their free ration. Thus it would involve setting up exchange control in the sterling area and would operate as an actual deterrent to countries reducing our indebtedness to them by taking our goods.

Moreover, this objection is not accidental, but is part of the essence of the proposal. For if this condition was waived, which at first sight might be plausible, so that a sterling area country could use any part of its sterling balances for use in the sterling area, then, corresponding to the reduction in one country's sterling balances, there would be an increase in the balances of another member of the area, which under the formula would at once become available to the second member for expenditure in dollars or elsewhere outside the sterling area, since it would make this expenditure without reducing its own balances below their zero hour figure. Thus whenever one member of the area sold goods to another member of the sterling area against their existing sterling balances this would have the effect of creating an equal dollar liability to some other member of the area; whilst if one member of the area bought from us and we bought an equal amount from another member of the area, this triangular trade would also involve us in an equal dollar liability.

I daresay you have concluded before now that the Bank's suggestion is not worth pursuing. But I should like in conclusion to draw attention to one feature of my proposal which is highly attractive to other members of the sterling area but which is not, I think, always appreciated.

This is the feature by which in the early part of Stage III exchange arrangements remain precisely as at present so that any member of the sterling area can use any part of its sterling balances without restriction to make payments elsewhere in the sterling area. They would merely be rationed in dollars and other outside currencies. This makes sterling very much more attractive and available than the Bank's proposal. During Stage III, however, before we should feel strong enough to accept convertibility, we should in fact have had to persuade other members of the area to fund in some appropriate way a large part of these floating balances. Nevertheless, subject to the eventual necessity of this, at no time or in principle would any part of the sterling balances which were not so funded cease to be available for expenditure within the sterling area. I therefore claim that the general basis of my plan is much more attractive to other members of the area than the Bank's plan. For the Bank's plan, apart from the free ration which we should almost certainly not be able to afford, completely blocks the whole of the zero hour sterling balances of a member of the area, and strictly limits the Stage III expenditure of each one of them to the amount of its current income, plus its ration, if any.

The Bank's plan cannot be regarded as a variant of mine but strikes at the roots of mine because it departs radically from the idea that we tie repayment of our war debts to our own exports.

[copy initialled] K

13 August 1944

While Keynes was at Bretton Woods, he of course kept up his interest in the progress of planning for Stage II. At the end of the Conference, before going on to Ottawa for discussions on the extent of assistance from Canada under mutual aid, he wrote to the Chancellor.

From a letter to SIR JOHN ANDERSON,[10] *21 July 1944*

Ronald is flying back to London this evening. I am therefore taking this opportunity to send you a few reflections more easily written in a letter than cabled. I am writing after two discussions with Law,[11] both before and after his conversations with Stettinius and Hull. And also in the light of the telegrams he has exchanged with London.

When we came here your idea was, I think, that we should take advantage of the presence in Bretton Woods of many of the high-up Americans who are concerned with our own problems to begin a bit of an educational campaign to en-

[10] John Anderson (1882–1958), K.C.B. 1919, 1st Viscount Waverley, 1952; entered Colonial Office, 1905; Secretary, Ministry of Shipping, 1917–19; Chairman, Board of Inland Revenue, 1919–22; Permanent Under-Secretary of State, Home Office, 1922–32; Governor of Bengal, 1932–7; M.P. (Nat.C.) for Scottish Universities, 1938–50; Lord Privy Seal, 1938–9; Home Secretary and Minister of Home Security, 1939–40; Lord President of the Council, 1940–3; Chancellor of the Exchequer, 1943–5.
[11] Mr Law had been in America for preliminary discussions concerning Stage II and other lend lease matters. For the remaining material on Bretton Woods see *JMK*, vol. XXVI.

lighten them about the realities of our position. In fact we have done nothing of the kind. In the first week Acheson and I tried to find spare time for a private talk, but the pressure of affairs here always made it impossible. I soon saw that it was not only physically impossible, but in fact inadvisable, since one could never have got their undivided or concentrated attention for any subject outside this Conference. In spite therefore of our being in daily and almost hourly contact with several of those with whom we had intended to talk, not even the smallest beginning has in fact been made.

In the light of subsequent developments I fancy that this may have been very fortunate. For with the prospect of your coming at an early date, and after judging the general atmosphere here, I am now inclined to think quite decidedly that the programme of infiltration which we were contemplating before we left London will be nothing like as good as a shock attack by yourself, provided always that the latter can be delivered pretty soon.

My best up-to-date view is therefore as follows:–

1. We shall be leaving here on July 23rd for Ottawa, taking a few days for some rest to recuperate from our excessive exertions before we start conversations with the Canadians. (Malcolm Macdonald[12] is sending his car for my wife and myself and we shall travel slowly; Eady visits his brother at Cornell; Brand pays a short visit to his office in Washington.) We shall be ready to leave Ottawa in the first week of August and can, of course, easily spend there a day or two more or less according as to how best suits the rest of the programme. I could also spend a short time in New York usefully and agreeably, getting the atmosphere there and talking to the groups with whom I have contacts and which are largely apart from the people we have been seeing here. In any case, it

[12] Malcolm John Macdonald (b. 1901); Labour M.P. for Ross, 1929–45; Secretary of State for Colonies, 1935, 1938–40; Minister of Health, 1940–41; U.K. High Commissioner in Canada, 1941–6.

would be desirable that we should reach Washington a few days before you do. But I do not think that there ought to be any considerable gap between our arrival and yours. That means that we shall be ready for you August 10th at latest and a little earlier if necessary; and the sooner the better. For reasons indicated below, it is, I think, some time between August 10th and August 30th that your operations will have to be conducted if they are to have the maximum effect.

2. The movements of the President are somewhat veiled in mystery. You will know more about them than I do. But if I understand rightly, it is between the dates I have named above that he is most likely to be available. Unless you can finish in the course of August serious delays may be involved, and the only lull when our financial matters can receive patient consideration may have passed by. I understand that Hull and Stettinius and most other people who matter will be more or less continuously available in Washington during August. Morgenthau, for reasons mentioned in my telegram to you, will not be back in Washington before the second half of the month. But it might in fact be quite convenient that you should begin operations before his return. For that would allow you, after seeing the President, to start in with Hull and Stettinius, taking up matters with Morgenthau a little later on without any discourtesy to the latter since he will not have been there to talk to.

3. The month of August is also rather essential because it is during that same lull that the policy of the American Administration in its relation to Stage II will be crystallising. The Export White Paper, the status of lend lease during Stage II, and the programme of the Ministry of Production cannot be delayed many days beyond the end of August.

4. Some communication from the Prime Minister to the President, by whatever means offers the most convenient opportunity, would, everybody agrees, be the right way to start the ball rolling. In this case, on your arrival here you

would be able to start off with the White House, putting our position before the President in a general way and asking him to instruct his leading appropriate officials to sit down with you and go into the matter in the fullest possible detail, we being prepared on our side to put on the table everything we know. You could then aim at sitting round the table, if possible several days in succession, with whose whom the President might designate. On the first day you could explain the bare facts of our position. No doubt a good deal is already known about this by some of the American technicians and of course Stettinius has been given an inkling. Nevertheless, I fancy that you could put this side of the matter in a way which would strike the Americans profoundly. Moreover, it will produce a more formidable effect if there has been no preliminary discussion. I am, therefore, no longer in favour of Eady, Brand and myself making a beginning of the educational campaign before you arrive. On the second day you could elaborate our own ideas of general policy for Stage II and afterwards. (On the production side it is easy to make a fairly clear distinction between Stage I and Stage II. But on the financial front the set-up we require in Stage II is essentially determined by what we shall need in Stage III, so that the argument must necessarily embrace both periods.) The second day could also be occupied by the thesis that it is to the general interest that we should not be forced into a down-and-out position by the end of Stage II, and that it is greatly in the interests of both countries that a way of preventing this should be found. On the assumption that the Americans are brought round more or less to this view, which should not, I think, be too difficult, the third day could be devoted to a general discussion of the ways in which they could help us once they are persuaded that it is their interest that they should do so. You could put forward some of our own suggestions, but naturally the choice between these and other alternatives is essentially for them, according to what they judge to be practically feasible and politically acceptable in their own conditions. My distinction between these three days is, of course, highly artificial. In fact the discussion could not be prevented from ranging over all three phases at each meeting. But that might not interfere too much with a general intention to guide and deploy the argument on the above lines. After the conversation had made as much progress as seemed possible, then unquestionably another interview with the President would be called for. I am in favour of making the action as continuous as possible. People in this country so easily lose interest and a subject which begins by being exciting turns stale in no time. It is very far from easy to engage their continuous attention, and that in the past has always been one of our greatest handicaps. But you, I think, might be in a position to get that continuous attention, and in that event the greater the momentum that the discussions can attain the better.

5. After some progress had been made with the people in this country corresponding to Ministers, then more or less simultaneously the rest of us can undoubtedly begin useful conversations and an educational campaign in the ranks of the officials who will be actually carrying out policies and will, of course, largely determine their details and advise those higher up what is possible. The point is that I no longer believe that this is the right place in which to start. The initial impulse must come from the White House, and we must not waste our ammunition prematurely in mere skirmishing.

6. None of us here see any reason, in the light of the local atmosphere, to modify in any respect the main lines of strategy which we were discussing before we left London. That does not mean that you will not be faced with great difficulties. Nevertheless, the existing plan still seems the soundest open to us to pursue. Indeed, on one aspect I am now expecting less difficulty than I did previously, namely, the proposed blocking of post-war sterling balances in favour

of our own exports. Wide circles in America are beginning to appreciate quite clearly that we can only meet our war debts out of our own exports. And they will feel it up to them not to attempt to frustrate this, even though they may not like it. I am sure that the right approach is that we seek no assistance for clearing up the past, which we shall do as best we can out of our own resources. The help we want is solely related to our future current expenses, which should and must be regarded as a sequel of war expenditure proper and necessarily handled in the same spirit of mutual aid, whatever particular technique it may be most convenient to employ for the purpose henceforward.

You should appreciate that you will be coming into an atmosphere of the greatest possible friendliness and good will. The Americans are inclined to be intolerably tiresome in method and in detail and with the execution of plans and in the mode of pressure they bring to bear. For these reasons one simply cannot help, in London, forming rather a false picture of the real emotional background. In none of my visits to this country have I felt it more strongly than on this occasion. One can and should approach them as a band of friends and brothers. They have their own difficult psychology and a dreadful tendency to suspicion and all the rest of it. But underneath, what I have just said is the real truth.

I fancy also that they are becoming increasingly aware that of all their associates we, and only we, are inspired, as they also genuinely are, with some measure of altruistic motive, and are prepared to sacrifice something for a better order in the world. When they are convinced of that, and in so far as they can feel confident that, when we are acting in our own special interests, we do so without concealment and only after their approval has been won over in favour of our being allowed to grind whatever axe we are grinding, then there is almost nothing they will not do for us.

All this applies not least to Congressmen, irrespective of

party. That is certainly one of the things one has been able to learn up here, and it is something of a revelation.

All the above is on the assumption that you can make your visit round about the date suggested. If not, then something quite different has to be worked out. I am sure that no other Ministerial representative can conceivably take your place, and that only you can hope to produce the necessary effect and attain the necessary results. If, therefore, you are not coming, we should have to return to something more like our original programme, namely, infiltration. The main plot cannot possibly wait beyond the end of August. But as I have said, I am more and more convinced that infiltration is a bad second best. So do please come.

Keynes's journey to Ottawa in August 1944 arose from problems that had arisen over the 1944–5 mutual aid appropriation announced in March 1944. At that time the anticipated sterling area deficit with Canada for 1944–5 was $1,475 million, while the appropriation came to $450 million. While London began planning a possible diversion of orders from Canada so as to reduce the deficit, discussions began at Bretton Woods to ease the position. When those did not leave the position on a more satisfactory basis Keynes and Sir Wilfrid Eady went to Ottawa to exercise their persuasive powers—and also to prepare the ground for the Stage II discussions.

In the course of the talks which followed, the delegation handed several documents over to the Canadians. Of particular interest was a revised version of Keynes's June Cabinet paper. A covering note to the Chancellor outlined the changes.

To T. PADMORE, *7 August 1944*

This is the final version of the paper which we have handed in to the Canadians giving them the statistical background of our financial situation, from which I have spoken at various meetings.

This is very similar to earlier versions which I sent to London. But we have tried in this final version to get rid of any phrases or sentences which would be unsuitable for rather wider circulation. The Chancellor may like to look through a copy, since with a few changes this might well form the basis of anything used in Washington. The statistical basis is a good deal wider than in the Cabinet paper, particularly by the inclusion of sections relating to mutual aid, the loss of capital assets and the reduction of consumption. The details relating to the growth of our balances are also a good deal fuller.

I am sending separate copies to Sir R. Hopkins and Sir D. Waley.

KEYNES

7 August 1944

STATISTICS BEARING ON THE DIMENSIONS OF THE UNITED KINGDOM'S PROBLEM OF EXTERNAL FINANCE IN THE TRANSITION

1. It is generally recognised that the problem of British external finance after the war will be greatly aggravated compared with 1919, because (1) the absolute amount of our overseas indebtedness is much greater, (2) the loss of our foreign investments available as a reserve is more complete, and (3) the current adverse balance of overseas trade which we shall have to meet by an increase of our exports is much larger.

2. It is not so generally recognised that, in addition, two considerable mitigations which were present last time will be absent. The policy of restraining the rise of prices has many advantages, but it will greatly increase the real burden of indebtedness as fixed in terms of money. The other outstanding difference is that last time we borrowed money from the United States which we used to meet our requirements in all parts of the world, so that we ended the war without abnormal indebtedness to any other country; whereas this time the United States has only aided us with goods she could

76

Total expenditure	£ million		Total of receipts	£ million	
I. Expenditure not met out of L/L and M/A			I. Receipts outside L/L and M/A		
General imports	590		General exports	300	
Overseas war expenditure on munitions and U.K. forces abroad	750		Earnings from Dominion contributions to war expenditure and American forces in U.K.	280	
Other 'invisible' payments	250		Other 'invisible' income	360	
	——	1,590	Net overseas indebtedness and loss of assets	650	
				——	1,590
II. Expenditure met out of L/L and M/A					
General imports	560		L/L and M/A received	1,710	
Munitions and ships	1,150		Less M/A accorded	500	
				1,210	
			M/A accorded by U.K.	500	
	1,710			——	1,710
	——				——
	3,300				3,300

herself supply and has not furnished us with cash to buy goods from elsewhere. Thus, nearly the whole of our 1914–18 external debt was canalised into the American debt—and that we shuffled out of. On the assumption that this time we intend to pay, the fact that we owe money all over the place has, as we shall see, some important offsetting advantages to our export trade. But it means that the effort required to emerge without loss of honour, dignity and credit will be immensely greater.

3. The Government's post-war domestic policy is based on the assumption that we shall be able to import all the raw

materials and foodstuffs necessary to provide full employment and maintain (or improve) the standard of life. This assumption is, at present, an act of blind faith. No means of making it good has yet been found. The object of this memorandum is to analyse the dimensions of the problem, reserving, for the moment, the means of solution.

4. So long as lend lease and Canadian mutual aid continue, the true situation is masked. The following [above, p. 77] is an approximate balance-sheet of the British overseas position in 1943.

5. This table can be re-arranged as follows:–

I. General imports	1,150		I. General exports	300	
'Invisible'			'Invisible'		
payments	250		income	360	
		1,400			660
II. Overseas war			II. Receipts for		
expenditure on			war expenditure		
munitions etc.			on behalf of		
and U.K. forces			Dominions and		
abroad		1,900	U.S.	280	
			Mutual aid		
			accorded to		
			Allies	500	
			L/L and M/A		
			received less		
			M/A accorded	1,210	
					1,990
			III. Net deficit	650	
		3,300			3,300

If all military expenditure were to cease tomorrow the imports of food and raw materials which we should require, whilst to some extent changed in character, would not be reduced in amount, since there will be more, not fewer, men in the country to consume food and to be employed in working up raw materials. Provisional estimates which have been made indicate that at the prices of 1943 that year's figure of £1,150 million for our imports would not be much below our import requirements in the first post-war year. Thus if overseas war expenditure and receipts, and lend lease, and mutual aid given and received were to cease immediately, the absolute amount of the net overseas deficit on current account would be actually greater than it is now by about £90 million a year, or say £750 million a year, unless and until it can be covered by increased exports and increased 'invisible' income from shipping, etc. Indeed, it is clear that there will be no time-lag in our import needs, except to the limited extent to which we can live on stock-piles, surplus stores and salvage. Perhaps the aggregate amount of the once-for-all relief from this source might be guessed at £300 to £400 million, but our stocks are so ill balanced that the enjoyment of this relief would have to be spread over a period. More accurate statistics bearing on this are expected from the Ministries of Supply and Food. On the other hand, there will be a considerable time-lag in the development of exports to fill the gap and a still longer lag in the date of payment for them. Even if the export deficit can be made to taper off over a fairly short period of years, the accumulated excess of imports over exports, before equilibrium is reached, will be very large. If we were to increase our overseas income, visible and invisible, by £250 million in the first year, by a further £200 million in the second year, by a further £150 million in the third year, and by a further £150 million in the fourth year, thus reaching equilibrium on current account in the fourth year, which would be a tremendous and, probably, impossible task, the cumulative deficit would nevertheless amount to £1,000 million in the first three years. At any rate, it is clear that this rate of progress is altogether out of the question, unless immediate active preparation is made for the recovery of export markets.

6. So far it has been argued that all overseas war expenditure will cease forthwith at the end of the war. In fact this will not be the case. For reasons both of security and of transport the demobilisation and repatriation of troops will necessarily be spread over a considerable period; and meanwhile heavy expenses will continue to be incurred overseas.

It is also believed that the British forces will be asked to accept a major responsibility for the occupation of enemy territory after the end of hostilities. Our cash expenditures abroad on military account, which amounted in 1943 to about £750 million a year, will not suddenly sink to zero when the war comes to an end. At present we can make no reasoned guess as to the rate at which or the period over which such expenditure will continue. Further, on the basis of our present policy (which has been entered upon more or less regardless whether we can afford it), relief and reconstruction abroad will be another large source of expense. To begin with, there is our contribution of £80 million to UNRRA. This does not (at present) include our share of the cost of relief to enemy countries or of relief during the military period elsewhere. The possibility of contributions to the projected Bank for Reconstruction and Development must also be taken into account. Finally, it is strongly argued in some quarters (and with considerable force) that there are important markets in which we shall not get a footing for our exports unless in the early years we are prepared to furnish a considerable volume of goods on credit. What the cumulative total of all this is likely to be in the early period, it is very difficult to guess. Would anyone care to put it at less than £500 million net in the first three years after the war, unless there is a considerable change in the present trend of policies?

7. The above makes no provision for the liquidation of overseas war indebtedness largely in the shape of demand-balances accumulated in London, which at present can be drawn upon with varying degrees of freedom. Finally, therefore, there is the question of the lowest rate at which we must allow these balances to be repaid and drawn upon, if we are to maintain our honour and credit. The largest elements in the total indebtedness, as for example, to India, are not, in this connection so dangerous in proportion to their amount as the smaller sums which we owe to a great variety of smaller creditors. Once we owe (say) £500 million to India, which is

far greater than we can possibly discharge in the early period, a further increase to £1,000 million does not really affect the dimensions of the early-period problem. Thus we have to regard the composition of the debt as well as its aggregate. In particular there are certain claims against us to which we shall have to accord a high priority. The Crown Colonies have lent to us the whole of their currency reserves. The populations of these countries are full of money and starved of goods. Can we by blocking the reserves held against the money, compel them to remain in this position for an indefinite period? We also hold the greater part, or the whole, of the currency reserves of Ireland, India, Egypt and Palestine.

8. Apart from the larger creditors and excluding certain less liquid liabilities, the following smaller and more dependent or necessitous countries held sterling resources in London at the end of March 1944 as follows:–

	£ million	
West African Colonies	76	
East African Colonies	72	
Other British Africa		
(excluding South Africa)	34	
Ceylon	39	
Malaya	95	
Hong Kong	32	
British West Indies	54	
Palestine	93	
Other Colonies and Mandates	79	
	—	574
Iraq	64	
Netherlands and Colonies	53	
Belgium and Colonies	17	
Free France and Colonies and		
French blocked balances	64	
Norway	43	
Greece	59	
Iceland	9	
China	21	
Persia	15	
	—	345
		919

9. There are, in addition, the following liabilities of more varying degrees of urgency:–

(*a*) the balances in the major sterling area countries whose currency reserves we hold—

	£ million
India	797
Egypt	297
Eire	93

(*b*) the balances of the sterling area Dominions—

	£ million
Australia	77
New Zealand	22
South Africa	24

(*c*) the secured loans, etc., from the United States and Canada—

	£ million
United States	79
Canada	162

and (*d*) the special account balances owing to South America and neutral Europe—

	£ million
Argentina	52
Brazil	23
Other South and Central America	12
Portugal (a gold liability)	62
Other neutral Europe	16

10. The grand aggregate, as at the end of March, 1944, stood at £2,670 million. By the end of 1944 the figure will exceed £3,000 million. Admittedly a considerable proportion of this, say, a half or even two-thirds, can be funded, or represents normal working balances and currency reserves which will be maintained and therefore, constitute no immediate danger. (Nevertheless even this half will add consider-

ably to our future burden if any significant amount of interest is payable on it.) It is the remaining one-third to one-half, i.e., £1,000 to £1,300 million as at the end of 1944, which is dangerous, because it represents entirely abnormal accumulations which the countries concerned will certainly seek to withdraw at the earliest opportunity. Unless, therefore, steps are taken to the contrary, it would be prudent to assume that during the transitional period as a whole attempts will be made to utilise at least £500 million, either in the shape of British exports or by demanding foreign currency in exchange.

11. As matters now stand and before reckoning any relief from the application of the various remedial measures open to us, we are left, therefore, with the following prospective deficit during the transitional period of (say) the first three years after the war.

	£ million
Excess of normal imports over exports (visible and invisible)	1,000
Overseas cash expenditure arising out of the war (i.e. liquidation of war expenses and demobilisation in overseas theatres, costs of occupation, relief, reconstruction loans, export credits, etc.)	500
Repayment of abnormal sterling balances	500
Total deficit	2,000

Nor is there any certainty that equilibrium will have been reached at the end of the three years. There is no need to stress the extreme precariousness of all the above estimates.

12. Nevertheless there are certain important reliefs from the above which it lies within our own power to make and which certainly will have to be applied in greater or less degree. In the first place it is evident that the scale of repayment of abnormal sterling balances, which we should probably be called upon to make if we put no special obstacles

in the way, estimated above at £500 million in the first three years, can, if necessary, be avoided. Some repayments will be unavoidable, but it may be possible largely to offset these by a further growth of balances in other directions. Thus, to take an optimistic view, a *net* repayment of the aggregate of these balances might be avoided altogether in the first three years.

13. In the second place, as mentioned above, there are certain abnormal stocks of commodities which can be drawn upon gradually. Unfortunately in terms of value far the greater part of these stocks consist of wool, which can only be liquidated over a much longer period than three years if the current clip is also to be properly looked after.

14. In the third place, the above estimate of import requirements is based on a normal scale of importation of manufactured and semi-manufactured goods as well as of food and raw materials. If necessary—and probably it will be necessary—whole classes of manufactured imports will have to be totally excluded during the transitional period.

15. By these various means the total deficit to be cared for might be brought down to (say) £1,250 million; and even less, if very stringent rationing of domestic consumption, continues to be enforced in certain directions, i.e. where consumption is at the cost of imports or loss of exports.

16. The weakness in this calculation lies in the assumption of so rapid and so large a recovery of exports within three years. The Board of Trade do not at present see their way to confirm the above estimates as being reasonably possible. Such as expansion will certainly be impossible unless the American Administration can be persuaded to regard an unfettered British export drive, beginning in 1945, as compatible with the continuance of lend lease or equivalent aid. In this respect, what is political play to them is a matter of life or death to us.

17. Apart from these special difficulties which we shall hope to overcome, it is essential that our degree of demobilisation

during Stage II must be sufficient, not only to allow the beginning of a return to more normal civilian standards, but also to provide an appreciable surplus for export. We have been fighting two years longer than the United States on a scale far more exhausting in relation to our resources, and we ought not to be asked to sustain much longer a proportionate effort so much greater measured in terms of sacrifice.

18. *The gold and dollar balances of the U.K.* A year before the outbreak of war our reserves were very substantial and stood at £1,043 million. The expectation of war led to a large-scale withdrawal of foreign balances, and at the outbreak of war we were reduced to £620 million. At the commencement of lend lease (April 1941) we were practically cleaned out, having gold and dollar reserves of £66 million with £63 million gold liabilities against them, so that our net reserves were down to £3 million. Thereafter came the Jesse Jones loan; the old (pre-lend lease) commitments had been substantially met; almost all our current requirements from United States were for a time lent leased; and the sterling area was beginning to gain substantial earnings from the United States troops; with the result that our reserves began to rise quite steadily. They are likely to reach a peak between £400 and £500 million before the end of 1944. Unfortunately, a livelier awareness by the United States Administration of this recovery in our reserves than of the much greater depletion of our net resources has led to a substantial curtailment of lend lease facilities, and at the same time a reduction of our earning power corresponding to the increase in reverse mutual aid, with the result that we are now mainly dependent on our precarious earnings from the United States troops in the sterling area to prevent our reserves from falling. When the war in Europe is over, our dollar account may be seriously on the wrong side, i.e. our reserves will begin to fall, even if lend lease continues as at present; whereas we have recently been warned that after the end of the German war the

continuance of lend lease facilities on the present scale must be deemed uncertain. Thus, as matters now stand, we shall be likely to emerge from the Japanese war with reserves materially less than the £500 million for which, at one time, we were hoping. Since reserves of about £300 million probably represent somewhere near the bed-rock figure below which we should not allow our reserves to fall except for the gravest cause and in extreme urgency, it follows that, unless there is a change in the situation, the relief we can obtain by drawing on our reserves in the transitional period is so small in relation to our possible requirements that it is hardly worth bringing into the picture.

19. Fuller statistics of the gold and dollar reserves in relation to our liabilities are given below:–

	31 Aug. 1938	31 Dec. 1939	31 Dec. 1941	31 Dec. 1942	31 Dec. 1943	30 June 1944
	($ million)					
	Reserves					
Gross gold and dollar reserves	4,365	2,335	500	930	1,722	2,171
Less gold and dollar liabilities	—	—	115	240	422	557*
Net reserves	4,365	2,335	385	690	1,300	1,614*
	Liabilities					
Quick liabilities (banking liabilities and liabilities of Crown Agents and Currency Boards)	3,143	2,000	4,585	5,805	9,750†	11,300*
Overseas loans	—	—	460	1,235	—	—

* Not yet available but estimated as above.
† Overseas loans not materially changed.

20. The increase in reserves in 1942 and 1943 was not the result of our receiving lend lease assistance on such a scale that our normal current earnings of dollars exceeded our requirements. The normal dollar earnings of the U.K. fell

short of our own dollar requirements by $287 million in 1942 and by $240 million in 1943; and our total dollar earnings, including pay of U.S. troops in U.K., fell short by $237 million in 1942 and $50 million in 1943.

The sources from which we obtained the increase in our reserves were as follows:–

	1942	1943
	$ million	
U.K. current a/c with U.S.	−287	−240
U.S. troops in U.K.	50	190
Rest of sterling area		
current a/c with U.S.	119	150
U.S. troops in rest of sterling area	194	365
Gold from South Africa for repatriation		
of South African sterling securities	15	167
Other gold and dollar movements (net)	214	−28
	305	604

Of the above items on the credit side, $828 million represent dollars acquired from the rest of the sterling area, which has involved a corresponding increase in our liabilities, and $182 million represent gold provided for the repatriation of South African sterling securities, which represents no increase in our assets.

21. A major improvement in our reserve position can only be achieved if the American Administration can be persuaded that it is as much in their interest as in ours to facilitate the growth of our reserves up to a level more commensurate with our responsibilities. As we approach the war settlement, it will not be convenient to either party that we should always have to plead *in forma pauperis* to be excused from full participation. It may prove politically difficult for the United States Administration to furnish us at a later stage with cash dollars, as distinct from assistance in kind, even though they may wish to do so; yet for many purposes it will be cash that we shall

need. It will be a cause of general embarrassment if one of the three Great Powers responsible for settling the world has no free cash at all. The seriousness of this prospect is not as yet fully realised by those who will be most hampered by it if it arises. On the assumption that we end the Japanese war with net gold and dollar reserves not much above £300 million, not only would the amount be negligible which we could regard as available; but our free resources would be entirely out of proportion to those of our associates. The United States would have sixteen times as much; Russia two to three times; France more than double; Belgium, Holland, Switzerland with comparable absolute amounts and much greater free amounts; and so on. Our position would be ludicrously out of proportion to our responsibilities. We should, therefore, aim at an end-war figure of at least £500 million net and refuse to undertake any post-war liability to Europe or to anyone else until it was assured to us.

22. In the immediately preceding paragraphs, a continuing restriction on imports and on the level of domestic consumption has been indicated as a necessary ingredient in the solution. To understand the difficulty of this, it is necessary to appreciate the severity of the present restrictions and to experience at first hand the measure of cumulative strain and fatigue from which everyone in England is now suffering. So far as consumption is concerned, this is well illustrated by the following comparison worked out on the basis of the material provided in the British Budget White Paper and in the U.S. Survey of Current Business for April 1944 [see p. 89]. This table shows that in real terms the intenser labour effort has been accompanied in U.K. by a reduction of 21 per cent in real consumption, whilst in U.S. it has been accompanied by an increase of 15 per cent. In other words, the war effort has allowed an improvement in the position of the American consumer relatively to that of the British consumer of nearly 50 per cent.

	1939	1940	1941	1942	1943
United Kingdom (1939 = 100)					
Expenditure at current market prices	100	103	109	116	119
Expenditure at constant prices	100	88	82	81	79
Market prices (including indirect taxes)	100	118	133	143	150
United States of America (1939 = 100)					
Expenditure at current market prices	100	106	121	133	147
Expenditure at constant prices	100	105	113	112	115
Market prices	100	101	107	119	129

23. *Mutual aid accorded by U.K.* Mutual aid accorded by U.K. is now running at about one-third of the aggregate mutual aid and lend lease received.

Figures relating to British mutual aid trickle in months after the event and even now the record up to the end of last year remains incomplete. The following table, however, gives almost the whole story to 31 December 1943.

	Goods and services (£ million)				
	Up to 30 June 1943	July/Sept. 1943	Oct/Dec. 1943	Total cumulative through Dec. 1943	Jan/Mar. 1944
U.S.A.	114·0*	30·0	56·0	200·0	65
Russia	179·0	21·6	29·3	229·9	—
China	—	—	—	7·0	—
Czechoslovakia	12·4	1·8	1·7	15·9	—
Greece	7·0	1·4	2·0	10·4	—
Turkey	6·4	6·6	3·5†	16·5	
Portugal	—	8·6	1·0	9·6	
Total	318·8	70·0	93·5	489·7	—

* Smaller by 10 than White Paper figure owing to downward revisions by M.W.T.
† Excludes Air Ministry aid.

In the case of the U.S.A. the above falls considerably short of the grand total up to March 1944 since it excludes the following which have also to be added in: (1) capital expenditure in U.K. afforded as reciprocal aid £155 million; (2) goods and services outside U.K. afforded as reciprocal aid £50 million (particulars of which are received seriously in arrear).

24. Assuming aid in recent months at approximately the same rate, total aid to the U.S. up to 30 June 1944 was not far short of £600 million, and to others about £400 million, making a grand total approaching £1,000 million. Mutual aid to the U.S. on this great scale (which would be still greater if converted to equivalent American costs) has undoubtedly played a major part in creating a political and psychological background in which much else has been made possible. Nevertheless it has been, and is currently, far in excess of the U.K.'s net capacity to supply out of its own resources. The U.K. has had no net current overseas surplus out of which to make this return contribution towards the war expenditure of the U.S. From the balance sheet point of view she has had to borrow it where she could from almost every country in the world and thus incur a greater overseas war debt than would have been incurred otherwise. The balance sheet of international payments in paragraph 4 above shows that at the present time the major part of the overseas war debt, which the U.K. is now incurring, is in order to make the above contribution to the war expenditure of the U.S. This balance sheet aspect of the mutual aid (or reverse lend lease) accorded to the U.S. must not be lost sight of, however necessary and inevitable it may be that, on the one hand, we should have to borrow in all parts of the world to balance our account in order, on the other hand, to keep up good appearances for political reasons in the U.S. It is certainly not an example of the joint pooling of war expenses according to capacity.

25. In the same context as mutual aid, it should be remarked that, apart from specific mutual aid, we have seldom charged the Dominions the full cost which we have incurred on their behalf for that part of the war effort which purports

to be their own. Rather than bargain with those who have done so much for us, we have preferred to give way before any complaint which had any plausible ground behind it, even though it left us, in fact, out of pocket.

26. *The loss of pre-war overseas assets.* The above aggregates of war indebtedness incurred by the U.K. take no account of loss of pre-war overseas assets disposed of during the war in order that the growth of war indebtedness may be correspondingly less. The amount of such disposals was estimated by the Chancellor of the Exchequer in his Budget speech at about £1,000 million. The balance which remains is largely unmarketable and it is not easy to estimate its capital value. A recent attempt, however, has been made to estimate both what has been lost and what still remains on an income basis, as follows:–

Net income from investments abroad (£ million)

1938		1943	
Lord Kindersley's estimates of amounts distributed as interest and dividends to U.K. residents, including income tax thereon. (Lord Kindersley's estimates do not include any income from Eire)	185	Bank of England provisional estimates on a similar basis to Lord Kindersley's, but including Eire 122 less Eire 8 114	
Undistributed profits, U.K. office expenses, etc.; believed to be estimated by Board of Trade at some	30	Undistributed profits, U.K. office expenses, etc., as in 1938; in addition:– E.P.T. and N.D.C. paid by U.K. registered companies; dividends unpaid, or paid to the Custodian. In all, probably some 20-30, say	26
	215		140
Less payments to non-residents on their investments in U.K. (in the case of Eire, a net payment) believed to be estimated by Board of Trade at some	15	say	10
U.K. net income	200		130

27. It would be unwise to capitalize the income for 1938 and for 1943 at the same rate. Dividends on equities are probably now higher than in 1938, and the fall in capital outstanding no doubt somewhat greater than simple comparison of the two incomes would indicate. Nevertheless the broad conclusion seems to be that about one-third has been disposed of or otherwise lost as a result of hostilities. If the pre-war value was round £3,500 million, the remaining value is now round £2,500 million.

28. Against this, we have to reckon with a net indebtedness on short term of £3,000 million as at the end of 1944. The year 1945 might add £500 million to this, and the post-war transition, on the basis of the most optimistic assumptions, will add not less than another £1,000 million. (This calculation neglects both the small excess of reserves over net short term liabilities at the beginning of the war and the unpredictable level of reserves at the end of it.)

29. Thus the U.K. will have begun the war with a net creditor position of (say) £3,500 million and will have ended it with a net debtor position of (say) £2,000 million (i.e. £4,500 million liabilities less £2,500 million assets). Nearly the whole of this loss she will have incurred in favour, not of neutrals but of her own Allies and Associates, as the price of their assistance in the common effort.

30. Now that the concluding stages are, we hope, in sight, weaknesses, which formerly it was necessary to conceal, it is now proper to confess. The object of doing so is to help all those concerned to view the position realistically. The object is not to make complaint. Whether wisely or unwisely, we have waged the war without regard to financial consequences deliberately and of set purpose. For better or for worse, it has been our own fault, as anyone who has spent the war in the service of the British Treasury must be well aware. The final outcome is the result of several ingredients. In the financial field we have never escaped from the consequences of the

Dunkirk atmosphere, when we felt alone: that this is *our* war; that if anyone helps it is very nice of them, but we cannot, of course, expect that it should be otherwise than on their own terms; that so far as we, but not they, are concerned, the future must be entirely sacrificed to the overwhelming needs of the present; and that if anyone wants a *douceur* he must, in the interests of getting on with the war, have it. Of course this was never the whole truth, – in relation to the other members of the Commonwealth, for example. Nevertheless, our financial policy was vitally influenced by this ingredient of appeasement, right and inevitable once, not so clearly necessary now. Next there is our position as a Great Power, equal in authority and responsibility and therefore equal in the assumption of burdens. This is the ingredient of pride and prestige—easily understandable, but, too long continued, nevertheless short-sighted if price and prestige are, in fact, to be preserved. And, finally, the most sympathetic and natural of all the ingredients, the habitual and almost un-thinking open-handedness of a family which has always felt rich and for whom the acceptance of liabilities had become not so much a sacrifice as a convention.

31. Our own set habits are, in fact, the greatest obstacle in the way of changing the atmosphere. All our reflex actions are those of a rich man, so that we promise others too much. Our longings for relaxation from the war are so intense that we promise ourselves too much. As a proud and great Power, we disdain to chaffer with others smaller and more exorbitant than ourselves. Having been so recently in dire extremity, our financial diplomacy is rooted in appeasement. Above all, the financial problems of the war have been surmounted so easily and so silently that the average man sees no reason to suppose that the financial problem of the peace will be any more difficult. The Supply Departments have demanded of the Treasury that money should be no object. And the Treasury has so contrived that it has been no object. This success is the

greatest obstacle of all to getting the problems of this memorandum taken seriously. And when we come to exports, no one ever seems to suppose that we need expect to be paid cash for them in full – exports for relief purposes, exports on credit, exports for prestige and propaganda, exports below world price so as to gain satisfied customers five years hence; never exports so that we can live.

32. *The principles of solution.* It is not the purpose of this memorandum to offer, or to debate, the solution. Nevertheless there are certain general principles to which we must hold henceforward with the utmost resolution, if we are to escape the natural consequences of the overseas financial policy which we have adopted hitherto. In conclusion, therefore, it may be useful to indicate one or two of them.

33. We do not intend to seek outside assistance in meeting the war debts which we have incurred to the other sterling area countries and to neutrals. We propose to meet these over a period of years in the shape of British exports and perhaps, in the case of certain neutrals, by a further disposal of our pre-war investments in their territories. But we shall ask those concerned to agree that, in view of the origin of the debts, the interest element shall be reduced to a minimum or altogether extinguished. That is to say, it is the capital sum which we shall endeavour to repay in full. Furthermore, subject to only minor exceptions, repayment must take the form of direct British exports, mainly additional to the normal course of trade, and cannot take the form of free exchange, of which we see no prospect of possessing a sizeable surplus in the foreseeable future. The abnormal war balances can be made available to those who own them only by instalments and only subject to these conditions. During the transitional period we may be able to arrange to allow certain transfers of indebtedness between our creditors within the sterling area. But in no case shall we agree to borrow outside currencies in order to make sterling war indebtedness available to buy exports from outside. All this is rooted in the inescapable necessities

of the case. In so far as we find ourselves in a position to make exceptions, it will be the Crown Colonies which will have the first claim on us. That criticism and complaint is bound to arise on the part of other exporters, we cannot help.

34. To Canada and the U.S. which lie outside both the sterling area and the special accounts system, we owe so far no war debts, except certain secured loans of relatively small amount (£79 millions to U.S. and £162 million to Canada), of which the debt to Canada carries at present no interest. We shall urge with all the force in our power that ways be found by which this freedom from war debts can be maintained for the remaining period of the war, and that uncovered indebtedness to Canada and the U.S. begins only with the peace.

35. What good reasons can we offer for asking from those who have been especially generous to us so to continue when we are not cavilling at incurring further war indebtedness in favour of those who have been less generous? Have we any better reason than the obvious one that a good deed breds the expectation of another? Yes, it can be argued that we have a better reason. For an analysis of those to whom we are incurring further debts shows that there is no true analogy. For let us consider in detail to whom are we incurring further war debts:–

(1) *Latin America.* The amounts are moderate and fall far short of what they still owe us. If we liquidated our assets there on the scale on which we have already liquidated our assets in Canada and U.S., there would be less than no war debts left.

(2) *European Allies.* The amounts are not large and do not represent any net gain by them, since they will be immediately engulfed for reconstruction.

(3) *The Crown Colonies.* Here our position of trusteeship and our over-riding authority put it out of the question that we should, by our own decision, exact large sums from them.

(4) *India, Egypt and the Middle East.* Egypt is neutral. The

others have never accepted the same unlimited liability to participation in the efforts of the war which we and certain others of our partners have accepted.

(5) *The other Dominions.* Here we are in fact incurring no war debt in excess of the sterling government securities remaining to be repatriated (a process already complete in the case of Canada). On the contrary New Zealand has no prospect of abnormal balances and, if Australia accumulates a small surplus through her earnings from U.S. troops, this would only enable her to make a small beginning of the repatriation of sterling government debt which Canada has completed.

36. There is, moreover, a further important respect in which there is no analogy between the position of the sterling area countries and that of Canada and the United States. Most of the sterling area countries (the important exception is South Africa) have lent the U.K. the whole of their currency reserves and have accumulated no outside resources whatever against the large volume of outstanding currency which their consumers will doubtless wish to turn in part into imported goods as soon as the war is over. India, for example, has turned over to the U.K. the whole of her large dollar earnings. Australia is doing the like in respect of her current considerable receipts from the U.S. troops. Thus an appreciable part of the sterling owed by the U.K. to the rest of the sterling area is simply the counterpart of the dollar earnings and other external receipts which they have turned over to us. Some indication of the magnitude of these receipts is given in the table in paragraph 21 above. This table shows that in 1943, for example, the U.K. received from the rest of the sterling area in actual gold and dollars no less than $515 million, which were added to the U.K. gold and dollar reserves at the expense of the gold and dollar reserves of the rest of the area. No aid parallel to this has been afforded by the two North American countries lying outside the sterling area. The two

methods of financial aid are widely different in character and it is not easy to make a useful comparison between them.

37. With the advent of peace we hope to borrow both from Canada and from the U.S. in so far as we still have expenses to meet which are a sequel of the war and can be properly regarded as part of the same story. Our purpose will be to keep this residual aid to the smallest possible dimensions. Terms, which lie within the capacity of repayment which we reasonably foresee for ourselves, must be fixed at the outset. We are not prepared to take a chance on the question of repayment, whatever view others might be prepared to take. Rather than accept terms which we can doubtfully satisfy, we shall prefer to do without and live perforce as best we can within our own temporarily limited means. We are fearful, lest, in the spirit of the greatest goodwill, there may be pressure on us to accept too much on conditions which we cannot clearly fulfil. If war debts begin to accumulate before the transition from war to peace is reached, we see little possibility of being able to accept on these conditions what we shall sorely need.

Keynes also reported to the Chancellor on the progress of his talks.

To SIR JOHN ANDERSON, *10 August 1944*

My dear Chancellor,

I take the opportunity of a vacant day, during which we are marking time, to send you a general report of the position up-to-date, although what I say is, of course, very likely to be superseded by a cable before you get this letter.

Our apparent task here, as set to us before we arrived, was to persuade the Canadians to bridge a gap in mutual aid during the current financial year estimated to amount to about $600 million. We also knew that there was a sum of $200 million held in suspense in respect of the first Air Training Scheme for the period prior to 30 June 1942, which, although the sum had been ascertained and not yet paid, we had never ourselves regarded as falling into the category of an agreed war debt.

On arrival here we discovered that Mr Ilsley[13] was quite confidently regarding this $200 million as a war debt due to Canada. And what was worse, we also discovered (rather late on in our negotiations) that there was also another debt, of about $200 million, carried in suspense in respect of our share of the cost of the *second* Air Training Scheme for the period from 1 July 1942 to 31 March 1945. Of this actual and potential debt we had no previous knowledge whatever.

Thus altogether there was a matter of $1,000 million to be cared for, if we were to emerge at the end of this financial year without any war debt to Canada (except the secured $700 million loan, now reduced by (the interest earned on)* the pledged securities to a somewhat lower figure).   It was soon clear to us that for domestic political reasons there was no possible chance of any increase in the Mutual Aid Appropriation by anything approaching this amount, and the chance of any increase at all pretty poor.

On the other hand, the Canadians were taking the line that, of course, it was up to them to meet the full charges which we have incurred on behalf of their overseas forces, and that any unpaid charges on their behalf, which we could substantiate, would be properly chargeable on their Defence Appropriation. (It is quite likely that there is enough margin in their Defence Estimates to cover this; and if not, a supplementary Defence Appropriation would be very much easier politically than a supplementary Mutual Aid Appropriation.) Accordingly we set ourselves to present our case on this head as convincingly as we knew how, on the basis of the material provided from London. The claims we felt able to justify in

[13] James Lorimer Ilsley (1894–1967); Minister of National Revenue, Canada, 1935–40; Minister of Finance, 1940–6.
* This should read 'sales of' K. 25/8.

principle amounted, on an approximate and highly provisional estimate, to the substantial figure of $800 million.

It is, perhaps, rather astonishing that we should be able to put up a plausible claim to such a huge undercharge. But our methods of financial appeasement hitherto have been so all-embracing and we have got so much into the habit of giving the financial case away in our dealings with Allies and Dominions, both of these tendencies being greatly aggravated by our War Office having abandoned close accounting so that we never know in time, or can substantiate at any time, the right figure, that one should not, I suppose, be surprised. On the other hand, it is very fair of the Canadians not to complain of our reopening so late in the day matters already actually agreed otherwise or at least acquiesced in over a long period.

To fill the gap between this $800 million and the $1,000 million required we had two other claims in our portfolio. The first, worth no less than $200 million, was a claim for tax refunds in a matter where the Canadian practice has been highly inconsistent and arbitrary. They have been charging on munitions sold to us through mutual aid, sales and other taxes, of a character which would normally be refunded on exports, at varying rates which in the case of tanks may run as high as 20%; whereas in the case of food they have chosen to remit all such taxes.

The second is the capital cost of ships ($250 millions) which is charged on mutual aid in spite of the fact that the ships do not pass into our possession.

The prior task, however, which we had to accomplish before our chance of getting the above claims accepted could be reckoned good, was to persuade the Canadians that it was neither reasonable nor to the mutual interest to begin loading us up with war debts. The argument here was, first, the general background of our financial position; second that if we were to exhaust our capacity to repay by borrowing before the end of the war, we could not afford to buy Canadian produce in Stage III even on credit. Our case here, which I had to rehearse three times before different audiences, produced a considerable effect. The greatest resistance, which has kept on popping up again and again after I thought I had disposed of it, is based on the question why we should resist incurring debts to Canada during the war, when we are blithely piling them up with every part of the sterling area.

In spite of this difficulty the result of these discourses was, I think, to put the Canadian civil servants and Ministers concerned into the mood of wanting to find a way to meet us in so far as they can do so without involving themselves in political and parliamentary difficulties.

This is how the matter still stands. We do not yet know how far our claims will be accepted.

The tax refund we shall, I have some confidence, get. It really is a bit of a swindle.

The ship refund we shall, in my opinion, not get. The justice of our complaint here is admitted in several quarters; but there is no disputing that it would create great difficulties for Ilsley and Clark[14] if they had to attempt to undo what, rather naughtily and unnecessarily, they have done somewhat irrevocably in the terms of their mutual aid legislation.

The claims for the refund of costs incurred for the overseas forces are, I think, admitted in principle. But when it comes to the amount of them, we have to admit that some of our claims are based on highly conjectural and unsubstantiated estimates, certain of which we have had to invent for ourselves here on the spot.

I do not myself believe that we are opening our mouths too wide. If a sufficient number of accountants were to work for a long enough time, I believe it more likely that the total would come out above our figures than below it. But undoubtedly we are asking the Canadians to take a good deal on trust.

[14] William Clifford Clark (1889–1952); Deputy Minister of Finance, Canada, 1932–52.

That is, if they also accept our plea that they should *not* insist on justification by elaborate accounting, but should agree to a broad settlement on the basis of both sides crying quits as on 31 March, 1945, neither owing anything to the other. At the same time, their Service Departments and their Treasury also are considerably attracted to our 'quits' proposal. For they, like us, are bored to death by the idea of a long-drawn-out chaffering over details of accounts, which might last for years and is not appropriate to the general background of the financial relations between the two countries.

Of course the crying of quits is not essential to a fairly reasonable solution. I have told Clark privately that if his Minister will agree to the tax refund and to the principle of our not being left out of pocket in respect of the costs we incur on behalf of the Canadian forces in the three respects we have specified, I will cease to hang about, as we all are doing now, heavy on his conscience, and will not commit suicide on his doorstep but will go home quietly. For I am convinced that this would give us, at long last, by far the greater part of what we are asking.

Indeed I feel very confident that at the worst we shall be able to cover the deficit of $600 million which we originally set out to cover. The doubt is how far we shall also manage to liquidate on this particular visit the two overhanging debts, of $200 million each, for the old and new Air Training Schemes.

The reason why all this is still hanging fire is for no lack of good will and is not the fault of Ilsley or Clark. It arises out of (*a*) the parliamentary, (*b*) the Cabinet and (*c*) the political situations.

We could not, in truth, have arrived at a more unsuitable and inconvenient date. Ottawa is in a hectic last fortnight of a parliamentary session which may, conceivably, be the last before the General Election. The spate of measures which they are trying to force through, though some of them have been under debate for months, is almost entirely financial, with the result that Ilsley and Clark are occupied in the House (particularly with the Canadian convention that the Minister in charge *never* leaves the Bench) all and every day. These measures include *inter alia* a vast programme of social reform (doubtless with an eye on the impending election) much on the same lines as ours but proportionately two or three times as lavish in terms of money. In the brief period of our visit Ilsley has been concerned with putting through (1) a colossal Children's Allowances Act, (2) a huge housing programme, (3) a brand new export credit guarantee scheme much more ambitious than ours, (4) a brand new banking industrial development scheme for loans to businesses which the existing banks do not cover, (5) the new Chartered Banks Act, a highly controversial measure, which will settle the status of Canadian joint stock banks for the next ten years, (6) a war veterans' bonus, furlough, vocational training, educational scheme on a scale which would cost us, I should say, about £1,000 million. All these matters are contentious and their parliamentary methods lend themselves to obstruction. Some of them are contentious in the Cabinet as well as in the House.

Well! You can imagine that the Canadian Treasury have not much spare time over to give serious consideration to our problems. Add that both Ilsley and Clark are tired and indeed ill to the point of physical collapse, and that the temperature is frequently over 90 and in the neighbourhood of 100; and you have a picture of the scene where all we can do half the time, as I have indicated above, is to lie heavy on their conscience, whilst they, on their side, are as kind and considerate and hospitable as they have the strength left to be.

The second set of difficulties concerns the Cabinet. We think these may be over-estimated. It is the line taken by Mr Mackenzie King[15] which will be decisive. We hope to gain his

---

[15] Rt. Hon. W. L. Mackenzie King (1874-1950), Prime Minister of Canada, 1921-6, 1926-30, 1935-48; Secretary of State for External Affairs, 1935-46.

serious attention shortly (his chief advisers, Norman Robertson[16] and Hume Wrong,[17] are amongst our firmest friends and advocates); but of late he too has been continuously occupied with his external policy estimates, a big speech on this, the jubilee of his political leadership, and intricate political problems. But Ilsley argues at times that this moment, when he is incurring vast financial obligations in other directions and is in difficulties with his colleagues about various matters with which we are in no way concerned, is not the best time to choose for fighting our case through his colleagues. This might be true if his colleagues were taking up a line against our claims, but we have no reason whatever to believe that this is so. It is really an argument from fatigue; and we here all think it would be fatal to allow him to postpone altogether any settlement with us. For one thing this would certainly get the 1944/45 finance mixed up with the impending Stage II controversy (see below).

The following is an illustration of what happens. I had a long meeting with the Ministers who make up the Cabinet Committee known as the Mutual Aid Board; and the discussion was judged by those present to have gone very well. But we were told subsequently that, after we had left the room, there was an awkward controversy between Ilsley and some of his colleagues about various proposals for rewarding men demobilised from the services, which quite upset the atmosphere.

Finally, there is the political situation, which is obviously of the greatest possible interest and complication, but about which I am probably rash to say anything at all after so brief an experience. Nevertheless here is the bird's eye impression

[16] Norman Alexander Robertson (1904–68), Under-Secretary of State for External Affairs, Canada, 1941–46.
[17] Humphrey Hume Wrong (1894–1954), Associate Under-Secretary of State for External Affairs, 1944–46; special economic adviser, Canada House, London, 1939; Minister Counsellor, Canadian Legation, Washington, 1941; Assistant Under-Secretary of State for External Affairs, Ottawa, 1942; Canadian Ambassador to U.S., 1946–53.

which the visitor gets in the first flush of his interest and before he knows enough to have become confused.

As you well know, whilst we in Europe are fighting a war, anywhere in this Continent in which you may find yourself they are much more absorbed in fighting general elections. There have been two here this week, both of them thrilling, one (in Quebec) particularly so. There will be a General Election throughout the Dominion very shortly after the end of the German War, and the present Cabinet, now winding up the Session, may never face a House of Commons again.

Mackenzie King's Liberal party which previously held Quebec by a large majority was defeated this week by a small margin, and the French will probably resume power. The election was fought bitterly with a very large poll (women voting for the first time), partly on the issue of Provincial *versus* Dominion rights, partly on the issue of full participation in the war; and the anti-participationists have won. They have here, in truth, a super-Irish question always at their door. That the anti-British party should have won just at this juncture cannot be overlooked by politicians. Canada feels great pride in her own war effort. But the above makes it still more necessary to represent any expenditure as arising out of this effort and not as financial assistance to us.

All this will affect Canada's participation in Stage II much more than the subject of our present discussions, – though it also has its repercussions there. The average man in Canada tends to look on the end of the German war as, substantially, the end of everything. Quebec will certainly take less than no interest in Stage II, and Quebec's representative in the Cabinet, St Laurent,[18] warned us that we must not expect too much. No one can say on what lines Mackenzie King will fight the Dominion election, but clearly he may have to suffer forfeits if he is to retain power.

[18] Rt. Hon. Louis Stephen St Laurent (1888–1973), Prime Minister of Canada, 1948–57; Minister of Justice and Attorney-General, 1941–6, 1948; Minister of External Affairs, 1946–48.

The strength of his personal position is immense; his prestige and popularity unrivalled; and all parties alike regard him as Canada's G.O.M. He also, undoubtedly, occupies the centre of gravity of Canadian political opinion. The question is what is to happen to his party political following, the Liberals. Of the four other parties in Canada which count, two are to the right of the Liberals and two are to the left. These four parties now command the provincial legislatures. Of the two to the right one is the reactionary anti-war French party of Quebec, and the other is the intensely pro-war, pro-British conservative party of Ontario; and they both hate one another more than either hates the Liberals. Of the two to the left one is the socialist C.C.F. which has swept Saskatchewan, and the other is the passionately anti-socialist Social Credit Party which has swept Alberta. These two also hate one another more than they hate the Liberals. So it is, you will see, a pretty kettle of fish. Doubtless Mackenzie King will use all his experience and astuteness. But what price may he not have to pay to the powerful forces in Quebec?

Our friends are loyal in the extreme and would not flinch from their full share in Stage II. But their first duty, even to us, is to remain in power!

Well that is the picture as we, rightly or wrongly, see it. The High Commissioner and Munro[19] have been immensely helpful with good advice and the right contacts. They have won a general confidence here which makes everything much easier for us. We are all enjoying ourselves and greatly exhilarated by our first contact with the Canadians, in many ways so much more sympathetic than the Americans, and with the vast and justifiable hopes of Canada. Eady is in great form. And after the first few days when there was much to do,

[19] Gordon Munro (1895–1967); Deputy Director, Prisoners of War Department, British Red Cross, 1939; Admiralty Liaison Officer, 1940–1; Financial Adviser to U.K. High Commission in Canada, 1941–6; Treasury Representative in U.S.A., and Minister at British Embassy, Washington, 1946–9; U.K. Executive Director and Alternate Governor of International Bank for Reconstruction and Development, 1947–9.

we are all taking something of a holiday with not above half a day's work, in great comfort, abundant hospitality and brilliant, enjoyable summer weather (even if it does get a bit hot sometimes); though such experiences in these easy, remote and excessively prosperous regions makes our hearts go out with very great emotion to those in London.

Yours ever,

KEYNES

P.S. There is one consideration of some importance which I find, looking this through, that I may not have emphasised sufficiently. It is quite vital to Canada's agricultural programme to be able to sell to us on a large scale in Stage III. No one is more conscious of this than Mr Gardiner.[20] I fancy that the part of my argument that went home most deeply was when I pointed out that if they load us up with war debt in Stage I and Stage II then assuming we hold to the policy of not borrowing more than we see our way to repay, we shall not be able to buy agricultural produce from them in Stage III even on credit. Eady and I both think that it is very important for the Ministry of Food to be taking every opportunity of making this clear. We ought to involve ourselves in no firm contracts in respect of food in Stage III except subject to a perfectly clear financial reserve. This reserve is double-barrelled. The scale of our Canadian purchases immediately after the war must be limited by Canada's ability to lend but also by our ability to borrow having regard to our capacity to repay.

As a result of the negotiations, the Canadians accepted four major British claims for payment: higher capitation payments to correspond to the actual cost of the Canadian army backdated to the invasion of Sicily; payment for advanced training given in the United Kingdom to Royal

[20] James Garfield Gardiner (b. 1883), Minister of Agriculture, Canada, 1935-57, Minister of National War Service 1940-41; Imperial Privy Council, 1947.

Canadian Air Force personnel backdated to 1 April 1943; payment for reserve and transit stocks attributable to Canadian forces; rebates of Canadian sales taxation on mutual aid contracts. The total sum involved was $655 million, which appeared to be enough to cover the rest of the financial year and leave $160 million to spare. In return, Britain agreed to sell $80 million in American dollars to Canada to cover the Canadian-American balance of payments position and to use any surplus Canadian dollars at the end of the financial year to settle certain claims. Over and above these arrangements, officials in Ottawa agreed that from a 'public relations' point of view the Keynes–Eady visit had proved as useful as any British official visit so far in the war.

On completing his business in Ottawa, Keynes returned to London after short visits to New York and Washington, taking the opportunity to have conversations with bankers on Bretton Woods, H. D. White on Bretton Woods and related matters, and British officials in Washington on Stage II procedures.

Meanwhile, preparations for Stage II continued. As noted above (p. 69), Mr Law had visited Washington in July to make preliminary soundings. Also, early in August Mr Morgenthau and Mr White had been in London for discussions on financial matters, including the post-war treatment of Germany. After these soundings and discussions, it was agreed that as a part of the Octagon meetings in Quebec in September, the Prime Minister and President would set out the guidelines for the Stage II discussions. The negotiations themselves would then follow in a joint committee in Washington. Although the Chancellor was to be the nominal head of the British side of the joint committee, Keynes, as his deputy, was to represent him. Morgenthau wholeheartedly supported Keynes's appointment.[21]

Keynes reached London after his American and Canadian travels on 24 August. Almost immediately he was involved in Stage II preparations.

In the course of these preparations, Keynes sent a report to the Chancellor.

[21] Mr White was more disturbed by Keynes's appointment. As he told Mr Morgenthau, 'Shouldn't monkey with a buzz saw'. To which Mr Morgenthau, replied, 'Not as long as the saw can keep turning. Sometimes its teeth get kind of dull'. See J. M. Blum, *From the Morgenthau Diaries, Years of War 1941–1945* (Boston, 1967), p. 316.

To SIR JOHN ANDERSON, *25 August 1944*

The origin of the attached paper is as follows:–

As you are aware, Mr Harry Hopkins has been gradually evolving certain proposals aimed at getting an agreed lend lease programme for Stage II. The essence of his proposals is that the President should issue at a fairly early date, after discussion with the Prime Minister, certain directives, which would result in clear cut recommendations by a Joint Committee being available immediately after the election (those of particular urgency being handed down, if necessary, at an earlier date).

In order that this plan should be satisfactory, it is evident that all will depend on the right directives being given in the first instance. Mr Harry Hopkins was fairly vague about this. Indeed, like Mr Morgenthau, he had not clearly distinguished between the problems of Stage II and those of Stage III. Shortly before I left America, therefore, Mr Brand and Mr Lee had a long discussion in New York with Sir Wilfrid Eady and myself as to the lines along which preparations could be most properly guided. This resulted in my being asked to prepare a brief paper.

As my plane was delayed, there was an opportunity for us to see Mr Brand again in Washington last Sunday. He took the opportunity to arrange a meeting under the Ambassador, at which, apart from Mr Brand, Sir Wilfred Eady and myself, Sir Ronald Campbell, Sir Henry Self[22] and General Macready[23] were also present. At this meeting the paper I had

[22] Sir Henry Self (1890–1975); civil servant; on Air Missions to Canada and U.S.A. 1938, Head of Mission, 1940: Director-General of British Air Commission, Washington, 1940–1; British Joint-Staff Mission, Washington, 1942; Permanent Secretary to Ministry of Production, 1942–3; Deputy for Minister of Production, Washington, 1943–5; Deputy Chairman, British Supply Council, Washington, 1945; U.K. member, Combined Raw Materials Board, 1944–5; Permanent Secretary, Ministry of Civil Aviation, 1946–7.

[23] Lt.-Gen. Sir Gordon Nevil Macready (1891–1956); Deputy Director, Staff Duties, War Office, 1936–38; Chief, British Military Mission to Egyptian Army, 1938; Assistant Chief, Imperial General Staff, 1940–2; Chief, British Army Staff at Washington, 1942.

prepared was considered and amended, and I was entrusted with the task of carrying it back to you as representing a first shot at what our people in Washington thought might be the right line of approach.

Immediately after our return here the paper was fully discussed in the Treasury under the chairmanship of Sir Richard Hopkins and further amended. After that it was discussed with Sir Robert Sinclair[24] and other representatives of the Ministry of Production, and finally, last night, with the Minister of Production. This resulted in still further amendments. All the above amendments, however, are essentially questions of presentation and do not materially alter the general form and purpose of the paper I have brought back from Washington. The Minister of Production has not yet seen the final amendments made at his instance, but I think it is likely he will be satisfied with the version attached. The chief matter left open is the question of the composition of the proposed Joint Committee, about which I will speak when I come to see you on Monday morning.

It was felt in Washington that, if this method of approach were to commend itself to the Prime Minister, there is something to be said for allowing Mr Harry Hopkins to have either the paper itself or a summary of it so that he could prepare the President before the meeting. But it is thought that, in that case, the communication to Mr Hopkins should not be made earlier than some three days before the meeting.

You will see that the purpose of the paper is to obtain sufficiently clear directives on general matters of policy to protect us from undue interference at lower levels, whilst, at the same time, not asking the President to give final decisions on matters of detail, which he cannot reasonably be asked to

[24] Sir Robert Sinclair (b. 1893); 1st Baron of Cleeve, 1957; Chairman Imperial Tobacco Co.; Prime Minister's Advisory Panel of Industrialists, 1939; Director-General, Army Requirements, War Office, 1939–42; member, Supply Council, 1939–42, Army Council, 1940–2; Deputy for Minister of Production at Washington, 1942–3; Chief Executive, Ministry of Production and Board of Trade, 1943–5.

accept until they have been subjected to prolonged examination by his advisers.

KEYNES

25 August 1944

Sir W. Eady and I view with considerable scepticism the estimate of $4 billion for our minimum munitions requirements. The biggest risk is that this figure will not be able to stand up to cross-examination. We have tried to introduce some protection against this contingency in paragraph 3 below.

A NOTE ON THE METHOD OF APPROACH
WHICH MIGHT BE ADOPTED AT THE
FORTHCOMING HIGH LEVEL CONVERSATIONS

1. The Prime Minister would explain that the general strategy contemplated for the war against Japan and the military commitments we have undertaken in Europe and elsewhere will require a supply of munitions, to equip the forces for which we are responsible, equal to about 75 per cent of our present requirements during the first year of Stage II, falling to about 60 per cent by the end of the year.

2. If the whole of this supply were to be furnished by ourselves (which would, in any case, be impracticable for many types owing to the time-lag required to supply types hitherto produced only in the United States), it would be impossible to release any of the manpower now mobilised for munitions at home. In view of the physical and material exhaustion of the country after five years fighting, and having regard to the urgent needs of the civilian population, the continuance of mobilisation for war purposes on the above scale would be insupportable. It is suggested, therefore, that the same proportion of our munitions requirements should

be furnished under lend lease as at present, namely 75 per cent of present supplies on the average of the first year, falling to 60 per cent at the end of it. This would allow the minimum relief of manpower which is calculated to be essential, and would leave the margin of manpower available for civilian purposes in the United Kingdom far less than it is likely to be in any other of the Allied countries during Stage II. The President would be asked to agree that at least this measure of relief was reasonable. The value of the munitions to be furnished under lend lease in this case is estimated at about $4 billion.

3. If, as a result of any change of plan, the number of men required from us in the fighting and occupation forces were to fall below the figure assumed above their munition requirements may be assumed to fall in about the same proportion. It is suggested that, in this case, the relief thus made possible should be shared in the same way, i.e. that the munitions furnished to us on lend lease should fall in the same proportion. The President would be asked to accept the principle that the supply of munitions available under lend lease should be not less than is required, in conjunction with what can be furnished from British Empire sources on the basis of the above uniform reduction, to fulfil the requirements of the forces for the equipment of which the British are responsible.

4. The President would also be asked to agree to such programme of non-munitions supplies on lend lease as can be shown to be required to enable us to maintain the desired degree of war effort against Japan, having regard to our general economic position, full particulars of which would be made available to the Joint Committee proposed below. Here again some 75 per cent of the present programme is the provisional estimate of what is required, namely a total of $3 billion, which would not, however, have fallen below this figure at the end of the year.

5. Lend lease assistance has been regarded hitherto as *residual* and has aimed at satisfying our justifiable requirements in excess of those which we can furnish ourselves in conditions of full mobilisation of manpower for war purposes. If it is accepted, for the reasons explained above, that lend lease assistance in Stage II should be maintained in the same proportion as our own effort, this criterion of lend lease availability will no longer be applicable. The appropriate criterion henceforward must necessarily be one of absolute amount. The President should be asked to recognise this change in conditions by agreeing to the preparation of a firm agreement specifying the amount and character of the assistance on which we can rely up to an aggregate value provisionally estimated at $7 billion, as the only effective way of establishing a criterion of lend lease assistance which will allow us to proceed with our preparations with certainty and security.

6. It is suggested, therefore, that a Joint Committee should be appointed with power to appoint technical sub-committees in order to draw up a list of the amounts and categories of the assistance to be covered by the firm agreement.

7. Since it is unlikely that the Committee could complete its deliberations before, say, November, it is essential that a directive should be given meanwhile which would prevent any steps being taken during the intervening weeks likely to be prejudicial to the carrying out, should they be approved, of any proposals which we are bringing before the Committee.

8. The instructions to the Committee should cover the whole ground of munitions, non-munition lend lease, mutual aid and export policies, and might be somewhat as follows:–

(*a*) It would not be competent for them to question the decisions in 1 to 5 above, and their task would be to draw up an agreed programme which would have the effect of implementing the decisions implicit in these clauses.

(*b*) So far as munitions are concerned, it would be the duty of the Committee to draw up a programme capable of fulfilling the above conditions in the manner most convenient and efficient from the point of view of the supply departments of the two Governments.

(*c*) So far as non-munitions are concerned, the Committee would examine the British position with a view to determining the justification of the scale of assistance in 4 above, and should in this connection consider the advisability of possible modifications in the fields to be covered by lend lease and mutual aid respectively with a view to simplification and concentration.

(*d*) So far as exports are concerned, it should be an instruction to the Committee to propose the principles which should govern henceforth the relationship between lend lease and mutual aid assistance and the export policies of the two countries with a view to minimising the measures of restriction and regulation; and in arranging in detail the character of the aid to be furnished under the above lend lease programme they should bear in mind the object of facilitating and simplifying the application of the principles, which they are proposing, in a manner likely to interfere with the respective export programmes of the two Governments to the least possible extent.

25 August 1944

Chapter 2

THE STAGE II NEGOTIATIONS

On his way to North America, Keynes took the opportunity to look at the post-war prospect in a broader framework.

DECISIONS OF POLICY AFFECTING THE FINANCIAL POSITION IN STAGES II AND III

A day or two before leaving for U.S.A. I mentioned to Sir R. Hopkins that I was uncomfortable about the possible cumulative effect of certain current decisions of higher policy (or, in the case of exports, lack of decisions) on our prospective financial position, especially in Stage III. He asked me to prepare a few notes and to ask Sir D. Waley to consider a more detailed examination of the case.

It will be convenient to begin with the latest estimate prepared in the Treasury (dated 1.9.44) of our overseas expenditures and receipts in the first year of Stage II, which I shall assume in what follows to be co-terminous with 1945. I shall argue subsequently that this estimate is in some respects too optimistic and in other respects too pessimistic. (In particular, a significant improvement will result if the Prime Minister's latest man-power directive is actually carried into effect.) But it will serve as a text to bring out the main points which I have in mind.

(1) The Chancellor should know that this latest estimate of our net overseas disinvestment in the first year of Stage II (say 1945) is *higher* than for any year of the war up to date, even on the assumption that lend lease and Canadian mutual aid continue on the same lines as heretofore. The following is a summary of it:–

Requirements	£ million	Receipts	£ million
Imports f.o.b.			
Food, civilian	556		
Food for U.K. forces	95		
Materials	448		
Oil	158		
Tobacco	45		
Other imports	55		
Food, materials and oil		British exports	450
for reciprocal aid	49	Diamonds	10
Total imports (f.o.b.)	1,406	Total exports (f.o.b.)	460
Shipping	350	Shipping	125
Interest, profits and		Interest, profits and	
dividends	45	dividends	145
War expenditure (cash,		Military receipts from	
overseas)	550	Empire Governments	65
Other payments	125	Other receipts	
		(unidentifiable)	100
	2,476		895
		Deficit	1,581
			2,476
This is before allowing for			
Lend lease estimated at			647
Canadian mutual aid estimated at			117
Receipts for U.S. and Canadian troops			
in U.K. highly conjectural (say)			50
			814
which reduces the net overseas disinvestment to			767

In this case our overseas obligations at the end of 1945 will not be far short of £4,000 million.

(2) The above, if it is correct, has a direct bearing on the first year of Stage III which is the main theme of this paper. (I am assuming a duration of one year for Stage II.) We must reckon that lend lease and mutual aid cease at the end of Stage II. We enter Stage III, therefore, running an overseas deficit at the fantastic rate of £1,500 million per annum. This figure can only come down gradually and there is an inevitable time-lag of appreciable length in escaping from expenditures in far-distant theatres. But what is particularly disturbing is the indication, as we shall see below, that present

policies will require a continuance of some important items of expenditure well into Stage III and that there is no present intention of bringing large-scale overseas military expenditures to an end when Japan is defeated, any more than there is when Germany is defeated.

(3) First of all, however, let us consider certain of the assumptions on which the above Treasury estimate is based. Let us begin with exports. It assumes that exports in 1945 will be nearly *double* what they are in 1944, that is £500 million compared with £267 million, but that there will be a time-lag in getting payment for £50 million, which reduces the prospective receipts to £450 million.

This conclusion is *solely* based on the fact that the Prime Minister's man-power directive would release sufficient man-power to produce this amount of exports. It assumes that exporters will have prospective orders all ready, that the period of conversion and production is not more than (say) three months, that the man-power released will find its way into the appropriate industries, that the raw materials will be available, that the stuff when produced will be exported and not consumed at home, and that (apart from a time-lag of a month or so in payment) none of it will be on credit. Clearly it is most unlikely that all these conditions will be substantially fulfilled. The estimate of £450 million cash receipts from exports in 1945 is, therefore, preposterously optimistic at any rate, unless we introduce a more deliberate planning policy for exports than is at present in sight. This is a field where it is the *absence* of decisions which is disturbing.

Nevertheless, there is a great deal we could do, if we were to set about it at once, to make the facts come reasonably near to the estimate. The kind of planning and procurement required involves the type of work for which the Ministries of Production and Supply, rather than the Board of Trade, have been primarily responsible hitherto. The execution, therefore, of the second category of suggestions made below should be handled by the technique of the Ministry of Production (in collaboration with the Ministry of Supply), either acting as a separate Ministry or (preferably perhaps) absorbing, or being absorbed by, the Board of Trade.

The task of getting a maximum volume of exports falls into two main categories:–

(i) The first is a matter of *announcement*. We should aim at informing exporters as soon as possible and certainly before the end of the year—

(*a*) that there are no longer any White Paper strings on exports whatever;

(*b*) that exports to all destinations within and without the sterling area are equally welcome (I hope the Treasury will come to the conclusion that this is highly advisable and that it is not worth while to tease exporters into being selective), but these must be for cash within three months unless a longer credit is approved by an organisation set up for the purpose;

(*c*) that a manufacturer who can show or guarantee that his produce will be exported will receive priority for raw materials and directed man-power;

(*d*) that key-men for export trading will be eligible for release in Class B;

(*e*) that the banks will be asked to give special consideration to applications for credit to provide working capital for the production of exports;

(*f*) that the Government will be prepared if necessary to guarantee a minimum price to any manufacturer of standard goods for export, so as to enable him to get ahead with planning production in advance of actual orders, i.e. it will underwrite output giving the manufacturer a free option to put goods on the Government if he cannot dispose of them overseas to better advantage;

117

(g) that exporters must not profiteer but are expected and encouraged to obtain the full, proper price in overseas markets;

(h) that a target will be set and communicated to manufacturers for each main class of exports.

(ii) The second category is a matter of *direction and procurement*. The existing technique of the Ministries of Production, Supply and Labour should be employed to direct raw materials and labour to manufacturers who can show that they require them for export. And, where necessary, it should also be used to procure (or, rather, underwrite the procurement of) standard export goods as suggested in (f) above. It should also assemble large-scale continuing contracts and allocate suitable firms for conversion so as to undertake them. For example, it should invite orders for locomotives for a period of 5 or 10 years from India, Egypt, South Africa, Argentina, Brazil, etc. and then see that they were suitably placed. It might place orders for so many millions of bicycles, so many sewing machines, so many tractors and ploughs, etc., etc., for each of the next five years. The field for such activities by an enterprising department is almost unlimited.

The vital necessity for *direction* of labour and raw materials becomes obvious when we examine the classes of goods in which we can reasonably hope for an expansion of exports. The Board of Trade hopes for a total increase of £233 million in 1945. Rather less than half of this relates to industries which already have the labour and should be becoming slack from the falling-off in munitions, e.g. iron and steel, non-ferrous metals, electrical industries, engineering, chemicals and vehicles. This should be an easy task for the Ministry of Production. Indeed it may well be that the target for these industries should be put considerably higher. But rather more than half relates to industries which have been drastically reduced and industries, moreover, where export orders will have to compete severely with orders for the home market. For example £15 million is expected from coal and coke, £6 million from pottery, glass, etc., £82 million from the textile industries, £5 million from paper and books. Surely there is not a hope of getting enough labour back into these particular industries quickly and also making sure that the output is exported except by using the war-time technique of direction at which we are now expert. Take, in particular, the textile industries. The Board of Trade export programme involves bringing back next year fully 100,000 workers even if home civilian demand absorbs no more capacity than the Government itself is releasing. This is largely localised female labour of a not very popular type. How can this be achieved unless the Ministry of Production uses its war-time methods, and, in particular, aims at cutting down munitions orders absorbing female labour especially in the areas where they compete with textiles?

Provided that we decide to move at once along these lines, then, perhaps, we can hope that the estimate of £450 million from exports in 1945 will not be too wildly wrong. But this result will not come to pass of its own motion.

(4) The next item in the Treasury estimate which invites attention is the figure of £550 million for war expenditure overseas. This relates to cash expenditure on the spot and is entirely additional to the stores and food consumed by the forces which reach them by sea. The figure seems still more formidable when we discover that it contains nothing whatever for expenditure in Europe, and relates only to India, the Middle East and Imperial lines of communication. It is made up as follows:– [see p. 120]

No doubt the expenditure in India is directly concerned with the Japanese campaign. But there remains a gigantic local expenditure on the lines of communication, which suggests the same disregard of financial consequences which was inevitable and right before Germany was beaten. One must needs wonder how long our financial solvency can hope to stand up to this.

	£ million
India	340
Egypt 90	
Palestine 25	
Persia 15	
Iraq 10	
Total Middle East	140
Australia	40
South Africa	20
Other	10
	───
	550

A leading example is our projected expenditure in the Middle East. At the present time the U.K. personnel in the Middle East (excluding Allied and Dominion forces) number 280,000 and our military expenditure there, which covers all outgoings including Allied and Dominion forces and the keep of prisoners, is at the rate of about £100 million per annum. According to the plans, on which the Treasury estimate is based, the numbers of U.K. personnel at the *end* of the first year of Stage II, say on 31 December 1945, will have *increased* to 342,000. This seems to be partly in replacement of Allied and Dominion personnel which will be considerably reduced, and partly to provide a central strategical reserve of 150,000 (though not, so far as we have ascertained, for use against Japan). As a result of this our military expenditure in this area in 1945 is estimated, as we have seen, at the *increased* figure of £140 million. Now what hope is there for expecting a drastic reduction of this expenditure in 1946? If these numbers are necessary on the last day of 1945 and if it is true that they are not primarily concerned with the war against Japan, the situation supposed to require them will presumably change very gradually. Unless there is a change in policy, will not the corresponding estimate for 1946 remain very large indeed? And how are we going to support this when lend lease ceases except by borrowing more than we can hope to repay? For what chance is there, when goods and shipping are available, that we shall be allowed by the countries concerned, particularly Egypt, just to add these sums to the already inflated sterling balances of the countries concerned?

Fortunately, however, a considerable mitigation should ensue from the operation of the Prime Minister's directive on man-power the effect of which in detail was not available when the Treasury estimate was made. This directive requires in Stage II a further reduction of 700,000 in the three Services or about 20 per cent. No information is available as to the areas in which the curtailments will be effected. It would seem probable, however, that the area we are considering could most easily bear the brunt of the reduction. Thus the Prime Minister's directive should have the incidental result of reducing the cash overseas cost very materially. But it is worth remarking that this directive was the consequence of the need to release more man-power and that the need to economise foreign exchange did not (so far as I know) play a part.

Aside from the results of the Prime Minister's directive, I cannot but think that the Treasury estimate is considerably too high. It appears to amount to more than £400 overseas cash expenditure per head of all the British personnel involved. Even after deducting recoverable expenditure for Dominions personnel, the figure seems most improbable. Taking everything into account, I should be disposed to substitute £70 million and perhaps less for £140 million.

The estimate of £340 million for India also remains a mystery to me. It appears to work out at about £700 per head for the British personnel based there. No doubt it includes large amounts for stores and munitions and also payments to the Indian forces. But surely it could be severely cut under criticism? Is it necessary to continue to produce munitions in India? Other contributions necessarily required of her by reason of the increasing number of American forces there will strain her resources excessively and is itself a reason for cutting down any avoidable demands.

The comparatively minor item of £20 million for South

Africa deserves attention. South Africa has, most certainly, not carried anything like her fair share of the financial burden compared with any other part of the Empire. I suggest to the Chancellor that the time has come to re-open this matter and frankly to ask South Africa to bear as mutual aid the whole of our (comparatively trifling) expenditure within her territory. It must be remembered that this would bring us in an additional £20 million in gold per annum, which is not to be sneezed at.

If we do not find one way or another of reducing the total figure of £550 million for 1945 to something nearer £300 million, we shall certainly start Stage III with an incapacitating handicap. Should not this task be tackled *specifically*? Is it advisable that we should continue into Stage II the principle that, in war decisions, financial considerations do not count at all? After all, to save £100 million foreign exchange is at least as good as to have another £100 million exports.

(5) As already remarked, the Treasury estimate of overseas military expenditure includes *nil* for Europe. There is no entry of liability in respect of payments in military currency; nor is there any entry for Europe under any other head, relief or other. Surely in this respect the estimate is unrealistic. For it is assumed, in effect, that throughout Europe (including Allied Europe) we shall live on the country so far as local supplies and expenses are concerned and incur no indebtedness of any kind. This is not likely to be realised, as our experience in Italy has shown. We are already committed to the pay of our troops in Allied countries although it is paid in military currency in the first instance, also to 25 per cent of military relief in all countries (which has cost £150 million in Italy up to date alone), and to our UNRRA contribution. In practice, to conquer and occupy Europe is likely to cost a very considerable sum in foreign exchange and overseas liabilities.

(6) This leads me to our current policy towards Germany

so far as it is known to me. For we seem in this field to be seeking the maximum, rather than the minimum, liability. In discussing German reparations my maxim in the Treasury has always been this time exactly what it was in the Treasury last time, namely that the chief thing to bear in mind is that it should not be *we* who pay them, an outcome extremely difficult to avoid. We did not avoid it last time and it looks to me at the moment that this time it will cost us even more, unless we change our ideas.

We are proposing to provide large numbers of occupation troops for a prolonged period, instead of taking the line that this should be primarily the duty of Germany's neighbours, —the French, Dutch, Belgians, Poles and Czechs. Furthermore, we are eagerly insisting on taking responsibility for the most difficult part of the country. Apart from any proposals for deliberate de-industrialisation, the devastation in this area by the end of the war is likely to deprive millions of workers in the area for which we are taking responsibility of any possibility of an early livelihood. To suppose that all this will not cost us a brass farthing is not sensible. How is it supposed that we are going to support the resulting heavy burden on us over what (we must assume) will be a considerable period of time, getting heavier rather than lighter as we move into Stage III?

Here again, however, a constructive suggestion will be more in place than vain criticism. I suggest that there are two fundamental principles affecting the settlement with Germany which we should unfalteringly demand and on which we should insist in season and out of season.

The first is that the first charge on Germany's resources ranking in front of everything is the *full* cost of the occupation, meaning by this the *full* cost and not merely the local expenditure. The second is that the next charge on her is the cost of any permitted and agreed imports into the country, so that there can be no question of allowing credit to Germany for her imports at the same time that she is paying reparations in any shape or form in other directions. Otherwise the maxim that it is not *we* who pay the German reparations will be broken. Yet it will be a miracle if we succeed in maintaining these principles without compromise.

The only other remedy is to avoid involving ourselves in the occupation of Europe to more than the least possible extent. We shall not see it through since it is beyond our capacity, but we shall waste considerable resources by discovering this later rather than sooner.

(7) The Treasury estimate allows nothing for relief either during the military period or through UNRRA. (Perhaps it is true that this will come largely out of stocks.) It allows nothing for relief and reconstruction in Burma and Malaya. It allows nothing for credits to Russia, Czechoslovakia and others. It assumes that our exports are all on a three-month cash basis. Setting one thing against another, I am still hopeful that this estimate is too high rather than too low, and that we may get away in 1945 with a total disinvestment below, rather than above, £700 million. Nevertheless even this reduction is not sufficient, in its repercussions on Stage III, greatly to affect or moderate the force of the general argument.

(8) The financial prospect is very greatly better than it was a short time ago before the Prime Minister's new directive on man-power and before the Departments were instructed to work on the assumption of an eighteen months' duration, instead of a two years' duration, for Stage II. But even after these decisions is there a right balance in our preparations between war and peace?

The vast cost of Stage II is partly due to the cumulative effect of the double effort of striving our utmost to shorten its duration and of providing at the same time for the assumption that we shall in fact fail to shorten it. Perhaps this is right and inevitable. Nevertheless, just as on the military side, we should be prepared for either alternative, so also on the non-military side we should be prepared for either alternative. If the Japanese affair were to crumple up quickly, the Board of Trade would be taken unprepared. Let paper plans, therefore, be authorised now, which are based on the assumption of a much shorter duration than eighteen months before Stage II. In this way, if all goes better than our expectations, the substantial reduction of the time-lag in conversion may be worth much.

(9) The prospective expense not only of Stage II but, on an even greater scale, of Stage III is, however, largely determined by another decision of policy, the financial results of which must be particularly emphasised; namely the decision to maintain an army overseas of about 1 million British personnel over and above the forces which will be fighting Japan. Is there any prospect of our being able to afford this in the first year of Stage III? And if not, is it not a waste of resources to behave during Stage II as if we could? I ask, therefore,—are we not, after the greatest conquest in our history, perhaps in danger of a *manie de grandeur*? Should there not be more balance in our purposes, at any rate until we can see our way more clearly?

We cannot police half the world at our own expense when we have already gone into pawn to the other half. We cannot run for long a great programme of social amelioration on money lent from overseas. Unless we are willing to put ourselves financially at the mercy of America and then borrow from her on her own terms and conditions sums which we cannot confidently hope to repay, what are we expecting? Are we looking forward to a spectacular bankruptcy (not, altogether, a bad idea) from which we shall rise next morning without a care in the world? Or are we following some star at present invisible to me?

Milton wrote:– 'War has made many great whom peace makes small. If after being released from the toils of war, you neglect the arts of peace, if your peace and your liberty be a state of warfare, if war be your only virtue, the summit of your praise, you will, believe me, soon find peace the most adverse to your interests.'

KEYNES

The Stage II negotiators had as their instructions a record of a conversation between Mr Churchill and President Roosevelt at Quebec and an agreement based on that conversation, both dated 14 September, amplified, to some extent, by a letter from Lord Cherwell to Mr Morgenthau two days later. The two documents appear below for reference.

I. QUEBEC CONFERENCE

Agreed Record of Conversation between Prime Minister and President on 14 September 1944

The Prime Minister said that when Germany was overcome there would be a measure of redistribution of effort in both countries. He hoped that the President would agree that during the war with Japan we should continue to get food, shipping, etc., from the United States to cover our reasonable needs. The President indicated assent.

He hoped also that the President would agree that it would be proper for lend lease munitions to continue on a proportional basis, even though this would enable the United Kingdom to set free labour for rebuilding, exports, etc., e.g., if British munitions production were cut to three-fifths, United States assistance should also fall to three-fifths. The President indicated assent. Mr Morgenthau, however, suggested that it would be better to have definite figures. He understood that munitions assistance required had been calculated by the British at about 3½ billion dollars in the first year, on the basis of the strategy envisaged before the 'Octagon' Conference. The exact needs would have to be recalculated in the light of decisions on military matters reached at the Conference. The non-munitions requirements had been put at 3 billion dollars gross, against which a considerable amount would be set off for reverse lend lease. The President agreed that it would be better to work on figures like these than on a proportional basis. The Prime Minister emphasised that all these supplies should be on lend lease. The President said this would naturally be so.

The Prime Minister pointed out that if the United Kingdom was once more to pay its way it was essential that the export trade which had shrunk to a very small fraction should be re-established. Naturally no articles obtained on lend lease or identical thereto would be exported or sold for profit,* but it was essential that the United States should not attach any conditions to supplies delivered to Britain on lend lease which would jeopardise the recovery of her export trade. The President thought this would be proper.

be a Joint Committee. It was held that it would be better to appoint an *ad hoc* Committee for this purpose on an informal basis, in the first instance, which could be formalised in due course. Pending its report the United States Departments should be instructed not to take action which would pre-judge the Committee's conclusions, e.g., production should not be closed down without reference to lend lease supplies, which it might be held should be supplied to Britain. The President thought that the Committee should be set up and suggested that Mr Morgenthau should head it representing him, and that Mr Stettinius who had taken such a large part in lend lease should also be a member.

Text of Agreement between Prime Minister and President

1. We have discussed the question of the scope and scale of mutual lend lease aid between the United States and the British Empire after the defeat

---

* The meaning of the phrase sold for profit occurring in paragraph 3 of the agreed record of the conversation between the Prime Minister and the President was later clarified in a letter dated the 16th September from Lord Cherwell to Mr Morgenthau, which reads as follows:–

> As you suggested I am sending this note so as to clarify the meaning of the phrase 'or sold for profit' in the record of the conversation between the President and the Prime Minister on the 14th September. According to my recollection you explained that it merely meant that our Government should not sell lend lease goods for more than the price at which they are entered in your books plus a reasonable allowance for transport and similar charges. I should be grateful if you could let me know whether this is correct. Though I do not know whether we are informed about the price at which lend lease goods stand in your books—thanks to your generous desire to keep the dollar sign out of lend lease—I feel sure that we habitually keep well within this limit and that we shall therefore find no difficulty in meeting the President's wishes in this respect.

The following reply was received from Mr Morgenthau, dated the 20th September, 1944:–

> This is in reply to your letter of the 16th September, 1944, concerning clarification of phrase 'or sold for profit' as it appears in your notes of conversation between President and Prime Minister on the 14th September.
>
> Without attempting a precise restatement, I have assumed that agreed principles which have heretofore governed sale or other disposition of lend lease goods in United Kingdom would be retained unless changing circumstances should make reconsideration desirable. In the latter event subject could be reopened for discussion between our two Governments.

of Germany and during the war with Japan. We have agreed that a Joint Committee shall be set up to consider this question with the following membership:–

American Members: Morgenthau.   British Members:
                     Stettinius.
                     Crowley.

2. The Committee will agree and recommend to the Heads of their respective Governments the amount of mutual aid in munitions, non-munitions and services which is to be provided for the most effective prosecution of the war. The Committee is instructed to obtain from the various branches of the Government whatever pertinent information is necessary for the preparation of their recommendations.

3. Pending the recommendations of the Committee to the heads of the respective Governments, the appropriate departments of each Government shall be instructed not to make any major decisions with respect to the programmes of lend lease aid for the period referred to above without the approval of the Committee.

4. In reaching its conclusions the Committee will be guided by the conversation between the President and the Prime Minister on the 14 September, 1944.

                    (Initialled)   F.D.R.   W.S.C.

On his arrival in North America, Keynes summed up the position at the beginning of the negotiations in two letters to the Chancellor.[1]

To SIR JOHN ANDERSON, *1 October 1944*

Dear Chancellor,

Spending the day here between trains, I found Cherwell also passing through and had an hour's conversation with him. I have also had an up-to-date report of the position in

[1] The references in both letters to the Morgenthau Plan for the post-war treatment of Germany pick up another strand of discussion current at the time. For additional material on Keynes's views on reparations, see *JMK*, vol. XXVI. The reference in the second letter to the discussions of the plan with Mr Morgenthau and Mr White probably reflects the fact that after a meeting with White on 20 August during which Keynes suggested that he favoured the post-war partition of Germany, White regarded him as a supporter of proposals of the Morgenthau type (*Morgenthau Diaries*, vol. 764, pp. 89–90).

Washington from Weeks[2] of the Ministry of Production, who is here with Gordon Munro from Ottawa. As Weeks returns to London tomorrow, I take this oportunity to send you some early reflections about which it may not be easy to cable to you.

I am considerably disturbed about the course matters are taking at Washington. I gather that Brand and most of the Washington representatives of our Departments are also unhappy.

Morgenthau's conception is that he and Cherwell should get together in a corner, that we shall submit to him full particulars of what we want and of our financial background in writing, that he and Cherwell will then reach decisions, and that these decisions will then be rail-roaded through the Committee, which shall be allowed the least possible opportunity to discuss them. Cherwell thinks this is a good idea. All, or nearly all, of our representatives in Washington fear this course may be disastrous. I share that view.

Morgenthau will be dealing with matters which he does not thoroughly understand and over which he has little or no control. All the decisions will have to be implemented by *other* Departments and none by the Treasury. It is feared that unless we can convince and carry with us and, where necessary, compromise with the *Departments concerned*, we shall get nowhere.

It is, I should add, part of Morgenthau's conception that there should be no elaborate organisation and no expert sub-committees to prepare the details for the main Committee, such as we were contemplating. So far *nothing has been done* in Washington to set up any such joint organisation.*

[2] Sir Hugh Weeks (b. 1904); Research and Statistical Manager, Cadbury's, until 1939; Director of Statistics, Ministry of Supply, 1939–42; Director of Statistics and Programmes, and member, Supply Council, 1942–3; Head of Progress and Planning Division Ministry of Production, 1943–5; Representative, Ministries of Supply and Production of Mission to North America, 1941–5.

* British Departments in Washington, however, who greatly want a proper organisation, have set up a shadow organisation on the British side so as to be ready.

If in the course of reaching a decision, we get across Morgenthau at some point, we are cooked. On the other hand, if agreement is reached over the heads of the Military and Supply Departments and the State Department and F.E.A., they may all unite to thwart the result.

Morgenthau (and Cherwell) attaches enormous importance to our submitting our case in writing as the first step. Something we can and should submit. But I cannot believe it is wise to deliver too much until one has sounded the ground.

The above may be—probably is—both too gloomy and too clear-cut a picture. Better, therefore, take little or no notice of it before Brand and I report from Washington. I write this because it may make what we cable more intelligible.*

Cherwell is now off travelling on an inspection of scientific establishments and will not (after tomorrow when I expect to see him again) be in Washington again for about ten days.

My anxiety is very greatly increased by another matter which ought to be (but I fear is not) irrelevant. I am told that at Quebec the P.M. began by pooh-poohing Morgenthau's proposals for the de-industrialisation of Germany. He (the P.M.) eventually accepted them as a result of Cherwell's strongly supporting them. This is the basis of the alliance between Cherwell and Morgenthau. M. was so pleased with this support and with its outcome, that he is undoubtedly very much inclined to greet with favour what Cherwell may propose. So far, so good.

But, as you will probably know, Morgenthau's proposals are violently opposed in the State Department and, I gather, in almost all other quarters in Washington. Thus an agreement between M and Cherwell based on this alliance may not assist elsewhere as much as one might have hoped. What is worse, Brand (I gather, and, as I should expect) is strongly opposed to M's. German proposals; so am I; and so, I believe, is everyone else in the British missions in Washington.

* Weeks will be reporting to Sinclair and Lyttelton along lines similar to the above.

Harry White is reported as main author of M's. proposals, though I do not *a priori* feel quite sure of this.

So you can see what a pretty kettle of fish there might be.

If, as is probable, M is being defeated by the other Departments on his German plan, he will (as is his habit) turn morose on *all* issues however disconnected; and if he suspects Brand and myself of sympathising with his opponents, —!

According to [Hugh] Weeks M's proposals are even balmier than I thought. The alleged gain of £400 million to our exports is not the consequence merely of the de-industrialisation of the Ruhr. It emerges because according to M. Germany is to be allowed no exports whatever!*

Two cuttings, which I enclose, will indicate the public reception of M's. plan—which like everything else is already public. That from *Time* gives the low-down. Walter Lippmann's article gives (what seems to me) the commonsense of the case. I had a most agreeable and restful journey.

Yours ever,

KEYNES

To SIR JOHN ANDERSON, *4 October 1944*

My dear Chancellor,

On arriving here I found the position very much as I had described it to you in the letter I wrote in Montreal.

In the first place Cherwell's position is a little embarrassing both to himself and to the others concerned. He believes himself to have been appointed by the Prime Minister to be in charge of the whole proceedings, and was not aware that the matter had been considered by the Cabinet on the lines recorded in the Minutes, from which I brought with me an extract. Ben Smith is a bit perplexed as to the relationship between himself and Cherwell, and his position is made much

---

* Of course the above *may* be a travesty of the plan. I am told that the Morgenthau plan is a voluminous document worked out in detail. A copy was available at Quebec but I am not aware that any of our people have a copy, though perhaps Cherwell has.

more difficult by the fact that Cherwell has been in a minority of one amongst all those taking part in the discussions as to what is our best line of procedure. Moreover, he (C.) takes the line that he is not prepared to be overruled and rather than that he would throw his hand in and depart home, which he constantly declares is what he has wanted to do from the beginning. I am told also that in matters of detail our experts find it very difficult to make any lasting impression on his mind.

That is on the debit side. On the credit side it is clear that Cherwell has established invaluable contacts with Morgenthau and Harry Hopkins, and that he has got Morgenthau into a state of mind in which he is prepared to do his damnedest (and that is just about what it is) to help us. Also, as I have always found, no personal difficulty arises between him and me, the difference is entirely limited to the merits of the case and we are, so far as I can judge, getting on very well (he constantly affirms that, if we think we can do better without him, nothing would please him more than to slip away, and, if this has to come about, he will do it in a manner which is entirely free from any suggestion of a row or difference of opinion, so as not to interfere with our inheriting his good relations with Morgenthau.) It is in my opinion essential that he should stay on until October 16th and for some days thereafter so as to get the first stage of the proceedings properly launched, but it might well be better after that that he should find some good excuse for going home, which I believe he would genuinely prefer.

Faced with this situation, and especially after I had seen Morgenthau and Harry White, as reported below, I felt it was essential to maintain a concordat and that the adherents of both points of view had something valuable to contribute. We therefore agreed on the programme set forth in the long telegram drafted by myself which went off today and will have reached you before this letter. Cherwell himself goes off today on a tour of scientific establishments and will not be back for ten days or so.

I took an early opportunity to visit Mr Morgenthau. He was exceedingly cordial and I had a long and satisfactory tête-à-tête on the same friendly basis as we had established at Bretton Woods. He expressed himself, as also did Harry White, as delighted that I had come, adding that he had hoped that you would send me. Harry White even went so far as to claim that he thought I probably owed it to Morgenthau's initiative that I had been selected!

So far as our immediate business was concerned, I was entirely brought round to Cherwell's point of view that we must at this stage fall in with Morgenthau's wishes. My only difference with Cherwell is in his believing and my doubting that Morgenthau's tactics can ultimately prevail or be successful. So long as we leave ourselves entirely in his (M.'s) hands we can, I feel sure, be confident that he will do his very best for us, and means to implement the Quebec agreements in our favour up to the hilt.

I must now mention that, just as I feared would be the case, both Morgenthau and Harry White were considerably more interested in their plan for de-industrialising Germany than in anything else. Morgenthau started off with this before coming to our main business; said that he would like me to see their full proposal in the form in which he had presented it to the President, provided I would regard this paper as something to be seen by no one except myself, though he agreed to my passing it on to you. He said that he would like a later date to have a round table talk with me about it. All this was, of course, most embarrassing and I had to preserve an unwonted and uncomfortable reticence. I discovered that he by no means considers himself defeated on this issue, and is still on the warpath. Everyone else here believes that Hull and Stimson, who are furious at his having slipped up to Quebec and put across the President behind their backs a plan which he knew they bitterly disapproved of, have been successful in persuading the President to throw over his plan. But it seemed clear that he has not yet accepted defeat, nor, so far as one can judge, is he particularly rattled about the storm which has blown furiously through the Press during the weekend. When Harry White broached the same subject I took the line that all plans relating to Germany which I had seen so far struck me as equally bad, and the only matter I was concerned with was that it should not be the British Treasury which had to pay reparations or support Germany. I gathered that the plan is not quite as crude as it appeared in the reports from Quebec. All the same it seems pretty mad, and I asked White how the inhabitants of the Ruhr were to be kept from starvation; he said that there would have to be bread lines but on a very low level of subsistence. When I asked if the British, as being responsible for that area, would also be responsible for the bread, he said that the U.S. Treasury would if necessary pay for the bread, provided always it was on a very low level of subsistence. So whilst the hills are being turned into a sheep run, the valleys will be filled for some years to come with a closely packed bread line on a very low level of subsistence at American expense. How I am to keep a straight face when it comes to the round table talk I cannot imagine. I try to prepare and sustain myself by repeating every night the three vows which I always make before a visit to America, namely, one that I will drink no cocktails, two that I will obey my wife, and three that I will never allow myself to be betrayed into speaking the truth; loyally striving, as a rule without much success, to deserve Sir Henry Wotton's epigram 'An Ambassador is a man sent to lie abroad for the good of his country'.

Well, you see it is a pretty kettle of fish. I am told on all hands that Morgenthau and White stand worse with their colleagues than at any previous time. The German episode has raised the temperature in some Departments, particularly in the State Department, to boiling point, some wiseacres even going so far as to say that Mr Hull will make it a condition of his participation in the forthcoming Administration that M. is dropped. Yet Morgenthau is quite clearly filled with the utmost goodwill and the very best intentions towards us, and the White House entourage advises us that we should go on regarding him as our best friend.

I should not forget to add that in Morgenthau's mind his goodwill towards us is emotionally and otherwise strongly bound up in his attitude to Germany. 'In the long run', he said to me, 'it is a question of a strong Britain or a strong Germany, and I am for a strong Britain.' That at any rate was a sentiment with which I was able heartily to agree. Liberality to us is at the bottom of his mind part of his revenge against Germany.

Is it fair to send a poor official, whose cynicism about politicians is already more than it should be, into such a boiling?

Yours ever,

KEYNES

As the letters above suggest, Keynes's arrival in Washington immediately involved him in discussions of the best procedure to be followed in the negotiations. In his approach Keynes emphasised the need for a general conviction amongst the Americans in the agencies involved with Lend Lease questions that the British requirements eventually agreed were just. This could not come from a series of orders from above. Rather, he saw the need for a full, frank and detailed discussion of the situation with the officials responsible for policy formulation, appropriations and administration. Nevertheless, he accepted Lord Cherwell's view that they must fall in, at least in the first instance, with Mr Morgenthau's preferred procedure of a small high-level committee, to avoid alienating him, while leaving the way open for wider discussions.

In the interim, Keynes and the rest of the British delegation worked at preparing the full statement of Britain's needs for the first year of Stage II for delivery to the Americans. This 'book of words' as Keynes called it, entitled *British Requirements for the First Year of Stage II*,[3] set out the needs agreed in Keynes's instructions from lend lease material for civilian and military use and export freedom. However, after receiving a cable on 13 October indicating that Britain's gold and dollar reserves at the end of 1945 would be below their previously expected level, Keynes went beyond his instructions in preparing a chapter asking for additional items to safeguard Britain's reserve position (Chapter 3). Emphasising that short-run financial embarrassment would hinder fruitful post-war collaboration, it raised the possibility of restoring previous cuts in lend lease and reimbursing Britain for certain transactions undertaken in the past (some of the old commitments). The memorandum also contained appendices on Britain's external financial position, civilian living standards in the U.K. and manpower problems. The completed document was passed to the Americans on 17 October. The day before, he sent copies to London for the Chancellor, the Governor of the Bank, Sir Richard Hopkins, Sir Wilfrid Eady, Sir David Waley and Mr Harmer.[4] His covering letter for the Chancellor set out his feelings at the time.

To SIR JOHN ANDERSON, *16 October 1944*

Dear Chancellor,

I enclose with this a copy of the book of the words which we shall be handing to Morgenthau tomorrow. I call particular attention to Chapter 3, which is, in my judgement, the kernel of the problem. I do not anticipate financial difficulties on the rest of the programme, though there may be supply difficulties about certain food and munitions items. I am also confident that we shall get rid of the Export White Paper. The telegram recently received about the prospective decline of our reserves in 1945 indicated, however, that if we did no better than get through the programmes we were instructed to get through, we run the risk of ending 1945 in parlous condition so far as liquid reserves are concerned. I therefore felt, as has been explained in a telegram, that we must con-

[3] A copy is available in the Cabinet Papers in the Public Record Office.
[4] Sir Frederick Harmer (b. 1905); entered Treasury, 1939; temporary Assistant Secretary, 1943–5; served in Washington, 1944, 1945, for economic and financial negotiations; resigned, December 1945; subsequently government director of British Petroleum Co. and chairman of P. and O. Steamship Co.

centrate on getting either additional lend lease assistance, or the refund of some of our half-dead claims, or preferably both, feeling confident that this would be in accordance with your wishes. My idea is to be very discontented unless we get a relief in one shape or another to the tune of $500 million, which would, if the forecasts are correct, just about keep our reserves where they are now.

The telegram forecasting the great reduction in reserves should not have taken me by surprise, since it is almost exactly what I predicted six months ago. Nevertheless, one had been forgetting recently the situation which was bound to arise as soon as we enter a period in which the extension of reciprocal aid and the curtailment of lend lease assistance would coincide with the falling away of earnings from U.S. forces in the sterling area. I think the forecast as telegraphed may be a bit on the pessimistic side, but the details do not strike me as unreasonable or unplausible.

This forecast only serves to confirm the feelings which I voiced in the memorandum written on the boat which I sent you a fortnight ago. The policy of keeping a vast army overseas has not yet been brought into proper relation with our financial capacity.

I hope you will like the document itself. It is certainly the fullest presentation of our case yet prepared, and I trust that there is not much in it which would have been better omitted. Every line had to pass the heads of Missions here, which, as you may suppose, added considerably to the job of getting the thing done in the time.

Yours ever,

KEYNES

P.S. Your telegram LLAMA 68 about the conjectural character of the forecast of gold and dollar balances reached me just in time to allow some drafting changes in the document. We had, in fact, already emphasised in several places the precarious and conjectural nature of the estimates. But after getting your telegram, I made some further last-minute changes in the same direction.

I am afraid, however, that we ought not to build too much on the forecast being wrong. In my judgment, the probable error in the forecast of reserves is much smaller than the error in our overall balance of trade. The latter includes two very precarious items, namely, our war expenditure in India and the Middle East, and our receipts from exports, neither of which much affect the estimate of our reserve position. The conjectural element in the latter is the earnings from U.S. troops, which the American Treasury are in as good a position —indeed in a better position—to estimate as ourselves. But it does not seem likely that we can get greatly increased receipts from that source. The forecast is in the main the inevitable and safely predictable consequence of our running into a period in which (*a*) the extention of reciprocal aid to raw materials, (*b*) the curtailment of the field of lend lease, and (*c*) the falling off in earnings from U.S. troops, are simultaneously effective over a whole year.

After a general discussion over dinner with Mr Morgenthau and Mr White on 18 October, the formal negotiations started in the former's office on 19 October. Keynes reported the mood of the early discussions on 21 October.

To SIR JOHN ANDERSON, *21 October 1944*

Your telegram No. 9033, which reached me just as we were going off to our first discussion, was most comforting. As you will have gathered from other telegrams, progress so far is mostly negative. We have discovered what some of us expected from the outset, namely, that Morgenthau would have no authority to settle anything, and that our several demands would be referred almost immediately to the Departments primarily concerned with them. When it came to a question of action, Morgenthau inevitably had to accept the role of almost completely passive transmitter. The general atmosphere however remains very friendly all round, and the only reason for any disappointment so far is that the Main Committee is at present reluctant to transmit any general decisions of policy to those considering details lower down the line. There is the intelligible reason for this that the Americans have not yet had our paper long enough to be able to clear up difficulties in their own ranks, and are therefore not yet in a position to agree principles with us. Accordingly we decided not to press the pace, and to allow them three days or so for further examination of our document among themselves. Neverthless Morgenthau was emphatic that there would be no question of re-opening Quebec decisions and we are in a good position to bring back to the Main Committee any particular case of action lower down which seems to us to be a departure from them.

2. The old claims in chapter 3 for which my nomenclature of half-dead cats has been generally accepted, has been badly received by Morgenthau. This is rather what I had expected. They will have served their intended purpose if they bring it home that if we are to grant that these items are better forgotten, something must be found to replace them.

3. Morgenthau, in private conversation with Cherwell and myself, fully accepts this. He says however that he would much rather find some novel way of providing us with a large lump sum of new money than play about with complicated methods of picking up a few dollars here and there, or resurrecting the claims which were the subject of earlier controversies. We are agreeing with him that [?it] would be vastly better to replace half-dead cats with a new live dog. But in what kennel is he to be found? Morgenthau says that with so many clever people around we ought to be able to think up something. When I ask White what the Secretary has in

mind and how it is to be done, White replies that he does not know. Nevertheless, Cherwell and I feel that Morgenthau is on the right track here. What we want is some entirely new ticket, yielding more than half a billion and anything up to a billion dollars. If we could make any reasonable proposal, now is certainly the moment at which it would have a favourable reception. The President himself will of course have to be brought in if we travel outside the narrower ambit within which we have hitherto confined ourselves. I will take an early opportunity of sounding White with Harry Hopkins.

4. Cherwell and I have been wondering whether the means could be found through the old idea of a lump sum American contribution to our expenses in the Middle East and India. It would help us to know which [*sic* ?whether] you would favour our exploring this ground very tentatively and cautiously. Our estimate of cash expenditure in the Middle East and India in 1945 is £440 million. If the United States were to reimburse half of this to us in dollars, it would nicely fill the bill. On the other hand an offer to assume a share of our sterling guarantees to India, Egypt and Palestine would not assist our present necessities.

5. An alternative which has occurred to us is to suggest, or rather get them to suggest, some retrospective lend lease to reimburse us part of our expenses before lend lease was effective. This would not encroach unduly on the Stage III possibilities, whereas certain other ideas floating about here would clearly do so, and might use up prematurely what is better kept in reserve for a later date.

6. You should be aware that there is no such clear distinction in the minds of the Americans as there is in ours between Stage II and Stage III of financial problems. If suggestions come up, as is quite likely, which we feel more appropriate to Stage III it will not be easy to decide how to receive them. Perhaps dividing line should be that any proposals for credits however easy and convenient terms must be

reserved for Stage III. But retrospective lend lease might be a suitable way of winding up the remaining lend lease period during Stage II. I should add that the above should not lead you to suppose that there is any reasonable expectation at present of any such thing. We are merely trying to think up suggestions in response to Morgenthau's request that if there is any plausible source of quite new money we should advise him about it.

7. Without risking any new bright ideas, we might build up (say) 300 million dollars by restoring various items to lend lease and in odds and ends of ways without raising the more controversial items. If taking everything into account you would prefer this less venturesome course may I have instructions?

8. At a recent private meeting with Stettinius, he again spoke hotly about Argentine meat contracts. Here I should like to venture on [?one or] two observations. In spite of telegram No. 5584 reporting that Armour rejected the idea of even a one year contract, I adhered to the opinion expressed in my previous telegram No. 5571, that a compromise on basis of a one year contract could be reached. This is confirmed by the Ambassador's conversation with Stettinius reported in telegram No. 5660.[5]

9. The second observation is to emphasise what is indeed obvious, that to continue contract conversations currently would be regarded here as in the worst of faith. I mention this in view of last paragraph of telegram No. 8966 to the effect

[5] American attempts to eliminate enemy activities in the Western Hemisphere stumbled repeatedly on Argentina, which remained neutral until almost the end of the war, was a major supplier of foodstuffs for Britain and allowed German sympathisers and agents to operate with impunity. Throughout the war, American attempts to take economic action against Argentina by freezing her American assets and the like stumbled on the fact that their impact would be blunted if Britain did not follow suit, which, owing to the foodstuffs position plus Argentine willingness to accumulate sterling balances in return, she was reluctant to do. However, in June 1944 the United States had frozen Argentine assets, had ordered American ships to boycott Argentine ports and had recalled her Ambassador. Britain recalled her Ambassador but did little else.

that we here need not excite ourselves unduly since something like two months would be likely to elapse in any case before negotiations reached finality. The concluding passage of Prime Minister's telegram that we were free [?to] re-open the matter again in two months, might be taken in conjunction with this to allow negotiations to go on provided no conclusion is reached for at least two months. It must be remembered that the State Department are convinced, however unjustifiably, that an important part of our motive in meat negotiations is to curry favour with the Argentine and nothing we can say is likely to disabuse them of this idea if we persist with the negotiations for contracts exceeding one year.

The Chancellor replied to Keynes's cable on 24 October.

From SIR JOHN ANDERSON, *24 October 1944*

1. For the moment I must content myself with acknowledging your telegram 5722 with its account of your first discussions with Morgenthau and also the remarkable document which you have put in. All of us here would like to send you and your team our congratulations and our thanks for the very full and frank way in which our case has been presented despite all the difficulties of time and shifting figures which may have handicapped you. I should personally like those who have shared your toils in the preparation of this document to know how much I appreciate the result.

2. I rather agree with the view you express in paragraphs 2 and 3 that if we find a new live dog, it will be preferable to a synthesis of half dead cats, especially as Morgenthau may reject some of the larger cats.

3. As for a live dog, my first impression is that the political difficulties over there and over here which would arise from a big cash contribution to our expenditure in India, would be troublesome, for we should have a continuing relationship with the U.S. Treasury and other U.S. Departments over the whole field of our expenditure in India. I agree that as India is recognised as a major base for the Japanese war there is something to be said for the Americans helping us in the cost of the organisation and maintenance of the base. But in fact the strategic plan of their Forces will scarcely be operating from India and they may take that point at once.

4. One idea which has been adumbrated here is that the Americans might

make an appreciable contribution towards the cost of the physical destruction in this country. This might make an appeal to responsive sentiment over there but apart from that it has little else to commend it. The sums at issue are not large enough for a reasonable American share of the cost to be of much use to us. The benefit would be for this country only whereas the weakness of our financial position affects the whole Commonwealth. Also our position as recipients of this gratuity would not be very dignified.

5. Of the various suggestions which have been canvassed the most promising is for a grant in aid of retrospective lend lease. That for two reasons. As events have shown, our efforts and our expenditure in the days when America was neutral contributed not a little to the defence of America and American interests. Moreover a substantial part of that expenditure set up a war potential in the United States, particularly in the aircraft industry, which certainly saved a full year in the development of the striking power of the American Air Forces. Therefore a substantial contribution from them in respect of that period would be a recognition of facts.

6. We assume that your intention is that any assistance on these lines should be a grant in aid, and not a loan, even interest free. Otherwise these expedients would impinge upon possible policies for Stage III.

7. I repeat that these are only first suggestions to add to all the others that you no doubt are considering. If you think either of them might be translated into a live dog we will supply you with such supporting evidence as you want. We will also go on thinking of other methods.

During the inevitable lull in the negotiations that would accompany the American elections in early November, Keynes had planned to go to Ottawa to prepare the ground for Stage II. However, he found himself unable to go and instead began to prepare the ground by letter.

To DR C. CLARK, *27 October 1944*

My dear Clark,

As you will have heard, Sinclair and I had a project of coming to Ottawa from November 3rd until about November 9th. This period over the Election is going to be the only possible period during which we can get away from Washington. I hear from Munro, however, that this would not have been at all convenient at your end. We have decided to give up the idea of an early visit, and wait until our work here is at an end. It is very rash to surmise when that will be, but provisionally in my own mind I am putting the date some time between November 15th and 20th.

Meanwhile, I am enclosing for you personally a copy of the Introduction and the Annexes to the Statement of British Requirements for the First Year of Stage II which we have handed to the Americans.[6] This contains the whole of the material except the chapters which give the details, military and otherwise, of our lend lease applications for the coming year. This is, you will appreciate, a top secret document. The High Commissioner will be handing copies officially, I believe, to the Prime Minister and Mr Ilsley.

By the time I reach Ottawa I shall be in a position to give you can account of the outcome of our American negotiations. The atmosphere is extremely good and could scarcely be more friendly. On none of my visits here have I been working in so forthcoming an environment. There is certainly a clear will in all quarters to meet us to the fullest extent practicable. But no actual decisions have yet crystallised, and it is too soon to show final confidence. I may mention that I am very hopeful indeed of the old question of U.S. dollar freights on Canadian mutual aid supplies being settled in our favour.

I am planning to bring my wife with me, and we are both very much looking forward to another visit to Canada.

Sincerely yours,
KEYNES

Keynes's enclosure ran as follows.

---

[6] Not printed. [Ed.]

ARRANGEMENTS FOR SUPPLIES FROM CANADA IN STAGE II

1. We (His Majesty's Government in the United Kingdom) have been considering the magnitude of the supplies which will be needed after the German armistice in order that we may play our full part in the war against Japan, and to carry out our military commitments in the occupation of Europe and elsewhere. During Stage II (by which we mean the period between the German armistice and the final end of hostilities) we have three major military commitments, that is to say

(*a*) the Japanese war
(*b*) the occupation of Germany, and
(*c*) the protection of Imperial lines of communication and the maintenance of order in areas of British responsibility.

At the same time we have to maintain the civilian standard of living in the United Kingdom—indeed we feel that after five years of war and privation, it has become necessary to make provision for some slight increase in these standards. In particular, it has now become essential to release some manpower for the rebuilding and repair of houses. It is also our intention to release sufficient manpower to enable us to make a substantial beginning in the recovery of exports during 1945. The results of our stock-taking, particularly in relation to manpower and overseas finance, will be communicated to the Canadian Government in a comprehensive form before that Government is asked to reach final conclusions.

2. We also hope at an early date to lay before the Government of Canada a series of detailed proposals concerning the supply and financial relationships between the two countries during Stage II. Meanwhile, the purpose of this paper is to suggest a general principle which might govern these

relationships, and to give a preliminary indication of the scale of assistance which we shall be proposing.

3. The general principle underlying our proposals is broadly as follows:–

We propose the adoption of a pooling plan, by which, incidentally, the financial relationships between the two countries will be greatly simplified. Under this Canada will supply us freely with munitions and war services, and the United Kingdom will supply freely to the Canadian Forces all supplies and services obtained from the sterling area (except pay). The scope of mutual aid to the United Kingdom will then be limited to food and ancillary services and certain raw materials to be mutually agreed upon.

4. This proposal represents a radical change in the basis of accounting between our two countries, but we believe that it follows the foundations of partnership in a common enterprise much more realistically than our arrangements in the past; it avoids much inevitable arbitrary accounting; it should prevent the periodic crises in our financial relationships which have always in the past been resolved by an act of generosity by Canada but which we cannot always ask to be so resolved; it is, moreover, thought to be of a nature which will commend itself to the Parliaments and to public opinions of the two countries as a fair and realistic sharing of the physical and financial burden of the Japanese war. The following will give some idea how this proposal might work out in practice.

5. An examination of the probable balance of payments with the sterling area reveals a gap greatly in excess of the current level of mutual aid. It is true that throughout the European war this gap has existed. In the first two and a half years it was filled by payments of gold and dollars, by repatriation of securities, and by the 700 million dollar loan— in this period Britain parted with capital assets and incurred debts to Canada to a total of $1,670 million. In 1942 and 1943 the gap was financed by the billion dollar gift, and we also

advanced U.S. dollars to cover the deficit. In 1943–44 and 1944–45 the gap was financed partly by mutual aid. But Canada also undertook to bear a larger part of the cost of her Forces overseas, with the result that the gap left to be covered by mutual aid was kept down.

6. But if this system were to continue during Stage II the gap to be covered by mutual aid would be much greater. Paradoxical as it may seem, the bigger Canada's fighting effort, the smaller is the gap since she has then to make larger payments in respect of her forces overseas. On the other hand, if Canada's part in the war effort becomes primarily one of munition and food supply, the gap is then very wide indeed. During the European war, we have been able to rely on Canada's generosity and sense of what is right, and the gap has always been filled. But we are aware of the problems which confront the Government of Canada during Stage II, and we do not wish to place before them proposals which on the present financial basis, can mean only one of two things —increased mutual aid appropriation or the incurring of war debts by ourselves.

7. We suggest, therefore, that:–

(a) Canada should provide munitions freely for the pool to the extent set out in the table (to be supplied) of estimated requirements. Canada would also provide freely all war services incurred in Canada on our behalf, e.g. inspection and inland freight on munitions.

(b) The United Kingdom should provide freely for the Canadian Forces overseas all supplies and services (except pay) which on shipping and supply grounds can most conveniently be obtained from within the sterling area.

(c) Canada would limit her mutual aid assistance to the United Kingdom to cover food requirements, together with the ancillary transport services connected with this food, also certain raw materials to be determined as mutually convenient.

(d) The financing of the Air Training Plan would be the

subject of separate arrangements, as has been the case in the past. We think, however, that these arrangements should be settled in general conformity with the above proposals.

(*e*) Other transactions between Canada and the sterling area, apart from such mutual aid as Canada may accord to other parts of the Commonwealth, would be financed on a cash basis.

(8) The cash transactions between the two countries would thus be in respect of the pay of Canadian troops within the sterling area and in respect of materials, manufactured goods and services together with certain miscellaneous payments (e.g. NAAFI) not covered by mutual aid. We do not think that this would lead to any substantial problem between Canada and the sterling area and, so far as we can see, any residual deficit during Stage II should be manageable, provided that we are able during Stage II to increase our exports to Canada from the present very restricted level. The amount of orders which we can afford to place in Canada will inevitably have to be limited by the amount of mutual aid plus the cash income of the sterling area in Canada.

9. It is suggested that the supplies and services referred to in 7(a) above would be met from Canada's War Appropriation and would in addition to Canada's own expenditure on her Forces in Canada and on the pay of her Forces overseas represent Canada's financial contribution to the common fighting and munition pool. At the same time, Canada would be drawing freely from the pool all the supplies which were needed by her Forces overseas from sterling area sources.

10. We believe this to be in financial terms, a true representation of the war efforts of the two countries. It avoids all the complicated and arbitrary Service accounting which will become increasingly difficult in the conditions of the Japanese war; it states firmly and clearly what contribution each country is making, and charges it to the appropriate place in each country's internal accounts.

11. We hope this plan will commend itself to the Government of Canada. For five years we have in fact been pooling our resources in the war against the common enemy. In physical terms, there has been a complete pooling of man-power and of supplies but this has never been openly endorsed in our financial arrangements. In this new stage of the war, it is surely right to bring our financial affairs into line with the physical realities of our respective war efforts.

12. We had originally intended to furnish full details of our requirements as appendices to this paper. The adjustments necessitated by the recent decisions on strategy taken at Quebec, however, have not as yet been fully determined by the Service Departments. Our needs for raw materials in Stage II are also under re-consideration in the light of the revised supply programme. We believe, therefore, that time will, in the end, be saved if we are left free to take another three or four weeks in the preparation of these programmes, presenting them to the Government of Canada at the second stage of these discussions.

Nevertheless, the Government of Canada may like to have at this stage a rough indication of the probable order of magnitude of our proposals. As regards non-munitions, there is likely to be a considerable reduction in requirements for metals, partly offset by some increased requirements for agricultural and forestry products. On balance, we estimate that the sum to be charged on the Mutual Aid Appropriation might amount to $600 million, and that the cost of providing munitions and other supplies and services referred to in paragraph 7(a) above on the War Appropriation would be of the order of $800 million.* Against this Canada will be receiving benefits under paragraph 7(b) above as reciprocal aid.

* The munition requirements for the United Kingdom and other Empire countries will not exceed in total 70 per cent of the 1944 level and may well be lower. Taking the Department of Finance's estimate for 1944/45 less internal taxation we calculate that 70 per cent would amount in round figures to $800 million.

Mr Morgenthau's Committee met twice more, on 25 and 30 October, to discuss British Dominion and Indian requirements, before Keynes sent the Chancellor another reporting letter.

To SIR JOHN ANDERSON, *30 October 1944*

Dear Chancellor,

This week we are coming to grips with the additional requirements in Chapter 3, and with the programme of the Dominions. It seemed to us that in both these respects the original statement of our case was capable of being improved and expanded. We have, therefore, prepared a supplement to our original statement, of which I enclose a copy.

The Dominions case as here set forth seems to me exceedingly strong, and I am hopeful that we shall be able to overcome some resistances which have been experienced in the past.

Chapter 3 is now a pretty comprehensive list. Any last minute thoughts are not likely to add much to it. Including the dead cats mentioned in the previous statement, if we got our maximum suggestions under every head, the additions to lend lease would come to about $380 million, and the outstanding claims to another $377 million. I am afraid that a fair proportion of these are only very moderate starters indeed, and the really good ones do not add up to much. However, you will probably have heard by cable how things are looking before you get this letter.

I am not pursuing any of the larger ideas until after we see what our changes are along these lines, though here also I shall probably have cabled to you before you get this letter. I am more and more inclined to the view that if we can get anything substantial along the lines of Chapter 3, it would be wiser to put off the other lines of approach, which would inevitably entangle us in Stage III considerations. I think it not unlikely that we may be able to take up Stage III not later than next February, and there is much to be said for not using up prematurely any of the expedients which might serve us for that later purpose. There is also the difficulty that almost any expedient, except those given in this supplement to Chapter 3, would require new legislation.

Meanwhile we can only live in hope—not too confident a hope. This qualification does not apply to our normal programme, which will, I think, make good progress. There are, so far as I can see, only three [four] major difficulties there:–

1. Lend lease for Indian rolling-stock.

2. The allocation we are asking for carcass meat.

3. Whether we can be allowed to keep such large oil stocks as we propose.

4. The obtaining of the coastal vessels on lend lease without any present raising of the question of end value.

None of these points, however, has yet been decided against us.

Yours ever,
KEYNES

To SIR JOHN ANDERSON, *31 October 1944*

My dear Chancellor,

Morgenthau asked Cherwell and myself to visit him this morning to discuss certain major issues.

He began by telling us that, in his capacity as the Chairman of the Combined Committee, he had been warned by Stettinius that the agreement of the State Department to the matters now under consideration in our current negotiations must be subject to a reserve on their part so long as the Argentine meat issue is unsettled. Clearly this was intended to be taken as a formal declaration. I asked whether it was to be understood as applying to the negotiations as a whole, or only to the meat items in the food programme. I said that the latter had clearly a certain relevance to the Argentine question, but that I should be sorry to have to inform you that the negotiations as a whole were in any way mixed up with this extraneous matter. To this I received no clear answer.

If this stood by itself, we should be entitled to be indignant at what is in the nature of a blackmail. Nor is it consistent with the Quebec decisions that the State Department should make matters decided there between the President and the Prime Minister dependent on an issue with a third country which has come up since. Unfortunately, however, I am pretty sure that the justification of such tactics in their own minds is that they believe we are double crossing them in the Argentine. I am not sure whether all the Argentine telegrams come your way. But I assume you will have seen the Ambassador's telegram to the Foreign Office 5842 of Oct 28 proposing a visit from Llewellin, in which the position is set out fully. All the same, perhaps I had better recapitulate the substance. It appears that before the Prime Minister made the promise to the President, which is interpreted by the State Department to mean that we agreed to break off the negotiations for a couple of months, the Ministry of Food had already made an oral offer to the Argentines of a four-year contract. After the Prime Minister's decision had been received, the Foreign Office decided, nevertheless, not to withdraw this offer but to wait until the Argentines accepted it, and then to consider what to do next, thereby hoping, I suppose, to gain perhaps a few days or weeks' breathing space during which they could indulge the pastime of not making up their minds. Accordingly, no action whatever was taken on the Prime Minister's instructions. The position remains that we have made an offer to the Argentine and that we have not withdrawn it. Just as the Foreign Office proposes to keep this dark from the Americans, so it proposes to keep dark from the Argentines so long as possible the fact that the Americans have pressed us to break off and that we have agreed to do so. Unfortunately, late last week the Argentine Government decided to accept. The position is being held currently (or was when I last heard of it) by our representative in Buenos Aires locking himself in his bathroom and being inaccessible to the Argentines seeking to accept the offer. There, I understand, he proposes to remain, not answering knocks on the door and not opening letters for another three weeks. What the Foreign Office hopes to gain from this period of enforced seclusion is not very clear, unless perhaps they think Mr Dewey[7] is going to win the Election. Not only is the fact that we have made an offer of a four-year contract to the Argentine Government and that the offer has not been withdrawn well known to the meat companies in the Argentine, it is also, we believe, well known to the State Department's sources of information. Stettinius, therefore, though he is too polite to say so in so many words, has reason to believe that, whilst we have led them to think that the negotiations are broken off, there remains in fact an outstanding and not withdrawn offer for a four-year contract.

How reasonable people can lend themselves to such monkey tricks, beats me. But if they do, they must take the consequences. And the formal statement made to Cherwell and myself this morning by Morgenthau is one of the consequences.

Morgenthau then went on to say that for his own part he entirely shared the view of the State Department on this matter, except that, speaking personally, he would go a great deal further. He was at pains to explain that all which I am reporting in this paragraph and the two following represents merely his personal view and must not be taken as coming either from the State Department or from the Administration, pointing out that there was no sort of joint Cabinet responsibility over here such as exists in London. With this preface he went on to explain that he did not agree with the State Department that it would make a significant difference

---

[7] Thomas Edmund Dewey (1902–71); lawyer; Governor of New York, 1942–54; Republican candidate for President, 1944, 1948.

to the Argentine position if instead of a long contract we were to continue to buy meat on a month-to-month basis. His own view is that, shortly after the Election, it is desirable to declare a complete economic boycott of Argentina, affecting both imports and exports. He shared the view prevalent in Administration circles that the United States cannot afford to continue to countenance a Fascist government in South America very much longer. He thinks that a complete blockade would bring the present Argentine Administration down. He is not, I should judge, at all closely acquainted with the issues which would arise from a complete blockade either on the political or on the supply side, as affecting food for liberated Europe generally as well as for ourselves. The point is that his feeling is strong and emphatic, and is most unlikely to be changed. I would add that there is no evidence that the State Department go, at present, so far as this. Nevertheless, the meat contract issue can no longer be regarded as a private fad of Mr Hull's. Mr Hull himself is in hospital and not likely to be back in charge for some weeks. In his absence all the members of the State Department and everyone else here on the American side with whom I have been in contact speak with the same voice. The P.M. when in Moscow asked Harriman[8] to look into this matter and Harriman reports to Cherwell that the Administration must be regarded as absolutely solid on this issue.

Mr Morgenthau was, however, equally clear that there should be no question whatever of our suffering in our meat ration. He said that he was entirely in favour of the meat programme we have put forward. He told us that surely our right policy was to put it squarely up to the Americans

[8] William Averell Harriman (b. 1891); Chairman, Union Pacific Railroad, 1932–46; Chairman, Business Advisory Council for U.S. Department of Commerce, 1937–9; Chief, Materials Branch, Production Division, O.P.M., 1941; special representative of President in Britain with rank of Minister, March 1941, in Russia, August 1941; representative in London of Combined Shipping Adjustment Board, February 1942; member, London Combined Production and Resources Board, July 1942; U.S. Ambassador to Russia, 1943–6, to Britain, April–October 1946.

whether they are prepared themselves to introduce sufficient rationing arrangements to allow us to get just as much beef without the Argentine as we have any hope of getting with it. Tell us, he said, that you must have your meat ration and cannot compromise on that, but that you are not crazy on the Argentine and that you put it squarely up to us whether we are really prepared to take the necessary measures to make good any deficiency of supplies from the Argentine. If, he added, we are not prepared to meet you on that, then certainly we can make no complaint whatever if you continue to make such arrangements with the Argentine as you think are necessary.

He believes that to supply us would not involve a curtailment of more than 10 per cent in the present American meat consumption. I am told that it would in fact require a 20 per cent curtailment of their beef consumption. But, of course, even 10 per cent would require administratively a rationing system such as they do not at present possess. To this he merely repeated:– 'Put it squarely up to us. If we admit we cannot supply you, then your hands will be free. Meanwhile you should give us a chance to see if we cannot take this opportunity, whilst public opinion is entirely favourable to drastic action and we are mobilised for war, to clear up the Fascist nest once for all.'

I duly report the above; it does not need any comment from me, except that if the Minister of Food agrees to the Ambassador's proposal that he should visit this country, it is desirable that he should come forthwith. There is the additional reason for this that Stettinius has misunderstood what the Ambassador has proposed to London (you may take it as a general rule that Stettinius always gets everything slightly wrong). He has told Morgenthau that Llewellin is coming over here and might arrive any day. It was rather a second thought on our part suggesting that he might defer three or four weeks, and the Ambassador has now telegraphed recommending a visit at the earliest possible moment.

Having got that out of the way, Morgenthau then passed on to another matter more directly germane to our negotiations. He said that his colleagues had now turned over entirely to him the question which of our various extra items should be conceded, e.g. whether tobacco should be put back on to lend lease, etc. This means, I fancy, that Morgenthau, having seized the final authority not with their entire approval, must also take full responsibility for measures that may be difficult to defend before Congress. Morgenthau is slightly scared, I think, of having to take the sole responsibility, but is not intending to shirk it. He considers, however, that this makes it necessary for him to be yet more fully informed as to our case and as to its full justification. He, therefore, asked for further break down of our expenditures, showing just how they were responsible (*a*) for the growth of the sterling balances, and (*b*) for the depletion of our dollar reserves. He does not really know what he wants. I shall try to supply him with the best I can cook up. We are to resume this talk tomorrow morning. He has, I am afraid, got it into his head that the responsibility he is now to assume requires him to look into our position and ask for proof of justification on all sorts of heads. He says that he cannot take the responsibility for telling Congress that our case is fully substantiated unless he is satisfied that we are making all proper economies, and that there is no direction in which we are wasting money. Why, he wants to know, do we go on spending so much in the Middle East; why so much in India, and so forth. I made him rather dangerously angry at one point of the conversation by saying that very likely some of these matters were open to legitimate criticism. Indeed, that I myself was disposed to be one of the critics. But nevertheless all these questions, and the best allocation of our manpower, had been the subject of intensive Cabinet enquiry, that the figures as given to him were the consequence of Cabinet decisions, and that we must be master in our own house. I do not think, however, that he really wants more than to be furnished with yet more statistics which will enable him to say that he has profoundly examined the position and is satisfied. Nevertheless, in this country, one is always on the edge both of pressure politics, as exemplified by the Argentine question above, and of undue interference, as in the matters just mentioned.

Here again I am just reporting what happened, and am taking advantage of Cherwell's early departure to say in a letter what it is not so easy to put frankly and fully in a cable.

I also detect a growing tendency in some quarters to cut the Gordian knot of trying to help us in Stage II by an attempt to run the Stage II questions into the Stage III questions. I shall resist this as long as possible.

At a lower level the evidence is that the Americans are striving their utmost to find items they can properly put back on lend lease, or pay us in some other way. The question is whether, when they have made these concessions—we shall know more about this by the end of the week—it will add up to enough. I am more and more inclined to take what we can get, struggling hard to make it as much as possible, and be content with that, rather than to be lured prematurely into Stage III topics.

One other matter I may as well take this opportunity to report. All through the Treasury, the State Department, and the F.E.A. there is intense interest in the operations of the sterling area, and unlimited ignorance as to what our arrangements are. I therefore delivered a lecture this morning in Dean Acheson's room to a considerable audience drawn from the State Department and F.E.A., and also from our own Missions, the Ambassador, Mr Ben Smith and most of the heads of our Missions being present. I hope I did more good than harm. I spoke with complete candour and lack of reserve on the whole subject. I had no script. If I had had a script and had submitted it to all the proper authorities, I fear, God forgive me, that months would have passed before the form of words would have been approved. I think that there can be no question that this frank account did a great deal of good. I hope also it did no counter-balancing harm by premature and unauthorised indications of the way we are thinking about these things. I was, of course, in fact more guarded in my utterances than was in all cases fully apparent to the audience.

I am sure the clue to act on here is to assume one is amongst friends, and that they do genuinely intend to do what they can within the queer limitations put upon them by their public and their politics, and their own methods so different from ours.

Yours ever,

KEYNES

On 6 November, he gave another estimate of the progress of the negotiations to Sir Richard Hopkins.

To SIR RICHARD HOPKINS, *6 November 1944*

My dear Hoppy,

Your letter of October 24th arrived very quickly.[9] I have got into such bad habits about writing that a point is rapidly arriving when it gets impossible to write at all. However, I have sent a great number of telegrams which will have kept you up-to-date on the immediate business. The pressure arising out of this and all the social engagements connected with it, has been pretty overwhelming. So much of one's work here is done in conversations behind the scenes that half the luncheon and dinner engagements one takes are just as much a part of public duty as formal meetings.

I was most delighted that you and the others also liked the big paper we put in. I was in some indecision whether to put so much on paper. My first intention had been to expound

[9] Hopkins' letter of 24 October concerned the 'book of words

much more orally. Nevertheless, it has turned out to be wise, I am sure, to put so much down. The more formal meetings in Morgenthau's room have not offered the right atmosphere, or the right audience either, for continuous exposition. They would not have heard one patiently. Also, many of the people whom it was most important to convince here, from high officials right down the line, would not have been present at an oral exposition.

The danger on the other side was, of course, that one would appear to crystallise one's own thought, and consequently their thought for them, prematurely; and might be making suggestions which would cause annoyance before one had sufficiently explored the ground. There was a particular danger in Chapter 3. And some items of Chapter 3 have in fact caused slight annoyance in some quarters. On the other hand, I believe I was right to deploy all our claims and suggestions, partly because, as it has turned out, there is scarcely a cat so stale that it has not found a fancier in one or other of the U.S. Departments concerned; and also the more they turn down, the more it is on their conscience not to turn down the rest.

In the result we can, I think, claim that the paper has had a really remarkable success in all quarters here. There have been many congratulations on all hands, and the result has been, particularly amongst the junior people, that they spend their time exercising their wits to work out notions on our behalf.

It is too soon to know what will emerge. The usual rumours which reach us from behind the scenes are pretty good. They are certainly doing their damnedest to work out enough items to fill the bill. There is even a possibility that they will offer to take some raw materials off reciprocal aid. I have been determined that this shall be solely on their initiative and not on ours. My latest guess is that we shall get, in one form or another, the equivalent of an extra $250 million, and I have not by any means given up hope of something more like $400 or $500 million.

If this turns out correct, then it will be better to postpone any major new items we may have for large scale assistance. After discussing the question in many quarters behind the scenes, I am sure that the Chancellor's opinion in paragraph 5 of his Telegram 9282 of October 24th [above p. 143] is right, namely, that some kind of grant in aid for retrospective reciprocal aid is the most promising, and indeed the only really promising one. On the other hand, this is much best kept back for Stage III. If it is made part of the Stage III settlement we might get as much as $2 billion on this ticket. If we were to trot it out now, we should certainly not get as much as $1 billion, and perhaps less.

At the moment, there is a lull in our affairs on account of the Election; everybody is away voting; and everybody is in such a dither of nerves and excitement that they cannot concentrate. So it is only after Thursday that export freedom and Chapter 3 will come finally to a head. As regards export freedom, the substance of the battle is already won. But as you will have seen from recent telegrams, we have not given up hope of a solution so complete that even difficulties about identical articles are overcome.

It has been impossible not to give a good deal of attention to the Election. Dewey is one of the most miserable rats ever brought to birth, and falls lower and lower even in the estimation of his own supporters every time he opens his mouth. It would be the greatest possible disaster if he were to get in. My own view is that he has not the smallest chance. You will know all about that long before this letter reaches you. My own hunch is that it will be a landslide for the President.

The climate here ever since we arrived has been marvellous. Almost unbroken sunshine, and a temperate air outside of 65 or 70. The place is incredibly beautiful with the changing colours of the trees, and you would have called it a paradise on earth. Nevertheless, it makes everybody ill. Half of the population have the most devastating colds, and the other half have headaches. What snake's venom there is in this paradisaical air I cannot diagnose. I escape better than most and so far I have had nothing more than a toothache.

According to present plans we ought to get off from here to Ottawa on November 20th, or soon after. After that I should like two or three days in New York, and then, if enough strings can be pulled, a passage back by sea. Since the British authorities seemed helpless in the above matter, Morgy has been most kindly busying himself about it, with War Department and State Department. And he is such an obstinate man that I do not think he will give up until he has succeeded. That means we shall be back somewhere towards the end, or very soon after, the first week of December. We have seen a great deal of Morgy, both officially and socially, and the skies are still clear. He has unquestionably been as good as his word up-to-date, and has fought our battles with the Departments with all the vehemence one could possibly have hoped. A day or two ago the Navy Department was completely obstructive and threatening us with a unilateral decision. For several days they had broken contact, and all was in the worst order. So I took Sinclair around to Morgy and we laid a formal complaint. He immediately declared that he would right the matter before the sun had set. And so he did. There was a full meeting of the American group a few hours later, Morgy read the Riot Act and ordered the Navy Department to comport themselves on the same lines as the other Departments. They refused, some brisk telephoning took place during the meting with high authorities, and the Navy Department collapsed. I was told by Americans present that this was almost the first recorded occasion on which the civilian Departments had an all-out victory over the military.

Speaking of Morgy, Lydia has certainly earned her passage money (let alone her maintenance of my good condition).

Oh, one other matter of shop before I close. I was most

delighted to get the news about the 1¾ per cent Bonds. I am sure that the psychological consequences of this will be just as valuable as the financial. Now it remains to consider the reduction of the Treasury Bill rate to ½ per cent. I hope you will give thought to that. It would save us quite a lot of foreign exchange. I should predict that it is bound to come after the war, and if so, I doubt if we are serving much purpose by keeping the 1 per cent rate during the war. The reasons which justified it originally have quite disappeared.

Well, there are thousands of other matters I would like to gossip about.

Ever your affectionate
[copy initialled] MK

The same day, 6 November, Keynes gave to the Governor of the Bank of England more details of his sterling area lecture, the first major attempt by a senior British official to remove American apprehensions on the subject.

To LORD CATTO, *6 November 1944*

My dear Governor,

Following on my telegram AMALL 84,[10] I duly gave my lecture at the State Department on the sterling area. It was largely attended by our own missions, including the Ambassador, as well as by the Americans. And I think I did good.

My theme was that the sterling area was a brave attempt on our part to maintain the advantages of multilateral clearing to the utmost possible extent, and that its maintenance as near as possible on the present lines for as long as possible was as much to American as British interest. This is quite contrary to the line people have been taking here. They think that the sterling area dollar pool is a nefarious device by which

[10] AMALL 84 was a request for information and a statement of his intent to give the lecture.

American exporters are deprived of markets. I pointed out that ideally it was a means by which the impediments on trade could be reduced to a minimum, so American exporters could continue business with those parts of the sterling area which do not have adequate dollar earnings. If, for example, India was to be allowed to leave the pool and accumulate her own dollar reserves, that would simply mean that there were fewer dollars available for American trade to other parts of the area. They could be perfectly certain that all the dollars the sterling area pool earns would subsequently be disbursed.

I think this produced a considerable impression. I explained how we should try and ride the sterling area system with as light a rein as possible, and surely they ought to help us in every way to do this, not least by making sure that we had enough dollars in hand to keep the rein light.

I also emphasised the voluntary and informal character of the sterling area arrangements, and the autonomous character of the various exchange controls. I explained that nothing could possibly suit the Americans better than that we should continue the sterling area during the transitional period on just the same lines as during the war. On the other hand, this would almost inevitably be beyond our powers, so that some measure of rationing of dollars to the various exchange controls of the area would probably become inevitable.

I am hopeful that all this met with sympathy and understanding. Certainly the air was cleared. I was told by Dean Acheson that many who had come with awkward questions to ask, found their questions answered in advance and so held their silence. So I hope I did more good than harm. All the same, thank God that no one from London was present, since I should have been scared to death as to what you thought about the freedom of my utterance. This freedom, which was not perhaps quite so great in essence as it appeared on the surface, was based on the ever-growing belief that we are amongst friends here, and that if only we can make them see the facts of the position as we see this ourselves, they will reach the same conclusions.

Yours ever,
[copy initialled] K

After the break for the elections, held on 7 November, the negotiations began again in earnest. In the course of these, Keynes provided Mr White and Mr Morgenthau with more details as to Britain's external economic position.

To DR H. D. WHITE, *13 November 1944*

Dear Harry,

I have now got from London the particulars for which you asked, giving the break-up of the gold and dollar liabilities which make the difference between our gross and net reserves, as regularly reported to the U.S. Treasury; and also the exact terms of those liabilities which are not immediate.

Taking the gold liabilities figure of 332·8 at the end of September 1944 as an example we have the following breakdown. (Gold is valued at 35 dollars per fine ounce.)

(A) Immediate		
(1) Bolivia	1·2	
(2) Sweden	1·8	
(3) Persia	10·4	
(4) Turkey	13·3	
		26·7
(B) Others		
(5) Portugal	284·6	
(6) Norway	6·5	
(7) Sweden	15·0	
(8) Turkey	Nil	
		306·1
Grand total		332·8

Items (1), (2) and (3) under (A) are recurrent liabilities, settlement of which for (1) and (2) is monthly, and (3) is quarterly. In other words, the figures represent the accruing gold liabilities which will become immediately payable in specie as soon as the month or the quarter, as the case may be, comes to an end. In the case of (4), the sum accumulated to date in favour of Turkey, she has a right to take in gold on demand.

The liability to Portugal is to deliver gold not later than five years after the end of the war with Germany. A gold price guarantee is also operative. The agreement with Norway, under which the gold liability was incurred, has been in abeyance since the German occupation; but we expect to wind it up shortly and to settle in gold. The liability to Sweden materialises on termination of the payments agreement. As regards Item (B) (8), certain Turkish funds are by agreement convertible into gold at four-monthly intervals (April, August and December), but there was no balance on the account in question at the end of September.

The breakdown of dollar liabilities at the end of September last is as follows—

(1) U.S. registered accounts	122·7
(2) U.S. 'M' forms outstanding	4·0
(3) U.S. finance officers' accounts in Australia	58·2
	184·9

(1) and (3) are convertible on demand into U.S. dollars. (2) represents invested sterling funds eligible for recredit to registered accounts.

These figures of gold and dollar liabilities cover only firm commitments accrued to date. I understand that even in this limited context they are not comprehensive and exhaustive. For instance, we have not yet included Australian pound accounts of individual members of the U.S. forces as a dollar liability, although these in fact enjoy the guarantee of convertibility, and at the present time U.S. army authorities are engaged in collecting such currency from the members of the forces with a view to turning them back again into dollars.

We do not, of course, make any allowance for possible demands of other holders of sterling balances, which may ultimately have to be met in gold, although there is no contractual obligation.

Yours sincerely,
[copy initialled] K

To H. MORGENTHAU, *16 November 1944*

Dear Mr Secretary,

I am sorry that I have been so slow in letting you have the further break-up of British war expenses abroad, which I promised you some little time ago. The reason is, of course, as you are only too well aware, that your people and ours have been kept busy up to almost the limit of possibility. I have thought that the most convenient way might be to arrange my reply in a series of short annexes, each dealing with a particular matter.

You will see that I have partly devoted myself to giving you some further figures for your own information, not suitable for general use, and that here and there I have suggested very briefly one or two lines of argument which might be useful, if later on you have to go up to the Hill on our behalf.

Perhaps I might sum up a few of the salient points:–

1. As you will see below, our indebtedness is largely due to our military expenditure in the Middle East and India. For five years we, and we alone, have been responsible for practically the whole cash outgoings for the war over the vast territories from North Africa to Burma. Without these expenditures we should never have held Rommel at the critical moment of the war.

2. Quite early in the war, the Treasury control over war expenditure overseas was virtually abandoned. If Treasury control over expenditure had continued, unquestionably

many economies could have been made. But these economies would not have been possible without setting up a machine of control which would have impeded the prosecution of the war. One has to choose. The principles of good housekeeping do not apply when you are fighting for your lives over three continents far from home. We threw good housekeeping to the winds. But we saved ourselves, and helped to save the world. Too much financial precaution might easily have made just the difference when, as at one time, the forces were so evenly balanced. It is easy to argue that a method set up in an emergency has been continued too long. Very probably that is the case. But the obstacles in the way of re-imposing detailed control when it has been long absent are very great.

3. We ourselves receive no reverse lend lease whatever from the British Commonwealth, apart from Canada. As is shown below, we have made far less favourable financial arrangements with our own Dominions than has the United States. We pay Australia, for example, for the same goods and services which the United States receive without payment. Even when lend lease is brought into the account, the United States has with these countries more favourable arrangements than we have.

4. We have not thought it right to ask for any contribution to the war from the Crown Colonies, where we are in a position of Trustee. We have paid them for everything we have obtained, and consequently owe them vast sums. We even pay them for the goods which they send as reverse lend lease to the United States, so that this contribution also falls on our shoulders.

5. We abandoned our export business in order to devote to the war the whole of the manpower which could by any means be made available.

6. We paid over nearly the whole of the gold reserves with which we started the war to the United States, and spent the money to build up the American munitions industries from

small beginnings, with the result that when America came into the war, the time-lag in the expansion of production was very greatly reduced.

No doubt the above makes up collectively a story of financial imprudence which has no parallel in history. Nevertheless, that financial imprudence may have been a facet of that single-minded devotion without which the war would have been lost. So we beg leave to think that it was worth-while for us, and also for you.

If there is anything further I can do whilst I am here, I am, of course, always at your service.

Sincerely yours,

KEYNES

I. *British war expenses overseas*

The incurring of overseas debt and loss of overseas assets has been going on at the rate of $2½ to $3 billion a year, since the beginning of the war, amounting to something over $12 billion over the period as a whole up to the end of 1944.

By far the greater part of this is due to military expenditure which we have had to meet in cash overseas, mainly in India and the Middle East. This has been running at an aggregate of about $2 billion a year. The nature of this expenditure is set forth in some detail below, on the basis of 1944.

For 1945 present estimates are nearly as high as for 1944. In Annex A of the Statement of Requirements, these were given (Page 12) as follows:– [see p. 169]
The break-up of this expenditure on the 1944 basis is given below. Since the above preliminary estimates for 1945 have been built up mainly on the 1944 basis, the 1944 break-up would be broadly similar. I understand, however, that the Chancellor of the Exchequer considers that these estimates may be unnecessarily high, and he is at present engaged in

	$ million
India	1,360
Egypt	240
Australia	160
Palestine	100
South Africa	80
Persia	60
Iraq	40
Others	40
	2,080

having enquiries made as to how best economies can be made. The final expenditure will partly depend on economy in detail, partly on broad decisions to be made by the War Cabinet. The above estimates are based on certain provisional decisions, but these decisions are not to be regarded as final. The Chancellor of the Exchequer hopes, therefore, that in fact our overseas expenditure in 1945 will be reduced below the figure given. If it should prove possible to reduce the expenditure by (say) half a billion dollars, then the expected disinvestment in the current year, which otherwise would approach $3 billion, will be that much less. It will be appreciated that it is very difficult to estimate long in advance the rate of expenditure over many far distant countries in war conditions subject to continuous change.

1. In 1943–44 the expenditure of the United Kingdom in India amounted to $1,132 million, made up as follows:– [see p. 170]

The expenditure in 1944–45 is expected to be at the somewhat higher aggregate rate of $1,312 million. The distribution of this expenditure between the different items will be broadly the same as in the previous year. It is often inferred from the magnitude of the U.K. expenditure that the Government of India is not itself bearing a very heavy burden of charges. This

A. Personnel charges (excluding rations, clothing, equipment etc.)	
1. Combatant units and ancillaries	$90·4 million
2. Supply and store depots, war hospitals etc. in India	56·4
3. Share of establishment costs of training and other formations treated as joint liabilities	34·0
4. Transportation charges of personnel	24·0
5. Provision of cash for payment of forces overseas (including S.E.A.C. payments in India)	90·0
Total A	$294·8 million
B. Acquisition of stores	610·8
C. Transportation charges on stores	59·6
D. Works expenditure in India on buildings, roads, airfields, etc.	135·2
E. Prisoners of war	16·8
F. Share of capital outlay on projects for expanding India's industrial capacity for production of stores for war purposes	16·4
Total	$1,133·6 million

is not in fact the case. The Government of India bears the whole of the local charges of the Indian Army when it is in India. As a result of this and of other expenditure arising out of the war the Government of India's expenditure in 1944–45 is estimated at $1,250 million, which is about four times the peace-time budget. Thus in addition to what the British Government bear, the Government of India is spending not far short of a billion dollars a year on war expenditure. Moreover, they are covering nearly the whole of this by taxation, which has been raised to nearly three times the pre-war level. Their loan programme is mainly to finance the loans which they have been making to the U.K.

The contribution of the United Kingdom Government consists of supplying the Indian Army with munitions made in the U.K. without payment, with the cost of Indian forces when operating outside India, and with the cost of British forces in India. It will be observed that more than half of the expenditure relates to the acquisition of stores. These stores are for use not only in India, but in various theatres where geographical considerations make India the best source of supply.

2. *Expenditure in the Middle East.* On the basis of our latest available figures of current expenditure, the aggregate rate during 1944 will work out at about $576 million, covering Egypt, Palestine, Persia, Iraq and Syria. For 1945 this is estimated at the reduced figure of $400 million. The main items were as follows:–

	$ million
Pay of troops	96
Work services	144
Provisions	48
Conveyance of troops and stores	48
Petrol, fuel and light	36
Wages of civilians, R.A.S.C. and Ordnance Departments	36

3. *Australia.* The total war expenditure by U.K. and Australia in 1944 is estimated at $267.2 million (the estimate for 1945 is at the reduced figure of $160 million).

Based on the expenditure of the first half of 1944, the major items making up the total were as follows:–

	$ million
War Office expenditure	24.0
Admiralty	32.0
Air Ministry	22.4
Ministry of War Transport	32.8
Ministry of Supply	146.4

The Ministry of War Transport payments are refunds to the Australian Government of freight received on sterling oil carried in lend lease tankers. This is, therefore, not a genuine net expenditure, and might more properly be excluded from the total. Payments by the Ministry of Supply are principally for munitions supplied by Australia under the munitions assignment procedure, and supplies for the Eastern Group Supply Council. It will be seen that our payments in respect of munitions produced in Australia is, as in the case of India, rather more than a half of our total expenditure.

II. *Financial relations between U.K., U.S., and the Dominions*

It is not commonly understood that the United States has made much more favourable financial arrangements with the British Dominions, apart from Canada, than the British Government has. In the case of Canada, as is well known, Canadian contributions in the shape of mutual aid and in other ways have produced broadly the same effect as the lend lease arrangements with the United States. With the other Dominions, however, the United Kingdom has no reciprocal aid arrangements; and the net result of the arrangements is that much more is paid to them than is received from them. India and Australia can be taken as leading examples.

In the case of Australia, as has been seen above, the United Kingdom pays for all her expenditure from Australia, both for supplies for the troops and for all raw materials. As against this, Australia makes certain capitation payments to the United Kingdom in respect of munitions and other services provided by the U.K. to the Australian forces. In the year 1944 military expenditure paid by the U.K. to Australia amounted to $184·4 million, whilst similar war expenditure paid by Australia to the U.K. came to $138·8 million, leaving a balance adverse to the U.K. of $45·6 million. In addition to the above, the U.K. paid Australia for all meat, other food, and raw materials obtained from them, leading to a very large adverse balance in the aggregate, whereas the U.S. receives meat on reciprocal aid terms.

This may be compared with the financial arrangements made with Australia by the United States. Reciprocal aid supplied to the United States forces by Australia in 1944 is estimated by $360 million. As against this, Australia is expecting to receive under lend lease non-munitions to the value of $103·4 million. This is exclusive of oil, shipping freights, aircraft supplied under direct lend lease, and munitions included in the U.K. programme. When allowance is made for these there remains a balance of about $100 million in favour of Australia.

As regards India, the comparison is still more striking, since the U.K. supplies the Indian Army with munitions without charge, which is not the case with Australia. The result is, as we have seen above, that in 1944–45 British payments to India on account of the war will amount to no less than $1,312 million, with no significant counter balancing payments the other way.

Turning to the American comparison, the reciprocal aid afforded by India to the United States exceeds by a significant amount what they themselves obtain on lend lease. Broadly speaking, the volume of reciprocal aid afforded by India is at the rate of $260 million. Whilst lend lease assistance, including both non-munitions and munitions furnished to the Indian Army, has fallen slightly short of the above.

III. *Unfavourable trade balances with other countries*

1. The remaining part of the British overseas indebtedness is the result of her abandoning her export trade, which has meant that imports necessary for carrying on the war can only be obtained by incurring debts. For example, imports from South American countries in 1944 will so much exceed exports

to them, that a large adverse balance of payment, which can only be covered by an increase of debt, necessarily results. The following are some illustrations covering the year 1944:–

	British exports to	British imports from
	($ million)	
Argentine	11·2	163·2
Brazil	15·6	92·0
Rest of South America (Bolivia, Peru, Chile, Uruguay, Paraguay)	15·6	92·0

The above is an absolutely inevitable consequence of the abandonment of British export trade and the diversion of manpower to direct war service. Much the same sort of figures could be supplied relating to the Crown Colonies. The Crown Colonies are mainly inhabited by native populations at a low standard of life, for which the British Government is in a position of Trustee. It has not been thought right to ask them to make any direct contribution to the costs of the war. Since imports from these Colonies have greatly exceeded exports, the present position is that the United Kingdom owes the Crown Colonies (doubtless to their great advantage in future years) the sum of about $2 billion. The British Government meet out of their own pocket the cost of the raw materials furnished to the U.S. from the Colonies, for example, rubber from Ceylon, thus increasing our debt to them.

2. *The dollar expenditure of the United Kingdom.* It is commonly believed that, as a result of lend lease, practically the whole of the British Government's dollar expenditure is covered. In fact this is far from the case, as has been shown in detail in the British Statement of Requirements. British cash expenditure in the United States, on the basis of the existing scope of lend lease, will exceed $800 million in 1945. In addition there are certain expenditures which are

unavoidably incurred in terms of dollars in third countries, bringing the total dollar expenditure of the U.K. outside lend lease to about $1 billion a year.

3. *British gold reserves.* The United Kingdom started the war with net gold reserves of about $2½ billion. In the period before lend lease, the whole of this was expended, the net gold reserves of the U.K. at the end of April 1941 having fallen to $3 million. By far the greater part of the $2½ billion of gold thus lost was paid to the United States. This money was spent in building up the munitions industry of the United States, so that there was a very much shorter time-lag in the expansion of munitions output after Pearl Harbor which would otherwise have been inevitable. More recently, the British gold and dollar reserves have been somewhat increased, largely as a result of earnings from the pay of American forces in the sterling area, a source of income which is rapidly falling off. At the end of this year the reserves may amount to $1½ billion, that is, a billion less than at the beginning of the war. During this same period, however, the overseas liabilities of the U.K., which were more than covered by their reserves at the beginning of the war, will have risen to $12 billion, which is eight times the figure of the reserves.

As a result of the war, the U.K. will have parted with much of its gold to the United States, as mentioned already, and will, for reasons also summarised above, have incurred indebtedness to almost every other Allied and Associated Nation and to every neutral.

This great burden of indebtedness has not been due to wastefulness or failure to economise. It has been due to our extreme single-mindedness in devoting all we have to the war. We have never allowed financial prudence to impede the prosecution of the war. This policy will have shortened the duration of the war for us and for everyone. But the burden will remain.

As the negotiations drew to a close Keynes's letters to Lord Halifax and Mr White revealed their progress, while his letter to Mr N. Robertson gave further details of his mission to Ottawa.

To LORD HALIFAX, *15 November 1944*

Dear Ambassador,

The Chancellor of the Exchequer having asked me to take on another little job in Canada (concerning the release by the Canadians of French gold and balances), which, if I am to be of any use, requires that I should be in Ottawa not later than November 20th, I took the opportunity of a lunch with Mr Morgenthau yesterday to find out whether he thought we could finish this week, so that I could aim at leaving Washington on Sunday.

I then discovered for the first time that instead of Tuesday of next week being the dead-line, set by his departure from Washington, as he had led us to believe hitherto, the old rascal actually contemplated this Friday afternoon, or Saturday morning at the latest. He has an engagement to speak at Chicago on Saturday in a War Loan drive alongside Admiral King,[11] and does not want to come back here before Thanksgiving, when he proposes to start a short holiday.

Since Sinclair wants to go away on Friday at midnight, it would obviously suit all of us if we aimed at having the last formal meeting on Friday. Unless they have some nasty surprises in view for us, I think this should be possible. Indeed, I believe we have now reached a point where an early date of termination is rather essential to bring things completely to a head.

We shall know the best, or the worst, today and tomorrow. There may be disappointments ahead. If so, one may conceivably have to consider the possibility of coming back here. But I very much hope not. Meanwhile, the programme is to

[11] Ernest Joseph King (b. 1878); Vice-Admiral in command of Aircraft Battle Force, U.S. Fleet, 1938-9; member, General Board, Navy Office, 1941; Commander-in-Chief, Atlantic Fleet, 1941, U.S. Fleet, 1941; Chief of Naval Operations, 1942-5; Fleet Admiral, 1944.

have meetings of the Technical Committee today and to-morrow, and probably Friday as well, and in addition to have meetings of the Morgenthau Main Committee on Thursday and Friday.

The very last day that Dill[12] was active he had asked me to speak to the Combined Chiefs of Staff about our financial position. That in fact is now to take place this Friday afternoon at 2.30 p.m. at the meeting of Combined Chiefs of Staff, Morgenthau and Admiral Leahy having given the idea their blessing.

Yours ever,
[copy initialled] K

P.S. We had rather a bad meeting this afternoon and made slow progress. The meeting lasted several hours, during which few of the Americans remained in the room for more than a quarter of an hour continuously. None of them had read the papers we had sent to them, even those we had sent a fortnight ago. I am told that Crowley and F.E.A. are trying to retard progress because it annoys them that Morgenthau should be trying to expedite it. The result is that my pro-gramme as set out above is in jeopardy.

To DR H. D. WHITE, *18 November 1944*

My dear Harry,

You asked me to let you have a note of the various out-standing items which need tidying up, that might be brought before a very small committee such as I suggested, which would act as a clearing party for the purpose, and where necessary refer particular items to the experts more par-ticularly concerned.

1. The final text of the covering letter to the non-munitions programme. This is the document which, as we understood,

---

[12] Field-Marshal Sir John Dill (1881–1944), Chief of Imperial General Staff, 1940–1; went with British Chiefs of Staff to Washington with Prime Minister, 1942, re-mained as Head of British Joint Staff Mission, 1942–4.

Mr Crowley particularly wanted to reserve for the purpose of looking through it himself. Apart from any changes he may want to suggest, there are a few points, not many, where we have not finally agreed the text with those concerned. It might also be necessary to consider an alternative way of handling this, namely, to make the covering letter itself much shorter and bring in some of the absolutely essential passages in that covering letter as comments to the particular programmes to which they relate. In some cases indeed this would look the more appropriate place for them.

2. The list of agreed Chapter 3 items which you gave us on Friday appeared to deal with those matters which it had been possible to look into carefully in the short time available. There remain other items which our experts are either in course of examining with yours, or would like to have an opportunity to examine. The possible additional items (reserving tobacco and sugar for higher authority) are the following:–

(i) Oil. Here our people have sent in a document with new proposals which has not yet been examined.

(ii) Shipping. There has not yet been any opportunity for our shipping experts to discuss with yours various items which we think might be eligible, apart from freights on non-lend lease government cargoes.

(iii) We do not feel that we have ever yet properly developed our case why certain supplies for the Colonies should not in present circumstances be made eligible. Some of our Colonies, for example, British East and West Africa, are contributing as much according to their means to the fighting effort of the Allies as other parts of the world which are reckoned fully eligible. The East African troops have in the last week had an important success in Burma. Apart from this, the present rulings as to non-eligibility were given in the main before the Colonies were according reverse lend lease. It seems to us unreasonable that Colonies which are supplying the United States with a substantial amount of reverse lend lease should be regarded as less eligible for lend lease than other parts of the Empire.

(iv) There were certain cases of machine tools originally purchased by us and subsequently in your use where we began a discussion but never carried it through to a conclusion.

3. On the question of coastal vessels, Maclay is currently in touch with the Maritime Commission and F.E.A. But we are not clear as to where we shall have to go for a final decision. This also affects one clause in the covering letter to the non-munitions programme.

4. At a recent meeting it was indicated to us that there might be an agreement by which machine tools, for which we have currently to pay cash, nevertheless might be the subject of subsequent consideration at the end of the lend lease period, or at the end of the war, with a view to returning to us the difference between the original cost and the estimated end value. This seemed to us a valuable and helpful suggestion which we should like to carry further in the appropriate quarter.

5. Closely analogous to the question of the machine tools is the formula to be selected in estimating the lend lease value of Indian rolling-stock. Very likely Currie has this in hand. But for the sake of completeness, I should include it in this list.

6. We are particularly anxious to agree at as early a date as we can the lines of the proposed statement by the President of the Board of Trade on export policy. At Friday's discussion there was, I think, a little misunderstanding about what we are after among some of those present. Though we were aiming at an early release, there is no question of any publicity before November 29th. We merely wanted to be in a position to submit to the Minister as soon as possible, for his consideration, the general line of approach which would cause the least difficulty here.

7. We should like to have some further conversation, with whoever is the appropriate person, on the waiver procedure provided for in the agreed statement of principles on export policy, to avoid, as was agreed on Friday, the continuous and detailed scrutiny of exports.

8. The question of reciprocal aid from the Dominions is not yet out of the way. We are having a meeting with the Australians on Monday, and hope to be able to produce for you something which may be satisfactory. But when we have prepared such a statement, we want to know to whom we should submit it.

9. Frank Lee has had some conversation with Coe from time to time as to the form the end document should take, in particular whether it should be a jointly agreed document, or whether we should make a report to our Prime Minister in terms of which you have agreed, whilst you would make a report to the President in terms which we had accepted as representing the facts of the position. It is very important that before Wednesday we should have cleared our minds about what we want in this respect.

Yours sincerely,

KEYNES

P.S. This letter is not as formidable as it looks. In my opinion, all we need at this stage is a meeting of half-an-hour to hand out these various items to the appropriate quarters, and make sure that someone, not ourselves, is attending to each of them.

To N. ROBERTSON, *14 November 1944*

My dear Robertson,

We are very much obliged to you for holding your hand on the question of the French gold balances for so long. We at this end have been doing our utmost to get London to make up its mind, but it is only today that we have got a definitive telegram. I understand from Munro that you are not making any communication to the French until November 22nd, but that you must be in a position to speak to them not later than that date.

Since the Chancellor of the Exchequer has asked me to take up the details of the question with you, I am aiming at leaving here on November 19th, so as to be available in Ottawa on November 20th and 21st for a conversation to fit in with your timetable of declaring your policy to the French on November 22nd.

In the telegram received from the Treasury referred to above, they accept the view that we cannot reasonably ask you to withhold the gold belonging to the Bank of France. From all points of view it is probably not only inevitable but right that this should be freely released. What I shall be wanting to discuss with you is the question of the balance of about $158 million which we voluntarily paid over in the early days after the collapse, which seems to us to be in an entirely different position. Since you may like to have an opportunity of thinking this over before I arrive in Ottawa, perhaps I had better give you an outline of the story immediately.

The total value of the munition contracts taken over from the French for delivery after the collapse of France has worked out at $694,440,000. Of this total, the French had already paid to the contractors as initial down payments on the signature of the contract about $228 million, leaving a balance of $466,440,000 to be paid on delivery. In respect of the amount payable on delivery, we paid $423,943,000 to the U.S. contractors on French account, and we furnished the French in free United States funds with $32,400,000, which was, I understand, for substantially the same purpose. There remain certain items you need not bother yourself with on balance, which were for some reason not recoverable or are in dispute. I give you these figures of the amounts we paid on delivery merely that you may have the whole story; they are not relevant to what follows.

Turning back to the amount of $228 million paid out by

the French before their collapse as initial down payments,—we started by paying the appropriate proportion of this over to an earmarked account with the Bank of Canada whenever we took delivery of the munitions in question. After we had paid over about $158 million in this way, we came to the conclusion that there was no earthly reason why we should go on doing this, and accordingly we stopped. The sum of about $70 million which we did not pay over is in the same moral and legal position as the $158 million which we did pay to the earmarked account.

Now we are intending to take up this question with the French in the near future, along with a number of other matters which we shall have to settle with them in order to get clear on the various items due from them to us, and from us to them. We think it would prejudice these negotiations if the $158 million already paid were regarded otherwise than in suspense. This should remain in your hands pending a final settlement of the whole matter.

When I reach Ottawa I shall be able to give you a little more background to this. But I have said enough to indicate the nature of our plea, namely, that the $158 million should be regarded as in suspense account to be left where it is until the whole issue has been amicably settled between the parties concerned.

Sincerely yours,

KEYNES

P.S. Since writing the above, we have heard further from Munro. We understand from London that the Treasury will soon be sending a small financial delegation to Paris, but the authority of this delegation is being deliberately limited to a discussion and possible settlement of an exchange agreement on the lines of the Anglo-Belgian agreement. They will explain to the French that there are a number of questions relating to claims and counter claims which we shall wish to discuss with a view to arriving at a mutually satisfactory settlement. But I understand that Monick has told us unofficially that the French themselves are not quite ready for this, and would like us to put off. This, too, I can explain more fully when I see you in Ottawa in a few days' time.

The final meeting of the Committee actually took place on Wednesday 22 November, although Keynes foresaw a few days of tidying up afterwards. After seeing the President for tea on 26 November and clearing final details with Mr Morgenthau and the President the next day, Keynes finally left for Ottawa early on the morning of 28 November. He described the final stages of the negotiations in a letter to the Chancellor.

To SIR JOHN ANDERSON, *30 November 1944*

My dear Chancellor,

I shall probably be back home almost as soon as this letter. And meanwhile I am too busy here to write you any proper account of anything beyond what you will get by telegram. But there are one or two reports I might make to complete the story you will have had by telegram of the last lap at Washington.

On the Sunday I went to tea with the President just after he had come back from his concluding talk with Mr Hull. He gave me well over an hour tête-à-tête conversation, in the course of which all manner of things were discussed. He was in grand form, I thought. I do not think that anything he told me will be particularly new to you, but I will try to make a note of some of the more important and interesting matters on the boat. There was nothing in our talk which required immediate report, except perhaps the fact that as regards the post-war treatment of Germany, he seemed to be in very much the same state of mind as he had been in Quebec. Subsequent representations from the State Department and others had not appeared to have taken much effect. On the other hand, his mind is obviously extremely fluid over the whole question. He has not really made up his mind about anything, and in my judgement (indeed, at one point he actually said so) he does not intend to make up his mind even on the more fundamental issues for quite a bit yet. At present all is fluid, what the Americans call thinking out loud, and no premature importance ought to be attached to anything which reaches you at the present stage about his plans or intentions. At least, that was the impression very strongly produced on me.

I hope you were as pleased as I was with the Americans agreeing in the end to make so excellent a public statement about what had been happening. That seemed to me to wind up the business in a most satisfactory way, and to give a very pleasant feeling after the various comings and goings which had preceded it. It was only obtained, however, after an immense struggle on the very last day. On Monday morning there was still the most vehement opposition on the part of F.E.A., and particularly Oscar Cox, to your making any statement whatever, apart from the bare announcement prepared for the President of the Board of Trade. And they were equally opposed to any announcement on their side. I attacked this position with all the vehemence in my power, urging that this was not only bad politics on their side of the Atlantic, but would most certainly be a great mistake on ours, and could only lead to misunderstanding, suspicion, and God knows what. It was a stormy meeting, and we left in considerable quarrel. Apparently, however, as often happens in Washington, the scene produced its effect. At a meeting amongst themselves in the afternoon I fancy that Morgenthau and Stettinius, whom I had been preparing along these lines, shared our views as to the importance of a public announcement. When I went round later in the afternoon, all was peace and amity. They produced their excellent draft and withdrew their opposition to what I had prepared for you.

As you will have learned by telegram, the political situation here in Canada will probably prevent us from reaching finality. But we shall have had time to get the facts agreed and the principles thoroughly explored. There is no question, in my mind, that Ilsley and Howe,[13] and also Dr. Clark, mean to do their utmost to meet our requirements in full by hook or by crook. We shall do well, in my judgment, to give them a few weeks in which to achieve this by their own methods. There can be no certainty, with the political situation what it is, about this, but I do not believe that we shall be disappointed.

Yours ever,
[copy initialled] K

Keynes summed up his American experiences, achievements and problems in a report to the Chancellor which he wrote aboard ship on the way home from America. This report went to the War Cabinet on 9 January 1945. However, slightly earlier, Mr F. G. Lee of the Treasury's Washington delegation summed up Keynes's achievement and situation in a letter to Mr F. E. Harmer.

To F. E. HARMER, *from* F. G. LEE, *6 December 1944*

My dear Freddie

'This is the way the world ends
This is the way the world ends
Not with a bang, but a whimper'

Now that the campaign is officially over, the general staff has gone away, and only the second line troops are left to deal with tedious mopping up operations, it may be of interest if I send you some brief personal impressions of the struggle. I am not, of course, going to attempt in any way to write a history of the negotiations—that would take more time and historical perspective than I possess. So you must be content with a hastily dictated and incoherent letter. (Of course, in so far as it is incoherent it is in a style appropriate to much of the negotiations. You will remember

---

[13] Clarence Decatur Howe (1886–1960), Minister of Munitions and Supply, Canada, 1940–6; Minister of Reconstruction and Supply, 1946–8; Minister of Trade and Commerce, 1948–57; Minister of Defence Production, 1951–7.

someone's comment on Carlyle's French Revels—that most of the events described in it appeared to be taking place at night amid dense smoke and complete confusion. Perhaps you ought to advise Hawtrey to reread his Carlyle before he comes to deal with this particular segment of financial history.)

The main difficulty in writing you this letter is to know where to begin. I think, however, that I can best give you an idea of the atmosphere if I say that for most of the time there were no negotiations in the ordinary sense of the word at all. That is to say, we scarcely ever had, or even approached, a proper discussion with the American team on the questions at issue. The setting in which the meetings of the so-called Main Committee took place was such as to preclude anything in the nature of a discussion. There was never any agenda: the two groups sat round the wall in Mr Morgenthau's room and made speeches at each other: once the question before the meeting became at all complicated, it was obvious that it had passed beyond Mr Morgenthau's comprehension and it was impossible in such a setting to try to make him understand what it was all about. It is true that with some difficulty Mr Morgenthau was persuaded to agree to joint Sub-Committee meetings under Harry White's chairmanship. But although Harry White proved an admirable chairman, the meetings were nearly always much too large, there was great difficulty in getting any agreement beforehand on an agenda, while the Americans found great difficulty in keeping a team in the field for as much as ten minutes at a stretch. People were always being called away to the telephone, to see the Secretary, to see a man about a dog, and so on. Consequently proceedings were always being held up while Mr Currie or Mr Acheson was found and persuaded to come back to the meeting.

The great misfortune was, in my view, the failure to establish at the beginning of the negotiations a small high-powered combined Committee at the 'official' level to act as a clearing house for the negotiations generally, to deal with points of principle, and to act as a channel through which really important issues could have been submitted to the 'Ministerial' Committee presided over by Mr Morgenthau. Admittedly, on our side this would have meant some overlap since presumably Keynes would have figured on both the 'Official' and 'Ministerial' Committees but I do not think that that would have mattered: and if there could have been a body consisting of, say, Keynes, Sinclair and Brand on our side and Acheson, Harry White and Currie on the American side—I believe that much more rapid and more satisfactory progress would have been made. As it was, for a very large part of the time we were completely in the dark about what the Americans were doing. It usually transpired that they were having prolonged, exhausting and difficult meetings among themselves about points in regard to which, if only they had consulted us informally beforehand, we could probably have saved them a great deal of needless anxiety nd trouble. As it was, they usually emerged from these meetings breathless but proudly bringing out as a trophy a document drawn up by one of their lawyers—which we at once rejected as either irrelevant or unacceptable or both. They then had to begin all over again.

The trouble largely arose, of course, from Mr Morgenthau's determination to remain in personal control of the negotiations. In the event, I think that the fact that he did so and that we were at great pains always to regard him as the leader on the American side, redounded to our advantage in the negotiations and will continue to help us in the future. But, as I have said, it meant that devolution to an effective combined body at the official level proved impossible. The chances of getting such a body established were in any event weakened by what one may call the Cherwell delusions on our own side. As you probably know, Cherwell persisted in believing that if only Mr Morgenthau and he could be left in a room together for about five minutes, untrammelled by officials and 'legalistic' documents, he (Lord Cherwell) would emerge with a definite promise of $5–6 billion and no questions asked. I cannot tell you what an immense relief it was to all of us here when the Cabinet decided to send Maynard out: until he came we were little better than disorganised rabble. The news of his coming made all the difference to our spirits: *Et l'espoir, malgré moi, s'est glissé dans mon cœur.*

Even given the initial failure to establish an effective Combined Committee at the official level, a great deal of the confusion could have been avoided had the Americans had a really effective Secretary for their group. But Frank Coe must, I think, be written off as a failure. He is never exactly a ball of fire—Maynard at one time said that the trouble with Coe was that he was bone lazy and in addition his glands were wrong. Certainly he is the only secretary I know who was falling fast asleep at a meeting of which he was supposed to be taking the minutes and had to be woken up by the Chairman. The main trouble was that he himself was very elusive and, when finally tracked down, had very little real knowledge of what was going on or was likely to happen on the American side. It was here that we missed Denby so badly—in fact the absence of Denby throughout the negotiations was one of our greatest handicaps. I feel that if Denby had been here, we could have ascertained from him informally what were the snags immediately ahead and could have suggested ways and means of by-passing them. As it was, the only *effective* off-the-record contacts we had with the American side was when Maynard used to get hold of Harry White informally.

Otherwise there was no one at what I may call the second-eleven level who was sufficiently in the know to be able to tell us what was going on behind the scenes. I ought perhaps to make it clear that in saying this I am not in any way criticising the way in which the actual discussions of the programmes themselves were conducted. I was not present at any of these, but my impression is that (apart from the difficulties with the Navy Department) the discussion of the military programmes was admirably conducted, while Griffin,[14] Appel[15] and others did their best to expedite discussions of the non-munition programmes and in general were co-operative and reasonable in their attitude.

Who then were the heroes of the negotiation—accepting the thesis that it was an episode which had its heroes. On our side, of course, one name stands quite alone. Maynard's performance was truly wonderful. I think that occasionally he over-played his hand and occasionally wore himself out in struggling for points which were not worth winning. But in general he was an inspiration to us all: it is no exaggeration to say that we felt like Lucifer's followers in Milton, 'Rejoicing in their matchless chief'. His industry was prodigious, his resilience and continuous optimism constant wonder to those of us more inclined to pessimism, while I doubt whether he has ever written or spoken with more lucidity and charm. And, of course, the impression which he makes on the Americans gives us an enormous initial advantage in any negotiation in which he participates. Take Harry White, for instance—that difficult nature unfolds like a flower when Maynard is there, and he is quite different to deal with when under the spell than he is in our normal day to day relations with him. I think that everyone on the United Kingdom side would agree that we could not have hoped to have got anywhere near the results which have actually been achieved had it not been for Maynard's genius and inspired leadership.

There are three other people on the U.K. side whom I should like to mention briefly. The first is Charles Hambro.[16] He was not officially a member of our Main Steering Committee. He was given the rather tiresome job of being Chairman of the Non-munitions Committee. This involved protracted discussions with F.E.A. often on boring points of detail and wording. Charles devoted himself to this work with great industry and

[14] William Vincent Griffin (1886–1958); company director and chairman; Director, Lend Lease, British Empire Branch, 1942–5.

[15] George F. Baer Appel (b. 1903); lawyer; member of Staff, Office of Lend Lease Administration, Washington, 1942–4; Foreign Economic Administration, Washington, 1944–5, London, 1945.

[16] Sir Charles Jocelyn Hambro (1897–1963); banker; Colonel, General Staff, War Office, 1940–3; member, U.K. Combined Raw Materials Board, and Head of British Raw Materials Mission, Washington, 1944–5; Director, Bank of England, 1928–63.

constant good temper. His was, I think, a very notable contribution. Secondly, I think that Helmore[17] did an extremely good job for the Board of Trade. He did so by assiduously attending every meeting he could. He kept the export question where it ought to have been—right in the middle of the picture. He got on excellently with Maynard and worked most harmoniously with us in the Treasury Delegation—always being ready to help us out in odd jobs if we were pressed for staff or time. I cannot believe that any other possible representative of the Board of Trade (certainly neither Magowan[18] nor Stirling) could have achieved for himself the position that Helmore did. Lastly, I should like to say what an excellent job, in my view, was done by Stevens[19] and the Secretarial staff under him. For the most part they simply had purely humdrum work to do, but they were always cheerful and ready to rally if we wanted some extra copying done late at night or some long telegrams despatched on a Sunday. Keynes paid a tribute to them at one of the official steering committees but I hope very much that it will be possible for the Treasury to give them a separate pat on the back for what they did.

On the American side I think that Morgenthau is definitely entitled to a place. It is quite true that for a large part of the time he had very little idea of what was going on. But his discussions with the Chancellor and subsequently with Keynes had left him with the clear conviction that the United Kingdom must be helped to make the first steps towards economic recovery, and he cast himself for the role of U.K. champion. And although he was on occasions both tiresome and timorous, I think that he sincerely stuck to that role in the face of opposition from other quarters in the U.S. Administration. He had one great triumph—when after terrific efforts he brought the Navy Department into line and made them discuss details of our Naval requirements with the Admiralty Delegation. This great effort plus the excitement of the election and of the 6th War Bond Drive left him exhausted, and in the last battle (about the date from which export freedom should begin) he was worsted by Crowley. But the willingness to help us is, I think, now definitely there. Here again, of course, we owe a very great deal to the charm of Maynard and the memories of Bretton Woods.

[17] James Reginald Carroll Helmore (1906–72); entered Board of Trade, 1929; private secretary to President, 1934–7; Under-Secretary, 1946; Second Secretary, 1946–52; K.C.B. 1954.

[18] Sir John Hall Magowan (1893–1951), Commercial Adviser to Ambassador in Washington from 1942; Commercial Secretary, British Embassy, Washington, 1931–4, Berlin, 1937–9; at Treasury, 1939–40; Deputy Controller, General Export Credits Guarantee Department, 1940–2.

[19] Roger Bentham Stevens (b. 1906); entered Consular Service, 1928; Secretary, British Civil Secretariat, Washington, 1944–6; Foreign Office, 1946–8; K.C.M.G. 1954.

A second figure who stood out on the American side was Harry White. I have already referred to his unwonted geniality. But apart from this he was most impressive on the occasions when he acted as Chairman of the Combined Sub-Committee. Admittedly he did not succeed in making the meetings very coherent, but he showed great ability in getting to the heart of the issues and in something of the action to be taken on them.

Dean Acheson played a comparatively minor role, although he saved the situation on one most tiresome question—that of the so-called 'reciprocal aid' clauses in the military agreements. In this case he presided over a meeting with the War Department and insisted upon their accepting as satisfactory the assurances which were given on behalf of Australia, New Zealand and India, instead of their sticking grimly to clauses which we had constantly declared to be unacceptable. The primary trouble with Acheson has been, of course, that he has been greatly overworked and that his subordinates are pretty poor. Collado, who deputised for him during most of the discussions is only mediocre, while Fetter, formerly of F.E.A. has strong claims to be regarded as the dullest inhabitant of North America.[20]

Lastly I would add, but with a good many reservations, Oscar Cox. He did not play any very prominent part in the earlier negotiations since he was pre-occupied with preparations of the President's lend lease report. In the later stage of the negotiations his political judgment was, I think, very definitely at fault, and it was he who was primarily responsible for urging Crowley to come out in opposition against the proposal to give us export freedom as from the 1st January, 1945. In short, I think that Oscar has again shown that he is willing to subordinate any question of principle to political expediency. But I think that when all has been said, he gets pretty high marks for the statement F.E.A. finally issued (Amall 163) which he drafted at great pressure and against his own will. Helmore will confirm, too, that during the course of a difficult discussion on our export statement (Amall 156) he was consistently both helpful and ingenious.

Finally, what can one say about the outcome of the negotiations? For my part, while life in Washington naturally makes one more and more a believer in what Sir Thomas Browne would call the mutability of any human arrangements, I think that the negotiation was an unqualified success. Certainly if one contrasts what we achieved at the end of November with what some of us hoped to achieve at the end of August, I think that we

---

[20] Emilio Collado; trustee, Export-Import Bank, Washington, 1944–5; engaged in Reconstruction and Development, 1946–7; Delegate, Bretton Woods Conference, 1944.

Fetter, Frank Whitson (b. 1899); economist, Office of Lend Lease Administration, 1943; Foreign Economic Administration, 1944; Department of State, 1944–6; Professor, Haverford College, 1934–48; Professor of Economics, North Western University, 1948–57.

can be well satisfied. In particular, I think that we achieved success in four definite directions:–

(*a*) The fact that the military programmes were accepted to the extent that they have been was a significant success, despite our failure to get protocol status. You will be aware that there was a good deal of near isolationism in both the International Division of the War Department and in the Navy Department which, before these negotiations, looked as if it might succeed in truncating, on one pretext or another, the military supplies which we should draw from this country in Stage II. These people may conceivably try to rear their heads again, but they will find it pretty difficult to argue their way around the signed agreements.

(*b*) I think that at the U.S. Treasury there is now a pretty clear recognition that the U.K. dollar balance position is serious and that we have got to be helped, if possible, to safeguard it. I will not go so far as to say that that will result in very positive action (thus our Chapter 3 hopes have, as you know, been rather disappointed) but it should, I think, prevent attacks on us because of the size of our dollar balances and should enable us, too, to appeal to the U.S. Treasury if some other U.S. Department puts forward a proposal which looks like involving us in a serious loss of dollars.

(*c*) On the question of export freedom—which was, to my mind, very largely the crux of the negotiation, we have achieved a settlement which is at least a long way better than anything that appeared likely to emerge from the abortive negotiations of the spring and early summer. And it is surely an immense advance to have it agreed that if and when we come across the 'vulnerable' items, the effect will be reflected not in any restrictions on our exports but in a possible circumscription of our lend lease programmes and an obligation to pay cash for the 'vulnerable' items in question. And, of course, it is something of a triumph to have been able to maintain the substitution principle in the case of cotton.

(*d*) Lastly I think that in what I may call the intermediate ranks of F.E.A.—I mean people of the level of Jim Angell[21] and George Appel—there has been something like a rally to our side and a recognition that we have had less than a square deal over lend lease during recent months. This is not to say that we shall not continue to have trouble with F.E.A. when the time comes to implement some of the agreed arrangements, particularly while Crowley and Currie survive. But our general bargaining position is, I think, immeasurably stronger.

As I said at the beginning, I am afraid that this is a very incoherent letter

[21] James Waterhouse Angell (b. 1898); economist; Office of Civilian Requirements, W.P.B., and predecessor units, 1941–3; Foreign Economic Administration, 1943–5; U.S. representative with rank of Minister, Allied Commission on Reparations, Germany, 1945–6; technical adviser, U.S. delegation to Bretton Woods, 1944.

which I have had to dictate (and which Miss Hughes has had to type) in the intervals of rather urgent work. But you may find it of some interest as a humdrum supplement to the brilliant, racy accounts of the negotiations which you will no doubt get from Maynard.

Incidentally, Charlie Noyes took no overt part in the negotiations at all, but was, I understand, concerned to some extent behind the scenes.

Yours ever,

FRANK

To SIR JOHN ANDERSON, *12 December 1944*

THE WASHINGTON NEGOTIATIONS FOR
LEND LEASE IN STAGE II

I have sufficiently reported in telegrams the positive conclusions of the Washington negotiations in October and November 1944. But there remain certain supplementary incidents and observations which may be worth further comment.

2. Prior to the conversations between the Prime Minister and the President at Quebec three dangerous tendencies, one newly emerging, the other two of old standing, were influencing the attitude of Washington towards the scope of lend lease in Stage II.

3. The first of these was directed to a considerable curtailment of the scope of lend lease after the defeat of Germany. There were, we believe, various proposals passing during the summer in and between Washington Departments, more particularly in the War and Navy Departments, but also in F.E.A. (the Foreign Economic Administration), lacking indeed any final authority but representing what some service and civilian officials might be found pressing on final authority at a suitable opportunity.

4. In the field of munitions these proposals were for limiting assistance to those of our needs required solely for the war against Japan and capable of being produced only in the United States, without regard to our overall requirements or

to our need to release man-power. It is likely that the requirements of the Admiralty would in any event have been subjected to particular scrutiny and curtailment. But if these proposals had been acted upon, only a part of our ground and air requirements would have been considered and the rest rejected out of hand. In the field of non-munitions lend lease would have been restricted, according to the more extreme school, to foodstuffs. I much doubt, however, whether the potential threat in this field was nearly so serious as in the case of munitions.

5. These ideas were logically defensible up to a point, if the scale of lend lease in Stage II were to be restricted, as broadly speaking it has been in Stage I, to our *marginal* requirements over and above what we could provide for ourselves when completely mobilised for war and drawing on all other sources to the maximum extent. They were also conformable to the fundamental principle of the Lend Lease Act that aid under it must be 'for the defence of the United States' which was held, and still is held, by some precisians to exclude the provision of any dispensable easements for the inhabitants of the British Isles. During the brief visit of Sir Wilfrid Eady and myself to Washington in August after Bretton Woods and Ottawa, it was made clear to us by the heads of the Washington missions that we must somehow secure that this limitation to merely marginal aid should cease to apply in Stage II. It was also clear that so vital a change as this could only be secured and held fast by a decision reached by the President at the instance of the Prime Minister. The Prime Minister took the opportunity of the Quebec meeting in September to discuss and agree with the President a brief outline directive, sufficient for this purpose, and requiring F.E.A. to have in view the objectives of permitting after VE Day some release of British man-power, some improvements in the standards of civilian consumption, and a broad resumption of the freedom to export. This directive was entrusted

to Mr Morgenthau and Lord Cherwell for further discussion and implementation with the United States Departments concerned.

6. Some difficulties and dangers remained. For this directive was of the briefest character and was capable of different interpretations, both in principle and in degree, when it came to working it out in detail and in practice. Nevertheless, the Quebec decision plainly rejected the principles underlying the proposed curtailments which, as mentioned above, were previously floating about in some quarters in Washington, and gave us a firm basis of clearly expressed general intention upon which to work. In addition, Mr Morgenthau, with whom Lord Cherwell had established an intimate and very helpful understanding, had become a convinced advocate of a strengthening of our financial and economic position. Sir Robert Sinclair and I, with other officials (amongst whom Mr Austin Robinson of the Ministry of Production, Mr Reader of the Ministry of Labour, and Mr Bridgeman of the Ministry of Fuel and Power deserve particular mention for their skilled help in essential details), joined Lord Cherwell in Washington. On the American side a Committee of three was established under Mr Morgenthau's chairmanship, including Mr Stettinius and Mr Crowley the Foreign Economic Administrator, with the addition of Mr Patterson and Mr Lovett of the War Department and Mr Gates of the Navy Department, where service questions were under discussion. On the technical Sub-Committee, as it was called, the principal American members, with whom all our detailed work was conducted on the non-munitions and export questions, were Mr Harry White of the United States Treasury (in the chair), Mr Dean Acheson an Assistant Under-Secretary in the State Department, assisted by Mr Taft, and Mr Oscar Cox and Mr Currie, principal officers of F.E.A. On the munitions side, however, Sir R. Sinclair pressed from the outset, wisely and with success, that our Service representatives, General Weeks, Air

Chief Marshall Courtney and Admiral Waller, should be put into direct touch with their opposite numbers, and many difficult points were discussed in a preliminary way with the Service Departments in the week before the formal presentation of the case.

7. It had been my original intention to depend to a much greater extent, as I had done in Canada, on oral exposition. But Sir Robert Sinclair favoured from the outset a full statement in writing and he proved correct. In view of the shortness of time, he had originally in view a document which would be mainly an elaboration of W.P. (44) 419. I felt, however, that if we were to have a written exposition, the only satisfactory solution would be a complete re-writing of the document. The preparation of this statement was a heavy task for all concerned, but in the end everyone accepted the advisability of attempting it and, after a week's very intensive work, the task was accomplished. There was never at any time an opportunity for continuous or coherent oral exposition to the right audience. A Washington meeting has to be experienced to be believed. At the Main Committee any continuous argument or indeed more than a dozen simple sentences were always out of place. At the technical and other Sub-Committees there would be twenty-five or more persons present at any one time, but their composition would be continually changing as they flocked in and out of the room to attend telephone calls and other business, so that we were seldom addressing the same audience for more than ten minutes together. One would suddenly discover that even the chairman had disappeared without explanation to return half an hour later, and the actual spokesman on the American side would break off his remarks at any moment to answer a call from without. Indeed in Washington the Ancient Mariner would have found it necessary to use the telephone to detain the wedding guest. For it is only on the telephone that one can obtain undivided attention. If you seek an interview, your

American friend will spend half the time talking on the telephone to all the quarters of the compass, until in despair you return to your own office and yourself ring him up, when you can expect to secure his concentrated mind for as long as you like, whilst someone else wastes his time keeping a date with him in the chair which you have so wisely vacated. No! Sir Robert Sinclair was right that a written document is best.

8. Moreover, there is no place where ample documentation is more appreciated than in Washington. There is an unquenchable inquisitiveness which quickly turns into suspicion if it is not satisfied. Nor is there, as a rule, any reason to fear dangerous purpose when a piece of information is pressed for. Attached to every Department in Washington there is a cohort of researchers, economists and statisticians, who will take unlimited trouble to understand your case and whose business it is to think objectively. If your case is a good one and if they feel that you have given them the material for a thorough understanding of it, they will become your best friends and advocates. In the long run, their influence is considerable; most certainly their criticism can be dangerous. I am convinced that in the past we have made a great mistake, and handicapped our representatives in Washington, by an economy of information. So-called 'reasons of security' must be reckoned at least as one of the minor, if not sometimes a major, inefficiency of the machine of war. The statement of our position won over to our support an army of honest thinkers and clever heads scattered all over the administrative area.

9. The munitions programme was given priority in our agenda. It was, in fact, agreed with remarkable ease and celerity. Sir R. Sinclair was able to present and justify exact details of requirements over a wide field. General Weeks and Colonel Sallitt from the War Office and Air Chief Marshal Courtney and Mr Hindley from the Air Ministry came over from London with full and up-to-date knowledge of all rele-

vant matters and presented the military case to the United States War Department with unfailing authority and skill. They seemed soon to acquire an ascendancy over their American colleagues and were never defeated on any matter to which they attached critical importance. The representation of the Supply Departments—Mr Willison from the Ministry of Production, and Mr Devons and Mr Taylor from the Ministry of Aircraft Production—were of the greatest assistance on the production side. With the Navy Department, on the other hand, there was much more difficulty, although our Admiralty requirements (apart from the Fleet Air Arm programme which was dealt with separately) were of a relatively unimportant character compared with the rest of our needs and, being an insignificant proportion of total American output, could not present great difficulty on the supply side. Early in the discussions the United States Navy Department broke contact with Admiral Waller and gave us to understand that we should be faced with a unilateral decision presented to the Main Committee without our experts having previous knowledge of its content or an opportunity for explanation and discussion. We, therefore, judged it advisable to lay a formal complaint about this procedure before Mr Morgenthau. He immediately promised us redress, saying that he saw no reason why the Navy Department should not follow the excellent precedent which had been set up by the War Department. We understand that, at a meeting of the American members of the Main Committee which was summoned immediately, the Navy Department after an initial show of strong resistance was in the end, and with some difficulty, brought to yield, after which fracas the essential items of the Admiralty programme were accepted without much further ado. Before sunset, as he had promised us, Mr Morgenthau was as good as his word. This opportunity may be taken to record that Mr Morgenthau was, throughout the discussions, as good as his word within the limits of his powers.

On two occasions—in particular, that just mentioned and the last-minute attempt to withhold our export freedom—he interposed on our behalf with vehemence and with success. Throughout the proceedings he maintained with Lord Cherwell (who had, however, left Washington before the turmoils of the last fortnight recorded below) and with myself unbroken relations of confidence, cordiality and intimacy, and he never failed to give us all the support that he could.

10. In one respect, the discussions on the munitions programme were particularly satisfactory, namely that the American side accepted our requirements with much less question than on previous occasions as being the proper and necessary consequence of the strategic decisions of the Combined Chiefs of Staff. Indeed, Sir R. Sinclair and the Service representatives did not have to accept any curtailments of the demands we had brought from London except where they were themselves satisfied that a reduction could be made safely or where there were genuine supply difficulties at the American end.

11. In another respect, however, we were defeated of our best hopes, inevitably in my opinion, though to Sir Robert Sinclair's disappointment. Our original idea had been to secure, without using the word, something approaching protocol validity for our requirements when once they had been passed by Mr Morgenthau's Committee. This proposal, however, aroused great wrath in the United States War and Navy Departments. We should have quickly exhausted our rather limited stock of goodwill in those Departments if we had pressed it. Moreover, there were sufficiently good arguments from future inevitable changes in the strategical position and in supply conditions in America why the Americans should reserve for themselves an ultimate discretion. The truth is that, not being at arm's length, as the Russians are, we have to suffer the inconvenient familiarities of our proximity as well as its broad advantages. Nevertheless, so far as phrases

are worth anything, they have in the covering letters accepted the basis of our military needs; they have said they will do their best to make available the quantities accepted in the agreements; and they agree that the production of our requirements will rank *pari passu* with their own. This is better than anything we have had hitherto; though there remain, as before, not only the continuing supervision of the Combined Munitions Assignments Board, which we readily accepted, but also all the usual jokers by which there is very little on which they cannot run out on us hereafter on one pretext or another, if they are so minded. In practice, those who have had experience of the system will, I think, agree that our failure to secure protocol procedure is not as bad as it sounds.

12. There is, however, some reason for caution arising out of this. Not too much attention should be attached to what follows, but it should not escape notice altogether. We have reason to think that the War and Navy Departments did not accept with any enthusiasm either the Quebec directive or the procedure of the Morgenthau Committee on which they were not represented formally or as of right. Mr Morgenthau was too clearly armed with the President's personal authority to make any overt resistance advisable. Moreover, his position was undoubtedly strengthened and the whole course of our negotiations made less difficult by the preliminary understanding he was able to reach with Mr Patterson, the Assistant Secretary of the War Department. Our case was presented to Mr Morgenthau on the 17th October. Within the hour a copy was in the hands of the War Department. Discussions with our representatives began at once, and by the morning of the 23rd agreement on the War Office and Ministry of Supply items had been reached and a report made to the Main Committee. The Air agreement did not lag far behind. All this undoubtedly gave great encouragement and reassurance to Mr Morgenthau as well as to ourselves. Nevertheless, the dissident elements may find some later and more favourable

opportunities for bringing the situation a little nearer to what they had been aiming at before Quebec. One is told that the Service Departments in Washington include certain less friendly elements such as are scarcely to be found, if at all, in the State Department, the Treasury or F.E.A. A certain number of quondam Isolationists dressed up in uniform are seated there. These Departments are admittedly the stronghold, not only (particularly in the Navy) of service jealousies but also of the unco-operative imperialistic ambitions and expansionisms into which the xenophobe passions of isolationism and America-first are suffering what can be literally called a sea-change. These minority and opposition elements are not strong, but they are capable of mischief; though it must be remembered that the discussions on the munitions programme preceded the Election, the outcome of which has served to diminish the practical significance of these elements, at least for the time being. We had hoped at one time to obtain some security against later back-sliding by keeping the Morgenthau Committee in being with a measure of continuing authority. In the confusion and habitual Washington disorder of our winding up it was not possible to make any formal proposition to this effect. Nevertheless, I think we might proceed on the tacit assumption that the Morgenthau Committee still continues in existence, for all we know to the contrary; and if the occasion should arise (which is, one hopes, unlikely) when there is some clear case of back-sliding from what this Committee had approved, the notion of bringing the matter formally to the notice of Mr Morgenthau and his colleagues should certainly be considered. If the Prime Minister decides to make any communication to the President, possibly there might be a suggestion along these lines; on the other hand, the tacit assumption suggested above may be the safer line, since it is perhaps not very likely that any general agreement could be obtained in Washington at the present time to put on a permanent footing a committee for this purpose with Mr Morgenthau in the chair.

13. Our non-munitions programmes (apart from the extra new items to be dealt with below) went through more slowly than the munitions but with no less ultimate success. They were handled entirely by the Washington missions on the spot dealing, under general direction, with their usual opposite numbers. We created a good impression by ourselves taking the initiative in cutting out a number of items, more particularly steel and non-ferrous metals and a wide range of miscellaneous manufactured articles, which were likely to interfere with our export freedom. By distinguishing between items for consignment to this country and items consigned direct to other areas, we found that we were able to effect this at a surprisingly low cost, perhaps $40 million. This also had the effect of making our lists look a cleaner and more straightforward affair.

14. We had to admit some compromises in the way of accepting a prospective reduction of our stocks, more particularly oil and certain foods, where, however, there was admittedly a good deal to be said for the American argument. The old question of the coastal vessels, which there had been pressure on us to agree in advance to take over for cash at the end of the war, was satisfactorily settled on the financial side, only to come unstuck on the allocation side—a bad business, due to a blunder for which our Shipping Mission was not responsible, which will, I hope and believe, come right in the end. The provision of the necessary lend lease finance, which is all we could concern ourselves with at this stage, does not, it must be remembered, always guarantee a corresponding allocation of supply, for example in the case of meat where we may have difficulty later on in getting from the Combined Food Board the full amount for which, if we can get it, we made sure that a lend lease appropriation would be available. Subject to these qualifications, in every case our Missions were sufficiently satisfied with the treatment they received not to think it necessary to call in further assistance or appeal to the Main Committee.

15. No doubt this was partly due to the better and more expansive atmosphere which the Quebec directive and the statement of our case had created. But it should not be overlooked what great credit is due for the result to the quality and skill of our Washington Missions and the standing they have acquired with their American colleagues. After an intermittent experience of Washington extending over the whole of the lend lease period, I venture to say that we have never had a more brilliant and effective team than were assembled there this autumn under the captaincy of Mr Ben Smith. There was not a weak spot. If it is not impertinent of me to say so, the present members of the British Supply Council have been serving the State in exhausting and exacting conditions with a mental and moral stamina which is beyond all praise. Without any doubt it is there that the credit is due. Mr Harry White remarked to me one day: 'I think Whitehall has no conception of what the chaps you send out here are up against.' Washington is a place frantic with frustration in every quarter. It is all very well to stick it for a few weeks, seeking daily comfort from the familiar adage of the British Ambassador three-quarters of a century ago (was it Lord Lyons?), who said, that in Washington it is not a question of how much you can do but how much you can stand. But a saintly patience and a strong character are required to persist for months with a clear head and without loss of temper. Yet our fellows manage, not only to keep their heads above the encircling flood of personal and political and departmental jealousies and indecisions and uncertainties which never are and never can be resolved or finalised, but also, so it seemed to me, to have gained, as time goes on, a genuinely increasing affection for those who torment them so, friendship and exasperation advancing hand in hand. So may a bird of passage record with particular admiration and respect and grateful thanks the names of Halifax, Ben Smith, Macready, Self, Brand, Lee, Goschen, Opie, Maclay, Hart, Hambro,

Archer, Penson, Hutton, Roll, Helmore, Symon, Wilkinson and Stevens.

16. The second of the influences mentioned in Section 2 was the objective accepted in the F.E.A. of the progressive contraction of lend lease and the progressive expansion of reciprocal aid, which had its origin in the United States Treasury criterion that lend lease aid was excessive if it led to our gold and dollar reserves rising from the figure of *nil*, at which they stood in April 1941 (when lend lease began) to anything materially above 1 billion dollars. This Treasury criterion, which was a unilateral pronouncement never accepted by us, ante-dated the entry of the United States into the war and the growth of our overseas liabilities. Nevertheless, it had been pressed for more than three years, and it was only after Mr Morgenthau's visit to London in the late summer of 1944 and his conversations with the Prime Minister and the Chancellor of the Exchequer, which greatly impressed him, that the United States Treasury Department were of a mind to depart from it. This, however, was not enough. For meanwhile the doctrines, originally based on the above criterion, had acquired an independent life of their own and a complicated but coherent body of dogma had been built up, which, in matters of detail, remained to the end our greatest practical obstacle. Vice and virtue had to have their positions reversed in the F.E.A. Commandments, a matter not to be accomplished in the twinkling of an eye, and right up to our last Sub-Committee meeting in Washington one was met by genuine well-wishers with the reply that that what one was proposing would be all very well if the opposite principle had not been established a year before. The very fact that this resistance was derived from what was in original purpose upright, being in mere accordance with instructions from above and in no way the child of ill-will or jealousy, made it all the more difficult to overcome.

17. Nevertheless, we can fairly claim that by the end of the

negotiations this heresy had been rooted out and that the avowed purpose of F.E.A. henceforward is to increase, and not abate, the scope of lend lease assistance, with a view to strengthening our general reserves so far as is possible within the legal limitations of the Act and without risk of giving rise to plausible (and, I would add, unplausible) criticisms in the press and in Congress, when, in the near future, the Lend Lease Act comes up for renewal and, a little later on, new appropriations under it have to be voted.

18. Unfortunately the outcome of our negotiations measured in hard cash fell considerably short of the change of mind and heart, and must be deemed, to this extent, unsuccessful. Mr Morgenthau and Mr Stettinius (Mr Crowley, though quite well disposed in principle, never attained the same level of consciousness of what it was all about, his ear being so near the ground that he was out of range of persons speaking from an erect position) were fully convinced that it was both advisable and desirable that new and special relief should be given us to the extent of some $400 to $500 million. Mr Morgenthau was determined at the outset to secure for us something of this order; fought valiantly to the end; and, being only too conscious of defeat, was appreciative, I think, that no useless word was said to rub the disappointment in. He was always open to hear new suggestions which might meet the case; but, in the light of your telegrams, I judged it better to refrain from any of the larger ideas which might trench on what is in hand for the purposes of Stage III.

19. In the end, our major proposals under this head fell through for the reasons explained below, and we had to be content with building up what we could from a variety of minor items as follows:– [see p. 205]

20. All this, however, is not worth its full face value. The direct cash relief, excluding (vi) above, is likely to work out ultimately at about $200 million more or less, against which we shall have sacrificed about $40 million by taking items off

	$ million
(i) New rulings on lend lease eligibility (definite)	
Oil	48
Ocean freights	14
Food items	7
NAAFI (including food)	14
Emergency housing	
Raw materials	28
Equipment	10*
Houses	50*

Sundry items for the Dominions and
    India (Australia 7, New Zealand 1,
    India 11)
	19

Maize (in lieu of Argentine supplies)	40†
	230
(ii) Reimbursement of old capital items	51
(definite)	
Definite	281
(iii) Contingency lend lease funds for capital equipment	
Contingency funds for Dominions and India	28
Ultimate lend lease proportion of Indian rolling-stock perhaps	15

(iv) New rulings on lend lease eligibility
    (not yet finally determined and
    still problematical).	

Freights on non-lend lease
    Government cargo
    Sundry items for Crown Colonies
    lend lease proportion of machine
      tools for United Kingdom (perhaps
      worth with luck a maximum of)
	20

(v) Reimbursement of old capital items (still under examination)	8

(vi) Relief to reciprocal aid by taking
    foodstuffs off the list either by
    their action or by ours
    (still under examination)
	46

Very uncertain	117

* Not necessarily a relief to our reserves, since if we could not have obtained these items on lend lease, we should probably have had to go without.
† At United States Prices, excluding freight, but freight will also be lent leased if shipment is on American vessels. At Argentine prices 17 also excluding freight. This relieves our Argentine liability but does not increase our dollars.

lend lease to secure export freedom (this, however, I reckon a cheap price, which might have been much higher). Indirect financial aid (emergency housing, maize and deferred recoveries for capital goods) should be worth another $100 million. If we can manage to get food-stuffs taken off reciprocal aid, which we understand Mr Crowley and F.E.A. would welcome if a way can be found, $46 million can be added to the direct cash relief. The right approach to this needs immediate and careful thought.

21. The relaxation of lend lease eligibility in favour of emergency housing deserves a special mention of grateful appreciation. We had no expectation of this when we left London, but we managed to argue successfully that no form of aid was likely to commend itself more sympathetically to the peoples of both our countries. It certainly represents a stretching on their part of the strict interpretation of the Lend Lease Act, and we must be careful, in availing ourselves of it, not to go beyond a reasonable gloss on what is properly 'temporary' or 'emergency' or 'replacement of bombed-out houses'. It was still uncertain when I left Washington how far suitable types of prefabricated structures would be obtainable. But I understand that the representatives of the Ministry of Works have been successful in discovering a suitable type and that we can now hope for the delivery of 30,000 houses in the course of 1945, which should prove a very helpful supplement to our own programme. I suggest that the attention of the Minister of Education might be directed to obtaining under this provision second-hand temporary structures suitable for emergency schools, which may be available in large quantity from the surplus stocks of the United States Administration and would probably be reckoned up against the lend lease appropriation at a very moderate price.

22. Since several of the items catalogued above would have fallen outside, and have been additional to, Mr Morgenthau's proposed relief of $400–500 million, I feel that we have fallen

$200 million short of our best and justifiable hopes. The reasons for this are to be found in a chapter of bad luck as follows:–

23. There were from the start two alternative means of giving us what we wanted, and in the end we fell between the two stools. The first expedient was to restore off-shore sugar and civilian tobacco to the lend lease eligibility which had been allowed to these items in the first phase of lend lease. Sugar always presented difficulties from our point of view as well as theirs. Existing contracts of ours in United States dollars, but in the Caribbean, not in the United States, were involved. But a further obstacle came, I think, from the current shortage and the prospective still greater shortage of sugar available for civilian consumption in United States. It was, moreover, this same obstacle, namely the reluctance to supply on lend lease any article of civilian consumption where it could be represented that lend lease was operating to the disadvantage of the American consumer, which stood in the way of our getting tobacco back into the list. This item presented no technical difficulties whatever. At the beginning of our conversations both Mr Morgenthau and Mr Harry White expressly declared themselves in favour. At that moment, cigarettes mysteriously disappeared from all the drugstores although supplies, perhaps falling slightly, remained at about 60–70 per cent above pre-war. I do not believe things went so far that anyone was ever actually without a cigarette. Everyone, however, from the President downwards, immediately concluded that it became out of the question to lend lease civilian tobacco. It was useless to argue that lend leasing the tobacco would not make the smallest difference to the volume of supplies we should receive, which were already contracted for and set aside. It was useless to point out that, if there was a shortage, it was a shortage not of leaf, of which there was eighteen months' supply in stock, but of labour and packaging for cigarettes, aggravated by bad

distribution, and that what we wanted was not cigarettes, but leaf. These were subleties, we were told, far beyond the comprehension of Congress or the possibility of explanation to the public. The unfriendly press was already showing pathetic cartoons of Uncle Sam reduced to a state of nervous breakdown through being deprived by a leering Britisher of his daily pack of 20. There cannot be any doubt that the unlucky synchronisation of our discussions with this spontaneous and unheralded outbreak of cigarette hoarding cost us $100 million.

24. This is an unattractive aspect of American habits. But what is more alarming is the ease with which policy can be deflected by irresponsible comment wildly off any recognisable mark. This is partly a result of the extreme sensitiveness of civil servants, right down the line, to unfounded and calumnious criticism by columnists, of which they may be at any time the personal victim without effective redress. On my last day Laughlin Currie, the civil service head of lend lease, sought to explain and justify to me the difficulties he had been putting in our way, some of which he knew I had thought unnecessary, by showing me an issue of *The American*, a weekly of Mr Hearst's, about to appear with numerous charges of alleged lend lease abuses without a vestige of foundation, of a character which we should no more ask than the Americans would concede. This only shows, I replied, how vain it is to protect yourself by refusing reasonable measures when the grounds on which you are attacked invariably relate to alleged crude acts of quite a different order which neither you nor we have ever contemplated; to which he rejoined that the Lend Lease Administration had survived unscathed so far precisely because it had been able to show that every plausible charge made against it was based on falsehood. Shortly before, I may add, in a nationwide radio address during the campaign, Mr Dewey himself had gone out of his way to denounce Mr Currie by name as a crypto-

communist who had been investigated by the Dies Committee, contrary to the facts and without a vestige of evidence, on no better ground than that he had been one of the original group of New Dealers, whose services the President had always retained, and was also believed to be an intimate of the Vice-President, Mr Wallace. I often had to complain, as a consequence of all this, that I was turned down not only when there was a good reason, but also, just as likely, for a reason which everyone admitted to be bad; and that it was hard luck to be caught both ways.

25. One certainly learnt the value of our excellent system of professional scapegoats, known as Ministers, with skins thickened by experience or natural endowment, whose duty it is to suffer vicariously for the sins of all the administrative tribe. American officials are open to press abuse and Congressional criticism. Yet they are without any real responsibility or adequate opportunity to reply; and it saps their nerve. This lesson was reinforced by another experience. One of the last matters, on which with characteristic willingness to take trouble Field-Marshal Dill concerned himself very shortly before his death, was to arrange a meeting of the Combined Chiefs of Staff to give me an oportunity to explain the nature of the financial burdens we had assumed, so that the American Service Chiefs might better understand that our requests for the relief of man-power were not made without good reason. General Marshall, who presided, followed my remarks with a discourse, only indirectly relevant to what I had said, on the theme that there was scarcely a General or an Admiral present who, with little or no experience of such a situation, might not find himself faced at any time with the task of defending his executive acts before a Congressional Committee, and that it was essential for us Britishers to understand that fact if we were to appreciate rightly what might from time to time befall us.

26. Escaping from this long digression, I return to the

other alternative by which we might have been given what we wanted. When the United States first came into the war they were, as is well known, fatally deficient in certain types of aircraft, which were coming forward to our order as a result of our having spent about 2 billion dollars, which was almost the whole of our gold reserves, in building up the American munitions industries from small beginnings. We therefore agreed to transfer to them a useful quantity of the aircraft which we had ordered and paid for. On the first occasion, when a matter of some $80 million was involved, they very properly reimbursed us. On the second occasion, which was arranged between Air Chiefs without waiting to formalise the financial provisions (the Arnold–Porter Agreement), when aircraft, which had cost us more than $200 million of our pre-lend lease reserves, were transferred, we expected a similar reimbursement. This time, however, the United States War Department decided just not to pay, and the United States Treasury did not press them to do so. Sir Frederick Phillips never accepted this position or agreed to it in any way. After he had vainly presented the bill on several occasions, it was put into cold storage with hope that a better opportunity might come later. There were also further similar but smaller items of later date, due to our agreeing to transfer certain munitions which had cost us cash dollars to the United States at their request to help them fulfil their protocol obligations to Russia. These brought our total claims to the order of $250 million. The United States contention is, presumably, that we either should give them these munitions as reciprocal aid (which, however, did not exist as an agreed arrangement at the date of the major transaction) or should regard them as replaced in kind by aircraft and other supplies which we have received subsequently on lend lease. Nevertheless, until we have agreed to one or other of these alternatives, the United States cannot put either of them into force by unilateral decision and, meanwhile, there can be little doubt that they owe us the money. They can, of course, at any time force us to waive our claims by making this a condition of further lend lease assistance; and, in all the circumstances, we could not object to this very strenuously. If, on the other hand, they are looking for ways to help us, here, on the face of it, was an easy means.

27. Mr Morgenthau began by showing considerable irritation at the revival of a claim which reminded him unpleasantly of a phase of shabby behaviour, the occasion of some friction at the time between Sir Frederick Phillips and himself, which he much preferred to forget. At a later stage, however, when it appeared that it would be very difficult to fulfil those hopes on our part which he had encouraged, he was, I understand, sufficiently magnanimous to change his attitude (partly, I guess, under the influence of Mr Harry White, who gave me the impression from the start that he thought this an easier way out than the alternatives). F.E.A. definitely favoured this solution which, from their point of view, was much preferable to restoring difficult items to the lend lease list. The State Department was of the same opinion. Accordingly the United States members of the Main Committee, namely, Mr Morgenthau, Mr Stettinius and Mr Crowley, referred the claim, so we were informed, to the War Department, out of whose funds the claims would have to be met. We were not made privy to the American discussions behind the scenes, but I have reason to believe that the United States members of the committee were genuinely disappointed at the outcome and felt quite bad about it. For the War Department referred the matter to their lawyers, who ruled that the appropriations out of which these claims might have been met had now expired, so that nothing could be done without asking Congress for a new and specific appropriation for the purpose. Mr Lovett, the Assistant Secretary of the War Department, informed the Morgenthau Committee that his Department did not think it opportune or politic to ask for

such an appropriation at the present time, a decision which was formally conveyed to us by Mr Morgenthau. Mr Harry Hopkins, in private conversation, expressed a doubt whether a certain lack of sympathy in the War Department (which we never had the same opportunity to penetrate with the full force of our case as we had with the civilian departments and which is, moreover, along with the Navy Department, the stronghold of the less friendly elements) did not play a part. But Mr Oscar Cox, counsel to F.E.A. and lately Assistant Attorney-General, told me that he felt little doubt that the ruling was formally correct. Whether, all the same, there may not have been some way round, we shall never know. I have thought it advisable to put this incident on record to the best of my understanding of what occurred; but, as will be seen, it is based, in part, on conjecture.

28. This was not the only issue on which at the last moment we were defeated by the lawyers, with whom every American Department is infested. A Sub-Committee, consisting mainly of lawyers, recommended that we should be allowed retrospective lend lease facilities for certain oil and shipping items worth about $30 million, and this was approved by the Main Committee. On my last day in Washington I was informed by Mr Crowley that some additional lawyers had found this to be impossible on account of a principle of law, which sounds very odd, that F.E.A. cannot take over an existing liability from another party but can only assume a newly created liability. Surely the plague of lawyers in Washington is a worse plague of Egypt than Pharaoh ever knew. It is only by a rare and lucky coincidence that what is administratively sensible is also lawful. The late Lord Hewart should have visited Washington to discover what the substitution of administrative law for administrative discretion means in practice. The place only carries on at all because of the wide reserve of discretionary power which becomes vested in the President in time of war, and what will happen when peace returns, with all its complications, heaven only knows.

29. There was, however, a further contributory cause, in my opinion, for our failure to win the missing $200 million. The strengthening of our reserves had not entered into the Quebec conversation, and the force of our case under this head, and probably even its existence, never reached the President. He had, I feel sure, no effective word of our proceedings until we were almost at the last lap of our course. Mr Harry Hopkins, consulted at the outset, decided that it would cause difficulties if Mr Morgenthau were to find that any reports were reaching the President except from himself. Mr Morgenthau has been criticised in some quarters for not keeping the President in closer touch with our discussions from the beginning. But, in fact, the President's complete preoccupation with the Election campaign and its immediate political consequences made this inevitable; besides which, Mr Morgenthau has easier access to his presence than to his mind. Anyhow, the necessary word to Mr Crowley to do his best to strengthen our reserves and not to be unduly timid never came. On the contrary, an impression of the President's mind, which produced a quite opposite tendency, reached Mr Crowley and ran right through F.E.A., namely, that the President wished nothing to be done which could be represented in Congress as involving any present change in the lend lease set-up and practice. The consequences of this are dealt with further below.

30. So, in the end, we were disapointed of our best hopes and duly fell between the two stools. But we put up a good fight and can claim as consolation that the half-measures (or kittens) we brought home from what came to be known as the Chapter III cats were all a bonus over and above the expectations we set out with instructions to realise when we left Whitehall. I would like to mention the keenness and skilled aid of Mr Lee and Mr Goschen in the pursuit, without which tens of millions less dollars would have been recovered.

31. There is also the thought that the atmosphere left

behind is one in which our American friends feel that they have done less for us than they intended; which may be better for future discussions than if, in retrospect, there was a suspicion in their minds that they had allowed us to overreach them. Mr Harry White and Mr Oscar Cox, in particular, were emphatic in private conversation in attaching much more importance to a good settlement in Stage III than to anything we could settle now. They were constantly urging me to be content now with the least that would do, and not to press for anything which might have the effect, even indirectly, of prejudicing the later discussions. Their own policy throughout was dictated by this thought, acting, as they believed, in our interests. And the same lies, I think, behind the President's tactics, as, in what follows, I surmise them to have been. I never had reason to doubt the basic friendliness, the intention to help and the genuine frankness of advice of all the American officials with whom I was in touch. I would particularly mention Mr Harry White for the unvarying fairness and helpfulness which he showed as Chairman in his own aloof and independent way, and the intimate advice, the truest to be had in Washington, on which I could rely in case of need; and Mr Dean Acheson for what I believe that he did, without confessing it or blabbing in the too frequent Washington way, behind the scenes.

32. If there is one wrinkle worth handing on to my successors, which I have picked up after spending nearly a year out of the last four stepping like a cat over the hot tiles of Washington, it is this. Remember that, in a negotiation lasting weeks, the situation is entirely fluid up to almost the last moment. Everything you are told, even with the greatest appearance of authority and decision, is provisional, without commitment, 'thinking out loud', a kite, a trial balloon. There is no orderly progression towards the final conclusion. Thus you must not believe that a man is not your loyal friend, merely because he has raised false hopes, or run out on you,

or even, from a strict point of view, double-crossed you. Equally, do not become faint-hearted against opposition. You may be able, when things look worst, to gain a sudden reversal in your favour. All this is a process, unfamiliar to us, of discovering by open trial and error what will go and what will not. I liken them to bees who for weeks will fly round in all directions with no ascertainable destination, providing both the menace of stings and the hope of honey; and at last, perhaps because the queen in the White Hive has emitted some faint, indistinguishable odour, suddenly swarm to a single spot in a compact, impenetrable bunch.

33. I come finally to the third of the dangerous tendencies of § 2, namely the temptation to use lend lease to satisfy trade rivalry by hampering our export trade. To avert this was our biggest political problem, yet the purpose most easily accepted on its merits by the officials with whom we were dealing. We had no difficulty in obtaining acceptance in the Treasury, in the State Department, in the F.E.A. and in the White House of the proposition that we ought to receive the widest possible export freedom at the earliest possible date. The task was to find a formula to achieve this which would escape political criticism, and, above all, to find an agreed procedure for communicating the substance of this formula to our own exporters on the one hand and to the American public and pressure groups on the other.

34. I affirm with emphasis that there is no ground for supposing any desire or policy on the part of the three departments with which we were dealing to hamper our export trade. On the contrary, they are as conscious as we are that our recovery of trade is the only way out and is almost as necessary to the solution of their problems as of ours. We can safely assume this (with a reserve in respect of the Commerce Department of which I have no evidence either way) in all our future dealings. Indeed, the United States Treasury (as was also the case in Canada) was much more

inclined to complain that we were taking advantage of lend lease (or mutual aid) to send *less* exports than we could to United States (or Canada). On the other hand, their political timidities in relation to pressure groups, other elements hostile to the Administration in and out of Congress, and the chatter of columnists was infuriating; and, in my private opinion, largely unnecessary, as I think the final outcome went some way towards proving. Surely this was a nettle, which, if it was grasped, would cease to sting and soon wither. Nothing of what I subsequently experienced, as related below, led me to change this conviction.

35. As a result of their so easily accepting the main proposition, we began gaily enough. We, on our side, discarded and never produced the more timid proposals we had prepared beforehand during our first week (and we largely owe our avoidance of a mistake here to the wise insistence of Sir Henry Self). They, on their side, bent their best wits to find words which would give us in practice virtually complete freedom. Then silence and a veil descended, and we could learn nothing for certain from our opposition numbers. We comforted ourselves that, if the Election turned out well, the mists would disappear. Exactly the opposite happened. After the Election, timidities mysteriously multiplied (on other parts of our front also, as well as on this). From the best possible source I was warned that dark forces, of which I knew nothing, were bringing to bear in the neighbourhood of the White House. Mr Morgenthau complained to me that advices from sources he could not identify were reaching the President. I never learnt what the mysterious scare was which ran through every corridor of that Byzantine Court within a few days *after* their electoral triumph. But the result was that things began to slip.

36. The President gave a press conference in which he pretended to be unaware that anything of the smallest importance or novelty was going on in our discussions. He even

went so far as to maintain that he had no idea what was meant by Stage (or, as the Americans call it, Phase) II about which the journalists were enquiring—he had never heard the expression, so he said. Nothing whatever is happening, was the impression he sought to produce, we are all just churning along as usual; which was certainly a second-degree method, so to speak, of lulling suspicion in the minds of the well-informed sleuths present. Yet he did, in fact, get away with it.

37. This gave the cue to Mr Crowley; though the precise rôle which he played at this time, especially during a vital week when he purported to be absent from Washington, I cannot say. After, as I gathered, considerable controversy with Mr Acheson and Mr Morgenthau, who, in face of this cloud on the horizon, though no bigger than a man's hand, had to yield in the end, Mr Crowley announced at our very last formal meeting that our whole programme which had been discussed hitherto on the basis of beginning on the 1st January was put back to the indeterminate date of VE Day. The same afternoon I was told on his authority that we must not even assume that the export arrangements could be considered as agreed after VE Day and that Mr Crowley also considered himself free to revise, as he thought fit, any item in the non-munitions programme which had been already accepted at the official level. There was also trouble and inconclusive conversations about Ministers at home being allowed to make any worthwhile statement to Parliament. In short, I was put on notice that they were, or might be, running out on us all along the line.

38. This was *after* the final meeting of the Main Committee from which we were entitled to suppose that we had had a decision. There was, therefore, nothing to be done except to see behind the scenes all our friends in high places one after another and more than once, and beg them to rally round. (And even so I got in temporary trouble with Mr Morgenthau

at one point because, for the excellent reason that he was (as usual) absent from Washington, I had not shown my draft of a statement to him first but had already cleared it with Mr Harry Hopkins and Mr Stettinius!) Fortunately Mr Crowley had altogether over-reached himself, and was compelled under severe pressure from his colleagues to recede back to the position which had been accepted by the main committee.

It ended in a recommendation to the President signed by all three of them (Mr Morgenthau, Mr Stettinius and Mr Crowley), the text of which I have not seen, but which gave us, I was led to understand, the certainty of complete export freedom after VE Day and, by administrative action, the substance of it from the 1st January next. In spite of this episode (and other peculiar information which I need not relate) I believe that our Tammany Polonius, Mr Crowley, neither meant nor wished us any harm, but conceived that he was playing the President's political game on the principle of political safety first.

39. My own conversation with the President, whilst it convinced me that he never intended things to go so far, nevertheless indicated how easily Polonius could have come to believe that he was doing what was wanted. The President declared to me without qualification that we must have our export freedom. He made no objection to a public announcement and accepted the position that Parliament must have this. But he also made it clear that it must all be so expressed that he would be free to confirm that there would be no change whatever in the general conditions of lend lease before VE Day. He told me that it was essential to prevent any premature raising of lend lease issues in the present lame-duck Congress, with which, he said, he might have considerable trouble. With the new Congress, he added, it would be another matter. We all know that in these matters the President attaches primary importance to *timing*—and that he is generally right. He put it clearly to me that from

his point of view the time is *not* now, but he was ready to go as far as possible to meet the dilemma that from the point of view of Ministers in London the time *is* now. I had to draft poised between these two horns and to warn you of the inadvisability of altering words which had been agreed with so much difficulty. (I did not trouble the President with the actual text, but he particularly enquired whether Mr Harry Hopkins had approved the wording, which fortunately I had had an opportunity to correct with his help immediately before I saw the President.)

40. Quite apart from any special warnings of trouble brewing somewhere, I can see strong justification in our own interests (and I am sure he so intended it) for the President's caution, provided it was not pushed too far. In the course of next year he may have to go to Congress three times on our financial behalf, first to obtain a renewal of the Lend Lease Act, next to seek fresh appropriations under it, and finally (if all goes well) in connection with Stage III. Naturally at this moment he wants to play the issue down and keep the waters smooth. But there was also another and perhaps more compelling reason for extreme care. In fact reconversion is proceeding in the United States much too fast to suit W[ar] P[roduction] B[oard]. Strong efforts were being made, whilst I was in Washington, to retard this tendency, which was beginning to interfere seriously with the output of munitions. If there were to be any suggestion that British exporters were to be released from restrictions as from the 1st January, whereas the official date for reconversion in the United States is VE Day, there would be no holding American manufacturers and W.P.B.'s task would be dangerously aggravated.

41. In fact we were successful in straddling the position. It was, indeed, only on the last afternoon, and as the result of strong assaults, that it was agreed to issue fairly full statements on both sides. In the result all fears were falsified. The reaction in Congress and in the responsible press was

excellent; whereas an attempt at concealment or a more partial statement would, I am convinced, have bred suspicion and a swarm of utterly false stories. The handsome way in which the Americans at the eleventh hour met our views and the success which resulted left for all of us a pleasant flavour in the air, which in the turmoil of the last week was becoming sullied; and we parted better and more intimate friends all round than before it.

42. I find that I have left to the end any mention of what I believe to have been the decisive factor in our favour. The Quebec conversation and Lord Cherwell's initial steps with Mr Morgenthau played an essential part in starting the business along the right lines and with the right general directive. The main statement of our case caused a much-needed enlightenment all down the line. But the real underlying reason why the wicket was so much easier than on previous visits to Washington and why a better measure of success than London, perhaps, anticipated, was certain from the start, is the ever increasing and ever deepening conviction in the minds of all responsible Americans that a strong Britain after the war is a vital, indeed an indispensable, requirement of American policy. I have a very strong impression that the recent course of events has somehow had the effect of causing this old notion suddenly to hit the sub-consciousness of the American people with the impact of certitude. It has become an unspoken premiss, which, whatever the momentary, superficial reasons to the contrary, cannot be questioned. Further acquaintance with Russia does not increase intimacy or confidence. The illusion of China has faded. Central Europe is a dreaded cavern of misery and chaos. The Governments of Western Europe are wished well but are doubtful quantities. The little Latin nephews are all very well but not what Uncle hoped. There is nothing to be found reliable or homely in the habitable globe outside Britain and the British Commonwealth. This, to-day, is America's deepest, least alterable conviction—a sure rock upon which, whatever may

appear on the surface, we can build with safety. They want to be told, not that we have sacrificed more than we can afford, but that we are stable, healthy and competitively strong. If, therefore, we can control our suspicions, even though they have some foundation, and our exasperations, for which there will be every excuse in the world, if we can overlook their inevitable jealousies and unwarrantable aggrandisements and indefensible intrusions, and if they can do the like, as I think they can, in respect of our not less objectionable faults, the only brotherhood by which civilisation can be held together, already sealed with blood, will become in due time a decent, commonplace, workaday affair, which is taken for granted, as anything must be which is to be good and durable. On no temptation or provocation or pretext must we allow ourselves to stray, even in thought or hypothesis, along another path than this.

43. And having said all that, I should like to return to earth and add something on a lower level which may look like the opposite of the above, but in fact is the safe means to the same end; though it might be more pertinent to the separate report which I hope to make on the impressions I have formed about the shape which the solution of our financial problem in Stage III might assume.

44. I have been designated this autumn to travel in North America seeking large-scale financial aid on the basis of a hard luck story about how we held the fort when we were almost alone, how we have conducted the war with the utmost financial imprudence, first to win it and then to shorten its duration in the interests of all alike, with the result that we have not now very much left; and, moreover, apart from grounds of fairness requiring a more equal sharing of the burdens, it is in the general interest that the United Kingdom should emerge from the struggle, not with a Pyrrhic victory, but economically, and financially strong. This story can be based on vivid and unanswerable evidence; though I am not sure how far the story of our past effort would carry us if

it were not supported by the very strong conviction, upon which I have been dilating above, that our future strength is an objective of major concern to the United States and to Canada.

45. Fortunately this same story, supported by the same underlying conviction, will carry us up to a point through the financial difficulties of Stage III—up to a point exactly the same considerations apply as in Stage II. But only up to a point. There are enough hostile or critical elements in the countries concerned to make it important that our friends, though in the majority, have a rock-bottom case to present. I notice already a tendency in the United States Treasury to enquire whether it is really necessary that we should continue such vast expenditures overseas after Germany has been defeated. I believe that we shall receive the support necessary to see us through those transitional difficulties which have been genuinely caused by what we suffered and accomplished at the height of the danger and by the part which we shall be expected to play in the settlement; and that we shall receive it on terms which will not burden the future unduly. Our chief trouble will be to prevent the attachment of inconvenient strings. If once the suspicion gets abroad that the scale of the assistance we seek is partly caused by our undertaking, for reasons of power and prestige, new liabilities and responsibilities both beyond what we are able to support out of our own resources and also beyond what our Allies and Dominions are asking and expecting of us, these strings will multiply and toughen.

46. Even to-day the United States Departments are on the brink of showing signs of an implied right of interference into what we should wish to consider our own business. It was necessary to be continuously aware of this tendency and to take what precautions one could. A position can very easily arise when no precautions will avail. In that case friction and ill-will are likely to occur between the two countries which will undo the best hopes of the future. I am certain that I shall

have with me every British official who has any intimate experience of Washington when I urge with vehemence that, in spite of their genuine good-will and magnanimous aid to us, financial independence of the United States at the earliest possible opportunity should be a major aim of British policy. This is, indeed, an indispensable condition of the right sort of workaday relationship. There are very few objects of policy beyond the demands of victory over the enemy to which that should be subordinated. A mighty Empire in financial leading strings to others will not be mighty at all, and we shall have sacrificed real power to show and sham.

47. His Majesty's Ministers would, I think, do well to assume that we shall not be freely or unconditionally assisted, except within a narrow field, to undertake foreign and imperial responsibilities at other people's expense for a sufficient length of time to bring such policies to fruition. Because we have been able so to contrive that we could wage the war as though money were no object, it will not be safe to conclude that post-war policies or even Stage II policies can be safely conducted that way. If the attempt is made, waste, ill-will and frustration are to be expected. There is a much more limited supply of cloth to cut our travelling coat than what we wear at home.

48. Following my previous precedent of getting one of our statesman-orator-poets or provide me, Chancellor, with a peroration for the reports I write to you on board ship, I offer you, after the intensive experience of seeking props described above, a familiar line, written at a time of this country's adversity, but containing a moral very applicable to the next few years, especially for the holder of your office to enforce—

That we must stand unpropped, or be laid low

KEYNES

S.S. Nieuw Amsterdam,
12 December 1944

Keynes's arrival in Ottawa coincided, as the letters above have indicated, with a political crisis. The crisis concerned the sending of conscripts overseas. Prior to the end of 1944, largely in deference to views in Quebec, conscripts could not be sent overseas without their consent. Casualties in Europe in the summer and autumn of 1944 made the continuance of this principle seem incompatible with the maintenance of the strength of the forces on active duty. The prospective change in policy resulted in a political crisis within the ruling Liberal party, which diverted the attention of Ministers from the problems of Anglo-Canadian war finance.

In its several discussions with the Canadians, the Mission outlined the scale of Britain's requirements for the first year of Stage II, which looked very large to the Canadians concerned, raised certain outstanding difficulties concerning mutual aid such as capitation payments and cancellation changes, and discussed sterling area import policy and French gold deposited in Canada. The Mission also discussed a pooling plan, which had come up earlier, whereby Canada and Britain would pool supplies for their armed forces and keep no accounts. This proposal would leave mutual aid to cover food and some raw materials, thus keeping the total for such aid, covered by a separate appropriation, down. The Canadians did not take well to the pooling proposal as they thought it might look to the world at large as a camouflage for a larger mutual aid appropriation. In the discussions, the Canadian Ministers suggested an interest-free 30- to 50-year loan as a means of keeping mutual aid down to manageable proportions, but the Mission rejected this solution as a possibility before the Stage III transitional period. In the end, the discussions solved few problems, but they laid the groundwork for the subsequent Stage II discussions early in 1945. They also continued the process of mutual education through such devices as a repetition of Keynes's Washington talk on the sterling area and the dollar pool. After the discussions, Keynes returned by sea to London.

On his return to London Keynes again became immersed in day-to-day Treasury matters. In the course of this involvement, it was agreed that work on Stage III planning, with its implications for the treatment of sterling balances, would begin early in 1945.

In the course of the month, Keynes continued his campaign against Lady Bountiful, striking a particularly effective blow when the Dominions Office proposed that Britain should make available funds to cover the maintenance charges on a $100 million reconstruction programme and take over Newfoundland's liability for a previous issue of securities, the sum involved being just over $3 million per annum.

To T. PADMORE, *18 December 1944*

NEWFOUNDLAND

I have not had time to study this thick file as carefully as I should. But I had a brief discussion about this problem with Mr Gordon Munro when I was in Ottawa, and it runs, of course, pretty closely into the financial negotiations. So I venture the following observations, very much on the lines of Sir Bernard Gilbert's note, on what seems to me to be a somewhat frantic proposal.

1. The population of Newfoundland consists of somewhat less than 300,000 poor fishermen. A grant of $100 million, therefore, represents per head the same amount as a grant to us from the United States of $15,000 million. When I first saw this, I thought that $100 million must be a misprint for $10 million. I still think it is better so regarded. This, however, is not the end. We are also to take over an annual liability of $3 million, which represents a further sum of $100 million. Thus the true comparison with a grant to ourselves would be $30 billion. Even if we were stuffed with money, this would seem to be somewhat out of proportion.

2. In fact we have no such dollars (Newfoundland is not, of course, in the sterling area, but uses Canadian currency). We have been busy informing the Canadians that we have no resources we can make available in Canada during the war and that, after the war, we shall need the utmost limit of what we can afford to borrow from them for the purpose of buying Canada's agricultural and other exports. We should, therefore, look extremely silly if we were suddenly to produce the above sum or take on such a commitment, even though it be spread over a number of years, since it is precisely our capacity to meet the service of a loan from Canada over a number of years which I have been arguing sets the limit to the amount we can borrow from them. Thus the above difficulty applies scarcely less to a proposal to Canada to lend

us the money, since, on the basis of the argument we have been using, this would mean that we could buy that much less of their agricultural exports.

3. The political argument by which this bounty is justified seems odd. It is agreed that the right long-term solution is for Newfoundland to be taken over by Canada. The argument seems to be that the Newfoundlanders will overcome their reluctance to leave us and put themselves in the hands of Canada if we give them these great sums. It would have been natural to conclude the exact opposite namely that, after this signal mark of our favour, the Newfoundlanders would be still more reluctant to part company with us.

4. In any case, as the Dominions Office point out, the first step would be to put all our cards on the table for a frank discussion with the Canadian Government. This would be a ticklish matter, both on the political and on the financial side. I need not enlarge on the extreme sensitiveness of Canadian feeling, particularly in the Department of External Affairs, to our dealings with Newfoundland. On the financial side, as I have pointed out, we should come very near admitting that we were trying to fool the Canadians with the stories of our financial position and prospects on the basis of which we had been talking to them.

5. Nevertheless, if we went into a discussion with the Canadians as to what on earth is to be done about Newfoundland entirely free from prejudice, it is possible that something might emerge. Canada's interest is, of course, at least as much in Labrador (which by a historical accident belongs to Newfoundland) as in Newfoundland itself. Labrador is an immense tract of country on the Canadian mainland, which has very lately become the centre of the prospective air traffic which takes the Arctic route. Canada, as the Chancellor will remember in connection with the Goose Bay discussions, has recently sunk great sums of money there. It also has, I believe, great timber reserves of ultimate value and also

important mineral deposits. It is conceivable, therefore, that some arrangement with the Canadians about Labrador might form the bridge. For example, I should not be at all surprised if Canada would not be prepared both to pay Newfoundland the $100 million in question and also take over their sterling debt (which they would then set off against credits to us), if Newfoundland would transfer Labrador to them. That is just an idea. A frank and full discussion with the Canadians might lead them to suggest something more suitable. What does seem fantastic is that we, not having such huge sums, should, nevertheless provide them, partly out of no doubt most valuable philanthropy, but also on the extremely sketchy political justification which is the best I can discover below.

If a deal over Labrador is politically impracticable, then surely Sir Bernard Gilbert is right that some way should be found of making Newfoundland at the earliest possible date the responsibility of Canada. Newfoundland's reluctance to the Canadian connection is well-known. Is it not common sense to suppose that it is not for us to make an unconditional grant as proposed, but for the Canadians to exercise comparable financial generosity on condition that the Newfoundlanders waive the objection they have felt hitherto?

[copy initialled] K

At the close of the year, Keynes, reflecting on his recent experience in America, attempted to make some recommendations for handling the British press during Anglo-American negotiations. Press reactions and reporting had proved a perpetual problem in the past and some have argued they were an important source of friction in Anglo-American relations.

To SIR DAVID WALEY *and others, 31 December 1944*

Over the holidays I have been reading some of the press cuttings of what was being reported in this country about our activities in Washington whilst we were away. They convince me that we must find some better means of handling the press.

The British correspondents in America were naturally particularly interested in trying to glean some news to send to this side. The result is that they picked up even more false stories than I was aware of whilst I was in Washington. They picked up *canards* from the more obscure press, which did not even come to my notice whilst I was over there and which I now see for the first time. The result is that nearly the whole of the British press was filled on three successive occasions with completely false stories, which were not merely inaccurate or incomplete, but utterly without any foundation; and in each case these were reported to the British public as though they were based on reliable information.

One's experience in Bretton Woods was much the same. I fancy that Lord Swinton's[22] [civil aviation] negotiations in Chicago were gravely injured in the same way. In his case the American argument was widely and tendentiously reported in the American press, whereas a fair and clear statement of the British case never once appeared.

It seems to me that, whatever the Americans may urge to the contrary, we should do well to handle our own press on our own responsibility and not pay too much attention to advice to the contrary or remain so inhibited.

Nevertheless, when one comes to consider what one can actually do, it is extremely difficult to make a sound recommendation, especially as one must, in spite of what I have just written, exercise extreme discretion and regard for American susceptibilities. On reflection, my conclusions can be summed up as follows:–

1. A British negotiator on the other side must regard the press, and more particularly the British section of it, as his

---

[22] Swinton, Viscount (1884–1972); Philip Lloyd-Graeme, assumed the name Cunliffe-Lister in 1924; 1st Earl, 1955; Unionist M.P. for Hendon, 1918–35; President, Board of Trade, 1922–3, 1924–9, 1931; Secretary of State for the Colonies, 1931–5; for Air, 1935–8; Minister of Civil Aviation, 1944–5.

own direct concern and must not take the line of withdrawing the hem of his garment.

2. It would be advisable to let two or three of the leading British representatives be aware from the start that you would welcome a gossipy visit from them, say, once a week, in which they could at least enquire of one whether reports which had reached them had any foundation. For example, one could treat Sir Wilmott Lewis of *The Times*, Robert Waithmann of the *News Chronicle* and probably one or two others like this. Even if one could not tell them much, one could at least prevent them from sponsoring unfounded stories.

3. It would be a great advantage to have an occasional press conference with our own people. I doubt, however, whether that is possible without creating dangerous jealousy amongst the American journalists. The convention is that a press conference has to be open to all and sundry. Indeed, I was even at one moment in danger of getting into slight trouble with the American correspondents at Bretton Woods because they saw Sir Wilmott Lewis lunching with me in the restaurant. Perhaps, however, the same purpose could be effected through our own press representatives. The trouble is that the latter seldom know enough about what is going on to be able to give safe guidance on their own. They either say too much or say it wrong. All the same, they might act as a link, so that one could be in contact at one remove. I think our own publicity people should see the British journalists at least once a week, as much with a view to correcting false stories as giving true ones, and be in touch with the head of the British delegation concerned both before and after such meetings, so as to get all the guidance they can. I know that our own publicity people are only too anxious to act like this. The difficulty, I have found, is that those I have been in contact with are personally so little suitable for their jobs.

4. One should try to persuade one's American opposite number to agree to give a joint press conference from time

to time. I am afraid that there will be jealousies which stand in the way of this. And, apart from jealousies, one is always overwhelmed with American advice to have no contact with the press whatever. And perhaps this advice is not always entirely disinterested. Indeed, the general plea of this paper is that we should be readier than we have been hitherto to take our own line.

I wish I could propose something more satisfactory than the above. But I am sure that the existing state of affairs is most unsatisfactory and, indeed, capable of being really dangerous. I do not know whether anyone in the F.O. or the Ministry of Information has been able to reach any clear views as to what is best.

Chapter 3

THE LAST MONTHS OF LEND LEASE: PREPARING FOR STAGE III

Although the day-to-day problems of war finance overseas continued to intrude, more and more of Keynes's time during 1945 was spent on post-war financial problems, in particular those of the transitional period after the end of lend lease, or Stage III. Throughout the period prior to the end of lend lease in August, Keynes, in addition to several memoranda, minutes and Treasury discussions of the situation, kept up an extensive and lively correspondence with R. H. Brand, head of the United Kingdom Treasury Delegation in Washington. Brand, along with others including F. G. Lee, kept Keynes informed of the twists and turns of Washington opinion and provided advice on procedure.

This mixture of wartime and post-war concerns came out clearly in two letters to the Canadian Deputy Minister of Finance.[1]

To DR C. CLARK, *16 January 1945*

Dear Clark,

Gordon Munro is taking to you in a separate letter some rather lengthy results of the further researches we have been making into the problem of how to avoid a re-adjustment between you and Washington on lend lease elements in the supplies to your Forces. But I should like also to write to you,

[1] Canada's liability for lend lease supplies mentioned in both letters arose from Canadian desire to avoid receiving direct American assistance under lend lease. At the same time Canadian politicians and officials were extremely worried about the apparent waning of the British commitment to multi-lateralism that had appeared to exist at the time of the Law Mission. This apparent belief in a backing away from multi-lateralism by the British was strengthened by official contacts and ministerial speeches. For further details see *JMK*, vols. XXV–XXVII. For a Canadian perspective on events see R. Bothwell and J. English, 'Canadian Trade Policy in the Age of American Dominance and British Decline, 1943–1947' *Canadian Journal of American Studies*, VIII(1), Spring 1977.

briefly in this case, about another matter, which I know is preoccupying both you and Towers,[2] namely, the type of exchange arrangements with the sterling area which are likely to be practicable in Stage III.

Naturally we, on our side, are not less preoccupied with this problem. I hope that we shall within two or three months have got it anyway clearer in our own minds. But I do not see how we can hope to get definite on the matter until after some progress has been made with Washington. Our present view is rather decidedly that we should not even begin to take this up there until after the end of the German war. In the course of the next few months the President has to go to Congress twice on our behalf—once to get the renewal of the Lend Lease Act, and again to obtain appropriations under it. In a conversation I had with him whilst I was in Washington it became quite clear to me that his sense of timing, which is usually right, is altogether against bringing up any matters, even in the most private conversation, until the above questions have been cleared out of the way.

To judge from the reports in the papers here, our good Mr Hudson[3] has caused some disturbance of mind in Ottawa. Since this is a private and personal letter, and since I am not a civil servant, I may make bold to say that you should not take him unduly seriously. Particularly if he gave the impression that any Cabinet decisions have been reached already along the lines he was taking, he was misleading you. On the other hand, I would also add rather emphatically that neither must you treat his point of view too lightly. It represents an attitude of mind which has some support in the

---

[2] Graham Ford Towers (1897–1975); banker; Assistant General Manager, Royal Bank of Canada, Montreal, 1933–4; Governor, Bank of Canada, 1934–54; Chairman, Foreign Exchange Control Board, 1939–51; Chairman, National War Finance Commission, 1943–5.

[3] Robert Spear Hudson (1886–1957); 1st Viscount 1952, Unionist M.P. for Whitehaven, 1924–9, for Southport, 1932–52; Minister of Pensions, 1935–6; Secretary to Department of Overseas Trade, 1937–40; Minister of Shipping, 1940; Minister of Agriculture and Fisheries, 1940–45.

Cabinet and a great deal of support both in Parliament and in the press. It is an attitude very difficult to upset until we have something better to offer in concrete terms, which, with the help of you in Canada and our friends in Washington, we hope to be able to produce in due course. Meanwhile, we are in dead water. That has many disadvantages and allows too freely the unchecked growth of half-informed opinion, but I doubt if there is any effective remedy at this stage. The discussions on the Bretton Woods plan will, however, bring a certain amount of this to a head, and such attempts as are possible will have to be made to deal with it.

The general conclusion which Eady and I have reached as a result of the above considerations is that it would be a very great advantage to us, and we believe of some usefulness to yourself, if you could pay us a visit sometime in the course of the next three or four months,—indeed, if you were to bring an informal party for oral discussion. As I have said, it seems most unlikely that we shall be in a position to discuss definite plans, but this would give an opportunity for us to share our thoughts with you. I think there is a great deal in the whole complication of the position which you would only see in perspective through a personal visit. For example, there are arrangements with Europe, which are occupying us a good deal just now. There is also the problem of India, and the problem of the Middle East. A young Treasury official, Davidson, who has just returned from the Middle East, has made a very good beginning there with an agreement, a copy of which will be reaching you officially. It appears to me that you might be amused to read a personal report he produced on his return here, which may serve to give you some idea of the complications of life through which we have to try to thread our way.

Very best wishes to you and all friends in Ottawa.

Ever sincerely yours,

[copy initialled] ĸ

ACTIVITIES 1944–1946

To DR C. CLARK, *19 January 1945*

Dear Clark,

You will remember the discussions we had in Ottawa about the possibility of finding some way round the perplexing problem of the dollar payments to U.S., for which you may be becoming liable on account of the lend lease elements in military supplies which the Canadian Forces receive out of the Empire pool.

Since I came back, we have been making some further research into the facts of the situation. I am afraid that these present an even more difficult problem than was suggested by the incomplete information, on the basis of which we were talking in Ottawa:– not only as regards the amounts involved, but also the degree of implied commitment to the United States.

I am still hopeful that we may be able to devise some satisfactory settlement, as a result of which no money passes. I shall return to this at the end of the letter. My primary purpose, however, is not so much to discover or discuss a solution as to try to establish an accurate statement of the position as it now is, so that we know what we are talking about.

I

1. I had better take first, though it is a subsidiary issue, the question of the amount of the refund of Canadian dollars which are due from us to you on account of the provisional payments we receive being in excess of the net amounts properly chargeable after the lend lease elements have been taken out. As regards the Air Ministry and the Admiralty, the problem is relatively straightforward. All your payments are determined on a gross basis, and it only remains to assess the lend lease element, the estimated value of which represents the refund we have to make.

In the case of the War Office, however, there is a further

234

complication. You will remember that provisional capitation payments have been made to date on the basis of a rate of 25*s* for both the North West European and Mediterranean theatres of war. The War Office are now completing their calculations and, as a result, they arrive at rates of approximately 40*s* for the Mediterranean theatre and 35*s* for the European theatre. These rates, which are on a gross basis, have not yet been finally settled in the War Office nor, of course, discussed with your Service people.

Thus, for the War Office, we shall have to calculate the estimated amount of the lend lease element, based on the capitation rates as finally determined and agreed between us. On the other hand, there will be a further amount due to us, assuming the above rates are accepted by your Service Departments, since the provisional payments made to date have been based on a much lower rate.

The final position between us can perhaps be best understood by reference to the accompanying statement Annex A.[4] This has been prepared to show the total estimated amount which should be deducted from the initial calculation on a gross basis, up to 31 March next, in respect of the lend lease element. For the sake of clarity, the statement is based on the assumption that all payments are made initially on a gross calculation (i.e. without deduction in respect of the lend lease element), since that conforms with existing accounting machinery between the Service Departments and your Forces. On this basis, the total to be deducted from the gross to arrive at your net liability to us, cumulative to the 31st March next, would be approaching $250 million. But, as the statement shows, your provisional payments to the War Office (assuming that their revised calculations of the capitation rates, as mentioned above, are accepted on your side) fall short of the amount of your liability calculated on a gross basis of $179 million in total. Thus, if we start from the figures of

[4] This and the enclosures mentioned later are not printed. [Ed.]

our receipts from your Forces which we worked on when I was last in Ottawa, there would only be a net sum of $70 million due from us to you at the end of the year, representing the difference between the amount of the calculated lend lease adjustment and the additional amounts due from you to the War Office on a gross basis. As you will see from the above, this amount is considerably less than the amount of the lend lease adjustment (namely $250 million), for which theoretically you may be liable to the U.S.

2. I take this opportunity to call attention to another unsettled item, which has only just been brought to our notice by the War Office and of which we were entirely unaware when I was in Ottawa. You will remember that your Forces were originally equipped with Ram tanks, which had been produced in Canada itself and which would, therefore, have given rise to no financial transaction if used by yourselves. During 1943 and 1944, however, your military authorities decided to equip your Forces with Sherman tanks in place of the Rams. In consequence you took over from us during the period up to 30 September 1944 over 1,000 Sherman tanks of U.S. lend lease origin, estimated to cost in the neighbourhood of Can.$110 million. These represent by far the largest part of the items of Army initial equipment for which you were liable to the U.S.—see paragraph 4(b) below. When your Forces changed over from Rams to Shermans, the Rams with which they were already equipped and which were in this country, became available, and some 780 of them have been, or are being, taken over by the War Office, partly for training purposes and partly for conversion to other operational uses. We have never made any payment to the Department of Defence for these tanks, which, as I have explained, were originally intended for your own use; nor has there been any discussion on the basis of value to us on which such a charge might be calculated.

The unsettled liabilities hanging over us are, therefore,

very substantial. For to the two items mentioned above we have to add our old friends, the outstanding liabilities on the two Air Training Schemes.

II

3. The basis of the calculation of the lend lease element in the military supplies to your Forces is extremely complicated and not easily understood. I had better, therefore, try to set it out in somewhat full detail.

4. There are three categories of supplies to be considered, as follows:–

(a) There is the lend lease element in reserve stores. It is only since the agreement of last August that you have begun to pay us for these. The payments you make when the figures are finally determined will exclude the lend lease elements. Our understanding is that the lend lease elements thus excluded do not give rise to any problem of adjustment between yourselves and the United States. The argument is as follows. In so far as the flow into the reserve stores equals the flow out, those same lend lease elements will remain at the end of the war unimpaired and can be dealt with by the Americans under their recapture clause. In so far as this is not the case, your receipt of such stores will have been dealt with under one or other of the headings below. This argument seems to us, as to you, satisfactory. In what follows, therefore, no further account is taken of any lend lease elements in reserve stores.

(b) Next comes what is known as 'initial equipment'. I understand that this is the description given to equipment supplied to units on formation and to initial issues to units of new types of equipment. At this stage, what is furnished to your Forces is for the most part fully identifiable. Leaving on one side minor items, which may not have been identified, all significant supplies of lend lease origin have been segre-

237

gated for accounting purposes at this initial stage. We have not charged you for them. On the other hand, you have aimed at a settlement with the U.S. It was precisely for this 'initial equipment' (together with issues of American-type aircraft —see sub-paragraph (d) below) that you have paid over the $140 million. It is true that the date at which you made this settlement is now a year old. But we understand that at the date when you made it the payment was a full one and looked a little bit ahead. Thus some provision was made for similar issues of equipment received subsequent to the date of the settlement. We believe that, whilst this conclusion may not hold good permanently, your liability to the U.S. under this heading is at present fully covered by the amounts you have already paid.

(c) We come finally to the lend lease elements in what is known as 'maintenance'. The War Office accounting procedure ceases at Base Depots; stores are written off upon issue from the Base to a more forward depot or area, and no further accounting record of them is kept. But it is not possible to judge at the stage of issue from a Base depot whether or not a particular item is ultimately going to be used by a Canadian unit or formation. There is, therefore, and can be, no detailed recording of issues of supplies to Canadian Forces in the field of equipment of lend lease origin, even where major items are concerned. Thus, even where equipment is identifiable when issued as 'initial equipment', it ceases to be, from the War Office point of view, identifiable when it is issued as 'maintenance'. For example, Sherman tanks issued for 'maintenance' are in themselves just as identifiable as Sherman tanks issued as 'initial equpment'. But they are, for the reasons given above, not so recorded.

(d) The two foregoing sub-paragraphs deal with War Office procedure. The position with the Air Ministry is somewhat different. There, as I understand, the distinction between 'initial equipment' and 'maintenance' does not exist and a different system of recording issues and calculating values applies. The Air Ministry keep a record of *all* issues of aircraft, from which particulars of the issues of lend lease aircraft can be readily determined. Your payments are, however, made on a gross basis, so a deduction falls due in respect of lend lease aircraft included in the total. With regard to other types of stores issued, no such identification of lend lease items is possible and an estimate of the lend lease element must be calculated on a percentage basis, as in the case of 'maintenance' payments to the War Office.

I should perhaps mention, though I do not propose to go into the point in detail, that the identification of an aircraft as being of lend lease origin is somewhat arbitrary. In practice, any aircraft received probably has a good deal of equipment put into it, or modifications made, before it is put into service. Against this there may be substantial items of lend lease equipment—e.g. aero–engines—in British types. I mention this point again in paragraph 15(iv).

(*e*) I have left the Admiralty to the last because no major point arises. The amounts of your payments to us are small in comparison with those for the other Services and there are no major lend lease items involved. Your payments are made on a gross basis, and we estimate the lend lease element by a simple percentage calculation.

5. No doubt, a good general idea could be formed of the amount of major items, such as tanks, which reach your Forces subsequently. But, if an accurate estimate has to be made for accounting purposes, it must be on the basis of an over-all percentage adjustment of the total supplies furnished to the Canadian Forces, based on the percentage of the lend lease element in the issues from the Empire pool as a whole. The only refinement which is possible is to calculate this adjustment separately for the main categories of supply. To a limited extent this has, I understand, been done; we have made calculations on the basis that particular main categories

of supply (e.g. A.F.V.s or aircraft) are wholly excluded. But to make a detailed calculation for each separate main category would, in our view, need a prohibitive amount of time and labour. We see no advantage in undertaking such a task, moreover, and it is most unlikely that, as applied to your particular problem, the result would be to reduce the total amount of the adjustment.

6. You will see that it follows from the above that, so far as the War Office is concerned, 'maintenance' includes not only lend lease elements, which are strictly speaking unidentifiable because they have become merged in larger final products, but also supplies which are in a sense identifiable, though not in fact identified by the actual accounting procedure. The case already mentioned of Sherman tanks issued, not as 'initial equipment', but to make good wastage, is an example of this.

7. The annexed statement shows the best indication we can make at this date of the technically unidentifiable lend lease elements supplied to your forces out of the Empire pool up to 31 March next. The figures cannot, of course, be finally determined until the actual payments up to the end of the period are known, but—if the assumptions are accepted on which we have based our calculation—this statement should be pretty nearly correct. You will see that, up to 31 March 1944, the cumulative total was of the order of $70 million, that the amount for 1944/45 is of the order of $150 million, and that currently, and so long as the German War continues, the cumulative total is increasing at the rate of about $150 million per annum. These figures exclude aircraft, which I have dealt with in paragraph 4(d) above. Thus the bill, strictly calculated on the above basis, may be as much as $250 million by the end of June 1945.

III

8. I turn next to the *de facto* position vis-a-vis the Americans. The above figure of $250 million, which is merely an estimate to give you some indication how you probably stand, has, of course, not been communicated to them; not even in an approximate form. Nor, so far, have they asked for it. In the early days of lend lease, the procedure for recording or obtaining consent for re-transfers of lend lease equipment to third Governments was very sketchy. Agreed recommendations as to retransfer procedure were, however, issued by C[ombined] M[unitions] A[ssignments] B[oard] towards the end of 1943. New procedure was then put into operation by the Service Departments to ensure that wherever possible lend lease stores were treated as identifiable, and records of retransfers were kept, consent being obtained in advance or the retransfer reported after the event as appropriate. For example, the L[ondon] M[unitions] A[ssignments] B[oard] issued instructions covering War Office stores after discussion and, as we understood, agreement with the Americans on detail of procedure. Copies of the C.M.A.B. recommendations and the L.M.A.B. instructions are annexed for your information.

9. It will be noted that, broadly speaking, there is no obligation under this procedure even to report any retransfers to Dominion units under British operational control, much less to obtain prior consent. Thus the agreed retransfer procedure does not call for any particular form of recording of issues to the Canadian Forces.

10. We were, of course, not a party to your discussions with the Americans about 'initial equipment', which resulted in your paying over $140 million, and we do not know how far, if at all, you conceded the principle that you would also be liable for adjustments in respect of 'maintenance', or, if so, from what date.

11. However this may be, the detailed working out of the above principle has never been completed. As stated above, we are under no formal obligation to the Americans to keep records for this purpose, and we do not in fact do so generally. On the War Office side the records of issues of 'initial equipment' (see paragraph 4(b) above) are obtained from the Canadian Army. The Air Ministry, however, as explained in paragraph 4(d) above, do keep records of complete aircraft, but not of any other types of stores.

12. Nevertheless, we had some discussion on this question with F.E.A., last April in Washington. These discussions arose out of a request by the U.S. War Department to General Macready for all particulars of all issues of lend lease equipment to Canadian Forces, whether 'through the L.M.A.B. or otherwise'—Colonel Boone's letter of 21 March 1944, annexed. (It will be seen from this that the Americans asked for particulars of 'maintenance' as well as 'initial equipment' issues.) Accordingly, after consultation with your Service representatives, we indicated that records of certain issues were available and that some rebate calculation would be made over the field not covered by such records. The principle of a lend lease rebate was, of course, well known to the Americans, and we have furnished them with particulars of the rebates allowed to the Australian and other Governments (NOTE: The latter rebate calculations are, of course, merely designed—

(a) to ensure on our part that we do not put ourselves in the position of receiving cash on resale of lend lease equipment;

(b) to ensure to the third Governments concerned the benefit without payment of the lend lease supplies; and

(c) to enable the Americans to keep more correct records of the actual recipients of lend lease if they so desired.)

13. As regards Canada, F.E.A. indicated that in principle they accepted the proposed procedure and were prepared to leave it to us and to you to work out details.

14. You will see, therefore, that we are to some extent committed to producing a calculation for the Americans' benefit, but they have never shown any inclination to press the question. The only further action that has been taken, so far as we know, is that the War Office sent to the B.A.S., on 18 November, a report of identifiable lend lease issues (of initial equipment) covering the period to 31 March 1944, with a covering memorandum instructing B.A.S. to forward this report to the U.S. War Department. This was done, but the matter afterwards came to the notice of the U.K. Treasury Delegation who, in view of our recent discussions on this question in Ottawa, asked B.A.S. to persuade the War Department not to take any action for the time being. This the War Department have agreed to do. No report as to issues of lend lease aircraft has yet been given to the Americans so far as we are aware.

15. The above will suffice, I think, to put you in possession of all the information at our disposal. The next question is what to do about it. As I am not myself at all clear what the wisest course is, perhaps the best plan would be to set out below a few of the possible considerations and alternatives.

(i) As you will see from the above, we are not quite sure what commitments you have yourselves entered into *vis-à-vis* the Americans. In particular, would it be possible to maintain that the settlement you made last year, resulting in the payment of $140 million, completely cleared you, not only in relation to initial issues, but over the whole field up to the date at which that settlement took place? If so, the sums involved for maintenance might be of the order of $50 million less.

(ii) It is not clear that we are under any definite undertaking towards the Americans in respect of items which are not strictly identifiable. Unfortunately, as you will have seen above, what the Army accountants reckon as unidentifiable goes beyond what can be properly claimed as such in the last resort. If such items as the Sherman tanks for maintenance

243

were taken out and treated in the same way as initial equipment (though as I have explained above, this appears to be impossible in practice), it might reasonably be argued that all the rest could be forgotten. But we very much doubt if this would alter the figures in your favour. The fact is that, as it happens, the issues to your Forces of A.F.V.s are so much more heavily weighted with American types than the over-all average of the Empire pool that refinement of the calculation helps us not at all. And if we have to make a calculation we, for our part, would believe that it is better in principle, and practically no more disadvantageous, to work on the broad over-all basis that I have used above.

(iii) Apart from the problem of the specific American types of equipment, we may be able to press on the Americans the 'substitution principle', claiming that this principle should operate in respect of unidentifiables, at any rate over a considerable field. That is, we could treat issues to your Forces as coming out of our own production (which in every normal case would exceed Canadian requirements) and treat lend lease supplies as having gone wholly to meet our own needs. If we could find some satisfactory way of dealing with the American types, we could reasonably claim that the above principle is applicable to a wide field of miscellaneous stores.

(iv) We could also claim that, provided we have set up procedure for recording as far as possible the issues of identifiable lend lease stores, the principle of requiring a lend lease adjustment from you need not be carried further. Very few stores in practice are 100 per cent American; that is, American types may be subjected to a good deal of alteration or re-equipment on this side. Thus, in treating issues of such stores as 100 per cent U.S., we should be slightly weighting the figures against ourselves in that no allowance is made for the cost of adaptation, etc. This helps to justify our ignoring any lend lease element in the unidentifiable items.

(v) We might further claim that, in instituting a recording

procedure to the maximum extent possible we had done all that could be reasonably required of us and that the fact that no recording was possible over the rest of the field justified the lend lease element being ignored by all parties. It has always been clearly understood that transfers must take place freely in the field of battle and that records of such transfers cannot be kept. It is not perhaps an unreasonable extension of this principle that the Commander of, say, the First Canadian Army, should be regarded as free to allocate Sherman tanks to a U.K. or Canadian formation under his command as circumstances required without the question of cash settlement arising.

(vi) Finally, it might be possible to claim that all this lend lease equipment remains in principle under our operational control, and that it will remain in our hands when the Canadian Forces are repatriated so that we remain the lend lease obligors. This might require some change of the present Canadian position, which is that all your equipment, once you receive it and have settled as necessary with the U.S., is absolutely yours, and you are free to deal with it as you wish. But, in the circumstances, it seems possible that you would wish to accept this change. There would be a parallel with the equipment issued to South African units under our operational command, where likewise we have claimed that we remain the lend lease obligors and that there can be no question of cash payment by the South Africans to the U.S. While the South African question has dragged on for some time without final settlement, the latest indications are that the Americans are coming round to accepting our contention.*

* The details of the proposed South African arrangement are given in an annex [not printed]. Unfortunately, during the negotiations the Americans pressed the question whether this would be regarded as a precedent for Canada and, in response, we argued that there were material differences in the situation. This, however, might be overcome by the argument that we were not proposing an identical settlement and that the differences in the Canadian position were, in fact, being looked after by the making of certain dollar payments.

16. There are two other thoughts of rather a different order, of which a brief mention might be made here so as to complete the story. If some adjustment on one or other of the lines suggested above is practicable, well and good. If not, your dollar liability must be approaching the impracticable. If so, it has to be taken in conjunction with the possibility of your becoming liable for large quantities of American equipment for your air arm in the context of the Pacific War. When I was in Ottawa Mr Howe was obviously much alarmed lest strategic plans might require you to pass over from British and Canadian types to the use of American types. If so—and particularly if this liability had to be added to the liability which is the main subject of this letter—then, however disappointing, might it not become inevitable for you to re-open with the Americans the whole matter?

17. The possibility of an entirely different way out has crossed our minds here as a just conceivable possibility. I will not attempt to enter into the details of this and will do no more than just put the thought into your mind. We have certain claims against the Americans, which, for various complicated reasons, they have found it difficult to meet, but about which some of the American Departments have an uneasy conscience, relating to pre-lend lease equipment for which we had paid cash dollars, but were ultimately put by us at the disposal of the American Forces. The order of magnitude of these claims is U.S. $250 million. In fact, there can be little doubt that, until some specific arrangement is made to the contrary they do owe us this money. This sum is of the same order of magnitude as the claims which might be sustained against you for lend lease elements in maintenance. It is decidedly smaller than the various claims you have against us in suspense, referred to in paragraphs 1 to 3 above, but is nevertheless not of a very different order of magnitude. It might be a sensible and friendly thing to do, if a triangular settlement could be made, by which all these demi-semi claims

could be thrown into a common furnace of extinction, each party forgetting its claims against the other on the principle of knock for knock.

18. That sort of broad settlement would be much easier for you and for us than for the Americans, who are tied hand and foot by legalisms. On the other hand, their legalistic system often means that, whereas a lawyer can always find some reason why something is impossible, if that is wanted, the sophistries of the profession also allow him to find a way out observable to no outsider, if *that* is what is wanted.

19. We shall, of course, breathe no word to the Americans on any of these various matters, except with your knowledge and approval and after further discussion with you. Nevertheless, you should be prepared for a request from them to us to tell them at short notice what the position is. We think there is a real risk of their returning to the statistics of the matter in connection with preparations next month for the next Lend Lease Appropriations. This would relate, of course, only to the statistical aspect, and not to the possible ways out. Nonetheless, it would be important to present the information in a way which did not prejudice wider considerations. If any such request comes, we shall give you all the notice we can. But our experience is that the lend lease authorities are apt to spring on one these demands for information at the very last moment.

Yours sincerely,
[copy initialled] K

Brand had told Keynes of conversations with Oscar Cox concerning increased American lending for trade and reconstruction purposes. Cox's statements suggested American plans for an omnibus reconstruction bill which would be an extension of lend lease and allow the President to lend or grant supplies or services to foreign countries subject only to a global total sum. Such a proposal, he thought, would go forward during hostilities, when it would look small relative to other current expenditures. It would be proposed as a good business proposition. If it went through, it would preclude special bilateral Anglo-American talks followed by additional legislation. After receiving two letters on the subject, dated 16 and 18 January, and a further letter dated 8 February from Lee suggesting that arrangements precluding a special Anglo-American settlement were inevitable, Keynes wrote what Sir Wilfrid Eady called 'a very wise letter'.

To R. H. BRAND, *15 February 1945*

My dear Bob,

I have never answered as fully as I intended those passages in your letter of January 16th which dealt with the Stage III negotiations and Oscar Cox's attitude to them. The need to say a word about this is reinforced by a letter from Frank Lee of February 8th, which has just arrived.

My general view is as follows:–

F.E.A. and the U.S. Treasury will obviously have to work out some sort of general formula for post-war loans to various European allies, e.g. France, as a good, sample case. These, whilst no doubt generous both in the matter of interest and in terms of repayment, are likely to be of a more or less normal character. Nor is there any reason why they should not be. None of the countries in question has any important external obligations at present, and some of them have substantial gold reserves. All this is right and proper. And we, of course, will be doing something similar, though the credit element in our arrangements will have to be kept down to the minimum.

It is, however, altogether out of the question that terms appropriate to this type of loan should form a precedent for our own case. We should not, therefore, show any inclination to look at or criticise these European discussions as though they had any bearing on the settlement with us. Any legislative provision under which such loans can take place will either be inapplicable to us or will have to be drafted in such wide terms as to cover almost any kind of assistance. No doubt, the latter would be the ideal. But if, as is likely, that is impracticable, then let the legislation be of purely European application.

Our approach, it seems to me, has to be on a totally different basis. It will be essentially an appeal for a reconsideration of the sharing of the costs of the war. To the least possible extent, if at all, should it contain any normal loan provisions, though one need not, of course, exclude an advance of some sort, of which the capital sum would be repaid eventually.

As to the exact nature of such an arrangement, probably the initiative would best come from them. On the other hand, they may easily be not sufficiently well-informed or fertile of mind to produce the right thing, so that the prompting and general idea may very well have to be put into their minds by us. I am, however, very much against making any conversational progress with this prematurely. For anything which is said will be canvassed, as is their way, in wide circles and suffer the obvious criticisms. It ought to come as a *coup d'état* from the President as a great surprise for everyone concerned.

I am hoping to get some general ideas on paper for intimate consideration here in the near future, and that will, of course, be passed on to you.

It follows from the above that one need not feel unduly interested in the form of assistance to Europe. Frank Lee says that he fears a separate U.K./U.S. arrangement is not a starter except under the umbrella of some general legislation. Personally I would resist that conclusion unless, as I have indicated above, the legislation in question is so general as to give the President powers to do practically anything he likes as regards terms within, perhaps, some limit of aggregate amount.

There is another matter on which I am in arrears in correspondence with you, partly because the position is changing and fluid, that is the question of UNRRA. Each day convinces me more firmly that the only right course is to re-condition that whole institution, indeed, re-order it from the beginning and make it what it was originally intended to be,—the body solely responsible for relief and for distribution in every quarter. Too many troubles are ensuing from our acceptance of the present imposture. However, this is too large a subject to embark on in this letter.

The Chancellor is seeing at the House of Commons this afternoon the first small party of M.P.s to discuss Bretton Woods. This particular party is under the leadership of Pethick Lawrence and, whilst not restricted to members of the Labour Party (for instance, it includes Schuster and Spearman), is on the whole Leftish.

As you will have heard, the latest news is that Rosenman[5] has left this country, apparently in order to intercept the President on his way home, so that we have not yet had a chance of seeing him.

Yours ever,
[copy initialled] M. K.

The problem of possible Stage III negotiating tactics had also arisen early in January 1945 as the result of a conversation between Mr Lee and Mr Coe of the Foreign Economic Administration, a note of which Lee sent on to London. In that conversation, Coe spoke of possible American foreign lending, including tied Export-Import Bank loans, the operation of British and sterling area exchange controls and the possibility of informal Anglo-American conversation on external financial and trade policies during the transition. On receiving this note, Keynes wrote:

To F. G. LEE, *23 January 1945*

My dear Frank,

Freddy [Harmer] has shown me the copy of the note dated January 3rd of your talk with Frank Coe. I should like to make

---

[5] Samuel Irving Rosenman (b. 1896); Counsel to Governor Franklin Roosevelt, 1929–33; Justice, New York Supreme Court, 1932; resigned to become Special Counsel for President Roosevelt, 1943; Special Counsel for President Truman, 1945–6.

a few comments on that, which perhaps you might pass on to Brand.

First of all, on a small point of detail. Coe is quite right in saying that at Bretton Woods we allowed it to be understood that we did not necessarily oppose tied loans in the case of a national lending institution. To take a concrete example, we felt that such a body as the Export Credits Guarantee Department is necessarily tied, and it would be difficult to draw the line. On the main issue, it is interesting to compare Coe's fishing enquiry with the rather analogous conversation which Opie had with some of his friends in the State Department. There is no doubt that they are as keen as mustard to get us gossiping about what might be in our minds.

My own feelings—and I think they are shared by others here—are that we just want them to worry themselves to death about it. The fact of their worry is indeed almost our only card.

Secondly, we do not want to put them out of their misery for sometime yet. If we have any private ideas, and perhaps we have, we most certainly do not want them to be hawked round Washington and receive the attention of the columnists for some weeks or months before they can be practical politics. The more completely we can politely keep them guessing, the better. I gather from White that, in his view, the right time to start will not be until after VE Day, but that it should take place within a month or two of that. This seems to us right —neither too soon nor too late.

Thirdly, when we do decide to open up, there is the question at what level we should do so. If one knew how to arrange it to be like that, clearly this is something which should start as high up as possible with the politicians and should not be left to the experts to take the initiative.

The most difficult chap to keep at bay will be, I should expect, Oscar Cox. When I was first in Washington, he was eagerly advocating a very early opening of the Stage III discussions. This, however, was before the Election and was

based on the belief that Congress would be particularly sub-
servient to the President in the two or three months immediately after the Election. In the light of experience he may
by now have become somewhat chastened, at any rate as
regards this argument. But he is intensely eager and interested in the matter and already has some ideas, which, although exceedingly well meant, are not, in my opinion, quite
along the right lines. If a way could be found to get him to
postpone thinking about this matter for a bit, one would be
more comfortable.

In the long run, however, his promotion to take Currie's
place must surely be to the good. His periodic political scares
will need handling, but, after all, he is surely very much easier
to deal with when it comes down to concrete matters. I think
he ought to be immensely helpful about Stage III in due
course, if only he can be prevented from going into detail
prematurely.

Yours ever,
[copy not initialled]

During the period, Keynes also had conversations with Judge Samuel
Rosenman, an adviser close to President Roosevelt, who had come to
Europe to enquire into the problems of civilian supplies for liberated areas
and to London to make soundings as to post-war financial and reconstruction problems. In the light of Judge Rosenman's report of the
conversation,[6] it is useful to print the Treasury account whose circulation
was limited to Keynes, the Chancellor, Sir Wilfrid Eady and Mr Brand.

[6] *Foreign Relations of the United States 1945*, Volume VI, pp. 28–9.

STAGE III

FINANCE

Note of a Conversation in Lord Keynes's room on Wednesday, 7 March 1945

PRESENT:

Lord Keynes	Judge Rosenman
Sir W. Eady	Mr W. H. Taylor (U.S. Treasury Department)[7]
Mr Harmer	Mr Phelps (State Department)[8]

JUDGE ROSENMAN said he had been charged by the President with the task of enquiring into a number of questions mainly concerning supplies to the liberated countries of North West Europe, but also with that of the U.K.'s need for financial assistance from the U.S.A. in Phase (sc: Stage) III. He realised that it was early to get to grips with this problem, and very likely ideas were not clear in London any more than in Washington. But the President knew that there was here a problem of the utmost importance which would have to be tackled sooner or later and wished to have some further idea of what might be involved. Judge Rosenman hoped therefore that we should be prepared to tell him anything we could of our present ideas on the subject so that he could report back to the President.

LORD KEYNES and SIR W. EADY said that this question was indeed in our minds, but we had not yet got our ideas clear about it, so that it was impossible at this stage to give even an official Treasury view—still less the views of His Majesty's Government, and there were many questions for Ministers involved. They hoped therefore that Judge Rosenman would regard this conversation as being purely personal and unofficial, and would take anything they said as representing the ideas which they had personally in mind at present.

The first point to be considered was that of timing. Lord Keynes, during his recent visit to Washington, had understood the view of both the President and Mr Morgenthau to be that this question could not be discussed between us until after the lend lease hearings (on the Extension and Appropriation Bills) were out of the way and the war in Europe was

---

[7] William H. Taylor; U.S. Treasury representative in London, 1944–5.
[8] Dudley Maynard Phelps (b. 1897); Associate Chief, Division of Finance and Monetary Affairs, U.S. State Department, 1942–3; Chief, Division of Foreign Economic Development, 1945–6; Acting Director, Office of Financial and Development Policy, July–August 1945, October 1945–November 1946.

ended. JUDGE ROSENMAN said he thought this was still the view in Washington.

As to the scope of the problem, it was practically impossible to make a good estimate at the present time. It depended very much on how long the war went on, both in Europe and the Far East. There was next the question of what would be done by way of winding up lend lease. This was largely a technical and administrative question, but it was highly important. There would be a large volume of lend lease supplies on the move when the time came, to say nothing of stocks in our hands of lend lease goods. It would make a great difference whether these items in the pipeline were dealt with under lend lease, or whether they were carried over to whatever new arrangements might be set up. In this connection it was important to remember that there was a very large administrative problem to consider; machinery had been set up to deal with all these supply arrangements under lend lease and reciprocal aid and that machinery could not be switched over to ordinary cash settlement at a moment's notice. Lord Keynes felt that this question ought to be given special consideration.

There was also the question of the President's right of recapture under the Mutual Aid Agreements. If this were exercised in respect of e.g. munitions, it would make very little difference to us, but might be a matter of vital importance for example in relation to our food stocks.

There are also a number of other factors which may materially affect the magnitude of the problem. The re-establishment of our position after the war depends on the restoration of our export trade, and the rate at which this can be achieved will depend largely on the rate at which we can transport our forces home from overseas, and release the manpower to industry. If shipping is scarce, this may take an inordinately long time. Moreover, our war expenditure overseas will not cease with the end of hostilities. At the present time we are spending something like $3 billion per annum in directly military expenditure overseas. This is comparable to the figure of our net disinvestment. In other words, thanks to lend lease and mutual aid assistance, our overseas position is not badly out of balance apart from this military expenditure; but when this is taken into account, the result is that our position is deteriorating at a rate which we cannot sustain indefinitely. If such expenditure drags on for some time after the end of the fighting and if—as is probable—there are substantial outstanding commitments to be cleared up at that point, the effect on our overseas liabilities may be appreciable.

A further point to consider is that there may possibly be additional calls upon us for relief, e.g. assistance to liberated countries. We shall have to meet large relief and reconstruction needs in our own territories in the Far

East, and it will have to be recognised that we shall not be in a position to give any assistance beyond our existing commitments to other liberated countries.

The existing amount of our overseas liabilities, coupled with the factors indicated above, makes it clear that the problem to be faced will be of very considerable magnitude. It will call for an entirely new approach on the part of the United States and ourselves. We do not consider that any of the international credit mechanisms, in existence or contemplated, provide the answer. What will be needed will be an act of statesmanship, perhaps on the initiative of the President himself just as he introduced the concept of lend lease at a time when some entirely new idea was necessary in order to ensure that we should go on fighting the war. We do not think that the lend lease idea is applicable to post-war problems. It has fulfilled its purpose during the war and we have always assumed that it would end with the war. (JUDGE ROSENMAN indicated assent.) It seemed to us that a new departure would have to be made, and it might perhaps be nece,sary to review the whole question of how the costs of the war had been borne by the United Nations. But we could not usefully put forward suggestions; it was very much a question of presentation and of politics. What we must emphasise was that we could not find the solution by attempting to dress up an arrangement in any ordinary commercial form of international credit.

It was clearly most important that discussion of this problem should, at any rate for the present, be confined to as small a number of people as possible, both here and in Washington. It would be fatal to the launching of any such new idea as is needed here that it should first have been widely discussed among officials, and very possibly leaked out to the Press, or to Congress or Parliament. We therefore propose on our side to confine all discussion of the matter within a very small circle. JUDGE ROSENMAN said he thought the President would entirely agree with that and will act likewise.

In conclusion JUDGE ROSENMAN said that he had been very glad of this opportunity of discussing the matter. He quite appreciated the informal and unofficial character of the talk. But it would be nonetheless very useful to him to report back to the President, so that the latter could be thinking about the problem in general terms, and considering how it should best be handled.

During March, Keynes also discussed Stage III problems with Lauchlin Currie. He continued to receive further advice from R. H. Brand.

By mid-month, however, towards the end of a ten days' rest in Cambridge, Keynes moved the discussions and conversations of the previous months on to a somewhat more formal plane with a memorandum, dated 18 March, entitled *Overseas Financial Policy in Stage III*. After brief discussions in the Treasury, Keynes revised the paper in late March and early April before it went into print for wider discussion. After informal discussions in Ministerial circles, the memorandum was circulated to the War Cabinet, revised slightly further, on 15 May. The Cabinet version with complete statistics appears below.

OVERSEAS FINANCIAL POLICY IN STAGE III

I

1. It has been a prime object of policy on the part of the Treasury and of the Bank of England, for at least the last two or three years, so to conduct their technical tasks that we should end the war in a financial position which did not leave us hopelessly at the mercy of the United States. This does not mean that we seek or prefer an international system after the war in which we depend on our own self-sufficiency, assisted by a chain of bilateral bargains with those countries which cannot afford to lose our markets, and by the maintenance of the present sterling area arrangements in their war-time severity for an indefinite period.

2. We cannot reasonably prefer such a system. A policy of economic isolationism and of economic rupture with the United States and Canada (and with a large part of the rest of the world also) could only be practicable if we had regained the financial reserves we have lost, and if we were prepared to live for several years after the war with rigid domestic controls and strict rationing of consumption, and with an organisation of foreign trade after the Russian model. It is certainly not compatible with a restoration of free enterprise. For only those countries would gang up with us which were prepared to denounce their commercial treaties with the United States and to forgo all prospect of borrowing easy money from that country. And who would they be?

3. The purpose of maintaining and preserving a measure of financial strength is not to enable us to fall back on so frantic and suicidal an alternative, but that in negotiation we should both feel and appear sufficiently independent only to accept arrangements that we deem acceptable. For it is one thing to take the initiative in rupturing economic relations and refusing an accommodation, and quite another to stand out for what is reasonable in itself and appropriate to the part we have played. Indeed, the bare possibility of an independent policy to be adopted in the last resort, if undue and improper pressure were to be exerted on the other side, may be, in the mixed politics and mixed motives of the United States, a useful and even a necessary inducement to them to reach a settlement with us which is, in a wide comprehension and in the long run, the justest and wisest in the interests of our two countries and of the world. Mr Walter Lippmann, whom I reckon a good judge in such matters, has always been insistent in private discussion that our American friends, who will have to advocate the right kind of settlement before their own people, will find their task much easier if they can point out that we do have an alternative, though an alternative very injurious to the principles of a free economy and very disagreeable to American ideas about post-war economic arrangements. The worse will be the best friend of the good.

II

4. The first thing is, therefore, to take stock of the situation as it stands today, and to examine how far we have been successful and how far unsuccessful in our aim. The successes, which have been considerable, can be summarised thus:–

(i) From the earliest days of the war we have tried to avoid incurring debts in foreign currencies or in gold. In this we have been successful beyond any expectation which would have been reasonable before the event. There is the Jesse Jones loan in United States dollars which we can liquidate at any time by selling the marketable securities hypothecated against it. There is the no-interest loan in Canadian dollars, corresponding to Canadian securities we ourselves hold, which can almost certainly be covered and embraced by our general post-war financial settlement with Canada. There is the gold set aside against our debt to Portugal, where at present there is a hitch in our negotiations but where the gold liability can probably be reduced and spread over a longish period. Apart from these we owe the outside world nothing but sterling; and it is pretty well understood by those concerned that they are in our hands and cannot successfully claim to use this sterling except in accordance with principles to be agreed with us hereafter (their chief anxiety is to learn as soon as possible what these principles are going to be, their present mood—and that is all to the good—being one which will, we hope, prove to be over-pessimistic). On such conditions, by cunning and kindness, we have persuaded the outside world to lend us upwards of the prodigious total of £3,000 million. The very size of these sterling debts is itself a protection. The old saying holds. Owe your banker £1,000 and you are at his mercy; owe him £1 million and the position is reversed.

5. (ii) We have striven, with the utmost concentration of purpose ever since 1941, to raise our liquid gold (and dollar) reserves to a substantial figure, though at the expense of a corresponding increase in sterling liabilities. This is partly on the ordinary banking principle of keeping more yellow balls in the air than you hold in your hand, which we learnt long ago to practise with unconscious ease. But it is even better than that; for such assets are fully liquid, which, as we have just seen, is not equally true of the liabilities. In this aim we now look like being more successful than seemed at one time probable. We started the war with reserves of £600 million. By April 1941 we had spent the lot and our reserves were literally nil. With the inauguration of lend lease we began slowly to recoup. But until recently it was a dogma of the

United States Treasury that reserves of £250 million would be as much as were good for us, and that lend lease aid should be reduced whenever we looked likely to reach that figure. In the Washington conversations last autumn we persuaded Mr Morgenthau that a goal of £500 million would not be unreasonable, although under the arrangements we then secured it seemed likely that our end-reserves would not much exceed £400 million. Subsequent events, particularly the prolongation of the German war bringing greater earnings from the expenditure of the American troops than we had previously estimated, suggest that at the end of 1945 our total net reserves may approach £500 million after allowing for an additional receipt of gold expected from South Africa towards the end of the year. If the Japanese war continues through 1946, the current position will deteriorate as a result of the falling off or cessation of American troop expenditure in this country. Nevertheless, if we take account of the gold to be received under the French Agreement and a possible release of some gold under resumed Portuguese negotiations, it is not impossible that we may, after all, retain the desired goal of £500 million as our end-reserves on the eve of cease-fire in Asia. The chief danger to the fulfilment of this hope, apart from a considerable prolongation of the Japanese war beyond the date when we cease to gain significant earnings from the American troops in this country, is the risk of a curtailment of lend lease aid in the last lap when the approaching end of the war and the relative size of our reserves are both apparent to the American Administration. If during Stage II we find ourselves quarrelling with the United States Treasury and State Department about the nature of exchange and commercial arrangements in Stage III, it will be the easiest thing in the world for them, by sharply curtailing their assistance to cause our reserves to melt away, so as to make us more tender to their touch (for our good, of course—so they would see it—as well as for theirs). Nevertheless, assuming that we do manage to reach and retain the goal of free net reserves of £500 million, that would provide the means (putting our bed-rock reserves, not to be touched except for the gravest cause, at £250–300 million) for greatly sweetening and alleviating the practical administration of the sterling area arrangements in the early post-war phase, in the event of our being forced to endeavour to maintain them in their war-time character with considerable rigour.

6. (iii) A third direction in which we can claim some significant success is in the quite recent measures for the evolution of the sterling area system in relation to Europe, as exemplified by the Swedish Agreement, the Belgian Agreement and the French Agreement (with Holland, Switzerland, Portugal, Turkey and Persia still to be brought into line and fair hopes of doing so on reasonably satisfactory terms). The recent generous offer by the Dominion of Canada (though half-baked and scarcely workable exactly in the form suggested) could perhaps be modified into a scheme by which Canada agreed to hold sterling, receiving in return the freedom of the sterling area and (in truth) half entering it. In combination with the special account system covering a large part of South America, all this means that we have gone far (and may soon have gone further) towards establishing a *modus vivendi* for carrying on trade without immediate financial embarrassment with almost the whole world outside the United States.

7. (iv) Before leaving the sterling area and technical questions of exchange, we should record amongst the successes our day-to-day handling of the other parties concerned. The sterling area and exchange control generally could have been so managed that everyone affected would by now have formed a firm determination to throw off the whole business at the earliest possible moment. In fact, the Bank of England and those occupied with exchange control in the Treasury have so contrived by consideration and reasonableness and traditional good manners, with scissors (in this context) ready

when the red tape began to bind, as to leave behind a sense of good temper and good feeling. Should financial hearts (if there are such things) be opened, I believe it would be found that those overseas would rather bank in London with blocked accounts than in New York with free ones. I reckon this a significant success, because it means that it might not be beyond our power to continue for a time, if need be, not perhaps the full rigour of the game, but a fairly effective version of the war-time sterling area. Political objections in India, by those who know nothing of how the system is carried on and therefore insuperable by considerate day-to-day handling, would be the chief obstacle.

8. (v) Finally, I record in the catalogue of success, the stabilisation policy for domestic prices and the management of the wage level. It can be argued that the former has, in fact, cost nothing, since it has been worked in practice by taxing certain branches of consumption in order to subsidise others; even, indeed, that it has been run at a profit, since the additional taxation of consumers has greatly exceeded the subsidies, without having given the consumer the feeling that prices taken as a whole are unreasonably high. As for wage-rates, they have, it is true, risen somewhat faster than the cost of living. Nevertheless, it must be conceded that the Ministry of Labour have, in the circumstances, done very well. The stabilisation policy of the Treasury and the utility programme of the Board of Trade (which also deserves a grateful tribute) gave them their solid foothold and they have taken good advantage of it. As a result, I do not think there is much wrong with our competitive position overseas based on an exchange of $4 = £1; at any rate the evidence is that a lower rate of exchange would harm, rather than help, us. It would have been a very serious thing if the somewhat artificial rate of exchange maintained during the war had landed us with an over-valued currency at the end of it. In fact, we have retained the benefit, or most of it, of the initial depreciation of 20 per

cent in 1939. The £ to-day is under-valued rather than over-valued in relation to most other currencies. All Middle East and Eastern currencies are over-valued through the comparative failure (in varying measure) to control inflation. The liberated European countries tend to begin with over-valued rates for reasons of prestige and internal social policy. The hourly wage today in this country is (broadly) 2s per hour; in the United States it is 5s per hour (reckoned at an exchange of $4). Even the celebrated inefficiency of British manufacturers can scarcely (one hopes) be capable of offsetting over wide ranges of industry the whole of this initial cost-difference in their favour, though, admittedly, they have managed it in some important cases. Perhaps the chief danger at any rate in the mass-production industries, is a cut-throat competition in export prices by the Americans loading them with less than their fair share of overhead costs (a practice which the much-abused international cartel is designed to prevent). The available statistics suggest that, provided we have never made the product before, we have the rest of the world licked on cost. For a Mosquito, a Lancaster, Radar, we should have the business at our feet in conditions of free and fair competition. It is when it comes to making a shirt or a steel billet that we have to admit ourselves beaten both by the dear labour of America and by the cheap labour of Asia or Europe. Shipbuilding seems to be the only traditional industry where we fully hold our own. If by some sad geographical slip the American Air Force (it is too late now to hope for much from the enemy) were to destroy every factory on the North-East coast and in Lancashire (at an hour when the directors were sitting there and no one else), we should have nothing to fear. How else we are to regain the exuberant inexperience which is necessary, it seems, for success, I cannot surmise.

9. These various favourable factors are, between them, perhaps just sufficient to make a policy of financial independence of the United States not quite unplausible, if the

financial burden of the overseas balance could be kept in the early post-war years within reasonable quantitative limits. We must, therefore, now turn to the other side of the account, and examine the aspects where we have to register failure, or, rather, where there is not as yet a sufficient expectation of success. So far the argument has run that we have a financial machine which is technically not too bad—at any rate we could not have hoped in our actual situation to have done much better. But it cannot carry an unlimited load. At present the prospective load appears to me to be far beyond our unaided powers, mainly for the four reasons set forth below. It is still necessary to repeat, almost without change, what was written in a memorandum prepared for the Chancellor of the Exchequer nearly six months ago. For in the meanwhile nothing much—certainly nothing sufficient—has been done to remedy the position.

10. (i) Our financial embarrassments have been, and still are, and look like being even after the war, mainly the result of the cash expenditure of the Service Departments in Africa, the Middle East, India and the Southern Dominions. Expenditure of every description in North and South America is under adequate Treasury control—at any rate we know in considerable detail what it is for. European expenditure falls into a special category and is dealt with separately under (iii) below. Treasury control over expenditure on imports which fell into partial abeyance for a time is now being recovered; here again we know in some detail how and why the money is spent. But there remains a vast cash expenditure overseas —local expenditure incurred on the spot—in the areas specified at the beginning of this paragraph which is poured out, not only with no effective Treasury control, but without the Treasury knowing either beforehand or afterwards, what it has been spent upon. At least that seems to be the case in a matter of two or three hundreds of £ millions. This generalisation must be partly qualified in the case of India because

of the proceedings of the recent Cabinet Committee on India which threw some dim light on the matter and produced a very broad analysis of the global figure of expenditure under a few main heads.

11. One need not doubt that most of this expenditure had a purpose once and resulted from the deliberate decision of some responsible person. In this context, however, I am chiefly alarmed by the apparent prospect (if nothing is done about it) of the appalling rate at which this expenditure will be running on the day at which the final cease-fire in Asia brings with it the end of American lend lease and Canadian mutual aid, a rate which it may be impracticable to reduce rapidly if we take account of the clearing up of arrears as well as of running expenditure.

12. The total cash overseas expenditure of British Government Departments, exclusive of the Ministry of Food and the Raw Materials Division of the Ministry of Supply, and also exclusive of *all* expenditure in Canada, United States, South America and Europe, is estimated by the Bank of England as follows (£ million): 1942, 584·4; 1943, 689·3; 1944, 716·3. Broadly speaking, practically no part of this expenditure is arising currently (or in 1944) out of the war with Germany; and it is likely to increase rather than decrease in Stage II. When we had thrown the Germans out of Africa, and the Middle East was no longer in danger, our expenditure in those parts remained much as before. The Major-Generals in Cairo look like becoming chronic.

13. It will be observed that this expenditure is currently exceeding, and over the whole period has been about equal to, our total net disinvestment throughout the world, which has been as follows (£ million): 1941, 661; 1943, 681; 1944, 651. Thus it is this expenditure which is *wholly* responsible for our financial difficulties.

14. Some further analysis is instructive. Included in the above in 1944 there were Treasury advances to Allied Govern-

ments of about £60 million. Ministry of Supply expenditure, presumably for munitions, came to another £60 million, almost wholly in Australia and South Africa (the Ministry of Supply's share of Indian expenditure is not separately analysed). Foreign Office and NAAFI and other miscellaneous items accounted for another £32 million. This leaves us with the hard core of War Office, Air Ministry and Admiralty expenditure which deserves analysis country by country and year by year as follows:-

Expenditure of War Office, Air Ministry and
Admiralty in certain areas

	1942	1943	1944
	£ million		
Ceylon	13·4	17·1	26·6
Australia	8·3	11·8	12·8
South Africa	20·7	24·0	32·9
New Zealand	1·4	1·9	1·1
Egypt and Sudan	97·1	92·0	76·3
Palestine and Transjordan	28·6	33·4	28·1
Iraq	13·6	30·2	11·1
British West Africa	14·4	15·5	12·1
British East and Central Africa	16·4	17·6	20·0
Malta and Cyprus	11·0	13·2	11·7
Miscellaneous sterling area	10·9	15·7	17·3
Turkey	1·4	4·4	1·5
Persia	11·2	13·7	8·8
	248·4	290·5	260·3
India*	222·1	281·2	313·8
	470·5	571·7	574·1

* Refund to Indian Government of recoverable war expenditure.

15. It will be noticed that over the three years the Indian expenditure to which so much attention has been directed (though with so little result) has only amounted to *half* the total, and that as much again has been spent in the neighbouring areas.

16. So far as I am aware, there is no detailed information in the Treasury concerning the nature of this expenditure. The bare totals have only been obtained through the assiduity of the Statistical Branch of the Bank of England and were not available until recently. Further examination would presumably show that its purposes are divided between—

(a) the war against Japan;

(b) the policing of the Middle East;

(c) the maintenance of lines of communication.

But whether the maximum of economy in regard to, e.g., (b) is being exercised, how far continuing expenditure is due to avoidable time-lags in revising decisions, how far general policies have been taken at home without sufficient (or any) knowledge of the cost involved, what pressure there is on local commanders to exercise maximum economy, whether we are not meeting expenditure which would be more properly a charge on the local government, and so forth—of all that I know nothing. In the context of this paper one particularly wishes to know what expenditure we shall still have to incur in these areas *after* cease-fire in Asia. In this connection it is disturbing to be informed that the British personnel in the Middle East (altogether apart from India and Ceylon) a year after the end of the German war will be considerably greater than it is now, and that this is not judged to be inconsistent with a recent directive from the Prime Minister for an immediate reduction of the personnel in this area by 23 per cent.

17. Obviously this is a large subject and one may go widely astray through ignorance. But the *prima facie* evidence of the global statistics is that unless it is advisable and practicable to bring this expenditure under drastic control at an early date (and perhaps it is not), our ability to pursue an independent financial policy in the early post-war years will be fatally impaired.

18. (ii) The second cause for anxiety is the state of preparation for the pre-organisation of our exports.

19. This is too large a subject to embark upon here. But it is necessary to emphasise that the financial machinery described in the earlier part of this section cannot work without fuel. In post-war conditions the existing sterling area arrangements can only function if we on our side can supply desired goods in satisfactory volume. Our main difficulty in financial negotiation already is the inability to promise in return any reasonable volume of goods. Meanwhile, it is fanciful and misleading to talk about an increase of 50 per cent or more in the volume of our exports, unless it is made clear that this does not apply to the immediate post-war phase. A recent calculation indicates that, without drastic changes of method not at present in view, a more realistic expectation is an increase of 22 per cent even in the post-transition period, with a much lower figure during the transition. This disturbing result, which would mean chronic insolvency, is due to the large part played by coal and cotton textiles in our pre-war exports and the likelihood of a decline, rather than an increase, after the war if these industries continue to be run as at present. Clearly the first step is to work out a better target than this, and the second is to hit it. In the present context it is the volume of exports which we can develop in the first three years after the war which is chiefly relevant. Yet the Bank of England statisticians no longer expect any improvement in the volume of our exports in 1945 compared with 1944. Indeed, their figure for the second quarter of this year, on which we are now embarking, is 7 per cent below the figure for the corresponding quarter of last year.

20. (iii) The burden on us of relief and reconstruction outside these islands, (*a*) through UNRRA, (*b*) during the military period and in areas not at present within the scope of UNRRA, (*c*) arising out of the occupation of Germany, (*d*) for our own liberated territories in the Far East, is at present indeterminate and menacing. We have already undertaken a liability of £105 million for (*a*) and (*b*). Proposals

have been prepared in the Treasury in respect of (*a*), (*b*) and (*c*) which might serve at any rate to keep our liability in excess of £105 million within determinate bounds, provided we succeed in insisting on their adoption without compromise. But shall we? The Colonial Office estimate the cost of (*d*) at £150 to £200 million. I would urge most strongly that this should be regarded as a liability to be carried by the Commonwealth as a whole and not by us alone. We all know about India. South Africa has profiteered out of the war remorselessly, for all General Smuts's fine words (perhaps because of them). Australia is beginning to tread the same path (she is finding herself rich enough to pay off a considerable volume of pre-war debt in this country).

21. (iv) Apart from their sharing in the cost of relief and reconstruction in the Far Eastern members of the Commonwealth, the basis of the financial sharing of defence by the sterling Dominions, both now and after the war, needs to be put on a new basis, as the Chancellor of the Exchequer has emphasised to us. The extent to which currently they are slipping out of financial responsibility, and the scale on which they are building up war profits at our expense, may not be generally appreciated (since it is a comparatively recent development), and deserves to be set out nakedly.

(*a*) *Australia*

In 1944 Australia made a net overseas profit out of the war of £94 million. This was after spending £45 million on overseas war expenditure, which, however, included some arrears. In 1945 they are expected to make a profit of £58 million. The decrease is more than explained by diminished receipts from United States forces; they will be making more out of *us* than before. For their total overseas war expenditure in 1945 is expected to shrink to £28 million. We, on the other hand, will be expected to pay them cash for our war expenditure in Australia to the amount of £69 million. If we had the same reciprocal aid arrangements with Australia that the United States has or that we ourselves have with France, we should be better off by £41 million in the year, and Australia would still be making a handsome surplus, such as she would have been well satisfied with in earlier years.

(b) New Zealand

This small country made a net overseas profit of £23 million in 1944 and is expected to gain another £18 million in 1945. Of this total of £41 million about half, namely £20 million, is due to our having agreed to make a supplementary payment to her of this amount on account of the difference between world prices and her local prices in respect of her supplies of food to us. At the same time, her overseas war expenditure, which was £18,500,000 in 1944, will shrink in 1945 to £6,500,000.

(c) South Africa

Including accretions to her gold reserve and repatriations of securities, South Africa gained £38 million in 1944 and is expected to gain £49 million in 1945. Against this her overseas war expenditure in 1945, excluding some arrears still due, will have fallen to the derisory figure of £11 million.

22. In short, whilst Canada is doing her full duty, the Southern Dominions are scarcely doing a thing. Observe this table:–

	1945 (estimates)	
	Overseas profit (+) or loss (−)	After meeting overseas war expenditure of
	(£ million)	
United Kingdom	−750	896
Australia	+58	28
New Zealand	+18	6½
South Africa*	—	11

* Excluding 10 arrears from both columns.

Out of our overseas war expenditure of 896, we shall be spending 69 in Australia, and 20 in South Africa. This is exclusive of what we spend in these countries on food and war materials.

23. I register, therefore, our financial arrangements with the sterling Dominions (let alone India) amongst our significant failures and a part cause of our financial weakness. The Chancellor rightly concludes that this small country is carrying a burden of Imperial Defence which she cannot continue to carry by herself. There is a time-lag in our perspective in this field as elsewhere.

III

24. What is the upshot? If matters go on substantially as at present, we shall be running an overseas deficit on the day of cease-fire in Asia at the rate of about £1,400 million per annum, assuming that lend lease and mutual aid for food and raw materials are then terminated, but that we have no further liability for any dollar expenditure in respect of munitions and war-stores, whether to be delivered or to be cancelled or as salvage in the sterling area. With our best efforts, current expenditure (which will have to include the clearing up of arrears) will only decline gradually. Assuming some improvement meanwhile in the unsatisfactory features just dealt with, an intensive economy drive to reduce overseas war expenditure, and a not less intensive export drive, we might get through the first year of Stage III with an adverse balance not exceeding £1,000 million. But we cannot prudently assume much less. Nor is this the end. Three to five years are likely to elapse before we reach equilibrium. There is no present warrant for putting the cumulative deficit before we reach equilibrium at less than £2,000 million. The bulk of this, and perhaps more than this, will have to be borrowed from outside the sterling area. For, whilst some sterling area

countries may run a surplus with the rest of the world, several of them, full of money and empty of goods and in certain cases devastated by the enemy, will certainly run a deficit. If the rest of the sterling area, taken as a whole, breaks even, we shall have done fairly well.

25. Let us hope that this will have proved to err on the pessimistic side. It may. Such estimates generally do; although other good judges fear that the above may err on the optimistic side. However that may be, if our most extravagant hopes were to come true, a deficit over the period as a whole in excess of £1,000 million seems a certainty. Thus this is not a well-chosen moment for a declaration of our financial independence of North America. Our necessities in the transition after the war will put a quantitative burden on the financial machine described earlier in this paper far greater than it can carry without further financial aid from the United States and Canada. At the very best, even assuming a fabulous improvement in the above weak spots, we should do well to assume that complete financial independence of the United States would require:–

(*a*) the continuance of war rationing and war controls *more* stringent than at present for (say) three to five years after the war;

(*b*) the national planning and direction of foreign trade both imports and exports, somewhat on the Russian model; and

(*c*) an indefinite postponement of colonial development and Far Eastern rehabilitation and a virtual abandonment of all overseas activities, whether military or diplomatic or by way of developing our trade, wealth and influence, which involved any considerable expenditure.

26. There remains a further, and in my judgment an overriding, consideration which, so far, has only been touched upon in passing. A policy of economic isolationism means acceptance—indeed, not merely the acceptance but the

advocacy—of a system of international economy after the war
of a kind to which all sections of opinion, not only in the
United States but also in Canada, are bitterly opposed. It is
foolish to suppose if we take this line that the North Americans will remain passive. They will regard us as having deliberately rejected a helping hand for reasons of envy and
ambition, and as recklessly disrupting the common Anglo-
American front which is the best hope of the world. We must
also expect strong opposition on the part of many of the
sterling area countries to gang up with us like this against
United States and we might end up with a greatly curtailed
sterling area. Outside the sterling area the United States
would use its lending power to persuade many countries,
especially in Western Europe and South America, to refuse to
fall in with our ideas. In short, the moment at which we have
for the time being lost our financial strength and owe vast
sums all round the world is scarcely the bright and brilliant
occasion for asking all our creditors to join up with us against
where financial power now rests, not for the purpose of
getting paid, but for the purpose of obliging us with a little
more.

27. All this is, of course, on the assumption that the Americans are in fact prepared to make us a fair offer, not so much
generous as just, using their financial strength not as an
instrument to force us to their will, but as a means of making
it possible for us to participate in arrangements which we
ourselves prefer on their merits if only they can be made
practicable for us. It would be a grave misdeed to prepare
for isolationism if any reasonable terms are open to us on
which we can walk with the Americans and the Canadians
along the path which surely, if we can keep to it, offers much
the best hope both for ourselves and for others. If, on the
other hand, no such terms are obtainable, if the hostile forces
in the United States overwhelm the forces of light and
friendship (which is possible but not probable), then the whole

situation is changed. By reason of this possibility, but also (much more to the point) as a matter of tactics it is necessary to keep alive the disagreeable, indeed the disastrous, alternative, without, however, disguising from ourselves its true character. Perhaps I run the risk of enlarging on the obvious. But a position of complete independence within our own family is so naturally attractive to those who are not in a position to see so clearly the other side of the medal that it might be a mistake to scamp the argument.

28. It is not merely in order to oblige the Americans (and the Canadians) and as the price of their assistance that it is in our interest to embrace the international, as opposed to the isolationist or etatist, scheme of foreign trade. The international system is, on its merits, in our interests, for two reasons. The nature of our trade does not lend itself to bilateral arrangements; what suits our exporters is to have the whole world as their playground without reference to the question what and where it suits quite another set of persons, namely, our importers, to buy. Moreover, the terms of trade under forced barter conditions are bound to be to our disadvantage. We could, I suppose, maintain a certain level of subsistence on a barter basis, but we could not expect to get fat. Nor should this system be advocated by those who in other contexts extol the advantages of free enterprise. For barter trade is the very antithesis to individual enterprise. Every bargain would have to be undertaken by a Government Department, and exporters, unless they were subjected (as they would have to be) to compulsion, would soon find that the game was not worth the candle. Indeed, planned bilateral trade, with a view to making sure that exports balance imports, is a feeble version of the Russian method of a state monopoly of exports and imports, and likely to be much less efficient. Indeed, if the free enterprise alternative breaks down (as it may), it is probably to the Russian model, in my opinion, that we shall have to look; and we may even have

to make some experiments in this direction in the near future. Indeed, planned bilateralism is being chiefly advocated in this country to-day (with a few notable exceptions) by the near-Communists.

29. The second reason is our position as the financial centre of the greater part of the British Commonwealth and also of a number of countries outside it. We built up the pre-war sterling area because we were bankers amiable to treat with and having a long record of honouring our cheques. It is a great mistake to believe that we can regain or retain this position except on the basis that sterling is a freely convertible currency. Bilateral proposals are sometimes advocated on the ground that they are the best means to preserve the sterling area. Nothing could be further from the truth. They are a sure means of disrupting it. There would be very little left, if anything, of the sterling area on the basis of making sterling a permanently inconvertible currency which could only be used to purchase goods over a limited field. Each member in turn would walk out on us. The proposals of this paper are, and are intended to be, the means to recover for London its ancient prestige and its hegemony.

30. The foregoing observations do not imply a lack of sympathy with the anxiety about our future balance of payments which underlies the bilateral approach in the minds of those of its advocates who are far from desiring on its merits a State monopoly of foreign trade. They ask themselves what hope is there of reaching equilibrium on any other basis. Is not the use of our position as a great consumer, to force our goods out on to the world in return for what the world wishes to sell to us, the only new weapon in our armoury and one we cannot do without? I do not claim that there is a conclusive answer to this. I am far from certain that we shall reach trade equilibrium in the post-war world by the methods of free enterprise. It is very possible, indeed, that the system will break down and that nothing short of a state monopoly of

foreign trade (for that is what planned bilateralism comes to in practice) will serve our needs.

31. No. The future is to be viewed with anxiety. The present argument does not flow from a blind faith in the blessings of free enterprise. The argument stands firm on four fixed points of conviction: First, in the actual position of this small island as the centre of an independent world system (so different in every respect from the position of Russia or of the United States) the freedom of trade is, on its merits, to our great advantage if it can be made to work. Second, at this stage of the evolution of thought and politics it is the only path along which we can walk as partners in a better hope with the United States and Canada. Third, the future is altogether unclear and unpredictable—there can be no sufficient evidence at this date of time for choosing the worse before trying the better. Fourth, if international trade on these principles breaks down (as well it may), we shall be in a vastly better position to justify a change and to ask others to join with us on new lines than if we were to go our own way now alone, and very much alone, without giving a trial to the alternative. Even if I were convinced that those will certainly prove right who believe that we can only live in the post-war world by a state planning of foreign trade, I should nevertheless think it wise statesmanship to act today on the other hypothesis.

32. I do not seek to conclude that the policy of isolation is, even in the last resort, utterly impracticable. On the contrary, as I have mentioned, we want to be able to pretend with sufficient plausibility that it offers a just possible alternative. But it might be expected to lead to serious political and social disruption at home and our withdrawal, for the time being, from the position of a first-class Power in the outside world. We should have to retire, as Russia did between the wars, to starve and reconstruct. We might, like Russia, emerge in good health half a generation later, but nothing much less than

Russian methods would have served our turn meanwhile. Indeed, the danger is that our dismay at the character of this alternative will make us weak negotiators and too willing to accept under pressure the other extreme, which is certainly the line of least resistance. For we shall need a robust spirit in negotiation and a willingness to face a breakdown, if necessary, in the first round. If the alternative just described is Starvation Corner, the other extreme, to which I now turn, should be called Temptation.

IV

33. What, then, is the amount of American aid which we are likely to need? It is impossible to quantify this with any degree of accuracy on the basis of what is now known. I put it at a probable minimum of $5 billion (£1,250 million) with up to (say) $8 billion possibly required to give us real liberty of action and to allow us to offer from the start the full multilateralism of trade and exchange which will be the best inducement to the Americans to fall in with our proposals. A larger sum might demoralise us and prevent us from ever reaching equilibrium again except after further crisis and some humiliation. We should certainly aim at getting through with $5 billion, but a call on a further $3 billion is very advisable if we are to have the full confidence and resources to develop our trade on far-sighted lines and to play our proper part in the world after the war.

34. Let us now turn to a closer inspection of Temptation. There is not much doubt that the Americans would be ready, and even eager, to lend us large sums *on their own terms*—$5 billion without doubt and perhaps the full $8 billion spread over a period. Nor will the terms they propose be, from their own point of view (whatever we may think), particularly unreasonable. I guess that the conditions which it would be easy to negotiate might be somewhat as follows:–

(a) A low rate of interest, certainly not higher than 2½ per cent, and perhaps as low as 2 per cent.

(b) Easy terms of repayment of capital, spread over (say) thirty years and not beginning for ten years, with provisions for postponement if, when the time comes, the burden appears too great for us.

(c) Free multilateral clearing within the sterling area from the beginning, i.e., the unfettered conversion into dollars of the current earnings of the sterling area countries even during the provisional period.

(d) Perhaps the same condition in respect of the pre-zero hour sterling balances.

(e) A pretty full implementation of the ideals of Article VII as understood by the Americans, with substantial concessions on our part to their point of view in the matters of preferences, cartels, bulk purchasing, etc.

(f) The wiping out of any remaining lend lease liability, but the inclusion in the above loan of various obligations arising out of the winding-up of lend lease.

35. A good many of those whom we reckon the more friendly will start out along some such lines as the above, and will consider in their own minds, that they are offering us a square, and even a generous, deal. I am afraid that, if we could do no better, most of us would, when we were right up against it, prefer this Temptation to Starvation Corner, which is not far from politically impossible, both at home and abroad, if Temptation is offering round the corner.

36. What then, without overstating them, are the objections to this version of Temptation?—

(i) Some part, perhaps a considerable part, of what we should otherwise owe to the sterling area and other countries, which are our natural customers, we should come to owe to the United States instead. Perhaps $2 billion might get thus transferred, as compared with the result of deferring free convertibility until the end of the provisional period.

277

(ii) We should owe the United States an annual sum of, say, $200 million in interest (assuming 2½ per cent on $8 billion), and, after an interval, say, a further $300 million for capital repayment, that is an annual service of $500 million a year, tapering away in the course of time. This would be in addition to a large outstanding debt of some $12 billion to other countries. It would be rash to say that this is impossible. Time and progress diminish the significance of what begin by seeming large figures. Moreover, we might find $5 billion sufficient. But we cannot be sure of shouldering such a burden with success, and we might find ourselves in a chronic condition of having to make humiliating and embarrassing pleas for mercy and postponement. It is interesting to note that the total war burden we should be carrying under the above assumptions adds up to exactly the same figure, namely, $20 billion, that the Russians think appropriate in the case of Germany (though they will not get it or anything like).

(iii) It would be wrong to expect us to make concessions in the field of economic policy under financial pressure.

37. But the main objection surely lies, not in these details, but in the whole proposed set-up being an outrageous crown and conclusion of all that has happened. The war would end by placing on Germany an external burden of $20 billion or less; it would end by placing on us a burden of $20 billion or more. It would end in Germany being forced into conformity with an economic policy designed from without; and the same here. She would plead to Russia from time to time for mercy and deferment; and so should we to the United States. It is not as the result of some statistical calculation about what we might be able to manage, that the mind revolts from accepting the counsels of Temptation. The fundamental reasons for rejection are incommensurable in terms of cash.

38. Nevertheless, before turning to the third line of approach, which I shall venture to call Justice, it is necessary to

examine the possible mitigations of a policy on the above broad lines which one might be able to secure in negotiation. It may be that a point comes when Temptation is sufficiently transformed to approach Justice. We must be clear in our heads about the best version of what we can perhaps fall back upon.

39. I have made bold to say that the above terms would be easy to negotiate. I think there are improvements on these terms which it might not be impossible to obtain, compatibly with accepting this general line of approach. For example, the annual service of the loan might be greatly lightened either by reducing the interest to a token figure or by deferring the final date of discharge or by both expedients. An annual service of 1 per cent would cost only $80 million a year even on a loan of $8 billion. It might be allowed that we need not release any part of the pre-zero hour sterling balances, but only their current earnings. It might be tacitly agreed that no element of financial pressure should enter into the conversations on commercial policy and other extraneous subjects.

40. Such a settlement would not be unduly onerous, financially or economically, on ourselves in relation to the United States, though it would leave us with the problem of the old sterling balances unmitigated. But it still fails to measure up to the criterion of Justice. The financial benefit to the United States would be next door to nothing, and worth less than nothing to the American economy. The sweet breath of Justice between partners, in what had been a great and magnanimous enterprise carried to overwhelming success, would have been sacrificed to some false analogy of 'business'. And even then Uncle Sam might quite likely remain under the conviction that he was Uncle Sap, a conviction which can only be removed by making him enter into the meeting-place by a different door.

V

41. What is this different door? It is not through the approach of relief such as is appropriate to Greece or Jugoslavia or aid in the finance of rehabilitation such as France or Czechoslovakia can properly ask; but through the approach of a general re-consideration of the proper burden of the costs of the war.

42. For a hundred good reasons we have had to accept during the war a post-war financial burden entirely disproportionate to what is fair. The theme is familiar. We did it in the interests of getting on with the war without a waste of time or loss of war-like efficiency. As a result, we, and we only, end up owing vast sums, not to neutrals and bystanders, but to our own Allies, Dominions and Associates, who ought to figure in the eyes of history as our mercenaries, unless the balance is redressed. This does not apply particularly to the United States; indeed, to them (and to Canada) proportionately least of all. It applies all round. Nevertheless, it is only through appropriate action by the United States and Canada that there is a prospect of an agreed general re-settlement. To which it should be added that the reward to the North Americans will not merely be that their action is contributory to the establishment of Justice, but also that, at very small cost to their economies, perhaps at less than no true cost at all, we shall be made able to be their partners and coadjutors in setting up a post-war international economy of the character on which they have set their hearts.

43. The President has often used words implying that he accepted in some sense the principle of equal sacrifice. We must ask him to let us take him at his word—at least to some extent. This does not mean that there is a clear logical conclusion to which we can press matters. Sacrifices are incommensurable. Apart from which we must be practical and work with a broad brush. There is a big gap between equality

of sacrifice and our being left with a heavier overseas financial burden than Germany, a burden which we shall owe to our *Allies*. Let us, therefore, consider a version of what we might accept as doing at the same time substantial justice and as allowing us to fall in whole-heartedly and sincerely with the American ideal of the post-war international economy.

44. The United States would be asked to play a part in this, but, as it will be seen, by no means an exclusive part. The method of redistribution of the burden and the rubric under which it is effected, which seem to me to be the best, after considering alternatives, both technically and politically and psychologically, is the following:–

(i) During the period before lend lease came into full operations we spent some $3 billion on purchases in the United States for what afterwards became a common war. Moreover, it was this expenditure which built up the munitions industries in the United States before they entered the war to their immense advantage after they entered it. This sum the United States would agree to refund to us as a sort of retrospective lend lease.

(ii) This payment, supplemented by the credit arrangements proposed below, would make it possible for us to undertake that we would accept *de facto* convertibility of sterling within a year after the end of the war (without necessarily waiving the other relaxations contemplated during the transitional period).

(iii) With this support behind us we would approach the various members of the sterling area with proposals for dealing with their sterling balances. These would not necessarily follow a uniform pattern, but might be, in general, except where there is good reason to the contrary, on the following lines:–

(a) Each member of the area would contribute a proposition of the final total of its sterling balances to the costs of the common victory.

(*b*) A proportion would be left liquid and would become fully convertible over the exchanges for the purpose of meeting current transactions in any part of the world.

(*c*) The remainder would be funded on terms to be explained below.

(*d*) Alternatively, if any member of the area would not accept such proposals, no part of their sterling balances would be made available except on the terms explained below.

(*e*) The figure of the sterling balances to be handled in one or other of these ways would include an appropriate allowance for the cost of our post-war demobilisation and terminal liabilities as well as the accumulations during the war.

(iv) In addition to the relief under (i) above, the United States to give us a call on dollars exercisable over (say) ten years up to a further $5 billion if required at a token rate of interest and on easy terms of repayment.

45. Let us now consider this in more detail. In the first place, it will probably be advisable to limit the above cancellation and funding proposals to the members of the sterling area and to leave outside this settlement the non-sterling area indebtedness to be dealt with otherwise. When one looks into the details this seems to be the only practicable arrangement. Moreover, we can probably manage to deal with the non-sterling area balances one way or another. In particular, we can, if necessary, fund certain of them on as large a scale as we choose, since we are not under the same moral or legal obligation as we are in the case of the sterling area balances, to make at least some part of them convertible into dollars. In fact, if the rest has been dealt with satisfactorily, we can probably manage (as it will be seen below) to make most of these miscellaneous balances fully convertible from the start.

46. At the end of 1944 net sterling area liabilities stood at £2,390 million, and liabilities to the rest of the world (including 'Resident' Allied Governments, Enemy Custodians, etc.)

at £781 million, making a total of £3,171 million. By the end of the war (should it come early in 1946) we might, without much error, assume sterling area balances as being £3,000 million and the rest £1,000 million.

47. The non-sterling area aggregate includes a number of items which need not, and could not appropriately, be included in the suggested settlement as follows:–

£ million

(i) *United States* (Jesse Jones loan, etc., covered by collateral out of which it will be discharged, and registered sterling which is already deducted in arriving at our net reserves)   78

(ii) *Canada* (Non-interest loan and sundry balances which will probably be brought into hotch-potch in any post-war financial arrangements with Canada)   139

(iii) *Portugal* (covered by gold and allowed for in reckoning our net reserves, which must in any case be the subject of special negotiation, leading, we hope, to a release of some of the gold)   72

(iv) Held by Custodians and Trading with the Enemy Department (which are safely in our hands and must be the subject of special arrangements; the largest item, France, has just been dealt with)   70

(v) European Allies and their possessions and China. (They will need all this to make purchases from the sterling area. Our task is to get as much of their future purchases as possible paid for in gold by those who have gold. Here also special arrangements are both possible and inevitable. The major items are Norway 73, Holland and possessions 64, Belgium and possessions 13, France and possessions 21, Greece 52, China 21)   253

     ——

     612

Deducting these items from the total of £781 million, we have only £169 million left. The greater part of this is Argentina (72) and Brazil (35), leaving no more than £62 million for the whole of the rest of the world, which can be reckoned as normal balances and present no problem. Argentina and Brazil, moreover, can be cleared by disposing of our investments in those countries which we should effect by a very tough bargain, when our hands are freer than they are now, securing the full value of our original investment.

48. These details confirm our previous conclusion that we can confine our attention in the present context to the sterling area balances. At the end of 1944 these were made up as follows:–

	£ million
Australia	122*
New Zealand	46
South Africa	28
India	1,004
Egypt and Sudan	356
Palestine and Transjordan	107
Burma, Malaya and Hong Kong	131
Other Crown Colonies	410
Eire	103
Iraq	69
Iceland	14
	2,390

* Against this we hold stocks of Australian wool, our payments for which are included in the above.

We must expect this total to have reached £3,000 million by the end of the war and perhaps not much short of £3,500 million if we make a proper allowance for expenses attributable to the war incurred during the phase of demobilisation. There are, however, here also a number of cases which need not be brought into the general settlement. Burma, Malaya and Hong Kong are special cases, which might be allowed their share of liquidity without cancellation of any part of their balances. South Africa, having gold, needs no free dollars, and the settlement here should consist in her making a substantial contribution in gold as will be suggested below. Thus we are left with a probable *post-bellum* aggregate approaching £3,000 million (as at the end of demobilisation) which is *prima facie* suitable for the proposed general settlement, made up (roughly) as follows:–

	£ million
India	1,500
Egypt	500
Palestine	130
Iraq	80
Australia	150
Eire	120
Crown Colonies (apart from Malaya and Hong Kong)	520
	3,000

49. The proposal is, then, that the above liabilities should be divided into three portions, one part to be made fully convertible, one part to be funded and one part to be written off. In determining the respective sizes of the three portions each country could be dealt with on its merits. For their individual circumstances and the causes behind the increases vary widely. The following circumstances, amongst others, would be relevant to the final determination:–

(*a*) In general an amount not less than the opening balances, as at the 30th June 1939, might be left convertible;

(*b*) The local price-level at which the indebtedness was incurred, relatively to United Kingdom prices, should be taken into account;

(*c*) In general an amount equal to the favourable commercial balance earned during the war, apart from United Kingdom war expenditure, after deduction of what has been already paid for in gold or by repatriation of securities, might be left convertible in addition to the opening balances under (a) above.

(d) The scale of lend lease assistance received, or reciprocal aid accorded and earnings from United States forces should be considered.

(e) The scale of war expenditure for which they have already made themselves responsible.

50. It will be found that in the cases of India, Egypt, Palestine and Iraq their receipts from our war expenditure exceed the increment of their sterling balances; that is to say, more than the whole of their commercial earnings has been paid for in gold or in repatriated securities. In these countries, moreover, we should be entitled to write down their balances by at least a third on account of the inflated local prices at which they have been acquired. (They could recover the whole of this writing off in terms of their local currency by depreciating their exchanges to the same extent, which perhaps they ought to be encouraged to do in the interests of the future equilibrium of their balance of payments.) Alone of the above countries India has borne a heavy share of war expenditure. The Crown Colonies may be felt to present some difficulty. But most of them have escaped any serious war expenditure so far, and they have earned substantial sums from our local war expenditure of exactly the same character as have India and Egypt. There is, for example, no reason in principle to discriminate in favour of Palestine compared with Iraq or Egypt; or in favour of Ceylon and the East and West African colonies compared with India, except that the appropriate scale in these latter cases would be, of course, much lower. Exact statistics are not available, but enough is known to enable broad justice to be done. The most difficult case is that of Eire, the whole of the increment in her sterling balances being due to her commercial earnings and a steady receipt of £11 million a year from Irish labourers in this country. Perhaps the right solution there will be to cancel nothing, but to fund a high proportion.

51. A first, quick glance at the relevant evidence suggests that the results might come out somewhat as follows:–

	Freed	Funded	Cancelled
		£ million	
India	250	750	500
Egypt	80	250	170
Palestine	25	70	35
Iraq	15	25	40
Australia	50	50	50
Eire	30	90	—
Malaya and Hong Kong	100	30	—
Other Crown Colonies	200	235	85
	750	1,500	880

52. It should be explained that the freed balances would be made convertible for the purpose of meeting a current deficit of trade. They could not, for example, be taken away in gold to set up a reserve at home or elsewhere abroad. The funded portion might be on the basis of 1 per cent interest which would be paid as liquid, convertible cash, and 2 per cent per annum of the capital released for special purchases of British goods, beginning 5 years after the war. On £1,500 million this would cost us £15 million a year at the start and another £30 million released per annum after 5 years, not all of which would be an additional burden on the balance of payments.

53. The writing off could be conveniently operated in most cases through the Currency Note Reserves by substituting domestic Treasury bills for British Treasury bills in the Currency Reserves, thus in effect creating a fiduciary issue to the corresponding amount or with other government or central bank funds or by the cancellation of loans advanced to His Majesty's Government during the war. In the cases of Palestine, Iraq and Eire some part of the privately held balances would have to be funded, which would probably mean in practice their having to be acquired by the central bank.

54. The countries in question would have the *option* to come into this settlement. If they declined the option, then we should fund the *whole* of the balances, let us say at ½ per cent interest in liquid, convertible cash, and the principal sum to be made available at the rate of 1 per cent per annum after five years and only for special purchases of British goods. No one would decline the option if they were convinced that this was the alternative.

55. So far we have asked for a retrospective contribution to the costs of the war of £750 million ($3 billion) from the United States and of about £880 million from the sterling area. But there remain certain further matters:–

(a) It was suggested above that we should also be given a call to borrow from the *United States* exercisable at any time during the first ten years after the war. The limit of this might be $5 billion at 1 per cent interest and a sinking fund of 1 per cent per annum of the initial amount, beginning ten years after the war, rising to 2 per cent per annum after a further ten years.

(b) How does *Canada* come into the picture? She, like the United States, would gain from the date of the settlement the full freedom of exchange within the sterling area which she so ardently desires. The final settlement with her might be as follows:–

(i) The no-interest loan, originally $700 million but reduced by now to a lower figure, should be confirmed in its present status, i.e., no interest and the proceeds of certain British-owned Canadian securities to be devoted to repayment, which might clear off the loan within ten or fifteen years.

(ii) The unsettled war outstandings amounting altogether to about Canadian $600 million, mainly the cost of the two Air Training Schemes, to be covered by a final Mutual Aid Appropriation.

(iii) A call on a loan, exactly on all fours with what is

proposed for the United States, of one-tenth the American figure; i.e., $500 million.

(c) There remains the case of *South Africa*, which has made so far a notoriously inadequate contribution compared with any other part of the Commonwealth. They should be expected to make a retrospective contribution of £50 million in gold to our costs of the war.

56. This would relieve us altogether of about £1,800 million of the burden of our war debt. On a further £1,500 million, the interest cost would be fixed at £15 million a year with capital repayment out of special exports of £30 million a year beginning five years after the war. Our gold and dollar reserves, after taking account of the proposed retrospective lend lease, would start at a level more than double what they were at the beginning of the war, though they would rapidly melt away in the first year or two after the war; and the excess of our liquid overseas liability over our reserves (after clearing up the position of the non-sterling area) should not be much greater than pre-war (and appreciably less in real value after allowing for the rise of prices). We should have lost (after dealing with the Jesse Jones loan, the Canadian loan and certain non-sterling area balances) about £1,500 million of our pre-war overseas assets. Altogether we might be about £100 million a year worse off in overseas income. This is apart from any further debt burden which we might incur by calling on the United States, and Canadian optional credits to cover an adverse position after the war. It also assumes that the war will not continue far into 1946 or beyond.

57. We might deem this to be sufficient justice. Nevertheless we should still remain the only country in the Alliance left at the end of the war with its overseas earnings heavily mortaged as a result of it—most of the others would still find themselves in substantial profit at our expense. We should still have fought, so to speak, as the only non-mercenaries. Nevertheless, with such a settlement as the above we could

face the economic future without any serious anxiety—except the perennial one of knocking some energy and enterprise into our third-generation export industries and of organising the new industries which our first generation is well qualified to conduct if the capital and the organisation can be arranged.

58. Unfortunately any such settlement is, as yet, far off. We can only hope to reach it by robust and unyielding negotiation which does not shrink from emphasising the claims of justice on the one hand and the nature of the alternative on the other. We must probably be prepared for the appearance of a break-down at the end of the first round. All concerned—the War Cabinet, the Treasury, the Dominions Office, the Colonial Office, the India Office, the Bank of England—must speak in the same, persistent tones which do not admit of a doubt.

VI

59. How can such proposals be presented with the best hope of conviction to the people of the United States and to the countries of the sterling area? This is a political, that is a psychological, question, and the best shape will only emerge, I expect, in the course of prolonged discussion. But the broad lines must be somewhat as follows:–

(i) We shall have been in the war and in the area of operations for longer than anyone else. In the interests of victory we freely abandoned financial prudence for the future. We and we alone supplemented our own resources by mortgaging the future through overseas loans. We and we alone did this.

(ii) It is precisely that expenditure which we incurred in the United States itself whilst we were holding the fort alone for which retrospective repayment would be made.

(iii) If, in the light of the final outcome and the full story, nothing is done to redress the position, we shall end by shouldering burdens incurred for the common cause, such as cannot be placed even on the defeated enemy. Our Allies will be seeking to obtain post-war reparations from this small country on a scale greater than it will be practicable to put on the enemy.

(iv) With such burdens upon us we cannot for several years to come participate in the free international economy upon which the Americans have set their hearts and which we also, no less than they, vastly prefer if it is made practicable for us.

(v) Some of our American friends are at present a little too much inclined to suggest to us that we should free ourselves from these burdens by a straight unilateral repudiation or what would amount to such, if it were to be enforced without the offer of a reasonable alternative (e.g. something like what is suggested above, for those countries which decline the option without, however, having first offered them the option). In our view we cannot do this—

(*a*) for reasons of honour;

(*b*) for reasons of justice, since the above would certainly not lead to a *fair* redistribution of the costs of the war;

(*c*) for reasons of practice, since it would not be practicable, for example, to deprive all the sterling countries of the liquid use of the whole of their currency reserves held with us.

So far from this course contributing to the solution of a free international economy, it would widen the field within which the strictest controls over foreign trade would continue to be necessary.

(vi) It is only by a more comprehensive settlement, which attempts to offer everyone what is reasonable, and so far as we can make it, fair, that the financial consequences of the war can be liquidated. This is the aim, namely, that as between the partners to the war, its financial consequences, in so far as they affect future economic intercourse between them, should be so far as possible liquidated. These words sum up the final purpose. Strict fairness will not be possible. On our own proposals we shall continue to carry burdens from which others will be freed. But the alternative mentioned in (v) above goes altogether too far and would shift unfairness at least as much as it diminished it.

(vii) The outcome of the war should not be such that the financial weakness of certain of the partners tempts other partners to use their financial strength to put on pressure to secure their own way.

(viii) Thus no fair solution can be reached without the participation of the Americans. The help asked from them is on relatively so small a scale that it costs them almost literally nothing. It enables them to dispose over a period of a foreign surplus far below what they are likely in any case to develop, a surplus of which in any case they will have to find means of riddance. The amount of the contribution proposed ($3 billion) is the cost of the war to the United States for a fortnight; to forgo good prospects for the sake of this saving would be surely to spoil the ship of Victory and Peace for a coat of paint. Is there any alternative way in which they can get better value? Under these proposals they can wind up the financial side of the war leaving behind a sense of justice between the partners; and all of us become free forthwith to participate in the free international economy which is one of the prime objects of American policy. They will never have a better chance of a wise act at so modest a cost.

(ix) It is essential that the settlement should not take the form of a unilateral decision on our part. It must be the result of a joint discussion and one which commends itself as fair to the general judgment of the Allied Nations. For only so can recrimination be avoided and only so can we, with a good conscience, make an enforced settlement on any, if there be any such at the last, who, being offered an arrangement which has commended itself as fair to the general judgment of the Nations, decide to stand out.

(x) It is not the money that the Americans will grudge. They will spill much more for worse causes. If, in spite of the confused vapours and incorrigible ignorance which surround and condition all public discussion in the United States, the people of the United States can be brought to see the thing in its true light, looking back to what has happened and forward to what should happen, we need not doubt their approval.

60. We could, I suppose, fall back on to a variant of the above by which the $3 billion from the United States was not freely contributed as retrospective lend lease, but was provided on the same terms as the proposed credit of $5 billion, which would then become $8 billion, all the rest of the settlement remaining the same. I do not think that the financial consequences of this would be insupportable. It will be noticed that this proposal approximates to the least dangerous version of Temptation outlined in paragraph 39 above. But politically and psychologically it would be greatly inferior. It would prejudice our approach to the sterling area countries for their contributions, which could no longer be represented as part of a general, agreed re-distribution of the financial burden of the war. I should expect that the grander version would be carried more easily with the general opinion of the world than the meaner version. The Americans would have lost the sense of magnanimity for a financial benefit which is useless to them and even perhaps injurious. This variant would only appeal to those who believe that their duty to God and to mankind requires that every action must be at least dressed up to look like 'business'.

61. The time for opening this discussion in Washington will not arrive until the German war is over, the San Francisco Conference finished, the Sixth Lend Lease Appropriation voted, and the Bretton Woods Plan through Congress. This probably means that the beginning of September is the earliest practicable date.

62. The most appropriate form of presentation will need very careful thought. The psychological mistakes of the Balfour Note after the last war must be avoided. For this reason the appeal to justice must not seem to imply that we have suffered injustice, or indeed anything but generosity, at the hands of the United States hitherto. The proposals must be presented, rather, as a means of liquidating the financial consequences of the war in a way which will allow the whole of the sterling area to enter, with the least possible delay, into a free international economy of the type which the Americans have put into the front of their desired policy; and as a means, also, of putting pressure on certain sterling area countries to collaborate by taking a juster share of the financial burdens of the war then they have yet accepted. If the Americans desire to make their contribution contingent on an at least equal contribution from the sterling area countries, we should welcome such a condition.

63. The advent of a new President and a new group of intimate White House advisers make it difficult to indicate the best channel of approach, until the new régime has settled down and we have learnt more about it. But, if it is possible, a paper should be passed in the first instance to the President and his principal advisers at the State Department and the Treasury, without any preliminary soundings at lower levels or in other quarters. It will be necessary in any case to discuss with the F.E.A. at an early date the many difficult problems arising out of the winding-up of lend lease and reciprocal

aid. The major Stage III discussions could perhaps take place conveniently under cover of the more routine lend lease conversations which will be required in any case with the avowed purpose of preparing the way for winding up the lend lease system with the least possible delay.

KEYNES

May 1945

Soon after his first draft on Stage III finance, Keynes raised the problem of overseas as against domestic expenditure in a comment on a paper by Sir Wilfrid Eady, 'The Cost of Defence in Relation to the Budget and our Foreign Exchange Resources'

From a letter to SIR EDWARD BRIDGES[9] *23 March 1945*

(3) I should make an even more emphatic distinction between the burden of overseas expenditure and the burden of domestic expenditure. We can always manage more of the latter, if necessary. Indeed, defence expenditure might prove one of the methods of reaching full employment and thereby, partly at least, pay for itself as compared with other alternatives, at least in the short run. Moreover, I at any rate would not be shocked by some borrowing, if the case for higher expenditure on defence in the immediate-ensuing years is overwhelmingly made out, hoping to cover this up later on by the buoyancy of the national income. Within reason anything is possible financially in the way of domestic expenditure, if the case for incurring it is made out with sufficient strength. Nothing of the kind, however, is true of overseas expenditure. There we might easily embark on policies involving costs which were entirely beyond our power. If we can solve our external financial position, I am sure that there is

---

[9] Edward Bridges (1892–1969), K.C.B. 1939, 1st Baron 1957; Treasury, 1919–38; Secretary of Cabinet, 1938–46; Permanent Secretary, Treasury, 1945–56; Fellow of All Souls College, Oxford, 1954–69.

enough productivity left at home to look after any reasonable domestic expenditure. But we must never lose sight of the fact that no kind of solution of the external financial position is yet in sight, and, in all probability, the most drastic economies will be required to make the problem soluble. I hope, therefore, that the Service Departments will be asked to divide the expenditure for which they are planning according to the place where it is spent as accurately as possible. In particular, it is very easy to overlook the large sums which the Admiralty spend overseas. For example, currently the Admiralty is spending at the rate of £50 million a year in the countries bordering on the Mediterranean, the Indian Ocean and thereabouts, excluding North America and Northern waters altogether.

Keynes himself was doing his best to prepare the ground for later Anglo-American discussions at the same time, in a conversation with Mr Harry Hawkins, who had been holding rather unsuccessful exploratory talks with officials in London on the next stages of the negotiations on commercial, cartel and commodity policy, and Dr E. F. Penrose.[10] Keynes emphasised, in the course of the talks, Britain's long-term commitment to multi-lateral trading arrangements, but said that much mutual tolerance would be necessary in the transition to normal post-war conditions. He emphasised the need for early agreement on long-term policy so that any temporary, transitional, deviations would appear in proper perspective and not become permanent as was the danger.

During the same period, worries about possible sterling area discrimi-

[10] E. F Penrose; economist born in England and educated at Cambridge; subsequently worked in Japan and at the Food Research Institute, Stanford University, U.S.A; International Labour Office, 1938–41; Special Assistant, U.S. Ambassador, London, 1941–4; U.S. Delegation, United Nations, New York, 1946–7.

The talks were rather unsuccessful because the British officials involved were effectively in straightjackets and conducting a stalling operation in the light of the defensive and limited directive for the negotiations that came from Cabinet. As had been the case since the spring of 1944 the Cabinet was deeply split over the commercial policy issue and the Prime Minister was attempting to delay a decision. At the same time, the Americans had altered their views since the Law Mission's understandings of the autumn of 1943 and were, as well, trying to plug any gaps that had been left in the Bretton Woods agreement on the IMF that would leave room for discrimination.

nation against Canadian exports during the transition, something that would affect Canada's traditionally delicate feelings concerning the balance of her relations with the United States and the United Kingdom, as well as her post-war trade prospects, came to the fore, both in an informal letter from Mr Gordon Munro and in cables from Mr Mackenzie King to Churchill and from Ottawa to the Dominions Office. In these circumstances Keynes wrote to Munro.

To G. MUNRO, *9 March 1945*

My dear Munro,

I have your letter of February 20th containing the report of Inglis' conversation with Clark.[11] Since then we have had the major telegrams[12] and you will have probably had the official replies to these before you get this letter.

On the Stage II issue we have no reason to be otherwise than very well contented. It is a bit tiresome that the decision between pooling and mutual aid is once again put off, that I suppose, is inevitable. It has, in particular, the disadvantage of leaving the question of cancellations unsettled, whereas as soon as the German war is over that is bound to become acute. Do keep reminding Clark that this is an issue that cannot possibly be shirked.

With the rest of the communications, I did not feel so entirely content. The Stage III financial proposal is, of course, exactly what Towers hinted at when I was in Ottawa. Beyond question it is generous and shows that in due course we can hope to have a satisfactory arrangement. But the general querulousness of some parts of the telegram seem to me unnecessary. However, I suppose they have their own domestic reasons for being a little on the irritable side. Also, there was, as it seemed to me, a tendency to want to jump

---

[11] Inglis, the newly appointed correspondent of *The Times* in Ottawa, had a talk with Dr Clark on 3 February.

[12] The Canadian cables had also assured Britain that she would receive the amount of mutual aid requested in the autumn of 1944 and that the forthcoming General Election would not interfere with the necessary appropriations. The cables also raised the possibility of a long-term loan to Britain for Stage III with deferred repayment arrangements and a waiver clause.

the tape. They did not, as you will see, strike me as being very wise or judicious approaches to the subject.

In particular, they entirely overlooked the fact that we cannot possibly have a settlement with Canada which completely frees the sterling area in relation to Canada and not have a more or less similar arrangement with the United States. That, naturally and rightly, was the immediate reaction of Brand. You will have seen, I expect, his telegram Remac 219, with every word of which I find myself in full agreement.

I was relieved, of course, that there was no suggestion of linking up unduly the Stage II financial assistance with other issues. Nevertheless, there was rather more suggestion of connection than entirely commended itself to us. After all, this is a joint war and on the financial side of matters we have certainly been bearing more than our fair share. That fact, or the consequence of that fact, should never be used by any of those concerned as a means of pressure. Quite the contrary. In fact, the Canadians have got us all wrong about this. It is not the case that we are pining and planning for a discriminatory bilateral world. Quite the contrary, we shall be venting our very best efforts to make future arrangements exactly what they want them to be. But it is a very long way from being easy for us to arrange this and it will have to be more or less on our terms. For that reason, as I think I mentioned in a previous letter, it may do no harm that they should be worrying quite a bit. But in fact, if Canada and the U.S. will each play their appropriate part, I have not the smallest doubt, if only they will be a little patient, all will turn out well.

I am sending a copy of this letter to Brand and letting him know how I feel about his own reaction to the Canadian telegrams.

Yours ever,
[copy initialled] M. K.

Throughout March, Brand continued to send Keynes suggestions on Stage III strategy and tactics, frequently emphasising the need for action sooner rather than later. Amongst his grounds for speed were a fear that the Japanese war would be lengthy and that, before the American public realised this, the moment of optimism after the German war would provide the best basis for a favourable reception of Britain's case; that many demands for assistance would increase the resistance to those coming at the end of the queue and that the deteriorating health of the American leadership would make delay dangerous. As he summed up the last matter on 1 April.

> [T]he President [Roosevelt] seems to be getting less and less robust. Oliver [Lyttelton] told me he was shocked to see him and w^d bet he w^{d}n't last 6 months more. Edward H[alifax] also agrees he looks much worse than a short time ago. Harry Hopkins is still in hospital. He is said to be coming out before very long. But how long he will last no one knows. If neither of them were available it w^d be extremely unfortunate. We would have to consider afresh the exact method of approach.

Keynes, meanwhile had sent Brand a first draft of his Stage III proposals. While Brand's comments of 5 April were making their way back to London, Keynes kept him informed of developments—a meeting with Mr Bernard Baruch[13] and reactions to the death of President Roosevelt on 12 April, as it affected timing.

To R. H. BRAND, *6 April 1945*

My dear Bob,

I have just received very promptly your particularly interesting and important letter of March 29th which, I fear, only confirms a good many feelings and suspicions we already had. There is nothing in it which really needs any comment from me except sympathy. The purpose of this letter is to report to you briefly (one cannot say very much in a letter) about a dinner given by the P.M. to Baruch at which I was present.

The object of the dinner was to have a full and frank discussion with him on the Stage III questions. The Chan-

---

[13] Bernard Marnes Baruch (1870–1965); in World War I, Chairman of Commission on Raw Materials and of Allied Purchasing Commission; member, Supreme Economic Council; American Delegate on Economic and Reparation clauses; in World War II, adviser to Byrnes; appointed to investigate and report on synthetic rubber and manpower; American Representative on Atomic Energy Commission.

cellor and Catto were there, also Cherwell. The Beaver [Lord Beaverbrook][14] and Brendan [Bracken] provided a carping chorus. Before we went the idea was to say as little as possible and not make any specific proposals. When it came to it, however, this was extremely difficult. The P.M. had apparently been advised by the President that it was most important to get Baruch to understand our problems deeply, and, in face of the P.M.'s pressing us to say just what we wanted, complete discretion became impracticable. Nevertheless, we did manage to keep down to very broad ideas. The course of the discussion is best summarised perhaps under the following heads:–

(1) Baruch started off from the point of view that we were greatly exaggerating our difficulties. He treated the British Empire, of course, as a single unit and urged that our performance in the war indicated that we had nothing in the world to be afraid of. He had been pumping all this hard into the P.M. during a week-end visit at Chequers. This did not mean, however, that he was not a sincere sympathiser and anxious and willing to do anything which was really and truly necessary.

(2) He asked us what the dimensions of our post-war requirements were likely to be. We mentioned $7 billion more or less according to the length of the war and other unpredictable circumstances. It was interesting that this did not take him at all by surprise. He said that $7 billion was exactly the figure which the President had mentioned to him as what the President had thought our requirements would be. Where exactly the President got this figure from I do not know.

(3) We pointed out that the question of terms was at least as important as the amount. It was the subsequent burden of the debt, taken in conjunction with our other existing obligations, which was at the bottom of our anxiety.

[14] William Maxwell Aitken (1879–1964), 1st Baron Beaverbrook 1917; M.P. (U.) Ashton-under-Lyme, 1910–16; Chancellor Duchy of Lancaster and Minister of Information, 1918; Minister for Aircraft Production, 1940–1; Minister of State, 1941; Minister of Supply, 1941–2; Lord Privy Seal, 1943–5.

(4) I then ventured on the proposition that the only practicable way out was a general reconsideration of our indebtedness, the United States facilitating this by a contribution, provided that the other countries concerned were also prepared to put up something substantial into the pool. It took a long time to get just what we meant into his head. He remained, I think, quite muddled whether, in the event of our needing $7 billion from U.S., we should need the whole of that as a free contribution and no part as a loan, or whether we could do with something smaller as a free gift, if others also contributed. I vaguely indicated that we should not necessarily need all that as an absolutely free gift, but I am not sure whether he took the point, and there seemed no harm in leaving a wide fringe of complete vagueness in his mind. In the general conversation he showed great interest in this and did not commit himself one way or the other. Just as he was leaving, in a private word with myself he said he thought it might be a promising idea and would certainly bear it in mind. So perhaps no harm was done.

(5) Several times in the course of the evening he emphasised that the various problems to be solved must be taken in due order. The first problem was the German question. He complained, and with complete justice, that there was no point of decision, no organ or committee of any kind, by which progress would be made with the various discussions which are going on in the different capitals. He emphasised that this was the only thing he really cared about at the moment. I do not think he knew anything about dismemberment ideas. One of his pet notions in relation to reparations is that no exports whatever should be allowed in manufactured goods. How on earth Germany's imports are to be paid for seemed too rude a question to ask. Cherwell is also on the line that Germany should be allowed no manufactured exports. Indeed, in Baruch's mind the idea that both Germany and Japan, our pre-war competitors, should be entirely forbidden to have manufactured exports hereafter

is part of his ground for extreme optimism about our post-war position. You can make your own mental comment on how much this is worth in a realistic world.

(6) Baruch emphasised that there was, in his mind, a strict order of priority—(i) the German problem, as already mentioned; (ii) the American domestic reconversion problem; (iii) support to the British post-war economic strength; (iv) the requirements of the liberated countries.

(7) One of the reasons why we had started by wanting to be very discreet was the fear that Baruch might take back to the President matters of which Morgenthau had previously heard nothing. There is still, I am afraid, a risk of this. On the other hand, Baruch went out of his way to point out that he was merely present as a private individual, that all these matters should be exclusively discussed with Henry Morgenthau, and that he was most unwilling to appear to be poaching on Morgenthau's business. As we were breaking up I begged him to be very discreet as to how he used the conversation, and I think he well understands the position and is quite likely to take pains to see that all is well on Morgenthau's side. But it is perhaps well that I should send you this letter so that you know pretty well what passed.

(8) Baruch, as you are well aware, is now stone deaf, though I thought in other respects in rather remarkable form. The consequence is that in a noisy conversation round a dinner-table, with several people talking at once, a very large part of what was said passed him by. In fact, it was only when the P.M. stopped everyone talking and gave his own summary of the upshot of the argument, delivering straight into the instrument, that one could have any confidence that it had registered. Thus, except in its broadest outlines, the story which registered may not correspond too accurately to what actually passed.

I should mention that Winston was quite magnificent

throughout, in his very best form, taking a profound interest in our Treasury problems for once, thoroughly understanding the points at issue and at every stage supporting the line taken by the Chancellor against the carping critics.

My long memorandum, of which you had an early draft, has now been revised after a preliminary discussion with the Chancellor and others. The next proof will be in print, and I shall either be sending you one along with this letter or immediately afterwards. All this, as well as the above, remains Top Secret for the present. The Chancellor's idea is to give Winston a copy and try to get him convinced and satisfied with it before it is given a more general circulation amongst Ministers, except that I am to be free to let Max [Beaverbrook] have a copy and do my best on the forlorn hope of winning him over to commonsense, since everything would be much easier should that, by a miracle, prove possible.

Winston showed himself very conscious of the weaknesses of the personal situation in Washington and the reasons for it, as emphasised in your own letter. I imagine that Byrnes'[15] resignation, which has taken place since you wrote, makes matters worse, if possible. However, Washington moves in a steeper cycle than one has ever experienced anywhere else. If we are now at the nadir, that probably means that everything will be lovely about six months hence.

This has a certain bearing on the timing of Stage III discussions. At one time we were thinking of the early summer. More recently we have not had any clear discussion on the matter. What are your views? My feeling now is that September will be quite soon enough. I do not like the idea of such discussions overlapping with San Francisco.

Yours ever,
[copy not initialled]

[15] James Francis Byrnes (1879–1972); Associate Justice, U.S. Supreme Court, 1941–2; Director, Office of Economic Stabilisation, 1942–3; Director, Office of War Mobilisation, 1943–5; Secretary of State, 1945–7.

P.S. The Chancellor tells me that he is sending, through Winant, a short letter to Morgenthau putting him wise to the fact that there has been a conversation with Baruch and that the above general subjects were touched upon.

To R. H. BRAND, *13 April 1945*

My dear Bob,

In the light of your letter of April 1, which you sent me from Greenwood, and of other information coming to hand, we have been giving a good deal of thought in the last week or so to the timing of Stage III discussions. I enclose a copy of the final version of my memorandum and will be grateful if you will destroy the two earlier texts you have.

Today's sad news, alas, disposes of one of your reasons for pressing on as quickly as possible. But other of your reasons remain. In addition to these, the view is expressed in some quarters that it will be very desirable to get a decision from the Cabinet before the Cabinet breaks up for the purposes of a General Election.

Finally, there is the ardour of the Canadians for an early solution. Hume Wrong, who is over here in connection with the Dominions discussions and San Francisco, was in the Treasury this morning. We gave him reasons for not being too impatient, and perhaps he was satisfied with them. But he still emphasised the political danger in Canada of delaying a solution, especially if this leads to the currency of rumours that our policy may very well be along lines extremely objectionable to Canada. He told us that he had just heard from Ottawa that there is now a prospect of Mackintosh[16] and Towers coming over here in three or four weeks' time for

---

[16] William Archibald Mackintosh (1895–1970); member, National Employment Commission, Canada 1936–8; Research Adviser, Royal Commission on Dominion Provincial Relations, 1938–9; served in Departments of Finance and Reconstruction and of Supply, Ottawa, 1939–46; Professor of Economics, Queen's University, Kingston, 1927–51; Principal 1951–61.

some conversations. That is a distinct gain and will probably enable us to hold the fort there for a bit yet.

The reasons for not attempting to start before the summer are mainly the undesirability of overlapping with San Francisco. Unless the hot weather comes to be considered the appropriate date, I should say that early September is coming to look the most likely time for opening up. Do you feel that that is too late? And, taking account of there being a new President etc., do you think that anything earlier is really practicable?

You must appreciate that, whilst there have been some preliminary conversations with the Prime Minister, the plan of campaign is not yet through the Cabinet. Moreover, one is sometimes too much inclined to overlook the fact that, when everything has been cleared on this side, it still remains somewhat wildly improbable (all the more so with the loss of the President) that we shall really be able to pull off anything like this. It will all depend on being able to keep the discussion with the Americans simple enough and on broad enough lines. If only the Americans will lead us along the sort of lines suggested, I shall be fairly optimistic about bringing along the sterling area countries. The Chancellor had a discussion this morning with the Dominion representatives now here and expounded our general situation to them without, however, being anywhere near giving possible solutions. The atmosphere was very good indeed. I do not doubt that they will all be willing to play their part when it comes to it, if the part they are asked to play is reasonable and belongs to a really comprehensive solution.

There is a good deal of gossip about the political position here, which I should like to impart to you. But I think the above gives you the bones of the situation.

Yours ever,
[copy not initialled]

P.S. The above was written before I had got your important letter of April 5th. I will be replying to that at length after a discussion with the members of O.F. on Wednesday. No reason meanwhile to hold up this.

Now that the final text has reached you, please be free to show this to Lee and Goschen,[17] though I should like to see no breath of the proposals at this stage to outside the Treasury Delegation.

Brand's letter of 5 April brought a reply from Keynes, drafted after discussions with members of the overseas finance section of the Treasury and Sir Wilfrid Eady. Owing to the interest of the exchange, both letters are given in full.

From R. H. BRAND, *5 April 1945*

Dear Maynard,

Stage III

Thanks for your letter of March 22nd. I have read your memorandum with the greatest interest and appreciation. It is very clear, and considering the magnitude of the subject, very concise. I have also read Eady's comments to you in his letter of 27th of March.

The problem is such a perplexing and baffling one and has so many sides that I shall limit my comments almost entirely to those which concern this country. On the other hand, while it is perplexing, one simple fact stands out, that we have to be given or borrow large sums from somewhere, and yet have to restrict our total borrowings to what we think, using a large admixture of optimism in our thought, that we can stand. I have not shown your memorandum to anyone else or discussed it with anyone. My comments are as follows:

1. The problem, as I see it, divides itself into three heads—

(a) Our Eastern and Far Eastern expenditure after the war. I take it the utmost efforts will be made to reduce this, but that in any case it must be very considerable. I take it further that this will not be financed in any event out of dollars, but that we shall make arrangements by means of which it is met through additional sterling borrowings.

---

[17] H. K. Goschen, temporary Administrative Officer, Treasury, 1944; Treasury Representative in Washington, 1945.

(*b*) Dollars required immediately by holders of sterling balances in addition to their current earnings of dollars. From what you say (see page 16) [above p. 277] I imagine you think that if a quarter of our sterling balances were left liquid the equivalent of $2 million [?billion] might be shortly remitted to the United States. My own feeling is that countries like Egypt and India, unless pressure were put upon them, would certainly try to transfer as large a sum as possible to this country.

(*c*) Lastly there is the gap between our imports and exports. This I take it you would propose to cover so far as dollars are used:

(i) By any balance of the $3 million [billion] gift not absorbed by our sterling creditors;

(ii) By drawing on the $5 billion credit;

(iii) Presumably out of such amount of our gold and dollar balances as we feel we could spare.

If the above analysis is wrong, perhaps you would let me know.

2. Your proposals are quite rightly based on Justice. Clearly it is Justice that we should be relieved from a large part of our intolerable burden. But in a situation like this I feel that the saying of the nigger that 'There ain't no justice nowhere' is amply justified. What you propose that the United States should do for us may well be Justice on the assumption that she *ought* to have come into the war when we did. But this will never be a popular argument here or one which is desirable to stress or one we can carry far without provoking serious reactions. We can say that what you propose the United States should do, plus what we ask the holders of sterling balances to do, is, taken as a whole, something like Justice to us, and that as for the part we assign to the U.S. we ask it from her not because it is just but because she is rich and well able to do so, and because it is very much in her interests. My point in saying all this is that I doubt whether it will be wise to stress to the American people that what we propose is not only Justice to us, but also Justice for them. There can be and would be endless arguments about this. I asked Fred Eaton, the General Counsel of W.P.B., a night or two ago, why we could not emulate Congressional Committees and before giving reciprocal aid appoint a Select Committee of the House of Commons which should investigate American witnesses and demand figures of their gold holdings and of any investments in the U.K. that U.S. citizens had, so as to see whether we were really justified in giving the U.S. any reciprocal aid. He replied that this would be a very unfortunate argument to use. I asked why? He said because the cases were not the same. All Americans knew they had saved the United Kingdom from absolute destruction, whereas the opposite was not the truth, and this made the two cases not in the least comparable.

307

While therefore we can justify ourselves on the grounds that our burden is intolerable, and that for our part in the war we are fully entitled to be given a helping hand, I myself would consider it unwise to base our case on what the Americans would consider was the assumption that they had not played their full part in the war. The American political leaders might well put a scheme forward before their own people as an act of Justice to us, but we could not do so, however true it might be.

3. For these reasons, I do not think it will be easy to get a free grant of money as a sort of restitution on the lines suggested by you at the top of page 20 [above p. 281]. If they were to give it, the Americans would certainly regard it as an act, not of justice, but of generosity. For this reason I should have preferred something that looked a little less like a free gift. Have you abandoned altogether the idea that the U.S. might take over a portion of our sterling balances? Supposing they were to take over $3 billions of them, this would in fact be not very different from our scheme, but their generosity would be mixed up as between ourselves and the holders of the equivalent sterling balances. The Americans might find it easier to be generous to others rather than ourselves, and personally I think it would suit us to have as little of their generosity as possible, though it is largely a question of dressing up. Many Americans seem exceedingly nervous about the effect of our huge sterling balances on our and their exports respectively, and certainly their exporters might well be pleased with such an arrangement. It would go far in any case to solve that part of our problem I refer to in section 1 (b) of this letter. Or possibly the U.S. might take over $3 billion of sterling balances and make a grant of $1 billion free to us.

4. There would then remain the import–export gap under section 1 (c) of this letter. I take it you intend the borrowing facility of say $5 billion at one per cent with a one per cent sinking fund after ten years to be utilised for this purpose. I do not know how far you calculate that we may have to call on this, or whether you have in mind possible other credit arrangements with other countries which might absolve us from the necessity of borrowing very largely in dollars. I would have thought myself that, if we borrow only from North America after the end of the war for means of payment of current imports, we should have to use a very considerable part of this facility, on the assumption that the rest of the sterling area would take at least $2 billion of your $3 billion referred to in above paragraph 3.

I don't know what estimates there are now as to the gap between external payments and receipts, but surely it must be very large to start with. Are there any figures which you take as a basis?

I recognise all the difficulties of borrowing elsewhere. From that point of view the world is a very small place. What one would wish would be that the countries supplying our bulk imports should be those which would finance them for us. For them to be able to do this they must, I fear, be prepared to give us long-term credit at exceptionally low rates, and they must be able to do so, i.e. their balance of payments position should be such as would enable them to do so. They would also be countries to whom we already owe a lot and with whom we must suppose we had just entered on some arrangement as regards existing debt in the manner described by you. This would hardly be an auspicious start to new borrowing. Nevertheless times are abnormal and our bargaining power in respect to imports should be, one might hope, considerable, though competition from Europe might diminish it for the time being. My detestation of borrowing huge sums from this country is so great that I would like to hope that the problem might be mitigated to some degree by borrowing elsewhere. But I am free to admit the difficulties are no doubt great. Nevertheless would not, for instance, Australia and New Zealand be able to do something considerable?

5. You must bear in mind that, notwithstanding your statements here about our $12 billion indebtedness, this country as a whole is entirely ignorant of the immensity of our problem. The Administration knows the facts from all the information that we gave them during the Stage II negotiations, but no one else does, and there would certainly have to be a lot of education, before the plan you suggest would get general approval here. Milo Perkins was telling me today that the vast propaganda campaign for Bretton Woods in his opinion is convincing the public that, if Bretton Woods passes, all is finished, and *our* problem, like everyone else's, is solved.

6. It is difficult for various reasons to make any very definite recommendations about timing and method of approach. I do not dissent from your view that in a matter of this importance the first approach may have to be from the Prime Minister to the President, but it is quite certain that the President would immediately pass it on to Morgenthau and, I suppose, the State Department. The President is immensely overburdened and he is ill. Harry Hopkins is ill. The latter may be back in about three weeks, but how well he will be then, I do not know. If he is back in three weeks, I think myself it would be a good thing if I were to sound Harry as to what he regarded as the best method of procedure. One could do that without indicating the nature of the plan. What is, of course, highly important, is that any negotiations with the President and his advisers should be absolutely secret.

The difficulties O. L[yttelton] and J. J. L[lewellin] are finding at this

309

moment in discovering anyone at all to deal with except Crowley is symptomatic of a serious disease in Washington. If the President gets worse and not better, the disease cannot but spread.

As to timing, my own view remains that, subject to your preparations being sufficiently complete, we should broach the subject not too long after the end of the German war. There is one big uncertainty in this. Your figures are, I gather, based on the assumption that the Japanese war ends at the beginning of 1946. It may end then or earlier or, in my opinion, a good deal later. If the Japanese are really going to fight to the death, it might well be a good deal later. Personally I have never yet seen any worked-out strategic plan for the final defeat of Japan. Admiral Leahy was emphasising to us the other day what an immense task was the invasion at 6,000 miles distance of Japan proper against say an army of 3 million Japanese stationed there.

7. I believe you are right that the United States will recognise that it is in its highest interests to help us on the road to financial and economic recovery, but the growing immensity of the demands on it from abroad is certainly beginning to affect public opinion here. You know what the psychology of the business world is. It is no good saying you can easily afford from the point of view of your exchange all this. What troubles them is the size of the national debt. About this they get more and more apprehensive, and will continue to do so, as long as the Japanese war continues. On the other hand at some point the question of unemployment will enter on the other side. All this may be an argument for our getting the facilities we determine upon before public opinion gets more alarmed about the burden of the debt than it is now. But on timing no Englishman's view would be anything like as good as H.H.'s.

Yours
R. H. BRAND

To R. H. BRAND, *24 April 1945*

My dear Bob,

Stage III

I have been giving close consideration to your letter of April 5th. On broad lines I am in agreement, but there are a good many details on which I should like to comment, including one or two important ones where I am not clear that our minds have, so far, completely met. My references are to the paragraphs of your letter.

1(*a*). Yes, the idea is that our Eastern and Far Eastern expenditure after the war should be met by sterling borrowings. But, if my proposals were carried out in full, it would be still better than this. In the estimates I have assumed for the various sterling area balances at the end of the war I have included upwards of £500 million for demobilisation and the clearing up and arrear expenditure which would actually be incurred after cease fire in Asia. My idea is that the proposed settlement should be reached on the basis, not of the actual figures of the balances at the date when it takes place, but on an assumed final figure. In other words, it would be implicitly covering further borrowings on an assumed scale.

1(*b*). Yes. My suggestion was that, if we made a certain part of sterling balances convertible on the lines suggested, we might expect to lose on balance in terms of dollars the equivalent of (say) $2 billion. But this would not necessarily mean, in my opinion, that the convertible sterling area balances would fall by the sterling equivalent of this. By making some part of the existing sterling balances and all accretions to them convertible we should make the holding of sterling attractive, and I should expect that, in certain cases at any rate, we should gain sterling. Thus, whilst we might have to find $2 billion out of our American resources, a part of this might be balanced by increased borrowings in the shape of sterling balances from the sterling area itself. Therefore, in terms of the U.K. adverse balance of trade with the outside world after cease fire, we could reckon a net loss of less than $2 billion.

I think it possible, however, (both here and in a later passage in your letter) that I have not made sufficiently clear what I mean by convertible sterling. I am using the term in a Pickwickian, that is to say Bretton Woods, sense. It does not mean that the sterling area countries can take their balances away for any purpose whatever, e.g. to turn them into gold or to set up a dollar reserve of their own in New York. The convertibility in question would be *de facto* convertibility for money required to finance current transactions. Thus, it would amount net to the adverse balance of the rest of the sterling area with the United States on current account. In fact, everything would proceed as at present, except that there would be no pressure from us on the rest of the sterling area to refrain from any purchase in the United States which they considered themselves rich enough to make, and equally no pressure to buy preferentially in the sterling area as compared with North America, except in gradual liquidation of their funded sterling debt. It will, however, be important to get quite clear in our own minds just what we mean by 'convertibility' in this context. Many technical difficulties are raised, and there is more work to be done before we can be precise.

1(c). Yes, this analysis is correct. I am assuming that our gold and dollar balances may be of the order of $2 billion. Thus, we should hold $5 billion ($2 + $3) in liquid cash without any obligation of repayment. My own advice would be that we should dip heavily into this and not make any use of the $5 billion credit until the $5 billion cash had shrunk to something more like $1½ billion, which we might treat as bedrock in the present context. I think the Treasury would be well advised to exercise the utmost pressure on the Departments and all others concerned before drawing on the $5 billion credit.

2. I have no doubt you are right here about the most advisable line of approach in U.S.A. You must remember that the present document is primarily addressed to critical members of the Cabinet here and is putting the case primarily from our point of view. I contemplate that a different sort of paper would be prepared and used for U.S.A. I should not by any means omit the appeal to Justice. If not in U.S. (though there also), certainly in the rest of the sterling area, the argument from Justice is a considerable element in our case. But certainly one should give more attention to empha-

sising the advantages to U.S.A. than I have given in this paper as compared with the advantage to the U.K. I feel one has to proceed on both lines of advance: There are some people to whom the argument from Justice will appeal. But, even they will be extremely anxious that there should be an argument from the self-advantage of the U.S.A. to which they can call the attention of less friendly critics. The remark you repeat from Fred Eaton is not only instructive but, I should say, representative, and tells us exactly what they do feel.

3. I myself started originally with something very much on the lines that you suggest, namely, that instead of a free grant the U.S. should take over sundry portions of our sterling balances. From the free gift point of view this comes, of course, to exactly the same thing. But, on further reflection, and that is I believe the view generally shared here, I have come to prefer very strongly the alternative set forth in the paper. And I believe that this alternative can be demonstrated to be better from the U.S.A. point of view as well as from ours. The point is this. Under my plan the $3 billion comes into the sterling area pool and, with that assistance behind us, we are able to offer convertibility to such part of the balances as are not funded or cancelled, and to all future accruing balances, which is the matter above all on which the Americans have set their heart. Whilst the Americans gain the freedom of the sterling area for their trade, we, for our part, hold the sterling area together intact and do not encourage even the beginning of the dangerous habit of their keeping separate dollar reserves. If, on the other hand, your alternative is suggested, this is dangerously near being the beginning of breaking up the sterling area and encouraging its members to hold reserves in New York as well as in London. Moreover, the money will not go nearly so far. We forthwith lose the $3 billion, some of which will probably not be required during the transitional period; whilst, on the other hand, some recipients will overspend their share of the $3 billion,

unless we forbid them to do so, and draw on our pool. In short, it means breaking up the whole conception of the dollar pool for the sterling area. I had not meant to go so far as this. It would certainly mean a greater likelihood of our having to draw on the supplementary $5 billion. It would also probably mean we should have to keep up a more rigorous exchange control than would otherwise be necessary and would find it difficult to accord to Americans that measure of convertibility, which is the main prize they can attain by falling in with our ideas. You will remember that we made some progress in persuading the State Department that the S.A. dollar pool was in their interest as well as in ours.

I do not go so far as to say that, if the Americans show a very great preference for your variant and would accept that, whilst rejecting mine, I would advise refusal. But I should regard it as very definitely a second-best, most certainly not to be brought to the front at the present stage. If they do bring it up, then I should certainly try for some further variant, such as that which you suggest in the last sentence of your paragraph 3.

4. In my own opinion, the supplementary $5 billion is rather an outside figure. We might well do with considerably less than this, and it might do us good to be compelled to do with less than this. If, therefore, in the course of negotiation, it got cut down to $3 billion, or even $2 billion I should not repine. All the same, it might be better to set out with a larger figure, which gave some margin. The object is not so much that we should borrow this—I would pray that we could do without it—but to give us that measure of confidence which we should need, not only to accept convertibility, but, having accepted it, to carry on without too much repression and control.

You ask whether we should contemplate borrowing from other countries. Certainly this would not be ruled out, but it would probably come to chicken feed compared with the North American contribution. You are not, of course, overlooking the proposed $500 million from Canada? I have already mentioned in relation to your 1(*b*) that we might well find ourselves borrowing some more from the sterling area, provided we were feeling strong enough to give them convertibility. In addition, there are the European neutrals, with whom we either have or intend to have agreements, which might have a credit clause to them; and the same applies to the South American countries. If necessary, I should suppose that all these sources could mount up to somewhere between $½ and $1 billion. There is, moreover, a constant trickle of resources from the liquidation or paying off of our remaining foreign investments. On the other hand, there is also the outward trickle of new foreign investments essential for the development of our industries and overseas enterprise generally. One of the reasons why one would wish to have a little elbow-room is that it is, I am convinced, to the very great advantage of the U.K. that we should feel free to be not unduly repressive to new overseas enterprises which require a capital contribution. I should like to see us investing abroad in the shape of new money or new credit at least £50 million a year. One of the greatest disadvantages of Starvation Corner, which I might have emphasised still more in my original paper, is that it will deprive us of this possibility.

You will see that I agree with you whole-heartedly that the borrowing of large sums from U.S. should be regarded as an absolutely last resort. The purpose of the $5 billion is not to use it, but to gain comfort and courage from the fact it is there to be used if necessary. I should measure the success of our overseas financial policy after the war by the smallness of the degree to which we called upon it.

5. God knows how we can best attempt the education of public opinion. I fear that what you say about Bretton Woods is only too true. In fact, from the point of view of getting through this further plan, we have to confess in the privacy of our own closets that nothing would suit us better than the rejection of Bretton Woods, though I am more and more

convinced that that will not happen, quite apart from the fact that good faith requires that we should lend the plan all the support in our power. If we could obtain general sympathy in high quarters in Washington, then there might be a good deal to be said in favour of taking Congressional leaders into the secret at an early stage. But, confessedly, I am out of my depth here.

6. The death of the President puts all this out of the picture. I shall be extremely interested to hear from you, as no doubt we shall be hearing before long, how the tactics ought to be adapted to the new set-up. Am I right in supposing that Byrnes will be the key figure?

On timing you will have had my previous letter of April 13th. Do you think that early September would be soon enough? Obviously the new Administration, or that part of it which is new, must be allowed to find its feet, and there are also Bretton Woods, San Francisco and the Lend Lease Appropriations to be got out of the way.

I now turn to your subsequent letter of April 9th to Eady on the same subject. You will see that I am entirely of your mind that we should borrow no more from U.S. than is unavoidable. I also agree that we shall have to indicate general sympathy with the Americans on commercial policy, though I shall be extremely surprised if this is in a sufficiently cut-and-dried form for any kind of commitment so soon as next September. The various elements in the policy of trying to march with the U.S. in the post-war economic set-up all hang together. A major argument would be that we were doing our damnedest to reach the greatest common measure of agreement with them on currency matters, on commercial policy and all associated issues. The proposed solution would enable us to march with them side by side. On the other hand, if they reject anything of this kind, then we should have to fall back on a second-best solution, as distasteful to us as it would be objectionable to them.

In fact, the doubts and hesitations which your letters suggest as a background to a general agreement to move along these lines are shared by me, and, I might add, by me not least. I regard the difficulty of putting all this across as quite enormous. What will finally come out is likely to be materially different, and it will be extraordinarily difficult not to be led into some unbalanced settlement, which we shall subsequently regret. Various versions of Temptation will always be lying round the corner.

But all such difficulties we must face when we meet them. The first step is to agree amongst ourselves what would do and to persuade the Cabinet and others concerned so that we can present a united front. That is the stage which we are at now. If this stage is successfully surmounted, that will be, of course, only one-tenth of the battle. In the later stage an elastic mind will be needed, but a mind not too elastic. We must never lose sight of what is fundamental and what is not.

Finally, there is your supplementary note of April 9th reporting your conversation with Milo Perkins.[18] I believe that Milo Perkins, as you report him, is entirely right. And the fact that the alternative is so extremely unsatisfactory is probably the biggest argument of all for the plan. Perhaps, however, as I have suggested above, you are exaggerating in your mind exactly what I mean by 'freeing the whole sterling area from exchange control at the end of one year'. The convertibility I have in view is, as I have explained above, qualified. The object is to give the Americans the substance of what they want without our undertaking a risk which might prove excessive.

Discussions of the paper here in Ministerial circles have just begun, and so far not without success.

Yours ever,
[copy initialled] M. K.

---

[18] The conversation had been concerned with American businessmen's fears that the existence of sterling balances and discriminatory exchange controls would affect their post-war sales prospects. [Ed.]

Another letter from Brand carried the discussion a stage further.

From R. H. BRAND, *25 April 1945*

Dear Maynard,

Thanks for your letter of April 13th just received, which I have read with the greatest interest. The timing of Stage III is a subject which is always in my mind, and I see no other course but to write to you from time to time putting the matter, as I see it, at any particular moment, but with possibly very changing views. If one waits, till one has some firm opinion on this extremely difficult matter, one may wait forever. I therefore send you some of my present thoughts. The main matters I want to touch on are: (*a*) the scope of any agreement with the U.S.; (*b*) procedure; (*c*) timing. I may say here that in general I fully support the main lines of your plan, subject to certain qualifications I made in my letter of April 5th. I feel myself that the only possible solution is a sort of general reconstruction plan. Even under 'Starvation Corner' we should have to carry out ourselves perhaps unilaterally a still more drastic reconstruction, so far as our sterling creditors were concerned. We have got to convince the world that what we are asking for is not generosity, for which we ought to feel undying gratitude, but only justice. But to put that over requires a vast deal of education, at least in this country, and I imagine not less in India and Egypt.

2. As regards (*a*), i.e. scope, I might perhaps start by saying that I have often thought particularly recently that to get a full and satisfactory agreement for the redistribution of the cost of the war, which you quite rightly think is necessary, we ought not to hurry our negotiations, and that there might be merit even in fixing up some temporary interim arrangement to carry us on for a year or more after lend lease, during which time we should have more leisure to make our full position understood by the world at large. So very few people in this or in any other country appreciate this now, or understand at all that, as you say, we might face a burden after the war of the same sort of order of magnitude as the Russians, for instance, would like to place on Germany, or that we should pay over many years the same reparations for winning the war as they would for losing it. The success of any negotiations here would be so much easier, if the impossibility from our point of view of settlements of a kind which might now be thought reasonable by many reasonable but ignorant people, was fully recognised by all concerned. Any such process of enlightenment and education would take quite a time, rapid as are the high pressure methods of 'selling' any ideas under the sun to this nation at any rate. Possibly when we start our negotiations with the Americans this idea of a

temporary arrangement to give us more time, might be worth pursuing. I put it forward for what it is worth. A further advantage in not being in too great a hurry to come to a financial settlement would be that we should know more clearly what our total position was likely to be by the end of the Japanese war. I should add a still further advantage. That it should become quite clear to American exporters, e.g. of cotton, tobacco, etc. that left to ourselves, the last place from which we should be able to buy such products would be the U.S., would be extremely salutary. Pressure groups would without question begin to press very hard. But it wants a little time for all this to sink in sufficiently deeply.

  If however we proceed to try and fix up the whole matter at one blow, then the scope of the first negotiations will have to be very wide. I limit myself to this country. It seems to me that a plan like yours may be compared to the drastic reconstruction of a company, and the putting in of new money. Even if they get a prior lien charge the parties who put in the new money are always concerned with the whole new set up since it is important to them that the company should be sufficiently cleared of all old dead wood, so that it can make its way in the future. But in this case the party putting up the new money is certainly not getting a prior lien charge; indeed exactly the opposite for the first $3 billion, and then only ranking equally with other creditors for the balance. The U.S. are therefore, or at least should be, and, I think, will be vitally concerned, particularly in view of their commercial policy ideas, in seeing that our reconstruction as a whole enables us to get along, enables us at some reasonable date to return to convertibility, and generally makes it possible for us to face the economic and financial future; in fact that the reconstruction plan should be a good one. I should imagine therefore that the U.S. Government would not agree to any such plan as yours without knowing what we should be able to do with all our sterling creditors. In fact I would hope that they might bring in some way or other very great pressure to bear on the sterling creditors to accept a reasonable plan, in the same way in which those putting new money into a company usually act towards old creditors (though ours are not very old!) It seems to me more than likely that the U.S. Government will want to say to Congress 'We have told the British we will do this and that, if all the rest of the world will do so and so'. Otherwise they might be in the position in which we may be, as you say, with regard to Germany, of putting money in on the one side and leaving the Russians to take it out on the other. You will remember that I have always thought that at some moment the U.S. and Canada will say 'Why hasn't the rest of the British Empire given at any rate to the utmost of their power lend lease like the U.S. and Canada have? Why should they expect to get all their money back when it is apparently assumed that we shan't get any of it back at all?' This makes the attitude that I describe above still more likely. I recognise that separate negotiations will be required with each sterling creditor, and therefore that no general plan can be imposed upon them all. But it may well be that we shall not be able to complete our U.S. arrangements, before we have tied up our other creditors and that the U.S. may ask—for our benefit—that they should accept certain conditions which otherwise we might find it difficult to impose upon them.

In another respect the scope of the negotiations must, it seems to me, to be very wide. I cannot conceive that the financial negotiations will be altogether divorced from the commercial negotiations. We are likely, therefore, to find ourselves in discussions which cover the whole both of our financial and economic policy in all quarters of the globe.

3. I now come to (b)—procedure. The advent of a new President, of course, changes the picture a great deal. His personality and background and his relative lack of experience, all indicate that the role of Congress will be very important. It would have been important even with the old President. It is likely to be much more important now. We have therefore to consider how to educate Congress, and also how to educate the public, since public opinion will greatly affect Congress. But before I come to that I should like to take up the question of how we broach the matter in the first instance. Your original plan was to go to F.D.R. and Harry Hopkins. Hopkins may still be of importance. (I enclose you a copy of a letter I received from him today.[19] I hope to see him shortly.) But how close he will be to Truman is still entirely unsettled. Morgenthau and White seem to be certain to be in office, at least until Bretton Woods is over, although many good judges doubt Morgenthau lasting indefinitely. The matter is of such importance that I would suggest that it would still have to be broached in the first instance somehow right at the top. Nevertheless we must assume that Truman would naturally immediately refer the whole thing to his advisers, and in this case the ones we should do best to rely upon seem to be Morgenthau, Harry White, and Clayton.[20] Crowley, if he stays, might have, I fear, to come in also to some extent.

Presumably the procedure would then be to have: (i) confidential discussions with the U.S. Administration; (ii) broad agreement on a plan; (iii) a campaign to 'sell' the plan to Congress and the country. This would be following the procedure now being adopted with regard to Bretton Woods.

[19] Not printed. This letter was a reply to Brand's letter of sympathy following President Roosevelt's death. [Ed.]
[20] William Lockhart Clayton (1880-1966); Federal Loan Administration and Vice-President, Export-Import Bank, 1940-2; Assistant Secretary of State, 1944-5; Under-Secretary of State for Economic Affairs, 1945-7.

It is with this last point, and still more with what (if anything) should precede it that I am concerned. We cannot put over Stage III in the private sort of way Monnet put over his lend lease negotiations. A great reconstruction plan for the U.K., a redistribution of the cost of the war, so far as we are concerned, all tied up as they are likely to be with commercial policy, will necessarily provoke wide discussion here, and a lot of education will be needed. We shall not get firm support for such a plan without a full public debate in Congress and in the Press in which our whole position will be canvassed, including our external sterling debt. This may have awkward repercussions, but I do not see how it is to be avoided. Our sterling creditors will necessarily get a clearer idea of our whole position than they have ever had before—for good or ill. If this is accompanied by a reasonable settlement with the U.S. and Canada, this should in the end do good.

Meanwhile should we do anything more to educate the completely ignorant public? I think we should, insofar as, in doing so, we do not embarrass ourselves. When you were at Bretton Woods you let out the amount of our external sterling debt. The main question, which remains to my mind, is whether we should say things, or allow other people to say things, which indicate the sort of order of magnitude of our adverse balance of payments in the first few years of the transition period. You will have seen I was very careful in dealing with this point in my speech to the Bond Club, though anyone who took the trouble to read it carefully could gather a good deal. It is this point, plus the external expenditure, which we are *necessarily* incurring in fighting Japan, which are the important ones. It is also important to explain at this juncture that if the Bretton Woods plans go through this does not wholly solve all U.K. problems. This is a very generally held opinion. I should like to have the Treasury's views and yours on how far one can go in these directions.

If the idea of some education now in the facts is agreed to, my idea would be to get some articles written in, say, *Foreign Affairs*, *Atlantic Monthly*, *Yale Review*, etc., which will indicate to those who can easily understand the character of our problems. If the elite understand, the knowledge will fairly soon begin to trickle down over a wide area covering many of those, who make public opinion. A more ambitious line would be to have a really good article, say, in *Life*. In addition one could stimulate Walter Lippmann and a few others to take the right road, and take steps to see some leading Congressmen and Senators.

4. Lastly there is (*c*), i.e. timing. We must certainly wait till after Bretton Woods, San Francisco and the Lend Lease Appropriations. The attitude of Congress with regard to these latter will give a good indication as to their

present very uninformed attitude. Their general idea appears to be that with the end of the German war lend lease practically comes to an end. Who can blame them much, since they know nothing of our story at any rate? It may well be that the situation will not be a very favourable one for beginning the conversations even as early as September. I do not think we can decide at the moment. But I would say now that anything before September is likely to be too early. A good deal will depend on how Congress behaves in the next few months. The Administration is very jittery, but it always is at this time of year. Nevertheless the accumulation of claims on the U.S. gives them some ground for a little nervousness. They have to face Bretton Woods, Export/Import Bank, lend lease for still more countries, UNRRA, Military Relief (Germany and Italy in particular), Russian and Chinese reconstruction, and the Japanese war. The position is all the more awkward, since we shall as far as possible be limiting our liabilities while still expecting to be full partners, e.g. Military Relief. It is thus a bad time to come forward with additional huge demands. This is an additional reason why I have turned over in my mind some temporary carrying over of the position.

In the same connection I would like to ask you a question. I take it you do not see any great difficulty in opening negotiations because of the indefiniteness of the end of the Japanese war? Clearly we are going to be involved still in immense expenditure abroad as long as that war lasts, and we shall have to get more and more into debt, at any rate with part of the sterling area, while it continues. We shall not know therefore what our whole position is going to be at the end of the war. On the other hand it remains true that even when we do know the end of the war is near we shall not know what our whole position during the next two or three years after that will be. So perhaps waiting till we know the whole story is a hopeless quest. I note you make a certain provision as regards our sterling indebtedness for the Japanese war going on, but whether it is enough, heaven only knows! However I hope to write you some further comments on your amended plan itself shortly.

As against the above I understand Stettinius has committed himself to call an International Trade Conference this year, though whether this means 1945 or within a year from now, I do not know. If I am right that we cannot settle commercial policy without knowing how we stand in surmounting the transition period, this commits us to beginning discussion of this latter problem before very long.

5. All this is pretty tentative. To some extent everything seems to me to depend on how long we can continue our rake's progress of getting facilities from lots of countries and crediting them with blocked sterling.

On this I have no opinion worth anything. If we cannot, that would change everything. If, as I am inclined to assume, we can, provided the Japanese war does not go on too long, there is something to be said for continuing the rake's progress and merely making the final bust-up bigger, just as a banker, living on his credit, has to continue in his too big house and travel first-class, when he knows he can't afford it. We are certainly in a very difficult position here to negotiate, when we continue to spend oceans of money in the Far East, when we have to continue to pose in occupying Germany, Italy, in looking after Saudi Arabia, etc. etc., as equal partners with the U.S. and the U.S.S.R., but have to tell the former we can't pay our bills.

Yours,

R. H. BRAND

To R. H. BRAND, *3 May 1945*

My dear Bob,

Stage III
Your letter of 25 April

1. I would rather accept some temporary, interim arrangement, in the hope of getting something fully satisfactory later on, than accept an unsatisfactory solution in a hurry. On the other hand, there would, I think, be great inconveniences in putting off any longer than we need if we can help it. For example, our import programme, particularly food, could not be arranged on other than extreme austerity lines until we had the satisfactory solution. We should also have to discriminate against American exports in a way which might create friction as well as pressure. Generally speaking, we should have to carry on the war-time regime during a period when there would be special pressure for its alleviation. And whether the psychological atmosphere will improve as time goes on for this purpose is a matter of opinion. The view is also held that we need to strike whilst the iron is hot, and that a really imaginative and far-reaching settlement will be impossible unless we can get on quickly.

None of this, however, qualifies what I began by saying,

namely that we should reject an unsatisfactory solution in the hope that the logic of events and a practical demonstration of what the position would be in the absence of a solution might bring about a better offer later on.

2. I agree with what you say about specifically linking up anything that the U.S. Government is asked to do with what the sterling creditors are at the same time asked to accept. If the Americans made their assistance contingent on certain action by the sterling creditors, I should regard this as positively an advantage. In our conversation with Baruch, which I reported to you, it was obvious that he immediately thought along those lines. It would not be possible to stipulate exactly what the others would do, because it is a matter of great complexity, and the plan could not be uniform. But, in broad terms, it could be provided that the $3 billion from the U.S. should be matched by cancellations by the sterling creditors of an at least equal amount.

3. I also agree with you that the scope of the negotiations must inevitably be wide. I would urge that as an additional reason against any avoidable delay. I hope we can avoid anything in the nature of a specific bargain. But we, on our side, must expect that the Americans will only play if we have reached satisfactory arrangements with them on Bretton Woods, on the commercial talks and probably on other matters also. Equally, if we do not get the financial settlement we consider we need, we might find it necessary to put off final conclusions on all the other matters, and that would be productive of great confusion and dispute.

4. The procedure would have, I think, to follow the general order you indicate in your paragraph 3. I am sure you are right that we cannot get the settlement we want in any hole and corner way. We must expect, and even welcome, a full public debate. And, as you say, it will be extraordinarily difficult to handle that wisely.

Meanwhile, I rather doubt whether it will be advisable to

do much more in the way of publicity than we have been doing in recent months. There is a danger of exhausting one's ammunition. There is also the danger of their getting unduly accustomed to our plaints so that repetition loses its effect. I think it would be useful to take opportunities of bringing up to date the sort of material you gave in your speech to the Bond Club, though there are great difficulties in giving any reasonable kind of forecast of the magnitude of our adverse balance of payments in the early transition period. I should hesitate to attempt that. If one is found to have over-stated one's case it does no good, whilst an under-statement may have an insufficient impact. Yet any estimate one could make now would be based on such inaccurate data that one or other of these alternatives would be almost inevitable.

On the other hand, I have probably, I think, made a sufficient allowance, unless the progress of the Japanese war disappoints us a great deal, in giving an end figure of £4,000 million for overseas indebtedness, including in this the cost of winding up operations as well as carrying them to a conclusion.

I fancy that the Canadians may be able to help a good deal in the matter of education. We all of us here have been much impressed by a recent address given by Rasminsky at Harvard.[21]

5. For my own part, I feel extremely doubtful whether Stettinius will bring off an International Trade Conference this year. For one thing, it will obviously depend on his success with the present measure before Congress. But, even if that goes through, there is a vast amount of frightfully difficult preliminary work to be done before such a conference could have a hope of success. I hope this is not wishful thinking, for it would certainly be better from our point of view that

[21] See L. Rasminsky, 'Anglo-American Trade Prospects: A Canadian View', *Economic Journal*, LI (2–3), June–September, 1945.
　　L. Rasminsky (b. 1908); Chairman: Foreign Exchange Control Board, Canada; delegate to Bretton Woods Conference, 1944; Governor, Bank of Canada, 1961–73.

such a conference should take place next year, after we have had an opportunity of promulgating our own Stage III arrangements, than in the autumn of this year.

6. In reply to your paragraph 5, I have no doubt that we can successfully continue our rake's progress of living on the sterling area so long as the war lasts. But, as soon as goods and transport become more freely available, I much doubt whether we could carry on except at the cost of allowing our gold and dollar reserves to run down somewhat rapidly.

Yours ever,
[copy not initialled]

Very nice letter from Harry Hopkins, of which you sent me a copy. I do hope he will still be able to play a part. If his health holds, I should have thought it quite possible that he might; not, of course, quite in the old way, but nevertheless with significant effect.

P.S. Commenting on the draft of this letter, Eady has noted that, in his opinion, we should not contemplate an 'interim arrangement'. He points out that it is not easy to see it taking any other form than some credit line, e.g. like the Canadian scheme. Despite the risks and inconveniences, he thinks we ought to contemplate coming away without a solution unless we have a satisfactory one. We must remember that the Americans will not like leaving the situation as it is because we should have virtually to block the sterling balances. On further consideration, it seems to me that there is a great deal in this. I had not really thought of an interim arrangement as including temporary borrowing, but surely Eady is right that this is what it would mean. It is much better that we and the Americans alike should be forced right up against the realities of the situation. Thus our right line would be to say that, if they cannot fall in with our plan, then we must do our best to live on our own resources. Maybe that the Americans will not welcome the consequences. But nor shall we ourselves.

A revised print of my main memorandum on Stage III is now being prepared. Certain passages have been omitted which it was thought might cause alarm and despondency in the minds of certain Ministers, e.g. the President of the Board of Trade and the Secretary of State for War, or the Dominions Secretary. Apart from the omission of these peccant passages, there have been no changes except that the 7th Section has been re-written in the light of the later circumstances, as in the attached text.

The Canadians are arriving at the end of next week, though, unfortunately, without Clifford Clark. We are all of us going off to Cambridge for the weekend, where we shall hope to get a couple of days quiet and continuous conversation. The idea is that we shall expound pretty frankly our whole line of thought as set forth in the Stage III memorandum.

As noted above (p. 303), before Keynes's Stage III paper received general ministerial circulation, the Chancellor sent copies to Lord Beaverbrook and Cherwell. At the evening meeting with Mr Baruch (above p. 300), Keynes suggested to Lord Beaverbrook that they have 'a long quiet conversation ...about it so as to get down to fundamentals, and see whether, after all, there is much more common ground than appears on the surface'. Beaverbrook agreed to have a talk after he had read the paper. On reading it, Beaverbrook sent Keynes two letters, the second of which asked a series of questions, which Keynes answered at a meeting they had on the evening of 19 April. Keynes described the meeting to R. H. Brand, in another letter, dated 3 May, as follows:

This passed off amicably and successfully. He was in a quiet and reasonable mood, admitted the force of the arguments, and agreed that, if we could get such a plan, he would favour it, although, in his opinion, it would mean that we should have to sacrifice many points which he holds dear.

After the meeting, Beaverbrook wrote to Keynes.

From LORD BEAVERBROOK, *20 April 1945*

My dear Keynes,

I fear that we shall concede the Bretton Woods situation with all its implications. We shall then be required to go on with the commercial policy with all its limitations.

We shall find ourselves (1) tied to the Gold Standard; (2) committed to a limitation of agriculture; (3) sacrificing Imperial Preference; and (4) bringing about a change in the status of the sterling bloc.

And after all that, we shall not be able to get our bargain through with the U.S.

If we could be sure of the bargain with the concessions, I should be in favour of it. Yours ever,

B

To LORD BEAVERBROOK, *27 April 1945*

My dear Beaverbrook,

Thank you for your letter of 20 April and especially for the last sentence. If the Americans reject any plan on the proposed lines and also any reasonable variant on it, assuredly we shall all have to think again—somewhat furiously.

But there will be plenty of opportunity for that. What we should be offering under the plan would be an undertaking of *de facto* convertibility within a year, instead of waiting, as we are entitled under the Bretton Woods Plan, for a transitional period of indefinite duration. If they reject the plan, they certainly cannot expect the transitional period to come to an end until we have managed to recover our equilibrium in the very adverse circumstances which would inevitably result from this rejection. In other words, they would fail to get, here and now, the kind of post-war world they want.

To that extent what we should be offering is unquestionably in the nature of a *bargain*. Moreover, we should not, in my opinion, commit ourselves irrevocably to the policies you mention until we know that the Americans accept the necessity of their finding means to make such policies possible for us. But in point of form I believe that we should be wise, in general, to try to keep one thing separate from another. It is conceivable that the Americans with whom we shall be dealing, or some of them, may think fit to introduce various extraneous issues into the picture in some rather crude way; but I do not think we should encourage that.

As you know, I do not interpret the effect of the policies under discussion just as you do, although I sympathise whole-heartedly with the anxieties in your mind. I am not less adverse to the gold standard than I was when I was fighting to destroy it; it is essential that we retain exchange elasticity. I am passionately in favour of keeping what agriculture had gained during the war. I value Imperial Preference and would sacrifice no more than is inevitable on account of the changed views of the Dominions and their anxiety to come to terms with U.S. A primary object in my mind is to restore the strength of the pre-war sterling area and regain London's hegemony, which, if we handle ourselves right, should be possible in spite of everything.

But, as you know, I believe that—

(1) Bretton Woods is far removed from the gold standard, as indeed the American bankers justly affirm;

(2) From what I hear, we shall have no difficulty in keeping all the protection we need for agriculture (the peasant-farming countries will need so much more than we need);

(3) I do not anticipate that we shall have to give up Imperial Preference as a principle, and large concessions are anyhow inevitable because the Dominions themselves are quite determined that their own interests require them.

(4) There is nothing in the status of the pre-war sterling bloc which we are asked to surrender. On the other hand, no-one will go on banking with us if we cannot honour our cheques without qualification; and a renewed strength to do that is just what the plan would gain for us.

Thus I see no reason why you should be unduly anxious, provided the plan comes off. We have a devilish difficult row to hoe, and it is only by the most delicate and far-sighted handling that we shall manage. And if you look on the other side of the picture, is not the prospect, if we fail, a cause for far greater anxiety? Do you really favour a barter system of trade which would mean, in practice, something very near a state monopoly of imports and exports *à la Russe?* Do you welcome an indefinite continuance of strict controls and (probably) severer rationing than we have now? Will you applaud the retrenchment of colonial development? Do you look forward to our stepping down, for the time being, to the position of a second-class power which entirely lacks the financial resources for playing a part in the outside world?

I set all this against your (1), (2), (3) and (4).

> Yours ever,
> [copy initialled] K

Throughout May, Brand continued to correspond with Keynes on Stage III, reporting on the personalities of the new American administration. As he put it on 3 May,

> You will see, therefore, that everything is likely to be in a considerable flux for some months here, but that the keynote of the whole show is also likely to be mediocrity and generally somewhat provincial views. This is not likely to suit us.

From this, Keynes concluded, in a letter to Brand on 11 May

> that we must give the new [Truman] Administration time to settle down before we crystallise our own plans. But my general conclusion remains that we want to proceed exactly as we have been contemplating, facing what is a probability that, in the first round, we shall not have much success. We must be prepared for rebuffs and not be too willing to alter our plans in the face of them. With enough persistance we shall get our way...But, as you point out only too clearly, we are likely to be dealing with provincials who will be slow to see the picture in a wide perspective.

Both returned to Stage III tactics and other matters with Brand's letters of 14 and 23 May.

From R. H. BRAND, *14 May 1945*

Dear Maynard,

Stage III

1. We have been so full up with 6th Lend Lease Appropriation troubles that I have not had any time to give to your letter of April 24th. You will have seen all the cables about those troubles, and you will be well aware that we have had a very difficult time with Crowley. We hope we have got to a point where our requirements will be covered, and that the arrangements come to will stick, but it all depends on F.E.A. having really available $700 million or so out of their 5th Lend Lease or earlier money. They say they have, although a very short time ago they said they were entirely out of money—for us at any rate. We shall do our best to get the situation clarified as soon as possible. Frank Lee, who leaves in a few days, will be able to tell you the story.

But you will also no doubt have seen about another difficulty on the munitions side connected particularly with the air programme. It appears that the late President gave an instruction that lend lease programmes (presumably only munitions) should be referred, before executive action was taken, to the Office of War Mobilisation, i.e. Vinson.[22] Thus we have still another authority introduced cutting across the Morgenthau Committee. Therefore Somervell[23] has now appealed to Vinson to get a ruling on future action. I do not believe there is anything we can now do on our side until Vinson replies, but, if the reply is inconsistent with or dangerous to the Stage II conclusions, we must go to Morgenthau.

2. Coming to your letter of April 24th, I am much obliged to you for the clarification that you give, particularly on the question of convertibility. I should, no doubt, have assumed that you were referring to *Bretton Woods convertibility*, but the fact that you expected to lose on balance the equivalent of say $2 billion made me think that 'convertibility' meant a still wider freedom to transfer from sterling into dollars. I understand that apart from technicalities what you have in mind is the following. Sterling area countries would be free to convert into dollars any part of the 'freed' sterling balances remaining to them in total, say £750 million, provided that the money was required to *finance current transactions*, e.g. for locomotives or

---

[22] Frederick Moore Vinson (1890–1953); Director, U.S. Office of Economic Stabilisation, 1943–5; Federal Loan Administration, 1945; Director, Office of War Mobilisation and Reconversion, 1945; Secretary of the Treasury, 1945; Chief Justice, 1946.

[23] Brehon Burke Somervell (b. 1892); Commanding General Army Service Forces, War Dept., Washington from 1942, and as such largely responsible for assignments of American ground munitions to the British forces.

any other current imports India wanted to make. Thus to this extent the U.S. would be giving money via us to the rest of the sterling area, we being released from an equivalent amount of sterling indebtedness. In so far as the dollar gift to us was used for this purpose, it would not be available towards the debit on our—i.e. the U.K.—balance of payments. Meanwhile you contemplate that the sterling area dollar pool would for the time being continue, so that, taking the rest of this area as a whole, the use of the free gift of dollars would, as you say, be measured by the adverse balance of the rest of this area with the U.S. on current account.

I suppose you have in mind the $3 billion gift would be a strong prop to the sterling area dollar pool. That is that any sterling area country would have to accept the scheme as a whole and could only exchange its free sterling balances for dollars, if it at the same time continued to support the dollar pool. Otherwise I should imagine the stronger countries, e.g. India, would like to have the use of any and all the dollars they earn as well as their proportion of the $3 billion. I am not clear whether you contemplate admitting their right to their own dollars if they feel strong enough to do away with all exchange control.

I might add that I hope as much as you do that our gold and dollar balances will be at $2 billion at the beginning of Stage III. We shall have to struggle hard to get them there. We may have increasing attacks on them, unless the course of the Jap war changes today's sentiments.

3. Generally I appreciate the strong arguments you use for a free gift as against a transfer to the U.S. of some part of the sterling balances. It will, however, as I say, require a very happy concatenation of circumstances to be within the bounds of realisation.

The $3 billion free gift is indeed the crux of the problem, and the core of the whole plan, although you do indeed contemplate with reluctance that if it could not be obtained as free retrospective lend lease, it might have to be accepted on the same terms as the $5 billion. My own feeling is that a free gift will in any circumstances be extraordinarily difficult to obtain. At any rate it would require an atmosphere totally different from anything like the present one. I do not say such a psychological moment might not arise, since as you know and say, the ups and downs of temperature in Washington are extreme! But it would require a sort of inner appreciation of our position and what would be in our case 'justice' in the minds of the American public, and of Congress, which they are very far from possessing now. Today the atmosphere is unfavourable. There is a reaction since the death of the President. The German war is over, and with it it was generally supposed that lend lease would disappear or be enormously reduced. Instead the demands of the outside world seem to be constantly rising. I need not enumerate them, as you know them well. At one of our meetings the other day Crowley said that if Congress found external demands totalling in all something between $25 and $30 billion, they would just throw them out. He added that, if when lend lease came to an end, the U.K. and Russia for instance had to have more money which could be found, say, from the Export/Import Bank, they would be well advised not to put their demands to start with above, say, $1 or $2 million, and, if that was not enough, go later for more. I made no comment on this, because it would have been useless to begin explaining to him that loans bearing the sort of interest that he had in mind would be no good to us. Nevertheless it is clear he thinks of the Export/Import Bank as the machinery we should use.

I might add that the U.S. will look much more closely at Russian demands in future. I understand that Averell Harriman, who has just been here, has been giving advice to, I believe, a large meeting of the military that the U.S. has got to be tough with the Russians in future and give them nothing without close examination. There is a growing anti-Russian feeling, or at least a growing feeling that the Russians are going to be extremely difficult people to co-operate with. The less reliance the U.S. place on Russia the more, of course, they will look in a political sense to us as allies. (N.B. Since I wrote this the announcement about stopping of Russian lend lease has appeared in the papers.)

4. The course of the Japanese war will, of course, be the most important influence in the near future. If it turns out to be short, we should be driven to make some plans very quickly. There is here a very optimistic feeling that the Japanese are likely to try to make peace very shortly, and this is leading people, like Crowley, to wonder what we intend to do in that case, if lend lease comes to an end very quickly. That we must do something sticks out a mile, and even Crowley and Bill Griffin obviously now see it. The Japanese war may, on the other hand—and this is the view I incline to—last a good long time. If it proves a difficult business, and still more if Russia does not come in, the Americans are likely to value our co-operation in it much more highly than they do now, and this would reflect itself, I should imagine, in a greater willingness to help us. But it is certainly not the case at present that they are actively looking for ways and means to help us. I put the question about a favourable time for Stage III talks to Harry White today. He said 'most definitely not now'. He thought possibly in two or three months' time.

We are in the next day or two going to discuss with F.E.A. some aspects of the problem, which would present itself if the Jap war finished suddenly. Frank Lee will be able to report to you. If the war looks like being fairly short, we shall undoubtedly be driven more and more to discuss problems pertinent to Stage III with F.E.A. and I expect others. We may well, therefore, be driven towards discussing some interim arrangements preparatory to a wider negotiation.

5. The gist of all this is that I have to repeat my advice that this would be a bad moment either to start formal negotiations, still more, of course, to come out into the open about Stage III. For either we want a change of atmosphere. This is not to say that we might not take a favourable opportunity to indicate something of our plans in secret to a few in authority here, but you know how difficult it is to keep things secret here, and how dangerous it would be to risk premature exposure. How any secret negotiations are to be conducted *here* I am not yet clear. I believe myself it is likely that we shall see Byrnes at the head of the State Department before long. Apart from the President, I suppose we should then have to rely on Morgenthau and Harry White at the Treasury, and Byrnes and Clayton at the State Department. The other way of commencing, which I have mentioned before, is to have some very private talks in London with one or two leading Americans. Clayton told me the other day he is going over to London in July, I suppose, for the UNRRA meeting. It might be advisable to open up with him to a certain extent. He is an entirely reliable man. Conceivably Harry White might be induced to go about the same time. If we pressed this, we would have to explain to Morgenthau that it was for the purpose of discussing our general situation. If they both came, you might expose to them as much as was thought wise of your ideas. The atmosphere here is not sufficiently favourable for any such discussions to lead very far at the moment, but they might be worth while, following on the Canadian discussions you are going to have. I hope to be over in July also.

6. What I cannot get out of my head is that Stage III will not be a case merely of agreeing a plan with the high-ups and then just putting it over. Jean Monnet's recent agreement is an example of the U.S. side being pushed to agree to something and then quickly repenting before they even get to Congress. We cannot incur that danger. There must be a period when the U.S. public becomes used to the idea of what has to be done; if possible a period when circumstances convince them as to what has to be done. We might have to wait for that period of education to begin till after the Jap war has ended. There *must* be at some stage such a period of education and enlightenment here, though it may well be that the enlightenment and propaganda ought not to be in the vague but connected with some particular plan, as in the case of Bretton Woods. My general feeling is that the great plan of redistributing the costs of the war cannot really be put

through till both wars are over. It must, so to speak, 'top-up' the whole of the fighting period. It must come when peace or such peace as might then exist reigns, when the dust has cleared a bit, and when things can be seen more or less in their real proportions, i.e. what the U.K. has done in the two wars on the one side, and the outrageous burden on her on the other.

7. Meanwhile we should do what we can to put ourselves in some sort of bargaining position. Maurice Hutton[24] tells me he has written to J. J. L[lewellin] about making plans to get as much food as possible from outside the U.S. I am all in favour of this course. This means in the main, I suppose, Canada, Australia, New Zealand, and Denmark. We shall rely greatly on pressure from exporting interests here, particularly farmers, and they won't at all like the idea we can go to other markets. The more we can reduce our dependence on this country the better.

8. Have you taken into consideration how far any dollar facilities we get here are to be tied to purchases here by us or the rest of the sterling area? If the sterling area is included, the U.S. would certainly expect, that the great bulk of the money would be tied.

Yours,

R. H. B.

From R. H. BRAND, *23 May 1945*

Dear Maynard,

Stage III

1. I should like to send a few more comments on your Stage III memorandum to continue the process of feeling sure that I understand your ideas correctly. In para. 24 you estimate that the accumulated deficit on the U.K. balance before we reach equilibrium is not likely to be less than £2 billion, or calculated in dollars—$8 billion. You give no details of how you arrive at this figure, and no doubt it would be difficult to do so. Presumably it takes account of the £500 million or so of additional sterling balances to be included in the settlement, which are supposed to be sufficient to clean up the immediate post-war situation in the Middle East and India, etc. I suppose it includes the $2 billion which you calculate the rest of the sterling area will call on us to provide by our allowing them to convert into dollars their 'freed' sterling balances of £750 million referred to in para 51. That

---

[24] Sir Maurice Hutton (1904–70); company director; Ministry of Food, 1939; member, British Food Mission in North America, 1941, Head of Mission, 1944–8; Head of British Supply Office in U.S.A., 1947–8; British member, Combined Food Board, 1944–6; International Emergency Food Council, 1946–8; International Wheat Council, 1944–8; U.K. Executive Director, International Bank for Reconstruction and Development, 1946–7.

would leave £1,500 million, or $6 billion as representing the U.K.'s own cumulative deficit which seems to me on all that you say a very moderate figure. I presume you anticipate that this cumulative deficit would be financed partly out of gold and dollar balances, partly out of the moneys obtained in the United States and Canada under your plan (of which $2 billion would have been *ex hypothesi* absorbed by the rest of the sterling area), and partly by obtaining credit through the post-war increase of sterling balances, which you anticipate, or by facilities obtained from other countries who supply us with their exports.

As I calculate, if we were to get our $3 billion, and if, which is doubtful, we end the Jap war with $2 billion gold and dollar balances, and if, further, the rest of the sterling area use $2 billion while we intend to keep $1½ billion as a reserve, we are left with $1½ billion for the U.K. itself plus any drawings on the $5 billion plus any credits we can pick up elsewhere. It seems to me we should have to be very lucky not to have to draw very largely on the $5 billion.

2. In your letter of April 24th, page 2, you say that everything would proceed as at present, except that there would be no pressure from us on the rest of the sterling area to refrain from any purchase in the U.S. which they *considered themselves rich enough to make*. I take it to the extent they wished particularly to buy American goods they would certainly consider themselves rich enough to make such purchases to the extent of the £750 million sterling balances which will have been freed, as that is free money for which they have neither to 'toil nor spin'. I gather this is your view also by means of which you arrive at the figure of $2 billion. In addition there would be the dollars that the rest of the sterling area would earn currently.

3. I take it further that what you have in mind, if your plan went through and sterling was convertible for current transactions, is that the sterling area would be run more or less as before the war, we being its bankers and providing each country with dollars or other currencies, as it wanted. How exactly the system worked then I am not clear. In fact I am not clear how the U.K. found the dollars to meet its own very heavy annual deficit as against the U.S.

4. With sterling convertibility I assume that there would be no pressure from us not only on the rest of the sterling area but also on any other country, e.g. the Argentine, to refrain from selling sterling for dollars. Ought we not therefore to add to the $2 billion any dollars we should have to find for these countries also? As long as we have exchange control we might, it seems to me, even when shipping and supplies get more plentiful, continue more or less to force the primary products countries to give us

credit, because their desire to sell to us may continue stronger than the dislike of holding blocked sterling. But of course, when sterling is fully convertible, they have the initiative and not we, and the amount of credit they give us is entirely a voluntary act on their part. On the other hand as you point out in your letter of April 24th, convertibility may lead to some of these countries leaving sterling in London, and thus go some way in terms of the U.K. adverse balances with the outside world to make our net loss less than $2 billion. But with the return of convertibility goes entirely our ingenious war-time plan, which you described so graphically to the State Department, of raising large sums of money without the lenders knowing what was happening. Our only two ways of getting external credit then must be (a) for any country concerned to leave some of its sterling voluntarily in London; (b) for us to make with it definite arrangements for long or short term loans. The amount of the latter that we would wish to arrange would necessarily I think be very limited.

Thus, as indeed is self-evident, convertibility depends entirely on some such plan as yours, or in other words everything in the end depends on getting what is sufficient for successful convertibility from North America, with perhaps something else thrown in from elsewhere. Eady described the plan as 'all or nothing' and it certainly seems to me that this describes it so far as the question of convertibility is concerned. We are like a man with a very high temperature, who tells the owner of a very strong drug that, if he will give it to him, he promises to go back at once to normal, and be able to work with and for him. But whether the drug is strong enough to keep us at normal, I don't feel the least able to say. But if the drug is only available on condition that we do undertake to return to normal at once, there is no doubt a great temptation not to resist accepting the offer.

The only other alternative before us is, no doubt, a wholly different one, namely to start by seeing to what extent we could possibly supply ourselves with imports from outside North America, or certainly from outside the United States. I believe that from the point of view of *supplies* there should be no great difficulty with the bulk of our requirements and that we could reduce our demands on this country, though no doubt with some austerity, to something quite small. But that still leaves out the question whether the rest of the sterling area would want to follow us. We may ourselves I should imagine from the political outlook find continued extreme austerity very difficult. Will the rest of the sterling area be prepared to practise equal austerity and limit their purchases from the U.S. merely for our sake? It seems to me very likely that this course would lead to the complete break-up of the sterling area, since in view of their hunger for goods, the countries with dollars would be likely to break away and go entirely on their own.

337

This danger however does not to my mind rule out the question whether we should in the next few months not insure ourselves as far as possible against the situation which would arise if the Japanese war came suddenly to an end, and lend lease supplies stopped, by making whatever long term arrangements we can now for the supply, particularly of foodstuffs, from other countries. I have been talking recently to Maurice Hutton on this matter, and he has been cabling to Jay Llewellin about it. In the normal course of nature we should, after a short time, buy very few foodstuffs from this country, unless the U.S. were prepared to subsidise them heavily. In any case the U.S. could not blame us for making long term arrangements with other countries, when they are warning us every day that lend lease is coming to an end. There seems much to be said therefore for making such arrangements as we can over a considerable period with the food supplying countries, to step up their production against an undertaking by us to buy so much, even if we do not see clearly at present how we shall finance the purchases. The danger that under convertible sterling this would give them an increased call on dollars is not very different from the danger of having in the alternative to find our own dollars for actual U.S. purchases. The risk, I suppose, is that if we were to diminish very greatly our call on U.S. food supplies they might be less disposed to give us the dollar facilities which we should want. I suggest, however, that you ought to consider whether we should not put ourselves in a better bargaining position as regards having an alternative with which to face the U.S. by securing as far as we can our future food supplies. If in the end we could not make any arrangement with the U.S. the food producing countries would presumably prefer to sell their supplies to us, partly against sterling exports, and partly against sterling balances, rather than not sell them at all.

I must confess, however, that the more one contemplates the problem the more difficult it seems to get in any sense free, as I so much wish to do, from financial dependence on this country.

5. I regard the statement in para. 13 that the Middle East–India expenditure is *wholly* responsible for our financial difficulties as extreme. If it did not exist we would have a great problem in filling the gap which will yawn before us when lend lease and mutual aid stop.

Yours,
R. H. BRAND

To R. H. BRAND, *30 May 1945*

My dear Bob,

Stage III and the twilight of Lend Lease

I put off replying to your letter of May 14th and Remac 389 of May 18th until we had had an opportunity of discussing these questions with Frank Lee. Yesterday the whole body of us spent the afternoon going through matters with him. No doubt he will be making a full report to you. This letter will deal only with one or two main issues and chiefly in reply to your letter of May 14th.

1. I will deal first with the various points which arise specifically on your letter.

(i) The interpretation in the first paragraph of your §2 is agreed. As regards the second paragraph, the idea is that the new current receipts of sterling area countries would be similarly convertible. That is to say, we should free a certain proportion of their existing balances and also new net accretions.

(ii) The prospects of our net reserves reaching $2 billion by the end of 1945 now look pretty good. Revised estimates were prepared a few weeks ago, but they did not seem quite sound enough to pass on to you. A further revision is now being made, which will be sent to you as soon as we feel it is good enough. The prolongation of the German war has, of course, made receipts from troops' pay considerably in excess of our earlier estimates. The upshot of the recent Food Conference means that we shall not be able to spend so many dollars on Caribbean sugar as we have been expecting.

(iii) The $3 billion free gift is, as you say, the crux of the problem. I do not doubt that you are right that this would be extraordinarily difficult to obtain, though the American political atmosphere changes quite as fast as the weather in this country. However that may be, you agree, I think, that it should be our opening gambit. There are two reasons why

339

I attach importance to it. I think that, if the plan of the Americans was to take this form, it would make the whole thing immensely more acceptable to public opinion in this country and far easier for us to get the sterling area countries to make the concessions required of them. If America insists on remaining on a strictly economic basis, that makes it harder for the others to depart from it. I attach predominant importance to this psychological atmosphere of the free gift.

The second objection is that, otherwise, the service of our various considerable debts will be too heavy for us. I attach considerable, yet nevertheless inferior, importance to this. I am very hopeful that we might not need more than $5 billion altogether. If the terms of this were in accordance with the suggestion in the Memorandum, then it would not be unbearable. I feel that the American counter-proposal might very possibly take the form of an offer of a loan of $5 billion on easy terms. If so, it will be extremely difficult to know whether or not it is wise to meet them. It is a matter, I fancy, on which one will do well not even to try to make up one's mind until the situation actually arises.

(iv) I notice that you are one of the pessimists about the length of the Japanese war. I rather incline the other way. Anyhow we clearly have to be ready for a sudden collapse, and that is what makes the timing of the whole thing so difficult.

2. That leads me to the next section of our conversation with Frank Lee, with particular reference to Remac 359. We were inclined to take the line that it was altogether unrealistic to suppose that lend lease can be suddenly brought to an end on or shortly after VJ Day. The early demobilisation must be considered as part of the operations of the war. It would be extremely difficult to terminate reciprocal aid and set up a proper accounting system for it at very short notice. Our feeling was, therefore, that we should refuse to debate with the lower quarters of F.E.A. on the basis of an early termination

being anything we could seriously consider. Put briefly, our conclusions were:–

(1) That we hope that the President would not declare the lend lease period at an end until at least six months after VJ Day. We thought we might ask the Prime Minister, on the assumption that he and the President meet in the near future, to seek an assurance from the President that he would not issue his decision about the termination of lend lease suddenly or without giving us plenty of opportunity for discussion.

(2) We should take the line with F.E.A. that the twilight arrangements inevitably run into more general arrangements for the transitional period. We do not think it would be fruitful to try to discuss them separately. As regards the post-war arrangements, we are ready to begin discussions in Washington at the earliest date which is generally felt to be convenient and advisable.

(3) A sharp distinction should be made between (a) supplies of which we have already accepted delivery, (b) supplies in the pipe-line, and (c) new procurement. (a) is subject to the recapture clause; we do not think that any other arrangement should be substituted for that. We should hope that (b) would be treated in the same way as (a) except where there was agreement to the contrary. (c) we should expect to taper off rapidly and any new procurements to be exceptional and strict. Probably the best plan would be to keep the financial arrangements relating to post-zero hour procurements in suspense with the idea that they would be subsumed by the general post-war arrangements. Meanwhile, we might agree (here I am interpolating something which has occurred to me since our discussion of yesterday) that they should be subject to reimbursement.

(4) We maintained our obdurate resistance to any loans under 3(c). As you will see, generally speaking, we are only too anxious that the twilight needs should be considered, but

would do our damnedest not to get entrapped into discussion in any detail in advance of provisional arrangements generally.

3. This leads me back to §5 of your letter. We were all rather attracted by the idea of some highly preliminary and private beginnings in London in July, on the assumption that you and Clayton and Harry White would all be here. We feel timid about any premature approach, but, on the whole, feel that would be as good a party as possible. We think it rather essential that Harry White should be one of the party and that we should not go any distance with Clayton behind the backs of the Treasury, although some conversation with him would probably be wise and inevitable. Certainly, if the Japanese war shows signs of collapsing, it will be a wise precaution to make some movement as early as July.

4. That there must be, at some stage, a period of public education and enlightenment we all agreed. My own view is that it would have to be a short and sharp campaign. This is a subject in which it would be impossible to keep up continuous interest, and it would be very liable to go stale on our hands.

5. We all agreed that the Ministry of Food should be pressed to draw up an alternative programme of supplies based on obtaining as much as possible from outside U.S. We must continue to take the Starvation Corner alternative seriously. We should all of us like to feel that, if our overtures are rejected, we can really fall back on this, at any rate for a spell.

6. Finally, there is your §8 about whether the dollar facilities would be tied loans. I do not myself feel very strongly about this. We shall in fact need all the dollar facilities for purchases in U.S. either by ourselves or by the rest of the sterling area. We shall probably have enough gold and other essentials to look after other parts of the world without drawing on the dollar gift or loan for the purpose. Possibly

a compromise would be to agree that the $3 billion free gift should be tied to purchases in U.S., but that the loan, so far as we draw upon it, should be free. At any rate, that might be our opening move.

Yours ever,
[copy initialled] M.K.

P.S. Since writing the above, I have had your further letter of May 23rd about Stage III. I am not, however, holding up this letter in order to deal also with the further points which you now raise. I will send another letter on this early next week.

To R. H. BRAND, *5 June 1945*

My dear Bob,

Stage III

Your letter of May 23rd arrived just before I sent off my letter of May 30th, and, as I mentioned in a postscript, I did not hold up my previous letter in order to comment on it. I will, however, now run through the chief points.

(1) I think I agree with the arithmetic of your paragraph 1. But there is one matter where I may be calculating differently. I am assuming that, if we have to provide, say, $2 billion to the sterling area countries, this does not necessarily mean that their pre-war zero-hour sterling balances will be reduced by anything like this amount. I am hopeful that, if we can allow them to convert their balances with some freedom, they will in fact, not individually perhaps, but in the aggregate, be willing to maintain their balances at the previous figure, new accretions of sterling offsetting the withdrawals through conversion into dollars. Thus the conjectural balance sheet would run somewhat as follows:–

Our accumulated deficit during the transitional period is 8 (all figures in billion dollars). But two of these are allowed for in the post-war sterling area settlement, leaving 6 to be provided for. Towards this we should have a loan of 2 from Canada and a free grant of 3 from U.S., leaving 1 to be met from other sources. If we took this 1 out of the suggested American credit, then we should have the possibility of using some part of our reserves, assumed to start at 2, and loans from other quarters, say, ¼, to meet any excess of the assumed 2 required for the rest of the sterling area over the new money left by the sterling area. You will see, therefore, that I am not assuming that we draw very much on the 5 credit. Indeed, I would, if necessary, be content with 5 altogether. That is to say, 3 free grant *plus* 2 credit. That would, you see, still leave a surplus of 1 on the basis of the above conjectures.

(2) I confirm your paragraph 2.

(3) I confirm your paragraph 3. Before the war I think we found the dollars we needed mainly out of the exports of India and Malaya, but there was, of course, also the surplus of payments from any other country having a convertible currency.

(4) With reference to your paragraph 4, I have already explained why I do not add the 2 for the rest of the sterling area to my estimate of our own adverse balance of trade. The rest of that paragraph of yours I confirm.

(5) I agree very strongly, and so does everyone else in the Treasury, with what you say towards the end of your paragraph 4 about our insuring ourselves as far as possible against the situation which would arise if lend lease supplies stopped suddenly. We are tackling the Ministry of Food on this, though I fear they will not be easy game. Early in the war we were buying hardly any foodstuffs worth mentioning from U.S.A., and that is the position we must return to at the earliest possible moment.

(6) With reference to your paragraph 5, in saying that the Middle East and India is wholly responsible for our financial difficulties, I meant our financial difficulties *up to date*. You

are, of course obviously right that, looking to the post-war period after the end of lend lease, it is the prospective adverse balance of trade largely arising from the excess of imports over exports which is the problem.

I repeat that I wholly share the pessimism which you and Frank Lee feel about the whole prospect. But of course, all sorts of variants, in fact, will turn up in the course of the discussion, if only the discussion can be started along right lines. I do not believe we shall get just what we are now talking about, but that we shall in the end get something not too unsatisfactory I do incline to believe.

Yours ever,
[copy initialled] M.K.

Between 19 and 29 May, Keynes and the Treasury had an opportunity to try out their ideas for Stage III on a delegation of Canadian officials in London to clear up some outstanding mutual aid problems. The discussions began in Cambridge on the weekend of 19 May. Keynes began with an exposition of his Stage III paper. The Canadians were pleased by the emphasis on a short transition and the long-term goals of the paper. However, they thought that a loan for Keynes's full sum was much more probable and they recommended flexible repayment terms. On the second day of the talks, the discussion had turned to outstanding Stage II problems, in particular to discrimination against Canadian exports to the sterling area. Keynes later took up the story in a letter to R. H. Brand.

To R. H. BRAND, *29 May 1945*

Dear Bob,

We finished today our discussions with the Canadians so far as they relate to Treasury matters as distinct from Board of Trade. Frank Lee has been present at the last lap and no doubt will be reporting to you. Nevertheless, it may be useful, as he is not going back at once, that I should let you know the broad upshot of what happened.

We began by a week-end at Cambridge, which I think everyone enjoyed and where we did a lot of quiet work. The first day was devoted to an exposition, mainly by myself, of the memorandum on the kind of Stage III plans which we contemplate putting to the United States. There was very little in that paper which I left out. But we did not actually give them the document to read. Today Towers asked if he might see it in confidence. I am not quite sure whether we shall in fact let him do so. The Canadians reacted to this quite favourably. Indeed, they were, I fancy, much relieved to see how genuinely we were tending towards the convertible and multilateral solution. They made no vital or important criticisms.

On the second day we passed on to a number of more immediate matters arising out of the fact that Stage II arrangements are not yet fully determined. The attached set of minutes will tell you roughly what happened.[25]

We left Cambridge without having finally settled the question whether we need do anything to meet them on not discriminating against essential Canadian goods in the sterling area on the ground that they could be obtained from elsewhere in the sterling area. It was quite clear however, that, if we could make a concession on this, it would make all the difference to the feelings with which our visitors went home and to the question whether or not they had felt their visit to be a success. On coming back to London, therefore, we decided to do our best to meet them. It was clear that financially there is not much in it and we could well afford to relax to the extent which would satisfy them. The whole difficulty, of course, was the question of a precedent with the United States. In the end we decided that there were enough differences between our relations with U.S. and Canada to justify a difference and that anyhow it would probably be worth while for us to take a certain chance in the matter. We all realised, I think, that this degree of relaxation may conceivably mean that, if the worst comes to the worst, we may have to do

25 Not printed [Ed.].

346

something on somewhat similar lines for U.S.A. If, as now looks probable, Stage II has not long to run and Stage III has to be on multilateral lines, then it may be we should not have lost much, even if we are driven to a concession. The result of these discussions was the attached paper, which we put to the Canadians yesterday, and with which they seemed to be extremely satisfied.[26] In fact, by limiting the concession to essentials strictly interpreted, we have given away much more in principle than in substance, and the maximum provision we have allowed, namely $25 million, is likely to prove considerably more than the concession will actually cost. (We felt, by the way, that this reference to $25 million would help us with U.S.A. For it would enable us to argue that the arrangement with Canada can be regarded as *de minimis*. We can do it because in fact it would cost us very little. Whereas, a sum so small as $25 million over a year could scarcely be of interest to U.S.A.)

In the Board of Trade discussions, where I have not been present, they have been put wise to the course of our commercial talks with U.S.A. in pretty full detail. The Board of Trade has also been tackling them about facilitating our exports in various ways, especially where they are interfered with by a price ceiling. But I am not in a position to report on the outcome of this in detail.

Yours ever,
[copy initialled] M. K.

At the end of the discussions, Keynes wrote to W. A. Mackintosh and Dr Clark.

To W. A. MACKINTOSH, *31 May 1945*

Dear Mackintosh,

The paper about Canadian exports to the sterling area, which we have already discussed with you, has now been

---

[26] Below, pp. 349.

approved by the Chancellor. I am, therefore, sending you half a dozen copies, which you may now take as the final official version from our side.

I am also enclosing a draft of the kind of circular which we should contemplate sending to the Crown Colonies, since we promised to let you see this. I would be grateful, however, if you could regard this as no more than a draft, since we have not yet had time to clear it with the Colonial Office, and it may be that some change of form may be necessary. As you will see, we have found it necessary, from our point of view, to stress both sides of the picture, and we hope this will not spoil its appearance when looked at from your side.

I am also enclosing a short note of certain other matters we discussed at Cambridge, where you may like to have a note of reminder.[27] We have not included in this list the question of the clean-up of last year and the possible application of any surplus which may result when there has been a final net settlement in respect of what is due from you to us in respect of stores and increased capitation rates, and from us to you to offset the lend lease element in the supplies we have furnished, since, as I think you agreed, we thought it better that this should take the form of a letter from myself to Clark, which will not be ready until early next week.

At the most recent meeting at the Treasury, I made use of a revised estimate, prepared by the Bank of England, of the prospective payments on both sides during the financial year 1945/46. I understand that this paper is still being worked at and may not be ready in time for us to give it to you before you go away. In this case, we shall send copies through Gordon Munro so that they will be in your hands in due course.

May I say how much we have enjoyed and appreciated the visit of all three of you. From our point of view, at any rate, we feel fully justified in having pressed so strongly that some

[27] Not printed [Ed.].

representatives of the Dominion Government should be here for oral discussions at this early juncture. The nature of our talks at Cambridge will have made it clear to you how much easier it has been for us to speak freely than it would have been, at this stage, to put anything down on paper.

Please give my best personal greetings to Mr Ilsley and also to Clifford Clark and Bob Bryce.[28]

Sincerely yours,
KEYNES

CANADIAN EXPORTS TO THE STERLING AREA

1. The deficit in the balance of payments on current account between the sterling area and Canada during the fiscal year 1945/46 is provisionally estimated at Can. $1250 million. This estimate assumes the continuance of the principles of import and exchange control currently applied. The Canadian Government have however requested a modification of these principles so as to remove the discrimination which they entail against essential imports from Canada into the sterling area as compared with essential imports from one sterling area country to another.

2. In order to meet the wishes of the Government of Canada the U.K. Government are prepared, on the assumption of a Mutual Aid Appropriation for 1945/46 sufficient to cover the deficit as estimated above, to modify their own import policy to the extent of adopting henceforward the principle that where Canada is a normal source of supply no distinction will be made on exchange grounds between Canada and the sterling area countries, subject to paragraph 5 below, as sources of supply for essential imports. That is to say, the existing criterion that the goods may be imported

[28] Robert Broughton Bryce (b. 1910); economist, Department of Finance, 1938–45; Executive Director, World Bank, 1946–7; Secretary to the Treasury Board, 1947–53; Secretary to the Cabinet, 1954–63; Deputy Minister of Finance, 1963–70.

from Canada only if they are not available in the sterling area would no longer apply in such cases.

3. The U.K. Government would have to retain discretion to exclude imports of any category of goods, and to determine the quantity of imports of any particular category to be regarded as essential. Where a category of goods is excluded or limited quantitatively on the criterion of essentiality, the U.K. Government would retain freedom to admit, or accept increased imports of, such goods from particular sources; any such additional imports would be regarded as non-essential and the principle of non-discrimination would not apply in such cases. In particular, imports of non-essential goods from a European country whose economy had been disrupted by the war might have to be permitted as a measure of assistance in the reconstruction of its economy, or as the only means of collecting payment from such a country.

4. As regards the rest of the sterling area, the U.K. Government would be prepared to take the following action—

(a) *The Colonies.* Instructions would be given to Colonial Governments to apply the same principles in relation to imports from Canada as the U.K. would itself apply.

(b) *Australia, New Zealand, South Africa, Southern Rhodesia and India.* These Governments would be advised of the policy adopted by the U.K. Government, and invited to do likewise.

(c) *Neutral and non-British countries, members of the sterling area.* The U.K. Government will not be asked to alter their present arrangements with these countries.

In the case of *Egypt and Iraq,* a defined sum is allocated in foreign currency out of the sterling area pool to cover all the expenditure of each country in the currencies of the U.S.A., Canada and certain other countries.

Where sterling area countries have large sterling balances, the United Kingdom Government feel that freest possible use of these balances in the sterling area must be allowed in order to give sterling a real value. It would be understood therefore that sterling area Governments would be free to admit from the U.K. additional quantities of goods of which a limited quantity only would be admitted as essential imports.

5. The U.K. Government recognise that the adoption of these principles would result in an increased import of Canadian goods into the sterling area over and above the amount budgeted for under the existing formula and that this amount would not be covered on the current estimate of Canadian dollar funds available to the sterling area (including the projected mutual aid appropriation). They would wish therefore to reserve the right to ask the Government of Canada to review the matter at any time during the course of the year, if it should appear that the resulting demands on their gold resources were more than in their judgement they could allocate to this purpose (say Can. $25 million).

Draft circular telegram to the Colonies

Import Control. H.M.G. in the U.K. have been discussing with the Government of Canada the effect on exports from Canada to the sterling area of the existing policy of import and exchange control. The basic principle operating, as you are aware, has been that goods should not be imported from outside the sterling area unless (a) they are essential, (b) they cannot be obtained within the sterling area.

The effect of this policy has been to impose a measure of discrimination against essential imports from Canada, as compared with essential imports from other British countries.

2. This policy has been dictated by the imperative necessity of conserving, during the war period, the foreign exchange resources of the sterling area to cover essential requirements. The need to conserve such resources will continue beyond the war period itself. But H.M.G. in the U.K. are anxious, in

consultation with the Government of Canada, to ensure that the pattern of post-war trade is not dictated by the perpetuation of controls set up for purely war-time purposes, and they desire therefore to take such steps as they are able to minimise the discrimination between Canadian exports and those of the countries in the sterling area.

3. They have therefore indicated to the Government of Canada that they are prepared henceforward to adopt, in regard to their own import policy, the principle that, where Canada is a normal source of supply, no distinction will be made on exchange grounds between Canada and the sterling area countries as source of supply for essential imports. That is to say, the existing criterion that essential goods may be imported from Canada only if they are not available in the sterling area would no longer apply in such cases.

4. This is to be regarded as an interim measure. The further development of trade between Canada and the sterling area must naturally depend on the settlement of wider questions. Moreover H.M.G. have reserved the right to reopen the matter with the Government of Canada, should the demands on their foreign exchange resources resulting from this change of policy prove too onerous.

5. Colonial Governments should henceforward apply the principle stated in para. 3 above in regard to essential imports into their territories from Canada.

6. Since this represents a substantial change of principle in the operation of sterling area controls, it is important that it should be fully understood by all those concerned with the administration of import controls and the programming of essential imports.

7. It is not proposed that any public announcement should be made at this date. But you should reply to enquiries from commercial interests affected in the terms of the principle as stated in para. 3 above.

8. You should note that the principle applies to essential

repeat essential imports where Canada is a normal source of supply. It will remain within your discretion to determine, subject to consultation with me where necessary, what imports you regard as essential to the economy of the Colony, both as to category and as to amount. In the case of Canada you should accordingly continue to exclude all imports of any particular category which are judged inessential, and admit imports as essential only in limited quantities. Where no imports, or a limited quantity only, are admitted as essential, you have discretion to admit additional imports of the same category, subject to supply and shipping availabilities, from the U.K. without thereby being required to admit such additional imports from other sources on a non-discriminatory basis. H.M.G. in the U.K. have explained to the Government of Canada the necessity for this provision, in view of the importance for both the Colonies themselves and the U.K., of allowing the freest possible use of the substantial sterling balances which the former now hold.

9. Special cases may also arise where it may be desired to admit imports from particular sources which could not be justified on a strict basis of essentiality. For example, in order to maintain normal trade relations with contiguous territories. The admission of such imports would not necessarily conflict with H.M.G's understanding with the Canadian Government, but before deciding on such cases you should refer to me.

You should also refer to me if any special cases of difficulty arise in relation to local Canadian interests, on the application of the principle stated above.

To DR C. CLARK, *4 June 1945*

Dear Clark,

In the course of the discussions we have been having with Mackintosh and his colleagues, a number of matters relating to the main issue were mentioned. Among these was the question of the final adjustment of last year's accounts. This was felt to be so peculiarly a concern of your Treasury that it would be better for me to write to you rather than discuss it in detail with Mackintosh.

Briefly, the point is this. When we discussed last August the arrangements for the fiscal year 1944/45 we worked on estimates which showed that, after the proposals then agreed upon were put into effect, there should result a fairly substantial balance in our favour at the end of the year (provisionally estimated, if I remember right, at somewhere between $150 and $200 million). This, we agreed, should be applied in the first instance to discharging our debt of Can. $200 million on the first Air Training Scheme. Anything further left over would go towards the second Air Training Scheme, though it did not seem likely that the balance would stretch so far as this.

In the final outcome our estimates were not far wrong, although in detail there have been some important differences between the estimates and the actuals. In particular—

(1) War Office capitation payments are likely to be much higher than was then estimated, although the final rates are not yet agreed; but

(2) against this the adjustment in respect to lend lease is also likely to be much higher.

The actual cash balance at the close of the year does not, however, reveal the real result, inasmuch as no final payment had yet been made in respect of the Canadian share of reserve stores and the revised capitation rate less the lend lease adjustment. In addition, we are hoping for payments to be received in respect of prisoners of war and of Joint Inspection Board charges, proposals both of which were received sympathetically when I was in Ottawa, but neither of which, I understand, has yet been finalised.

I believe that the actual balance on the U.K. Cash Receipts Account at the end of the fiscal year was Can.$89 million.

But some of this may have have been earmarked against deliveries made in the last financial year not yet paid for, if I understand your accounting system correctly, and I do not know the final net amount available. In any case, it will only correspond to what we were estimating last August when the factors mentioned above are balanced out and paid for.

Meanwhile nothing has been paid out against the first Air Training Scheme. It would seem, therefore, that some deliberate action will be necessary if our original intention is to be carried out; for otherwise it must be presumed that the outstanding payments by your Departments referred to above would go into the Cash Receipts Account so that they, together with any available free balance on that account at the close of the year, would then be liable to be drawn upon to meet the current outgoings of the new financial year. This raises a question of machinery which I discuss below. But, before doing so, I would like to go a little further into the statistical position as we see it.

In our stocktaking the following are the outstanding items to our credit—

	Can. $ million
Balance on the U.K. Cash Receipts Account	?
Adjustment on a/c of capitation payments (say)	180
War Office Reserve Stores (say)	140
Air Ministry Reserve Stores (balance) (say)	30
Prisoners of War Inspection Board (provisional) (say)	55
Total (say)	450

From this a lend lease adjustment, which we provisionally estimate at 200, falls to be deducted, leaving a net balance of, say, 250. For the lend lease rebate I have used a revised estimate based on the results of the recent discussions between your Service representatives and ours. But the new figure is still highly tentative. As I say, we are not in a position to know the free balance on the Cash Receipts Account. The figure for the capitation payments is the same as I used when I wrote to you last January, but my latest information is that it may be somewhat on the high side. The figures for reserve stores have not yet been agreed with your Service Departments, and I have merely used the estimates of our own people. The estimates for prisoners of war and for the Joint Inspection Board are those which we mentioned in Ottawa; I have no more accurate figures, but your Departments will have the exact particulars.

But, in any case, it would appear that, when all this has been finally settled, the sums due to us in respect of last year may be of the order of Can. $200 million, though this figure is subject to a large margin of error. On the other side of the account, however, there are also very substantial liabilities outstanding.

These are as follows—

		Can. $ million
Ram tanks, etc.		?
Air Training		
1st E.A.T.S.	200	
2nd E.A.T.S. say	225	
Current, say	50	
	—	475
Surplus disposals		?
		—
Total	(unknown, but say 550 or upwards)	

I have not attempted to set a figure for the Ram tanks, etc. As you know, these were estimated to cost originally somewhere around $100 million, but a lower value—how much lower I do not know—would no doubt be placed upon them for these purposes. This would have to be discussed between our Service Departments in the first instance.

I have included with the Air Training liabilities a figure of 50 for the current year. This, I hope, is too high since we must make every effort to cut down demands on you for this purpose from now onwards. But I have assumed, in the light of previous discussions, that you would wish to treat any liability that does arise as on all fours with the E.A.T.S. liabilities, rather than as a charge on our current Canadian dollar resources.

Finally, you will see I have referred to surplus disposals. This is a new item in our accounts, and I would not attempt to guess a figure. Nor do I want at this stage to enter into this very difficult question in detail. But it seems to me probable that some liability to you will arise under this heading, and it is well, therefore, to bear it in mind in considering the position as a whole.

At this point I would like to turn again to the question of machinery. As I have indicated, there are substantial sums on both sides of the account. But none of these have yet been ascertained exactly, and it may yet be some time before they are settled. I would like you, therefore, to consider whether in principle it would not be desirable to handle all these items apart from the ordinary machinery of the U.K. Cash Receipts Account and to set up some separate accounting machinery for holding them in suspense until our receipts on the headings concerned can be offset, as far as they will reach, against these liabilities. In other words, I suggest some sort of Suspense Account and that you should—

(a) transfer into it any free balance on the U.K. Cash Receipts Account as at 31st March last, (b) instruct your Departments to pay into it any amounts arising from time to time in respect of capitation and reserve stores, together with any retrospective adjustments in respect of prisoners of war and the Joint Inspection Board, up to 31st March last.

As the balance on the account so accumulates, it might be applied against the liabilities in the following order—

357

(*a*) we would first return to you the whole of the lend lease adjustment as finally ascertained,

(*b*) next we would pay the amount owing in respect of the Ram tanks, etc.,

(*c*) as between Air Training and Surplus Disposals, we have no strong views and would be content to leave the question open for the time being.

Would you think this over and let us have your views? There would no doubt be other ways of achieving the same result in substance, and we do not hold strongly to any particular form of settlement. But I believe in principle the approach I propose would be the right one in the light of our earlier discussions.

Yours sincerely,

[copy initialled] K.

Meanwhile, discussions on aspects of the Stage III approach to the United States continued within Whitehall. On 29 May Keynes and Sir Wilfrid Eady met Messrs Munro, Lee, Harmer, Grant and Thompson-McCausland in Keynes's room at the Treasury. They initially discussed the possible curtailment of reciprocal aid in raw materials, not to gain financial advantage in terms of the reserves, but to restore materials to private trade and ease the problems of the post-war settlement if Stage II lend lease ended suddenly. They then turned to the possibility that lend lease would end immediately after VJ day, which they thought might come in the course of the summer. Keynes thought that such an abrupt end would be unrealistic, given the problems of repatriating troops and dealing with goods in the pipeline. However, other members of the meeting were more pessimistic. In the end, it was agreed that this was a problem tied up with the prospective Stage III talks and although it might be possible to raise the problem in a preliminary way when American officials came to London for the August meetings of UNRRA, in the interim Britain would have to run the risk of an early VJ Day and termination of lend lease.

The discussion then turned to Stage III itself. Mr Lee, who had just returned from Washington, suggested that the atmosphere there was not right for an approach at that time, given American officials' commitments during the passage of the Bretton Woods agreements through Congress and the need to educate opinion as to Britain's needs. When Keynes outlined his preferred method of approach, Lee suggested that the sombre alternative to generous assistance would prove effective with the State Department, but not with Congress and he doubted the possibility of Justice as a solution to Britain's problem. Thompson-McCausland also raised the problem of the loan and gift arrangement in Keynes's proposals, for he thought that only the loan part of the arrangement would come into the discussion, if the proposal went forward in that form. In the end, however, the meeting took no decision on Keynes's Stage III proposals. However, it agreed with a suggestion of Mr Grant's to look more closely at the details of Starvation Corner.

At the same time, the Treasury began discussions with the Board of Trade on the treatment of sterling balances. Sir Arnold Overton[29] suggested tying some of the balances to expenditure in the United Kingdom, especially as Britain would be slower to re-enter export markets after the war than the United States. On this suggestion Keynes noted.

To SIR DAVID WALEY *and* SIR WILFRID EADY, *28 May 1945*

Clearly we must have a discussion. But this goes to the root of the matter. I do not see how we can reasonably expect both to get liberal assistance from U.S. and retain effective discrimination.

I do not think that Overton's suggestion of a gradual releasing of the balances would help. We could scarcely avoid releasing in the first year a sum at least equal to the requirements of that year. In that case we should have spoilt the overall picture without having effectively protected ourselves.

One cannot, of course, deny that Overton is right in pointing out that the removal of discrimination will not be as helpful to our exports as its retention. But, as I have said, that is the heart of the matter. And perhaps one can comfort him with the reflection that in the early years markets will be so

[29] Sir Arnold Overton (1893–1975); Board of Trade, 1919; on Secretariat of Ottawa Conference, 1932; delegate of U.K. Government to negotiate Anglo-American Trade Agreement, Washington, 1937–8; Permanent Secretary, Board of Trade, 1941–5.

good that it will be our capacity to supply which will be the limiting factor.

KEYNES

28.5.45

Throughout the rest of June, Keynes's comments on letters from R. H. Brand indicate the way his mind was moving.

To SIR WILFRID EADY, *and others, 13 June 1945*

There are some matters in the attached letter from Brand[30] about Stage III which deserve thought. My comments on the passages I have numbered are as follows:–

1. His arithmetic here is not quite right, but a subsequent letter he had not received when writing this, puts it straight.

2. In my opinion Brand is right up to a point that references to justice should be avoided, but only up to a point. The appeal to justice does not necessarily suggest any lack of generosity on the part of U.S. It is a wider conception about the way in which the financial consequences of the war should be liquidated. Just as he thinks that this sort of line of approach is to be avoided, so I, on the other hand, think that too exclusive an appeal to American self-interest will be misjudged.

3. You will see from this passage that Monnet had originally obtained $2·6 billion on lend lease from Crowley, but was fearing so recently as June 5th that it would be cut down to $2 billion or $1·8 billion. In fact, since the date of Brand's letter, a telegram has arrived to the effect that the faithless Crowley has applied to Congress for a total of 0·9 billion for France, Belgium and Holland, all added together. Thus, it looks as if Monnet's $2·6 billion has been cut down to $0·6 billion. Undoubtedly, Monnet was unduly successful in the first instance. But it is a pretty stiff example of Crowley's faithlessness.

---

[30] Not printed [Ed.].

4. Evidently this was before Crowley's staff had discovered that he had double-crossed and betrayed them. The actual reduction was made by Crowley on his own initiative without consulting or informing his staff and was put through by a deliberate deception of the Director of the Bureau of the Budget. A later telegram indicates that Denby, Crowley's best and ablest assistant, has resigned. Nevertheless, I hope he will not press this, since without Denby we shall be vastly worse off.

5. You will see that Brand half suggests that the opportunity of the next meeting of the Three should be used to begin the education of the President on financial issues. I am rather doubtful about this. My feeling would be that, on the occasion of his first meeting with the Prime Minister, these matters should not be put into the foreground. It is unlikely that there would be time to do the work properly. If there is a chance of any discussion of the financial issues, my suggestion would be that no attempt should be made on this occasion to deal with Stage III problems, but it might be prudent for the Prime Minister to ask the President that there should be no sudden, unilateral termination of lend lease when the Japanese war comes to an end, but that the arrangements for the twilight and for liquidating lend lease should be the subject of discussion between us. The fact that reciprocal aid is even more difficult to terminate suddenly than lend lease would be a good and sufficient reason for this.

[copy initialled] K

To SIR WILFRID EADY *and others, 21 June 1945*

The papers below,[31] and more particularly Brand's two letters of June 12, provide the beginning of a basis for a discussion on Stage III procedure—as soon as Brand arrives or perhaps a preliminary talk sooner (§6 below is urgent). My present half-formed impressions are as follows:–

[31] Not printed [Ed.].

1. Camer 435 expresses a doubt whether, in view of the political uncertainty here, Stage III discussions can begin early in September. Obviously we cannot see our way clearly as yet. But it is very desirable not to postpone if it is by any means avoidable—for these reasons:

(*a*) I am sure that we cannot safely delay discussions about the twilight of lend lease and mutual aid, which will be intricate and difficult. Yet it is most undesirable that we should embark on these as an issue separate from Stage III. This is all the more important because the whole pressure on the American side will be to get them regarded as separate. Brand reports Clayton as agreeing with him that we cannot wait beyond September.

(*b*) It must be a matter of some doubt how long into 1946 the Japanese war will persist. If the end catches us without our having made any serious progress with Stage III finance, it will be awkward.

(*c*) Discussions on Stage III in the very early autumn will enjoy the great advantage of *preceding* our final commitment to Bretton Woods which cannot reach Parliament before October or November; and also of preceding the next stage of the commercial talks which is now scheduled, I think, for very early next year.

(*d*) We have to be prepared for a failure at the first round, and must allow time for this. It will be fatal to leave matters so late that we have no option but to accept the best we can get.

(*e*) Assuming a measure of success sufficient to enable us to proceed to discussions with the several S.A. countries, we still have a very long row to hoe, where also any delay much beyond the end of the Japanese war will be, at the least, highly inconvenient.

2. My Stage III memorandum is dated last April. Presumably it cannot now be usefully brought before the Cabinet sooner than August 1. But that would still give time, if

Ministers can be brought to give their attention to it, for us to aim at beginning in Washington soon after September 1. Could not the Chancellor tell his colleagues that this must be the time-table? (If the Cabinet prefers something materially different from the proposals of the memorandum, all the less time to spare. If broadly they accept them, it need not take much time.)

3. Brand's letters and telegrams show that the projected talks in London during July with a few picked Americans (Clayton, White, Cox) must now be given up. I am not altogether sorry. A definite approach, fully panoplied, may be better than a gradual, vague and more tentative handling. Nevertheless, if in the end Clayton (and not Acheson) turns up for the UNRRA Council, I think a very private talk on fairly general lines would be advisable.

4. As Brand points out, the newly established 'National Advisory Council on International Monetary and Financial Problems' provides us with the same sort of forum (and perhaps a better one) for these discussions as the Morgenthau Committee did for those of a year ago. The membership is very suitable and the majority are old friends.

5. Nevertheless, as Brand also points out, it will be very advisable to begin at the White House level and to obtain some preliminary general blessing or at least some directive from the President. He might instruct the new Council to discuss Stage III financial arrangements with the British and to report to him personally the result of such discussions. The fact that Harry Hopkins has survived into the new regime may make all this a little easier.

6. This leads me to a matter which is immediately urgent. Should the opportunity of the forthcoming meeting be taken for an immediate approach to the President by the Prime Minister? Here again the presence of Harry Hopkins might be helpful. If so, the approach might be on the following lines:—

(i) We expect no material assistance from lend lease after

the end of the Japanese War. Nevertheless it will not be possible to liquidate the vast system of lend lease and mutual aid at very short notice. The Prime Minister would, therefore, appreciate an understanding with the President that there will be no sudden or drastic action which has not been the subject of prior mutual discussion and agreement.

(ii) The sooner such prior discussion begins the better. We should like to start conversations at a very early date on the modalities of liquidating the lend lease and mutual aid system as quickly as possible after the end of the Japanese war.

(iii) But, from our point of view, such discussion is unavoidably bound up with the question of what happens next. Our formidable running deficit on overseas account will not cease suddenly or even quickly with the end of the Japanese war. The way in which we are able to handle it will largely determine the part we can play in Stage III and the extent to which we can hope to collaborate with the U.S. in the early establishment of an international economy of the type which both of us believe to be to the best general advantage of the world.

(iv) There is no time to lose because the type of solution, which we propose to suggest to the President in the hope that he will approve it, will require the collaboration of the many countries to which, as a result of the war, we now owe excessive debts. What we shall be aiming at will be American assistance as a basis for a joint handling of the problem with a view to a liquidation, so far as possible, of the financial consequences of the war in so far as they affect and distort future international relations. The President will readily agree that the unmeasured contribution of this country to victory should not result in our being burdened with overseas war debts much in excess of the maximum which we can hope to lay on Germany. We fully endorse the view, taken emphatically by Congress (as we have done from the beginning), that the question of the war debts problem lies entirely outside the scope of the Bretton Woods plans. It is a non-recurrent problem which requires its own special solution, but one which we cannot solve satisfactorily without the help of the U.S., though no doubt we can find some way, albeit an unsatisfactory way, if we are left to solve it alone.

(v) If, therefore, the President agrees, the Prime Minister would propose to invite the Chancellor of the Exchequer to send a party to Washington at the beginning of September to lay proposals before the President personally in the hope that he will refer them, with all the blessings he feels he can give, to an appropriate Committee with which the British party can discuss them in detail, this Committee to report to him the upshot of the conversations.

7. I do not think that we need feel *too* pessimistic about the eventual outcome. The ideology behind our proposals should have a powerful appeal to the State Department. Mr Dewey's remarkable speech in New York on June 7 (see 286 Saving attached) suggests that the Republicans are more likely to support us than to rebuff us. For U.S. the money at stake is of no consequence whatever. It is *entirely* a question of approach and of atmosphere, in short of diplomacy. If the Prime Minister could get the initial sympathy of the President (to whom the subject matter may be very unfamiliar) the battle would be half won.

KEYNES

21.6.45

The Treasury, taking up Grant's suggestion of 29 May, meanwhile began to think more seriously about Starvation Corner. An attempt to think of a non-dollar bloc to deal with conditions of dollar shortage by Sir Wilfrid Eady and Mr R. W. B. Clarke[32] drew the following comment from Keynes.

[32] Richard William Barnes (Otto) Clarke (1910–75), K.C.B. 1964; served in Ministries of Information, Economic Warfare, Supply and Production, 1939–45; member, Combined Production and Resources Board, Washington, 1942–3; Assistant Secretary, Treasury, 1945, Under-Secretary, 1947, Third Secretary, 1955–62, Second Secretary, 1962–6; Permanent Secretary, Ministry of Aviation, 1966; Ministry of Technology, 1966–70.

What these figures show, to express the substance of what in his § 2 Sir W. Eady says in another way, is that, if a tidal wave were to overwhelm North and South America, our subsequent financial problems would not be too bad and nothing worse than starvation would supervene.

They do not help me with my essential difficulty, which is as follows:

If, having failed to get financial assistance from U.S.A., our overall adverse balance of trade remains as before, from which countries can we expect to borrow what we have failed to obtain from U.S.A.? Deprived of the free use of their existing sterling resources, most of the countries suggested for the sterling group cannot expect to have an over-all favourable balance after the war out of which they can lend to us. Indeed, half the problem is that they also will have a large adverse balance with the Americas.

That is why I put the essence of the situation in the following form. If we have an overall adverse balance of trade, Plan II will not work. If we have not, any plan will work.

My next difficulty is that I see no prospect of the proposed members of the sterling group accepting membership of the club under Plan II conditions. They have everything to lose by doing so and nothing to gain. It would have to be part of the plan that they cut themselves off to the greatest possible extent from trade with U.S.A. just like ourselves. What motive have they to rupture trade relations with U.S.A. in order to lend us money they have not got?

On the secondary question of the distribution of the foreign-owned dollars, I agree that a very large part is in the Americas, though I should add Canada and Mexico to the South American countries.

Nevertheless, in the present context, what we have to think of is the total value of dollars and free gold. In addition to the American countries, France, Belgium, Holland, Switzerland, Sweden, Russia and China possess very large resources. China alone, including privately owned balances, is said to hold $800 million in U.S.A. After taking account of American contributions to UNRRA, the Export and Import Bank, the two Bretton Woods Plans, etc. etc., I do not think there is any serious risk of an overall shortage of gold and dollars in the first three years.

KEYNES

9.7.45

Discussions with the Board of Trade, and by this time the Economic Section of the War Cabinet, on the treatment of sterling balances also continued. The Board of Trade and Economic Section, realising, after the earlier discussions, that the tying of the release of sterling balances to purchases of British exports might upset the commercial policy talks under Article VII of the Lend Lease Agreement, suggested that the schedule for the release of sterling balances change so as to give British exporters time to meet the expected demand. When Sir Arnold Overton made the proposal to reduce the initially convertible balances, Keynes replied

To SIR ARNOLD OVERTON, *10 July 1945*

Dear Overton,

Many thanks for the suggestion you sent me with your letter of July 9th. Perhaps it would be useful to have a round table talk about it sometime next week, when Eady will be back and Brand will be here. For example, sometime on the 18th, 19th or 20th. I shall be away myself for a few days preceding the 17th and will get in touch with you then about a time.

Meanwhile, I should say at once that I think there is a great deal to be said for the amendment you propose or something on those lines. I had already been reaching the conclusion that the immediate freeing of £750 million might be unnecessarily generous, and perhaps even dangerous. But I had not got to the point of marrying this idea with an off-setting arrangement for releasing larger sums absolutely year by year hereafter. I have no doubt that what you propose would be in the interests of this country. The question is how much in this direction one can get away with, on the one hand with U.S.A. and on the other hand with our sterling area creditors. But I do not see that they can reasonably object to a modification in this direction.

In my own opinion, the advantages would be more financial and arising out of general caution than to help our export trade, though no doubt the larger the amount immediately released, the more willing will the sterling area creditors be to spend their rather ample resources outside this country.

Several of the paragraphs in your note relating to the suggestion of allowing 'special purchases' of British goods mistake, I think, what I had in mind. (My own fault; I did not develop this at all). What I had in view would not really be open to most of the comments in your paragraphs 6–10. The observation, however, in your paragraph 11, that what is in view would be analogous to the use of tied loans, is just. That is exactly what the arrangement would be. And whilst I should agree that there would be great advantage to us in outlawing tied loans, I regard that as altogether out of the question. To begin with, it would mean that we should have to abolish our Export Credit Department, and the Americans the Export-Import Bank, on which, in their present mood, they propose largely to depend. Indeed, it is not practicable to outlaw every version of a connection between trade and finance. My conception of the 'special purchases' would be precisely that we should release some of the blocked funds to finance certain contracts in exactly the same circumstances as in happier conditions we should have found ourselves financing them with an *ad hoc* loan. There is nothing new or, in my opinion, vicious in providing finance to pay for particular capital goods furnished from this country, and that is what it would be.

Nevertheless, I foresee some difficulty in making the Americans see the matter in this light. For, whilst they will never dream of outlawing tied loans themselves, they will certainly do all in their power to prevent us from having them. Thus, whereas the first part of your proposal may not be as acceptable to the Americans as my version, your second feature they would undoubtedly prefer.

I am sending a copy of this letter to Robbins.

Yours sincerely,

[copy initialled] K

With R. H. Brand's return to London, the discussions of the British approach to Stage III became much more intense. Before they began, Keynes wrote to Brand in reply to the latter's letter of 23 June. Both appear below.

From R. H. BRAND, *23 June 1945*

Dear Maynard,

Stage III

I have been thinking further over the way to put your plan to the American side. I may, in what I say now, repeat myself, but the best course seem to me to express my thoughts to you from time to time as they occur to me.

1. The whole plan in its outcome, if we are successful in persuading the U.S. Government to support it, can be defended here as justice to the U.K. in the sense that it is just (*a*) that the U.K. should be relieved largely of its war debt burden and (*b*) not be forced to incur an additional very large post-war debt which in essence will also be a war debt.

What we cannot put to the American people is that it is justice that they should give us a free grant on the ground that they should have entered the war before they did and that therefore they owe us the $3 billion we spent here.

2. There is no reason why, if we 'sell' the plan thoroughly to the U.S. Government, they should not use such an argument in their own way, if they dared. That would be for them to decide. But it would be fatal for us to do so. This is all the more so, since the U.S., no doubt, would claim that since they came into the war, they with lend lease had seen that justice was done to us far more than all the nations which had merely lent us money.

3. The only argument we can use is that there is no way by which we

369

can have justice done to us except by the U.S. helping on the largest possible scale out of its superabundant wealth, simply because there is no one else able to do it. The rest can play their part in forgoing claims but they cannot provide the free cash needed. Moreover, since the whole scheme has for its object to put the U.K. on an even keel, it would be foolish to provide us with the means to do so on terms which would prevent this from happening by re-imposing a burden on us certain to prove intolerable.

4. We could in addition, of course, use all your arguments about the psychological effect on our sterling creditors, about the immense benefit to the U.S. from our joining the ranks of the convertible and so on. At very small cost they would be making a new world.

5. I dislike, I confess, putting forward a request such as this. Whatever we may say, the Americans will always regard it in the future as a great act of generosity on their part, for which we must always be grateful. There may be in fact little difference between a gift and a loan on exceedingly easy terms, but it will always be considered that there is a difference. Therefore, I think that the proposal cannot be pressed, if the U.S. authorities are against it. We have to get the U.S. authorities to support the plan whole-heartedly and it is they who must put it forward as their own idea and support it with all their strength.

6. If, of course, the U.S. Government were to accept the plan whole-heartedly, a very strong case can be made; and on their side the U.S. Administration might equally assist us to make a very strong case with the sterling creditors. They could show it was of vital interest to the U.S. if they did put up a lot of money for us, that concessions by others should be sufficient to restore us to something like normal and so that then we should be strong enough to be able to sustain convertibility and generally act as a good partner.

7. The vital question, therefore, is whether the idea can be thoroughly 'sold' to the Administration before any knowledge of it reaches the public. It wants to be thrashed out in absolute privacy with the people at the top and then that they should persuade the President. From all I hear, he wants orderly arguments presented to him by those in whom he trusts. If those arguments are convincing, it might not take long to convince him.

8. The great leap in the dark seems to me to be the immediate return to convertibility. The more one thinks of it, the more advantages this has against the transitional period. Inconvertibility during that period means, if I am right, forcing inconvertibility on all the other parts of the sterling area. The temptation for them then would be to break away. If we had to buy as much as we could from them on credit and on the assumption

370

that we can not provide more than a proportion of their imports, they would themselves have to borrow dollars to buy imports from the U.S. and elsewhere. Thus against a sterling obligation from us they would enter themselves into dollar obligations to the U.S. This would not be at all a tempting prospect for them.

With convertibility for all current transactions what would matter would be the overall balance of payments of the whole sterling area with the rest of the world outside the U.K. Insofar as there were a deficit we should see sterling to an equivalent amount sold to provide dollars and other currencies. Thus the exports from the rest of the sterling area into the U.S. would be a matter of the greatest moment to us. Thus convertibility would be the very best means of keeping the sterling area together.

You in London, however, can judge much better than I what our chances are of maintaining convertibility. I should take it to be a gamble, even if the world goes moderately well. If it goes badly, the chances surely would be greatly against us. Nevertheless clearly the promise of convertibility at once would be an enormous inducement to the U.S. to fall in with our proposals. How it would react on our internal economic policy, Beveridge plans, housing, very large reconstruction schemes and so on is another matter. We should have to walk on a tight rope. We *must* have our exports. That, I feel, is the first *sine qua non*. But we must also, to get them, have industrial reconstruction and beyond that is the necessity for 'homes for heroes', security for all, etc. It will be a tremendous undertaking, requiring presumably lavish expenditures.

9. I enclose you a cutting from the *Washington Post* of today, which has a bearing on all this. I should assume that what John Williams says comes from himself, and that what Taft says comes from Baruch.[33] I can at least say that nothing whatever of this kind has been said outside this office by any member of the Treasury Delegation.

I would regard what was said by Taft as encouraging except that he is so often, in fact nearly always, wrong.

Yours sincerely,

R. H. BRAND

[33] The *Washington Post* clipping reported statements of Professor J. H. Williams, Vice-President of the Federal Reserve Bank of New York, and Senator Robert Taft favouring a $3 billion grant to Britain for the transition. Senator Taft had also suggested that British officials were asking for $7–8 billion in grants.

To R. H. BRAND, *11 July 1945*

My dear Bob,

I am off this evening for a few days at Tilton and expect to be back on the morning of July 17th. I am sticking to this plan in spite of our expecting you in a day or two, partly because Eady is also away this week, partly because you may like to have a week-end clear before settling down to public affairs in this office, and partly because this seems the only lull in the near future when it will be convenient to be away from Whitehall. I hope this will suit you all right. Bridges is off to 'Terminal'[34] on Saturday so that you might do well to get a talk with him before he goes. Waley and others in Moscow are already on their way to Berlin, so that there can be no further developments for the moment on that front. In fact, as I have said, this is the best expectation of three days lull.

As I shall be seeing you so soon, I need not go into too much detail. But it may be useful for me to note down one or two things about the present situation so that you can have a chance to think them over.

I am afraid you have been having a hectic time[35] in Washington lately. But you have held our end up magnificently, and no harm has been done in my opinion. At any rate, on the F.E.A. front. We were rather surprised to learn a day or two ago that the Chiefs of Staff were in a great flurry about frustration on the War Department front. Of course, the ultimate weakness of their case is that their demands are in

[34] The Potsdam Conference.
[35] Brand's 'hectic time' had concerned a change in American policy over Stage II. American officials, reacting to President Truman's directive that military supplies under lend lease were only available for the war against Japan, began cutting back on the Keynes–Morgenthau Stage II agreement. Supplies outside the direct needs of the Japanese war became inadmissible, as did munitions that Britain could produce. The definition of war in the Administration's new policy excluded the costs of occupying Axis countries. This change in policy had been the subject of contacts between the Ministers concerned and the Prime Minister and the President. It had then become a matter for discussion at the highest level during the Potsdam Conference.

fact largely phoney, and nothing much would really happen if they were rejected. That is, in my own judgement, the reality of the matter. But, of course, on paper they have an absolute case, and we have to do our best for them. Jacob[36] has drafted a paper for the P.M., which looks to me on right lines. Sinclair is, of course, taking the lead in all this, and Harmer is in close touch. I think Harmer would rather like to have a talk with you to hear the latest from your side as soon as you get here.

We were all extremely pleased with the report of the Senate Committee [on Bretton Woods]. Bernstein[37] certainly did a grand piece of work. Nothing could have been more sympathetic or a better preparation for our Stage III proposals. I daresay you were right to get him to strike out the specific figure of $4 billion. There were indeed dangers in it. On the other hand, it would not have been a bad figure to have got down in black and white as something which the Senate had heard mentioned without being shocked.

With your letter of June 23rd about the line of our approach I am largely in agreement. I have had in mind during the next few days at Tilton to start drafting something which would not conflict with your advice and may have a first shot to show you when I am back next week. (In fact, I ought to have mentioned the opportunity to start drafting on this before we confer with you as one of the reasons why I had wanted to get away for a few days at this point.) In a short preliminary talk we had the other day, the Chancellor took the line that he regarded a free grant, supplemented by a possible call on a loan up to a further amount, as an entirely different proposition from our depending on a loan for

[36] Lt. Colonel Edward Ian Claud Jacob (later Major-General Sir Ian Jacob, G.B.E.) (b. 1899); Military Assistant Secretary, Committee of Imperial Defence, 1938; Military Assistant Secretary to War Cabinet; Director-General, B.B.C., 1952–60.

[37] Edward Morris Bernstein (b. 1904); Assistant Director of Monetary Research, U.S. Treasury, 1941–6; Assistant to Secretary of the Treasury, 1946; Director of Research, International Monetary Fund, 1946–58.

certain and from the start. As at present advised, he would resist the latter somewhat vehemently. But a loan which we did not have to take up and, in fact, thought we might by good management avoid, taking the form of an option so that we could feel confidence and security, was another matter. You, I know, are none too optimistic about our avoiding a loan in the long run. And it would be rash to contradict this forecast. On the other hand, it does seem to me, and I gather to you also, that as time goes on a prospect of an approach on the lines we contemplate looks a great deal more hopeful than it did when I first put it forward.

I think it is your paragraph 8 about the risks of a return to convertibility which hits the nail on the head. As I shall be able to tell you, all efforts towards reasonable economy so far have had the smallest possible result. Save in those moments when I am feeling exceptionally buoyant, it seems to me that we cannot be trusted with $3 billion in our pocket. We should just run through it in the first year or two, and then where should we be? I believe we could manage on the $3 billion, possibly calling on another $2 billion loan. But we shall *not* manage it unless we change our ways very considerably from what they are now. Indeed, the art of government all round seems at the moment to be at its lowest ebb. On the other hand, there is a reason for looking at the issues another way. If, in the course of two or three years, we are able to overcome our overseas deficit, then we shall certainly have been wise to have adopted convertibility and all will be well. If, on the other hand, we fail, then no alternative plan would have been in any degree better. No doubt convertibility would break down, but so would any conceivable arrangement. It may be true that we cannot be trusted with a little easy money. Nevertheless, that is the only possible route. If we do not pull ourselves together, there will be a financial Dunkirk anyhow. If we do, then the projected plan is a good one. However, perhaps because I live in London and you in Washington, my anxiety of late has been much less whether we can put this sort of thing across the Americans than whether, having done so, we can be trusted with the money.

I enclose an interesting suggestion from Overton, which seems to me to have a great deal in it. This would, to some extent, mitigate the risks of accepting convertibility, since it would greatly reduce the fund in respect of which we should be accepting it in the early period. You will see that I am suggesting a round table talk on this when you and Eady are available again.

I have also been discussing with Harmer and Grant the material which should be prepared. Here again we must have a further talk with them when you are here.

The Prime Minister has been provided with a note to the effect that he should tackle Truman about arranging for Anglo-American talks on the wind-up of lend lease and what should follow as soon as possible. Bridges will certainly be there and Cherwell may be for part of the time. I rather understand the arrangement is that, if these kind of questions come to a head and are discussed otherwise than perfunctorily, the P.M. will send for the Chancellor to join him, the Chancellor holding himself in readiness for this. My own best bet would be, however, that they would never get down to any Anglo-American issues which are capable of a week-end or two's postponement. The P.M. intends to be back in London for the declaration of the General Election, so that there will be barely ten days, in fact very definitely not ten days, at Potsdam from start to finish. I believe that the whole of this time will be spent on issues arising out of Germany, frontiers, machinery of government and reparations. There will be no time for matters which can be just as well, or better, discussed when there are no Russians down the passage. Either there will be a second session of Terminal after the General Election results are out, which would be very inconvenient indeed for the P.M., or, having cleared up the main

German questions, there will be an adjournment to London to clear up the outstanding Anglo-American issues. Thus I shall be surprised if anything significant develops during the meeting in the course of the next ten days.

As you will have observed, the General Election here was a ghastly and even shameful business—not, I admit, quite as bad as the Presidential election in U.S.A. last year, but nevertheless beneath the dignity of human nature. Beaverbrook and the P.M. between them have done their damnedest to lose it. On the eve of the poll the general impression was that the Conservatives would have a large majority. Later information from the constituencies casts considerable doubt on this. I regard it as probable, but by no means absolutely certain, that the Conservatives will have a working majority over all other parties combined.

You have been a great correspondent over the last few months. It has been an enormous help to have so much of the background and to feel that one has known what is in your mind. I have given a limited and discreet circulation to some, but not all, of your letters to the three or four most closely concerned. But it is high time that you should come here in person. And it looks as if the psychological moment has been chosen. You will have seen the telegram about Clayton's intention to come to London in the first week of August with a view to opening up Stage III discussions. We shall have to give a good deal of careful thought to the question how deeply it is prudent to enter into the matter with him at this point. Our proposals will not have been before the Cabinet so early as that. And, if it should happen that the result of the election leads to complicated conclusions, it would be quite impossible at that time to obtain anyone's ear.

Yours ever,
[copy initialled] M. K.

Before the discussions started, Keynes set his thoughts down in a memorandum entitled *The Present Overseas Financial Position of the U.K.*, dated 23 July. This paper, along with others from the Bank of England,[38] were the subject of discussions in the Treasury on 20, 23 and 30 July.

In the light of these discussions, Keynes revised his paper, circulating both it, and another paper entitled *Our Overseas Financial Prospects*, on 13 August. The revised paper was circulated to a limited group of Ministers before they discussed the situation with Keynes (below p. 420).

(This is a first draft, following a series of discussions in the Treasury, of the substance of the argument and proposals which we might present to the Americans at the first stage of the proposed oral discussions in Washington in September.

KEYNES, 13.8.45)

I. *The Present Overseas Financial Position of U.K.*

1. On the assumption that lend lease and Canadian mutual aid would continue to the end of 1945, recent estimates indicate that our net gold and dollar reserves at the end of 1945 would be of the order of $2 billion. The movement of our reserves and their composition are shown in detail in Appendix A.

2. British liabilities to overseas creditors at the same date are expected on the same assumption to stand at about $14 billion, so that the net reserves of $2 billion represent a

---

[38] The Bank of England suggestions came in the form of papers by Mr C. F. Cobbold, dated 12 July, and Lord Catto, dated 23 July. Cobbold's paper, which opposed any uniform solution for the sterling area and suggested that bilateral settlements with sterling area creditors should wait until the balances reached a peak, advocated approaching the United States for a grant for essential requirements for food and raw materials for Britain but nothing for the sterling area. With this grant in hand, Britain would develop her existing payments agreements and only move gradually towards convertibility.

Lord Catto, who was also uncertain of the desirability of a commitment to reach multilateral convertibility for current earnings at an early date and also opposed a loan, proposed that Britain submit an itemised claim for retrospective lend lease of about $1·5 billion and a proposal for a secured credit of $4 billion. The credit would have no sinking fund and bear no interest, but if Britain failed to repay drawings within, say, 10 years, she would give up the security deposited (overseas assets outside the United States such as Argentine railways and perhaps some West Indian islands such as the Bahamas).

proportion of 14 per cent of the liabilities. The distribution of the liabilities is shown in detail in Appendix B.

3. Assuming that Lend Lease and Mutual Aid have been terminated not later than the end of 1945, the excess of current overseas expenditure over current income of 1946 may be expected, apart from major changes of policy, to reach a figure not far short of $4 billion. Thus, in the absence of new solutions not yet in sight, the existing reserves would be entirely exhausted before the year was out even if further substantial aid could be obtained from the sterling area. The large deficit incurred during this first post-war year should be regarded as an unavoidable part of the total costs of the war. Estimating further ahead is not much better than guess work, but an additional deficit not far short of $3 billion seems probable in the ensuing period before equilibrium has been reached. The detailed evidence on which these estimates are based is given in Appendix C.

4. The gold and dollar reserves of the U.K. are the reserves of the whole of the sterling area in the sense that it is only out of these reserves that the sterling balances of the sterling area can be released for dollar purchases in excess of the current gold and dollar earnings of the area. No part of the sterling area holds any significant gold reserves apart from the Union of South Africa. Since the central reserves must be maintained above a certain minimum level except in extreme emergencies, it is evident that, if the sterling area as a whole (including the U.K.) has a running adverse balance with the rest of the world in the early years after the war, which is the general expectation, no significant part of the overseas sterling balances, as they stand at the end of the war, can be released for expenditure outside the sterling area, and the size of the running adverse balance outside the area will have to be strictly controlled, unless facilities are provided such as are not yet in sight.

(Appendices A, B and C are not yet ready.)

II. *The Character of the Problem*

5. The problem clearly falls into two parts, the size of the accumulated sterling balances at zero hour and the running adverse balance after zero hour.

6. The former is the less urgent problem. For no one can make us release these balances faster than is materially possible. Nevertheless they directly react on the latter problem in two ways.

7. In the first place, our existing debts affect what additional amounts we can borrow to help the current position. Our considered view is that we cannot be expected, and will not agree, to pay a commercial rate of interest on war debts, incurred in the common cause. Nor shall we undertake to repay the capital sums at a greater rate than lies within our reasonable capacity. But we are not prepared to repudiate by unilateral action any part of our capital liability to those who came to our financial assistance without security and on a vast scale when we were in dire straits, or to allow priority of repayment to debts incurred subsequently. Nor is it advisable for us to substitute for sterling debts, due to a great number of countries which are our natural customers, a dollar debt due to a single country which may involve an obligation beyond our power to satisfy.

8. We ask our American friends to agree that this is a proper attitude and that they will not ask us, or seek to induce us, to depart from it.

9. In the second place, it would cause very great disturbance to the national economies of some of our sterling area creditors if we could not begin from the start to release a marginal instalment of their sterling balances. The Union of South Africa holds a large independent gold reserve, and what follows does not apply to her. Nor does it apply to our creditors outside the area. But the rest of the area (apart from small amounts of gold and dollars held by India and

Australia which are not large enough to affect the position) hold no gold or dollar reserves whatever, either in their currency reserves or central banks. Their sterling balances in London comprise the whole of the ultimate external reserves of their banking systems and of their note issues, which, more perhaps from habit and good will than from prudent calculation, they have been willing to entrust to us during the war. If in the early years we block these balances entirely within the sterling area, we shall throw their trade relations with countries outside the area into serious confusion and will have been guilty, if there is any means of avoidance, of an abuse of confidence. This applies more particularly to the currency reserves of the Crown Colonies, which have not been entirely free agents in the matter. We have obtained their produce during the war, for our own use or (in some cases) to present it as reciprocal aid to the U.S., largely in return for bits of paper, i.e. by expanding their note issues. The expectation has been that after the war, when supplies and shipping are again available, these bits of paper can be used to pay for essential imports.

10. Thus there is a certain marginal part of the sterling balances which we are under an honourable obligation to treat in the same way, and at least *pari passu*, with our own current adverse balance after zero hour. There must be from the outset, that is to say, some minimum addition to our own current requirements for a marginal release of the pre-zero-hour sterling balances of certain sterling area countries.

11. Nevertheless it is our own running adverse balance after zero hour which constitutes the major part of the urgent problem. This is greatly aggravated in the first year or two after victory in Asia, by the fact that our military expenditure overseas will not sink to nothing at the hour of Japan's defeat but must unavoidably continue at a heavy rate for an appreciable period thereafter; and also by the fact that we have incurred obligations to UNRRA, to our own liberated terri-

tories in the Far East, and arising out of the occupation of Germany and the pacification of Europe and Asia.

III. *The First of the Alternative Solutions*

12. It appears to us, after the most earnest study, that we are confronted, broadly speaking, with two alternative courses of action, both of which would require the good will of the rest of the world, but one of which we can carry out or attempt to carry out chiefly on our own initiative, whilst the other would only be possible by a general plan on the part of all the chief countries concerned and could not be executed without the understanding aid of the U.S. There are, of course, certain compromises which are possible between the two alternatives set out below, partaking more of the one or more of the other. But for clarity of exposition it will be better to stick at the start to the clear-cut alternatives.

13. The first alternative is to develop, and modify according to circumstances, the system of the sterling area as it has been evolved during the war supported by payments agreements (on the model now existing with several European and South American countries) with countries outside the area. Under this system there would be full convertibility of exchange of sterling balances for current payments within the sterling area and between the sterling area and those outside countries accepting unrestricted payments agreements. Imports into the area from countries, setting a strict limit to the maximum amount of sterling which they are willing to accumulate or requiring some proportion of such accumulations to be paid or guaranteed in gold or dollars, would have to be strictly controlled and limited so far as possible to essentials, except to the extent that they were covered by exports to such countries from the area. With a country declining a payments agreement altogether trade would have to be still more restricted; and the excess of

imports from it into the area over exports to it from the area would have to be limited, necessarily, to what could be paid for by drawing on our gold and dollar reserves. A payments agreement would be offered to every country including the U.S. (It should be explained that under a payments agreement the U.S. would undertake to accumulate in sterling in the hands of the Bank of England an amount equal to the favourable balance of payments between the dollar area and the sterling area, either with or without limit of amount. During the transitional period this sterling could be freely employed on current purchases within the sterling area. At the end of the transitional period the accumulated sum would fall to be dealt with as described below).

14. Under such a system we could not rely on maintaining intact the sterling area dollar pool as it has existed during the war. Sterling area countries having a favourable current balance with the U.S., or some of them at least, would very likely insist on retaining their dollar surplus for their own use and would not agree to hand it over to the pool, as they have done hitherto. The partial break-down of the dollar pool, with the sterling area arrangements continuing unchanged in other respects, would not, however, be to the general advantage and would certainly operate to the disadvantage of the United States. For it would not increase the dollars available to pay for American exports and would merely mean that the sterling area countries having a running deficit with the U.S. would be forced to limit their purchases still more strictly. Moreover the countries having a dollar surplus might turn some part of these dollars into gold or hoard them, in which case American exports would not merely suffer more rigorous regulation but would be actually reduced in aggregate. The maintenance of the dollar pool is a way of ensuring that all the available dollars are in fact spent within the dollar area with the minimum of discrimination.

15. In theory such a system would have to be more rigid

in relation to a country unwilling to enter into a payments agreement than it has been during the war. Hitherto (apart from certain very recent exceptions) the exchange control of any member of the sterling area has been entitled to obtain from the central pool any dollars required for imports considered essential and not obtainable within the sterling area. This measure of liberality was, however, only made practicable through the limitations set by difficulties of supply and transport. In peace-time conditions the above practice would have to be replaced by an annual dollar ration (as is already the case with Egypt). Individual members of the area would, of course, be free to supplement their ration by borrowing from dollar sources but without any guarantee of the availability of their sterling resources for eventual repayment of such dollar liabilities. The principle underlying this procedure is simple and inevitable. *All* the dollars available from American imports and loans and from drawing within the limits of safety on the central reserves, would be made available in payment for American exports, and no more than all is possible.

16. This system, especially if the United States would accept a payments agreement, has certain advantages. The war-time system could slide off into it without any break in continuity. It might provide a highly elastic instrument for dealing with the unpredictable quantities of credit which will be required during the transitional period. It would offer some initial help to British exports which might accelerate the date at which equilibrium in the balance of payments could be achieved. Nor would it be essential, though highly convenient to the trade of both parties, that the U.S. should accept a payments agreement without limit of amount.

17. Moreover there would be no intention of maintaining such a system in its full rigour indefinitely. It is obvious that any system must break down eventually unless those concerned (more particularly the United Kingdom in this

instance) can find means of reaching equilibrium in their balance of payments within a reasonably short period. When this equilibrium has been achieved, the transitional period will have come to an end and there will be no longer any obstacle to the adoption of general multilateral convertibility in respect of the proceeds of future current trade. There is nothing in the above arrangements, provided they are limited to a transitional period, which would prevent the U.K. from accepting forthwith the obligations of the International Monetary Fund. The possibility of a transitional period having the above character has been strictly preserved in Article XIV, as indeed was essential pending the definite provision of any practicable alternative. Furthermore under the Bretton Woods Plan we should be entitled to put special restrictions on the subsequent use of the sterling balances accumulated before the end of the transitional period.

18. It would also be our intention to follow faithfully the provision of the Bretton Woods Plan that during the transitional period 'members shall have continuous regard in their foreign exchange policies to the purposes of the Fund, and, as soon as conditions permit, they shall take all possible measures to develop such commercial and financial arrangements with other members as will facilitate international payments and the maintenance of exchange stability'. It would be our purpose to allow and arrange as free an exchange of sterling between special accounts under payments agreements as was mutually acceptable to the other countries concerned. And with the improving trend towards equilibrium, the necessary degree of restriction would be progressively reduced. If we have to adopt this system we should hope that it would be with the good will and close collaboration of all concerned. We on our part would do our utmost to minimise causes of friction and to use no more discrimination than is inherent in a system where trade is limited and conditioned by the separate availability of payment facilities.

19. Nevertheless on closer examination this alternative is seen to involve some serious difficulties. It is probably the best we can do if we have to solve the problem by ourselves and on our own initiative. It is not, in our judgment, impracticable for us to make the attempt to enter on the post-war period along these lines. But candour forces the admission that it is not as good as it has been made to look in the preceding paragraphs.

20. It will almost inevitably lead, in practice, though that would not be our deliberate intention, to a greater degree of bilateral trade negotiation than is in theory inherent in it. For countries, whether inside or outside the area, having a favourable balance of trade with the rest of the sterling area, would be reluctant to receive payment in terms of sterling, the future availability of which would be uncertain. They would, therefore, attempt (signs of this are already apparent) to link their sales to us with a definite undertaking as to the scale on which we would export to them. The paradoxical situation would arise that our customers would tumble over one another to obtain as large as possible a quota of our limited supply of desired exports—obviously a situation in some ways highly attractive to us, yet no less obviously capable of producing very great frictions in international trading relations. The allocation of the dollar quota in the absence of an unrestricted payments agreement with the United States would provide another scramble. The whole object of the system would be to make the rest of the world lend us more money than they were inclined to lend and sometimes more than they possessed as a voluntary surplus; and the whole object of each other country, whether inside or outside the sterling area, would be to try to distort its operations so that they in particular carried as little of the aggregate burden as possible.

21. In short, the system would be forcing an unnatural pattern on international trading relations, though perhaps

one advantageous to British short-term interests, over the whole of the formative post-war period, when as rapid a return as possible to normality is in the permanent interest of peaceful and profitable trade between nations. Moreover, we might reach an equilibrium in the balance of payments in these hot-house conditions in ways which we should be incapable of sustaining when we were deprived of them.

22. Above all, this alternative is open to the major objection that it is merely postponing the solution of the intrinsic problem to the end of the transitional period, without there being any reason to suppose, indeed the contrary, that it would be any easier to solve then than it is now. By the end of the transitional period the British overseas debt would have risen under these arrangements to $20 billion or more. Even payment of interest at 1 per cent, without any repayment of capital, would strain our immediate resources. Yet, for reasons already explained, many of the countries concerned would be in serious straits if the whole of their sterling resources became frozen. Yet this is how it would have to be. At the end of the transitional period the trade of a considerable part of the world would be thrown into sudden disorder. For it must be remembered that during the transitional period members of the sterling area and countries having payments agreements with it would have the free disposal over a wide area of their accumulated, and not merely their currently acquired, sterling balances. It is only at the end of the transitional period that they would suddenly lose any effective use of their standing sterling reserves.

23. In fact, when the transitional period came to an end (meaning by this the period before the U.K. had attained equilibrium in its own balance of current payments), there would be, as there now are, only two alternatives, and they would be the *same* two. Either it would be necessary to continue more or less permanently the sterling area system supported by payments agreements as heretofore (though in

the much more favourable conditions for its operation which would exist when the U.K.'s own balance was in equilibrium). In this case the zero-hour overseas holdings of sterling would become a sort of international fiduciary currency, the amount of which outstanding would remain more or less constant, slowly declining in so far as we became capable of repayment, though the holders of it would change in accordance with the fluctuations of international surpluses and deficits, a state of affairs better for the holders than freezing—in short, a grand verification of the Law of Sir Thomas Gresham (the first British Treasury official who played with the management of foreign exchanges), the very inferiority of sterling having ensured its final triumph. Or, alternatively, we should have to fall back on the second alternative, the explanation of which is about to follow. When this explanation has been read, it will be clear enough that, if something of this kind is inevitable in the long run, it will be vastly easier to put it through now than when the common emotions and close collaboration of the war are five years behind us in the valley of forgetfulness.

24. This is not to say that we should not decidedly prefer an essay in cunctation, which is what this first alternative really is, to accepting an unsatisfactory expedient or putting our name to what we have no sufficient confidence that we can honour.

IV. *The Second Alternative*

25. The other alternative is to organise, so far as may be, a liquidation of the financial consequences of the War amongst all those chiefly concerned who have won a common victory by a common effort. Not a complete liquidation—that would be asking too much. The British people are prepared to accept for themselves and their posterity, as the price of deliverance, a burden of external indebtedness to their Allies which no one else will be expected to carry, not even the defeated enemy. The peculiar war-time system of the sterling

area has been a great success; for one may doubt whether the war would have been won without it. But it has resulted in the economic and financial affairs of half the world becoming inextricably intertwined with our own. Thus, unless means can be found to bring our burden within the limits of what is practicable, immeasurable and lasting confusion to the world's international economy cannot be avoided.

26. We ask our American friends, therefore, to join us in a realistic appraisal of the facts and to aid the acceptance of what, sooner or later, inevitably arises from them.

27. We have been expecting that. Including some allowance for overseas expenditure arising out of the war after the war is over, the actual and prospective gross overseas indebtedness of the United Kingdom will be of the order of $16 billion. The earlier termination of the Japanese war may perhaps make a downward revision of $1 billion reasonable. Nevertheless in what follows it will be assumed that the gross aggregate to be handled is $16 billion, taken as a round figure.

28. We seek to persuade you that it is right and proper and advisable to divide this aggregate into two parts. One part, say $4 billion would be cancelled; the other part, say $12 billion would be made freely available to the holders by instalments, and also all subsequent current earnings of sterling in full, for current purchases in any country without discrimination, this being made practicable in addition to our meeting our running adverse balance in the early post-war period by a sum of $5 billion being allowed by the U.S. as an addition to our reserves. The plan would enter into force as soon as possible after the end of the war, say at the end of 1946. By this means, whilst the Bretton Woods transitional period could not be formally terminated so soon, we should dispense immediately with any element of discrimination in the use of available sterling balances as between the sterling area and countries outside the area. Whilst the sterling balances accumulated before zero hour could be made available

to the holders only by instalments, whatever was available from time to time would be available without discrimination. In particular, the existing arrangements governing the sterling area dollar pool would be forthwith dissolved.

29. Thus it is proposed that a total relief of $9 billion should be provided to the extent of (say) $4 billion by our sterling creditors and of $5 billion by the United States. We also hope for some aid from Canada. The relief allowed by the sterling creditors would take the form of the writing off of a part of their sterling balances. The relief afforded by the United States would be in the shape of a reserve of dollars which could be called upon, partly to finance our dollar purchases during the transitional period and partly to give us the resources to implement our offer of general availability by instalments to the remaining uncancelled portion of the sterling balances and to all current earnings of sterling after zero hour.

30. Before returning to the details of the proposal as affecting the United States, it will be convenient to develop in greater detail the character of the plan which would be offered to the sterling creditors, as follows:-

(i) A figure would be established for each country fairly representing its cumulative war-time accretions in sterling. The amount of its purchases or repatriations of sterling securities and of any gold supplied during the war would be added to its sterling balances at the end of the war, and also an estimated figure for net war receipts from the British Government accruing after the end of the war as a result of clearing up war accounts, movements of troops and demobilisation; whilst the pre-war figure for the balances and other special receipts of a capital character would be deducted.

(ii) We have already made sufficient study of the particular cases to convince us that a uniform all-round formula would not work out fairly. There would, therefore, be separate discussions with each country concerned.

(iii) We should set out from the starting point that a writing off of one-third of the net resulting war gains as estimated above would be generally appropriate except in so far as there were sufficient reasons for a lower figure. Account would be taken of the local price level at which the expenditure had been incurred, of the burden of war expenditure and war strain undertaken in other ways, how far the accumulated sterling balances include the surplus of normal trade due to war-time impediments to normal importing and how far they are due to special receipts from overseas which would never have accrued apart from the war, and any other relevant circumstances. We think that after making allowance for exceptional treatment, justifiable and necessary in certain cases, there would remain an amount of about $4 billion appropriate for cancellation.

(iv) The negotiations with those concerned would be on a voluntary and agreed basis in the following sense. There would be no unilateral writing off of debt. It would, however, be represented that the possibility of freeing in the near future any significant portion of the sterling balances wholly depended on some measure of agreed general liquidation of the financial consequences of the war and in particular on assistance from the U.S. Those countries which were not prepared to take a fair share of the burden could not expect to benefit from the facilities afforded by the U.S. for freeing sterling balances. That is to say, countries unwilling to come into the general scheme (after receiving all proper allowances under (iii) above) could not participate in its benefits.

(v) Let us assume that the plan proves generally acceptable and that the aggregate appropriate writings-off add up to $4 billion out of an initial aggregate of $16 billion, leaving $12 billion still owing. We would then propose to free (say) $1 billion, divided between all the holders of sterling, to be available forthwith to meet their current adverse balances of trade without discrimination. It is obvious that this also could not be shared on a general formula—the amount of the immediately available proportion would have to depend *inter alia* on the proportion cancelled, on the scale of the country's external requirements and on the size of the country's pre-war sterling balances.

(vii) The balance of $12 billion would be similarly released by instalments over a period not exceeding 50 years. Such subsequent releases (in addition to the initial $1 billion and the whole of net current earnings) might commence in the fifth year at a rate of (say) $200 million a year with the faithful intention, though without a premature obligation, gradually to step up the rate of releases as time and opportunity permit.

(viii) In addition to these normal arrangements, if in subsequent years it were to suit us to make loans overseas for any purpose or in any context, including loans through the International Bank for Reconstruction and Development, we should be free to offer a holder of unreleased sterling to release instalments in advance of the due date suitably discounted; so that in this case earlier *ex gratia* releases of this character might come to play the same part in our economy as, for example, the Export-Import Bank or loans to the International Bank in the case of the United States. The effect of such releases on the British economy will be much the same as our former regular foreign investment, and the time may come when it will prove a useful help to our policy of full employment to have the equivalent of such foreign investment always at hand without having to trouble about the credit of the borrower or the problem of subsequent payment of interest and capital. In fact we should be obtaining at some future date the same kind of advantage as the United States will be obtaining now if they fall in with this plan!

(ix) It is not proposed that the unreleased portion should carry interest. The more rapid ultimate liquidation made possible by the complete elimination of interest on the portion temporarily frozen seems better in result and more appropriate to the character of loans which have not gone to the creation of commercial assets capable of earning interest. On the available sterling balances interest could, of course, be earned by the holders at (say) Treasury bill rate, if they were retained in a liquid form, or at a higher rate, if they were to be invested in the U.K., becoming liable in this case to any restrictions in force on capital withdrawals.

(x) It should be made clear that this offer to the sterling area holders of sterling balances would have to be made contingent, for the time being at least, on their remaining members of the area for certain purposes. We could not safely afford to undertake the releases of the balances on the scale indicated above if we had to assume that the whole of the amounts so released would be immediately withdrawn. The amounts released would in some cases amount to the whole or the greater part of the free external resources of the countries in question, and would constitute, so to speak, their ultimate reserves which it would be as much in their interest as in ours not to expend imprudently or at too great a rate. Thus there would have to be an understanding that the releases of pre-zero-hour sterling were to be used solely to meet any adverse balance of trade on current account accumulated after zero hour and not to acquire gold or foreign assets; but when required, they would be equally available, just like pre-war sterling, to pay for imports from any source without discrimination. Any net favourable balance arising out of current trade which they might earn after zero hour, would, on the other hand, be available for any purpose including the purchase of gold and foreign assets; so that we should be accepting this part of our post-transitional obligations under the International Monetary Fund as soon as the proposed scheme came into operation. Furthermore even where we were retaining the ultimate discretion in our hands, we should endeavour to interpret the rules in any particular case in as free and liberal a manner as the state of our overall resources permitted; and we believe that the recent experience of the members of the sterling area of the way in which we have handled our relations with them even in times when we were in the greatest possible difficulties will have given them confidence in the value of such a general understanding. In particular we should consider it our duty to release sterling balances in advance of the due date, to the full extent that our own resources and other liabilities would permit, to any member of the sterling area finding itself in temporary, unforeseen difficulties. Our object throughout is to avoid any absolute obligations beyond what we have confidence we can carry, with the full intention of being better than our word whenever our resources allow and the other party has need.

(xi) The arrangements outlined above are given as a specimen of what the separate negotiations might evolve. They are not intended as a binding model in matters of detail. We should endeavour to work out separately in collaboration with each particular country involved a technique which involved the least possible interference with their normal banking arrangements and the interests of private persons. Here again we believe that we can operate *in practice* a much better and freer system than any to which it would be safe for us to commit ourselves as a binding obligation.

(xii) We believe that the other countries in the sterling area can be made to see that their acceptance of this general scheme is as much in their interest as in ours. This does not mean that each will not strive to the utmost to get out of it as much as possible for themselves; and it will need resolute diplomacy and great determination on our part to achieve a fair and balanced all-round settlement. Nevertheless they are all of them keenly aware of the limitations on what is within our power and that there is no means on earth by which they can get more than is within our power. If, therefore, the

United States is prepared greatly to increase our capacity on condition that the sterling area countries also play their fair part in liquidating the financial consequences of the war so as to bring the burden which we (and we alone) will continue to carry within tolerance, they will understand that the choice for them can only lie in the last resort between coming in to the plan and sharing its benefits or staying out and foregoing them.

(xiii) If, nevertheless, there are any countries in the area which finally reject a settlement which seems fair in relation to ourselves and to the other participants and to the ultimate governing conditions of the whole plan, we should invite them to withdraw from the area. Henceforward they would be entirely free to make their own arrangements. But their zero-hour sterling balances would not share in the initial release of available sterling, nor would they carry interest. It would be our purpose and intention to discharge them in due course, but they would have, necessarily, to rank behind our other commitments, and we could give no prior undertaking as to the dates of release. Here also, however, we should accept the principle of non-discrimination. Either the balances would not be available at all, or they would be available for spending in all areas equally.

V. *The Second Alternative in relation to the United States*

31. Our gold and dollar reserves of \$2 billion, of which not more than \$1 billion could be drawn upon except in the gravest emergency, are so small in relation to the other quantities in the picture that no plan can be built upon them otherwise than as a minor and secondary support. In the absence of any other support we should run through the whole of the available gold and dollar reserves within less than a year after the end of the war.

32. We are not prepared to borrow new money for our own

purposes, the repayment of which is put in front of the money which has been freely and liberally entrusted to us and our safe-keeping during the war. Nor are we prepared to borrow new money for the purpose of our present creditors which would canalise a proportion of our present widely spread indebtedness into the hands of a single creditor or substitute a liability in gold or foreign currency for a liability in sterling.

33. These must be regarded as final decisions which we hope will be accepted with sympathy and approval as fundamental to a wise and just approach to our problem.

34. Nevertheless there remain a variety of technical solutions which could be proposed within the ambit of these general conditions. If we put forward a particular solution which would obviously be the ideal one from our own point of view, that must not be taken to mean that we regard it as the only possible solution of the *genus* Alternative II. We do not, at this stage, enter into any technical details.

35. Our suggestion is that the United States should place at our disposal as a grant-in-aid to help to solve the international problem of the liquidation of war-time indebtedness a sum of $5 billion in three instalments—$2 billion in the first year and $1½ billion in each of the next two years. This figure has not been arrived at, and cannot be justified by, any exact calculation, and is based on a broad judgement of the necessities of the case. We should have liked to have kept to a lower figure of (say) $3–4 billion, but the prolongation of the war and the greater obligations now facing us lead us to feel that with less than $5 billion we could not accept the responsibility of fulfilling the obligations to make sterling available on the scale suggested above or of terminating the existing sterling area arrangements so soon as the end of 1946. On the other hand, a larger sum than $5 billion might make us sufficiently comfortable to relax from full pressure without which we shall not recover equilibrium as soon as we should. Hence a mean of $5 billion. If it proves insufficient, as it

possibly may, we must face the resulting problem in the light of the surrounding facts as and when they arise. On the basis of $5 billion we should be ready to face the risks and responsibilities of a settlement on the general lines indicated above.

36. On what grounds can we make such an unprecedented suggestion to the Administration of the United States?

37. Under lend lease we have already enjoyed an extraordinary measure of liberality. In fact, in so far as our difficulties arise out of war-time accumulations of sterling and not out of our running deficit immediately after the war, they are precisely due to the fact that we have not had the benefit of similar arrangements with other countries; though we must remember that most of these other countries are poor countries or undeveloped countries and countries not so rich as ourselves and, in some cases, heavily indebted to us, and that they have in fact given us invaluable and even decisive assistance in the war through their having been willing to entrust all their resources to us without security or guarantee and to continue doing so after their sterling balances had vastly exceeded any figure even in the remotest anticipation when the arrangements were first made. Moreover, the proposed plan would in fact require of them contributions to the common cause not disproportionate to the contributions of others, if regard is had to their relative wealth and real resources in proportion to their populations.

38. The only main point on which we can commend these suggestions to the United States is that they may be a sufficient, and perhaps an indispensable, condition of establishing after the war the type of commercial and financial relations between nations which they wish to see established, and which we, too, wish, if it can be managed.

39. The object is, as already stated, to facilitate the liquidation of indebtedness arising out of the war on a scale sufficient to allow a return to normal practices at an early date. Not ourselves only are concerned in all this. The financial

arrangements of half the world are, as we have seen, so entangled with our own, that the pattern of world trade and finance as a whole is deeply involved.

49. But there is also an immaterial element. For nearly two years the United Kingdom with her small population, having no support except the steadfastness of the distant members of the British Commonwealth, held the fort alone. Everything we had in energy, man-power and possessions was thrown into the furnace, with an intensity and eager agreement by the generality which, as it now appears, did not, fortunately, exist in the camp of the enemy. The effort and the sacrifice were successful. It cannot then appear to those who have borne the burden of many days that it is a just and seemly conclusion of this sacrifice to be left, as the price of what has happened, with a burden of future tribute to the rest of the world beyond tolerable bearing. Our people would not accept with a quiet mind what was coming to them, when the full meaning of all this came to be felt in the burdens and privations of daily life after the war; and it is by man's feelings, and only so, that the stable foundations of society within and without countries are disturbed.

41. Yet in relation to the vast expenditures of war the sums involved are a trifle. In fact it is inconceivable that the people of the United States can be influenced in their decision, one way or the other, by the sum of money at stake. It cannot be the money that matters. What they need is to be convinced that the thing is right and justifiable when the nature of the decision is frankly explained and understood without reserve.

42. If it is thought useful to analyse more deeply how the problem has arisen, all possible data will, of course, be made available. But the explanation can be summed up very completely in a few sentences. The financial difficulties of the United Kingdom during and immediately after the war are more than fully accounted for by three factors:–

(i) In the period before lend lease, or rather before lend

lease came into full effect, some $3 billion, which constituted almost the whole of the British gold and other reserves, was expended in the United States to pay for munitions (which involved the building up of a largely new munitions industry in the U.S.) and other purchases required for the war.

(ii) Throughout the war the U.K. has been mainly responsible, without any significant assistance from any other quarter except the Government of India, for the local cash expenditure required for military operations over a wide area of Africa and Asia, extending from Tunis to Burma through Egypt, the Middle East and India, which has already amounted to $10 billion and will be substantially higher before the last bills have been paid. Yet it was this expenditure which threw one enemy back on the gates of Egypt and the other on the gates of India:

(iii) It was the very face of lend lease from the United States, mutual aid from Canada and the arrangements with the sterling area which made it possible for us to abandon our foreign trade and support a total concentration into the war industries and the armed forces which would otherwise have been impracticable. If it had been our role to maintain and expand our foreign trade with a view to the assistance of others, we should find ourselves in a vastly better position today to recover post-war equilibrium, even if we had given away the whole of the net proceeds of our war-time exports.

OUR OVERSEAS FINANCIAL PROSPECTS

1. Three sources of financial assistance have made it possible for us to mobilise our domestic man-power for war with an intensity not approached elsewhere, and to spend cash abroad, mainly in India and the Middle East, on a scale not even equalled by the Americans, *without having to export* in order to pay for the food and raw materials which we were using at home or to provide the cash which we were spending abroad.

2. The fact that the distribution of effort between ourselves and our Allies has been of this character leaves us far worse off, when the sources of assistance dry up, than if the roles had been reversed. If we had been developing our exports so as to pay for our own current needs and in addition to provide a large surplus which we could furnish free of current charge to our Allies as lend lease or mutual aid or on credit, we should, of course, find ourselves in a grand position when the period of providing the stuff free of current charge was brought suddenly to an end.

3. As it is, the more or less sudden drying up of these sources of assistance shortly after the end of the Japanese war will put us in an almost desperate plight, unless some other source of temporary assistance can be found to carry us over whilst we recover our breath—a plight far worse than most people, even in Government Departments, have yet appreciated.

4. The three sources of financial assistance have been (a) lend lease from the United States; (b) mutual aid from Canada; (c) credits (supplemented by sales of our pre-war capital assets) from the sterling area (including credits under payments agreements with certain countries, especially in South America, which are outside the area, but have made special agreements with it).

5. In the present year, 1945, these sources are enabling us to overspend our own income at the rate of about £2,100 millions a year, made up roughly as follows (these figures were compiled on the assumption that lend lease and mutual aid would continue on the basis of recent provisions until the end of 1945):–

	£ million
Lend lease (munitions)	600
Lend lease (non-munitions)	500
Canadian mutual aid	250
Sterling area, etc.	750
	2100

(The mutual aid, amounting recently to about £500 million a year, which we ourselves are according is here treated as part of our own domestic expenditure. From some, but not all, points of view this should be deducted from the above.)

6. This vast, but temporary, assistance allows us for the time being to over-play our own financial hand by just that amount. It means, conversely, that others are under-playing their hands correspondingly. How vividly do Departments and Ministers realise that the gay and successful fashion in which we undertake liabilities all over the world and slop money out to the importunate represents an over-playing of our hand, the possibility of which will come to an end quite suddenly and in the near future unless we obtain a new source of assistance? It may be that we are doing some things which are useless if we have to abandon them shortly after VJ, and that our external policies are very far from being adjusted to impending realities.

7. To sum up, the overseas balance of 1945 is estimated as follows:–

	£ million		£ million
Imports excl. munitions	1,250	Exports	350
Munitions received under lend lease and mutual aid	850	Net invisible income and sundry repayments, etc.	100
Other Government expenditure overseas	800	Government receipts from U.S. and Dominions for their forces and munitions	350
Total expenditure overseas	2,900	Total income overseas	800
		Deficit	2,100
			2,900

These estimates have been compiled on the assumption of a continuance of the Japanese war and Lend Lease to the end of 1945. But the early termination of the Japanese war is likely to reduce lend lease aid by more than it reduces our expenditure; so that, apart from some new source of aid, the financial position is more likely to be worsened than improved in the short run.

8. What happens on the morrow of VJ Day? We are led to expect that lend lease and mutual aid (amounting this year to £1350 million altogether) will cease almost immediately. The sterling area arrangements in more or less their present form are, we hope, rather more durable, but they will become increasingly less productive of finance as supplies and shipping become available, and before long will become a burden instead of an aid;—for the credits in our favour accrued on account of its being physically impossible for the sterling area countries to spend what they have been induced to lend us. I shall assume below that we can continue to expect substantial aid from the sterling area for a year after VJ, but no longer. We also have fair assurance of some subsequent assistance from Canada.

9. On the other hand, certain sources of expenditure will also dry up almost immediately, more particularly the munitions which we are obtaining from North America under lend lease and mutual aid. We shall no longer need them and we are entitled to cease taking them. This will save us expenditure which is running currently at the rate of about £850 million a year.

10. Nothing else will cease automatically or immediately on the morrow of VJ Day. But there will, of course, be a further substantial economy in Government expenditure overseas which can be obtained more slowly, say in the course of a year. There is likely, however, to be a considerable time lag in reducing such expenditure, for three reasons. In the first place, bills for much of the expenditure are received considerably in arrear, and we are responsible in India and Australia (as we are not in the case of lend lease supplies) for winding up our munition contracts just as at home. In the second place the withdrawal of our forces will be

protracted on account both of lack of transport and of the slowness of the administrative machine. In the third place (and above all) a substantial part of our existing Government expenditure overseas has no direct or obvious connection with the Japanese war and will not, therefore, come to an end merely because the Japs have packed up;—retrenchment in these other directions will require quite a separate set of Cabinet decisions. Merely as a personal judgment, based on a general knowledge of the breakdown of the expenditure in question, I should guess that without any change in policy good and energetic management might bring down the annual rate of £800 million to (say) £300 million by the end of 1946, although the cost during that year as a whole may be not much less than £450 million. Any further substantial reduction will require drastic revisions of policy of a kind which do not automatically ensue on VJ.

11. Unfortunately there are also certain items of *income* which arise out of the war and will fade away with it. In reckoning the current overseas balance, credit has been taken (see §7) for income of £350 million a year arising partly out of the personal expenditure of the American forces in this country (£115 million in 1944 and probably as much as £60 million in 1945) and mainly out of the contributions made by the Dominions towards the equipment and maintenance of their own divisions which had been provided by us in the first instance. These sources of income will have disappeared almost entirely within a year of VJ, but, allowing for time-lags in meeting old bills, and for possible repayments from the North Western European Allies, they may amount, on optimistic assumptions, to as much as £150 million during that year.

12. We must next allow for possible economies after VJ in other overseas expenditure for goods and for increased earnings from our shipping and from the expansion of our exports in 1946. To correct for these factors we have to

embark on difficult guesswork, and the range of reasonable estimating is very wide.

13. In the cost of imports of food and raw materials an increase, rather than a reduction, is in sight, if the public are to be fed reasonably and employed fully and taking account of the fact that stocks are being currently drawn upon. We are budgeting (unless circumstances force us to restrict, as is quite possible) for more rather than less food in 1946 than in 1945. The raw materials required to provide employment, though not always the same in character as those we now import, are unlikely to be reduced in aggregate, since the numbers to be employed in industry will, after demobilisation, be more rather than less. On the other hand, some miscellaneous economies should be possible. One way and another our import programme might be kept down to £1300 million. Even this, assuming prices at double pre-war, means considerable austerity. For our pre-war imports were £850 million, that is (say) £1700 million at the assumed post-war price level. Thus the above figure assumes a reduction of 23 per cent below the volume of our pre-war imports and therefore presumes strict controls, in the absence of which an appreciably higher figure is to be expected as soon as supplies are available.

14. As for exports there seems a reasonable hope of increasing them from an aggregate of £350 million in 1945 to £600 million in 1946. Extreme energy and concentration on this objective should do better still. Net invisible income in 1946, allowing for some recovery in commercial shipping receipts, might be put at £50 million.

15. On the assumption of an export and import price level double pre-war, and no major changes in present policies, the position in 1946 can, therefore, be summed up as follows:– [see p. 404]

16. When we come to subsequent years, we are in the realm of pure guess-work. If, to cheer ourselves up, we make bold

	£ million		£ million
Imports	1,300	Exports	600
Government expenditure		Net invisible income	50
overseas	450	Government receipts from	
		Allies and Dominions	150
			800
		Deficit	950
	1,750		1,750

to assume that by 1949 we have reached the goal of increasing the volume of exports by 50 per cent, the value of exports in that year, at double pre-war prices, would be £1450 million. If we suppose further that we can keep the further growth of imports within very moderate limits, if we can steadily curtail Government expenditure overseas and if we can steadily increase our net invisible income, we can produce the following pipe-dream, showing an eventual equilibrium in the fourth year after VJ, namely 1949:-

		Government expenditure overseas	Total	Exports	Net invisible income	Total	Deficit
	Imports						
1947	1,400	250	1,650	1,000	100	1,100	550
1948	1,400	200	1,600	1,300	100	1,400	200
1949	1,450	150	1,600	1,450	150	1,600	nil

(£ million)

It should be emphasised that imports can be kept down to this figure only by strict regulation.

17. Combining the above assumed deficits in 1947 and 1948 with the estimated deficit of £950 million in 1946, we have a total deficit of £1,700 million for the three years taken together.

18. Where on earth is all this money to come from? Our gold and dollar reserves at the end of 1945 will stand at about £500 million. We might, if necessary, draw on this to the tune

of £250 million but certainly not more. In 1946 we might conceivably increase our net borrowing from the sterling area by (say) another £300 million by stipulating that the further expenses in those countries strictly arising out of the war should be added to the war debts. But there will be chaos in the trade relations of the sterling area and a breakdown of the whole system unless we are prepared to release at least £75 million a year to these and our other creditors in each of the years 1947 and 1948, leaving a net gain of £150 million over the period as a whole. These two sources together bring the cumulative deficit down to £1,250 million, i.e. £5 billion.

19. The conclusion is inescapable that there is no source from which we can raise sufficient funds to enable us to live and spend on the scale we contemplate except the United States. It is true that there are sundry resources which have not been taken into account in the above. For example, we still have some capital assets which could be gradually realised; and we have an expectation of some further aid from Canada. But the above calculation assumes that we have reached equilibrium by the end of 1948, which we have no convincing reason to expect, and also that we have by that date drawn down our ultimate reserves to the minimum. Moreover the reader may have noticed that I have almost altogether omitted any reference to the vast debt of between £3,000 and £4,000 million which we shall be owing to almost every country in the world. In other words, it has been tacitly assumed that we have found some way of dealing with this which allows us to discharge nothing in the three years 1946–1948 taken together and in fact to add £150 million to it. Moreover the assumed rate of growth of exports is wildly optimistic, unless our methods change considerably. The conclusion holds, therefore, in so far as any firm conclusion can be based on such precarious material, that there remains a deficit of the order of $5 billion which can be met from no other source but the United States.

20. It is sometimes suggested that we can avoid dependence on the United States by a system of semi-barter arrangements with the countries from which we buy. This, however, assumes that the limiting factor lies in the willingness of overseas markets to take our goods. Whatever may be the truth a few years hence, this will not be the position in the early post-war period which we have in view here. The limiting factor will be our physical capacity to develop a sufficient supply of export goods. Barter arrangements assume that we have goods to offer in exchange; and that is precisely what we shall lack in the next two years. At present the boot is on, and pinching, the other leg;—the countries from which we buy are trying to make their sales to us contingent on our accepting barter terms, under which we supply goods which they want but which we unfortunately are unable to provide.

21. What it does lie in our power to do in mitigation falls under two headings. Even to attain the assumed expansion of exports, and certainly if we are to improve on it, we must stop forthwith making munitions which are not wanted and re-convert industry to peace-time production at a much greater pace than is at present in view. Hitherto the assumed continuance of the Japanese war until the end of 1946 has provided a magnificent camouflage for carrying on as though the end of the German war did not make all that [much?] difference. To suggest acting on the assumption that we might beat the Japs before 1947 has been regarded by all the Major-Generals as a brand of defeatism. Perhaps the time has now come when we can re-convert ruthlessly and with no regard to anything but speed and economy. It is not sensible either to keep men idle at the works or to use up valuable raw materials on producing useless objects merely to avoid statistical unemployment.

22. The second heading probably presents much greater difficulty. We still have a vast number of men in the three Services overseas, and the Government cash expenditure

outside this country, which this involves, is still costing more than the value of our total exports. It might be supposed that the defeat of Japan would bring most of this rapidly to an end, subject, of course, to the inevitable time lags. Unfortunately that is a long way from the truth. Out of the £425 million cost of the Services overseas in the current year the South East Asia Command is responsible for only £100 million. We have got into the habit of maintaining large and expensive establishments all over the Mediterranean, Africa and Asia to cover communications, to provide reserves for unnamed contingencies and to police vast areas eastwards from Tunis to Burma and northwards from East Africa to Germany. None of these establishments will disappear unless and until they are ordered home; and many of them have pretexts for existence which have nothing to do with Japan. Furthermore we are still making loans to Allies and are incurring very large liabilities for relief out of money we have not got.

23. Broken up broadly between purposes, I believe that the 1945 expenditure outside North America is distributed as follows:–

	£ million
The Services	425
War supplies and munitions (mainly India, South Africa and Australia	300
Reciprocal aid, loans to Allies, relief, Foreign Office, etc.	75
	800

Of this total about £450 million was incurred in the first half of the year before VE and £350 million was expected in the second half after VE. The effect of VJ on the rate of expenditure in the last quarter of 1945 has not yet been estimated.

24. Broken up between areas, the expenditure of £725 million on the Services and war supplies is made up broadly as follows:–

	£ million
India, Burma and Ceylon	410
Middle East	110
S. Africa, Australia and New Zealand	110
B.W., B.E. and Central Africa	20
Malta and Cyprus	10
Europe	40
Other	25
	725

25. To an innocent observer in the Treasury very early and very drastic economies in this huge cash expenditure overseas seem an absolute condition of maintaining our solvency. There is no possibility of our obtaining from others for more than a brief period the means of maintaining any significant part of these establishments, in addition to what we shall require to meet our running excess of imports over exports and to sustain the financial system of the sterling area. These are burdens which there is no reasonable expectation of our being able to carry. Yet there are substantial items within the £800 million which will not be automatically cut out merely as a result of the defeat of Japan.

26. Even assuming a fair measure of success in rapidly expanding exports and curtailing Government expenditure overseas, it still remains that aid of the order of $5 billion is required from the U.S. We have reason to believe that those members of the American Administration who are in touch with our financial position are already aware that we shall be in Queer Street without aid of somewhere between $3 and $5 billion and contemplate aid on this scale as not outside practical politics. But this does not mean that difficult and awkward problems of terms and conditions do not remain to be solved. The chief points likely to arise are the following:–

(i) They will wish the assistance to be described as a *credit*. If this means payment of interest and stipulated terms of repayment, it is something we cannot undertake in addition to our existing obligations with any confidence that we can fulfil the obligations. It would be a repetition of what happened after the last war and a cause of further humiliation and Anglo-American friction, which we should firmly resist. If, however, the term *credit* is no more than a camouflage for what would be in effect a grant-in-aid, that is another matter.

(ii) The Americans will almost certainly insist upon our acceptance of a monetary and commercial foreign policy along the general lines on which they have set their hearts. But it is possible that they will exercise moderation and will not overlook the impropriety of using financial pressure on us to make us submit to what we believe is to our grave disadvantage. In fact the most persuasive argument we can use for obtaining the desired aid is that only by this means will it lie within our power to enter into international co-operation in the economic field on the general principle of non-discrimination. We should not seek to escape our obligations under Article VII of the Mutual Aid Agreement, but should, rather, ask for the material basis without which it will not lie in our power to fulfil them. In my opinion we need not despair of obtaining an agreement which provides sufficient safeguards and will not seriously hamper the future development of our economy along lines freely determined by our own policies.

(iii) Bases, islands, air-facilities and the like may conceivably come into the picture.

27. Nor must we build too much on the sympathy and knowledge of the members of the American Administration with whom we are in touch. It will be a tough proposition, perhaps an impossible one, to sell a sufficiently satisfactory plan to Congress and the American people who are unacquainted with, and are never likely to understand, the true force of our case, not only in our own interests but in

the interests of the United States and the whole world. For the time being Ministers would do well to assume that no arrangement which we can properly accept is yet in sight; and that, until such an arrangement is in sight, we are, with the imminent cessation of lend lease, virtually bankrupt and the economic basis for the hopes of the public non-existent.

28. It seems, then, that there are three essential conditions without which we have not a hope of escaping what might be described, without exaggeration and without implying that we should not eventually recover from it, a financial Dunkirk. These conditions are (a) an intense concentration on the expansion of exports, (b) drastic and immediate economies in our overseas expenditure, and (c) substantial aid from the United States on terms which we can accept. They can only be fulfilled by a combination of the greatest enterprise, ruthlessness and tact.

29. What does one mean in this context by 'a financial Dunkirk'? What would happen in the event of insufficient success? That is not easily foreseen. Abroad it would require a sudden and humilating withdrawal from our onerous responsibilities with great loss of prestige and an acceptance for the time being of the position of a second-class power, rather like the present position of France. From the Dominions and elsewhere we should seek what charity we could obtain. At home a greater degree of austerity would be necessary than we have experienced at any time during the war. And there would have to be an indefinite postponement of the realisation of the best hopes of the new Government. It is probable that after five years the difficulties would have been largely overcome.

30. But in practice one will be surprised if it ever comes to this. In practice, of course, we shall in the end accept the best terms we can get. And that may be the beginning of later trouble and bitter feelings. That is why it is so important to grasp the reality of our position and to mitigate its potentialities by energy, ingenuity and foresight.

31. Shortage of material goods is not going to be the real problem of the post-war world for more than a brief period. Beyond question we are entering into the age of abundance. All the more reason not to mess things up and endanger the prizes of victory and the fruits of peace whilst crossing the threshold. The time may well come—and sooner than we yet have any right to assume—when the sums which now overwhelm us may seem chicken-feed, and an opportunity to get rid of stuff without payment a positive convenience.

KEYNES

13 August 1945

The beginning of August brought Messrs Clayton, Collado and Hawkins of the State Department to London for discussions on UNRRA, post-war commercial policy and Britain's current and prospective financial position. Keynes, along with Brand and Eady, met them on the morning of 3 August for an informal discussion of Britain's position. The discussion was informal because the change in Government during the Potsdam conference, following Labour's victory at the General Election, had not given officials time to discuss the situation with the new Chancellor, Hugh Dalton, or other Ministers. In fact, Ministerial discussions, Keynes suggested, would prove difficult to arrange before 15 August, the date of the Speech from the Throne for the new Parliament. Keynes suggested that the Americans set a date, not later than 15 September, for the start of discussions in Washington. This would allow Ministers time for decisions before the Parliamentary recess and Ministerial holidays began on 1 September. Keynes then spent the rest of the meeting outlining the facts of the British financial position. In the afternoon, other American officials joined the discussions, which centred on commercial policy, the twilight of lend lease, and UNRRA. Further meetings on trade policy took place on 4 and 9 August; Keynes was present at the first.

On 14 August, Keynes took part in another financial meeting, whose subject matter had become more urgent following the fall of Japan on that day. At this he strongly pressed for the avoidance of any sudden or unilateral modification in lend lease, and agreed that reciprocal aid should continue, until discussions had occurred on the next stage. The meeting also discussed the timing of changes in lend lease deliveries, Britain's financial position and hopes for the post-war settlement and the links between financial and commercial policy. A final meeting on trade matters occurred on 15 August.

Keynes's views on these subjects at this stage appear clearly in a note he circulated in the Treasury following a conversation with Mr Bevin, the new Foreign Secretary.

To SIR WILFRID EADY *and others, 16 August 1945*

I

My conversation with the Foreign Secretary led me to think that the policy he would prefer, left to himself, would be somewhat as follows:

We should ask the Americans for financial facilities to cover the transitional period, but we should not agree to commit ourselves to any monetary or commercial arrangements, not even Bretton Woods, until we could see our way more clearly. The matter would be kept under continuous review during the transitional period, and we should decide later, in the light of experience, how far it would be safe and advisable for us to commit ourselves along the multilateral and free trade lines upon which the Americans have set their hearts. A recent conversation with Mr Aldrich[39] had encouraged him in the idea that such a policy might not be unacceptable to American opinion.

Obviously there are many advantages in such a plan, if there were good reason to believe that it is practicable. I told him that Mr Aldrich would naturally sympathise with such suggestions, since he had been fighting the American Administration on these lines for the past twelve months. But, not only had Mr Aldrich been thoroughly defeated, but in the course of the campaign, which for some six months had been a nation-wide effort, the Administration had committed

[39] Winthrop William Aldrich (b. 1885); banker, lawyer; President, Chase National Bank, 1930–4; Chairman of the Board, 1945–53; Ambassador to Britain, 1953–7

themselves absolutely to the view that Mr Aldrich's policy was mistaken and that it was essential to reach definitive understandings forthwith, not indeed as to what would happen during the transitional period itself, when there will be safeguards, but as to what was to happen when the transitional period was at an end. To retreat from Bretton Woods at this stage would involve such terrific loss of face for the Administration that the idea is, I am sure, altogether untenable. Commercial conversations have, of course, not reached anything like such a degree of crystallisation, and we have much more room for manoeuvre there. Nevertheless, in this field also I do not think there would be any chance whatever of persuading the State Department that they should abandon their present ideas *in toto* and should just sit by like good children to see what the future brings. Moreover, it is asking too much of human nature, and certainly of American nature, to suppose that the United States would give us large-scale financial assistance without any present commitments on our part whether, having escaped from our immediate difficulties through this aid, we should or should not walk in step with them so far as international economic policies are concerned for the future.

Nevertheless, I found myself in complete sympathy with what was in the Foreign Secretary's mind and what lay behind his attitude. He is rightly convinced that we must exercise the utmost caution in the giving of commitments, which might limit our autonomy in domestic economic policy and force us into courses we thought mistaken or disastrous, as the result of international engagements entered into as the price of obtaining enough cash to escape from our immediate embarrassments.

This seems to me, however, not to be a sufficient reason for rejecting all commitments, but only for examining them with considerable care. I feel this all the more because a very large part of the American policy is, I believe, in our own interests as much as in theirs and that they are urging it on us sincerely and believing that we also have much to gain from it. We can safely walk with them a very long way. There are only a few elements in their projected policies which are dangerous to us. On those we should stand firm, but there is no need as yet to abandon hope of persuading the Americans to be moderate. I think they are quite genuinely anxious not to use financial pressure to force us into policies which we believe to be to our disadvantage and, whilst not necessarily able to avoid altogether temptation along these lines, know well enough that to use such pressure would be wrong.

Turning to the principal points of policy concerned, I am quite satisfied that Bretton Woods contains sufficient safeguards to be safe. If America embarrasses the rest of the world by running into a slump, I am convinced that the Bretton Woods plan will improve, and not worsen, a bad situation. We have effective autonomy over our rate of exchange; we can walk out of the plan at an hour's notice; the basic obligation we are undertaking under the plan is one which we have believed it to our advantage to maintain, even during the war, namely, that whenever we allow an import into this country we allow it to be paid for in the currency of the vendor. Not even during the war have we blocked dollars in the sense of refusing convertibility for dollar credits arising out of the value of what we have imported from the United States.

Turning to the commercial agreements, I admit there is more difficulty. But here also more than three-quarters of the proposals the Americans have put before us seem to me to be, not only acceptable, but helpful. The only matters which are not acceptable in their present form are the following:–

(1) *The treatment of preferences.* Nevertheless, if the Americans will allow the preference negotiations to be brought in exactly on all fours with the tariff negotiations, there is no present reason to think that we cannot arrive at a mutually satisfactory result.

(2) *State trading.* Even the present wording is not unsatisfactory. The Americans recognise that they have to make a draft which the Russians can accept. I have little doubt, therefore, that no obstacle of principle will be placed in the way of State trading. The discussions will turn only on the question what safeguards are required to ensure that state trading should be of a non-discriminatory character.

(3) As regards *exchange control*, the State Department would like to improve on Bretton Woods and deprive us of some of the safeguards we have obtained under Bretton Woods. We shall have the full support of the American Treasury in resisting this. I feel confident that these ideas will be dropped.

(4) We are not adequately protected against unfair American competition through dumping, export subsidies and, more particularly, shipping subsidies. Here it is a question of finding the right technical protection. On the question of principle the State Department are on our side.

(5) Finally, there remains the biggest snag of all, namely, the objection on the part of the Americans to the continuance of import programming or quantitative restriction or quota regulation, or whatever name one chooses to call it by, after the end of the transitional period. At present the Americans are only prepared to accept the re-imposition of such controls after the transitional period, if an international body has satisfied itself that there exist balance of trade difficulties which cannot be solved otherwise. To accept any such arrangement would be, in my judgement, to incur the Foreign Secretary's just censure on the grounds indicated above. Neither in our case, nor in that of any other country, is it consonant with the present progress of thought and policy on these matters for us to commit ourselves to a return to nineteenth century *laissez-faire* in import programming. This is where we should dig ourselves in. If we have a right to restrict the volume of imports, then it is quite safe under the Bretton Woods plan to agree to pay in the appropriate

currency for those imports which we have voluntarily accepted. If the control of imports is taken entirely out of our hands, then I should agree that the Bretton Woods commitments might be dangerous. To secure what we want here will undoubtedly mean a stiff tussle with the Americans. But, in very truth, they are talking nonsense, and out-of-date nonsense. Moreover, there is scarcely any other country in the world which would be more ready than we to accept the American conditions. I believe, therefore, that we can win that battle. The only point which we might have to yield would be that import programming should be on non-discriminatory lines. It is not easy to implement that in practice, but in principle a non-discriminatory commitment is probably to our own interest, provided other countries enter into a similar engagement.

Our right policy is, therefore, I suggest, not to refuse to walk with the Americans in these matters, but to walk, though willingly, carefully. We must dig in in the right place and choose the right issues for resistance. The right issues are, of course, those that are fundamental to our future position and where we have an irresistibly strong case. If we stick to those, we shall win.

II

I would, however, urge most strongly on the Chancellor and on his colleagues that it is not necessary to have cut-and-dried Cabinet conclusions on these matters at the present stage. Unless we enter into financial negotiations with the Americans forthwith, we cannot certainly rely on the continuance of lend lease for above another thirty days at most. But, if we enter into conversations, it would be reasonable to expect that there should be an opportunity for the conversations to make progress before the axe falls. These negotiations need not, however, involve any of the above matters in their initial stages. We should begin by discussing the terms and technique for winding up the lend lease and reciprocal aid systems. We should then expound in considerable detail the facts of our existing financial and economic position and prospects. Thirdly, we should seek to engage the Americans in discussions of the solution, and we should begin by putting forward proposals which were self-contained and did not offer any premature commitments concerning future commercial policy.

At that stage, if not at an earlier stage, in the discussions we must take it as certain that the Americans will raise, on their side, our acceptance of Bretton Woods and of certain general principles relating to commercial policy. Some further discussion at the official level may serve to narrow the area of difference of opinion. It is at that stage that the Cabinet will have to make up their minds. It would be a great convenience if the matters could have been given attention during the intervening period, so that by the time these matters are coming to a definite head it will be possible for a representative of the Board of Trade to join the talks at Washington with a fairly clear idea of what the sticking points are so far as the Cabinet is concerned. But it is neither possible nor necessary to delay the opening of the financial discussions until after a provisional decision has been reached as to exactly how far we are prepared to meet the Americans about the conditions.

Apart from the monetary and commercial understandings, which the Americans will seek as a condition of assistance, there remains one matter of extreme difficulty, namely, the form which the assistance shall take. The Americans will certainly begin by offering us something in the nature of a credit, no doubt on generous terms, which is repayable at due dates and ranks, to a considerable extent, ahead of our other creditors. They will not readily understand the honourable character of our obligations to many of the sterling area countries. There will be the utmost difficulty in persuading

417

them to agree to a form of credit or grant-in-aid of a kind which we can safely accept. I think there may be more difficulty about the form of the credit than its amount. They will begin by offering $3 billion, whereas we need $5 billion. But, if everything else can be settled satisfactorily, it may be not much more difficult to get $5 billion than $3 billion.

The first stage of the negotiations should, I suggest, be conducted on conditions which allow the negotiator a considerable elasticity of thought and conversation, in the light of the situation as it develops, but extremely little latitude to give way on those matters which are regarded as fundamental to our future position and to our ability to meet our commitments. He must, therefore, to quote the Foreign Secretary, 'have the gift of breaking off' and be ready, if necessary, to come home unsuccessful. That means that the Chancellor the Exchequer must be prepared, if necessary, to draw on our gold reserves for what one hopes would be a brief period. If it proves impossible to get a sufficiently satisfactory solution, that would be the time for the Cabinet to consider with anxiety and concentration of mind the exact character of the alternative to giving way. We should not yield on any of the basic points until these matters have been meditated upon with that concentration of attention which is possible only when we are right up against it. It would then be for Ministers to visit Washington, in the light of the final decisions reached, with a view to discovering whether we cannot, at the last lap, get sufficient of what we want. It is very possible indeed that at this last lap success would be achieved.

III

Meanwhile time presses, and it is essential to begin the first stage immediately. I repeat that that needs no more immediate decision on the part of Ministers than that they view with sympathy the nature of our opening bid. There we ought to make up our minds in the next few days whether it is in any respects a little too generous and should be further refined. But, broadly speaking, almost everyone would agree, I think, that its chief fault is that it is too good to be true. It certainly would not involve dangerous commitments for the future on the commercial side. Nevertheless, it would be very advisable, if Ministers could reach a conclusion at as early as possible a date in the negotiations whether they agree with the view that the Bretton Woods Plan contains sufficient safeguards. And it would also be useful if, with the least possible delay, certain broad conclusions could be reached as to what our sticking points are in commercial policy.

16.8.45

KEYNES

Initially, Washington sources suggested to London that lend lease might continue for thirty days on the civilian side and even longer on the military side. However, on Friday 17 August President Truman decided, in line with a strict reading of the requirements of the legislation, to end lend lease immediately.[40] The decision was formally communicated to Britain on 20 August. Stage III had begun.

[40] The suggested American terms for termination were: (a) no new contract commitments; (b) supplies in the pipeline to be available against payment; (c) supplies already transferred or in stock to be retained against payment; (d) lend lease supplies to enter the pipeline in return for cash for sixty days from VJ Day. The Americans suggested that payment for items in (b) and (c) above should take place over thirty years at $2\frac{3}{8}$ per cent interest.

Chapter 4

THE LOAN NEGOTIATIONS

Three days after Britain received formal notification of the termination of Lend Lease, Keynes attended a meeting of Ministers. Prior to the meeting, the Ministers had received copies of Keynes's proposals of 13 August. The Secretary reported the meeting as follows.

FORTHCOMING DISCUSSIONS WITH
THE UNITED STATES

Record of a Meeting of Ministers held at No. 10 Downing Street,
on Thursday, 23 August 1945 at 10.15 p.m.

PRESENT

The Rt Hon. C. R. Attlee, M.P.,
Prime Minister

The Rt Hon. Herbert Morrison, M.P., Lord President of the Council	The Rt Hon. Ernest Bevin, M.P., Secretary of State for Foreign Affairs
The Rt Hon. Hugh Dalton, M.P., Chancellor of the Exchequer	The Rt Hon. Sir Stafford Cripps, K.C., M.P., President of the Board of Trade

The Rt Hon. Lord Pethick-Lawrence,
Secretary of State for India

The Rt Hon. the Earl of Halifax, H.M. Ambassador, Washington	Lord Keynes
Sir Edward Bridges	Sir Robert Sinclair
Sir Wilfrid Eady	Mr Robert Brand

Mr Hall-Patch[1]

[1] Edmund Leo Hall-Patch (b. 1896), K.C.M.G. 1947; Assistant Secretary, Treasury, 1935–44; Financial Commissioner in Far East, 1940; Assistant Under-Secretary of State, Foreign Office, 1944; Deputy Under-Secretary of State, Foreign Office, 1946–8; Head of British Delegation and Chairman of Executive Committee of Organization for European Economic Co-operation, with rank of Ambassador, 1948; U.K. Executive Director of International Monetary Fund, 1952–4.

THE PRIME MINISTER invited Lord Keynes to make a statement as to the lines on which he thought the negotiations should be handled.

LORD KEYNES said that his first point was that he thought that our negotiators should be given no discretion on the main issues and that everything they did should be *ad referendum.*

Some questions would have to be settled about cleaning up lend lease. He thought that we ought to try and persuade the Americans to agree that lend lease and mutual aid should continue for military supplies for a limited period. Nearly half of the food which we were at present receiving from American lend lease was in fact being sent to our troops. He thought that we should also stipulate that the terms of credit on which we continued to receive lend lease supplies should be left to be dealt with as part of the general Stage III negotiations. On this part of the negotiations he thought that points of detail were more likely to arise than points of principle.

In reply to a question he said that Australia had a separate agreement with the United States, and it would probably pay her to cut clear altogether at once.

Stage III negotiations. On what terms would the Americans offer us help? The terms offered might vary from an out-and-out grant-in-aid, to a commercial credit. He thought that he should not be authorised to agree to anything except an out and out grant. Help on any less favourable terms should not be accepted except after very long thought on the part of Ministers in London. He thought that the first American proposal would be quite unacceptable from our point of view. We would then give our point of view and they would make counter-proposals and the discussion would so continue. Lord Keynes thought that this point, namely the nature and financial terms of any help to be afforded to us, would constitute the greatest stumbling block.

The next point concerned the amount of the credit. We wanted $5 billion (including whatever was necessary to clean up lend lease) in order to put us in a comfortable position. The Americans were thinking in terms of $3 billion, rising possibly to 5. It was fairly clear that Mr Clayton had come over here instructed to talk in terms of $3 billion, but was now becoming sympathetic to a higher figure. It was just possible that we could manage on $4 billion, but $3 billion would not enable us to make any commitments as to how we should use the help given to us.

This led to the question of what we should give as *quid pro quo* for this help. On this, the first point was a settlement of our indebtedness to the sterling area. If the Americans gave us $4 or 5 billion, we could then go to the sterling area countries, and ask them to cancel part of our indebtedness to them and agree that the remainder should be made fully convertible by instalments. This point was of great importance, both to ourselves and the United States, and would be so regarded by the United States State Department and the United States Treasury. Lord Keynes thought that this was the only constructive proposal which he should put forward at the outset.

The United States authorities would certainly ask about Bretton Woods. He would start by pointing out that the Chancellor of the Exchequer had recently re-affirmed the pledge given by his predecessor that we would enter into no commitments before Parliament had considered the matter in the Autumn.

They would then ask what the Government proposed to advise Parliament to do. His own view was that Bretton Woods was a carefully prepared document which contained adequate safeguards and that we could undertake the obligations contained in it, provided they were not coupled with dangerous concessions under the heading of commercial policy.

Commercial policy. Lord Keynes emphasised that there was no question of our being asked to agree to a detailed commercial treaty at this stage. What we should be asked to do would be to sign a joint invitation with the United States to 15 other countries to attend an international conference next year, on the understanding that the terms of the invitation represented the policy of our two countries.

Most of the United States document was acceptable to us and indeed valuable. There remained, however, four points of specific difficulty which he would refer to. Provided however, that the Americans felt that we were substantially in agreement with them, he thought that they might give us reasonable satisfaction on these points.

The first of the four points concerned preferences. On this our line should be that this was inseparable from tariffs and could not be handled on an a priori basis before the tariffs talks started. We should not yield an inch from this attitude.

The second point concerned state trading. The document on this point was innocent, but not unambiguous. Since the document had to be acceptable to Russia, there should not be any serious difficulty under this head. The Americans would make the point that state trading should be non-discriminatory. This suited us quite well.

The third point concerned the programming of imports. Here we must stand on the ground that we must be able to programme imports, not merely as a temporary expedient in times of difficulty, but as a normal part of our policy. He thought that Mr Clayton would be prepared to agree on this point, subject to such programming being non-discriminatory. It was also worth bearing in mind that most of the other 15 countries to be invited to the conference would share our views on this matter.

The fourth and last point of difficulty on the commercial side concerned the Bretton Woods provisions about exchange control. Here the United States State Department thought that the United States Treasury had conceded too much to us at Bretton Woods and wanted to recover part of the concessions then made as part of the commercial agreement. To this we should not agree.

Finally, Lord Keynes referred to a number of other questions which might arise in the discussion. He said that Mr Harry White in their talks a year or so back had asked whether it would not be possible to throw something into the negotiations which was incapable to monetary measurement. This necessarily led to the question whether we had not some island or islands which we could make over as part of the deal. Lord Keynes added that he thought that a settlement of this matter would require a Bill in Congress and that the United States might well wish to deal in the same Bill with consideration under lend lease and also of formal cancellation of the old debt.

Discussion followed.

THE PRESIDENT OF THE BOARD OF TRADE raised the question whether it would not be best to go straight for a grant-in-aid, and to do our best to dress it up effectively, and to stand on this line. LORD KEYNES said that this had been his first instinct, but that he had been rather pushed off this in the course of discussion. Thus Mr Clayton was clearly not thinking on these lines.

SIR ROBERT SINCLAIR favoured the grant-in-aid as the one solution which was really right on merits and made good sense; but he agreed that means would have to be found to dress it up in such a way as to make it acceptable.

MR BRAND said that he agreed with Lord Keynes, but perhaps was rather less hopeful. He thought, however, that it would be undesirable that the United Kingdom representatives should ask for a grant-in-aid. There was the danger that if we did, there would be a leakage and that it would be stated in the United States Press that we had made such a request. This might well be represented to our disadvantage. He thought that we should let it appear from the strength of our case, as we developed it, that this was the one really satisfactory way of dealing with the situation, but that we should let the Americans come to this, rather than make the suggestion ourselves.

This met with general approval.

LORD HALIFAX agreed with this view, and made three further points.

(i) That Mr Cordell Hull was still very influential in the background,

(ii) That the chance of our getting a large sum from the Americans depended less on the size of the sum, than on its being wrapped up in attractive appurtenances,

(iii) That it was important that we should be able to concede some points, and take up an attitude which would strike some spark of enthusiasm or emotion from the Americans. He mentioned the suggestion that he had made some time back that we should say that at the peace conference we would take an unselfish attitude about bases. He also mentioned the suggestion that we should make a gift of the island of Tarawa to the United States in recognition of the noble feat of arms there of the United States Marines. THE FOREIGN SECRETARY said that he would like to follow up this suggestion.

THE PRIME MINISTER asked with whom the negotiations would be carried on. LORD KEYNES thought that they would be carried on by a Committee of the United States Cabinet presided over by Mr Vinson, but it would be very helpful if Lord Halifax would at an early stage ask the President to designate a specific body with whom we should negotiate on this matter.

Discussions followed as to whether it would be appropriate for us, when the Bretton Woods Agreement came before Parliament, to follow the Congress procedure and to signify our assent subject to an interpretation of one or two points by the governing body organisation. It was generally felt that although the Americans would not welcome this, they could hardly object to it.

THE PRIME MINISTER summing up the meeting said that he thought that the general conclusion of his colleagues was that the matter should be handled by Lord Keynes and his colleagues on the basis that he had outlined that evening; and that the negotiations should be *ad referendum*, reports being made to Ministers in London as and when necessary.

Statement in Parliament. The question was then raised whether the Prime Minister should make a statement in Parliament on the following day on lend lease and reciprocal aid. A copy of a draft statement had been circulated to the Ministers present at the meeting. The great importance of such a statement for United States opinion was stressed.

On the other hand it was felt that a debate on this matter on the adjournment might be embarrassing.

The conclusion of Ministers after discussion was that the statement should be made subject to one or two drafting amendments, but that the

Leader of the Opposition should be approached and informed of the Prime Minister's intention to make this statement and asked to do his best to handle the matter in such a way as to avoid debate.

Keynes's mission to the United States was announced in the House of Commons the next day. The mission left Southampton by sea on 27 August for Quebec City.

Keynes arrived in Ottawa on 2 September. During the next few days the mission discussed matters connected with the termination of mutual aid on 15 August with the relevant Canadian ministers and officials. The result was to meet British supply requirements until the end of 1945 through a series of devices. The visit also gave Keynes an opportunity to try out his ideas on Stage III and commercial policy on the Canadians to get some indication of possible American reactions. The results were encouraging.

From Ottawa, Keynes sent the Chancellor a further revision of his August paper. This received general circulation in London on 12 September. Keynes's covering note set out the changes he had made.

To SIR WILFRID EADY *and others, 4 September 1945*

I attach, in duplicate, a revised version, prepared on the boat, of the draft you saw before I left. There has been no important change of substance, but the form has been touched up throughout. The most significant changes are the following:–

1. The preliminary matter has been re-written and the prospective adverse balance of trade presented in a more tentative form.

2. The third section presenting 'the first alternative' has been re-introduced.

3. The concluding section concerning the terms of the 'credit' has gone over more completely to Brand's preference, and virtually nothing is said about the terms at this stage. On further reflection the choice seemed to me to be between saying more or saying less and that the latter was the preferable alternative.

Nevertheless, although even vague references to the terms of credit have been omitted I gave a good deal of reflection to this matter whilst on the boat. I am increasingly doubtful

425

about the prospects of a straight grant-in-aid. There will have to be some camouflage. Moreover, the best way of introducing this question now seems to me to be on the lines that our aggregate undertakings to all our creditors as a whole will be as high as we can safely promise. If, therefore, the U.S.A. want to share in priority to the sterling area creditors this means that the latter will get that much less. In the extreme limit where the U.S.A. has complete priority the whole scheme for releasing the sterling area balances would be frustrated. It is therefore in the general interests to go as near as is politically practicable to the opposite extreme.

I have been working at a short paper on a version of what could represent a 'credit' but on lines which it would not be unsafe for us to accept. I will send this shortly for your comments. There is, of course, no question at present of going beyond what is in the attached paper.

Moreover, I am still quite uncertain whether it will be advisable to present this document, at any rate until the discussions have made some progress. My feeling is now rather in favour of trying to get the Americans to show their hand before we attempt to be constructive. It may be politic that as many as possible of the points on which we can yield should appear to have been given away under a good deal of pressure rather than that they should be voluntarily preferred at the start.

As you will have gathered from recent telegrams the atmosphere is not particularly good at the moment. I am therefore keeping a very open mind as to the best means of approach until we have actually gone into the talks.

KEYNES

PROPOSALS FOR FINANCIAL ARRANGEMENTS IN THE
STERLING AREA AND BETWEEN THE U.S. AND THE
U.K. TO FOLLOW AFTER LEND LEASE

I. *The present overseas financial position and
prospects of the U.K.*

1. *Gold and dollar reserves.* Before making allowance for any additional cash outgoings in the last four months of 1945 as a result of the partial or complete suspension of lend lease assistance and Canadian mutual aid, recent estimates indicate that the British net gold and dollar reserves at the end of 1945 might be of the order of $1·9 billion. The movement of these reserves since the beginning of the war and their composition are shown in detail in Appendix A [not printed].

2. The gold and dollar reserves of other parts of the sterling area are also shown in Appendix A. It will be seen that the dollar reserves are insignificant and present no more than a daily working balance. Gold reserves, apart from the substantial holding of South Africa and an amount held by India which is slightly in excess of the statutory minimum, are also insignificant. Thus, in the main, the gold and dollar reserves of the U.K. are the reserves of the whole of the sterling area (except South Africa) in the sense that it is only out of these reserves that the rest of the area can be provided with dollars to meet purchases in excess of their current dollar earnings.

3. *British liabilities to overseas creditors* at the end of June 1945 stood at $13·4 billion. They are likely to approach $14·5 billion by the end of 1945, apart from any consequences of the end of lend lease. In this event, the estimated net reserves of $1·9 billion at the same date will represent about 13 per cent of the liabilities. The distribution and composition of the liabilities are given in Appendix B [not printed].

4. *The current adverse balance of the U.K.* In 1945 prior to VJ Day the annual rate of overseas expenditure and income

was running as follows, exclusive of munitions received under lend lease and Canadian mutual aid:–

	$ million		$ million
Imports excluding munitions	5,000	Exports	1,400
Government expenditure overseas	3,200	Net invisible income and sundry repayments, etc.	400
		Government receipts from U.S. and Dominions for their forces and munitions	1,400
			3,200
		Deficit	5,000
	8,200		8,200

This deficit was being covered roughly, as follows:–

	$ million
Lend lease (non-munitions)	2,000
Sterling area credits, etc. (net)	3,000
	5,000

The mutual aid accorded by the U.K. which might either be entered on both sides of the above account or, alternatively, like the volume of the munitions received under lend lease and mutual aid, excluded from both, was running at the rate of about $2,000 million a year. The net effect of the termination of lend lease (non-munitions) on the prospects of the last four months of 1945 has not yet been worked out with sufficient accuracy to be worth quoting.

5. *The prospective current adverse balance of the U.K. in 1946.* There are far too many uncertainties in this picture to allow any close estimates. But the broad results of our preliminary study of the prospects are given in the following paragraphs.

6. In the cost of imports of food and raw materials etc. an

increase, rather than a reduction, is in sight compared with 1945, if the public are to be fed reasonably and employed fully, taking account of the fact that stocks are being currently drawn upon and that prices will be somewhat higher. The raw materials required to provide employment, though not always the same in character as those we now import, are unlikely to be reduced in aggregate, since the numbers to be employed in industry will be increased as a result of demobilisation. On the other hand some miscellaneous economies should be possible. One way and another our import programme (c.i.f.) might be kept down to £1,300 million which would be much the same volume as in 1945, excluding munitions and allowing for some rise in prices. Even this, with sterling prices at double pre-war, means considerable austerity. For our pre-war imports were £850 million, that is (say) £1,700 million at the assumed post-war price level. Thus the above figure assumes a reduction of 23 per cent below the volume of our pre-war imports and therefore presumes strict controls, in the absence of which an appreciably higher figure is to be expected as soon as supplies are available.

7. There will, of course, be a substantial economy in Government expenditure overseas but there is likely to be a considerable time lag in reducing such expenditure for three reasons. In the first place, bills for much of the expenditure are received considerably in arrear, and we are responsible in India and Australia for winding up our munition contracts and for meeting cancellation charges. In the second place the withdrawal of our forces will be protracted on account both of lack of transport and of the slowness of the administrative machine. In the third place a substantial part of our existing Government expenditure overseas is concerned with policing and occupation tasks and the protection of lines of communication over a wide area, some of which is likely to continue throughout the year. It should, however, be possible to bring the annual rate of cost down to $1,200 million or less before

the end of 1946, although the cost during that year as a whole may be not much less than $1,800 million. The cost of UNRRA and other relief and rehabilitation overseas is included in these figures.

8. There are also certain items of *income* which arise out of the war and will fade away with it. In reckoning the current overseas balance, credit has been taken for income of $1,400 million a year arising partly out of the personal expenditure of the American forces in this country ($460 million in 1944 and probably as much as $240 million in 1945) and mainly out of the contributions made by the Dominions towards the equipment and maintenance of their own divisions which has been provided by us in the first instance. These sources of income will have disappeared almost entirely by the end of 1945, but, allowing for time lags in meeting old bills, and for possible repayments from the north-western European allies, they may amount, on optimistic assumptions, to as much as $600 million in the year following VJ. Thus we put the net Government expenditure overseas in 1946 at (say) $1,200 million. But this estimate is very uncertain.

9. Turning to exports there seems a reasonable hope of increasing these from an aggregate of $1,400 million in 1945 to at least $2,400 million in 1946. It is dangerous to exaggerate the probable rate of recovery. The processes of demobilisation and reconversion will present acute difficulties. The demands of civilian consumption will be pressing and must be met in some measure. Two industries, cotton textiles and coal mining, which made large contributions to the volume of our pre-war exports, will meet many obstacles in regaining their pre-war level and cannot be expected even to approach this level for some time to come. We must also allow for the time lag in actual receipts from exports. Extreme energy and concentration on the objective of exports might succeed in bringing our receipts to double the 1945 figure which would be $2,800 million. It will be safer, however, to base our

present estimates on a figure of $2,600 million whilst aiming at the higher figure as a target area hoping to do even better.

10. We also hope for a considerable increase in the net income from our shipping and also for some steady improvement in other items of invisible income. It will be seen that the cost of imports has been reckoned above c.i.f. It follows that the earnings of our own shipping in bringing in our own imports has to be taken into account in assessing our invisible income. We are inclined therefore to put our net invisible income at the increased figure of $600 million.

11. On the assumption of an export and import price level double pre-war in terms of sterling, the prospects of 1946 can be summed up, subject to every possible reserve, as follows:–

	$ million		$ million
Imports	5,200	Exports	2,600
Government expenditure		Invisible income (net)	600
overseas (net)	1,200		
			3,200
		Deficit	3,200
	6,400		6,400

12. The precariousness of this estimate must be again emphasised. If we are sufficiently hard pressed, we can do better. For this does not reflect the maximum possible austerity in domestic consumption or the maximum possible reduction in Government expenditure overseas by limiting, or contracting out of, our international commitments. Also it is extremely difficult to predict the rate of export recovery. Perhaps the minimum deficit in 1946 which it would be possible to organise is $2,500 million and the maximum we need fear is $3,500 million.

13. *The later years of the transition.* When we look beyond 1946 we are in the region of pure guesswork. If by 1949 we can reach the goal of a volume of exports 50 per cent above

pre-war, they will be worth $5,800 million in that year. Assuming that we can combine this state of export business with keeping the volume of imports comfortably below the pre-war level, and that we can gradually curtail Government expenditure overseas, we shall about break even in that year. But this still makes no provision for any repayment of debts.

14. Assuming this result by 1949, which is, it should be emphasised, a hypothesis and not a forecast, and a gradual progress towards this from the 1946 deficit in the intermediate years 1947 and 1948, we are left with a cumulative deficit from the end of the war of (say) $4 billion as a (most unlikely) minimum and (say) $6 billion as a maximum which we ought not to allow ourselves to exceed. More probably the transitional period will be drawn out over a longer period than three years without the cumulative deficit, however, being necessarily outside the above range of figures though longer drawn out.

II. *The character of the problem*

15. It will be seen that the financial problem falls into two parts (a) the treatment of the sterling balances accumulated during the war and (b) our running adverse balance after the war and before we have fully restored our domestic economy.

16. The former is the less urgent problem if we consider only ourselves. For no one can make us release these balances faster than is materially possible. Nevertheless, they directly react on the latter problem in two ways.

17. In the first place, our existing debts affect what additional amounts we can borrow to help the current position. Our considered view is that we cannot be expected, and will not agree, to pay a commercial rate of interest on the sterling war debts incurred in the common cause. Nor shall we undertake to repay the capital sums at a greater rate than lies within our reasonable capacity. But we are not prepared to

repudiate by unilateral action any part of our capital liability to those who came to our financial assistance without security and on a vast scale when we were in dire straits, or to subordinate them entirely to debts incurred subsequently.

18. We ask our American friends to agree that this is a proper attitude and that they will not ask us, or seek to induce us, to depart from it.

19. In the second place, it would cause very great disturbance to the national economies of some of our sterling area creditors and especially to their trade relations with the United States, if we could not begin from the start to release a marginal instalment of their sterling balances. For many countries in the sterling area will have a dollar deficit on current account as soon as supplies and transport are available. Since the Union of South Africa holds a large independent gold reserve, what follows does not apply to her. Nor does it apply to our creditors outside the area. But the rest of the area, as we have already explained have no significant gold or dollar reserves available either in their currency reserves or central banks. Their sterling balances in London comprise substantially the whole of the ultimate external reserves of their banking systems and of their note issues, which, more perhaps from habit and good will than from prudent calculation, they have been willing to entrust to us during the war. If in the early years we block these balances entirely within the sterling area, we shall throw their trade relations with countries outside the area into serious confusion and will have been guilty, if there is any means of avoidance, of an abuse of confidence. This applies more particularly to the currency reserves of the Crown Colonies, which have not been entirely free agents in this matter. We have obtained their produce during the war, for our own use or (in some cases) to present it as reciprocal aid to the United States, largely in return for bits of paper, i.e., by expanding their note issues. The expectation has been that after the

war, when supplies and shipping are again available, some at least of these bits of paper can be used to pay for essential imports.

20. Thus there is a certain marginal part of the sterling balances which we are under an honourable obligation to treat in the same way, and *pari passu*, with our own current adverse balance. There must be from the outset, that is to say, some minimum addition to our own current requirements to provide for the essential needs of certain sterling area countries, the financial systems of which are wholly centred on London.

21. Nevertheless it is our own running adverse balance in the period of three to five years after the war which constitutes the major part of the urgent problem. This is greatly aggravated in the first year or two after victory in Asia by the fact that our military expenditure overseas will not sink to nothing at the hour of Japan's defeat, but must unavoidably continue at a heavy rate for an appreciable period thereafter; and also by the fact that we have incurred obligations to UNRRA, to our own liberated territories in the Far East, and arising out of the occupation of Germany and the pacification of Europe and Asia.

III. *The first of the alternative solutions*

22. It appears to us, after the most earnest study, that we are confronted, broadly speaking, with two alternative courses of action, both of which would require the good will of the rest of the world, but one of which we can carry out or attempt to carry out chiefly on our own initiative, whilst the other would only be possible by a general plan on the part of all the chief countries concerned and could not be executed without the aid of the U.S. There are, of course, certain compromises which are possible between the two alternatives set out below, partaking more of the one or more of the other but for clarity of exposition it will be better to stick at the start to the clear-cut alternatives.

23. The first alternative is to develop, and modify according to circumstances, the system of the sterling area as it has been evolved during the war, supported by payments agreements (on the model now existing with several European and South American countries) with countries outside the area. It should be explained that under payments agreements a country agrees to hold in sterling, with or without limit, any favourable current balance it may accumulate with the sterling area, whilst we enter into corresponding obligations to it if the balance proves out to be the other way. Under such a system all sterling balances would enjoy full convertibility of exchange for current payments within the sterling area and between the sterling area and those outside countries accepting unrestricted payments agreements. Imports into the area from countries, setting a strict limit to the maximum amount of sterling which they are willing to accumulate or requiring some proportion of such accumulations to be paid or guaranteed in gold or dollars, would have to be more strictly controlled and limited so far as possible to essentials, except to the extent that they were covered by exports to such countries from the area. With a country declining a payments agreement altogether trade would have to be still more restricted; and the excess of imports from it into the area over exports to it from the area would have to be limited, necessarily, to what could be paid for by drawing on our gold and dollar reserves. A payments agreement along the above lines would be offered to every country including the U.S.

24. If the U.S. were to stay outside such a system, we could not rely on maintaining the sterling area dollar pool as it has existed during the war. Sterling area countries having a favourable current balance with the U.S. or some of them at least, would very likely insist on retaining their dollar surplus for their own use and would not agree to hand it over to the pool, as they have done hitherto. The partial break-down of the dollar pool, with the sterling area arrangements continuing unchanged in other respects, would not, however, be to

the general advantage and would certainly operate to the disadvantage of the United States. For it would not increase the dollars available to pay for American exports and would merely mean that the sterling area countries having a running deficit with the U.S. would be forced to limit their purchases still more strictly. The maintenance of the dollar pool is a way of ensuring that all the available dollars are in fact spent within the dollar area with the minimum of discrimination.

25. For this and other reasons such a system would have to be more rigid in relation to a country unwilling to enter into a payments agreement than it has been during the war. Hitherto (apart from certain very recent exceptions) the exchange control of any member of the sterling area has been entitled to obtain from the central pool any dollars required for imports considered essential and not obtainable within the sterling area. This measure of liberality was, however, only made practicable through the limitations set by difficulties of supply and transport. In peace-time conditions the above practice would have to be replaced by an annual dollar ration (as is already the case with Egypt). Individual members of the area would, of course, be free to supplement their ration by borrowing from dollar sources though without any guarantee of the availability of their sterling resources for eventual repayment of such dollar liabilities. The principle underlying this procedure is simple and inevitable. *All* the dollars available from American imports and loans and from drawing within the limits of safety on the control reserves, would be made available in payment for American exports, and no more than all is possible.

26. This system, especially if the United States would accept a payments agreement, has certain advantages. The war-time system could slide off into it without any break in continuity. It might provide a highly elastic instrument for dealing with the unpredictable quantities of credit which will be required during the transitional period. It would offer some initial help

to British exports which might accelerate the date at which equilibrium in the balance of payments could be achieved. Nor would it be essential, though highly convenient to the trade of both parties, that the U.S. should accept a payments agreement without limit of amount.

27. Moreover there would be no intention of maintaining such a system in its full rigour indefinitely. It is obvious that any system must break down eventually unless those concerned (more particularly the United Kingdom in this instance) can find means of reaching equilibrium in their balance of payments within a reasonably short period. When this equilibrium has been achieved, the transitional period will have come to an end and there will be no longer any obstacle to the adoption of general multilateral convertibility in respect of the proceeds of future current trade. There is nothing in the above arrangements, provided they are limited to a transitional period, which would prevent the U.K. from accepting forthwith the obligations of the International Monetary Fund. The possibility of a transitional period having the above character has been strictly preserved in Article XIV, as indeed was essential pending the definite provision of any practicable alternative. Furthermore under the Bretton Woods Plan we should be entitled to put special restrictions on the subsequent use of the sterling balances accumulated before the end of the transitional period.

28. It would also be our intention to follow faithfully the provision of the Bretton Woods Plan that during the transitional period 'members shall have continuous regard in their foreign exchange policies to the purposes of the Fund, and, as soon as conditions permit, they shall take all possible measures to develop such commercial and financial arrangements with other members as will facilitate international payments and the maintenance of exchange stability'. It would be our purpose to allow and arrange as free an exchange of sterling between special accounts under payments

agreements as was mutually acceptable to the other countries concerned. And with the improving trend towards equilibrium, the necessary degree of restriction would be progressively reduced. If we have to adopt this system we should hope that it would be with the good will and close collaboration of all concerned. We on our part would do our utmost to minimise causes of friction and to use no more discrimination than is inherent in a system where trade is limited and conditioned by the separate availability of payment facilities.

29. Nevertheless on closer examination this alternative is seen to involve some serious difficulties. It is probably the best we can do if we have to solve the problem by ourselves and on our own initiative. It is not, in our judgement, impracticable for us to make the attempt to enter on the post-war period along these lines. But candour forces the admission that it is not as good as it has been made to look in the preceding paragraphs.

30. It will almost inevitably lead, in practice, though that would not be our deliberate intention, to a greater degree of bilateral trade negotiations than is in theory inherent in it. For countries, whether inside or outside the area, having a favourable balance of trade with the rest of the sterling area, would be reluctant to receive payment in terms of sterling, the future availability of which would be uncertain. They would, therefore, attempt (signs of this are already apparent) to link their sales to us with a definite undertaking as to the scale on which we would export to them. The paradoxical situation would arise that our customers would tumble over one another to obtain as large as possible a quota of our limited supply of desired exports;—obviously a situation in some ways highly attractive to us, yet no less obviously capable of producing very great frictions in international trading relations. The allocation of the dollar quota in the absence of an unrestricted payments agreement with the United States would provide another scramble. The whole object of

the system would be to make the rest of the world lend us more money than they were inclined to lend and sometimes more than they possessed as a voluntary surplus; and the whole object of each other country, whether inside or outside the sterling area, would be to try to distort its operation so that they in particular carried as little of the aggregate burden as possible.

31. In short, the system would be forcing an unnatural pattern on international trading relations, though perhaps one advantageous to British short-term interests, over the whole of the formative post-war period, when as rapid a return as possible to normality is in the permanent interest of peaceful and profitable trade between nations. Moreover, we might reach an equilibrium in the balance of payments in these hot-house conditions in ways which we should be incapable of sustaining when we were deprived of them.

32. Above all, this alternative is open to the major objection that it is merely postponing the solution of the intrinsic problem to the end of the transitional period, without there being any reason to suppose, indeed the contrary that it would be any easier to solve then than it is now. By the end of the transitional period the British overseas sterling debt would have risen under these arrangements to $20 billion or more; and, for reasons already explained, many of the countries concerned would be in serious straits if the whole of their sterling resources became frozen. Yet this is how it would have to be. At the end of the transitional period the trade of a considerable part of the world would be thrown into sudden disorder. For it must be remembered that *during* the transitional period members of the sterling area and countries having payments agreements with it would have the free disposal over a wide area of their accumulated, and not merely their currently acquired, sterling balances. It is only at the end of the transitional period that they would suddenly lose any effective use of their standing sterling reserves.

33. In fact, when the transitional period came to an end (meaning by this the period before the U.K. had obtained equilibrium in its own balance of current payments), there would be, as there are now, only two alternatives, and they would be the *same* two. Either it would be necessary to continue more or less permanently the sterling area system supported by payments agreements as heretofore (though in the much more favourable conditions for its operation which would exist when the U.K.'s own balance was in equilibrium). In this case the zero-hour overseas holdings of sterling would become a sort of international fiduciary currency, the amount of which outstanding would remain more or less constant, slowly declining in so far as we became capable of repayment, though the holders of it would change in accordance with the fluctuations of international surpluses and deficits, a state of affairs better for the holders than freezing; in short a grand verification of the Law of Sir Thomas Gresham (the first British Treasury official who played with the management of foreign exchanges), the very inferiority of sterling having ensured its final triumph. Or, alternatively, we should have to fall back on the second alternative, the explanation of which is about to follow. When this explanation has been read, it will be clear enough that, if something of this kind is desirable in the long run, it will be vastly easier to put it through now, than when the common emotions and close collaboration of the war are five years behind us in the valley of forgetfulness.

34. This is not to say that we should not decidedly prefer an essay in cunctation, which is what this first alternative really is, to accepting an unsatisfactory expedient or putting our name to what we have no sufficient confidence that we can honour.

IV. *The second alternative*

35. The peculiar war-time system of the sterling area has been a great success; for one may doubt whether the war would

have been won without it. But it has resulted in the economic and financial affairs of half the world becoming inextricably intertwined with our own. Thus, unless means can be found to bring our burden within the limits of what is practicable, immeasurable and lasting confusion to the world's international economy cannot be avoided. The other alternative is therefore to organise, so far as may be, as being in the general interest and not only in our own, a liquidation of the financial consequences of the War amongst all those chiefly concerned who have won a common victory by a common effort. Not a complete liquidation—that would be asking too much. The British people are prepared to accept for themselves and their posterity as the price of deliverance, a burden of external indebtedness to their Allies which no one else will be expected to carry, not even the defeated enemy.

36. We ask our American friends, therefore, to join us in a realistic appraisal of the facts and to aid the acceptance of what, sooner or later, inevitably arises from them.

37. Including some allowance for overseas expenditure arising out of the war after the war is over, the actual and prospective indebtedness of the United Kingdom to the other countries in the sterling area* will be of the order of $12,000 to $14,000 million. We think that it is right and proper and advisable to divide this aggregate in two parts. One part say $4 billion, would be on one ground or another, written off; the other part, say $8 billion would be made available to the holders by instalments for current purchases in any country without discrimination. To make this practicable in addition to our meeting our own running adverse balance in the early post-war period, we estimate that it would be necessary for the United States to provide a sum of $5 billion as an addition to our resources. The plan would enter into force as soon as possible after the end of the war, say at the end of 1946. By

---

* Debts outside the sterling area, which will have to be dealt with separately, amount to nearly $4,000 million, making $16,000 to $18,000 million altogether.

this means, whilst the Bretton Woods transitional period could not be formally terminated so soon, we should dispense immediately with any element of discrimination in the use of available sterling balances as between the other countries of the area and countries outside the area. Whilst the sterling balances accumulated before the end of the war could be made available to the holders only by instalments, whatever was made available from time to time would be available without discrimination, though this would not preclude additional special arrangements under 39 (viii) below. In particular, the existing arrangements governing the sterling area dollar pool would be entirely withdrawn.

38. This would afford a total relief of (say) $9 billion, provided to the extent of (say) $4 billion by our sterling creditors and of $5 billion by the United States. We also hope for some aid from Canada. The relief allowed by the sterling creditors would take the form of writing off of a part of their sterling balances. The relief afforded by the United States would be in the shape of a dollar credit which could be called upon, partly to finance our own dollar purchases during the transitional period and partly to give us the resources to implement our offer of general availability by instalments to the remaining uncancelled portion of the sterling balances and also to the current earnings of sterling by the sterling area countries after the end of 1946.

39. Before returning to the nature of the proposal as affecting the United States, it will be convenient to develop in greater detail the character of the plan which would be offered to the members of the sterling area, as follows:-

(i) A figure would be established for each sterling area country which fairly represented its cumulative war-time gains. The amount of its purchases or repatriations of sterling securities and of any gold supplied to it during the war would be added to its sterling balances at the end of the war, and also an estimated figure for net war receipts from the

British Government accruing after the end of the war as a result of clearing up war accounts, movements of troops and demobilisation; whilst its pre-war sterling balances and any special receipts of a capital character would be deducted.

(ii) We have already made a sufficient study of the particular cases to convince us that a uniform all-round formula would not work out fairly. There would, therefore, be separate discussions with each country concerned.

(iii) We should set out from the starting point that an average writing off of rather more than one-third of their net war gains as estimated above would be generally appropriate except in so far as there were sufficient reasons for a different figure. Account would be taken of the local price level at which the expenditure had been incurred, of the burden of war expenditure and war strain which they had undertaken in other ways, how far the accumulated sterling balances represent the surplus of normal trade due to war-time impediments to normal importing and how far they are due to special receipts from overseas which would never have accrued apart from the war, and any other relevant circumstances. It might be appropriate to bring various assets and counter-claims of our own into the settlement with certain countries. We think that after making allowance for exceptional treatment, justifiable and necessary in some cases, there would remain an amount approaching $4 billion appropriate for writing off.

(iv) The negotiations with those concerned would be on a voluntary and agreed basis in the following sense. There would be no unilateral writing off of debt. It would, however, be represented that the possibility of freeing in the near future any significant portion of the sterling balances wholly depended on some measure of agreed general liquidation of the financial consequences of the war and in particular on assistance from the United States. Those countries which were not prepared to take a fair share of the burden could

443

not expect to benefit from the facilities afforded by the United States for freeing sterling balances. That is to say, countries unwilling to come into the general scheme (after receiving all proper allowances under (iii) above) could not participate in its full benefits.

(v) Let us assume that the plan proves generally acceptable and that the aggregate appropriate writings-off add up to $4 billion out of an initial sterling area aggregate of $13 billion, leaving $9 billion still owing to the sterling area, apart from our debts outside the area. We would then propose to free sterling to the equivalent of (say) $800 million, divided between all the holders of sterling, to be available forthwith to meet their current adverse balances of trade without discrimination. It is obvious that this also could not be shared on a general formula—the amount of the immediately available proportion would have to depend *inter alia* on the proportion cancelled, on the scale of the country's external requirements and on the size of the country's pre-war sterling balances.

(vii) The balance of about $8 billion would be similarly released by instalments over a period not exceeding 50 years. Such subsequent releases (in addition to the initial $800 million and the whole of net current earnings after the plan comes into effect) might commence in the fifth year at a rate of (say) $100 million a year with the faithful intention, though without a premature obligation, gradually to step up the rate of releases as time and opportunity permit.

(viii) In addition to these normal arrangements, if in subsequent years it were to suit us for any purpose or in any context to make the equivalent of loans overseas, including loans through the International Bank for Reconstruction and Development, we should be free to offer a holder of unreleased sterling to release instalments in advance of any due date suitably discounted; so that in this case earlier agreed releases of this character might come to play the same part in our economy as, for example, the Export-Import Bank or

444

loans to the International Bank in the case of the United States. As in the case of the Export–Import Bank such additional releases might be for the purpose of financing British contracts, but in so far as they were for use overseas they would be available without discrimination. The effect of such releases on the British economy will be much the same as our former regular foreign investment, and the time may come when it will prove a useful help to our policy of full employment to have the equivalent of such foreign investment always at hand without having to trouble about the credit of the borrower or the problem of subsequent payment of interest and capital. In fact we should be obtaining at some future date the same kind of advantage as the United States will be obtaining now if they fall in with this plan.

(ix) It is not proposed that the unreleased portion should carry interest. The more rapid ultimate liquidation made possible by the complete elimination of interest on the portion temporarily frozen seems better in result and more appropriate to the character of loans which have not gone to the creation of commercial assets capable of earning interest. On the available sterling balances interest could, of course, be earned by the holders at (say) Treasury bill rate, if they were retained in a liquid form, or at a higher rate, if they were to be invested in the United Kingdom, becoming liable in this case to any restrictions in force on capital withdrawals.

(x) It should be made clear that this offer to the sterling area holders of sterling balances would have to be made contingent, for the time being at least, on their remaining members of the area for certain purposes. We could not safely afford to undertake the releases of the balances on the scale indicated above if we had to assume that the whole of the amounts so released would be immediately withdrawn. Thus there would have to be an understanding that the releases of the war-time accumulations of sterling were to be used solely to meet adverse balances of trade on current account accumulating after the plan comes into operation and not to acquire gold or foreign assets; but when required, they would be available to pay for imports from any source without discrimination. Thus we should be accepting this part of our post-transitional obligations under the International Monetary Fund as soon as the proposed plan came into operation. Furthermore, even when we were retaining the ultimate discretion in our hands, we should endeavour to interpret the rules in any particular case in as free and liberal a manner as the state of our over-all resources permitted; and we believe that the recent experience of the members of the sterling area of the way in which we have handled our relations with them even in times when we were in the greatest possible difficulties will have given them confidence in the value of such a general understanding. In particular we should consider it our duty to release sterling balances in advance of the due date, to the full extent that our own resources and other liabilities would permit, to any member of the sterling area finding itself in temporary, unforeseen difficulties. Our object throughout is to avoid any absolute obligations beyond what we have confidence we can carry, with the full intention of being better than our word whenever our resources allow and the other party has need.

(xi) Any favourable sterling balance arising out of current trade which a sterling area country might earn after the plan comes into operation would be similarly available, on the same conditions, without discrimination.

(xiii) The arrangements outlined above are given as a specimen of what the separate negotiations might provide. They are not intended as a binding model in matters of detail. We should endeavour to work out separately in collaboration with each particular country a technique which involved the least possible interference with their normal banking arrangements and the interests of private persons. Here again we believe that we can operate in practice a much better and freer system than any to which it would be safe for us to commit ourselves as a binding obligation.

(xiv) We believe that the other countries in the sterling area can be made to see that their acceptance of this general scheme is as much in their interest as in ours. This does not mean that each will not strive to the utmost to get out of it as much as possible for themselves; and it will need resolute diplomacy and great determination on our part to achieve a fair and balanced all-round settlement. Nevertheless they are all of them keenly aware of the limitations on what is within our power, and that there is no means on earth by which they can get more than is within our power. If, therefore, the United States is prepared greatly to increase our capacity on condition that the sterling area countries also play their fair part in liquidating the financial consequences of the war so as to bring the burden which we (and we alone) will continue to carry within tolerance, they will understand that the choice for them can only lie in the last resort between coming into the plan and sharing its benefits or staying out and foregoing them.

(xv) If nevertheless, there are any countries in the sterling area which finally reject a settlement which seems fair in relation to ourselves and to the other participants and to the ultimate governing conditions of the whole plan, we should invite them to withdraw from the area. Henceforward they would be entirely free to make their own arrangements. But their existing sterling balances would not share in the initial release of available sterling, nor would they carry interest. It would be our purpose and intention to discharge them in due course, but they would have, necessarily, to rank behind our other commitments, and we could give no prior undertakings as to the dates or terms of release.

V. *The proposed plan in relation to the United States*

40. Our gold and dollar reserves of $2 billion, of which not more than $1 billion could be drawn upon except in the gravest emergency, are so small in relation to the other quantities in the picture that no plan can be built upon them otherwise than as a minor and secondary support. In the absence of any other support we should run through the whole of our available gold and dollar reserves within less than a year after the end of the war.

41. Our suggestion is, therefore, that, to help to solve the international problem of the liquidation of war-time indebtedness, the United States should place at our disposal a sum of $5 billion in three instalments, $2 billion in the first year and $1·5 billion in each of the next two years. This figure has not been arrived at, and cannot be justified by, any exact calculation, and is based on a broad judgement of the necessities of the case. It has to cover four distinct liabilities:–

(*a*) our own running adverse balance during the transition apart from what we can [obtain] from other sources, (*b*) the obligation to release instalments of their sterling balances to members of the sterling area, (*c*) the settlement of our war-time debts outside the area and (*d*) any liabilities to the U.S. arising out of war disposals and the final wind-up of lend lease. We should have liked to have kept to a lower figure of (say) $3–4 billion, but the magnitude of the various obligation now facing us lead us to feel that with less than $5 billion we could not accept the responsibility of the obligation to make sterling available on the scale suggested above or of relaxing the existing sterling area arrangements so soon as the end of 1946. If this proves insufficient, as it possibly may, we must meet the resulting problem in the light of the surrounding facts as and when it arises. On the basis of $5 billion we should be ready to face the risks and responsibilities of a settlement on the general lines indicated above.

42. On what grounds can we make such an unprecedented suggestion to the Administration of the United States?

43. Under lend lease we have already enjoyed an extraordinary measure of liberality. Moreover, our difficulties insofar as they arise out of war-time accumulations of sterling and not out of our running deficit immediately after the war, are precisely due to the fact that we have not had the benefit of similar lend lease arrangements with other countries; though we must remember that most of these other countries are poor countries or undeveloped countries and countries not so rich as ourselves and, in some cases, hitherto heavily indebted to us, and that they have in fact given us invaluable and even decisive assistance in the war through their having been willing to entrust all their resources to us without security or guarantee, including in some cases their net dollar earnings and to continue doing so after their sterling balances had vastly exceeded any figure even in the remotest anticipation when the arrangements were first made. Moreover, the proposed plan would in fact require of them contributions to the common cause not disproportionate to the contributions of others, if regard is had to their relative wealth and real resources in proportion to their population.

44. In the first place, we can commend these suggestions to the United States in that they may be a sufficient, and perhaps an indispensable, condition of establishing after the war, the type of commercial and financial relations between nations which they wish to see established, and which we, too, wish if it can be managed. The object is, as already stated, to facilitate the liquidation of indebtedness arising out of the war on a scale sufficient to allow a return to normal practices at an early date. Not ourselves only are concerned in all this. The financial arrangements of half the world are so entangled with our own, that the pattern of world trade and finance as a whole is deeply involved.

45. But there is also an immaterial element. For nearly two

449

years the United Kingdom with her small population having no support except the steadfastness of the distant members of the British Commonwealth, held the fort alone. Everything we had in energy, man-power and possessions was thrown into the furnace, with an intensity of purpose and eager willingness on the part of all our people. The effort and sacrifices were successful. It cannot then appear to those who have borne the burden of many days that it is a just and seemly conclusion of this sacrifice to be left, as the price of what has happened, with a burden of future tribute to the rest of the world, and mainly to our own Allies, beyond tolerable bearing. Our people would not accept with a quiet mind what was coming to them, when the full meaning of all this came to be felt in the burdens and privations of daily life for many years after the war, and it is by man's feelings, and only so, that the stable foundations of society within and without countries are disturbed. Moreover, we should be prevented from sharing, as we wish and intend, in the responsibility for the reconstruction of the ravaged world and in affording material support for the economic international institutions which are the best hope of a new order of peaceful intercourse between nations.

46. On what terms do we hope or expect such assistance? We would prefer to place our position without reserve before the Administration of the United States and discuss frankly what is right and reasonable without attempting to make any definite proposal in advance of such discussions. We do not yet know whether or how far the United States will favour the general principles outlined above for partially liquidating the financial consequences of the war in the interests of an early return to normal conditions on terms which, in the phrase of Article VII of the Mutual Aid Agreement, will not unduly burden international commerce.

47. Some further figures relating to the war effort of the United Kingdom and on the relation of mutual aid to lend

lease are given in Appendix C [not printed]. If it is thought useful to analyse more deeply how the post-war financial problem has arisen, all possible data will, of course, be made available. But the explanation can be summed up very completely in a few sentences. The financial difficulties of the United Kingdom during and immediately after the war are more than fully accounted for by three factors:–

(i) In the period before lend lease, or rather before lend lease came into full effect $3 billion, which constituted almost the whole of the British gold and other reserves, was expended in the United States to pay for munitions (which involved the building up of a largely new munitions industry in the United States) and other purchases required for the war.

(ii) Throughout the war the United Kingdom has been mainly responsible, without any significant assistance from any other quarter except the Government of India, for the local cash expenditure required for military operations over a wide area of Africa and Asia, extending from Tunis to Burma through Egypt, the Middle East and India, which has amounted to some $10 billion and may be higher before the last bills have ben paid. Yet it was this expenditure which threw one enemy back at the gates of Egypt and the other at the gates of India.

(iii) It was the very fact of lend lease from the United States, mutual aid from Canada and the arrangements with the sterling area which made it possible for us to abandon our foreign trade and support a total concentration into the war industries and the armed forces which would otherwise have been impracticable. If it had been our role to maintain and expand our foreign trade with a view to the assistance of others, we should find ourselves in a vastly better position today to recover post-war equilibrium, even if we had given away the whole of the net proceeds of our war-time exports.

Keynes left Ottawa by train on 6 September. On his arrival in Washington the next day, he began his final preparations for the negotiations. He was immediately also faced with the problem of lend lease supplies in the pipeline and commercial policy. At one time he had been attracted to the idea of paying cash for the former, but by 8 September he had concluded that the sum involved was too high for such a gesture. Although he favoured an interim credit which the final lend lease settlement might supersede and asked for permission to give way along these lines in negotiations, by 13 September the matter had become entwined in the general discussions. Meanwhile pipeline supplies continued as the result of a Presidential decision. New orders were paid for in cash.

On commercial policy, the delegation immediately faced a continuation of earlier American pressure to include the subject in the Stage III discussions, pressure which resulted in a London decision, taken over Keynes's objections, to send out additional experts, Professor Robbins and Sir Percivale Liesching.[2]

On 10 September, the day before the first formal meeting with the Americans to set up the various committees for the discussions, Keynes sent back his first impressions of the atmosphere.

To SIR WILFRID EADY, *10 September 1945*

My dear Wilfrid,

Very rashly, but so as to put you in as close touch as possible at as early a date as possible, I have prepared the attached note. It is based on fairly long talks separately with Vinson and with Harry White. But I shall not have seen Clayton until this afternoon. When I do I am hopeful that I can comfort him on the difficulty discussed in Baboon 21. I am assiduously sticking to the existing arrangements and at present feel some confidence that this is the right start, though quite possibly strengthening the team will be necessary a little later on.

---

[2] Percivale Liesching (1895–1974), K.C.M.G. 1944, K.C.B. 1947, K.C.V.O. 1953; Colonial Office, 1920; Dominions Office, 1925; seconded to staff of High Commissioner in Canada, 1928–32; Political Secretary, Office of High Commissioner in S. Africa, 1933–5; Official Secretary, Office of High Commissioner in Australia, 1936–8; Assistant Under-Secretary of State, Dominions Office, 1939–42; Second Secretary, Board of Trade, 1942–6; Permanent Secretary, Ministry of Food, 1946–8; Permanent Under-Secretary of State, Commonwealth Relations Office, 1949–55.

The top copy of this is intended for you, Bridges and the Chancellor. I am also enclosing a duplicate in case you may care to pass one on to the Bank for Catto and Cobbold.

As you may imagine, we had a pretty strenuous time in Ottawa to get through in three days and I had not a minute away from official or semi-official business. All the same, they were once again so jolly and truly warm in their approach that it was a pleasure from start to finish. And, once again, Gordon Munro was infallibly efficient and helpful.

About the position here, the only thing I would add to the attached note is that the atmosphere is perhaps rather too good. One's experience in Washington has always been that when things look beastliest all will be glowing three months hence, and vice versa. So perhaps it is dangerous for the Press to be starting off so forthcoming. There will, however, I think, remain the solid gain that the public will have got thoroughly used to the idea before we have to break it to them in concrete terms.

Yours ever,
MAYNARD KEYNES

SOME HIGHLY PRELIMINARY NOTES ON THE FORTHCOMING CONVERSATIONS: 9 SEPTEMBER 1945

I. *General atmosphere*

It is absurd to presume to make any comments so soon; but as one's first impressions are often more clear cut and for that reason sometimes more serviceable than the more complicated and hazier view that one reaches later, I may as well record at once the first impact of Washington on my mind.

In my judgment the result of the Prime Minister's statement about the way in which lend lease was terminated and the dramatisation of this in the House of Commons and in the Press has been wholly good and tremendously effective. We have seldom, if ever, in my experience, had such publicity on a financial and economic matter. There is something interesting and responsible on the matter in the newspapers every day, and most of it very favourable.

There is general approval for the underlying policy of the President in bringing lend lease to an early and clear cut conclusion, but the way the thing was done is very unpopular and has caused a noticeable reaction in our favour of doing something for us, as well as giving opportunity for the publicity just referred to, at any rate in the Eastern Press.

Crowley's position with his colleagues and people of influence with the Administration seems to be poor and deteriorating; probably much poorer than he himself realises since he believes, probably with good reason, that he has been carrying out the President's present intentions and he does not yet realise the impending strength of the influences which are exceedingly likely to change this as soon as the President becomes better informed about what is at issue. Crowley's line is that the U.K. must get the same terms as all the other countries who are on the doorstep, that is to any, a 3(c) credit for what is in the pipe line and an Export-Import Bank credit on the same (or worse) terms for anything else; no more than that and no special cases. The Treasury and the State Department, on the other hand, are perfectly clear that we are a special case which the above provisions go nowhere in meeting. It is also relevant that both Vinson and Clayton are believed to feel that he has recently double crossed each of them on separate occasions in matters arising out of our affairs. He secured the abrupt termination of lend lease contrary to Vinson's advice after Vinson had left the President's room under the impression that no such decision was going to be made; and in the matter of Clayton's letter to us, Crowley's disregard of it has put Clayton in a position which the latter feels to be rather humiliating and lays him open to having his good faith doubted by us (which would, in fact, be most unjust). White was emphatic that in the long run it would be the advice of Clayton and Vinson which would determine the President's action.

II. *The machinery of the conversations*

The nature of the committees to be set up has been explained by telegram. I gather that it is the intention both of Clayton and Vinson to sit in fairly continuously on the main committees in a way in which their predecessors never would. Vinson explained to me, on my first courtesy visit to him, that he wants to give close attention to the factual presentation of our case so that he feels he is thoroughly soaked in it. As a lawyer, he added, he felt that the judgment which must follow should be dictated by the facts. I told him that this was exactly what we looked for and would welcome. Vinson also clearly advised me, though not in quite so many words, that we should from now on cease to have any direct or separate contact with Crowley in any matters of principle relating to the winding-up of lend lease. He indicated that as soon as the conversations had started, the Top Committee would have full powers over all lend lease questions as over anything else and that any decisions should be handed down by the Top Committee and not separately discussed at any lower level. We shall certainly not give way at the start on the question of accepting Crowley's terms subject to the proviso. My telegram asking for discretion to give way, if necessary, was sent off before my conversation with Vinson and, in any case, was only intended to make provision so that we could act quickly on this point if a stand about it seemed likely to be futile and make unnecessary trouble, thus prejudicing the main negotiations. Our previous information was that on this particular matter Vinson and Clayton would support Crowley. If they do this I think that we should give way, but certainly not until the position is clear cut.

III. *The possible substance of the American plan*

It is evident that an elaborate plan has been or is being worked out in the U.S. Treasury. This is primarily White's plan with, I think, a good deal of assistance from Bernstein. When I saw him White was obviously burning to show it to me and only just managed to restrain himself from doing so. But reading between the lines of what he said and piecing things together, I should infer that the general lines of what they are thinking about are likely to be as follows:–

(*a*) I think that White himself has now come round to the view that we need something in the order of $5 billion rather than $3 billion. This was helpful since there was an earlier rumour that White was in favour of too low a figure. He added, however, that he thought the amount might prove a mater of some difficulty with the committee. The inference certainly was that he would support us in asking for the higher figure.

(*b*) The U.S. Treasury are thinking in terms of a 50-year loan without interest. But here again, White thinks that it will not be easy to get the 'no interest' principle through the committee. Whether a 50-year loan means a loan in which the capital is repayable by 50 annual instalments or whether nothing is due until 50 years hence, I have no indication, but I should imagine the former. If so, a $5 billion loan without interest would mean an annual service of $100 million a year.

(*c*) The tendency of White's thought which I found most disturbing was that he seems to have returned to an earlier idea by which the U.S. would take over as their liability a certain part of the sterling balances. We must, of course, press them very hard that the right way is to strengthen us so as to liberate some part of the sterling balances and that their plan, instead of assisting multilateral convertibility, would in fact impede it since, if the assistance to each sterling area country is segregated, this would be incompatible with rendering their remaining sterling balances either wholly free or wholly blocked. Our latest plan is so much better than this that we should have hopes of getting it through. Nevertheless, White's line of thinking on this matter is dangerous, since once he associates himself with a general proposition, he is not easily shaken from it.

IV. *Our initial tactics*

On this matter I had a very interesting and helpful conversation with Towers during my stop in Ottawa. He was emphatic in preferring our old plan of $3 billion grant-in-aid plus an additional option of $5 billion credit, with the intention of drawing on the $5 billion credit to the least possible extent. He is, of course, anxious that we should arrange a non-discriminatory use of sterling balances on the lines which we discussed with him in Cambridge and which is still part of the plan; and he thinks that this would be enormously attractive to the Americans. But he says that, if he were in our place, he would hesitate greatly before conceding this except in return for assistance which took the form of a grant-in-aid at least in substantial part. He thought that we ought to present our case at the start on something like the following lines.

We should say that one alternative would be to receive a dollar loan on semi-commercial terms. In this case we should try to keep the size of it down to the absolute minimum and in order to do this we should inevitably have to enforce a restrictive policy with regard to imports so far as we and the rest of the sterling area are concerned and also, in all probability, a discriminatory one. The alternative plan would be a substantial grant-in-aid which would leave us with at least some potential borrowing power still in hand in the event of the grant-in-aid proving inadequate to our needs. But in this event we could take far greater risks. If we had a substantial

457

grant-in-aid it might go a very long way in seeing us through the transitional period. Thus we could safely promise a far less restrictive policy and could accept the obligation of non-discrimination. To repeat the point, if our potential borrowing power is used up at the start so that we have nothing to fall back upon, we can take no risks and must be restrictive. We can only take the chance of a liberal and expansive policy if our immediate necessities are covered by a grant-in-aid so that we can still have some potential borrowing power in hand against contingencies. The ideal plan would therefore be my original proposal for a grant-in-aid for a substantial, nevertheless moderate, amount such as $3 billion with an option of $5 billion on generous credit terms in hand against contingencies. I should add that Towers was rather disturbed by the low level of imports which I told him we contemplated if we were to have any hope of breaking even within three to five years. He thought that such a low level of imports on our part must have a seriously restrictive influence on world trade as a whole and that we should certainly aim at a settlement which would not force on us such severe and lasting austerity. How far the above advice can be made compatible with the line of thought of the U.S. Treasury as indicated above, remains to be seen. But I feel that basically Towers' advice is very good indeed. (I fancy that Canada will not be less liberal in principle than the U.S.A. and might very likely follow the American model on the above lines, if we can secure it.)

KEYNES

10.9.45

On 12 September, the day before Keynes began his presentation of Britain's position to the Top Committee, the Mission held a press conference. After a short speech by the Ambassador, Keynes delivered a statement setting out the purposes of the Mission before carefully answering questions.

THE BABES IN THE BRETTON WOOD

*Cartoon by David Low by arrangement with the
Trustees and the London Evening Standard*

459

STATEMENT BY LORD KEYNES AT PRESS
CONFERENCE: 12 SEPTEMBER 1945

I am rather glad to have this chance of explaining the purpose of the present mission to Washington in its proper perspective as we see it. The British government had no reason to expect that lend lease would continue for a significant length of time after the end of the war or would be available for any expenditure except that which arose out of the war in its concluding phases. We had been contemplating for some time back that a Mission ought to come from London to Washington not later than the present month to discuss with your Administration the mutually convenient basis for winding-up lend lease and reverse lend lease and the financial and other arrangements to follow on, so as to cover the transitional period before normal conditions of trade could be re-established. We attached great importance to the avoidance, if possible, of an interregnum between the old arrangements and the new; and our intention was, therefore, to complete these conversations before the end of the war. You must remember that up to almost the other day the instructions of both our Governments were to act on the assumption that the war with Japan would last beyond the end of 1945. And even though some of us thought that we ought to be ready for a collapse by the end of 1945, the beginning of September looked last July soon enough for getting down to the matter in view of the very great difficulties in the way of an earlier date—in particular our General Election and a possible change of Government and the Potsdam Conference which caused the chief immediate concentration of attention of leading members and officials of both Governments on a different set of problems, namely, the defeat of Japan and the settlement of Europe. It had, however, been previously decided in London as long ago as last June that these Washington discussions ought to be started not much later than the beginning of September.

The atomic bomb and Japan's sudden collapse have thrown our time-table out and we find ourselves faced with the prospect of just that interregnum which we had hoped to avoid. Nevertheless, that is far from being the fundamental problem which faces us in the ensuing months. We have received far too much liberality and consideration in the famous Lend Lease Act to make any complaint about the clean cut. Speaking personally, I in fact, rather envy you your characteristically drastic methods which you are applying, I notice, no less to yourselves than to us. I wish sometimes that there was something more of that spirit in my own country. We are in some danger of reacting too slowly to a radical change in circumstances and of not bracing ourselves forthwith, as we must do, to the new efforts ahead of us. It has to be admitted that after a full six years of war accompanied, not only by intense effort and sacrifice, but also by considerable privation, people in England were expecting a little relaxation. You in this country can have no idea how tired we are and what a difference it makes in the long run on the top of all the other miseries of war to have your standard of life cut by 20 per cent and possess not nearly enough homes for the boys and evacuated civilians to come back to. Nevertheless, it may well be wholesome for us to be brought sharp up against the realities of our post-war position instead of being deceived, as well as comforted, by temporary expedients which would do little or nothing to solve the real problems of the transition.

Let me now turn to our particular difficulties and our fundamental problems. They have arisen out of the way in which it has been to the common interest to conduct the common war. Our role has been to mobilise a greater proportion of our population and for a longer period than in any other Allied country for actual fighting and the production of munitions. This has suited the common cause best. We have been enabled to do this mainly as I will now explain. Instead of having to expand our exports so as to pay for our own consumption and to provide for the consumption of our Allies we have been enabled and encouraged by lend lease from the United States, by mutual aid from Canada and by the equivalent of loans from the countries in the sterling area, to sacrifice two-thirds of our normal exports so as to employ the manpower thus released in direct, instead of indirect, war activities. This arrangement has had various consequences.

In the first place, we are much worse off in tackling the task of recovering our exports and paying our own way than we should have been if the roles had been reversed. The result is that much more time inevitably must elapse in our case than in yours before we can restore the level of our exports even to the pre-war level whilst in addition the loss of a considerable part of our assets, which helped us to pay for our imports before the war, means that we shall not break even until we have reconverted our industry so as to achieve a volume of exports more than 50 per cent above the pre-war level. To reach this is a colossal task.

In the second place, the financial technique adopted in relation to the sterling area, which has played an indispensable part in mobilising our common resources for the war especially in the early days, has had the effect that the financial and commercial arrangements of a considerable section of the world have become almost inextricably intertwined with our own financial and economic affairs in London. Most of the sterling area countries have in effect advanced to us substantially the whole of their external resources. The result is that they cannot continue to trade freely with the rest of the world in the post-war period unless we are in a strong enough position to release to them as available purchasing power some part of these resources.

There are therefore serious impediments in the way of the return of ourselves and of a number of other important trading countries to normal trading practices, as early as we should wish, and to the expanding world trade which is essential if standards of life throughout the world are to take the advantage they ought to take of the technical advances of our age.

The United States and we in Britain and the other countries concerned are faced therefore, broadly speaking, with two alternatives. Since trade is two-sided the problem is two-sided also.

The first alternative is for us to do the best we can with the resources we still command and aim at emerging slowly from our temporary difficulties with as little outside aid as possible, depending on the various defensive trade mechanisms which have been developed by war controls; matching the purchases we make from any country with the purchases that country makes from us and inevitably curtailing our overall import programme on the lines of the greatest austerity of which we find ourselves capable.

There are a good many people in England who think that this is really our best plan. Personally, I think that they greatly underestimate the disadvantages of it not only to ourselves but to the trade of the world as a whole and above all to the prospect of avoiding occasions of friction and difficulty between friends and former Allies.

The other alternative is to work out with you, and with your aid, some means of returning at the earliest possible date to normal trade practices without discrimination and to in-creased freedom and liberality in commercial and tariff policies; in the belief that the resulting general expansion of world trade will result in the final outcome that you and other countries as well as ourselves being much better off on balance than under the first plan. As the Ambassador has emphasised, we shall certainly not expect your Congress to approve any arrangements which have not been proved to their full satis-faction as being in the long-term interest of the United States itself.

Nevertheless, we have to face the fact that this second and, as it seems to some of us, far preferable alternative will not be at all easy to work out. We shall have to strive after it in a bold and constructive spirit with all the earnestness and concentration of purpose which the two sides to the discussion can command.

No doubt an easy course would be for you to offer, and for us to put our name, to a substantial loan on more or less commercial terms, without either party to the transaction troubling to pay too much attention to the question of the likelihood of our being able to fulfil the obligations which we were undertaking. But not only do I fear that the deception would probably have a very short life but it would be extremely shortsighted if the absence of friction and bad feeling between our two countries is—as I hope it is—one of our principal aims. However this may be, we shall not lend ourselves to any such soft and deceptive expedient. We are not in the mood, and we believe and hope that you are not in the mood, to repeat the experiences of last time's war debts. We would far rather, and here I know that I speak for all shades and sections of opinion and sentiment in my country, we would far rather do what we can to get on as best we can on any other lines which are open to us.

We hope for your understanding collaboration in finding the right way out of the transition. We are not concerned or anxious about the ultimate outcome. It is not only our fighting men who have proved themselves in this war. In relation to their numbers and our resources at home our administrators, our scientists, our manufacturers, our farmers and our workers have shown that they can hold their own with anyone. It would be absurd to suppose that the trouble a few years hence, either ours or yours, is likely to be due to an insufficient power to produce material goods. Our pains, ours and yours, are more likely to be due to our stomachs being fuller than our heads and our appetite weaker than our opportunity. Our immediate task and our first duty is to avoid an unnecessary mess meanwhile and a false start along the wrong path.

We have to look at the financial and commercial problem

of the world as a whole; and, moreover, build up a currency and commercial structure which is in the best interests not only of world prosperity (which our technicians will make easy) but of peace and goodwill amongst men (which does not come so easily); so as to avoid the violent disturbance of international commerce which are the road to discontents which can shake the social order and to maintain full employment and good wages everywhere by means that do not beggar but, on the contrary, enrich our neighbours.

I am sure that my country and yours have no conflict of purpose or of interest which need prevent us from working together in a common programme. But we, as well as a large part of Europe and Asia are being subjected to a violent disturbance of our economic equilibrium; at a time when men's spirits are exhausted, their patience and their tempers threadbare, and they are the prey to suspicion and fear and all uncharitableness. There was never more need of a truthful and objective judgment and of faith and faithfulness if the world is to harvest the fruits of what it has endured.

It is therefore at a bitter crisis of men's souls and minds, though the war itself be over, that we come 'as a faithful ally' in Winston Churchill's words, to take counsel with the Administration of the United States on the ways and means of restoring the economic strength of ourselves and of that considerable part of the world, the economy and finance of which has, as I have said, become inextricably intertwined with our own.

Before leaving London I participated in a series of fruitful conversations with Mr Clayton. We now hope to continue these in a wider framework and have an opportunity of putting the position without reserve, and exactly as we see it, before the leaders of your administration. There is no occasion here for secret diplomacy. Any proposals which the experts may work out amongst themselves will have to be justified before public opinion and the legislatures of our two countries and, indeed, of the whole world. There must therefore be no withholding of any part of the factual and statistical evidence on which they are based. But it will be desirable, in our opinion, that these should be presented in due course as a whole and not piecemeal prematurely.

On 13, 14 and 17 September, Keynes gave an oral exposition of the British post-war position to the Top Committee at meetings in the Board Room of the Federal Reserve Board. The agreed minutes of these meetings provide an indication of the ground covered, although they do not provide an exact guide as to what was said.[3]

U.S.–U.K. FINANCIAL AND ECONOMIC NEGOTIATIONS
TOP COMMITTEE

Minutes of a meeting of the Top Committee held at the Board Room of the Federal Reserve Board, Constitution Avenue, on 13 September 1945, at 3.30 p.m.

PRESENT

Mr Clayton (in the chair)

U.S. Representatives	*U.K. Representatives*
Mr Crowley	Lord Halifax
Mr Vinson	Lord Keynes
Mr Eccles	Sir Henry Self
Mr McCabe[4]	Mr Brand
Mr Amos Taylor[5]	Mr Hall-Patch

Mr Collado ⎫
Mr Early ⎬ *Joint secretaries*
Mr Lee ⎪
Mr Stevens ⎭

---

[3] The appendix tables are not reproduced here. Most were reproduced in the White Paper *Statistical Material Presented During the Washington Negotiations* (Cmd. 6707), December 1945.

[4] Thomas Bayard McCabe (b. 1893); Director, Federal Reserve Bank of Philadelphia, 1938–48; Chairman, Board of Governors, Federal Reserve System, 1948–51; member, Business Advisory Council, Department of Commerce, 1940, Chairman, 1944–5; Departmental Director, Division of Priorities, Office of Production Management, 1941; Deputy, Lend Lease Administration, 1941–2.

[5] Amos Elias Taylor (b. 1893); Assistant Chief, Finance Division, U.S. Department of Commerce, 1931–9, Chief, 1939–42, Chief, Division of Research and Statistics, 1942–3; Director, Bureau of Foreign and Domestic Commerce, 1943–7; member, Executive Committee on Economic Foreign Policy, 1944–5.

THE LOAN NEGOTIATIONS

1. *Press relations*

MR CLAYTON reminded the meeting that a decision on this subject had been deferred from the previous meeting. He had now, however, had a telephone message from Lord Halifax agreeing that it would be desirable to arrange for U.S. and U.K. press officers to attend meetings of the Top Committee.

LORD HALIFAX confirmed his agreement to the course mentioned by Mr Clayton, it being understood (i) that the press officers would exercise discretion in any statements made to the press in amplification of agreed press releases and (ii) that on occasions when particularly secret matters were to be discussed it might be necessary to exclude press officers from the meetings of the Top Committee.

MR CLAYTON said that the U.S. repesentatives fully concurred in the understandings mentioned by Lord Halifax.

2. *External financial position of the U.K.*

LORD KEYNES began his exposition of the external financial position of the U.K. in the transitional period. He said that the problem fell into two sections:

(*a*) the inheritance of the past—i.e. problems arising from the accumulation of sterling indebtedness—and

(*b*) the difficulties of the immediate future—i.e. the problem of the running adverse balance which the U.K. would have to face in the period before it could break even.

The second problem was more urgent and more onerous than the first. It was clearly more pressing to find a solution to the difficulties of meeting the U.K. cash outgoings over the next few years than to attempt to deal with accumulated indebtedness arising from the past. Therefore it appeared to him logical to begin his exposition with an examination of the future position.

3. *Overseas expenditure and income of the U.K. in 1945*

LORD KEYNES took as his text the two estimates given in the appendix to these minutes. He made the following comments on the first of the two tables—namely that showing the estimated annual rate of overseas expenditure and income of the U.K. prior to VJ Day. He explained that this could be taken as equivalent to the position of the U.K. in 1945 as it would have been had lend lease and reciprocal aid continued throughout that year. He thought that the outcome of the conclusion of hostilities might be that economies of the order of perhaps $300 million might be made in the expenditure figure, but these would be more than offset by the net deterioration of the position which would result from the termination of lend lease and mutual aid.

Lord Keynes proceeded to make the following detailed comments on items in the first table:

(a) Imports (excluding munitions)—$5,000 million
Lord Keynes thought that this figure was familiar to and accepted by most American statisticians.

(b) Government expenditure overseas—$3,200 million
Lord Keynes thought that this item represented that part of the U.K. war burden which had been most commonly under-estimated. It could be conveniently analysed under three headings as follows:

(i) *Munitions and other supplies.* This head accounted for approximately $1,200 million out of a total of $3,200 million. It represented sums paid out for the purchase of munitions from non-American sources, the greater proportion of which never came to the U.K. itself. Expenditure had been largely concentrated in India, South Africa and Australia, especially in India. It had been a deliberate act of policy to expand munitions production from Indian industrial capacity so as to relieve the stress on shipping, particularly during the period of intensive submarine activity. It could be expected that expenditure under this head would fall very rapidly since there had been a drastic cut-back in orders except in certain special cases such as tropical clothing required for British forces in the Far East. But the incidence of cancellation charges and the time lag in effecting payments would cause the rate of expenditure to remain substantial throughout 1945 and part of 1946.

(ii) *Expenditure of services overseas.* This was estimated at the very large figure of $1,700 million. It included not only the pay of British military forces overseas but the cost of employing local labour on the construction of capital works and on ancillary services. The bulk of the expenditure was again in India and the Middle East. But over the whole area of operations from Tunis to Burma the U.K. had, broadly speaking, borne the cash cost of all military operations. The expenditure involved had been colossal but it had stopped the Germans at a critical moment in our fortunes. Included in the figure of $1,700 million was the cost of getting munitions through to Russia, especially via Persia, and the heavy expenditure which the Admiralty had had to incur in expanding port facilities in all parts of the world in order to handle an abnormal volume of naval and other traffic.

Expenditure under this head could be expected to fall substantially, but the large establishments maintained overseas could not be reduced all at once and expenditure might therefore have to continue in the immediate future on quite a considerable scale.

(iii) *Foreign Office expenditure*. Under this head, which could be regarded as accounting for $300 million, Lord Keynes included such items as loans to allies, expenditure on UNRRA and relief measures, Secret Service expenditure, and other expenditures overseas such as the upkeep of missions. In reply to a request from MR VINSON, Lord Keynes undertook to furnish details of loans which were being currently made, or which had ben made in the immediate past, to foreign governments.

(c) *Exports—$1,400 million*
Lord Keynes said that he thought that this figure would be a familiar one. It represented a volume of exports at the rate of about 36 per cent of pre-war.

(d) *Net invisible income and sundry repayments—$400 million*
This estimate was based on the assumption that no net income would be received from shipping services in 1945. Indeed the estimate of $400 million was only as high as it was by reason of the inclusion of certain dollar income which had been regular at any rate during the war but which it was impossible to attribute to any specific source—such as movement of capital, miscellaneous personal expenditure by foreigners and the like.

(e) *Receipts from the U.S. and Dominions—$1,400 million*
This item was partly made up of receipts from U.S. forces, which at one time had been very substantial ($460 million in 1944) but which was now declining. The estimate for the whole of 1945 was $240 million. This latter estimate assumed that there would be no net accrual under this head during the rest of 1945, owing to the conversion of sterling balances held by U.S. paymasters which would be no longer required.

The balance of receipts under this head took the form of reimbursements by the Dominions for munitions drawn from the U.K. munition pool. The biggest source of income under this head was from Canada.

(f) Lord Keynes explained that in the calculation of the deficit and of the way in which it was being covered, munitions expenditure in Canada and mutual aid from Canada had been excluded from both sides of the picture as a matter of statistical convenience since for practical purposes these amounts could be regarded as balancing.

4. Estimated overseas expenditure and income of the U.K. for 1946

LORD KEYNES explained that the framing of this estimate necessarily involved a greater degree of excursion into the realm of guess-work. In making the calculations the basic assumption had been made that the prices of imports and exports would run in 1946 (in terms of sterling) at double pre-war prices. As regards imports the current official Board of Trade figure showed prices at 194% of pre-war. It could be expected that in 1946 shipping freight and insurance charges would fall, but this was likely to be offset by an increase in f.o.b. prices, a tendency which had become evident in certain recent cases such as the purchase of Argentine meat and Canadian wheat. As regards price basis for exports, it might be that the basic assumption of 200 per cent was a little pessimistic as the prices for certain exports (e.g. textiles) were currently running at somewhat over that figure.

In accordance with the usual practice the cost of imports had been reckoned on a c.i.f. basis.

Lord Keynes then proceeded to comment in detail on the heads of the estimates as follows:

(i) *Imports—$5,200 million*. He emphasised that this figure connoted the maintenance of austerity in the U.K. import programme. It would represent a reduction of about 23 per cent in volume over pre-war imports notwithstanding the degree of essential restocking which would be required. It allowed very little for imports of miscellaneous manufactured goods except essential machinery. It was mainly comprised of food and raw materials: the volume of food imports assumed a return only to the 1944 level of food consumption in the U.K. It was in this field that the major economy as compared with pre-war imports would be effected.

It was noteworthy that a recent estimate by statisticians in the U.S. Department of Commerce put U.K. imports in 1946 at a considerably higher figure—of the order of $6,400 million at current prices as compared with the U.K. estimate of $5,200 million. This assumed imports of the same volume as pre-war.

(ii) *Government expenditure overseas (net)—$1,200 million*. This estimate represented a considerable reduction from the estimated total of $3,200 million in respect of 1945. Conceivably it might be possible to secure an even larger reduction. But it had to be remembered that the U.K. was faced with very heavy responsibilities overseas which in many cases could not be discarded without the risk of detriment to world security. The U.K. responsibilities in the Middle East were of this character. In addition there would be the cost of rehabilitating British territories in the Far East; of maintaining the U.K. contribution to UNRRA, an increase in which was contemplated; of maintaining our share in the military occupation of Germany and Austria; and in the net cost of providing relief outside UNRRA in Northwestern Europe.

(iii) *Exports—$2,600 million*. It was very difficult to estimate at all accurately what the scale of U.K. exports in 1946 would be. This depended partly on the rate of conversion and partly on the extent to which it would be possible to stint the domestic consumer (particularly in such fields as household goods and clothing). It would be appreciated that to direct exports in the same way as munitions production had been directed under close Government control would not be at all easy, although there was a possibility of doing so to a limited extent by a differential allocation of raw materials. There were many impediments to the achievement of a rapid reconversion of industries to domestic and export production. There was a shortage of factory space due partly to competing storage claims; in the case of factories which had been closed during the war, plants had to be reconditioned and in some cases replaced; there were the demobilisation arrangements precluding the prior release of key men in advance of those who had served longer in the military forces; the shortage of houses made the reallocation of labour difficult; while in some cases, as with the textile industry, it was difficult to induce workers to return to their peacetime vocations.

On the other hand no question of market difficulties should arise in 1946 or in the immediately following period. The U.K. should be able to sell without difficulty anything that could be exported although net receipts might be diminished by the normal time lag in collecting payments due to the general system whereby exporters carried the burden of financing during the shipping period.

In the light of all the above factors, the estimate of $2,600 million probably erred on the optimistic side. It had been based on the assumption that exports would generally have the first priority call on U.K. production, but that this policy could not be pushed to extremes. The most optimistic estimate current in the U.K. was that exports might perhaps be double in volume those for 1945. On this basis the estimate would be $2,800 million. The estimate given in the appendix ($2,600 million) represented a small reduction on this: it was significant that in their recent study the statisticians of the Department of Commerce put the figure at $1,864 million only.

(iv) *Invisible income (net)—$600 million*. This was based on the broad assumption that on all items of account other than shipping the U.K. would break even. It was thought that the net earnings of U.K. shipping which would include earnings from the carriage of U.K. imports would account for nearly the whole of the estimate of $600 million. This figure might perhaps be on the low side, but it was necessary to remember that in certain areas (e.g. the Far East) the outgoings of U.K. enterprises for rehabilitation, etc., were likely to exceed any receipts from profits in the immediate post-war period.

5. *Outlook beyond 1946*

LORD KEYNES explained that he had not attempted to prepare any statement of the estimated balance of payments position in 1947 and succeeding years since this would involve entering into pure speculation. Broadly speaking it was estimated that the cumulative deficit which the U.K. would have to face in the period before equilibrium was recovered would be of the order of $6 billion, of which, as he had explained, about half was expected to occur in 1946. He did not think that it was conceivable that the cumulative deficit could possibly be less than $4 billion. It might be that the period over which the cumulative deficit would occur would be as long as five years, depending on the rate of recovery and expansion of exports and of the scale on which imports would be permitted. It was common knowledge that the export target was to increase the volume of exports by 50 per cent above pre-war, but that was a formidible task in any event and the difficulties of reconversion in the earlier years of the transitional period might be followed by difficulties of maintaining markets in the later part of the period. It was relevant to note that the estimate of the cumulative U.K. deficit made by the statisticians of the Department of Commerce was that this would be of the order of $8 billion. This estimate, however, assumed a much more extended programme of imports than had been envisaged in the estimates put before the Committee; indeed, the volume of imports was estimated at 15 per cent above pre-war levels.

6. *Conclusion*

At the end of his exposition Lord Keynes answered a number of questions on points of detail.

THE LOAN NEGOTIATIONS

Minutes of a meeting of the Top Committee held at the Board Room of the Federal Reserve Board, Constitution Avenue, on 14 September 1945 at 3.30 p.m.

PRESENT

Mr Clayton (in the chair)

U.S. Representatives	U.K. Representatives
Mr Amos Taylor	Lord Halifax
Dr White	Lord Keynes
Mr Thayer[6]	Sir Henry Self
Mr McCabe	Mr Brand
Mr Eccles	Mr Hall-Patch

Mr Collado
Mr Early
Mr Lee   } *Joint secretaries*
Mr Stevens

1. *U.K. financial position—gold and dollar reserves and liabilities*

LORD KEYNES continued his exposition of the external financial position of the U.K. He began by an analysis of the figures given in Appendix A to COM/TOP-3.

(i) *U.K. gold and dollar reserves.* Lord Keynes said that most of the figures in Statement I of Appendix A had been put before the U.S. representatives at the Stage II discussions in the autumn of 1944. The table had, however, been brought up to date to June 1945.

The low point of U.K. net reserves was reached in April 1941, when they fell to $12 million. A recovery took place following on arrangements for the grant of the RFC loan, the saving in dollar outlay brought about by lend lease, and later from the receipt of income from U.S. forces in the sterling area. Indeed, at one time consideration had been given to the question of whether the reserves were not reaching too high a figure, but

---

[6] Walter Nelson Thayer (b. 1910); lawyer, investment banker; Assistant U.S. Attorney, New York, 1937–8; Attorney, Lend Lease Administration, 1941–2; member, Harriman Mission, London, 1942–3; General Counsel, Foreign Economic Administration, 1945.

473

the U.S. representatives had accepted the view that in comparison with the enormous growth in U.K. liabilities the reserve could be regarded as not inappropriate. It would be seen that the balance had risen to $1,840 million at the 30th June last.

The figure for the end of July 1945 showed a further small advance to a net amount of $1,883 million. The advance gross figures which had been received in respect of August 1945 showed, however, a decline over the corresponding July figure of $47 million while there was a loss of $16 million during the first week of September. Given the fact that net accruals from U.S. forces had virtually disappeared, it appeared likely that the total of the U.K. balances would be less at the end of the year than the July 1945 peak of $1,883 million, though not perhaps by a great deal. On the one hand the U.K. would be losing income from U.S. forces and having to pay cash for requirements previously obtained on lend lease, but this would be offset to some extent by the receipt of additional gold from South Africa. (This would be gold against which South Africa had agreed to hold sterling balances to a limited extent.) All in all, however, it appeared likely that the target of $2 billion which the U.K. had hoped to achieve would not in fact be reached.

(ii) *U.K. gold and dollar liabilities.* LORD KEYNES briefly analysed the figures given in Appendix A Statement IA. In relation to Portugal, which accounted for by far the largest item in the figure of gold liabilities, Lord Keynes explained that the liability had resulted from an unfavourable financial agreement which the U.K. had had to conclude with Portugal during the war, coupled with the fact that very substantial expenditure had had to be incurred in that country on the purchase of essential commodities (including preemption at fantastically high prices) and on quasi-military expenditure. Negotiations were now in progress both for the revision of the agreement as regards the future and for the introduction of an arrangement which would reduce the amount of the accumulated liability payable in gold. In response to DR WHITE, Lord Keynes agreed to communicate to the U.S. representatives such further information as was available in regard to these negotiations and also to indicate precisely the terms of the gold payment prescribed in the current agreement.

The liabilities in respect of Norway and Sweden were non-recurrent. A new agreement had been made with Sweden whereby the U.K. no longer had to earmark gold against its requirements of Swedish crowns.

As regards the dollar liabilities, by far the largest items were in respect of U.S. sterling accounts in the U.K. which the holders could convert into dollars at any time, and Australian currency held by U.S. army finance officers and personnel which would also be eligible for automatic conversion. In reply to DR WHITE, Lord Keynes agreed that part of the figure of $124 million in respect of U.S. sterling represented the working balances of U.S. banks and commercial firms in the U.K. which would not normally be converted unless there was general anxiety about the future of sterling. The forward liability of $20 million shown in respect of India represented, in effect, a sum of dollars which it had been agreed India could call forward from the dollars in the sterling pool in order to finance expenditure on capital projects in the post-war period.

(iii) *Gold and dollar holdings of the rest of the sterling area.* LORD KEYNES explained that some of the figures in Appendix A Statement II in respect of the holdings of U.S. dollars were not perhaps very accurate. Thus it was believed that the U.S. Treasury had fuller figures in respect of Egyptian holdings of U.S. dollars, tending to show an amount in excess of the figure of $11 million given in the statement. The latter figure probably represented U.S. dollar holdings held by or disclosed to the National Bank of Egypt; the larger figure known in the U.S. Treasury might represent that figure plus private holdings of U.S. dollars undisclosed to the authorities in Egypt. The figure of $33.4 million shown in respect of India which also could not be regarded as completely accurate, included the sum of $20 million shown as a forward liability to India in Statement IA.

It would be seen that the dollar figures were all small and in effect represented no more than working balances.

As regards gold holdings, Lord Keynes said that the really significant figure was the very large holding of South Africa. The position as regards South Africa gold was briefly that South Africa had sold gold to the U.K. to the value of about $300 million a year, the cost of which had been devoted partly to the repatriation of debt and partly to the maintenance of working balances in London. Apart, however, from a recent decision to hold a limited amount of sterling in excess of working balance requirements, South Africa had not accumulated sterling in London. Hence its very large gold holdings. In considering the attitude of the South African Government in this field due weight should always be given to the great internal political difficulties which that Government faced by reason of its participation in the war.

In the case of India, the gold holding of $274 million represented the pre-war gold reserve. Any gold accruing to India since the outbreak of war had been sold to the U.K. against sterling. Of the total of $274 million, $245 million was held against the statutory minimum currency reserve requirements. This amount could not be reduced unless existing legislation were revised.

(In concluding his remarks in regard to the statement in Appendix A, Lord

Keynes said that the U.K. Government recognised that its gold and dollar reserves were in excess of the minimum which it would be essential to maintain unimpaired during the transitional period. But there would of necessity have to be inroads on the reserves which would cause the U.K. authorities serious concern.)

2. *External liabilities and disinvestments*

LORD KEYNES said that the figures given in Statement I of Appendix B, showing the external liabilities of the U.K., were by now familiar to the U.S. representatives. The total was likely to rise to $14,000 million by the end of 1945. The figure of $3,685 million which was the estimated total of the liabilities in August 1938 ought not to be regarded as an average pre-war figure, but was one which was swollen by an abnormal movement of funds to London. On the other hand the figure of $1,920 million for August 1939 was somewhat below normal: probably a figure of a little over $2 billion should be taken as the normal pre-war figure.

Lord Keynes then proceeded to explain that the expansion of the liabilities during the war represented, in effect, the means which had been adopted to ensure purchasing power for the U.K. within the countries in question without recourse to formal loans. To negotiate such loans in advance would have been a formidable undertaking: but the extension into the abnormal circumstances of the war of the normal practice of allowing sterling balances to accumulate in London had in effect enabled the U.K. automatically to obtain the credits necessary for war expenditure in the countries concerned. The accommodation obtained in this way was very cheap. The balances were mainly held by central banks or governments and employed for them by the Bank of England. The money was invested in Treasury bills or Treasury deposit receipts and earned interest at 1 per cent or 1⅛ per cent only. It had been made clear to the Governments concerned that it was not in the spirit of the arrangements concerning these balances that they should be invested in longer-term securities.

Lord Keynes then referred to the figure of $1,220 million shown in the statement as the total of overseas loans. He thought that these did not represent any very pressing problem. The two most important items under this head were (*a*) the outstanding balance of the RFC loan and (*b*) the outstanding balance of the interest-free loan from Canada of $700 million received by the U.K. early in the war to cover the cost of war expenditure in Canada. This loan was being amortised by the sale of U.K.-owned p477 securities in Canada but there had as yet been no decision as regards its treatment in the post-war period. It should not give rise to any pressing difficulties. These two loans together accounted for about $900 million: the balance of the total was largely represented by interest-free loans for war expenditure which had been made to the U.K. by Colonial Governments and private individuals overseas.

3. Analysis of liabilities to certain large holders of sterling balances

LORD KEYNES then proceeded to give an analysis of certain of the figures in Appendix B Statement II.

He said that in his view the holdings of the European allies (Belgium, Greece, Holland and Norway) did not represent a serious problem. Indeed, it was probable that by the end of 1946 the greater part of these balances would have been expended upon supplies and services from the sterling area although he agreed with MR ECCLES that insofar as this took place any new purchasing power accruing to the U.K. would be *pro tanto* reduced.

Broadly speaking, the balances of these countries represented their pre-war holdings plus the earnings of their shipping during the war and insurance payments. In particular, part of the holdings of the Greeks and the Norwegians represented balances held by their ship-owners who would seek to use those balances for the replacement of wartime shipping losses.

In general, Lord Keynes thought that it would not be reasonable to suggest any drastic action in regard to the balances of these countries, particularly in view of the losses which they had incurred in other ways owing to the war. He would prefer to see them free to use the balances in the sterling area in accordance with their needs, although if there were any general arrangements providing for the conversion of balances special conditions might have to be agreed as to the rate at which this should take place in the case of these holdings.

As regards the balances under Group 3, Lord Keynes explained that these represented largely the holdings of South American countries with which the U.K. had had payments agreements during the war. Broadly speaking these agreements provided that the balances could be used only in the sterling area, although there had been a number of recent occasions when the U.K. had agreed to allow such holdings to be used for expenditure in other South American countries. In the case of the two largest holders other than Portugal—the Argentine and Brazil—the U.K. still held substantial assets in both countries exceeding the total of the sterling holdings. Although, therefore, the increase in the Argentine balances was giving rise to some anxiety, there was the possibility of some arrangement for an offset of the holdings against the disposal of U.K.-owned assets in the countries in question.

As regards the sterling balances of countries within the sterling area

(Group 1) Lord Keynes said that the large holdings which gave rise to most concern were those of India, Egypt, other Middle East countries like Palestine, and Eire. It would not be reasonable to regard all the holders of balances in Group 1 as deserving or susceptible of identical treatment. Thus there were *prima facie* grounds for believing that in the case of Egypt the accumulation of sterling had been brought about largely by the excessive prices which the U.K. had been charged for goods and services. The same considerations had at one time been thought to hold good as regards India, but it now appeared after close and careful study that this was not so. Prices paid in South America had in general been reasonable. At the opposite end of the scale from Egypt were the Crown Colonies, which had not profiteered from the war and which had entrusted the whole of their currency reserves to the U.K. in the form of sterling balances. Some contribution to a final settlement could possibly be made by some of the Colonies, but not a large one.

Lord Keynes then illustrated the diversity of the problem by referring to Statement IIA in Appendix B, which contained an analysis of the form in which the balances of certain of the countries holding sterling were held. (The figures in the statement were not quite up to date, but the proportions could be regarded as still accurate.) He pointed out that whereas in the case of India out of a total holding of $3,737 million only $157 million was held privately, a much larger percentage of the balances held by Egypt, Palestine and Eire was in private hands. It might well be that measures to deal with these privately held balances would involve special difficulties. This indicated that no uniform overall method of handling the problem was likely to prove practicable. The U.K. certainly would not wish, in dealing with this problem, to adopt methods which might violently distort ordinary commercial and financial relations.

(In conclusion Lord Keynes said that the general impression of the problem which he would wish to leave was that while the total amounts involved were very large indeed, the question of dealing with them was a complicated one which would not admit of any uniform solution. It could be hoped that perhaps half of the balances would not present any really pressing problem. But it must be remembered that many political and other interests were concerned and that the problem was one which presented great complexities and diversifications.)

4. *Disinvestment by the U.K.*

In reply to questions from the U.S. representatives, LORD KEYNES explained that except in South America the U.K. had already liquidated its investments to a very substantial extent, particularly its holdings of Government debt and readily marketable securities such as those of public utilities. Thus nearly the whole of its investments under this head in South Africa had been liquidated, and a very substantial proportion of those in India. Substantial long-term debt was still owed to the U.K. by Australia and New Zealand in excess of the amount of their sterling balances. Owing to repatriation which had been proceeding to a marked degree before the war, U.K. holdings of marketable Egyptian securities had proved very small.

It was true that the U.K. still held valuable assets, in the form of equity holdings in industrials, mines, plantations, etc., which it would be very reluctant to sell since to do so would inevitably weaken the general position of the U.K. by diminishing its income from invisibles. Statement III of Appendix B showed that in the period January 1942—June 1945 disinvestment by the sale of external capital assets had amounted to nearly $2·5 billion. This was quite apart from the very substantial realisation of U.K. holdings in the U.S. which had taken place earlier in the war. The total realisation of external capital assets had been estimated at about $3 billion some time ago and would probably reach nearly $3½ billion by the end of 1945.

MR CLAYTON said that, in considering the problem of sterling balances, due weight would have to be given to the view held in many quarters of the U.S.A. to the effect that whereas the U.S. people had given very extensive assistance to the U.K. and other countries in the form of lend lease which would probably never be repaid in goods or money, other countries within the British Commonwealth, which had no less an interest than the U.S.A. in the defeat of the common enemy, had not seen their way to give assistance on other than monetary terms.

LORD KEYNES said that he sympathised with, and appreciated the relevance of Mr Clayton's remarks. He would wish to deal, however, with this aspect of the question when he came to the point of discussing possible means of dealing with the general problem of the sterling balances.

5. Future arrangements

LORD KEYNES said that he had now placed before the Committee the statistics dealing with the external position of the U.K. He had available certain other statistics of a somewhat different character which he would gladly bring before the Committee if the U.S. representatives wished to have them made available. These statistics were designed to illustrate the war effort of the U.K. (including a certain amount of comparative material)

479

and to give an analysis of lend lease and reciprocal aid. In short, they would illustrate the past rather than point to the future.

MR CLAYTON said that the U.S. representatives would be interested to receive such material and it was agreed that Lord Keynes should make it available and should review it at the next meeting of the Committee, which was arranged for 4 p.m. on the 17th September.

U.S.–U.K. ECONOMIC NEGOTIATIONS
TOP COMMITTEE

Minutes of a meeting of the Top Committee held in the Board Room of the Federal Reserve Board, Constitution Ave., on 17 September 1945 at 4 p.m.

PRESENT

Mr Clayton (in the chair)

U.S. Representatives	*U.K. Representatives*
Mr Vinson	Lord Halifax
Mr Wallace[7]	Lord Keynes
Mr Crowley	Mr Brand
Mr Eccles	Sir Henry Self
Mr Symington[8]	Mr Hall-Patch
Mr McCabe	

Mr Collado ⎫
Mr Early   ⎬ *Joint secretaries*
Mr Lee   ⎪
Mr Stevens ⎭

1. *The external financial position of the U.K.*

LORD KEYNES said that at the second meeting of the Committee he had quoted an estimate of the cumulative deficit on the balance of payments with which the U.K. would be faced during a period of years in the immediate future. He was anxious that it should not be inferred that that estimate, taken by itself, connoted the full measure of the problem of the

[7] Henry Agard Wallace (1888–1965); U.S. Secretary of Agriculture, 1933–40; Vice-President of U.S.A., 1941–5; Secretary of Commerce, 1945–6.
[8] Stuart Symington (b. 1901); U.S. Senator; Administrator, Surplus Property, Washington, 1945–6; Assistant Secretary of War for Air, 1946–7.

external financial position of the U.K. during the period in question. In order to arrive at a more complete picture regard must be had to other liabilities, counterbalanced by certain assets. Thus on the side of liabilities, there must be added to the cumulative deficit on the balance of payments such sums as would be due to be paid by the U.K. in respect of supplies drawn from the lend lease pipeline and inventories, together with a further sum (the magnitude of which might vary within considerable limits) in respect of the conversion of sterling balances if it proved possible to follow a liberal policy in this field. On the other hand such liabilities would be counterbalanced by withdrawals from the U.K. gold and dollar reserves, by the realisation over the next three to five years of certain remaining capital assets held abroad, and by assistance from other countries, the most important of which was likely to be Canada. Thus the true residual deficit to be faced by the U.K. in the post-war period would be represented by the difference between those two sets of factors.

THE COMMITTEE took note of Lord Keynes's statement.

2. *The U.K. war effort*

LORD KEYNES gave a general review of the statistical and other material, circulated to the Committee in paper COM/TOP-4, illustrating the burden on the U.K. economy of the war effort and the impact of mutual aid. He explained that wherever possible figures had been quoted which had already formed the subject of discussion and agreement with U.S. statisticians, e.g. in connection with the preparation of the combined report to the C.P.R.B. on the impact of the war on civilian consumption in the U.S., the U.K. and Canada. But in a number of cases there was still some degree of uncertainty about the figures quoted, and it would be much appreciated by the U.K. representatives if the calculations quoted in the paper could be critically examined by U.S. statisticians with a view to the production as far as practicable of agreed figures. The document had not yet been cleared with London, but it was hoped that after there had been consultation as to the details between the U.S. and U.K. statisticians it would form part of a general document which could be published.

MR CLAYTON said that the U.S. representatives would be happy to consider the question of arranging for consultation on the detailed figures, as suggested by Lord Keynes.

Continuing, LORD KEYNES said that in a number of cases comparative figures had been quoted of the U.S. war effort. This had not been done with any idea of drawing invidious distinctions between the relative war efforts of the two countries but in order to give greater vividness to the presentation of the facts concerning the U.K.

The following were the main points stressed by Lord Keynes in his review:–

(*a*) Wherever percentages could not be used, the comparison between the U.S. and U.K. figures had been effected by using the conversion factor of 2·9 to 1 for non-monetary magnitudes (the ratio of the populations of the two countries) and the factor of 4 to 1 for monetary amounts (the approximate ratio of the national incomes in 1944).

(*b*) Not only was a higher degree of mobilisation of manpower for war purposes achieved in the U.K. than in the U.S.A., but the U.S.A. had started with greater untapped reserves than the U.K. in the shape of substantial unemployment. This had materially affected the extent to which manpower had had to be withdrawn in the U.S.A. from civilian and export production.

(*c*) The figures of war damage to property in the U.K. were incomplete and would be revised. In particular the figure for the number of houses totally destroyed was too small and no account had been taken of the destruction resulting from rockets in the first four months of 1945 when an average of 20,000 houses a week had been damaged. The current shortage of houses not only constituted the greatest single cause of discomfort and complaint in the U.K. at present: it directly impeded reconversion and the reallocation of labour, while the need to import very substantial quantities of timber for building would add to the U.K. exchange difficulties.

(*d*) The position as regards merchant shipping was considerably more favourable than at one time was feared would be the case, although (leaving on one side the question of the actual composition of the fleets) a contraction of the order of 25 per cent in the case of U.K. contrasted with a four-fold expansion in the U.S.A.

(*e*) The wealth of the U.K. had diminished over the war period, by reason of actual damage and internal and external disinvestment, by approximately $25 billion, or 20 per cent.

(*f*) The decline from pre-war to 1944 of 16 per cent in the real value of per capita purchases of consumer goods and services in the U.K. contrasted with an increase of the same order of magnitude in the U.S.A. The position had probably deteriorated still further in the U.K. during 1945. The situation in this field was of particular significance in that it meant that a substantial part of the U.K. production would have to be diverted to giving some relief to the domestic consumer instead of being concentrated on exports.

In reply to MR CLAYTON, Lord Keynes said that he did not think that it was true that the standard of living among the poorer classes in the U.K. had improved during the war. There had been a great levelling up of incomes, especially after taxation, but consumption had been so strictly controlled, and supplies so limited that by far the greater part of the increased money incomes of the poorer classes had been saved. In any event the poorer classes inevitably felt the effects of certain forms of rationing—e.g. in respect of clothing—more severely than wealthier sections of the community. The overall reduction in consumption could not possibly have been achieved by the wealthier classes only, since families below the level of £500 a year accounted for nearly 90 per cent of the population of the U.K.

(g) In the field of exports the 1944 U.S. figures for commercial exports showed only a small decline over the pre-war figures while the U.K. exports had shrunk to 55 per cent of the pre-war value and 30 per cent of the pre-war volume. In addition the U.S.A. had very large lend lease exports, which might well result in lasting benefit to U.S. export trade.

3. *Mutual aid*

LORD KEYNES thought that the section of the paper on mutual aid would be found largely self-explanatory. The U.K. representatives felt that the extent of the reciprocal aid furnished by the U.K. and its impact on the U.K. economy had never been fully appreciated by the people of the U.S.A., despite the admirable presentations of the subject which had appeared in the periodic reports issued by FEA. The comparisons given in the paper showed that the percentage of lend lease and reciprocal aid to the national products of each country was 4·1 per cent and 3·5 per cent respectively. Lord Keynes agreed that the comparison was perhaps somewhat misleading in that the period selected for the U.S.A. included some months when there was only a small flow of lend lease supplies, but he thought that a comparison based on figures for peak periods of lend lease and reciprocal aid deliveries would not yield any very different result.

4. *Conclusion*

LORD KEYNES emphasised that the figures which he had been quoting, though they related to the past, were relevant to the general questions before the Committee, in that they revealed the extent to which the U.K. had concentrated its resources on the direct prosecution of the war, the burden of reconstruction with which it would be faced in the immediate future (including heavy overseas expenditure which could be regarded as being as clearly a part of the war as expenditure during actual hostilities), and the serious handicaps which would impede rapid recovery. The actual reequipment and modernisation of British industry would not directly affect the external position very substantially since comparatively little would have to be imported for that purpose, although there would certainly be some imports of machinery and there might be a temporary shortage of steel. In general, as would be seen, the external difficulties of the U.K. were the direct consequence of the absorption of the national energies in the prosecution of the war. According to recent discussions with Herr Speer, there had been an interesting, unexpected, and perhaps decisive contrast between the degree of concentration on the war effort and of limitations on civilian consumption in the U.K. as compared with the position in Germany. The achievements of the U.K. in this field were the direct consequence of the perils of 1940: but they would have their own consequences in the inevitable financial and economic difficulties which the U.K. would face during the immediate post-war period.

On 19 and 20 September, Keynes proceeded to outline the possible solutions to the situation he had discussed previously.

U.S.–U.K. ECONOMIC NEGOTIATIONS
FINANCE COMMITTEE

Minutes of a meeting of the Finance Committee held in the Board Room of the Federal Reserve Board, Constitution Ave, on 19 September 1945

PRESENT

Secretary Vinson (in the chair)

U.S. Representatives	*U.K. Representatives*
Secretary Wallace	Lord Halifax
Mr Clayton	Lord Keynes
Mr Eccles	Mr Brand
Mr McCabe	Mr Hall-Patch
Mr Angell	Mr Harmer

THE LOAN NEGOTIATIONS

Mr Coe ⎫
Mr Hebbard ⎬ *Joint secretaries*
Mr Lee ⎪
Mr Goschen ⎭
Mr Early—*Assistant Secretary General*

1. *Possible lines of policy open to the U.K.*

MR VINSON invited the U.K. representatives to open the discussion by outlining the problem as it appeared to them.

LORD KEYNES said that he thought that it might be of value to the Committee if he gave a sketch of possible alternative policies which the U.K. might follow in the period of years lying immediately ahead. Before, however, he did so he wished to emphasise that in any event the U.K. did not expect and would not seek to avoid having to carry for two or three generations a burden arising from the war of a kind not likely to fall on other countries. Some of the other allies would face grave problems in the reconstruction of their internal economic life. Happily the U.K. would not be in that position. The internal economic machine was, broadly speaking, functioning effectively. But the special problems arising in the field of external finance—especially those arising from the external liabilities due to most of the U.K.'s allies and associates in the war—would undoubtedly continue to impose a heavy burden on the U.K. even if assistance were granted. There was no thought that the U.K. would seek assistance on a scale which would eliminate that burden altogether. Moreover, in considering the question of assistance, the U.K. regarded the problem as one of liquidating as far as possible the financial consequences of the war. Seen in that context, the problem was clearly not one which concerned the U.S. and the U.K. alone: the U.K. representatives were at one with Mr Clayton in thinking that all the countries chiefly concerned should be invited to contribute to its solution in a manner which would best promote trade throughout the world.

Continuing, Lord Keynes said that the alternative courses which he proposed to propound would be presented in an extreme form for the sake of clarity. But it would be obvious that in practice many compromises between the two extremes would be feasible.

Under the first alternative, the U.K. would try to carry on with the minimum of pre-arranged assistance from the U.S.A. or any other country. It would depend primarily on the continuation of the system developed during the war for the financing of purchases from countries within the sterling area and countries with which payments agreements had been concluded. This system had not only had the advantage of enabling the U.K. to obtain accommodation which might have been more difficult to negotiate in the form of direct loans; it enabled the benefits of multilateral trade to continue over a very wide area. Thus no impediments whatever were placed on current transactions between countries within the sterling area. The arrangements in question had been extended over a still wider area by the conclusion of payments agreements with most of the important non-sterling area countries outside North America. These agreements provided, in brief, that the parties to the agreement would each be prepared to accumulate the currency of the other party arising from normal trade transactions and would not seek to obtain conversion of any balances into gold or spend the accumulated balances outside the currency area of the other party. The U.K. had successfully avoided having to agree to ceilings on the amount of balances held under these agreements. On the other hand most of them were terminable at very short notice and if a given country's holdings of sterling tended to rise substantially there would no doubt be a disposition to terminate the agreement. There was no obligation on the U.K. to assist countries with which payments agreements had been concluded (as distinct from countries within the sterling area) by the provision of foreign currencies to meet essential needs, although arrangements were made in certain cases permitting them to use sterling balances for expenditure in third countries.

It would be possible to carry on and to extend the same system in the post-war period. That is to say the U.K. would continue to operate the sterling area arrangements and to invite third countries to conclude payments agreements or to enter into special credit arrangements on a modest scale. This would enable the U.K. to obtain imports from a great many important supplying countries: in reply to a question by MR VINSON Lord Keynes thought that perhaps 75 per cent of the imports of the U.K. in normal times could be drawn from countries within the sterling area or with which payments agreements had been or could be concluded. With some distortion of channels of trade the percentage might be made an even higher one. The adoption of arrangements on the lines suggested would involve no violent break with the conditions which had obtained during the war. It would enable multilateral clearing to be maintained over a very wide area. Moreover, it might well provide a positive help for exports from the U.K. in the difficult period following upon the contraction of the seller's market occuring in the immediate post-war period. It would not be necessary to maintain such a system indefinitely: it could be modified or discontinued once the U.K. had reached equilibrium. It would be possible to maintain such a system within both the spirit and the law of the concessions permitted under the International Monetary Fund Agreement in respect of the transitional period. Indeed the U.K. Government would be continuously concerned to keep the restrictive elements in such an arrangement as small as possible so as to involve the minimum dislocation of trade and of friction with other countries. It could not be hoped, however that these dislocations and frictions could be entirely eliminated.

Thus a system on the lines proposed would have considerable advantages and it was certainly not without its advocates in the U.K. On the other hand, in Lord Keynes's personal view its disadvantages, not all of which were apparent at first sight, had usually been underestimated. Thus its advocates tended to underrate the difficulty of carrying on in time of peace a system which had worked effectively during the war but only because it had been helped to do so by the limitation on imports which had been occasioned by restrictions on shipping and shortage of supplies. In practice—though not in deliberate intent—the system would tend to give rise to a considerable degree of bilateralism. Pressure in this direction would not come so much from the U.K. as from the countries selling to the U.K. They would not want to continue to pile up large sterling balances but would demand goods. Thus there would be continuous pressure on their part to obtain as large a share as possible of U.K. exports. Indeed they would probably aim at making specific arrangements whereby sales of their commodities to the U.K. would be tied up with specific sales of U.K. exports to them. This would inevitably tend to dislocate the natural movement of trade and would multiply the occasions of friction. Moreover, in the case of sterling area countries the allocation of dollars and other foreign currencies from the central pool would become increasingly difficult if, as was probable, limitations had to be placed upon issues from the pool. This particular problem had been largely masked during the war when restriction on the availability of shipping and supplies, coupled with the instance of lend lease had greatly reduced the dollar needs of most countries within the sterling area. Moreover there must be a doubt as to whether the sterling area pool would readily hold together in the circumstances of the post-war period. There might be pressure on the part of countries like India, which would possess a surplus of dollars from its current earnings, to leave the sterling area. This would diminish the amount of dollars available to the pool and would increase the difficulty of allocating them in a convenient and equitable manner. In short, there would be a shrinking in the multi-lateral benefits accruing from the existence of the pool.

A further disadvantage was that if the U.K. reached equilibrium in its balance of payments by such means it would have done so by 'hothouse methods' and equilibrium might well be difficult to maintain when such conditions no longer obtained. Finally there was the difficulty (to which too little attention had been paid in the British Press) that a solution on the lines indicated would only put off the evil day so far as a settlement of the problem of sterling balances was concerned. Under such a system countries within the sterling area would be enabled to use these balances pretty freely within the area itself and in effecting purchases from countries with which the U.K. had payments agreements. But it would *not* be possible for the U.K. to take any really effective action as regards the great bulk of the past accumulation of sterling balances which would have to be frozen. Thus at the end of, say, 5 years time, the U.K. Government would face exactly the same problem as they were facing today, and it was not to be supposed that a solution of that problem would be any easier in five years time, when the memories of co-operation in a common war effort would have faded, than it would be today.

The other alternative solution—which Lord Keynes also presented as an extreme form—would have as its aim the complete elimination of the discriminatory elements in the sterling area system at any rate so far as current transactions were concerned.

Under such an arrangement all new sterling earnings of the sterling area countries could be freely used to finance current transactions in any part of the world; in other words they would automatically be freely convertible into dollars or any third currency to make current payments. The same would apply to any part of the accumulated sterling balances which was made liquid. The sterling area dollar pool would thus be dissolved.

In short, under such a solution the U.K. would be in a position to bring into force, say at the end of 1946, the major part of the permanent provisions of the International Monetary Fund Agreement and would cease to avail itself of the concessions in that agreement applicable to the transitional period. It was doubtful whether any date *before* the end of 1946 would be appropriate, since it would take time to conclude the new arrangements and moreover it would be clearly desirable that expenditure over say, the next eighteen months, which was essentially of a war character (e.g. the substantial payments which would be necessary in India on demobilisation and like measures) should in effect be added to the accumulated balances as they would stand at the date from which the special arrangements for dealing with them would come into force.

Lord Keynes envisaged that such arrangements would be threefold. Part of the balances would be made liquid and would be available for current expenditure anywhere in the world. Part would be released in instalments over a long period of years, although there might well be provision that in certain circumstances a more rapid release could be made than was envisaged under the instalment plan. Finally it would be reasonable to suggest to the countries holding such balances that as an integral part of the general arrangements for dealing with the balances they should of their own volition discuss the possibility of their making a contribution towards the general settlement by writing off part of their holdings. In other words, it would be made clear that the U.K. Government regarded the scheme as one in which advantages and obligations went together. If countries entered the scheme they would be expected to contribute as well as to receive benefits from it. If any individual country stood out, the U.K. would do its best to repay in course of time the balances held by that country, but such a country would clearly have to be content with a lower priority of repayment than others which came into the scheme.

Whether such a scheme would be practicable must depend upon the degree of strength of the U.K. exchange position. Clearly the stronger their position was, the more liberal the resultant solution could be made. The U.K. representatives were not authorised to put forward this alternative as a definite proposal. It was a matter for examination and discussion. But speaking personally, Lord Keynes said that he would like to see the U.K. get as near to it as possible. It was a mistake to suppose that the U.K. was wedded to a less liberal solution. On the contrary there was a very general recognition that it was neither in the interest of the U.K. nor in that of the world at large that the special defensive arrangements which had played so essential a part in the U.K.'s war economy and the continuation of which was implicit in the first alternative, should be allowed to gain ground and to become part of the permanent structure of trading and finance. If it were possible to achieve a wider solution on the lines indicated, not only would all countries in the scheme receive definite tangible benefits but an arrangement would have been achieved which must appeal to all men of goodwill. For this second arrangement would not only lead to an expansion of world trade but it would achieve the other very important objective of minimising friction between nations on economic matters.

Lord Keynes concluded by stating that he would welcome the comments of the United States group on his exposition.

MR VINSON replied that the U.S. representatives would appreciate a somewhat more specific statement. They could not feel that they were clear on the relative quantities involved in the threefold treatments of the sterling balances under the second alternative. LORD KEYNES replied that it was very difficult for the U.K. representatives at this stage to discuss the second alternative in terms of detailed figures. As he had explained, the degree to which the plan could be put into effect would depend on the strength of the U.K. exchange position. In the absence of knowledge as to the scale of assistance that might be made available and the terms applicable to it, that position must remain a matter of speculation.

MR CLAYTON pressed Lord Keynes to give some indication of the amount of the balances which in the U.K. Government's view ought properly to be written off. He reminded the committee of the widespread feeling in the U.S.A to the effect that at least part of these balances had resulted from the provision of goods and services of the same character as had been provided by the U.S.A. on lend lease in furtherance of the common war effort.

LORD KEYNES said that naturally the U.K. Government would like to see a substantial part of the balances written off. On the other hand there could clearly be no question of a unilateral repudiation on the part of the U.K. A settlement of the balances on the lines which he had indicated (i.e. a partial immediate release, the refunding and release by instalments over a period of years of another block, and the writing off of the balances in appropriate cases) could only come about as a result of negotiations with the individual countries concerned in the course of which the U.K. Government would have to persuade them that it was both equitable and in their best interests that they should participate in the general scheme proposed and contribute to it by writing down part of the balances. As he had previously indicated, no uniform solution would be justified or appropriate. Even in those cases where, on a *prima facie* view, a writing down appeared to be most justified there were often special considerations which might make negotiations to that end difficult. For instance, it was doubtful to what extent some of the largest accumulations, such as the sterling balances held by India, were the result of expenditure directly arising out of the war: in many cases they represented the accumulation of trade balances unfavorable to the U.K. at a time when U.K. exports could not be maintained at a high figure. Again there might well be obvious political difficulties in persuading Eire (which had remained neutral throughout the war) or Egypt (which was not a member of the British Commonwealth and which remained nominally neutral until the last moment) that they should in effect now make a retrospective contribution to the war effort. In the case of India it should not be inferred from the size of the balances that the issue was a clear cut one. India had made a gigantic effort during the war which had proved a heavy strain on her resources. Moreover, there was the political consideration that the present moment, when it was hoped that a further advance might be made towards Indian self-government by the appointment of a purely Indian Council under the Viceroy, was not perhaps an opportune one at which to suggest the scaling down of the U.K. debt to India. It would be out of the question to suggest to India that the price of a further advance towards complete self-government should be a concession by the new Indian Administration in the matter of the U.K. debt to India. In the case of Australia and New Zealand not only had those countries given very substantial assistance by way of reciprocal aid to the U.S.A. but their long-term debt to the U.K. still exceeded the amount of the sterling balances which they held. There would thus be a certain embarrassment in suggesting that they should agree to scale down the balances held by them in the U.K. while leaving the long-term debt to the U.K. untouched. In the case of the Colonies, special considerations arose in that the U.K. was committed to a policy of fostering to the utmost possible extent the welfare of colonial peoples under its protection: here again it would be, or at any rate appeared as being, at variance with that policy for the U.K. to insist upon a drastic reduction in the balances held by the colonies in the U.K. especially as in many cases these represented the whole of the colonies' currency reserves.

Lord Keynes said that he quoted the above examples not in order to demonstrate that the problem was insoluble or that the U.K. would not welcome and be prepared to press for the maximum possible scaling down of the sterling balances. He did, however, wish again to impress upon the U.S. representatives that the problem was a complex one, that it would involve separate and in many cases delicate negotiations with the individual governments concerned, and that no clean-cut and uniform solution would be practicable. LORD HALIFAX endorsed Lord Keynes's remarks in this respect and emphasised that in the case of India it would be disastrous for the U.K. to initiate any action which could be represented as a breach with the long-standing principle that there was no interference by the U.K. with India's independence in financial matters. There was no single point upon which all sections of Indian political opinion were more sensitive and more united than this.

MR WALLACE observed that the plan outlined was put forward in the interests of all countries, and should be so viewed by all of the countries which would be asked to participate.

MR VINSON stated that the U.S. representatives fully appreciated the difficulties involved in negotiating a solution to this complex problem, since they were not entirely absent from the viewpoint of the U.S. representatives themselves. MR ECCLES added that he thought that the American public would have difficulty in appreciating the full necessity of assisting in the solution of the U.K. problem, in the absence of an indication of a similar appreciation on the part of other countries. He was also interested in the manner in which the blocked balances could be made convertible without prejudicing the standard of living of the United Kingdom.

2. *Conclusion*

It was agreed that the Committee should resume its discussions at 3 p.m. on the 20th September.

U.S.–U.K. ECONOMIC NEGOTIATIONS
FINANCE COMMITTEE

Minutes of a meeting of the Finance Committee held in the Board Room of the Federal Reserve Board, Constitution Ave., on 20 September 1945 at 2.45 p.m.

PRESENT

Secretary Vinson (in the chair)

U.S. Representatives	*U.K. Representatives*
Mr Clayton	Lord Halifax
Mr Crowley	Lord Keynes
Mr Amos Taylor	Mr Brand
Mr McCabe	Mr Hall-Patch
Mr Eccles	Mr Harmer

Mr Coe
Mr Hebbard
Mr Lee   } *Joint secretaries*
Mr Goschen

Mr Early—*Assistant Secretary General*

1. *Possible plan for dealing with sterling balances*

At MR VINSON's invitation, LORD KEYNES gave details of possible arrangements for dealing with the sterling balances held in the U.K. by various countries. He emphasised that he must not be regarded as putting forward definite proposals. What he intended to do was to illustrate by the quotation of actual figures what might be arranged as regards the balances if certain assumptions were fulfilled. He did not propose to assume the most optimistic basis possible: the possible arrangements which he would indicate would be predicated on the basis that very favourable conditions would obtain but not optimum conditions. Finally, he wished to emphasise that the subject matter of his remarks was highly secret and that he therefore hoped that the utmost discretion would be used in any subsequent dis-

492

cussion or circulation of papers. MR VINSON said that orders would be given to regard the discussions of the Finance Committee and any of the papers connected with it as Top Secret.

LORD KEYNES said that he was proposing to confine his remarks to possible arrangements in connection with the balances held by countries in the sterling area. He proposed to assume that those balances would amount to $12 billion at the end of 1946. The actual rate of growth during 1946 was, of course, uncertain, but he thought that a figure of $12 billion was a reasonable one to take as a basis. It was his personal view that if a sufficiently attractive scheme could be put forward it might be possible to secure agreement to the cancellation of up to one-third of this total—in some cases perhaps against a surrender by the U.K. of certain assets or claims in the countries concerned. He emphasised that the scale of cancellation which he was suggesting had not been discussed either with the Governments concerned or with those Departments in London which dealt with the Governments in question, but *prima facie* he felt that a reduction of the order indicated would not be unreasonable from the standpoint either of equity or of self-interest. He hoped that the countries concerned would realise that it would be better for them to have assets totalling, say, $8 billion on which they could call under an agreed plan rather than larger assets of the order of say $12 billion from which releases would be very uncertain or non-existent.

An arrangement complementary to the reduction of the balances to, say, $8 billion would be the immediate freeing of a percentage of the balance, with the object of arranging that that percentage could be used to finance current transactions in any part of the world. It might be possible to free, say, 10 per cent of the written-down portion of the balances in this way. On the basis of a revised figure of $8 billion this would involve an immediate release of $800 million. This sum, together with current earnings, ought to suffice to meet the needs of the countries concerned for to 4–5 years at least. In fact there would be reason to hope that the recipient countries would not call upon all of it, especially if the knowledge that it was available bred general confidence. They would regard it as being, in effect, a reserve upon which they could draw freely, as and when required for the financing of current purchases, but not for other purposes.

The minimum release on the scale proposed would—on the basis of the illustrative figures quoted—leave amounts aggregating $7·2 billion, in respect of which there would be no immediate release for expenditure either in the sterling area or elsewhere. It would be the intention of the U.K. Government that no interest should be payable on the portion of the balances remaining unreleased, on the grounds that they were not primarily commercial in origin and that therefore interest payments would not be appropriate. Arrangements would be made for the release of the remaining balance over a period of years, beginning in, say, 4–5 years after the immediate release to which reference had been made. A rate of release of, say, 2 per cent per annum over a period of 50 years would involve payment of $145 million a year. It would be understood that both the minimum release and the subsequent instalment releases would be in addition to the current sterling area earnings of the countries concerned, which would be freely convertible into any currency for the financing of current transactions.

In any such scheme it would be necessary to protect the position of the U.K. by a clause permitting postponement of releases in certain contingencies. Conversely there might be a provision to the effect that releases could be anticipated in cases where a particular country holding sterling balances got into temporary economic difficulties such as might have called for assistance by way of loan from the U.K. in normal times.

Lord Keynes emphasised that the degree to which there could be fulfilment of arrangements on the lines which he had sketched would necessarily depend upon the scale of assistance which the U.K. was enabled to receive from the U.S. and upon the terms applicable to that assistance.

The scale of assistance required by the U.K. from the U.S.A. would involve the sum of three requirements:–

(a) an amount necessary to take care of the U.K. adverse balance of trade in the transitional period;

(b) the amount needed in order to deal with sterling balances on the lines indicated earlier in the discussion; and

(c) whatever net amount might fall to be paid by the U.K. to the U.S.A. as a result of the winding up of lend lease and reciprocal aid. It was not possible at this stage to estimate with any accuracy what might be the size of the third of the above amounts. Therefore it would be best for a figure to be stated which would be exclusive of that particular requirement and which would have to be increased *pro tanto* when the amount needed under that head had been clarified.

On this basis it was estimated that the U.K. would need to be able to draw upon a sum of $5 billion over the next 3–5 years. The limitation of assistance to that sum would undoubtedly involve the acceptance of considerable risks. Thus the cumulative adverse balance of the U.K. might itself be of the order of $6 billion. Moreover, other contingencies, including the release of some part of the sterling balances held by allied and neutral countries, might involve further requirements perhaps of the order of another $1 billion. Probably, however, it would be thought worth while taking the risks attendant on the limitation of assistance of $5 billion.

Lord Keynes emphasised that if assistance were accorded on the scale proposed the U.K. Government would have no intention of using the $5 billion unless it were clearly needed: obviously the assistance actually drawn would be kept down to the lowest possible amount consistent with the fulfilment of the obligation assumed by the U.K. and the maintenance of a minimum reserve. He thought, however, that a figure of $5 billion represented the smallest sum on which the U.K. would have a good chance of being able to face commitments on the scale which he had indicated without plunging beyond its means. Moreover, it would be of the first importance that third countries should be enabled to have confidence in the strength of sterling. Unless that confidence could be established and maintained the degree of assistance necessary would be still greater. Finally, assistance on the scale indicated should enable the U.K. to maintain as far as possible normal methods of trade without resorting either to the maximum degree of austerity in imports or continued and deliberate state intervention with the object of expanding and directing exports. If such methods were adopted it might be possible to put the figure of assistance required at a lower level: but this would inevitably be at the cost of the adoption by the U.K. of methods of procedure which would not be readily acceptable to the U.S.

2. *Supplementary information*

LORD KEYNES then proceeded to answer a number of questions put to him by the U.S. representatives.

In reply to MR VINSON, he stated that the external resources available to the U.K.—other than assistance from the U.S.A.—during the transitional period could be classed under three main heads. There were first the gold and dollar reserves, which would probably amount to a figure somewhat in excess of $1·5 billion at the end of 1945. The U.K. Government would be bound to regard a figure of about $1 billion as an absolute minimum reserve. It followed that an amount of perhaps half a billion dollars could be regarded as available from the reserves for use in case of need. Secondly, there were the U.K. assets in North and South America. The great bulk of the assets in the U.S. were pledged against the RFC loan. When this was paid off there would be a release of assets but the total amount available would not be of great significance, while a policy of disposal would be harmful in that the continuing balance of trade position of the U.K. would be worsened by the consequent loss of dollar income. In the case of South America it was hoped that the saleable assets held by the U.K. could be drawn upon as necessary to clear up what was owed by the U.K. to the South American countries, particularly the Argentine, Brazil, and Uruguay. Finally, there was the possibility of assistance from Canada and certain other countries. There had as yet been no discussion with the Canadian authorities as to the amount of assistance which might be forthcoming from Canada. But there was reason to believe that such assistance might be on a scale which would take care of the adverse balance of the U.K. with Canada during the transitional period. On this basis the assistance might be of the order of half a billion dollars. This assistance would almost certainly be greater than the assistance accorded by any other country, but a modest degree of credit should be forthcoming from Sweden as well as from certain countries within the sterling area.

MR ECCLES asked, in connection with the latter point whether he would be correct in assuming that further accommodation amounting to perhaps $1 billion would be necessary from the sterling area in 1946. LORD KEYNES thought that this estimate might be too high: possibly the figure might prove to be more like $500 million. He agreed with Mr Eccles in thinking that when negotiations took place with sterling area countries concerning a possible settlement of the balances an important factor would be the extent to which such countries could obtain goods from the dollar releases which would be made available to them.

In reply to MR ECCLES, Lord Keynes said that it would be wrong to assume that the amount of $800 million which he had mentioned as the possible amount of the initial release from the balances would be wholly absorbed by the working balance requirements of the countries concerned. If an alteration were made in the legislation of these countries so as to provide that the funded portion of the balances could constitute their currency note reserve, the actual working balance requirements could be kept at a comparatively low figure.

In reply to MR ECCLES, Lord Keynes said that, leaving South America out of account, it was possible that something like £500 million would be withdrawn at the end of 1946 from the sterling holdings of countries not within the sterling area. This would counterbalance the additional accommodation which he had assumed might be obtained from sterling area countries in that year. He explained that the European allied countries had not been accustomed to hold large balances in London and that it was natural therefore to expect a considerable withdrawal of their present balances during 1946, although he agreed that it would probably be prudent to ensure an agreement that the balances should not be withdrawn in excess of a prescribed rate. In so far as such balances were made convertible, the effect might be not so much to reduce the direct dollar needs of the countries concerned as to reduce those of some third countries which would receive convertible sterling in the course of ordinary trade transactions. It was not contemplated that it would be necessary to use part of the assistance from the U.S.A. to deal with the balances held by South American countries. The U.K. would hope to continue operating for as long as possible on the basis of the present payment agreements. But it might be expected that in the comparatively near future the U.K. might be obliged to negotiate some arrangements whereby the whole or part of the balances in, say, the Argentine, Brazil and Uruguay would be set off against liquidation of British marketable assets in those countries and whereby payment for supplies would subsequently be made in free sterling.

MR ECCLES asked whether the U.K. expected to obtain equipment and supplies from German reparations. LORD KEYNES said that in so far as the U.K. might obtain some deliveries of capital goods, these would be outside the picture which was being presented to the Committee. It was hoped to obtain from Germany certain supplies of timber and potash. But it was very doubtful whether these would be of any net benefit to the U.K. balance of payments position, since it had been agreed that German exports were to be sold so as to finance the German import programme. In point of fact, the U.K. might not break even in this field.

MR MCCABE inquired as to the extent of United Kingdom investments in foreign countries. LORD KEYNES replied that it was difficult and not particularly significant to set a capital value upon such investments. The annual income would be capitalised at some rate of interest to arrive at a capital figure, but this could not represent the amount which the United Kingdom could derive from the liquidation of those assets, since many of them were not easily marketable. Another factor to be considered was the cost of reconditioning investments and other reconstruction costs in the various areas which had not been included.

MR MCCABE asked where the largest investments were located. LORD KEYNES replied that there were considerable investments in Latin America, if measured by their face value. The United Kingdom still retains a considerable portion of its pre-war investments in Australia. Most of the marketable investments in India had been liquidated. The U.K. still held a fairly substantial investment in South African mines. There were not inconsiderable investments in Europe, but the present value of these was extremely questionable. Investments in Canada, perhaps amounting to $1

497

billion, were offset by Canadian loans to the United Kingdom; this would not, however, represent an offset on income account, since the Canadian loan was non-interest bearing.

Some discussion took place on the scale of exports which the U.K. would have to achieve in order to attain equilibrium in its balance of payments. LORD KEYNES referred to the generally accepted target of a volume of exports 50 per cent in excess of the volume pre-war, but pointed out that even if it were assumed (which was by no means certain) that the terms of trade did not turn to the disadvantage of the U.K., it would be necessary to achieve exports in excess of 50 per cent above the pre-war volume if it were hoped to take care of the sterling balances problem on the lines which he had indicated.

In reply to a question by MR MCCABE, Lord Keynes said that despite the immense difficulties of the external position he was hopeful concerning the prospects of maintaining the general standard of living in the U.K. in view of the significant increases in productive capacity which could be expected to follow continued technological advances.

3. Future arrangements

MR VINSON proposed that as a next step there should be joint discussions at the operating level on a number of points of detail in order that the U.S. representatives could obtain more precise and detailed information on certain questions than it had been possible for Lord Keynes to give in his general expositions. He had in mind such matters as the clarification of the issues which might affect the position of individual countries holding large sterling balances and further elucidation of the estimated balance of payments position of the U.K. in 1946.

LORD KEYNES said that the U.K. representatives would be happy to arrange for such consultations to take place, although he gave a warning against attempts to proceed to the framing of precise details of the estimated balance of payments position in future years. When so much was necessarily speculative, he believed that the only safe approach was to form the best possible judgment of the global magnitudes, viewing the problem broadly as a whole. To attempt to build up detailed supporting statistics was in his view liable to lead to highly misleading results.

On completing his exposition, Keynes cabled the Chancellor.

To H. DALTON (*NABOB 70*), *21 September 1945*

1. At our fifth session yesterday I completed the series of my opening discourses in which I have set forth the facts of our problem and the alternatives before us. The first three meetings were devoted to the statement of the facts of our position. The next two to the substance of paragraphs 22 to 39 of the revised version of my memorandum which I sent to you from Canada.

2. In the first of these last two meetings I refrained from giving figures of the amount of assistance we shall require and the scale on which we might hope to release sterling area balances assuming sufficient assistance. But I was strongly pressed by Vinson at the end of the meeting to come down to brass tacks and it was generally agreed on our side that this had become the right course.

3. In the second of these meetings therefore I stated the amount of assistance required as five billion dollars plus such amount as turns out to be due from us to pay for the cleaning up of lend lease. No reference has yet been made on either side to the terms of such assistance.

4. We have been given a patient and attentive hearing but, apart from a number of questions on points of detail, the Americans have refrained from comment except as reported in the next paragraph and have made no constructive proposals of their own. I fear that the delay in opening the commercial talks may mean that a considerable time may now pass before we receive any concrete reaction from the Americans. Nevertheless our impression is that they were satisfied with the proposals for liberalising the sterling area and were not shocked by the size of the sums mentioned.

5. Clayton and other members of the committee have repeatedly emphasised the importance they attach to the other members of the sterling area making a substantial contribution to the final solution. We are given to understand that this will be an indispensable condition of American

499

assistance without which they could not hope to approach Congress successfully. They wish to represent the plan as one to which all parties concerned are prepared to make appropriate contributions. We have not disputed the fairness of this approach but have urged them not to underestimate the practical and political difficulties of going too far in this direction and have emphasised the importance of our treating each case individually on its merits and the unfairness of any uniform solution. We have also argued that several of the countries affected, especially India, have made larger contributions to the common effort in proportion to their wealth than appears on the surface. Nevertheless a certain amount of pressure from the Americans in the direction indicated and the fact that they insist on associating jam for the sterling area with the pill may help us in the end to achieve a fair settlement all round.

6. Acting in accordance with your instructions we have handed over to them in writing nothing but the tables of figures of which copies have been sent to London. The proposals relating to the sterling area have been confined to oral exposition. The Ambassador and Brand and all of us here are very strongly of the opinion that the time has come when we should do well to give them in writing a statement more or less on the lines of paras 22 to 39 of my memorandum referred to above. Excellent minutes of the meetings have been prepared which have or will reach you. But these minutes have deliberately avoided giving any such details as would make them equivalent of a written statement. The result is that much of the detail including some of the safeguards we are preparing for ourselves have probably entered the minds of some or all of the listeners in a vague and inaccurate form: since they have already been given the substance it is better that they should have it before them accurately in a form which they can think over at leisure. May I now prepare a version of the above paras for them

which may need little editing here and there in the light of discussions we have had with the Americans but would not depart in substance from what you already know?

7. The *New York Times* stated today that it has obtained a copy of the statistical table we presented to the Top Committee some days ago and proves the accuracy of its statement by copious and exact quotations though these are all taken from COM/TOP 4 and not from COM/TOP 3 which is a much more confidential paper. I have pointed out to the State Department that this does not encourage us to let them have anything further in writing but they assure me that as a result of the Ambassador's having called attention to the excessive size of the gathering at the first three meetings very special precautions have been taken to guard the secrecy of the proceedings at the last two meetings which were with the Finance Committee and not the Top Committee. The papers of the Finance Committee will be treated as Top Secret and given a very restricted circulation. At the end of each meeting we called Mr Vinson's attention to the special need for keeping secret at this stage any discussions affecting other members of the sterling area and at each meeting he has given direct instructions to this effect to all present. Anyhow oral discussions are no more protected from disclosure than written papers and merely render one liable to disclosure in a less accurate form.

8. The Canadian Minister in Washington told Brand last night that Mr Clayton had mentioned to him in conversation that the American members of the Committee were well satisfied with the statements we made in our first five meetings and considered that we had proved our case but whether Congress would be similarly convinced was another matter. He also told Brand that according to Clayton the President had asked for a full statement of requests to the U.S. for assistance from all applicants including UNRRA and will take no decision until he has the complete picture.

On 20 September Keynes saw Crowley on the subject of the treatment of outstanding lend lease matters. They agreed, subject to Ministerial approval on both sides, that payment for pipeline goods and inventories were really one problem, that no basis of finance be agreed then, that supplies in the pipeline and inventory needs would continue to be met, that discussions would continue on the sums involved in the final clearing up of lend lease and that the final settlement could be in cash, 3(c) credit (thirty years at 2⅜ per cent), or part of the overall settlement agreed to by the negotiators.

On 26 September Keynes and Lord Halifax met Clayton and Vinson. In the course of the discussion, the Americans noted that they accepted the British proposals for the liberalisation of the sterling area and the scaling down of sterling balances. They emphasised that their case to Congress for any assistance must rely on the advantages to the United States of facilitating and liberalising international trade, and not on past sacrifices or comparisons of past efforts. The discussion also suggested that both sides were centering their estimates of the size of the necessary assistance on $5 billion, but that the Americans were certain that a loan with interest was the likely solution to be acceptable to Congress: a grant-in-aid was certainly impossible. At this stage, of course, no one gave ground on the terms of assistance.

However, both Keynes and Halifax believed that a loan without interest was a possibility then under consideration by Treasury and State Department officials. Keynes set this out more clearly in a letter to the Chancellor after the meeting.

To H. DALTON, *26 September 1945*

My dear Chancellor,

I attach a memorandum on the terms of American financial aid which needs your urgent and earnest attention. It should be read in the light of the Ambassador's private telegram of today's date about our conversation with Clayton and Vinson. Any guidance you can give us will be very welcome.

Nothing could have appeared more Rhadamanthine than the poker faces of those two noble Roman Senators. I believe them when they discard the project for a grant-in-aid since that agrees broadly with what reaches me from my other sources. It is certainly a good thing that we are represented as having been asking for that. But no kites have been flown suggesting that we should get it. On the other hand I feel confident that Harry White is advising Vinson in favour of a non-interest loan. The real difficulty there is Clayton. He is not only deeply imbued with business analogies but suffers in my opinion, obstinately and beyond cure, from honest intellectual misapprehensions about the ease with which American debtors can discharge their debts. He is an honest and most friendly man, but his very honesty makes intellectual mistakes on his part all the more dangerous.

You have to consider in this context both the political and financial aspect. From the political point of view I imagine you will attach great importance to a non-interest-bearing loan since that is easily understood. Of course, the fact that it is easily understood is precisely their difficulty. From the strictly financial point of view it is possible, as you will see from my memorandum, to dress up an interest-bearing loan so that it costs us very little more. At present, as the Ambassador has reported, we have not conceded even the remote possibility of your being willing to consider interest.

Yours

MAYNARD KEYNES

THE TERMS OF ASSISTANCE

1. Assuming that there is no hitch over the commercial talks we have now reached a stage where we can safely assume that the American side of the Committees will recommend to the President that we receive substantial assistance. Apart from points arising out of the commercial talks the conditions will be more or less as follows:–

(a) We liberalise the arrangements of the sterling area along the lines and on the scale I have indicated to them as possible, provided that they help us sufficiently.

(b) We accept the Bretton Woods Plan.

(c) Our principal creditors amongst the sterling area countries agree to make substantial contributions to the general settlement by scaling down their claims.

(d) If there are to be any associated demands, such as bases, we have still to hear of them. These are more likely to be raised, if at all, as 'consideration' for lend lease than in connection with post-war financial assistance.

2. There remain the questions of the amount of the assistance and its terms. The amount is likely to be less difficult than the terms. Our first bid has been $5 billion plus the cost of cleaning up lend lease (which, allowing for offsets, but including surplus disposals, might be of the order of another $500 million). Their first formal offer is likely to be $4 billion, but they, like us, are now thinking in terms of a figure in the neighbourhood of $5 billion.

3. The question of the terms is far less clear. The chief purpose of this note is to seek further guidance from the Chancellor. We have said nothing so far to prejudice our taking a stand on a grant-in-aid. If we had no-one to deal with except the State Department and the Treasury, we might have some hope. But the prospect of getting such a proposal across Congress and public opinion here is poor. The Americans would also be much embarrassed by the precedent created for other countries, though they do, we believe, accept us as a special case and intend, within limits, to treat us as such. They would much rather, therefore, call the assistance a credit and then dress it up so as to be as little onerous as possible.

4. I still hope that the offer of the U.S. Treasury will, or can eventually be made to take the form of a non-interest bearing loan repayable in 40 or 50 instalments of which the first falls due 5 or 10 years hence. They will consider that this goes a tremendous way to meet us—as indeed it does.

5. It will be difficult to argue that we could not meet this. On the basis of 50 instalments and $5 billion, the service would

be $100 million a year. Instalments of repayment to the sterling area might be another $150 million a year, making a total of £62,500,000 annually. Assuming an international price level double pre-war in terms of sterling, this is the equivalent of no more than £31,250,000 in pre-war values. Put another way the aggregate service for our war debts would be less than 5 per cent of the export target we shall have to aim at to break even apart from the debt. Either we can manage this or we are sunk anyhow. The American portion of the debt burden would be less than 2 per cent of our prospective overseas earnings and income.

6. I have tried to think of a plausible reason why, as suggested by Towers, we should receive part of the assistance as a grant-in-aid, even if part is to be on repayment terms. But without much success. Retrospective lend lease corresponding to what we spent here is, most certainly, not a good starter. What might be possible is a taking over by U.S. of sterling area balances to the tune of $1 to $2 billion, replacing our sterling obligation by a dollar obligation with no further liability to us. But there are obvious objections to this from our side. Should we think the avoidance of an ultimate repayment of $1 or $2 billion worth the disturbance to our sterling area arrangements through the sterling area countries holding individual dollar balances? If so, this is worth trying. If not, I see difficulties, perhaps insuperable, in the way of a grant-in-aid. May I have instructions?

7. Assuming that we do not reject a repayable non-interest credit and are prepared to take this as the basis of discussion, what mitigations can we seek to obtain?—

(a) First of all, we should press for 50 rather than 40 instalments, beginning 10 years, and not 5 years, hence.

(b) We might propose rising, instead of equal, instalments, so as to ease the earlier period;—e.g. $50 million as the first instalment rising by $2 million a year. Or we might accept a total service of $250 million of which $200 would go to the

505

sterling area in the first year, the sterling area instalment falling and the U.S. instalment rising by $2 million a year.

(*c*) We might defer settling the terms of repayment for 5 years (I do not like this).

(*d*) We might ask for an escape clause on the model offered us by Graham Towers; that is to say, in any year in which we are losing our reserves and have less than our quota left as defined under the Bretton Woods Plan, the instalment due in that year is postponed and does not become payable until it can be met without reducing our reserves below our quota.

8. The Graham Towers clause is based, it will be observed, on the measure of *our* poverty. It is open to the grave objection that any objective criterion of our poverty will leave us in semi-servitude for an indefinite period. I have, however, thought out an alternative escape clause which seems to me to be much preferable and also likely to be more acceptable, to which, after a good deal of reflection, I attach great value. I am sure that it deserves to be considered very seriously. It is as follows.

9. According to my new formula, no creditor country, whether a sterling area country or the United States or Canada, would be entitled to draw an instalment in repayment of the service of our war debts now under consideration in any year in which its monetary reserves (as defined by the Bretton Woods Plan) stood above its Bretton Woods quota and were *increasing*, the instalments in question being deferred in this event to the latter end of the period of amortisation which would be correspondingly extended.

10. It will be seen that under this formula payment depends on the need of the recipient country, and is deferred if the recipient is, in effect, demanding payment in gold. *We* cannot escape paying if the recipient has any current use for payment, either in the shape of goods or services or in order to lend it. But if the recipient has no current use for it whatever, then it must agree to defer its claim. *Our* credit is

in no way impugned by deferment; nor could we be charged, as we could under the Graham Towers formula, with so arranging our affairs as to avoid payment.

11. This formula also has the advantage that it can be generalised and would not apply to the U.S. in particular. All our war-creditors, including the sterling area countries, would be subject to the same (highly reasonable) terms,—we only make purchasing power available to those who can find a use for it. Moreover, it fits the Bretton Woods conception like a glove and could, indeed, be administered and certified by the Board of the International Monetary Fund.

12. At the same time it is a very considerable protection against those conditions which we have particular reason to fear, namely, conditions where the difficulty arises not out of our inability to produce goods for export but out of the creditor's unwillingness to receive them.

13. The above was drafted before the conversation with Mr Vinson and Mr Clayton reported in the Ambassador's private telegram. In the light of this conversation, I offer the following alternatives for consideration. They are all of them in terms of $5 billion and would include an escape clause as in (9) above.

(i) That we still seek to obtain a part, say $2 billion, as a grant-in-aid (which would be much facilitated if we would agree to earmark it to the sterling area), and $3 billion repayable as to capital but free of interest. Probably not a starter.

(ii) A grant-in-aid for $2 billion as above, with the balance of $3 billion at 2 per cent interest repayable over 50 years, beginning 10 years hence. An equal annual service for this of $100 million would pay it off in about 45 years.

(iii) A non-interest loan repayable over 50 years, beginning 10 years hence, of which the annual service would be $100 million. It might take the form of earmarking gold for us to this extent, this justifying no interest. The gold would never leave their hands since they would only release it as we needed it and as soon as we needed it we would return it to them.

(iv) A loan at 1 per cent repayable by an equal annual service of $100 million beginning 10 years hence, which would pay it off in about 70 years.

(v) A perpetual loan at 2 per cent, free of interest for the first ten years, of which the service would cost $100 million.

(vi) A loan at 2 per cent, free of interest for the first 10 years, with an annual service commencing at $100 million and gradually rising by (say) $5 million a year to a ceiling of $200 million a year, which would pay it off in about 45 years.

14. It will be seen that the proposal is (except in the case of (i) and (vi)) that the annual cost should be kept at $100 million. (ii) and (iii) are my own preferences. Failing these, is (v) or (vi) which would probably be more acceptable, out of the question? (vi) would probably be acceptable to the Americans but seems to us definitely too expensive.

KEYNES

Keynes and Lord Halifax continued their discussions with Clayton and Vinson on 27 September and confirmed their impression that, according to Keynes, 'a straight grant-in-aid of five billion is not on the map', but that an interest-free loan for the same amount might be possible. Keynes then asked for permission to discuss possible formulae for assistance that kept debt service at or below $100 million per annum.

Meanwhile, on 25 September, London replied to Keynes's request of 21 September to put forward in more detail the sterling area ideas he had discussed in general terms with the Americans. Worried as to the possibilities of leaks in Washington, plus the lack of previous consultation with members of the sterling area, London suggested that Keynes should attempt, initially, to get the Americans to make proposals. If these were leaked, they could be so labelled. London also suggested that Keynes obtain an American statement that assistance was conditional on some British action on the balances problem. Keynes accepted this line of approach on 28 September. He also told London that he had suggested that the new sterling area settlement come into operation at the end of 1946.

At this stage, Mr Crowley, the Baboon[9] to the negotiators, fell from power. As well as informing London by cable, Keynes wrote two notes to Sir Wilfrid Eady.[10]

To SIR WILFRID EADY, *28 September 1945*

My dear Wilfrid,

As you will already have learned by telegram, the Baboon is dead, deader than the cats we were trying to revive and he to bury, and the worms have got him.

I attach a cutting from the *Herald Tribune* which is, I should say, more or less right. Whilst nominally the end is on 15 October, we understand that in effect matters are out of his hands forthwith.

The reason is, of course, that we are not the only people he double-crossed. For ourselves we have had another example of this in the last week. I thought I had fixed up with him the arrangement mentioned to you by which the method of financing the pipe line and inventory would be postponed and the Committee would examine all the offsets we proposed to claim against them. The first thing to happen was that he endeavoured to make it a condition of this—a question never mentioned at our meeting—that we should take over the whole of the inventory without picking and choosing. Whilst this matter was still unresolved, he introduced a new condition entirely at variance with our conversation, namely, that the offsets would only relate to items arising after VJ Day. Howbeit, his enemies and our friends have got him down. Matters are now wholly in the hands of Clayton and Vinson and I think that the Secretary of Agriculture, Clinton Anderson,[11] recently a Congressman who has easy access to

---

[9] This nickname was so general that the cable series for instructions from London for the Mission was named, at Keynes's instigation, Baboon. It was the only six-letter cable series the Treasury used by itself during the war.

[10] The clippings referred to in these do not appear.

[11] Clinton Presba Anderson (b. 1895); Member at large for New Mexico in House of Representatives, 1941–7; Secretary, Department of Agriculture, 1945–8; Senator from New Mexico from 1948.

the White House, will also be brought into closer touch. He and Crowley were at daggers-drawn. I dined with Clinton Anderson last night and it was clear to me that the real access to the President on all our affairs in future will be through Vinson, Clayton and Anderson. Wallace, who is on our Committee, appears to all of us to be completely gaga. He seems to pass out within five minutes of the beginning of any meeting and appears incapable of concentrating his mind on anything.

The *Herald Tribune* article attached exaggerates, however, in my opinion, the improvement in our situation through the departure of Crowley except as regards lend lease. I do not think his aversion was carrying any weight whatever on the question of a grant-in-aid or an interest free loan. The trouble is, I am sure, just what Vinson and Clayton declared it to be, namely, the extreme difficulty of putting either of these propositions across Congress.

Nevertheless, our task in the rational settlement of lend lease will be immensely eased. My understanding is that the questions of policy about which I have previously visited Crowley, I shall now discuss with Clayton. The exact arrangements at the lower level are not yet clear to us. Unfortunately, it appears that much may be in the hands of a chap called McCabe with whom Frank Lee and others have had many dealings. In their opinion his personal incompetence and stupidity make him from their point of view even worse than Crowley. It may be, however, that he is not to play as important a part as they are expecting.

Well, I suppose the Baboon series ought now to come to an end and a new series begin. But I cannot think of a happy code. I wish, by the way, that you could more frequently give us an indication of the origin of the Baboons which reach us. You yourself have been very good and helpful in often indicating which telegrams were particularly from you to me. But, in general, we have no idea either from what Department they emanate or from what level. I suggest that you should more frequently begin them with 'From Treasury' or 'From Ministry of Production' or whatever the origin is. And that when the telegram is from a fairly high level it should begin 'From Eady' or 'From Sinclair' or in other cases some reference to Ministerial direction.

Yours ever,
MAYNARD KEYNES

P.S. Brand and Frank Lee were told at lunch today by Griffin and others that Crowley was 'hopping mad' (though not apparently with us) and that he had written a very angry letter to the President which would create a sensation if it were published. They were rather apprehensive lest Crowley should pose before the public as a man who had been flung to the wolves because he alone had attempted to stand out for sound business terms with the U.K.—and that he might take this line in any evidence which he might give to Congress at a later stage about the present negotiations. There is probably a good deal of force in this; on the other hand there is some reason to believe that Crowley is not fundamentally anti-British and that the people whom he really dislikes are the Russians.

To SIR WILFRID EADY, *29 September 1945*

I am assured that Crowley's dismissal was not connected with any difference of opinion between him and his colleagues on the treatment to be accorded to us, but that it is at least possible that the story in the attached cuttings [not printed] is being put out by him as an alibi for the real reason. It is unfortunate that the British Press is highlighting this episode as being a victory of our friends over this particular enemy since that is being cabled back to the American Press. The joke being passed round F.E.A. this morning was that today is for the British VC Day.

My information is that after having made almost everyone of his colleagues his bitter enemy, Crowley ended up by losing his temper with the President in such a fashion that the President's reaction could not be otherwise than it was. Those who have been working with him have said that of late his demeanour can only be described as pathological. No sane person, they say, could expect to get away for long on these lines. At any rate, his hour has now sounded and he is utterly and absolutely out of the picture. So you will see that our experiences with him have not been unique. Before having a row with the President, he had made deadly enemies of Vinson, Clayton, Dean Acheson and Clinton Anderson, who are some of the most powerful figures in the reorganised administration.

Nevertheless, whatever the exact occasion, good riddance to bad rubbish!

KEYNES

On 1 October, Keynes again asked for general instructions from London, following a telephone conversation with Sir Wilfrid Eady. He stated that a grant-in-aid was out of the question in any likely circumstances. If he pressed the Americans for a set of proposals in black and white, he thought the answer would be the offer of a loan at 2 per cent over fifty years. However, he thought that a non-interest-bearing loan with a ten-year waiver on starting repayments was a possibility and wished permission to discuss it more freely. If, however, Ministers insisted that a grant-in-aid was the only possible solution, Keynes thought it might be necessary to break off negotiations at a suitable point, after the talks on commercial policy discussions had made more progress. He also thought that the elimination of preferences might be made a condition of any American aid.

The same day he wrote to the Chancellor

To H. DALTON, *1 October 1945*

My dear Hugh,

Thank you for the comforting telegram you sent me after Ottawa. It was much appreciated. But of course, that was child's play compared with the task here. I have been meaning ever since I arrived to send you a letter with some gossip about the atmosphere. But I never seem until now to have had time and energy left.

There is no question but that we are working in an atmosphere of great friendliness and an intense desire on their part to work something out to our advantage. The governing group, as I see it, with ready access to the White House who can be pretty sure of influencing the President in the long run, very clearly intend to do their best for us. That is to say, Vinson, Clayton, Dean Acheson, and I think I can add Clinton Anderson, the new Secretary of Agriculture who was lately a Congressman. Even Crowley, in spite of stories to the contrary, I have never rated as outright hostile. His purpose as I have read it has never been to injure us but simply to appease Congress according to his lights and to provide what his friends there would think to be a businesslike settlement. Nevertheless, his disappearance in the latter days of last week does make a considerable difference for the better. In particular, it should be easier to obtain a reasonable financial settlement for the clean-up of lend lease. I should reckon that his departure should save us at least $100 million. There have been rumours, which I believe have been rather unfortunately repeated in the British Press, that he has gone because he differed with his colleagues about how we should be treated. I am sure that is not the real point. Now that people in his department can speak a little more freely they all say that his behaviour of late can only be described as pathological. By curious outbursts of temper he made deadly enemies of all his more influential colleagues and it is reported that he wound up his career by abusing the President personally. So, nothing to do with us, his hour has struck.

The problem as our American friends see it is essentially a question of dressing it all up. As I have said, they mean well if possible. But as I judge, they have not yet come to any conclusion in their own minds about the right formula. Meanwhile, there is a good deal of play acting, slow motion and poker playing. One must not, as I have learnt after having spent altogether more than a year in Washington during this war, one must not take anything either good or bad too seriously until the final sudden act of crystallisation, which always, when it finally happens, takes one by surprise. In particular they will not, I think, come out with any clear-cut offer until they see how the commercial talks are going.

The points gained are these:–

(1) It is agreed that we are a special case and are entitled to terms that no one else would get.

(2) Five billion dollars is not thought too much.

(3) The arrangements I have suggested for the sterling area are acceptable.

It follows that the terms of any assistance are now the essence of the matter.

Here I can, I regret to report, see no sign that a naked grant-in-aid for the full amount will prove practicable. Not even our best friends are thinking quite along that line. On the other hand I do not at present take seriously their equally categorical refusal to consider a non-interest-bearing loan. Nor do I think it impossible that some part of the assistance may take the shape of a grant-in-aid, though I am not at all optimistic about that.

I am hoping to hear from you shortly whether London would be too much shocked by some version of debt service, provided it did not cost us more than $100 million a year, which is the equivalent of the cost of a non-interest-bearing loan over 50 years. If you want something better than that these particular negotiations will have I guess to be broken off. As you know, I have always contemplated the possibility of that and would not repine if it comes to it. The resulting delay and friction and dissipation of good feeling would be serious. My advice would be to accept a settlement on these terms or better (for I am not yet in the mood to go the whole distance of the discretion I suggest). I should not be particularly keen on attaching to this an escape clause based on our inability to pay which we can very likely get, for I feel that willingness to draft such a formula would lay us open to the proposal of harder terms similarly protected. I should therefore stick to the escape clause I have already sent to you based not on our ability to pay but on the willingness of the creditor country to receive.

Our friends are not only troubled as to how to dress the business up so as to be acceptable to Congress, they are also faced with the difficulty that the Executive has no power to agree the terms and any terms they may fix up with us are liable to be amended by Congress. For this reason, one of my old friends here, Oscar Cox, who is acting as an adviser to the President, is playing with the idea of introducing a Bill very much on the analogy of lend lease which would give the President eight billions he could play with and transfer to us and others when he is satisfied that it is to the advantage of the U.S. more or less on any terms. The actual context runs as follows:–

'Such terms and conditions may include partial repayment and repayment in indirect as well as direct benefits in the event that the President determines that conditions have developed where such partial repayment or repayment in indirect benefits would be in the best interests of the U.S.'

You will see that this would cover either a grant-in-aid or a non-interest-bearing loan, or a bit of both. And the President would obtain the powers before he declares just how he would use them. I am sceptical whether such a proposal could get through Congress but clearly it has its advantages. So after criticising some of the details, I have not dissuaded him from putting an idea on these lines into the President's mind.

In spite of the late date it is very hot here. Last week crossing or approaching 90 most days and often humid. But the heat, however disagreeable, seems to agree with me and

I am in good health. The team here, as I knew it would be, is just about as good as one could possibly have. The Ambassador is immeasurably helpful and we are working together very closely. Brand and Lee and Harmer, Goschen and Self and the other heads of Missions provide, as I discovered a year ago, just about the finest group one could want to go into action with. It is, of course, all rather exhausting. We live in a blaze of limelight. There are a couple of articles about our goings on in every newspaper almost every day. The Press is of course extremely mixed but the more responsible organs quite satisfactory:- up to the point that we are a special case and should have five billions but not to the point of suggesting a grant-in-aid to that amount. To give you an example, I enclose two cuttings which were on my breakfast table this morning. The *Times Herald* is a local rag which Walter Lippmann always says no Britisher should be allowed to read since it merely creates unnecessary alarm and despondency. The cutting from the *New York Times* being by Crider, was probably largely inspired in the U.S. Treasury. In contact with the Press, which it is impossible to keep at bay, one is of course always in danger of saying too much or too little. It is a cat's dance the whole time. And then there are the endless social engagements to keep in touch with friends and influential people. The Ambassador gave last week what I think was a very useful small dinner to half a dozen of the leading Senators on both sides. They cross-examined me for three hours sitting on the porch of the Embassy on a tropical evening and seemed both interested and friendly, though incredibly remote.

Some people here say that the failure of the London Conference will make our task more difficult by driving American opinion towards isolationism. But it is also capable of working the other way. And that, in my private opinion, is how it will work.

You would be astonished, by the way, at the importance

given here to Laski. Even Senators and responsible columnists believe that for practical purposes he is the ruler of the country. It comes to me from people whom one can scarcely credit with not knowing better. The idea seems to be that he is Stalin with the Prime Minister in the position say, of Kalinin. They are quite staggered with surprise and still really rather incredulous when one tries to describe the actual position. You must not underestimate the enormous importance attached to his lightest utterance.

Yours,

MAYNARD KEYNES

P.S. The labour situation here is quite out of hand. I predict that basic rates of wages will have gone up 10 to 15 per cent before I leave and perhaps by as much as 25 per cent within a year. If we can manage better than this it will certainly help our competitive position very considerably.

I attach a Gallup poll result which you may have seen before this arrives. It is an indication of what our friends in the American camp are up against.[12]

It is interesting that the intelligentsia are relatively in favour of us and the manual workers overwhelmingly against us.

On 2 October, Keynes summed up the position and prospects of the negotiations on the clean-up of lend lease.

To the Treasury (NABOB 107), 2 October 1945

1. Our many telegrams show the sub-committees concerned with winding up lend lease are at present engaged in a mass of troublesome detail which suggests great loss of time and considerable friction ending up in an enormous bill. Taken at its face value this would be very depressing. But it is better

---

[12] Not printed. All the polls of the period indicated a low level of interest in foreign affairs and strong opposition to a loan to Britain.

regarded as a process we must go through rather than a true pointer to the ultimate conclusion, and you should not be unduly alarmed.

2. Time is not being wasted because the itemised and audited method of settlement is being shown to be impracticable and because both sides are becoming better acquainted with what it is all about and with the orders of magnitude involved.

3. In informal conversation with members of the Top Committee I find some reason to think that a global settlement of a reasonable amount is probably what they would like to end up with if possible. And indeed it is evident that any other method must occupy many months and perhaps years before finality is reached. The difficulty of a global settlement is of course the question how to reach a figure within our means which could be justified to Congress. For this reason Crowley was bent on what he called a business-like settlement. With his departure it is possible that more elastic principles may find favour.

4. I think of this settlement as covering:

(a) Requirements from the pipeline.

(b) Food and material end stocks.

(c) Military lend lease inventories having a civilian end-use, subject to any items recaptured.

(d) Durable goods and capital installations.

(e) Transport aircraft.

(f) Ships.

(g) United States military surpluses lying in the United Kingdom, and possibly those in some other parts of the sterling area.

5. The aggregate figure for which the Americans might be prepared to settle for all of these might be between $750 and $1000 million. Against this our offset for mutual aid inventory and in the pipeline up to 28 February next, and the various back claims which we should seek to keep alive might be worth at most $400 to 500 million and at worst 200 to 250.

6. I am not including in this the amounts due to us for lend lease shipping and oil reimbursements worth about $150 million. We are aiming to collect these in cash in accordance with the normal procedure which has existed hitherto, thus keeping them out of an overall settlement. But if we do not succeed in this they will presumably have to be brought into the settlement.

7. I do not propose at this stage to discuss in detail the possible scope of the offsetting arrangement or the manner in which it might be dressed up as a question of presentation. Ideas are not yet sufficiently crystallised on the United States side for this to be profitable. But I think we must proceed on the assumption that the ultimate outcome will be that we shall be asked to accept a commitment for a specific dollar amount which has to be added to the sum of the assistance which we require from the U.S.A.

8. For this reason I think it is not too soon for you to give thought to the question of what global settlement will be acceptable if we can get the principle adopted. My present impression is that the smallest amount covering all the categories mentioned above, of which there is any hope, is $250 to 300 million; that a settlement on these terms would be a very good bargain, but this is considerably better than what we at present have any reason to expect. On the basis of present estimates I should regard $500 million as the highest we should be willing to contemplate, but their starting figure is likely to be higher than this.

9. All this is half-baked and, as the Americans say, thinking out loud. But it would help us to have your first reactions.

10. We are sending by Saving a report on how the work of the lend lease sub-committees stands up to date, with a covering letter from me to Clayton summarising the points of principle on which we need to reach early decision with the United States side.

Ministers were to meet to discuss these developments, plus Keynes's memorandum of 26 September on 5 October. Prior to that meeting, an exchange of letters and telegrams between Sir Wilfrid Eady and Keynes summarised the situation and developing opinion.

From SIR WILFRID EADY, *28 September 1945*

My dear Maynard,

The Ambassador's Prisec telegram of 26 September arrived after I had sent you my letter of yesterday and therefore I had no chance to make any comment.

Although what you told us was not unexpected, and certainly at this stage, the news did little to lighten the encircling gloom.

The dilemma faces the Americans as well as ourselves. We cannot liberalise the sterling area and free additional markets to American exports for the sake of their employment policy unless we receive help from them on a very large scale, and that help is given on terms that puts no anxiety on us in the immediate years. If we had to pay interest, even at what they would regard as non commercially low rates, and even if they agreed, as they no doubt would, that the repayment of interest and capital did not begin for say five years, we should be haunted during that period by the problem of setting aside dollars or hypothecated reserves to meet the annual charges as they fell due. I do not need to say anything to you about the difficulty of providing interest and amortisation on a loan of $5 billion.

Indeed, there are knowledgeable people here who think that if we are to be honest, the only terms we could accept for a loan of this size are non-interest-bearing, capital to be repaid over 40 years beginning after the first ten years, i.e. 50 years in all.

If the present level of world prices were reasonably maintained, if our own productivity were increased as we hope, if the American export drive is on fair terms and does not attempt to shut us out of the immediate markets which are essential to the early creation by us of a favourable balance of payments, and if the Americans do not put pressure on us because of the loan to allow the importation into the United Kingdom of substantial amounts of dollar goods which are not essential to us, e.g. motor cars, various luxuries, additional petrol, films, etc., then the view I have mentioned may strike you as pessimistic. But quite frankly, in the immediate future, say the next two or three years, those 'ifs' must, I think, be treated not as dialectical 'ifs', but as real 'ifs'.

On the background position, you have of course to allow for certain changes of emphasis with the present Government. Influential members of the Government would clearly feel it very distasteful that after a victorious war, in which we have borne our very full share of effort and sacrifice, we should find ourselves under a loan obligation of an enormous amount to one of our two major Allies. I wrote something some time ago in connection with my alternative approach indicating that gratitude and generosity were explosive emotions to exist between us and the United States. There is no doubt that feeling is held in some quarters. The attitude of the United States Administration on certain major issues of foreign policy is rather unpredictable and is liable to be influenced by sudden turns of domestic American policy. When that happens it shows itself by a public attempt to put pressure on us, not so much in the hope that we will yield to the pressure, as to be able to announce that the pressure is being exerted. That sort of thing will inevitably, and in the best conditions, recur not infrequently in the next two or three years. But the acerbity of it might be sharpened if, underlying our relations, the U.S. Administration feel that they have behaved very generously to us, and we feel that we are obliged to remember that fact.

As regards the austerity consequences of anything less than complete success, I should judge the present Government to be much less frightened of the politics of that than their predecessors. Indeed, there is a risk that austerity for its own sake may become a little too fashionable, partly as a more noble way of life, partly as a psychological sublimation of disappointment. The practical dangers of that mood are that there will be a popular reaction, and also that in the process of seeking austerity we may damage incentives. It is quite likely that the right policy for today is for everybody to make as much money as they can by hard work, and enjoy themselves on the proceeds of their efforts.

As you will understand these are personal comments but they may be useful to you as pointers. I do not think the Government would be cynical about taking on obligations which they doubted they could fulfil. They would regard that as part of the old and bad tradition of international lending, and they would probably support you in saying that we would not take on an obligation that we did not see a reasonable expectation of fulfilling.

They will also not be frightened of austerity in regard to imports from the United States, or effective priority for exports. Finally, one or two of them, and those not the least influential, are extremely sceptical whether, in practice, the American contribution to international trade is going to live up to their promises, and whether in fact the Americans are going to permit other countries to trade in such a way that they will be able to accumulate a favourable balance of payments out of which they can repay obligations to America.

Three or four more comments. Ever since Atlantic City I have been haunted by a talk with Pasvolsky[13] on a theme to which he has referred more than once since then. He urged that we were exaggerating the difficulty of achieving equilibrium, and that our exaggeration was due to tactical motives. To the Americans the amount of our external indebtedness, or the more urgent prospective deficit on current account, does not seem so overwhelming as it is to us, for even the most intelligent of them have difficulty in translating the productive and organising effort it would mean for us into the equivalent effort for their own much more gigantic economy. In the papers you put in I was interested to see how you drove home the comparative size of the effort, both in terms of population and national income. That is a lesson which wants to be driven home I am sure in a number of quarters.

The second point is the awkwardness of a breakdown in the current negotiations. That does not mean that it is necessary, at all costs, to reach a settlement which clears up the whole situation. But against the political background of our present relations with the United States, in regard for example to Europe and to Russia, I fancy that our Government would be disturbed if there had to be public admission that on a matter of this kind we had failed to reach even a provisional or preliminary agreement. It may be therefore that we must take the matter in two stages, and provide for some way of ensuring supplies to us for this year and for a large part of next year, and leave the more comprehensive settlement you have in mind until somewhat later. We should of course be embarrassed if that is the outcome because all our dealings with the sterling area would continue to be on a hand to mouth basis. On the other hand the reality of the effort we must make to achieve equilibrium would become indisputably apparent. There are those who believe that we shall not get a united and continuous effort of this kind unless there is a danger imminent for us comparable with the situation after Dunkirk.

It is to be hoped that the Americans will not attempt to attach too many strings to the kind of settlement you have been discussing. If they appear to tie us up on commercial policy too much, or if they introduce extraneous

[13] Leo Pasvolsky (1893–1953), economist; U.S. Bureau of Foreign and Domestic Commerce, Department of State, 1934–5; Director of Trade Agreements, 1935–6; Special Assistant to the Secretary of State, 1936–8, 1939–46; Chief, Division of Special Research, 1941–2; Supervisor, Division of Political and Economic Studies, 1943; Executive Director, Committee on Post-war Programmes, 1944; delegate to Bretton Woods Conference, 1944.

political considerations, there is some risk I think of an impulsive reaction over here.

Finally there is the question of the nature of the financial assistance, i.e. whether even at this date the Americans could not be induced to see the political wisdom of starting us more or less right by applying the idea of retrospective lend lease. (You may remember that early on in the days of lend lease, Oscar Cox and one or two others thought that it might be wise to ante-date lend lease to the beginning of the war). Then on top of the retrospective lend lease we should of course have to borrow, but as you indicated in one of the later versions of your paper, we might, by great efforts on our own part, be able to keep the borrowing down to relatively low figures, perhaps not much more than $2 billion.

There have been other suggestions in the Press of building us up by a 'lend lease' gift of gold, presumably with some obligation to replace in specie over a period. It is a gamble but it might not be much more of a gamble than an obligation to repay across the exchanges.

I thought that was my final point, but there is another on which you and I have had previous talks—the way in which if, in the end, we take money from the Americans, we are to take it. Are we to have the whole sum paid over to us, or are we to receive it by instalments on demand, subject to some scrutiny by them of our position, and what escape clause is contemplated. I am not going to dilate on all this again because I am sure you have it well in mind.

It is quite likely that these wandering thoughts will be out of date when we receive the note mentioned in paragraph 9 of the Ambassador's Prisec telegram. You will understand that they are not, and indeed in the circumstances cannot be, either considered comments of my own or a reflection of any discussion with anybody else. They are just the first reactions, after brooding on the Prisec telegram, and may just be worth your while reading.

I am doubtful whether it will be practicable to settle this business by an exchange of cables. Ministers may want fuller consultation, either with you or with Brand or Halifax. Alternatively, though it is not really an alternative so much as a second best, I could come out and get the full story from you and bring it back.

Yours ever,
WILFRID

Since writing the above 6490 about your further private talk has come in. But my letter is sufficiently relevant to send it.

From SIR WILFRID EADY (*Telegram 9913*), *3 October 1945*

Your telegram 6549.

1. It may not be possible to give you considered guidance of Ministers in time for meeting on Friday. Your memorandum of 26 September which is important comment on discussions only arrived Monday and Ministers, despite other urgent preoccupations, will be considering it together with the Prisec telegrams sent at end of last week as rapidly as possible. At present I can only give you preliminary departmental view.

2. We should not think it reasonable to advise Ministers to insist upon a grant-in-aid or nothing.

3. But we could not recommend acceptance of any commercial principle such as interest even at low rates in a loan designed in great part to modify working of the sterling area. The position of the sterling area as it is after the war is not a commercial situation and application to its solution of commercial principle would be, we believe, entirely unacceptable over here. We must I suggest consider two per cent interest as commercial principle.

4. We note your view that a non-interest loan whose repayment begins after ten years represents the very best terms you have hope of getting. Departmentally, we are doubtful whether we can see certainty of transferring $100 million (hundred million dollars) annually even after ten years. Fuller explanation of our doubts will follow. Doubts would be still more acute if we are not free to restrict United States imports both into the United Kingdom and also those parts of sterling area dependent for external finance on United Kingdom. Power to restrict might be limited in time but might well be needed for five years. Is this necessity understood by Americans?

5. If, in the end, final American offer is $5 billion (five billion dollars) on those terms and without strings, Ministers will obviously have to consider it with our comments upon possible difficulties of undertaking regular repayment.

6. Meanwhile, we are more attracted to earlier version of your ideas. Most attractive proposition would divide assistance into two parts. First part, whether described as grant-in-aid, or preferably, repayment of part of our expenditure in U.S.A. during cash and carry period, would be devoted to modifying restrictions in sterling area. How much modification would depend on size of gift. Even $2 billion (two billion dollars) would take us some distance along lines which Americans desire. If Americans realise, as Harry White probably does, that part of American assistance must in fact be a gift, however wrapped up, we do not see why repayment of cash and carry expenditure should prove more difficult to Congress than other propositions.

524

7. We should need further assistance and should of course prefer not to have to pay interest. But it might on the whole suit us to have drawing rights up to a further $4 billion (four billion dollars) or so of untied credit as we require it and without any enquiries. It might be practicable to arrange 1 per cent interest on the credit in use. Such arrangement would keep visibly before us urgent need for securing all round equilibrium at earliest moment and might check too frequent application to the credit.

8. This is variation on (i) and (ii) of paragraph 13 of your memorandum. Would it not be practicable to try this out further?

9. I make no comment upon Imperial Preference issue. You can understand reaction over here if the abolition of Preference is taken out of tariff settlement and made condition of financial assistance.

10. We hesitate to advise you from here on present tactics. But general reading of your communications suggests that after your exposition of our case and your indication of general lines upon which we would propose to use American help, it might be convenient for you to seek indication from Americans how their mind is running. That does not mean black and white proposals as suggested in paragraph 2, and certainly they probably realise by now that 2 per cent interest on a loan of $5 billion (five billion dollars) for 50 years is likely to be regarded as unmanageable, and therefore contrary to principle that Ministers will not undertake obligations which they do not see a reasonable certainty of fulfilling. Apart from difficulty that at present we should hesitate to advise Ministers that $100 million (hundred million dollars) annually is manageable, we fear that if you now suggest that kind of figure it might be regarded as a first bid, and this might embarrass both you and us. If you judge that you should keep ball in play for the moment, we offer paragraphs 6 and 7 of this telegram as a suggestion.

3.10.45   W.E.

To H. DALTON, *4 October 1945*

Since I understand that Ministers will be considering shortly telegrams Nos. 6444 and 6490 and my memorandum of 26 September I should like to add following further observations:–

2. As we have already indicated a non-interest loan of five billion dollars repayable over fifty years and therefore costing twenty-five million pounds a year during the period of repay-

ment represents the best terms of which we here see any serious prospect. And of course nothing nearly so good as this is yet in sight. Nevertheless doubts will naturally be felt by all of us whether this is a burden we can safely accept. To point out that it is only an additional two per cent of the external income we shall need anyhow and is only a little more than what we spend on American films may be some comfort but it is not conclusive.

3. In weighing the alternative risks we have to run we have therefore to consider whether there is any other course open to us which will cost us less. Take for example the three following suggestions:

(*a*) A grant-in-aid of two billion dollars with a right to a further three or four billions credit at one per cent interest. This is an attractive alternative well worth considering but it will cost us nearly as much.

(*b*) Temporary arrangements with United States to carry us through next year with a postponement of the main settlement until we see our way clear. In effect this will cost us a good deal more without settling anything. For we should need as a minimum five hundred million dollars to clean up lend lease on 3(*c*) terms and another one thousand million on Export-Import Bank terms to see us to the end of 1946. On the terms at present standard for other borrowers, such as France, this would cost us more than one hundred million dollars a year in the early years beginning at once. It is therefore a far inferior and uneconomic expedient.

(*c*) To borrow what we need from the sterling area and other countries apart from United States. No one can suppose that they would continue to lend us on the same terms as during the war without security of any defined prospect of repayment vast sums they have not got and cannot spare except at crushing cost to their own post-war reconstruction. Before we had borrowed more than one-third or one-half of what we need we should have incurred a heavier burden than the equivalent of one hundred million dollars. It must be remembered that under a multilateral currency system one hundred million dollars due to the United States is no greater burden than a similar sum due to any other country.

4. I conclude that there is no means open to us of securing a sum of the order of five billion dollars at a lesser cost than one hundred million dollars a year. Thus, if it is true that this with or without a moratorium is the best that we can get from the United States, the only genuine alternative to accepting this commitment is to do without imports and curtail domestic consumption so as to spare more for exports and cut down our military expenditure overseas and political commitments abroad so as to avoid altogether expenditure equivalent to the greater part of five billion dollars.

5. It would be a brave man who says we can face this. It would mean that we should decline for the time being to the position of a second rate power abroad and we should not only have to postpone for at least five years any improvement in the standard of living at home but would have to ask the public to accept greater sacrifices than at any time during the war, and it would be a foolish man who says that this would be an easier and safer plan than to find ways of making a comparatively small economy five or ten years hence after we have got ourselves straight. To run tomorrow or the next day into major economic and political trouble of this order of magnitude with all its implications for the future of Anglo-American relations is surely a greater risk to the future of the country than to commit ourselves to make economies hereafter equivalent to two per cent of our future imports.

6. This does not mean that we can get the non-interest-bearing loan which is the basis of the above argument; only that it would be worth having on a balance of considerations if we could get it. Nor does it mean that we should not try to do better still if we see the smallest chance of success. The question of what political price it is worth our while to pay

is another matter which this telegram of course has made no attempt to assess.

To SIR WILFRID EADY, *4 October 1945*

My dear Wilfrid,

Your letter of September 28th arrived more promptly than usual and was quickly followed by your most helpful telegram 9913 (if, by the way you ever have again to get something to me extra urgently, if you will post it air-mail in the Parliament Street Post Office it will get here two days quicker).

We shall not of course have our meeting behind the scenes until tomorrow. But there are certain general points both in your letter and in your telegram not likely to be affected by what happens on Friday about which I began drafting you a letter. But I saw that if I wrote a letter it would not arrive in time for the meeting of Ministers. So I fired off a telegram containing in effect a supplementary memorandum for the Chancellor. That does not, however, make it altogether unnecessary to answer your letter:–

1. The arrangement you mentioned in the fourth paragraph of your letter as the only terms some people think we can accept is, of course—either in that form or its equivalent —just what we shall go for. We shall certainly not go an inch beyond that without your express instructions.

2. On a caveat you mention in your next paragraph about possible pressure to allow imports of American goods, I am glad to be able to say that there has been no hint of that. Indeed, Clayton has been quite explicit that he is thinking in terms of an untied credit. He, personally, is opposed to tied loans and said that he would make Export-Import Bank loans and all other American loans untied if he could.

3. An interim arrangement such as you suggest in the second half of your page 3 has its obvious attractions. But I am confident that it breaks down on arithmetic. I have dealt with this explicitly in the telegram. If we were to do what you

suggest it must mean accepting Crowley's credit for the clean-up of lend lease and an Export-Import loan for the balance of our urgent requirements. Our cost of the interim arrangements themselves would be over one hundred million dollars. Thus we should have accepted the burden without reaching a solution. I am convinced that there is no alternative way out which would not cost us more, and perhaps a great deal more, than one hundred million dollars.

4. In your last page you raise the question of the form of the loan. We have not yet got down to that; but my impression is that they, like ourselves, are thinking in terms of a system of instalments on demand. I am evading the question of an escape clause, for if we once admit the possibility of an escape clause they will use this as an argument why we should accept worse terms thus protected.

I turn now to your telegram 9913 which, as I have said, is very helpful and will allow us to make further explorations without undue commitments on Friday. You will see that in my telegram I have been trying in part to answer in advance your Treasury argument that the burden of one hundred million dollars scares you. Of course, it does not leave me comfortable. The only difference between us, if there is one, is that I am more scared, ten times more scared, by the alternatives and I was anxious that your very proper arguments should not be seen except against a background of the alternatives.

I think it quite worth while to explore a bit along the lines of your paragraphs 6 and 7. This is not really consistent with your hesitations about the non-interest loan for the whole amount since the proposed combination plan would cost as much. The only advantage of it is that, it being rather less precise than the non-interest loan, we are not talking so clearly in terms of one hundred million dollars.

I enclose a grand article by Walter Lippmann which is out today, which deserves to be printed on your side [not printed]. He wrote it in the light of the pretty full knowledge of the position which I thought it useful to give him in more than one conversation behind the scenes.

What is probably most difficult for London to appreciate is the frightfully difficult selling proposition which our friends here have. Congress is, of course, miles behind the Administration and on this occasion I fancy the public is miles behind Congress. The Press on the whole is pretty good;—half way, perhaps, between the Administration and Congress and nearer, on the whole, to the Administration, where, in fact, they get most of their inspiration. You must always bear it in mind that people like Vinson are not trying to do us down in any of the propositions they make. They are simply searching round for something which, in their political judgement, they can sell to Congress. Any feeling about preferences on merits is confined to the State Department; and Harry White remains entirely cynical on the matter and is convinced that the State Department plans have not the smallest chance of ever getting through Congress. He regards our talks with them as waste of time.

Lunching at the Federal Reserve yesterday I found them quite vehemently on our side. Governor Eccles, who is of course a member of our Top Committee, thought that we had more than made out our case; indeed, his concern was how we should get through even as it was. He thought pressure on us about preferences unfair and absurd. The only point, he says, about giving away preferences is that we should get more trade and you less and that can only make things worse. That, he said, was the general feeling in Federal Reserve circles. All the same that does not make the slightest difference to the universally prevailing belief that the elimination of preferences is a first class selling point. The short slogan is 'The British give up preferences and the dollar pool'. It is on that basis that they think they can get us what we want. However, we shall see. I am a very long way from despairing about finding a reasonably satisfactory compromise. It is becoming clearer to them every day that what they are suggesting is essentially unfair; and, to do them justice, they are fairminded people.

Yours ever,
[copy not initialled]

On the day of the meeting of Ministers, Keynes sent Eady another letter.

To SIR WILFRID EADY, 5 October 1945

My dear Wilfrid,

I enclose a copy of a rather fascinating contraption of Harry's and a spare one for the Bank. If you think anything can be made of it, let me know.

It seems to me to contain some good ideas. In particular, under our own plan some part of our outstanding debt to the sterling area might be expressed in the form of minimum irremovable working balances. This is, I think, rather in the line of Cobbold's thought.

Harry's point is, of course, to make the whole affair so complicated that the average Congressman has no idea what it amounts to and whether or not interest does or does not truly emerge. It can also be represented as a combined plan whereby each of the sterling area countries was taking its proper participation.

I hear rumours, but Harry did not mention it to me, that one of the conditions the U.S. Treasury would like to make is that South Africa make us a present of one hundred million pounds in gold. A grand idea. God bless him. But how it is done has not yet been divulged. They have, of course, their knife into South Africa and are intending to propose a very severe lend lease settlement which stings the Boers to the maximum extent. But again, I do not know how it is done. In this context I read that Mr Hofmeyr[14] is shortly

14 Rt Hon. Jan Hendrik Hofmeyr (1894–1948), South African Minister of Finance and Education, 1939–48.

going to London to discuss the final financial clean-up. If this is true, I hope you are collecting a vast assemblage of claims, complaints and every other inducement. The expenditure of our Admiralty on improving the South African ports is one of the most outrageous cases. Then there are the prisoners. But above all, of course, my conviction, which I think you share, that quite apart from specific details, the South Africans have grossly refrained from playing their full and proper part.

Yours ever,

MAYNARD KEYNES

P.S. Since I wrote the above I have come to attach rather more importance to Harry's proposals. For at our meeting yesterday, Vinson referred to them obscurely and invited my opinion whether I thought there was anything in them. I was somewhat embarrassed since, unless I had had my talk with Harry, I should have had no idea what Vinson was referring to. I replied, of course, that it was difficult to pass any judgement without knowing more of the details, but the general notion did seem to me perhaps worth further exploration.

DR HARRY WHITE'S PLAN

As I reported earlier in my visit, Dr White with his assistants in the U.S. Treasury, has had on the stocks a plan for our assistance which hitherto has not come out into the open. This is because Dr White has not been successful, so far, in selling it to Mr Vinson. Unintelligible fragments of it have leaked to the Press and have appeared in various quarters. The actual plan is not only more intelligible but more helpful than the leaks. After I had persuaded Dr White to tell me about it, my comment was that I thought it too fancy. He answered that that was just the reason that Mr Vinson had given for not taking it up. I do not think that Dr White has abandoned his notions. He would be especially inclined to revive them if we gave him any encouragement. I made no comment except what I have mentioned above. But they are worth reporting not only as a matter of interest but because they certainly do contain an idea and, apart from incidental disadvantages, might leave us with a smaller future burden than any alternative. The plan is as follows:–

1. The sterling area balances are taken as at the 30 June 1945, figure, say, eleven billions as the nearest round figure. This would be divided into three parts.

(a) Two billions would be unblocked but the countries in question would undertake to maintain minimum working balances in London of this amount.

(b) Four billions would be written off.

(c) Five billions would be funded and become repayable by capital instalments without interest over a period of years.

2. So far the plan does not differ essentially from our own proposals. The U.S. would then offer to buy from the sterling area countries the funded portion of their debt discounted as from the due dates at, say, three per cent interest. Let us assume that the present discounted value would be two and a half billions. If the sterling area countries accept this they would have two and a half billions in free cash put up by the U.S. Treasury to play with. I did not understand that this would be tied in any way to purchases in the U.S. but would be free cash and they could do what they liked with it. For example, though he did not say so in so many words, I imagine that they could, if they like (e.g. the Colonies) sell their dollars to us for free sterling. A sterling area country running a deficit would have no other external cash except these dollars out of which to meet it; but my understanding is that the dollars would be generally available for expenditure anywhere and not tied to the U.S.

3. We should then owe the U.S. not the original five billions

but the discounted two and a half billions. This we should repay to the U.S. over a period, and, if Dr White has his way, without interest. This would mean in effect that they would have made us a present of the three per cent interest representing the difference between the nominal value of the sterling area funded debt and its present discounted value.

4. The above would look after the sterling area debt. There would remain the question of our current adverse balance of trade. To meet this the U.S. would give us a further credit of, say three billions. This also would be repayable as to capital over a long period and, if Dr White has his way, it would be free of interest.

5. The recipe for justifying no interest might be to make the loan in both cases a gold loan which would allow a sophistry to the effect that it would cost the American Treasury no interest.

6. There still remains one feature of Dr White's plan to mention. The sterling area balances in the above have been struck as at 30 June 1945. We, however, have been talking in terms of what the sterling area balances are likely to be on 31 December 1946. The White plan would provide for this by requiring the sterling area countries to make us a new post-war loan of two billions to cover our expenditure during the eighteen months succeeding 30 June 1945. This would be funded and repayable over a period, without interest.

7. The final upshot is that we should owe five and a half billions to the U.S. instead of five billions, and four billions to the sterling area (of which two billions could not be taken away) instead of eight billions (of which eight hundred millions would be immediately free).

8. Thus the dollar liability is scarcely more than we should owe on the basis of a straight five billions arrangement whilst the sterling loan would be effectively two billions instead of about seven. The dollars directly at our own disposal would be three billions instead of five. But the dollars at the disposal

of the sterling area as a whole would be five and a half billions instead of five. Taken in conjunction with our new loan from the sterling area this might not be inadequate.

9. Now that I have seen the plan in detail it seems to me much freer than I had expected from the element of interference with the sterling area arrangements. But of course, some members, e.g. India, Egypt and Eire, would no doubt be encouraged to keep separate dollar reserves through finding themselves in the first instance with a substantial quota of dollars in their hands.

10. The worst technical snag that I can see is that in effect, from the bookkeeping point of view, the sterling area countries would have to find some way of caring for not only the initial four billions written off but also the two billions corresponding to the difference between the nominal and discounted value of the funded portion. In certain cases at least this might present a difficult technical problem.

11. When all is said, however, the plan is conceived on extremely generous lines. Dr White may quite well be right that this could be presented to the public and to Congress in an attractive form. It would be represented here that the sterling balances had been entirely wound up. It would also be represented that all participants were making a common substantial sacrifice. The close analogy between the new loan from the sterling area and the new loan from the U.S.A. with the former carrying no interest might make it easier that the latter should carry no interest also. It could also be presented in England on attractive lines. The very fact that it is fancy gives it an imaginative and not purely financial aspect which might prove attractive to the general public.

KEYNES

After the meeting of Ministers, Eady filled Keynes in on the background to the telegrams containing Keynes's instructions that would follow.

From SIR WILFRID EADY, *6 October 1945*

My dear Maynard,

I hope that an adequate telegram of guidance will reach you on Monday.

The meeting of Ministers was not altogether an easy one. They are very tired and the Foreign Secretary is of course really preoccupied with the results of the Foreign Ministers Conference. There is rather a natural resentment that in our external affairs we seem to be bullied in turn by the Russians and the Americans, and a certain emotional wish to say 'plague on both your houses'.

Also, and this you will remember at all times over the last two years, the issues at stake involve a certain amount of patient reading of figures, alternatives, supply position etc., and none of the Ministers at present likes this.

One thing is pretty certain. They do not want to be under an obligation to the United States for one dollar more than they need or for one minute more than is necessary. I behaved not too well because I had to intervene several times. I told them broadly that we could not possibly keep going without 2 billion dollars from the Americans to cover a clean-up of lend lease, purchase of ships, 1946 requirements, and 1947 requirements on the basis that somehow or other we would in 1947 have been able to secure supplies from other quarters. As the time comes nearer, to deal with the sterling creditors looks more and more difficult, and of course our general external position is not made much easier by the fact of the additional expenditure we will have to incur in Palestine and other parts of the Middle East.

If you find the telegram unintelligible in any part, don't hesitate to cable either personally to me or in the PRISEC series asking for elucidation. I told the Chancellor that we must do our best to keep you informed of how Ministers' minds are running even at the cost of a long message. He dislikes long documents on any subject.

I make a guess that Ministers will not say Yes or No without having you back here for consultation beforehand. It is really the background of the whole story that is important.

Pethick [Lawrence] was sensible about the manageability of $100 million, but he wanted you to extract a promise from the American Government that there would be no deflation during the next fifty years! Obviously we can't get that, and what we must have is escape clauses if things go wrong.

I am sending you a note by Rowe-Dutton which suggests that dollars will inevitably be short.

Forgive haste of this but I am under terrible pressure just now.

Yours

WILFRID

The telegrams which followed the meeting of Ministers made the following points:

(1) Ministers would not accept a large loan at 2 per cent owing to the difficulties of servicing it and the fact they believed it inequitable. They would instead borrow for the necessary imports and clean-up of lend lease on Export-Import Bank terms.

(2) They were prepared to give way on a grant-in-aid. If they did so, they would prefer a grant of $2 billion to offset British expenditures during the period of cash and carry before lend lease and a credit of $3–4 billion on which they would pay 1 per cent on the drawings made.

(3) If (2) failed, they would accept interest and amortisation commitments of up to $100 million per annum subject to a waiver on Britain's initiative if there was deflation in the United States, or if the American economy was not in overall international balance. If resort to the waiver meant interest and amortisation payments were missed, in no subsequent year should British payments exceed $100 million.

(4) Keynes was to make no suggestions to the Americans, for the moment, on the form of the financial settlement until they took the initiative.

(5) Keynes was to explain to the Americans that the tying of the issue of Imperial Preference to the financial settlement would make the selling of the latter to Ministers hopeless.

On 9 October, after receiving the Chancellor's cables on the meeting of Ministers, which, as Keynes put it, 'gave us just the guidance we hoped for', Keynes and Lord Halifax called on Vinson and Clayton.

At the meeting Keynes advanced a plea that $2 billion of the assistance come in grant form, but he failed to shift the Americans from the view that such a solution was politically impossible.[15] Both Vinson and Clayton also remained adamant that an interest-free loan was not practical politics, even though the sum involved was 'only peanuts' to the U.S. Treasury.

When Keynes and Lord Halifax pressed the Americans for an indication of what they had in mind, Clayton suggested an untied loan of $5 billion repayable in fifty annual instalments beginning in five years with an additional annuity of $50 million per annum to cover interest.[16] The scheme

---

[15] However, both Keynes and the Ambassador thought that this proposal, although likely to fail, was not completely out of bounds and they, therefore, proposed to keep it in reserve for the future.

[16] Here Keynes suggested, when reporting to the Chancellor, a variant of slowly rising payments starting at $100 million and rising to $200 million with an average of $150 million.

would have a liberal test of Britain's ability to pay, which would allow waivers on interest payments. Clayton said that he was prepared for a very liberal arrangement here, as he was an optimist over Britain's ability to pay such sums.[17]

The meeting then turned to the problem of future conditions in America, import demand and sterling area arrangements. Each side provided the other with favourable assurances.

The same day, Keynes and Sir Percivale Liesching reported to London on the general position in the discussions of Imperial Preference, where Americans demanded firm assurances from Britain as to the reduction and elimination of margins of preference before promising financial aid. The British negotiators, following instructions, had rejected such a link, but wished to be prepared for a possible way out of the impasse if that proved necessary. They suggested a reduction of preferences in agreed stages, with no increase in margins of preference in the interim, all general tariff reductions automatically reducing margins of preference, all margins of preference being open to individual negotiation, and a procedure for the reduction or elimination of preferences not otherwise reduced. They also suggested that Britain remove, if necessary in exchange for American concessions, all preferences on commodities where the goods from preferred sources were under 5 per cent of total imports of the goods concerned.

On 11 October Keynes made an attempt at drafting a waiver clause for submission to London. He suggested three grounds: a breakdown of multi-lateral clearing when under 75 per cent of the currencies earned by Britain were freely convertible into dollars, an international trade depression recognised by the International Monetary Fund as causing serious disturbance to international payments equilibrium, and a notification of dollar scarcity under Article VII (1) of the I.M.F. Articles of Agreement.

The same day, in a letter to Sir Wilfrid Eady, Keynes summarised the situation.[18]

To SIR WILFRID EADY, *12 October 1945*

My dear Wilfrid,

Your letter of 6 October reached me promptly and it was useful to have this background to telegram 10094. As I said

[17] Keynes advised the Chancellor that the time was not ripe to begin detailed discussions on such a proposal. However, unless London rejected the proposal out of hand, which neither he nor Halifax advised, the negotiators should prepare a possible formula.
[18] He sent a similar letter to C. F. Cobbold at the Bank.

in my reply, that telegram was very helpful indeed. It was, in fact, very much what I hoped.

The Ministers seem to me to be moving along the right path and it is very important for us here to know just what form their various anxieties are taking. There was nothing in the telegram which embarrassed the Ambassador or me in our conversation.

There was, I think, only one point which was not clear to me. But as this was of minor importance I ignored it in the telegrams. The phrase in question was at the end of paragraph 10 of your telegram, namely, the following:– 'Finally for the purpose of all our rights the currency unit must be the U.K. together with the Colonies.' This conveyed to me no meaning whatever. Perhaps it arrived corrupt.

Another telegram which came in most useful was 10095 from the Chancellor to me about Preferences. This seemed to all of us here a particularly well drafted telegram. It had the particular advantage that I was able to show Vinson the actual text. The literary experts here allege that the metaphor in the last sentence indicates your hand.

On the state of the negotiations I have little to add to the somewhat abundant telegrams which have gone off in the last few days. I am not myself seriously concerned about the Preferences hurdle. Nor is the Ambassador. We shall find a way round it which avoids going over it. Liesching is more cautious about the prospects but I think that he really shares this view too. Most of the other commercial talks are making very good progress indeed. We simply overwhelm the Americans in debate on almost every point. The lion drove the unicorn all round the town. Old Harry White sits there with a cynical grin admiring the virtuosity of our team and the others seem to have gone off to the sub-committees with a definite intention to take up a more tenable position.

I hope there are not going to be unnecessary ructions about civil aviation. But at present we are pretty well out of touch over here and can form no clear idea what the trouble is about, if there is any. Of course that has been the chronic position of all of us in relation to this particular topic.

Thus, as you will already have appreciated, it all boils down to the terms of the assistance. None of us think there is any chance at all of a straight grant-in-aid. It could not hope to get through Congress in that form. When Aldrich talks about it in the way in which I see he impresses the Ministers, he really does it only to tease. I am still hopeful, however that with sufficient tenacity we can get an arrangement which limits the annual burden to $100 million.

I have a feeling that crystallisation is about to take place on the American side. At present they are divided amongst themselves between various alternatives. My hunch is that Vinson will at the last lap come down heavily in favour of some contribution which limits the burden to $100 million. There has been a lot of play acting and poker playing and Vinson, in my opinion, has been pretending to be much tougher than he really is. Partly, I fancy, to get in the position of being able to intervene with his own colleagues on our behalf with some effect when he thinks the psychological moment for crystallisation is approaching. Harry White has been our most ardent advocate behind the scenes in favour of the no-interest principle.

When I first sent you Harry White's scheme I did not take it too seriously. But it is undergoing various changes and I should not be surprised if it does not come into our hands in some semi-official tentative form early next week. I am hoping, therefore, that you are giving serious thought to it. Brand and Robbins and others here are enthusiastic for it and believe it is the best yet. Partly on the ground that it is cheapest for us and partly because it is the best packaging for Congress. My own feeling is that it contains some extremely good ideas which might play an important part. But there is a good deal in the detail which I should like to alter and, as

I think, improve. In particular, it seems to me important that we should not set up the other members of the sterling area with independent dollar reserves and that the arrangements should take the form of liberating the sterling area balances rather than setting aside dollars. But, of course, this makes it less superficially attractive to American eyes and it is difficult to argue against the contention that since the dollars will be completely free and untied it makes no significant difference as to how they are used in the future which way round you put it.

Life here is, as you may well suppose, strenuous. But I imagine it is no more strenuous than your own worries. We have the benefit of great physical comfort and, as the Fall comes on, of exquisite, exhilarating weather (my first two or three weeks here the heat and humidity were truly terrific). I am standing up to it all right and have only had one bad evening with heart symptoms which were due to over-eating on the top of over-working. It is difficult in the face of so much temptation and perpetual banquets to keep sufficiently austere. It is, of course, the variety of duties one has to perform here which make the working day so terrifically long. There are the negotiations proper and the constant advocacy they entail. Then there is the heavy routine and detail chiefly arising out of lend lease clean-up. All that, however, would be easily managed. There is a magnificent team here and the work and organisation go through without the slightest friction and with really very great efficiency. What puts the lid on is the colossal task of public relations which I have never had on me so heavy in any previous visit.

Apart from the Press, contact with which has been a much more important part of my business than usual, the Ambassador has thought it prudent on this occasion, and I am sure he is right, to seek far more intimate contact than I have ever had before with members of Congress. I am continuously seeing both Senators and Congressmen in batches. I think there can be no doubt it does good. The Senate is a manageable body and I think I shall be able to meet something like a quarter of them before I leave. But as to Congress, one has to keep to those who are said to be more influential, including a fair admixture of critics. In themselves these parties are enjoyable. I have a much higher opinion of the members of Congress than I had before. It is also perfectly clear to me that both parties have an immense will to agree with us (from that point of view the Russian impasse has done no harm). They have an insatiable thirst for information and personal contact. If you give them both there is almost nothing they will not accept. I cannot but believe that members of the Administration exaggerate the difficulty of handling Congress in the matter of our affairs. I repeat that in Congressmen of all shades of opinion, including some of those alleged to be most hostile, I find at bottom an immense desire to agree and to help if the thing can be put up to them in such a way as to appear reasonably plausible.

In more than one of your letters you said that you have mentioned your feeling that I shall have to come home to explain before the Ministers agree. I greatly hope that this can be avoided. It would upset the timetable most dangerously. The plan of the Administration is to tackle Congress hot foot immediately we are through. The present moment is probably more favourable than usual. The whole of the Press and a good part of Congress is too warmed up. To let it cool off might lose all. Also the whole timetable in relation to Bretton Woods, the Commercial Conference etc. would be thrown out. So when we have reached the last lap and the final best offer, do persuade them to be convinced by the telegraphed word.

Yours ever,
MAYNARD KEYNES

Will you pass this letter on to Bridges?

P.S. Wonders never cease. I attach the *Baltimore Sun* article. Our Press Service told us that an enquiry from the *Baltimore Sun* elicited the fact that their representative had been shown a document in the Treasury and taken through it and that this constituted the last part of the article. The first part he had concocted himself out of the other information. This being so, I thought I had better drop round to the Treasury today and have a chat with Harry White about some features in the *Baltimore Sun* version which I did not particularly like. What was my surprise to find that Harry had never heard of the article in the *Baltimore Sun*. He began by saying that it was impossible that they could have had the document. After sending for the article and reading it, he admitted that the journalist must have seen the document but that it was a confusion between two versions which had been under discussion and in any case was quite out of date in relation to what he himself was now pressing on Vinson. What a world, in which your subordinates leak the wrong draft without telling! Whilst Harry surprised me with the above, I surprised him by saying that I regarded $5 billion as the now accepted amount of assistance. According to him the Treasury have been urging this figure behind the scenes but it more or less failed in getting it and he warned me about getting a nasty surprise about the amount. He indicated that this had been a matter of discussion as lately as yesterday. Nevertheless, I think he must be wrong. I am sure that both Vinson and Clayton have definitely assumed $5 billion in all their recent talks with me. And in fact in his Press Conference (which, of course, Harry had not seen) the day before yesterday, Clayton actually mentioned $5 billion as the agreed figure. Again, what a world!

The same day, Eady attempted to provide Keynes with more London background as the Chancellor was replying to his cable reporting the conversation of 9 October with Mr Vinson and Mr Clayton.

From SIR WILFRID EADY, *12 October 1945*

My dear Maynard,

It may help you to have a snapshot of the Ministerial background behind the answer to 6733.

Ministers are not involving themselves in the technical details of these financial discussions, although the time will obviously come when it will be the details that may decide the matter. On the whole it is helpful to the officials that Ministers should be taking the simple view at this stage.

They have deep feelings on the matter. This partly arises from the natural disappointment that as they come to review the position of the country they do not see any early prospects of large improvement in the general standard of living. Also they have been influenced by certain personal factors. At Potsdam I think there is no doubt that Byrnes ran out on Bevin. The attempt of Clayton to trade Imperial Preference for money has disturbed them. As you know there is a strong Empire feeling in the Party as it is at present, and in any case they dare not concede to a flustered Opposition the rallying cry that the Labour Party once again are endangering the Empire!

Finally Winant's stupidity in trying to force a civil aviation agreement as part of the financial talks has affected them and led to Bevin using the word 'blackmail' to Winant.

Further, they are reluctant to admit that we are in any sense dependent upon the U.S. to get ourselves out of our present difficulties. There is no question that there is more reason for their attitude than there was during the previous five or six months, for they are much firmer on the subject of control of imports and foreign expenditure than were the Coalition or the Caretaker Government; and, so far as we can judge, Cripps[19] is really making the export drive into something effective. As you know it always has been a problem of securing the initial momentum. In a sellers' market, once that has been obtained, very large results will come quickly and they will be cumulative.

Therefore, although at the Treasury we know that we cannot get out of the next eighteen months without incurring a substantial debt to the U.S. probably of two billion dollars, there is rather more prospect that we shall work our own passage home than there was a few months ago.

The risks are, of course, serious because public opinion may not continue

---

[19] Richard Stafford Cripps (1889–1952), K.C. 1927, Kt 1930; Labour M.P. for East Bristol, 1931–50; Solicitor General, 1930–1; British Ambassador to U.S.S.R., 1940–2; Lord Privy Seal and Leader of House of Commons, 1942; Minister of Aircraft Production, 1942–5; President, Board of Trade, 1945–7; Minister for Economic Affairs, 1945–7; Chancellor of the Exchequer, 1947–50.

to stand in the present conditions. But personally I am rather doubtful whether there would be any real revolt, for whatever happens things are likely to get slightly better each month.

Therefore you will see that the draft reflects both feeling and determination. I thought that this would be a useful guide to you in knowing to what extent you felt you were bluffing and how far there were cards in your hand. I should say that you could play your hand more strongly than we had expected when you went over.

Also I think that Ministers are impressed by the evidence in the United States that it is in their interests not less than our own to do something to unjam the present jammed gears. How far that impression derives from inspired articles I don't know, but the articles by Lippmann, of which you sent us copies, have been shown to one or two Ministers. As you said, they were grand articles and they went to the heart of the matter.

My own anxiety is really over the sterling area deal. There is still some astonishing ignorance about the underlying facts of the sterling area in America. If the extracts from the article in the *Baltimore Sun* which have appeared today are reasonably accurate, they impute suggestions that the sterling area should give us a credit 'in their own currencies' for all their exports to the U.K. during the next five years, and that the total financial contribution from the sterling area to the U.K. must be not less than the total financial contribution made by the U.S.

Our negotiations with the sterling area are going to be difficult enough even if we have a free hand. Pethick, for example, does not believe that the Government of India would ever reach an agreement with us to write down any part of the balances: it would be politically impossible. Bevin made the apt comment that in that case they had better keep their sterling balances.

But if Clayton either tries to introduce too rigid a sterling area settlement, or, for political reasons, purports to make the contribution from the sterling area larger than makes sense, all the influences which support the sterling area would, I think, be gathered together to reject the proposal.

I scarcely need to lecture you on the point for you will be able to stop Clayton if he is going to be nonsensical. But one or two of your sentences in your telegrams about the American attitude to what we are to fix with the sterling area made me slightly apprehensive.

Once again this letter has to be rather hurried, but it may be useful to you.

I sigh for the wings of a dove, a dove large enough, that is, to take me more rapidly over the Atlantic than B.O.A.C., for a long talk with you and Brand would help me to understand quite a lot of things at which at present I can only guess. All I assure you is that I read with the greatest care everything that obviously has come with your personal hand on it and I do my best to follow you in imagination after all the teaching on this subject that you have given me during the last two years. I wish I knew some way of arranging that you should telegraph to me in a really private series if you found any of our more important telegrams to you clearly deficient in appreciation of the facts over there. Inevitably the ultimate responsibility for advice rests largely upon me, though nothing that has come to you represents my personal view enforced upon anybody else. If you should ever want to telegraph privately it may be that the Ambassador knows a way of ensuring that a telegram can be sent which will be delivered only to me without the inevitable distribution of copies. But, as you have often said, the only way to secure adequate distribution of a document in Whitehall is to mark it Highly Secret and the only way to ensure that nobody reads it at all is to send it en clair!

Yours
WILFRID

You must take all my letters like a bet 'Time of despatch as on post mark'. Events change so rapidly that I can only photograph at a snapshot.

The Chancellor's telegram stated that a loan on Clayton's terms of 9 October was unacceptable as the Government could not 'without reserve present it to all parties in Parliament and to our people as an equitable settlement, that, in Keynes'[s] phrase, it has in it the sweet breath of Justice'. In addition he did not see that there was a reasonable certainty of discharging the obligations involved. He also disliked the waiver proposal because of the possibility of continuous friction it involved. In summing up, he still stated his preference for a grant-in-aid with an additional loan. If this proved impossible he would fall back on an interest-free loan repayable over fifty years with no repayment for the first five to ten years.

Keynes and the Ambassador tried the Chancellor's instructions on Clayton and Vinson on 15 October, but 'made no progress whatever'. The atmosphere they said was 'gloomy and unconstructive'. They also reported that Clayton's mind appeared to be moving towards a credit of under $5 billion with an annual service of $100 million.

After a further meeting on 16 October, Keynes set out the position for the Chancellor.

To H. DALTON (*NABOB 177*), *18 October 1945*

1. After five meetings on form of financial aid between Vinson and Clayton on their side and Ambassador and myself on ours, it may be useful to take stock. This telegram is after consultation with Ambassador, Brand, Self, Liesching, Robbins and Hall-Patch and represents our collective opinion.

2. We came here in hope that we could persuade the U.S. to accept a broad and generous solution which took account of our financial sacrifices before U.S. entered the war and of President Roosevelt's principle of equality of sacrifice as well as of the post-war advantages to the U.S. of a settlement with us which would enable us to share world responsibilities with them free from undue financial pre-occupation and to join them in shaping the pattern of world commerce and currency on lines which would favour expansion and general prosperity.

3. We thought of such aid as being at the best a free grant, failing that a partial grant, and at the worst an interest-free loan. A settlement on any of these lines would be intelligible to the British public as being free from commercial considerations and a grand gesture of unforgetting regard to us from a partner with whom our comradeship in the war has been of a very special intimacy. The difference between a settlement on any of these lines and one which tries to imitate, however feebly, a normal banker's investment is much greater than is represented by any increase in our future financial burden.

4. If we are to believe what we are told by Vinson and Clayton repeatedly and with great emphasis the American Administration has rejected any such settlement. They have done this not because they themselves would resist but because of their honest and considered judgement that Congress and the public are not in the mood to stand for it. No one pretends that public opinion is well informed about the real issues. But public opinion with the usual exceptions is not

hostile. There is widespread goodwill and a desire to help. But in this business country where it is a moral duty and not merely a self-regarding act to make any money which the traffic will bear and the law allow, some imitation of a normal banking transaction is necessary if the moral principles of the country are not to be affronted. If the elements of a trade are present, the American way of life requires that at least the appearance of a trade should emerge. Thus precisely those elements which will spoil the flavour to us are necessary to make the result palatable here. At the moment, moreover, there is a phase of withdrawal from the large-scale assistance all round which was under discussion only a short time ago. Retrenchment is in the air. Congress is also occupied with Vinson's proposals for tax reduction and, as it happens, the total cost of the relief to the general tax-payer now under discussion, namely five billions, is the same size as the aid for which we ask, so that the latter seems much larger than it would in other contexts.

5. There is so much goodwill in most quarters and such wide appreciation of the larger issues in all responsible quarters that it is difficult to believe they do not under-rate what bold and eloquent leadership could do. But you must understand that such leadership is just what is lacking in this present Administration from the President downwards. Their policy is to keep in close touch with the opinion and desires of Congress, following rather than leading, and flavouring to taste any pill which it is indispensable to administer.

6. We cannot demand what they tell us it does not lie within their power to give. It may be that the type of settlement which the late President would have delighted to invent and to put through is altogether out of character with the general lines which the present Administration feels compelled to follow. We must not be misled by hopes which only the gay, generous and brilliant spirit could have realised for us.

7. If this diagnosis is correct we must think again substituting prose for poetry. Our disappointment does not justify

us in doing perhaps irreparable injury to our own body politic and economic or in shattering the basis of day-to-day Anglo-American co-operation. We must do the best we can.

8. Before turning to the possibilities of prose, it may be well to break off to insert a necessary qualification to all the foregoing. In this country nothing is certain until the very last moment. We know that Clayton and Vinson and other leaders of the Administration are determined to bring these negotiations to a successful conclusion. The public is being deliberately fed through the Press with the expectation of success. Even a delay in settlement would seriously disturb their timetable and upset the Treasury Department policy of Bretton Woods and the State Department policy of a Commercial Conference on which each has set its heart. To satisfy us may lay them open to criticism.

But if they fail to satisfy us they may encounter even more criticism. If we stand our ground to the last, it is not impossible that we may not yet get an offer which at present does not appear to be in sight. Do not, therefore, suppose that there is any defeatism in your mission here. But we have to be prepared for either alternative. Time is now running short and all is set for a conclusion within about a fortnight. It will be useless and injurious to drag on much longer than that. It is, therefore, important that we should have your early guidance on whether prose will be acceptable in the last resort.

9. Clayton frankly admits the force of our case. His point is that he must dress the thing up to look as ordinary as possible, to escape notice wearing a business suit. Subject to this necessity he appeals to us to help him in finding a way which is as acceptable to us as possible. When we remark as we are constantly forced to do, that nothing will induce us to repeat the experience of last time's war debts and sign an obligation we have no confidence we can meet, he accepts our position and offers us any escape clause in reason to provide against this risk.

10. When we try to make precise the burden we think we

can support we find ourselves on treacherous ground. We have been again pressed recently to explain exactly how we arrive at five billions as the measure of what we need and what sort of balance of trade we expect to emerge with at the end of five years or whenever it is that the transitional period terminates. An outline of our answer is given in my next following telegram. It will be seen from this that an eventual balance requires that our external income from exports and net invisibles shall be of the order of nearly seven billion dollars or say six and a half billion at the very lowest. We say that we are able to assume a debt liability of 100 millions which is 1½ per cent of this but see no reasonable hope of being able to meet 150 millions which would require a further expansion of our overseas income or curtailment of our overseas expenditure by less than another 1 per cent. This obviously lays us open to the accusation of possessing extensive and peculiar information about the future.

11. Our best answer is, of course, that what really scares us is the possibility of owing to the U.S. an amount of money which is enormous in relation to our prospective exports to them in conditions where, for all we know now, multilateral clearings may have broken down. Very well, says Clayton, draft a clause to protect yourselves against this possibility. We admit that commerce in the post-war world either goes all right from our point of view or it does not. In the first case 150 millions may be practicable and in the second case 100 millions may be scarcely possible. Nevertheless failing the solution of a free grant one has to draw the line somewhere and they must not try to involve us in the fallacy of sorites. Very well says Clayton, draft a clause under which your liability will be related to your capacity. We do not want to embarrass you, he adds, but we want to be able to say that we have reached an elastic arrangement which duly protects the interests of both sides.

12. You will be aware how reluctant I have been to enter

on the slippery path of escape clauses. But we all think that the time has come when we cannot reasonably excuse ourselves from making some response to Clayton's generous and not unreasonable suggestions. In refusing to do so we are in truth still grasping at the inelectable poetry and refusing to come to earth in well-reasoned prose. Yet from his own point of view and from ours too when once we have accepted the inevitability of prose, Clayton is generous and is not unreasonable. If you had sat as many hours as the Ambassador and I have sat declaiming all our best poetry before an audience, not indeed unresponsive to those strains in their own hearts, but never deviating from the rejoinder that Congress, they feel quite sure, will be deaf to them, you would see our difficulty in persisting with a refusal to come down to earth.

13. Against the risk of a breakdown in multilateral arrangements and the scarcity of dollars, I have already sent a suggestion in paragraph 2 of telegram 6772 which for convenience of reference I repeat in the next paragraph.

14. The Government of the United Kingdom shall be entitled to approach the Government of the United States for a deferment of the annual instalment of payment due in any year in any of the following circumstances. In the event of deferment the amount due in respect of amortisation shall be postponed so as not to increase the amount due in the years immediately following but by an appropriate extension of the period of repayment.

(a) *A breakdown of multilateral clearing.* In the event of less than 75 per cent of the foreign currencies earned by British trade being freely convertible into dollars.

(b) *An international depression of trade.* In the event of general and prolonged depression of world trade acknowledged by the International Monetary Fund as constituting a serious disturbance of the equilibrium of international payments.

(c) *Scarcity of dollars.* In the event of the International

Monetary Fund having notified under Article VII (I) of the International Monetary Fund that a general scarcity of dollars is developing.

15. As a measure of our capacity to pay more than 100 millions I can think of nothing better than some version of what I have already suggested in paragraph 7 of telegram 6733. The terms might then be as in the next paragraph. I should add that Clayton has not yet seen this suggestion but we could offer it in response to his request that we should propose a suitable safeguard.

16. A loan of five billions of which the capital and interest would be repaid in 50 instalments of 150 millions a year commencing five years hence of which 100 millions in each year would be attributed to capital repayment and 50 millions to interest. Assuming that all fifty instalments of interest are paid this would work out actuarially at the equivalent of about 1·7 per cent interest per annum. But in addition we should receive the advantage of a waiver clause by which the 50 millions representing an instalment of interest would be finally waived in any year in which the volume of our visible home-produced exports did not reach a level of 750 million pounds in terms of pre-war prices. Alternatively and much better if they would accept it, the contract might say that the 50 millions for interest would only become payable in years when the critical figure had been reached.

17. Since we could in this case almost certainly afford the extra 50 millions, the plan is on the face of it reasonable as well as generous. When our exports did not reach the critical figure the loan would become interest-free. Moreover the criterion is definite and is not really open to the criticism of paragraph 13 of your telegram 10274. Can anyone honestly argue that the difference between this and a loan which is interest-free in all circumstances is so material that even in the last resort we should prefer a breakdown of the present discussions with all that means to our standard of life, to our

hopes of recovery, to our position in the world and to Anglo-American friendship?

18. The only alternatives which may still be worth considering are mentioned in the next two paragraphs. The first of these is before the Americans and has probably been finally rejected but we are not quite sure that it has been. The second is a new idea, not yet put forward.

19. A grant of 2 billions and a credit up to 3 billions at 2 per cent interest, instalments of capital repayment and of interest beginning five years hence.

20. A loan of 4 billions repayable by fifty-five annual instalments of 100 millions beginning five years hence which would cost, allowing for deferment, the equivalent of about 1 per cent interest, supplemented by a ten years' option on a banking credit of a further 1 (or 2) billion at 2 per cent interest.

21. The ball now lies with the Americans and they may make a counter-proposal shortly. We do not look forward to it with much hope. We fear that it may take the form of a reduction in the amount of the aid whilst keeping the annual service at 100 millions. But it is just possible that we shall be agreeably disappointed. We repeat that the American side are just as keen as we are to reach a satisfactory conclusion and are as depressed as we are at the deadlock.

22. In conclusion we have naturally given some thought to the question whether there is a way out for us by obtaining a moderate amount here and now to meet our immediate necessities on commercial terms without any commitment about Bretton Woods, commercial policy and sterling area. I have little to add on this to what I have said in my telegram 6610. Those of us here who in recent weeks have been studying intensively our balance of trade prospects believe

(a) That we cannot reduce our cumulative balance of trade deficit below 3 or 4 billions at the very lowest without great and almost insupportable sacrifices at home and abroad.

(*b*) That it is an illusion to suppose that the sterling area can carry on as in time of war.

(*c*) That we cannot hope, therefore, to get a net contribution on capital account much exceeding, say, 1 billion dollars at the utmost from all other outside sources put together.

(*d*) That our prospects are poor of even a small Government loan here without any commitment about Bretton Woods, commercial policy or the sterling area.

(*e*) That we should soon have involved ourselves in as heavy a debt charge as what we are now boggling at.

(*f*) That the measure of disruption of our economic life at home and of our external relations, which would be inevitable if a comprehensive settlement with America fails, can hardly be exaggerated.

23. An agreement for 5 billions would not in fact involve us in any excessive future burden if in practice we can get on with much less. For we should be under no compulsion to draw it all. Yet it would have given us the confidence and security which is indispensable if we are to restore our position in the world.

24. If our present friendly and intimate relations with the American side are brought to an end and we announce that we are tired of being pushed about and would prefer to stand by ourselves without the entanglements of Anglo-American partnership or agreement in the economic field, so much will be disastrously changed over so wide a field and for a period to which no-one can set a term, that we cannot bring ourselves to contemplate it. It may be as difficult to convey to you the complex atmosphere of Washington as it is to make vivid to the Administration here the disappointment of London. But the Americans would remain convinced that they had offered us aid on a scale and on terms which they would not dream of offering to anyone else, and which was only possible in remembrance of past comradeship and common sacrifice and in hope of furthering common aims in future. Our rejection

of it would undoubtedly be felt here as just one more reason for yielding to the temptation to withdraw into themselves with all the incalculable consequences of that to the future of the world.

To H. DALTON (*NABOB 178*), *18 October 1945*

My immediately preceding telegram.

1. Following are details referred to in my preceding telegram of the further revised explanations which we have given to the Americans why we need five billions. All figures in $ million.

2. Our pre-war balance on the average of 1936–8 worked out as follows:–

Imports	3,500	Exports	1,950
		Net invisibles	1,350
		Deficit	200
			3,500

3. Our target is a hypothetical post-war balance in the year immediately after the transition as follows:–

Imports	6,500	Export	5,750
Overseas Government expenditure	250	Net invisibles	1,250
Available to pay sterling area and U.S	250		
	7,000		7,000

Imports, exports and freights are at an assumed price level double pre-war.

4. Our estimate for 1946 also at prices assumed approximately double pre-war as follows:–

Imports	5,200	Exports	2,600
Overseas war expenditure (net)	1,200	Net invisibles	800
		Deficit	3,000
	6,400		6,400

5. On this basis our deficit may work out as follows:-

1946	3,000
1947	1,250
1948	500
1949 ⎫ 1950 ⎭	250
	———
	5,000

6. In addition to the above we have a liability for the settlements of lend lease, etc. to the United States say 500 and a net release of sterling balances to the sterling area 1946–50 of say 800 to 1,000, making grand total of say 6,500. Towards this we can perhaps look to Canada for 500 and 800 to 1,000 of the adverse balance in 1946 might be added to the aggregate of sterling area balances brought into the general settlement.

7. There remains the possible use of our gold and dollar reserves and our remaining capital assets. Also perhaps some small loans from Sweden etc. We argued, however, that we need all these to cover withdrawals of sterling balances held outside the sterling area. In particular withdrawals by European countries during the transition which we can scarcely refuse. Thus we could not reckon on any significant net contribution from these miscellaneous sources.

8. Accordingly our final requirement from the U.S. would be five billions. This represents some reduction on our previous request since we are in effect assuming that it will cover 500 for settlement of lend lease.

9. Admittedly if all goes well we may do better than this. The Americans claim that the final deficit should be at least one billion less. We reply that we hope that they are right and agree they may be. But we cannot enter into commitments about the sterling area etc. without a margin. We shall draw no more than we require but we cannot be expected to enter into the commitments they hope from us unless we have elbow room up to five billion.

On 20 October, Keynes reported another conversation with the Americans.

To H. DALTON (*NABOB 191*), *20 October 1945*

1. Ambassador, Brand and I have seen Vinson and Clayton again to hear their proposals. These took just the form which in para. 21 of NABOB 177 we warned you they might, only worse.

2. Vinson told us rather solemnly that there had been a further meeting of the Top Committee on the American side and also of the National Advisory Council under the Bretton Woods Act, of which the membership largely overlaps, and that both bodies were unanimously of the opinion that the best offer they could make us which they believed Congress would accept was as follows.

3. A loan of three and a half billions at 2 per cent interest plus whatever is required to clean-up lend lease on 3(c) terms. The first instalment of service on the loan could be deferred five years and subsequent instalments of service could be arranged if we wished on an ascending scale beginning say at 90 millions and not exceeding 110 millions before 25 years, provided the interest worked out in the end to the actuarial equivalent of 2 per cent. The lend lease accommodation on 3(c) terms would be at 2⅜ per cent, the capital repayable over 30 years beginning next year, that is to say the same as for other people.

4. In reply to my question whether they would expect us on the basis of this limited aid to enter into the same commitments in regard to the sterling area as those we had previously discussed, they answered that they would.

5. Some time was wasted in a confused discussion how they had arrived at three and a half billions as sufficient. The answer seemed to depend partly on sheer confusion in Clayton's mind, partly on double counting and largely on assuming that we could run down our gold and dollar reserves

557

from an assumed figure of one and three-quarter billions at the end of this year to the bedrock figure of one billion at the end of the transitional period. Thus we should leave the transitional period stript and without available resources for the precarious years beyond, but with our commitments unabated.

6. In spite of the air of finality with which this announcement was made I can scarcely believe that they expected us to accept it. I replied that we would of course report this offer to London. But Ambassador and I warned them that there could be only one answer. We could not imagine that an agreement was possible on these lines; yet a failure to reach agreement must have dangerous and even tragic consequences. I asked whether their advice would be that we should adjourn without more said, or that I should prepare for an early return to London or that we should try to think of something quite different. After an anecdote from Vinson about how hosts behaved to guests in his native Kentucky smiles returned to faces and there was a general agreement that we should try to think of something quite different.

7. I ventured therefore, and I hope that in all the circumstances you will not blame me, to return to Clayton's proposal of a five billion loan against a 50 year annuity of 150 millions beginning five years hence with a waiver clause for the interest.

8. As regards the amount I urged that in view of the commitments we are asked to accept we must start with a figure which was adequate in our own judgment. If we did not need so much we certainly should not draw it and they must trust us so to act. They replied that whilst previously they had talked in terms of five billions they were increasingly concerned about the difficulty of putting so high a figure through Congress. This was chiefly due, we think, to the remarks of Senator George already reported to you, who is chairman of the Senate Committee which will deal with the

legislation to provide aid to us, though they admitted they themselves were surprised that George had spoken that way. In any case it would help them a little if we could talk in terms of four and a half billions plus whatever is required to clean-up lend lease. No harm in this, provided it is clear that the lend lease addition is on the same terms as, and is incorporated with, the main loan. I emphasise this because Vinson mentioned that he was now hearing for the first time of any suggestion that the lend lease finance should be handled outside the 3(c) terms. When we reminded him that this had been already settled in our favour, he said that this was news to him but readily withdrew if the question had been already fixed otherwise. It is not unnatural that Vinson and also Clayton should know very little on the lend lease side. Angell, the last survivor of the senior F.E.A. officials who are acquainted with our affairs is leaving next week to replace Pauley on the reparations commission which is good for Waley but bad for us, all the others having resigned in the course of the month since I arrived. On the lend lease end our party faces a new audience every week. In other respects as well as in this you must take it as basic that your negotiators have to do their best in an environment which must be difficult to understand in London and will indeed again become unintelligible to us when we are back, although when one lives in it, deep in the heart of Texas, or rather in this case, half in Texas and half in Kentucky, it comes to seem part of the landscape and even to have some advantages.

9. They urged, therefore, that it would help them very much if we could keep the figure down to say four billions plus the clean-up of lend lease. If you can meet them on this, it will certainly help a good deal. For my part I think we need elbow room and would be reluctant to cut the figure at any rate at this stage. There is also a danger that the service of the lower amount would be kept the same as for the higher, though this risk may become less when we have

made more progress with drafting the exact terms. Perhaps in the end we might take an option on the last million on rather different conditions though this might not fit in with the waiver provisions discussed below.

10. We then turned to the nature of the waiver. They said that they had abandoned this line of settlement because I had so firmly rejected the whole idea of an escape clause. I admitted that this was so both on instructions from London and because we all felt a strong moral objection to such clauses if there was any means of avoiding them. I said that I was still under the same instructions. Nevertheless in an effort to break the jam, perhaps we might explore the possibilities a little further quite off the record.

11. First of all, they corrected their previous offer by substituting 159 millions for 150 millions as the fixed annual service on 5 billions. Clayton explained that their actuaries had worked out that this was the correct figure required in order to yield 2 per cent interest after presenting us with five years deferment. When Clayton spoke previously of 150 millions he warned us that this was subject to calculations on which his actuaries were at work and was his own first shot. Thus in using this figure as the basis of our own calculation, as in paragraph 16 of NABOB 177, we were giving it greater exactitude than has proved to be warranted. On the other hand we did not appreciate or allow in our calculation for the fact that no interest is debited against us in respect of the first five years. In fact, an annual service charge of 159 millions for fifty years, beginning after five years, is actuarially equivalent to an interest rate of 1·6 per cent over the whole term of the loan, which is slightly less than what we told you before.

12. After emphasising that I was going quite beyond my instructions, I then tried on them the type of waiver clause outlined in paragraph 16 of NABOB 177. They immediately expressed a lively interest and said that something on these

lines might be acceptable. The reaction against the strain of the first half of the interview seemed by now to be clearing the atmosphere. Having delivered their mouthful, they were now wanting to help if they could.

13. Clayton began by wanting to take our balance of payments as the criterion. But Vinson soon saw the serious objections to this and supported my alternative. Clayton remained emphatic, however, that the criterion of our external income must include our net invisible income. The absence of this item would lead to suspicions. Americans rely greatly on future tourist traffic for filling the gap. They calculate that with 100,000 Americans on the average of the year (presumably in Oxford) each spending at the rate of £500 a year, the whole problem of what we are now discussing is solved with something to spare. I replied that the only real objection to including our net invisible income was the lack of a sound statistical estimate for it but admitted that it might be good for us to have to improve our statistical departments.

14. The upshot was that they might be prepared to recommend and thought they could defend an arrangement by which we should repay the capital of a loan by fifty equal annual instalments, beginning five years hence, and would pay an additional fixed annual sum, by way of interest, over the same fifty years, calculated so as to be equivalent to 2 per cent over the whole period. But the latter sum would be payable in those years only in which our exports and net invisible income exceeded 7 billion dollars at a price level double pre-war, or say pounds 875 million at the pre-war value of money—this part of the annuity being finally waived in years in which this figure was not reached. This is only a way of splitting up a fixed annual service charge, which has the effect of deferring interest and speeding up repayment in the earlier years, and conversely in the later. Actuarially it comes to the same thing in the end as a normal sinking fund

table. Perhaps you may think it would suit us better to propose the latter, under which the capital instalment in the first year would be 59 and the interest 100 the former rising and the latter falling as time goes on, since in the earlier and, presumably, more difficult years, we should thus be entitled to waive a greater proportion of the annual payment. If so, I do not believe that they have yet formed any fixed views on the method to be followed so long as the total annual instalment is the same. On this please see the draft to be telegraphed later.

15. After consideration of the above the Ambassador and the others named in paragraph 1 of NABOB 177 have nothing to add to the reasons given in that telegram why we think this proposal deserves your consideration, except that we are now more convinced than before that nothing better than this is on the map. For example the alternatives in paragraphs 19 and 20 of NABOB 177 are now, in our opinion, out. The Americans seem quite convinced that they must offer Congress what purports to be a two per cent loan but think it quite defensible from their angle that the payment of this interest should depend on our full recovery in the sense of our having reached our post-transitional target of external income. Indeed who can argue that the extra amount we are now resisting will not be a very small matter when once we have accomplished the tremendous task of reaching the target. Moreover, we obtain subsequent relief in any year in which our position again deteriorates. I should add that the Americans propose over and above the waiver clause in the contract to take unilateral powers to themselves in the proposed legislation authorising the executive to waive or defer the capital instalments or otherwise modify the terms in our favour in any future circumstances in which they deem this to be advisable.

16. At the end of the meeting reported above Vinson and Clayton asked that we should put our ideas in writing. I said

that I could go no further without guidance from London and it was agreed not to meet again until we had heard from you. We recommend that we be authorised to continue discussion on the above lines, except that we shall put the target of our external income at not less than seven and a half millions [billions?] rather than seven. See my next following telegram. We should make it plain that the more precise version we were giving them in response to their invitation to explore the possibilities of a waiver clause was not a formal proposal from you and was in common with our negotiations on other issues without commitment.

To H. DALTON (*NABOB 192*), *19 October 1945*

My immediately preceding telegram.

1. Graham Towers came here yesterday at our suggestion since we thought his advice would be valuable. At a talk with Ambassador, Brand and myself we took him pretty fully into our confidence. He began by expressing great disappointment with the American attitude which seemed to him to fall seriously short of the requirements of the case. He entirely shared our view that this was a case for a grant-in-aid. He felt however, that to break off because we could not get a grant-in-aid would lay us open to great criticism by the public here. Nevertheless he would not for his part be inclined to go beyond an interest-free loan.

2. Subsequently however on hearing of Clayton's proposal for a waiver clause and my suggestion as to the form which waiver clause could take, he changed his opinion to the extent of advising that we should be on weak ground in refusing this provided the target figure for our external income was high enough.

3. In his view we should talk in terms of at least seven and a half for the aggregate of our exports and net invisible income rather than seven billions. Since the latter figure

would not even allow a return to our pre-war level of imports, he would argue that a settlement which assumed a level of imports below pre-war even after a substantial period could scarcely be described as a policy of expansion.

4. As on former occasions we all felt that Towers' advice coming from the background of his experience on this continent was invaluable. You will see that in the draft I am following his advice as regards the target figure.

5. This afternoon Towers is exploring the atmosphere behind the scenes and will be seeing amongst others White and Clayton. I am sure we can rely on his complete discretion in the light of the confidences we have given him.

Two days later he summed up the situation in a letter to his mother.

From a letter to F. A. KEYNES, *21 October 1945*

...We have reached a point in our negotiations where we can get no further without instructions from London and it seems likely that a few days will elapse before these instructions arrive...

This has been the roughest assignment I have ever had. We are now at the critical stage. On the face of it things don't look too good. But it is almost as essential for them as for us to reach an acceptable conclusion. So I remain fairly optimistic and, with the onset of senility, don't worry anything like as much as I used to...

On 22 October, Keynes set out the situation to the Governor of the Bank, who with the Chancellor's approval had sent Keynes a cable dated 16 October containing his own suggestions.[20]

[20] Catto's telegram, which R. H. Brand noted 'indicates how differently one can think about things in London and Washington', suggested that the Americans grant an interest-free credit for $5 billion repayable over fifty years, that Britain would repay at once to the United States her First World War debt liabilities, worked out free of interest and scaled down to $1 billion, that the two countries settle on a nominal figure for the settlement of lend lease, and that Britain promise to liberalise the sterling area as quickly as possible, begin sterling balances negotiations and negotiate with the United States on commercial policy.

To LORD CATTO, *22 October 1945*

Dear Mr Governor,

Many thanks for your telegram. I will bear your suggestion in mind if the problem looks like moving in a direction where it will be helpful. At present, rather surprisingly, our real difficulties are not along those lines. Not once has the problem of the old war debts been mentioned to me either by the members of the Administration with whom we are in conference, or by the Press with which I have had frequent contact, or by the many Congressmen and Senators to whom I have given the opportunity of asking me questions. Not once has this come up. And so I feel that this deeply sleeping dog one would let lie. It has not yet emitted a whimper, far less a bark.

On the other hand it is precisely on our agreeing to at least the appearance of interest that the Americans are adamant. For my part, I am not persuaded that bold leadership could not put through an interest-free loan. But that, one has to admit, is not their view and they must be the judges. Their whole loan tactics at the moment are that they must be in a position to declare that the loan is one at two per cent interest. Having done that, as you will have gathered from my telegrams, they are not unsympathetic to the conclusion that this must not be allowed to lead to a position where we are in fact in difficulties about paying.

Of all the various lines of argument the Ambassador and I have tried, the one to which I find them always readily responsive is that we must not repeat the experience of last time's war debts and they must not press us to sign a bond we are not confident we can meet. They never dispute this contention. They add, that for their own part, there is nothing that they are more anxious to avoid than any sort of appearance of default. They agree with us that that would be fraught with all sorts of evil consequences and could lead to nothing but bad. But, they go on, surely we can find ways to prevent this from arising. If you will draft your own version of an escape clause we will do our best to accept it. One is on difficult ground when one insists that we must have the liability fixed once and for all now, and that it should not be made dependent in any way on our future capacity. If we do obtain a grant-in-aid the question, of course, would not arise; but that, I am afraid, is simply off the map.

However, you will have seen the whole current state of the negotiations set out in much greater detail in my telegrams of a few days ago. My own feeling is that if we can get anything nearly as good as I am asking permission to discuss without commitment, we shall have done the best possible. I am a long way from being sure that we can carry them as far as that.

The above does not mean that I have departed from the view which I expressed before I left London that if necessary we must break off. The only qualification I would now add is that I believe that an interval of time would so upset the time table as to make our chance worse and not better, unless we are prepared to break off for quite an appreciable time. Even then, if we come back in a state of still greater emergency than we are in now, I should be surprised if we should get better terms. The main point that I now feel is this. If we do break off we must choose very carefully the grounds. We must be able to publish that we have offered and failed to obtain proposals which will strike, not indeed hostile opinion here, but the opinion of our friends as fair and reasonable. It would be only too easy to break off on grounds which in London would seem irrefutable but would be regarded here as fatal even by our best friends.

I should add, as I hope I have made plain in the telegrams, that I am not feeling at all a defeatist or unduly pessimistic. There is a lot of poker playing still going on. Unless we chose our ground badly they cannot afford to break off without success any more than we can. There will be an immense urge to agree with us and at the last moment everything may change quite suddenly. But that will be contingent on our having done our very utmost to meeting their genuine difficulties.

For after living here some weeks, one cannot doubt the genuine difficulties with which Vinson and Clayton will be faced when they try to sell the settlement to Congress. During the whole of my visit here there has not been a single major proposal that the President has put to Congress that Congress has accepted. Once we have come to terms with Vinson and Clayton they will have to fight on our behalf like tigers if they are to have any hope of victory. That is why they are so anxious both to know their case inside and out and also to have a case which they can put forward in a form which they judge to be not too vulnerable.

The outcome will turn on appearances and of course the curse is that appearances which help here do just the opposite at home.

I wish I could have a proper talk with you. If it were more practicable for me to fly I should have made the effort to pay a brief visit to London. But as it is, by sea with sailings as they now are, I should probably be away the best part of three weeks and that would hopelessly upset the timetable at which the Americans are aiming.

The strain on one's nerves and strength is of course considerable and it will be a great relief when it is all over. But I am standing it pretty well. Lydia exercises iron discipline about diet, ice-bags, rests and sleeping. She joins me in sending best love to you and your wife. To which I add affectionate greetings to all at the Bank. The great transmogrification seems to have gone through splendidly. My very great personal congratulations on the way you have handled it. Nothing could have happened with more dignity and less loss of what is real. I am hopeful that the Bank will be entering on a new career not less honourable or useful than what has gone before.

Yours ever,

[copy initialled] M.K.

On 23 October, Keynes reported that White's plan was showing no further signs of life and that London should not worry about it any longer. The next day he sent London a summary of a longer paper, doubting Rowe-Dutton's conclusion that the dollar would be scarce after the war. After several re-workings, the paper became Keynes's article 'The Balance of Payments of the United States'.[21]

On 27 October, after a meeting of Ministers the previous day, the Chancellor replied to Keynes's cables of 19 and 20 October. He suggested two plans which he believed might be acceptable to Parliament. The first, Plan A, was for a loan of $2·5 billion at 1 per cent for fifty years with an option on a further interest-free loan of $2 billion as backing for an offer to sterling area countries to make sterling freely available for current expenditures outside the area. This plan also foresaw some writing off of sterling balances as a contribution to the costs of the war, asked for a waiver along the lines of Keynes's earlier suggestions.[22] and committed the British Government to take the Bretton Woods Agreements to Parliament for approval and act as a sponsor of an International Trade Conference. The second, Plan B, suggested that Britain borrow $2·5 billion on commercial terms with no commitments beyond servicing the debt, commercial terms being 2 per cent for fifty years with repayment beginning after five years.[23] The Mission's instructions were to push for Plan A for all they were worth. They were assured that the Cabinet would accept 2 per cent interest on the $2·5 billion in Plan A, if the sterling area option was interest-free.

The London telegrams left Keynes, according to one of the other members of the delegation, 'white with rage and talking about resigning'. By the next day, according to the same source, 'M. had thought it out very well and after writing and destroying one or two vitriolic drafts produced very good ones'. Discussion followed as Keynes proposed simply to go ahead with Plan A and ignore Plan B, telling London it was a non-starter. Eventually Keynes and Halifax replied in more detail to the cables suggesting that 'the realities of the position B are fatally misunderstood in London'. The plan, they explained, was beyond the bounds of any practical possibility, as lend lease would come only on 3(c) terms (thirty years at 2⅜ per cent) and the only other assistance available was in the form of Export-Import Bank loans for twenty years at 3 per cent. Thus a credit

---

[21] *Economic Journal*, LVI (222), June 1946, *JMK*, Vol. XXVII. See above p. 536.

[22] The meeting of Ministers had deprecated any further discussion of the terms of a waiver.

[23] These terms were better than those currently offered by the Export-Import Bank. The figures suggested indicate that Ministers expected the lend lease clean-up to cost $500 million, as the meeting thought in terms of a total debt of $3 billion.

of $2·5 billion and a Lend Lease settlement of $500 million would cost $228 million per annum starting in 1946. However, they suggested that $2·5 billion was probably beyond the capacity of the Export-Import Bank and that the best London could hope for, if the Americans did their best, was the lend lease settlement plus $500 million at once with the possibility of another $500 million later.

However, Keynes and Lord Halifax pointed to the dangers of raising Plan B. If they did so, they continued,

we must expect a dangerous hardening of opinion in all quarters here. In American eyes we should be deliberately preferring the policy of separate economic blocs. Their first reaction might be just to sit, content to allow the financial pressure against us to develop under its own steam.

They agreed to put Plan A to the Americans, but warned London to be prepared to think of the next move.

Subsequently the mission put off seeing the Americans on Plan A until further elucidation was available from London on several points and Professor Robbins and Mr Hall-Patch, both of whom had returned to London, were able to provide a more detailed elucidation of the position. In particular, they questioned the advantage of the small change in British payments under Plan A as compared with Clayton's offer, $23 million per annum; as against the generous American waiver proposal based on ability to pay they suggested that the American waiver be preferred to Keynes's suggestion based on the United States' ability to receive payment. They also suggested that they be allowed to proceed with Plan A, so dressed up, as quickly as possible, so as to catch Congress before it adjourned, this being the time regarded as the Americans as the most propitious.

While the delegation waited for instructions, matters were more or less in suspense. Keynes summed up his mood in a note to his mother.

From a letter to F. A. KEYNES, *4 November 1945*

...Before the end of this week I shall know where I am. The crisis will come in the next few days. On the whole I am not unhopeful. But my difficulties in bringing London along to a reasonable compromise are not less than those in moving Washington. And our business, taken as a whole, is of enormous complexity. Last week was very worrying and I could not see how I was to extricate myself from all the nets of obstinacy and misunderstanding which were closing in from all quarters. But now it looks much better...

The team has pulled grandly together. Halifax and I work together like brothers. A week ago we sent two faithful ones back to London to handle the situation there. Obstinate and tiresome though the Americans are, they are full of good will and good intention and kind nature. What a country of optimists!

One of the matters under discussion while the Mission awaited further instructions from London was future arrangements for the sterling area. On 5 November, Keynes sent a proposal to Dr White, before London had fully agreed to its contents.

To H. D. WHITE, *5 November 1945*

My dear Harry,

As time is passing, I am glad to be able to say that I am now free to let you have the draft on sterling area arrangements which, as I mentioned to you the other day, I had prepared and sent to London. This has not yet been finally cleared with London; but I hope it will be in a day or two, though I gather from a telephone conversation that they may have some corrections. Meanwhile, in accordance with your suggestion, it may save time if you can look it through.

This draft follows very closely the arrangements I outlined in my original discourse on the subject, except that there is no longer a definite mention of the target for writing down the sterling balances. We have, of course, a much greater interest than you have in making this as large as possible. But London holds, very reasonably, that it is not possible to quantify the result before one begins discussions, and any attempt to do so might seriously prejudice the negotiations. A great variety of factors will have to be taken into account and one also has to allow, of course, for some members of the sterling area deciding to stand out; though, if this happens, it is more likely, in my opinion, to be on political grounds than on any sound calculation of self-interest.

I am enclosing half a dozen copies. Something on the lines of this might be incorporated in an exchange of letters, which should be the best way of handling it. If you have any points to raise on this I suggest I should come round for a talk as soon as you are ready for me,—say this afternoon.

Yours ever,
MAYNARD KEYNES

STERLING AREA ARRANGEMENTS

1. Under present arrangements the accumulated sterling balances of the sterling area countries and their current earnings outside the sterling area are available to be spent freely within the sterling area. But residents in the sterling area may only transfer their balances outside the area with the approval of the exchange control of their country of residence. Exchange controls in different parts of the area are autonomous and there are no written agreements between them; but they have agreed to pursue, broadly, a common policy. Transfers outside the area for capital purposes are, generally speaking disallowed. Personal remittances, including expenses of travel, are scrutinised in respect of their amount and their purpose. Exchange is provided to pay for any imports for which an import license has been obtained, and it is, therefore, through import licensing that control is effectively exercised over purchases abroad.

2. Since some foreign currencies have been in much shorter supply than others, it has been inevitable, if accounts are to be balanced, that the system of import licensing should be exercised so as to discriminate in favour of those currencies which are in free supply and against those which are in scarce supply. Intermediate between the sterling area currencies themselves and the so-called 'hard' currencies (especially the

U.S. dollar) which are in specially short supply or can only be obtained against gold, there are a number of countries chiefly in South America with which 'payments' agreements have been signed, whereby these countries agree to hold sterling balances without definite limit, and the currencies of which are, therefore, in relatively free supply. More recently a fourth class of agreement has been evolved, chiefly with the liberated countries of Europe, partly similar to the 'payments' agreements but with definite limitations to the reciprocal agreement to hold balances in one another's currencies.

3. Since the members of the sterling area have followed their long-standing practice of passing over their earnings of 'hard' currencies to the London exchange authorities and drawing their requirements of these currencies from London, in this way feeding and drawing upon a 'pool', this system, as it affects the U.S. has come to be described as 'the sterling area dollar pool'.

4. The U.S. Administration has represented to the British Government that this system, however inevitable in time of war, is seriously detrimental to the interests of U.S. trade and commerce, since it must be administered, inevitably, in a manner which discriminates against American exporters.

5. The U.K. Government agree that the system is liable to operate in time of peace in a way which is restrictive to international commerce, but that there is no avoiding it so long as the supply of dollars to the sterling area countries falls below their natural requirements. Under this system the U.S. dollars which accrue to the 'sterling area dollar pool' through the imports of the U.S. or in other ways are available for expenditure in the U.S. No more than this, supplemented by limited supplies of gold, is possible, however strongly the U.K. may wish to liberalise the working of the system.

6. Moreover, there is a further obstacle to complete equality of treatment. At the end of June 1945 the sterling area balances and other liquid resources in London, representing

the obligations of the U.K., amounted to $10·9 billion and the total gold and dollar reserves of the U.K. to no more than $1·8 billion, and the position is likely to deteriorate further during the ensuing twelve months with an increase in the sterling area balances to the neighbourhood of $12 billion. Thus the reserve resources available to the U.K. exchange authorities are entirely inadequate to allow the sterling balances to be freely withdrawn. The position of the holders of these balances would be seriously worsened if the whole of their accumulated balances were to lose their present availability. Indeed this would throw the commerce of a considerable part of the world into confusion and the field over which multilateral trade could be conducted would be greatly curtailed.

7. This does not mean that the Government of the U.K. would not wish, if it lay in their power, to return to the non-discriminatory arrangements which existed before the war, by which the group of countries, using London as the base of their external finance, were able to employ their available external purchasing power in all areas of the world with equal facility. Indeed the whole purpose of the exchange control of the U.K. has been to increase the availability of sterling and to enhance the attractiveness of their London balances to all holders of sterling.

8. The problem is, therefore, to find a means of making the earnings from all future trade available to be expended without discrimination and, in addition, to free a sufficient portion of the accumulated balances and further portions by stages, so as to provide a sufficient working balance for the restoration of freedom of commerce.

9. The Government of the U.K. would be prepared on the basis of aid on a scale appropriate to the size of the problem, to proceed not later than the end of 1946 to make arrangements under which the current earnings of all sterling area countries would be freely available to make purchases in any

currency area without discrimination, apart from any receipts arising out of military expenditure by the U.K. which it may be agreed to treat on the same basis as the balances accumulated during the war; and in addition to treat similarly a portion of the accumulated balances forthwith, and further portions by instalments in future years for the purpose of meeting current needs. This would require that a part of the accumulated balances should be retained until they become similarly available: thus unless the amounts released were reasonable in relation to the requirements of the holders, the position of the holders might be changed for the worse.

10. The result would be that any discrimination arising from the so-called 'dollar pool' would be entirely removed, in the sense that each member of the sterling area would have both its current earnings and its available sterling balances at its free disposition for current transactions anywhere.

11. The representatives of the U.S. Administration agreed that they would regard the carrying into effect of these measures as a matter of great interest and importance to the U.S. They would represent a decisive move towards the liquidation of the financial consequences of the war to commerce, over a wide area. Nevertheless it was the strongly held opinion of the U.S. representatives that they should not be the only contributors to a general settlement of this kind. The sterling balances had been largely built up during the war and represented gains in external resources which would not have accrued to the countries concerned if those countries had contributed to the common costs of the war on the same principles as the aid which the U.S. had afforded to her Allies under the Lend Lease Act. They regarded it, therefore, as an essential condition of such a general settlement, if it were to commend itself as fair and right to the public opinion of the U.S., and indeed of the world at large, that the other countries concerned should also make retrospective contributions in a degree related to the improvement during the

war in their external financial positions. They were of the opinon that the indirect benefits through freeing their balances which would derive from aid furnished to the U.K. by the U.S. should go only to those countries which were themselves prepared to make an appropriate contribution to the common settlement.

12. The representatives of the U.K. agreed that they would naturally welcome common action along such lines. At the same time they affirmed that they could not properly press a unilateral settlement on the countries which had shown such great trust in them during the war and had in this way given the U.K. essential support in contributing to the common victory. Any such settlement must be by mutual agreement. Nor would any settlement be a fair one which worked on a rigid formula or on cut-and-dried lines, since other factors ought to be taken into account besides the present size of the accumulated balances. They agreed, however that the principles underlying the thesis of the U.S. representatives were fair and constructive and in the interests of all parties. They would, therefore, be ready at an early date to discuss a re-settlement with those concerned on the basis of dividing the accumulated sterling balances of each country into three categories, one category being freed at once and becoming convertible into any currency for current transactions, one category being similarly released by instalments over a long period of years, and one category being written off as a contribution to the success of the scheme as a whole and in recognition of the benefits which the countries concerned might be expected to gain from it. For the countries in question would have to recognise that, failing such a settlement as that under discussion and without aid from the U.S., it would be physically impracticable for the U.K. to repay the balances except over a long period of years and at a rate about which it would be impossible to enter into any definite commitment in advance. Thus it might be hoped that the

sterling area countries would agree that it was in their own interest, as well as fair and reasonable, to come into such a general settlement, rather than to stay out of it.

13. The U.K. representatives would seek to arrive at voluntary agreements with the sterling area creditors varying according to the circumstances of each case by which each would make an appropriate contribution to the common plan by arrangements which would include a scaling down of the sterling claims. Of the sterling balances scaled down as above a limited part would be released immediately and the remainder by instalments over a period of years. As regards the subsequent releases it would be necessary to protect the position of the U.K. by a clause permitting postponement of releases in certain contingencies. Conversely there might be a provision to the effect that releases could be anticipated in cases where a particular country holding sterling balances was in a position such as might have called for assistance by way of a loan from the U.K. in normal times. More precise arrangements than the above could not be specified in advance of discussion with the countries concerned. The U.K. representatives however, agreed with the view that countries unwilling to enter into an agreement on these lines, which the U.K. would consider satisfactory and fair in relation to the contributions of others, could not expect to participate in the special releases which would become available to participants in the scheme and would have, out of the sheer inescapable necessities of the case, to accept a lower priority of release of balances than those countries entering into the common scheme and to depend on the U.K.'s future capacity to repay after the U.K.'s obligations under the common scheme had been fully met. Nevertheless all future sterling earned by members of the sterling area, whether participants in the scheme or not, would be freely available for the purpose of current transactions, subject to the qualification relating to military expenditure in paragraph 9 above.

14. The U.K. representatives called attention at the same time to the weight of the commitments into which they would be entering by acceptance of a comprehensive scheme on the above lines. They would be foregoing the advantages to British exports of the large volume of potential purchasing power in overseas countries which would otherwise be available on a discriminatory basis favouring the U.K. and they would be committing themselves to make substantial future payments in convertible currency without the assistance to their capacity to liquidate the sterling balances which they would otherwise have retained. They were not prepared to accept commitments which they did not see their way to fulfil on reasonably cautious estimates. Their acceptance of a plan on the general lines indicated above would, therefore, only be possible if the aid contemplated was on a sufficient scale, and of this they must be the final judges, to carry the weight of the commitments they would be expected to undertake.

At this point complications ensued as Keynes received further proposals from London over the first ten paragraphs of the draft of the document Keynes had sent White, which he had communicated to London on 23 October as Nabob 215.[24]

From E. ROWE-DUTTON (*BABOON 202*), *5 November 1945*

My immediately following telegram contains a shorter version of paragraphs 1 to 10 of NABOB 215.

2. This takes more than full advantage of the invitation in NABOB 276 to offer corrections to your draft, but we have felt the need to be very guarded, in a document which may form part of the official record, against using any phrase which might cause embarrassment in years to come.

3. In re-casting it in this form we had in mind a factual account of the century old and successful banking system and the imposition thereon for war purposes of a scheme of exchange control and import control. It is exchange control and import control, including Government purchase, which are and must be discriminating in war-time, and not the sterling area.

[24] Keynes had already removed the ninth and tenth paragraphs of the original draft.

4. The result is a different approach to the presentation from that which we think you had in mind. But we believe that starting from our text you could interpolate one or two passages for American consumption without altering the shape of our story. We hesitate to suggest these for we are not entirely clear what purpose you had in your presentation.

5. If you recast paragraphs 8 and 9 of NABOB 215 from the starting point of the discrimination involved in exchange control when dollars are more scarce in the area than sterling you would have a lead from our paragraphs to the argument in paragraphs 11 and onwards.

6. The last sentence of your paragraph 8 strikes us as economical of truth.

From E. ROWE-DUTTON (*BABOON 203*), *5 November 1945*

My immediately preceding telegram.

1. The sterling area is a trading and banking system which has, over a century and more, taken natural growth and shape from the free decision of British and other communities overseas to use sterling as their common external currency and as the currency of their monetary reserves. This natural evolution of the sterling area has entailed three practical consequences: First any foreign exchange which has accrued to banks in the area in the course of their business has been converted by them into sterling; secondly, as counterpart of this, the foreign exchange holdings and dealings of the entire area have been centred in London; thirdly, sterling countries have been willing to accept sterling itself without limit.

2. Until the outbreak of war in 1939 this system worked with the utmost freedom. Sterling could be used for payment to any country in the world or could be freely converted into any foreign currency.

3. When war broke out there was no change in the three elements of the system enumerated above. On the contrary there was an understanding between all members that these three characteristics should remain unchanged. Under the stress of war-time necessity exchange control was introduced throughout the sterling area as in virtually every other country of the world outside U.S.A. But the individual countries within the area have administered their own controls independently of London (though with a common concern to reserve scarce currencies for essential expenditure), and London has, without exception, provided foreign exchange for any expenditure authorised by any control in the sterling area.

4. Meanwhile the exercise of exchange control, tempered by the very substantial liberty inherent in the sterling area system itself, has enabled a situation of great difficulty to be administered to the greatest advantage of all concerned, both inside and outside the area. The effect of six years

of war has been at once to increase greatly the sterling balances which sterling area and other countries hold in London and to decrease greatly the foreign assets and export trade which provide London with foreign exchange and backing against expenditure of those balances outside the sterling area. In the absence of exchange control such a situation must have resulted in a scramble for the available foreign exchange for the purposes which were most profitable to the individual, but not necessarily most essential to the prosecution of the war, with disastrous results to currency and price stability and to supply.

5. But the control has not superseded the essential liberties of the sterling system. The sterling balances are not blocked. They can be spent freely anywhere within the area and, within the limitation imposed by shortage of foreign exchange, are available to make all payments approved by the local exchange control outside the area. As reconversion proceeds and exports can be increased, freedom to spend outside the area will be enlarged. But meanwhile it is inherent in the situation that freedom to spend inside the area is greater than freedom to spend outside. This discriminatory effect is not a result of policy or deliberate intention. Least of all is it the result of the sterling area system itself, which by centralisation of the gold and foreign exchange reserves of the entire sterling area enables such foreign exchange resources as are available to be used with the greatest economy and avoids their immobilisation in a multiplicity of individual reserves. It is the result of facts. Sterling is available; dollars are not. To disregard these facts in an effort to make sterling freely transferable or convertible outside the area at this stage would be to invite a drain on the central gold and foreign exchange reserves of the area that they could not support. Consequently, if liberalisation of sterling is not to wait upon the slow processes of reconversion and re-balancing of payments, the central reserves of the area must be fortified from outside.

To SIR WILFRID EADY (*Telegram 7406*), *5 November 1945*

1. I find myself in great difficulty over BABOON 203. A fortnight has passed since I sent you by NABOB 215 which this amends. If you had let me know sooner or if we had more time we could no doubt have managed to conflate the drafts to some extent. But we are all now working under great pressure on other matters which may legitimately be considered more urgent and important.

2. I venture therefore to send our frank reactions for your

strictly private consideration. Lee, Harmer and I began by thinking we could work a good deal of BABOON 203 into the framework of NABOB 215. But as we worked at it the stuff broke in our hand as being inaccurate, irrelevant or phoney. It will appear to the Americans as an inept piece of special pleading. You must remember its intended context, namely, in an annex to a bill before Congress, or in an exchange of notes referred to in the annex.

3. In particular, the note struck that the war made the least possible change in the sterling area arrangements will not only seem to readers here forced and untrue but is the wrong note. Surely the right note is that in war-time conditions we were compelled to make substantial changes compared with peace time and what we are now trying to do is to return to the peace-time situation.

4. The main purpose of the earlier paragraphs of my draft was to explain to Congress and to the public here how the war-time sterling area works since the all-prevailing ignorance on this matter has proved one of the greatest obstacles to rational consideration of our problems.

5. If, as may well be the case, there are some errors of description in NABOB 215 we should be glad to make the necessary changes. It may be that paragraph 2 of NABOB 215 is open to criticism from your point of view. If so, by all means let it be amended or considerably curtailed. We can also use with profit some part of BABOON 203 relating to the pre-war arrangements of the sterling area. We are not quite sure what criticism is intended on paragraph 8 by paragraph 6 of BABOON 202 but if this refers to the over-statement of the purpose of the United Kingdom exchange control we will water it down.

6. I hope, therefore, you will let me retain the framework of NABOB 215 which is undoubtedly much more suitable for my purpose, making any necessary corrections in it to conform to considerations of accuracy and caution. I am quite

clear that BABOON 203 will not do as it stands and I do not think that my time will be best spent in the next few days trying to make my draft look more like it. Apart from the main financial negotiations, we are now on the last lap of the clean-up of lend lease which means that any spare time that any of us have here to work up our case as completely as possible may be worth a considerable number of dollars.

7. A preliminary talk with White on the basis of the revised NABOB 215 went on the whole very well, though it was limited to elucidating the meaning and purpose of the draft. In particular we were very glad to find that White was most sympathetic to our desire not to quantify the scaling down of the sterling area balances. I think we can rely on his support. His chief disappointment seemed to be that our proposals covered only our arrangements with other sterling area countries and not with payments agreements countries. The payments agreements will undoubtedly need amendment and evolution when the sterling area system is modified. But I have never given the Americans reason to suppose that we were entering into any commitments at the present time except as regards the sterling area itself. At any rate, White is now under no illusion that we retain our Bretton Woods transitional rights in respect to our currency arrangements with non-sterling area countries.

From SIR WILFRID EADY (*Telegram 11187*), *6 November 1945*

Your telegram No. 7406.

I am sorry we did not send you earlier comments on paragraphs 1 to 10. We were preoccupied with paragraphs 11 onwards because I was led into a misunderstanding of your position on cancellation by the wording of paragraph 15. I agree that you should not devote your energies at the moment to the niceties of mythology. But you will remember that there is in many parts of the sterling area an emotional content in that conception comparable to that on Imperial Preference. The sterling area will continue even in its liberalised form, and it was on this account that we wanted to avoid the suggestion that the sterling area was necessarily discriminatory.

In fact it was not discriminatory before the war, and it is exchange control and the system of Government purchases and so on that has introduced the war-time discrimination. I must leave you a free hand to make as much use as possible of BABOON 203 in re-arranging your paragraphs. For this purpose I give you blunt comments on some important sentences which have disturbed us. All references are to the paragraphs in NABOB 215.

2. Paragraph (1), Sentence (1). It is not only the accumulated balances plus current earnings outside the area, but also current earnings inside the area, which are freely available within the area.

Sentence (2). For 'transfer their balances' read 'make payments to persons resident'.

Last sentence. Although you are right to shift the emphasis on to import licensing, it is probably system of government purchasing that has mainly controlled purchases abroad.

3. Paragraph 2. We hope you can cut this to a minimum. We have always sought to avoid listing currencies by degrees of hardness, and should prefer not to have this round the neck of import licensing in future.

4. Paragraph 3. This is not how the system works in practice. The rest of the area is much more likely to sell either direct or through a London intermediary for sterling which the foreigner acquires by selling his own currency to London. Thus, the members may never touch foreign currencies at all, and the conception of a dollar pool created by handing in dollars is a graphic but over-simplified version of what happens. I can understand that you may want to retain the phrase 'dollar pool' but you would have no difficulty in showing how the actual arrangements produce the impression of a dollar pool.

5. Paragraph 4. For the reasons explained in paragraph 1 above we should like to word this so as to bring out the point that it is not the sterling area system which is discriminatory, but the war-time necessities of exchange control. Following attempts this line:

(*Begins*) The United States Administration has represented to the British Government that the administration of this system in time of war, as distinct from the complete freedom which it permitted before the outbreak of war, is seriously detrimental to the interests of American trade and commerce, since there has inevitably been introduced an element of discrimination against American exporters. (*Ends*)

6. Paragraph 5. See paragraph 3 of BABOON 198. I must press you to revise the second sentence of paragraph 5 in the light of BABOON 198. We are not contemplating bilateral allocation of dollars, but non-discriminatory availability of sterling. Would you consider the following re-draft for the whole of paragraph 5?

(*Begins*) The United Kingdom Government point out that until the outbreak of war in 1939 this system worked with the utmost freedom, and without discrimination. Sterling could be used for payment to any country in the world, or could be freely converted into any foreign currency. It is not the system as such which is restrictive of international commerce, but the fact that the area as a whole has command over a supply of dollars, and other foreign currencies, which is far from adequate to meet its natural requirements. Increased liberalisation of the administration of the system can only spring from an increased supply of dollars and other foreign currencies, and in no other way whatever. The strong desire of the United Kingdom to effect such liberalisation will ensure that any such increased supply is utilised to that end. (*Ends*)

7. It is a matter of judgement whether it is wise to quote the figures of sterling indebtedness and liquid reserves. They are probably well-known, and I assume you want to use them to point your argument in the rest of the paragraph. I leave that to you to decide.

8. Paragraph 8. Last sentence. Our criticism meant that primary purpose of exchange control was to mobilise our resources and dispose of them in the way most suited to war needs, while doing as little damage as possible to status of sterling.

9. The above are the points to which we feel justified in calling your attention within the flexible limits of accuracy and caution suggested by you, and in the spirit of this telegram I agree with paragraph 6 of telegram No. 7406.

10. Paragraph 7 of telegram 7406. Your account of Harry White's preliminary attitude on cancellation is indeed cheering news to me. I beg you to shun debate about European payments agreements or special account agreements as you would shun the devil. Press reports some two weeks ago carried express statement that Americans had demanded complete revision of payments agreements. Noticeable flutter occurred in countries affected by the agreements, and sterling cannot afford unnecessary attacks of nerves at the moment.

11. I was very interested in the last sentence of 7406. We are constantly discovering new virtues in the dubious oracles of Bretton Woods.

To this series of telegrams, Keynes finally replied.

To SIR WILFRID EADY (*Telegram 7746*), *7 November 1945*

Very grateful for your telegram No. 11187 which completely meets my difficulties.

2. I have embodied, with only verbal changes, all the amendments suggested in 11187. I have also added additional paragraphs at the beginning on the lines of and embodying the greater part of the first three paragraphs of BABOON 203.

3. I do not think the theory is serviceable that it was merely the introduction of exchange control which changed the character of the sterling area. Indeed, it would be dangerous to put all the stress on this, for nothing that I am agreeing here will interfere in the least with our discretion to use exchange control during the Bretton Woods transitional period. Neither we nor any other member of the sterling area are undertaking to abolish exchange control. The source of complaint is the discriminatory character of the control as between the sterling area and countries outside the sterling area, and it is useless to try to gloss that over.

4. I have omitted the last part of the last sentence of paragraph 3 of BABOON 203 since this passage would cause surprise to the Americans in relation to Egypt and the Middle East. Perhaps they might even claim to behave as if it were true.

5. Some fig leaves which may pass muster with old ladies in London wilt in a harsher climate.

6. BABOON 221. It has not been made clear that these sentences come from the mouths of the Americans and not from us. That all members of the sterling area have given us aid comparable with lend lease is, however, a new one on me. Are you thinking chiefly of Eire?

7. The finally revised text of NABOB 215 as handed to the United States Treasury will be sent you in NABOB Saving.

After a meeting of Ministers on the evening of 5 November, which Professor Robbins attended, Keynes received his instructions. Plan B disappeared. Plan A remained London's first choice, especially if the $2 billion intended for backing the liberalisation of the sterling area came interest-free. The mission could accept 2 per cent interest whenever it thought appropriate and it could propose the interest-bearing loan element be only $2 billion, plus the lend lease settlement if the terms of the latter kept it under $500 million and not on 3(c) terms. The instructions also accepted the Clayton version of the waiver clause. If Plan A failed, London proposed a new Plan B with a line of credit of $1 billion with interest at 2 per cent on the amount used and an option on a further $1 billion at 2 per cent. Both plans assumed repayment over fifty years starting in five years.

Keynes, along with the Ambassador and Brand, met with Clayton and Vinson on 6 November. After the meeting, he wrote to the latter.

To F. M. VINSON, *6 November 1945*

Dear Mr Vinson,

Sorry to bombard you with letters, but the Chancellor of the Exchequer has given me such emphatic instructions to make as clear as I possibly can the importance he attaches to that part of the proposals which relates to the $2 billion interest-free loan, that I propose to repeat in writing some part of the argument which I gave you orally this afternoon. In case they may be of use to the other members of your group I am attaching some spare copies. I am also sending a copy direct to Mr Clayton.

In the first place our objective, and yours, is to ensure that world trade can be resumed on a non-discriminatory basis. The main obstacle that has to be removed is that during the transition period the U.K. balance of payments will be in deficit, and the countries with whom we trade will be receiving sterling which we are not in a position, without U.S. assistance, to make freely available for current payments throughout the world. In asking for such assistance therefore, we are seeking something which will benefit not only the U.K. but the whole of the world, and not least the U.S.A. itself.

I think we have made clear in our earlier discussions by what processes we should move towards this goal. Part of our balance of payments deficit will be incurred directly to the U.S.A.; and to that extent we have contemplated that assistance by the U.S.A. should take the form of an interest-bearing loan on the terms discussed today. But for the remainder, our need is to be able to ensure that the countries with whom we trade are free themselves to trade with the rest of the world, and the U.S.A. in particular, on a non-discriminatory basis. This we can only achieve if we are in a position to ensure that the sterling which the world receives from us can be used for current payments in whatever currency. In fact, the extent to which we should draw on the dollars made available to us for this purpose would be measured by the extent to which the world had need of dollars for current payments in multi-lateral trading conditions.

Thus, in putting forward proposals whereby the assistance furnished for this purpose would not bear interest, we are drawing a distinction between the assistance which is of direct benefit to the U.K. itself and that which is of general benefit to the world at large. While we must accept the principle that we must be the channel through which that assistance is provided, we do not feel it is unreasonable to urge that this distinction should be recognised in the terms of the assistance.

Finally let me add that, as you know, the situation with which we are confronted is one in which not only the U.S.A. but the holders of sterling balances must be asked to make their contribution in consideration of the benefits which they will receive. The Chancellor of the Exchequer has particularly asked me to emphasise the importance in presenting these large questions to the countries concerned, of showing that both you and we recognise that the assistance thus provided as it were for the general benefit should be on different and more liberal terms than that furnished for our own direct requirements.

Yours sincerely,

KEYNES

The Ambassador, Brand and Keynes reported the meeting to the Chancellor, adding the information that they had started the discussions on a 2 per cent basis for Plan A and had also proposed the Clayton waiver clause. The Americans replied that their formal offers had not yet gone above $3·5 billion and that they had not settled in their own minds the terms of the lend lease clean-up. They were extremely unhappy about tying the interest-free element of $2 billion to the sterling area. However they made no commitments, beyond agreeing to meet again.

At this stage another element entered the negotiations. In the course of discussing the sterling area settlement with Keynes early in November, White had raised the point that the British proposals excluded payments agreements with non-sterling area countries. Keynes replied that he had never intended to suggest that the arrangements for these countries would be other than those allowed under the Bretton Woods proposals for the transitional period.

However, on 8 November, Keynes reported to London that 'strong rumours are reaching us that the Americans are most disturbed by what is apparently a sudden discovery so far as they are concerned...that our sterling area proposals do not cover payments agreements'. He was uncertain as to the form of the American reaction but he warned London to prepare for it. He continued

From a cable to SIR WILFRID EADY (*Telegram 7491*), *8 November 1945*

3. The trouble is that the Americans know next to nothing about the nature and variety of payments and special account agreements and do not know either their good or less good points. Their attitude is largely doctrinal and consequently tiresome and unpractical. I think I can put up a good case showing that any cut-and-dried commitments by us at this date would be impracticable and might lead to all sorts of difficulties for us. I can also argue that some of the payments agreements are very much of the same character as their own tied loans. If however they raise this issue at the top level in a definite and determined way it will be very difficult to get away with nothing. We here have therefore been giving careful thought to the question if there is some general formula we could offer them which would at least pacify their doctrinal feelings.

4. In fact payments agreements and the like will undoubt-edly suffer evolution if the sterling area arrangements are themselves altered. What we cannot stand is a premature decay particularly of the South American payments agree-ments or a system which binds us in a way which does not bind the other fellow. In the new circumstances which would be created by an adequate American loan we are not likely, in fact, to tie up sterling earned after 1946 in a way which the Americans could object to. But we cannot safely move earlier than that nor can we enter into any undertaking about releasing accumulated balances. In the light of these reflec-tions the best general formula which we have been able to work out here is as follows:–

5. 'As soon as is practicable after completing the proposed arrangements for the liberalisation of the sterling area it will be the policy of the United Kingdom to provide by mutual agreement with countries outside the sterling area adhering to the International Monetary Fund that monetary agree-ments with them shall not be so operated in practice on either side as to involve discrimination in the use of a favourable balance arising from current transactions.'

6. We do not think that this concession to doctrine would do us any harm in practice. If we could offer this it might prove of vital assistance in getting us over a difficult hurdle. Will you think it over?

On 11 November, after putting it to the Americans, Keynes and Brand reported the rejection of Plan A and predicted that the American counter-offer would be $4·5 billion at 2 per cent with repayment over 50 years and a five-year moratorium. The $4·5 billion would include the Lend Lease settlement. They expected a semi-final draft on 15 November.

Although a preliminary draft did come on 15 November, certain clauses proved so unacceptable to the mission that the Americans asked for time to withdraw the draft and reconsider them.[25] Nevertheless, Keynes took

[25] Keynes on reading the draft, according to one member of the mission looked 'very shaken and white; and all that he could say was that we had better pack up and go home'. The difficulties arose over the sterling area arrangements and the waiver.

the opportunity to emphasise that a sum of $4·5 billion, including the clean-up of lend lease, would be necessary to allow the British to agree to the clauses they accepted.

By 18 November, after several days discussions, the contents of the American proposals were clear enough to cable to London. Before they met the Americans the next day, the Mission dispatched a series of telegrams on the basis of the discussions so far, prefaced by the statement

We should warn you that, as you may gather from the contents of our following telegrams, we are having heavy going and there may be further troubles ahead.

There then followed seven telegrams based on the discussions.

The telegrams outlined five important points at issue.

(1) The Americans proposed that the waiver would become operative if (a) British export earnings on current account net of war debt payments over the previous five years were on average below the 1936–8 average adjusted for price changes and (b) Britain's gold and foreign exchange reserves at the end of the previous year were less than 15 per cent of imports averaged over the previous five years or less than 25 per cent of British demand and short-term liabilities. The Mission recommended the rejection of alternative (b), but asked for instructions on a possible compromise formula as the American worry about reserve levels was strongly held.

(2) The American waiver proposals stated that there would be no waiver unless there was a proportionate reduction in the release of sterling balances and in the repayment of sterling balances and in the repayment of other post-1945 loans to Britain. In addition, the American proposals restricted the ability of Britain to accelerate repayments to others without doing so to the United States. The Mission's counter-proposal restricted the proportional repayment reductions to loans taken up in 1946 and sought to exclude Britain's colonial dependencies and other specified payments from the accelerated repayment clause.

(3) The American sterling area and payments agreement proposals suggested that the non-discriminatory availability of current receipts would begin by the end of 1946, except in the case of military payments which would follow at the end of 1948. The Mission recommended the rejection of these proposals as the general case for payments agreements and suggested that they should only operate where the agreements contained no restrictions on either party's freedom.

(4) The American negotiators proposed that British import controls should not discriminate between sources of supply, except where they were necessary to clear off blocked balances or aid war-devastated areas, as soon

as possible and definitely before the beginning of 1947. The Mission reserved its position, but recommended acceptance.

(5) The American proposals for the treatment of past sterling balances related to both sterling area and other countries and to all balances accumulated prior to the final settlement and post-war military expenditures. The British alternative proposals related to war-time balances and post-war military expenditures only in the sterling area, mentioned only discussions on the matter at an early date, and allowed for the early release of blocked balances in lieu of loans in particular cases. However the Mission recognised that the differences involved were not major, beyond the determination of the proportion of the balances written off or funded, an issue that still lurked under the surface.

On 19 November, Keynes reported the day's meeting with the American Finance Committee. The meeting did not result in the expected formal American proposals suitable for transmission to London. Rather, discussion centred on another rough draft[26] similar to those which had formed the basis of the previous week's discussions. However, it did provide some clues as to the American group's sticking points, on which Keynes and other members of the delegation expanded when they sent the draft to London on 21 November.

At that time, although the sum of the assistance did not appear in the draft, the mission believed it could obtain $4 billion and it asked for an instruction that this sum be the minimum on which Britain could carry out liberalisation arrangements of the type under discussion. It also asked for instructions not to give way on the need for a lend lease settlement on the same terms as the loan.

At this stage, in a series of cables and letters, Keynes set out the atmosphere.

From a cable to SIR EDWARD BRIDGES *and* SIR WILFRID EADY *(835 REMAC), 20 November 1945*

I send this to reinforce our plea for as quick a reply to our long series of NABOB telegrams as is practicable for Ministers. A firm reply will I believe be much more effective if it comes quickly.

There can be no doubt that the position here is deteriorating and that any further delay weakens our position. We started in a good atmosphere partly resulting from reaction

[26] This draft appears below (pp. 629–32) as Appendix I.

of opinion against the sudden termination of lend lease. The effect both of that and of the impact made by our original exposition has now largely passed away as a result of the long-drawn-out negotiations. The subject has gone stale and critics and sceptics of all kind and from all directions are recovering their courage.

From a letter to SIR WILFRID EADY, *21 November 1945*

As you may have surmised, life here for the past three weeks or longer has been absolute hell; though I doubt if you can have guessed quite how bad it has been.

Everything that we think we have settled with the Top Committee is then transmitted by them inaccurately to experts and lawyers, who have not been present at the discussion. The latter work without consultation with us and produce to their own top lads something which bears not the faintest resemblance to what we have agreed. This is then adopted by the American Top Committee and hurled at us in what looks very like an ultimatum. We then in a series of exasperated meetings have to throw out as much as possible to bring the text, not completely, but as nearly back as we can. This sort of thing does not happen just once but time after time after time.

The procedure not only causes actual fury in one's breast but also one can seldom make progress except by using diplomatic fury and every other means of getting one's way open to one in the Committees. And this, after ten weeks of it, not infrequently working more than ten hours a day is, as you may suppose, exhausting.

What really holds us together is the excellent ability and unanimity of our team. Each uses his appropriate gifts to the best advantage. I think it is the team work above all which impresses the Americans. Harry White is full of envy on that point in particular. And the absence of any friction within does, of course, make an enormous difference. All the same, towards the end of last week my physical reserves looked like giving out. But I have been nursing myself since then and am hopeful of being back again in full strength by the time we have the replies to our long telegrams to London. I doubt, however, as I mentioned in the telegram, whether it is advisable for me to make a rush visit to Ottawa. It would probably mean travelling for forty-eight hours out of seventy-two. If I can make the trip so as to get at least two nights in between, I shall try to do it. But that now looks distinctly unlikely if I am to get back by the *Queen Mary*.

We do not yet know what you will be thinking about our two long batches of telegrams. I can only say that they might have been a great deal worse. And what is so particularly maddening about it all is that the chaps here do not really intend to do us any harm. They simply cannot see our point of view and even at this late date, not one of them, with the possible exception of Harry White, has even the faintest conception of how we actually run the sterling area with the associated special accounts, etc. Thus they are constantly producing something exceedingly difficult and tiresome, without meaning anything bad. But, having produced it, they show, of course, all the pertinacity of the so-called expert.

One of the oddest things about the last fortnight, when all of us have been feeling that it was going to be next door to impossible to reach agreement, has been the absolute confidence of the other side that very little was at issue and that we might come to full agreement at any time in two or three days.

It is quite clear that they would be horror struck at any breakdown in the negotiations and that, at the last lap, will be our greatest strength.

Provided you give us just enough room to negotiate and compromise on a few important points, it is a firm reply that we hope for from you.

Will you pass this on to Bridges.

From a letter to F. A. KEYNES, *21 November 1945*

...The last three or four weeks have been exhausting and exasperating beyond description. I am enough at leisure to write to you today because there is a brief lull whilst we wait for further instructions from London in response to an enormous batch of telegrams we have got off to them in the last two days, telling them just how the offer here now stands. When one contemplates the wood, I still believe that we shall finally end up with something brought off; but as one moves into the trees one feels that one will never re-emerge again into day light.

They mean us no harm—but their minds are so small, their prospect so restricted, their knowledge so inadequate, their obstinacy so boundless and their legal pedantries so infuriating. May it never fall to my lot to have to *persuade* anyone to do what I want, with so few cards in my hand!

As you may suppose I am beginning to use up my physical reserves...

At this stage, according to one civil servant fairly closely involved
The Treasury and the Bank had hysterics—Instead of going calmly through the document and seeing what we could accept and what we couldn't, they seemed prepared to end the whole negotiations.
Suggestion of this came directly to Keynes, when Sir Edward Bridges and Sir Wilfrid Eady replied to Keynes's telegram on 22 November, for they said, 'We ought to warn you that we should expect the reply [of Ministers] to be that the draft memorandum...is quite unacceptable in anything like its present form.'
Meanwhile Keynes continued to emphasise the gravity of the situation in his cables to London.

From a cable to LORD CATTO (*Telegram 7816*), *22 November 1945*

3. You must appreciate that the long delays have caused a steady deterioration of the position. After I had made my

initial exposition of our case the atmosphere both with the American group and with the Press and Congress was at its best. For more than a fortnight after that we had to mark time waiting for the arrival of the commercial party. And when they arrived we naturally concentrated on their business. You know how quickly things go stale in this country. Then there was another gap of more than a fortnight whilst we were awaiting instructions from the Cabinet. All this was inevitable but the consequences were that the initial atmosphere was completely lost. The American side now seem convinced that they can get nothing past Congress which they cannot represent as hard trading out of which America gets as much future benefit as it concedes. They are also much concerned with the precedent for other countries which your proposal would not meet since other countries also have both old war debts and lend lease settlements. In particular it is because of their obstinacy that two per cent is the minimum rate of interest that half our difficulties have arisen.

4. All the old wiseacres and bogus older statesmen are now shaking their heavy locks to our disadvantage. Baruch, Jesse Jones, Crowley and the like are inserting insidious words.

To SIR WILFRID EADY (*Telegram 7825*), *22 November 1945*

Since our [telephone] conversation I have discussed position with Ambassador. He feels very strongly that it would be a grave mistake to start over again on new lines. Anyhow there is no way of by-passing the problems raised by the present draft. They have to be faced and solved. Apart from this, firstly we should fill the Americans with suspicions that we were going back on the previous discussion, however unjustified this reaction on their part might be; secondly, any course which involved serious delay would be thought by them, and plainly would be a menace to the Bretton Woods timetable which is already a major anxiety in their minds.

A great many countries are waiting on us and there must be time for them to act *after* us if Bretton Woods is not to fall down completely.

2. On the other hand, a stiff reply with counter proposals on the same pattern as their draft may well be the right move.

3. We could accompany such a replay with a renewed appeal to the Americans to think on bigger lines and with a better realisation of the profoundly significant underlying issues. Our purpose would be not to by-pass the technical details which must be squarely met but to urge them not to produce a deadlock by forcing their point of view to its logical conclusion on issues which in practice are so difficult and dangerous for us that even with the best of goodwill we cannot give way.

4. The Ambassador first thought of telegraphing as above to the Chancellor or the Prime Minister, but decided it would be better for me to send this to you. But he would be glad if you could see that the above is before Ministers when they are considering their reply.

The meeting of Ministers referred to in the previous telegram took place at 5 p.m. on 23 November. The meeting was notable for the strong attack on the Treasury by Herbert Morrison, the Lord President of the Council, for not giving Keynes enough of a free hand in the negotiations as well as considerable disagreement as to tactics. At the end of the meeting, it was agreed that the Prime Minister should send a cable to Lord Halifax setting out Ministers' views of the situation.

The telegram set out the areas of agreement and disagreement. The Ministers concerned stated that they were prepared to accept a credit of not less than $4 billion (including the lend lease clean-up) at 2 per cent repayable over fifty years with the first payment occurring in five years, the liberalisation of the sterling area along the lines Keynes had proposed to White,[27] a commitment to recommend to Parliament the Bretton Woods arrangements as soon as the financial agreement was concluded, and the commercial policy proposals already agreed by the mission. However, Ministers were not prepared to agree to the completion of the negotiations

[27] Above, pp. 571–7.

595

with creditors before the end of 1946, the abrogation at the end of 1946 of Britain's transitional rights to impose exchange restrictions on current transactions allowed under Bretton Woods, the priority of the American debt above all other external obligations and the reserve test under the waiver arrangement. The Ministers also proposed to raise the difficult points of the negotiations directly with the President.

On receiving these instructions Keynes and Halifax delivered the substance of their instructions in writing[28] to Vinson and Clayton on 25 November. Keynes's report of the discussions continued.

From a cable to H. DALTON (*Telegram 7895*), *25 November 1945*

3. Vinson and Clayton were considerably taken aback. Nevertheless they did not react too violently against the change in the general approach for which we were pleading. One lives on a see-saw here and there are several indications recently that we may have reached bottom point. There are quite a few on the American side who sympathise with us and are experiencing some revulsion of feeling against the legalistic binding provisions which they have been pressing on us lately. We had to go through this phase. But there is at least a chance that we shall escape from it. The Prime Minister's instructions gave us a grand chance and I hope you will feel that we have taken good advantage of it.

4. Unfortunately after we had delivered our case with supporting comments, Clayton who has been seedy for some time, had to tell us that he had fever and was not well enough to continue discussion. This is rather a disaster.

5. It will undoubtedly help us at the last lap to have your authority to reduce the figure to 4 billion including lend lease. But as they have not yet proposed a firm figure to us there is no need for us to offer this concession now. Moreover we see some danger in it if it can be avoided. The Americans are still asking $750 million net for lend lease and they can make a case difficult for us to resist on merits up to about $600 million. We still hope to settle for the latter figure but scarcely

[28] These appear below (pp. 633–6) as Appendix II.

for less. Since we first started, London's estimates of the inventory for which we are liable have steadily increased.

6. All of us here feel that to have no more than $3,400 million new money is to cut things dangerously fine. Certain statistics we have seen which might appear to justify such a figure are, in our opinion, misleading and based on fallacy.

7. As you will see from the text as telegraphed, we are fighting hard to retain a satisfactory waiver on the lines of paragraph 4 of the Prime Minister's telegram.

8. All of us here are greatly disturbed by the relatively small importance London now seems to attach to the waiver. The suggested reduction in the amount of the credit makes matters worse, since this may mean that we shall end the transition with inadequate reserves. In our view a waiver clause has inestimable value both practically and politically. This is especially the case if it creates a precedent for other settlements. We cannot face with equanimity an unqualified liability to external creditors which may reach £75 million sterling a year in the aggregate. We must not overplay immediate technical considerations to the disadvantage of the responsibilities of cautious statesmanship towards the future. We feel that such a settlement, half of which, if Canada gets the same terms, would cost 2 per cent interest, would be widely and justly criticised as too nearly a repetition of last time's war debts. I am asked by my colleagues here, and I share their view, to say that we would give up an objective waiver only on the most express instructions and we should ask to be excused from taking any responsibility for it.

The Ambassador also recommended against raising the issues of the negotiations with the President for the time being.

After Keynes and Halifax had met Vinson and Clayton, Keynes found himself invited to an American technical meeting at which 'the attitude seemed more conciliatory than at any meetings this delegation have attended since they came to Washington'. However, the drafting suggestions that resulted from this meeting were soon lost in an unexpected storm.

When Keynes and Lord Halifax's memorandum on the American proposals reached London, the Chancellor raised a point which suggested that Ministers and the Mission had misunderstood each other. He suggested that it was not the intention of Ministers to release all sterling area current earnings from the end of 1946. When Keynes received the Chancellor's instructions on this point, the delegation drafted a strong cable emphasising the long history of the current earnings commitment from its approval by the Cabinet before Keynes left London, through the emphasis Keynes placed on it in his presentation of the terms of assistance in September and his discussions with White, to Ministers' reaffirmation of the proposal to Professor Robbins in London in November. The cable concluded

We are unanimously and strongly of the conviction that it is impossible to withdraw our longstanding and frequently repeated undertaking to accept clause 6 of the American draft without what the Americans would regard, and in our judgement with full justification, as complete retraction on a vital matter, and that one in regard to which we have with your full authority made a perfectly express commitment.

You will understand our feeling that something like our own *bona fides* is here involved and accordingly the extreme difficulty in which your telegram has placed us. It would inevitably on the American side destroy the mutual confidence to which with your help we have just made appeal.

Moreover, if you were to insist on these instructions it would certainly be in vain. For in that event you may take it as assured that there will be no financial agreement.

Very troubled days followed. As one participant recorded soon afterwards.

M. at the point of extreme nervous tension and on the verge of physical collapse: Lydia in floods of tears at almost every occasion: and all of us in a pretty bad state of mental and nervous exhaustion. Telegrams passed to and fro: M's getting more desperate—he was more than once on the point of resignation but was persuaded not to: London is getting more curt, and completely uninformative.

One exchange between Sir Wilfrid Eady and Keynes provides an indication of the tension.

From SIR WILFRID EADY (*Telegram 11897*), *27 November 1945*

Referring to our telephone conversation please believe that we are not trying to sabotage your efforts or being more stupid than nature has made us. To settle such an important and complex document in a hurry by cables is very difficult for both sides, and we must be patient with each other. We are doing all we can to help you but we have to remember the impact of the document upon opinion here and elsewhere.

2. If you are in doubt about the meaning of any important paragraph in any telegram from here, Grant or I are ready, at any time of day or night, to answer a telephone call.

To SIR WILFRID EADY (*Telegram 7933*), *27 November 1945*

Grateful for your telegram 11897. We thought we were in sight of home and were, and indeed still are, dismayed at the revival of what must wreck things here when we believed it had been disposed of long ago. Referring to my NABOB telegram today to the Chancellor we have a real chance of a settlement in the next few days if you will give us just enough elbow room. If we miss taking advantage of the present mood, my judgement is that things will move backward and not forward. Once granted the inevitable that we have to pay 2 per cent, the rest of what we recommended in today's NABOB is not too bad.

Keynes's reference to his NABOB telegram was to a report of a meeting of the Top Finance Committee on 26 November. In the course of the meeting, Vinson 'in the most generous and sympathic language we have yet heard from him' withdrew the American proposal for specific reserve criteria in the waiver clause and proposed instead that the waiver discussions would take general account of the reserve position. The meeting also led Keynes to ask for approval for several drafting changes in the waiver proposals, and the clauses concerning discrimination, the sterling area and payments agreements outside the sterling area. Keynes also reported that the lend lease settlement would now be within the terms of the loan agreement, and that the sum involved would be $500 million so that a settlement of $4·5 billion appeared likely. He asked for permission to settle on these lines and concluded, 'A quick O.K. to this telegram, and we might be home in both senses of the word.'

Meanwhile the divergence of views between the mission and London over the exact form of previous understandings on the sterling area continued, caught up in a renewed series of Ministerial discussions. After a Cabinet meeting on 29 November, new proposals went to the delegation. These merely confirmed the gap in perceptions between London and Washington on many of the points at issue. As the delegation put it on the proposed sterling area arrangements (only one of the points still at issue with London):

From NABOB 419, 30 November 1945

4. Our concern is with the future. We fear the effect on the negotiations of the steps we are instructed to take, and we do not believe that the policy suggested is one which we can defend in argument.

5. So far as the effect on the negotiations is concerned, we can only repeat our unanimous conviction that the course we are told to take must be disastrous. We wonder whether it is appreciated in London to what extent our offer to liberalise the sterling area by a specific date has been one of the main attractions to the Americans throughout the negotiations. To approach them at this stage and to say that consideration of the difficulties involved compels the U.K. Government regretfully to retract this offer must create the very worst impression. We are all convinced that the Americans would not be prepared to accept a retraction of this kind.

6. We should be in a stronger position for reopening this question if we believed that it really was important for us and could produce a convincing reason. But all of us here, and we have given considerable attention to the matter, believe that the importance now attached to it by London is not only misplaced but definitely erroneous.

7. In the first place, we do not believe that we can argue that the liberty of action we should now demand to retain is of sufficiently real value to be material to our negotiations with the sterling creditors. We have repeatedly emphasised to the

Americans the fact that the sterling area arrangements are informal and voluntary and that there exist no agreements which compel the sterling area countries to surrender to us their current foreign exchange earnings. What is at stake here is whether they will be willing to continue trading with us in sterling which is not freely convertible into other currencies, and this over a period in which we shall not be able to satisfy all their demands for goods. Even apart from the question of settling the accumulated balances it seems to us that convertibility of current earnings is something which for the most part we shall have to give away *de facto* even if it is not given away *de jure*. Indeed it may be that convertibility will be the main inducement to some of the more difficult countries to continue to trade with us in sterling, and to increase their sterling holdings, at a time when such assistance may be of vital importance to us.

8. May we try to disentangle the issues:–

(*a*) We are not prepared to cancel any part of the accumulated balances unilaterally. Agreed.

(*b*) No one has ever supposed that we can release these balances except at a very slow rate. The pace of that release has always been our real bargaining weapon. Agreed.

(*c*) Whilst with luck we may persuade the sterling area countries to carry on with the present basis for another year, we have no power to compel them to do so when we have reached a state of disagreement or to use this as a threat to bend them to our will. We cannot force these countries to go on accepting restricted sterling. To forego what is an empty threat would seem, therefore, to be no great matter. Why not agreed?

9. But assuming for the sake of argument that we did in fact retain the power to refuse convertibility, might not its exercise give rise to consequences which would be much more embarrassing than the course which we here propose? If it were proposed that release of current earnings should, in the case of each creditor, only take place from a date to

be separately negotiated with each creditor, this would raise the difficult question of differential treatment for different creditor countries. The release date in each case would depend, not merely on the success or otherwise of each particular negotiation, but also on such fortuitous factors as the order in which we negotiated with the different creditors. It seems to us here that such differentiation would be very invidious and difficult to defend. The only way to avoid it (unless a common release date for all sterling countries is adopted) would be to delay release to any one of the creditors. But it would be grossly unfair to impose such delay on the rest of the creditors and would certainly raise serious political difficulties.

10. Moreover, if notwithstanding the foregoing, we proceeded to release each country's earnings as and when we reached agreement, then surely the position would be technically untenable? Australia's earnings for instance might have become convertible through a settlement, but negotiations with India were still hanging fire. Under existing arrangements, which we infer you would continue to apply to India, her sterling would be freely transferable to Australia where it presumably would appear as current earnings. Would not this lead to endless possibilities of evasion, and indeed the complete disruption of the existing sterling area arrangements?

11. Apart from the arguments on merits which we have attempted to set out above, we have to consider what the American attitude would be if we were to put your draft, with the arguments in BABOON 312, to them. In the first place, as we judge, they would ask, as they have repeatedly done before whether we intended to release each country's earnings upon reaching a settlement. In the past we have replied, and successfully, on the lines of paras. 9 and 10 above. If these arguments are sound, they would lead to the conclusion that there could be no releases until we had completed all the settlements, i.e. until some quite indefinite future date. This

would at once bring to light the fundamental difference between your attitude, and their and our understanding of the position hitherto. Next they might no doubt enquire what would happen in the event of our failing to reach agreement with any one of the countries concerned. Would this finally nullify the whole of our undertaking? Your draft does not cover this contingency. Again we are forced to the position that either a definite date must be given or the undertaking is of very doubtful value. Thus, even apart from the questions of good faith which we have referred to elsewhere, the position we should have to take up would be one which it would be impossible to defend.

12. There is a final argument which in our opinion deserves full consideration in any practical weighing of alternatives and that is the attitude to this question of Canada. On this point we have had the benefit of consultation with Munro who assures us that the Canadians are highly sensitive on this point and are certain to insist as a price of further assistance, that at an early and named date the current earnings of the sterling group shall be freely convertible. Should we not look very foolish if, having broken with the United States on our refusal to pursue this policy, we find that the Canadians, to whom we turn for aid are insistent on just the same point?

13. We urgently request that this matter be reconsidered. We believe that we are in sight of the goal of a satisfactory settlement. But we believe too that this will be denied us, if our instructions remain as they are at present; and, what is more, the failure of the negotiations on this point would leave a most painful impression and even more important issues would be in jeopardy.

The upshot was that, at the suggestion of Professor Robbins, the Chancellor sent Sir Edward Bridges to lead the delegation. Keynes again immediately threatened to resign, but changed his mind after talking to the Ambassador. When Bridges arrived on 1 December he was immediately drawn into the discussions with the Mission, as a meeting with the Americans was scheduled for the next morning.

In fact, the Finance Committee met twice on Sunday, 2 December to consider the American draft[29] of the financial agreement as well as the proposals from London. At the meetings, Vinson, suspecting that Bridges had come to Washington because of London's dissatisfaction with Keynes and other members of the Mission 'went out of his way to build up the actions of and effective negotiations by the older group'.[30]

The net result was, according to one of the British team 'exactly as expected, humiliation'. Most of the London proposals got nowhere; the sum became $3,750 million plus $650 million for lend lease and the sterling area and payments agreements arrangements were to operate for a year after the loan came into effect.

In two subsequent meetings on 4 and 5 December, the Mission on instructions from London attempted to gain an extension of the Bretton Woods transitional arrangements outside the sterling area. Except for a form of words allowing for the possible operation of the scarce currency clause, they failed. The Anglo-American Financial Agreement was signed at 10.30 a.m. on 6 December.

At the end of the negotiations, the Chancellor wrote to Keynes.

From H. DALTON, *5 December 1945*

My dear Maynard,

Thank you from the bottom of my heart for all you have accomplished in this long, hard fight—against great odds.

You have, I know, strained yourself, mentally and physically, to the very limit. And you have got us the dollars, without which—though I have more than once thought that a break might have to come—the near future would have been black as the pit!

I am very deeply grateful to you, and so are my colleagues. Even those who least like some details of the Agreement are loud in praise of your skill, resource and patience.

And now come home and rest.

I look forward very much to seeing you again, and shaking your hand.

Yours ever,

HUGH DALTON

[29] Reprinted below (pp. 636–40) as Appendix II.
[30] *Foreign Relations of the United States 1945*, vol. VI, p. 187.

At the end of the negotiations Keynes held a dinner party for the delegation, including secretaries and typists, 'in honour of a job finished by a team'. Then, after clearing up in Washington, including making a call on President Truman, on 7 December Keynes went on to New York. There he saw Federal Reserve and private banking friends to make arrangements for drawing the credit when the time came and he also collected a silver tankard for the Bank of England.[31] He left New York on the *Queen Elizabeth* on 11 December and arrived in Southampton on 17 December.

In London, news of the Loan Agreement had met with a hostile reception. The hostility was reflected in the Press and the House of Commons debate on the proposal to approve the arrangement. The linking of the loan with the commercial policy proposals and the Bretton Woods Agreement hardly helped in this connection. The Conservative leadership in the Commons and a majority of the party abstained when the proposals came to a vote, but many Conservatives defied their leaders and voted against the Government. Many Labour members were also unhappy with the arrangements even though they supported the Government in the division lobbies.

Except for a brief stop at Gordon Square, Keynes proceeded directly from Southampton to the House of Lords where a debate on the proposals was in progress. During the first day of the debate, Keynes intervened once to provide Lord Simon with a point of information, but otherwise he listened to the discussion which lasted over five hours.

However, on the second day, Keynes opened the discussions.

From House of Lords Debates, *18 December 1945*

LORD KEYNES: My Lords, two days in Westminster are enough to teach one what a vast distance separates us here from the climate of Washington. Much more than the winter waste of the North Atlantic and that somewhat overrated

---

[31] The late J. P. Morgan had bequeathed the tankard to the Bank in the following terms: 'In grateful recognition of the kindness and hospitality shown me during many years by the Governors and Directors of the Bank of England I direct my Executors to take from among the silver-ware in my possession the large tankard dated 1692 given by Queen Mary II to Captain Janszen as an expression of thanks for his exertions and skill in seamanship which were the means of saving the life of King William III on the occasion of his voyage to Holland and to present the same to the Governors and Directors of the said Bank as a memento of myself: and I give and bequeath such article accordingly.'

Although J. P. Morgan died in 1943 the tankard remained in America until December 1945 because of war-time shipping risks. It is now in the Bank of England collection.

affair, the Gulf Stream, though that is quite enough in itself to fog and dampen everything in transit from one hemisphere to the other. Yet I can well see that no one would easily accept the result of these negotiations with sympathy and understanding unless he could, to some extent at least, bring himself to appreciate the motives and purposes of the other side. I think it would be worth while that I should devote some part of what I have to say to that aspect. How difficult it is for nations to understand one another, even when they have the advantage of a common language. How differently things appear in Washington than in London, and how easy it is to misunderstand one another's difficulties and the real purpose which lies behind each one's way of solving them. As the Foreign Secretary has pointed out, everyone talks about international co-operation, but how little of pride, of temper or of habit anyone is willing to contribute to it when it comes down to brass tacks.

When I last had the opportunity of discussing the Bretton Woods plan in your Lordships' House, the plan stood by itself, and its relationship to post-war policy as a whole was not clear. This was responsible for the least easily answered criticisms. All one could say in reply was that the plan was not intended to stand by itself, but one must begin somewhere. The other aspects were not yet ready for proposals, though details would be taken in hand as soon as possible. Today the situation is different. A more or less complete outline for the re-ordering of commercial and currency policies in their international aspects and their reconversion to peace-time practice is now available. Each part is complementary to the rest. Whether it be well or ill-conceived, in the rounded whole which your Lordships have before you, the proposals fall into three parts: a blue print called long-term organisation of world commerce and foreign exchanges on a multilateral and non-discriminatory basis; short-term proposals for the early reconversion of the sterling area in the same direction; and an offer of financial aid from the United States to enable this country to overcome the immediate difficulties of transition which would otherwise make the short-term proposals impracticable and delay our participation and collaboration with the United States in getting the rest of the world along the lines of the long-term policy indicated.

Each of these parts has been subjected to reasonable criticism. The long-term blue print invites us to commit ourselves against the future organisation of world trade on the principle of tying the opportunity of export to import by means of bilateral and discriminatory arrangements and unstable exchanges such as are likely to involve in practice the creation of separate economic blocs. It is argued that this is premature and unreasonable until we have found means to overcome the temporary difficulties of transition and have more experience of the actual conditions of the post-war world, in particular of how a full employment policy works out in practice in its international aspects. The short-term proposals have been criticised on the grounds that they do not allow us enough time to liquidate the very complex war-time arrangements, or to arrange the onerous financial obligations which they heaped on us. Finally, a complaint is made of the terms of the financial aid from the United States, that the amount is insufficient and the burden of the interest too heavy.

It is not for one who has striven every day for three months to improve these proposals so as to lay them less open to these criticisms, and who perhaps knows better than most people how imperfectly he has succeeded, to take these criticisms lightly; nor on the day after my return to this country am I yet in a position to judge, with much accuracy, the mood which underlies the criticisms which are being made, and which is probably more significant than the particular complaints in which it has been finding its outlet. Nevertheless I wonder if this first great attempt at organising international order out of the chaos of the war in a way which will not interfere with the diversity of national policy yet which will minimize the causes of friction and ill will between nations, is being viewed in its right perspective. I feel sure that serious injustice is being done to the liberal purposes and intense good will towards this country of the American people as represented by their administration and their urgent desire to see this country a strong and effective partner in guiding a distressed and confused world into the way of peace and economic order.

Let me plunge at once into the terms of the loan and the understandings about short-term policy which are associated with it. Since our transitory financial difficulties are largely due to the role we played in the war and to the costs we incurred before the United States entered the war, we here in London feel—it is a feeling which I shared and still share to the full—that it might not be asking too much of our American friends that they should agree to see us through the transition by financial aid which approximated to a grant. We felt it might be proper for us to indicate the general direction of the policies which that aid would enable us to pursue and to undertake to move along those lines, particularly in terminating the discriminatory features of the exchange arrangements of the sterling area as quickly as circumstances permit and that, subject to those general understandings, we should be left as free as possible to work things out in our own way. Released from immediate pressing anxieties on terms which would not embarrass the future, we could then proceed cautiously in the light of experience of the post-war world as it gradually disclosed its lessons.

Clearly that would have given us the best of both worlds. How reasonable such a programme sounds in London and how natural the disappointment when the actual proposals fall seriously short of it. But what a gulf separates us from the climate of Washington; and what a depth of misunderstanding there will be as to what governs relations between even the friendliest and most like-minded nations if we imagine that so free and easy an arrangement could commend itself to the complex politics of Congress or to the immeasurably remote public opinion of the United States. Nevertheless, it was on these lines that we opened our case. For three days the heads of the American delegation heard me expound the material contained in the White Paper to which the noble and learned Viscount, Lord Simon, referred. He would have done it more eloquently, but I can fairly say that I was heard not only with obvious and expressed good will and plain sympathy, but also with a keen desire on their part to understand the magnitude and the intricacies of our problem.

I must, at this point, digress for a moment to explain the American response to our claim that for good reasons arising out of the past they owe us something more than they have yet paid, something in the nature of deferred lend lease for the time when we held the fort alone, for it was here that in expounding our case we had an early and severe disappointment. It would be quite wrong to suppose that such considerations have played no part in the final results. They have played a vital part; we could never have obtained what we did obtain except against this background. Nevertheless, it was not very long before the British delegation discovered that a primary emphasis on past services and past sacrifice would not be fruitful. The American Congress and the American people have never accepted any literal principle of equal sacrifice, financial or otherwise, between all the allied participants. Indeed, have we ourselves?

It is a complete illusion to suppose that in Washington you have only to mention the principle of equal sacrifice to get all you want. The Americans—and are they wrong?—find a post-mortem on relative services and sacrifices amongst the leading Allies extremely distasteful and dissatisfying. Many different countries are involved and most of them are now in Washington to plead their urgent needs and high deserts. Some have rendered more service than others to the common cause; some have suffered, voluntarily or involuntarily, a greater sacrifice of lives and of material wealth; and some of them have escaped from a nearer, more imminent or deadlier peril than others. Not all of them have had out of Uncle Sam the same relative measure of assistance up to date.

How is all this to be added, subtracted and assessed in terms of a line of credit? It is better not to try; it is better not to think that way. I give the American point of view. Is not it more practical and more realistic—to use two favourite American expressions—to think in terms of the future and to work out what credits, of what amount and upon what terms, will do most service in reconstructing the post-war world and guiding post-war economy along these lines which, in the American view, will best conduce to the general prosperity of all and to the friendship of nations? This does not mean that the past is forgotten, even though it may be beginning to fade, but in no phase of human experience does the past operate so directly and arithmetically as we were trying to contend. Men's sympathies and less calculated impulses are drawn from their memories of comradeship, but their contemporary acts are generally directed towards influencing the future and not towards pensioning the past. At any rate I can safely assure you that that is how the American Administration and the American people think. Nor, I venture to say, should it be becoming in us to respond by showing our medals, all of them, and pleading that the old veteran deserves better than that, especially if we speak in the same breath of his forthcoming retirement from open commerce and the draughts of free competition, which most probably in his present condition would give him sore throat and drive him still further indoors.

If the noble Lord, Lord Woolton, had led the Mission to Washington—as I indeed wish that he had!—I would lay a hundred to one that he would not have continued in the vein in which he spoke yesterday for more than a few days. Neither pride of country nor sense of what is fitting would have allowed him, after he had sensed from every sort of information open to him how Americans responded to it, to make an open attempt to make what every American well appreciated was well enough known in men's hearts the main basis for asking for a gigantic gift. We soon discovered, therefore, that it was not our past performance or our present weakness but our future prospects of recovery and our intention to face the world boldly that we had to demonstrate. Our American friends were interested not in our wounds, though incurred in the common cause, but in our convalescence. They wanted to understand the size of our immediate financial difficulties, to be convinced that they were temporary and manageable and to be told that we intended to walk without bandages as soon as possible. In every circle in which I moved during my stay in Washington, it was when I was able to enlarge on the strength of our future competitive position, if only we were allowed a breather, that I won most sympathy. What the United States needs and desires is a strong Britain, endowed with renewed strength and facing the world on the equal or more than equal terms that we were wont to do. To help that forward interests them much more than to comfort a war victim.

But there was another aspect of the American emphasis on the future benefits which were expected as a result of financial aid to Britain. Those on the American side wanted to be able to speak definitely and in plain language to their own business world about the nature of the future arrangements in regard to commerce between the United States and the sterling area. It was the importance attached on the American side to their being able to speak definitely about future arrangements that made our task so difficult in securing a reasonable time and reasonable elasticity of action. As the Chancellor of the

Exchequer has explained in another place, we ran here into difficulties in the negotiations; and we accepted in the end more cut-and-dried arrangements in some respects than we ourselves believed to be wise or beneficial, as we explained in no uncertain terms and with all the force at our command. We warned them that precisely those criticisms which have been raised would be raised, and justly raised, in Parliament. They on their side, however, were not less emphatic that we should render their task impossibly difficult in commending their proposals to their own public unless we could find ways of meeting their desire for definiteness, at least to a certain extent.

Yet I must ask Your Lordships to believe that the financial outcome, though it is imperfectly satisfactory to us, does represent a compromise and is very considerably removed from what the Americans began by thinking reasonable; for at the outset the peculiar complexities of our existing arrangements were not at all understood. I am hopeful that the various qualifications which have been introduced, the full significance of which cannot be obvious except to experts, may allow in practice a workable compromise between the certainty they wanted and the measure of elasticity we wanted. Negotiations of this character, in which technical requirements and political appeal must both be satisfied, are immensely difficult, and could not have been brought to any conclusion except in an atmosphere of technical collaboration between the two sides, rather than of technical controversy.

I must now turn to the financial terms of the Agreement, and first of all to its amount. In my own judgement, it is cut somewhat too fine, and does not allow a margin for unforeseen contingencies. Nevertheless the sum is substantial. No comparable credit in time of peace has ever been negotiated before. It should make a great and indispensable contribution to the strength of this country, abroad as well as at home, and to the well being of our tired and jaded people. After making some allowance for a credit from Canada, and for some minor miscellaneous resources, it represents about as large a cumulative adverse balance as we ought to allow ourselves in the interval before we can get straight. Moreover, it may not prove altogether a bad thing that there should be no sufficient margin to tempt us to relax; for, if we were to relax, we should never reach equilibrium and become fully self-supporting within a reasonable period of time. As it is, the plain fact is that we cannot afford to abate the full energy of our export drive or the strictness of our economy in any activity which involves overseas expenditure. Our task remains as difficult as it is stimulating, and as stimulating as it is difficult. On a balance of considerations, therefore, I think that under this heading we should rest reasonably content.

That the Americans should be anxious not to allow too hot a pace to be set in this, their first major post-war operation of this kind, is readily understandable. The total demands for overseas financial assistance crowding in on the United States Treasury from all quarters whilst I was in Washington were estimated to amount to between four and five times our own maximum proposals. We naturally have only our own requirements in view, but the United States Treasury cannot overlook the possible reaction of what they do for us on the expectations of others. Many members of Congress were seriously concerned about the cumulative consequences of being too easy-going towards a world unanimously clamouring for American aid, and often only with too good reason. I mention such considerations because they are a great deal more obvious when one is in Washington than when one returns here.

On the matter of interest, I shall never so long as I live cease to regret that this is not an interest-free loan. The charging of interest is out of tune with the underlying realities. It is based on a false analogy. The other conditions of the loan indicate clearly that our case has been recognised as being, with all its attendant circumstances, a special one. The Americans might have felt it an advantage, one would have thought, in relation to other transactions to emphasise this special character still further by forgoing interest. The amount of money at stake cannot be important to the United States, and what a difference it would have made to our feelings and to our response! But there it is. On no possible ground can we claim as of right a gesture so unprecedented. A point comes when in a matter of this kind one has to take No for an answer. Nor, I am utterly convinced, was it any lack of generosity of mind or purpose on the part of the American negotiators which led to their final decision. And it is not for a foreigner to weigh up the cross-currents, political forces and general sentiments which determine what is possible and what is impossible in the complex and highly charged atmosphere of that great democracy of which the daily thoughts and urgent individual preoccupations are so far removed from ours. No one who has breathed that atmosphere for many troubled weeks will underestimate the difficulties of the American statesmen, who are striving to do their practical best for their own country and for the whole world, or the fatal consequences if the Administration were to offer us what Congress would reject.

During the whole time that I was in Washington, there was not a single Administration measure of the first importance that Congress did not either reject, remodel, or put on one side. Assuming, however, that the principle of charging interest had to be observed, then, in my judgment, almost everything possible has been done to mitigate the burden and to limit the risk of a future dangerous embarrassment. We pay no interest for six years. After that we pay no interest in any year in which our exports have not been restored to a level which may be estimated at about sixty per cent in excess of pre-war. I repeat that. We pay no interest in any year in which our exports have not been restored to a level which may be estimated at about sixty per cent in excess of what they were pre-war.

LORD BARNBY: In volume or value?

LORD KEYNES: Volume. That is very important; I should have said so. The maximum payment in any year is £35 million, and that does not become payable until our external income, in terms of present prices, is fifty times that amount. Again I repeat, the maximum payment in any year is £35 million and that does not become payable until our external income—that is from exports and shipping and the like—is, in terms of present prices, fifty times that amount. In any year in which our income falls short of this standard, interest is fully and finally waived. Moreover, the instalments of capital repayments are so arranged that we obtain the maximum benefit from this provision in the early years. For at the start the minimum payment to which we have committed ourselves is no more than £13 million a year; that is to say, less than one per cent of the external income which we must attain if we are to break even quite apart from the cost of the American loan.

It is relevant, I think, to remind your Lordships that the maximum charge to us in respect of the early years is not much more than half of what is being charged in respect of loans which the United States is making currently to her other Allies, through the Import and Export Bank or otherwise; whilst the minimum charge per cent to which we have been asked to commit ourselves in the early years is only one-fifth of the annual service charge which is being asked from the other Allies. None of those loans is subject to a five-year moratorium. All the other loans which are being made are tied loans limited to payments for specific purchases from the United States. Our loan, on the other hand, is a loan of money without strings, free to be expended in any part of the world. That is an arrangement, I may add, which is entirely consistent with the desire of the United States to enable us to return as fully as possible to the conditions of multilateral trade settlements.

Your negotiators can, therefore, in my judgment, fairly claim that the case of last time's war debts has not been repeated. Moreover, this is new money we are dealing with, to pay for post-war supplies for civilian purposes and is not—as was mainly the case on the previous occasion—a consolidation of a war debt. On the contrary, this new loan has been associated with a complete wiping off the slate of any residual obligations from the operation of lend lease. Under the original Lend Lease Agreement, the President of the United States has been free to ask for future 'consideration' of an undetermined character. This uncomfortable and uncertain obligation has been finally removed from us. The satisfactory character of the lend lease settlement has not, I think, received as much emphasis as it deserves. The Secretary of State for India emphasised it in his opening speech yesterday, but it was not, so far as I noticed, taken up in any of the speeches which were made by other noble Lords.

VISCOUNT SIMON: I made express reference to it.

LORD STRABOLGI: I mentioned it, too.

LORD KEYNES: I am indeed glad that there is some part of the settlement which has commended itself to those on the benches on this side of the House. No part of the loan which is applied to this settlement, relates to the cost of lend lease supplies consumed during the war, but is entirely devoted to supplies received by us through the lend lease machinery, but available for our consumption or use after the end of the war. It also covers the American military surplus and is in final discharge of a variety of financial claims, both ways, arising out of the war which fell outside the field of lend lease and reciprocal aid. Is it not putting our claim and legitimate expectations a little too high to regard these proposals, on top of lend lease, as anything but an act of unprecedented liberality? Has any country ever treated another country like this, in time of peace, for the purpose of rebuilding the other's strength and restoring its competitive position? If the Americans have tried to meet criticism at home by making the terms look a little less liberal than they really are, so as to preserve the principle of interest, is it necessary for us to be mistaken? The balm and sweet simplicity of no per cent is not admitted, but we are not asked to pay interest except in conditions where we can reasonably well afford to do so, and the capital instalments are so spread that our minimum obligation in the early years is actually less than it would be with a loan free of interest repayable by equal instalments.

I began by saying that the American negotiators had laid stress on future mutual advantage rather than on past history. But let no one suppose that such a settlement could have been conceivably made except by those who had measured and valued what this country has endured and accomplished. I have heard the suggestion made that we should have recourse to a commercial loan without strings. I wonder if those who put this forward have any knowledge of the facts. The body which makes such loans on the most favourable terms is the Export-Import Bank. Most of the European Allies are, in fact borrowing, or trying to borrow, from this institution. The most favourable terms sometimes allowed as, for instance, in the case of France, for the purpose of clearing up what she obtained through the lend lease machinery, are 2⅜ per cent with repayment over thirty years, beginning next year; that is to say, an annual debt of 5⅝ per cent so that an amount equal to 34 per cent of the loan will have been paid by France during the six years before we have begun to pay anything at all. The normal commercial terms in the Export-Import Bank are, however, 3 per cent repayable over twenty years commencing at once, so that payments equal to 48 per cent of the loan would have been paid during the first six years in which we pay nothing. Moreover, the resources of this institution are limited and our reasonable share of them could not have exceeded one-quarter or one-fifth of what we are actually getting. Nor are they without strings. They are tied to specific American purchases and not, like ours, available for use in any part of the world.

What about the conditions associated with the loans? The noble and learned Viscount, Lord Simon, as have also several other critics, laid stress on our having agreed to release the current earnings of the sterling area after the spring of 1947. I wonder how much we are giving away there. It does not relate to the balances accumulated before the spring of 1947. We are left quite free to settle this to the best of our ability. What we undertake to do is not to restrict the use of balances we have not yet got and have not yet been entrusted to us. It will be very satisfactory if we can maintain the voluntary war-time system into 1947. But what hope is there of the countries concerned continuing such an arrangement much longer than that? Indeed, the danger is that these countries which have a dollar or gold surplus, such as India, and South Africa, would prefer to make their own arrangements, leaving us with a dollar pool which is a deficit pool, responsible for the dollar expenditure not only of ourselves but of the other members of the area having a dollar deficit.

This arrangement is only of secondary use to us, save in the exceptional war-time conditions when those countries were, very abnormally, in a position to lend to us. We cannot force these countries to buy only from us, especially when we are physically unable to supply a large quantity of what they require. It seems to me a crazy idea that we can go on living after 1947 by borrowing on completely vague terms from India and the Crown Colonies. They will be wanting us to repay them. Two-thirds of what we owe to the sterling area is owed to India, Palestine, Egypt and Eire. Is it really wise to base our financial policy on the loyalty and good will of those countries to lend us money and leave out of our arrangements Canada and the United States? And Canada, let me add, is not less insistent than the United States—if anything she is more insistent—on our liberating the current earnings of the sterling area.

I hope I shall convince the noble and learned Viscount, for I have not yet finished. This was, anyhow, a condition very difficult to resist, for the main purpose of a loan of this magnitude was for the precise object of liberating the future earnings of the sterling area; not for repaying their past accumulations. Some have been misled by the fact that that has been expressly emphasised. Our direct adverse balance with the United States is not likely to exceed during the period more than about half the loan. The rest of our adverse balance is with the rest of the world—

VISCOUNT SIMON: The noble Lord speaks of a proposal difficult to resist. May we be informed if the experts did their best to resist it?

LORD KEYNES: They did their best to resist so early a date, but I am giving the reasons why, in being forced to surrender, the magnitude of our surrender was not so very great. I have explained so far that it would be very difficult in any circumstances to carry on the arrangements beyond that for the reasons I have explained, and I am now passing to what was, I feel, a vulnerable part of our case. That was, that the precise object of having so large a loan was to make these very arrangements practicable. About half of it would be a direct adverse balance with the United States. The rest of the adverse balance is with the rest of the world, mainly the sterling area. Canada will be dealt with separately. The very object of the other half of the loan is, therefore, to provide us with dollars mainly for the sterling area. We are given not only the condition but also the means to satisfy it. I am afraid it would take more than my forensic powers to maintain that position in its most absolute form against an argument so powerful as that, if the Americans could say: 'You are going to borrow all this money by impounding the earnings of the sterling area. What is the necessity for so large a loan? The calculations have been based on the contention that we have to meet the major part of your adverse balance.' But this is not the end. I do not think we need repine too much.

The way to remain an international banker is to allow cheques to be drawn upon you; the way to destroy the sterling area is to prey on it and to try to live on it. The way to retain it is to restore its privileges and opportunities as soon as possible to what they were before the war. It would have been more comfortable to know that we could have a little more than fifteen months to handle the situation, but, nevertheless, the underlying situation is as I have described. I do not regard this particular condition as a serious blot on the loan, although I agree with the noble and learned Viscount that I would have preferred it less precise, as I would have preferred many other points to be less precise. Such a view can only be based on a complete misapprehension of the realities of the position, for apart from the question of debt, do the critics really grasp the nature of the alternative? The alternative is to build up a separate economic bloc which excludes Canada and consists of countries to which we already owe more than we can pay, on the basis of their agreeing to lend us money they have not got and buy only from us and one another goods we are unable to supply. Frankly this is not such a caricature of these proposals as it may sound at first.

In conclusion, I must turn briefly to what is, in the long run, of major importance—namely, the blueprints for long-term commercial and currency policy, although I fear I must not enlarge on that. In working out the Commercial Policy Paper, to which, of course, this country is not committed, unless a considerable part of the world is prepared to come into it and not merely the United States, and in the Final Act of Bretton Woods, I believe that your representatives have been successful in maintaining the principles and objects which are best suited to the predicaments of this country. The plans do not wander from the international terrain and they are consistent with widely different conceptions of domestic policy. Proposals which the authors hope to see accepted both by the United States of America and by Soviet Russia must clearly conform to this condition. It is not true, for example, to say that state trading and bulk purchasing are interfered with. Nor is it true to say that the planning of the volume of our exports and imports, so as to preserve equilibrium in the international balance of payments, is prejudiced. Exactly the contrary is the case. Both the currency and the commercial proposals are devised to favour the maintenance of equilibrium by expressly permitting various protective devices when they are required to maintain equilibrium and by forbidding them when they are not so required. They are of the utmost importance in our relationship with the United States and, indeed, the outstanding characteristic of the plans is that they represent the first elaborate and comprehensive attempt to combine the advantages of freedom of commerce with safeguards against the disastrous consequences of a *laissez-faire* system which pays no direct regard to the preservation of equilibrium and merely relies on the eventual working out of blind forces.

Here is an attempt to use what we have learnt from modern experience and modern analysis, not to defeat, but to implement the wisdom of Adam Smith. It is a unique accomplishment, I venture to say, in the field of international discussion to have proceeded so far by common agreement along a newly-trod path, not yet pioneered, I agree, to a definite final destination, but a newly-trod path, which points the right way. We are attempting a great step forward towards the goal of international economic order amidst national diversities of policies. It is not easy to have patience with those who pretend that some of us, who were very early in the field to attack and denounce the false premises and false conclusions of unrestricted *laissez-faire* and its particular manifestations in the former gold standard and other currency and commercial doctrines which mistake private licence for public liberty, are now spending their later years in the service of the State to walk backwards and resurrect and re-erect the idols which they had played some part in throwing out of the market place. Not so. Fresh tasks now invite. Opinions have been successfully changed. The work of destruction has been accomplished, and the site has been cleared for a new structure.

Questions have been raised—and rightly and reasonably raised—about the willingness of the United States to receive repayment hereafter. This is a large subject to which I have given a great deal of thought, but I shall not have time to develop it fully today. I am not, as a result, quite so worried as most people. Indeed, if in the next five or ten years the dollar turns out to be a scarce currency, seldom will so many people have been right. It is a very technical matter, very emphatically within their past experience, but not so easily the subject of future prediction. I am afraid I must content myself with a few headlines. First, it is not a question of our having to pay the United States by direct exports; we could never do that. Our exports are not, and are not likely to be as large as our direct imports from the United States. The object of the multilateral system is to enable us to pay the United States by exporting to any part of the world and it is partly for that very reason that the Americans have felt the multilateral system was the only sound basis for any arrangement of this kind. Secondly, all the most responsible people in the United States, and particularly in the State Department and in the Treasury, have entirely departed from the high tariff, export subsidy conception of things, and will do their utmost with, they believe, the support of public opinion in the opposite direction. That is why this international trade convention presents us with such a tremendous opportunity.

For the first time in modern history the United States is going to exert its full, powerful influence in the direction of reduction of tariffs, not only of itself but by all others.

Thirdly, this is a problem of which today every economist and publicist in the United States is acutely conscious. Books on economics are scarcely written about anything else. They would regard it as their fault and not ours if they fail to solve it. They would acquit us of blame—quite different from the atmosphere of ten or twenty years ago. They will consider it their business to find a way out. Fourthly, if the problem does arise, it will be a problem, for reasons I have just mentioned, of the United States *vis-à-vis* the rest of the world and not us in particular. It will be the problem of the United States and the whole commercial and financial arrangement of every other country. Fifthly—and perhaps this is the consideration which is least prominent in people's minds—the United States is rapidly becoming a high-living and a high-cost country. Their wages are two and a half times ours. These are the historic, classical methods by which in the long run international equilibrium will be restored.

Therefore, much of these policies seem to me to be in the prime interest of our country, little though we may like some parts of them. They are calculated to help us regain a full measure of prosperity and prestige in the world's commerce. They aim, above all, at the restoration of multilateral trade which is a system upon which British commerce essentially depends. You can draw your supplies from any source that suits you and sell your goods in any market where they can be sold to advantage. The bias of the policies before you is against bilateral barter and every kind of discriminatory practice. The separate economic blocs and all the friction and loss of friendship they must bring with them are expedients to which one may be driven in a hostile world, where trade has ceased over wide areas to be co-operative and peaceful and where are forgotten the healthy rules of mutual advantage and equal treatment. But it is surely crazy to prefer that. Above all, this determination to make trade truly international and to avoid the establishment of economic blocs which limit and restrict commercial intercourse outside them, is plainly an essential condition of the world's best hope, an Anglo-American understanding, which brings us and others together in international institutions which may be in the long run the first step towards something more comprehensive. Some of us, in the tasks of war and more lately in those of peace, have learnt by experience that our two countries can work together. Yet it would be only too easy for us to walk apart. I beg those who look askance at these plans to ponder deeply and responsibly where it is they think they want to go.

After Keynes's speech and another five hours of discussion, the resolution to approve the financial agreement was carried by ninety votes to eight. About 100 peers abstained. The Bretton Woods proposals were approved without a division.

After the discussion in the Lords, Keynes cleared up a few outstanding odds and ends in the Treasury before going off to Tilton to rest. During his time at Tilton, he wrote several letters to friends and others connected with the negotiations, often enclosing copies of his speech in the Lords. Two of these letters best set out his reactions to the situation in London on his return from America.

To SIR RICHARD HOPKINS, *6 January 1946*

My dear Hoppy,

It was very nice to get your line of greeting.[32] As you say, the public response (under, I should add, the careful tuition of their leaders) to what had been done was rather disturbing. But, on reflection, I am not worried. I am convinced that we did a good piece of work, which will be found to wear well

---

[32] Hopkins had written Keynes on 18 December, 'I am afraid you will feel that the public response is a poor reward but that seems inevitably to follow from the method of presentation [adopted by the authorities].'

and has been sufficiently thought out in detail to contain merits which will only be gradually discovered as time goes on. Anyhow, I am certain that by ramming the thing home to a conclusion we have avoided great dangers, far greater than Ministers and some of their advisers are in the least conscious of, and to avoid misfortunes is about all one can hope for in this world.

Moreover, can I not perhaps claim to have brought off a double event, which I have often tried at and never yet managed? I have regained my self-respect by finding myself once more in the minority, but this time actual events are being forced to follow the minority view, and Cassandra, though disbelieved, gets her way.

I am just at the end of a fortnight at Tilton and have recuperated completely; not that I have refrained from work —there was a frightful lot of non-Treasury matters to catch up with after four months—but I was free from *worry*, and that is what really matters.

Tomorrow I am going back to London. I will be seeking a talk with Bridges about what happens next. And, if you are about the place, I should very much like to have a talk with you. I am clear that advantage ought to be taken of this break, and that I should not from now on do whole-time duty at the Treasury. Whether I should slip out completely at once, or whether it should be a gradual operation, is what has to be settled.

> Yours ever,
> [copy initialled] M.K.

To LORD HALIFAX, *1 January 1946*

Dear Edward,

I have taken a fortnight off letter writing to attend to bran-pies (it was a great success) and such like matters. But perhaps, though late, you'd like to hear how I found the odd and disturbing Parliamentary position when I got back.

It was a mixture of ignorance and (on both sides) pure party politics. The ignorance was all-embracing. So far as the public was concerned, no-one had been at any pains to explain, far less defend, what had been done. And as for the insiders, so dense a fog screen had been created that such as the Chancellor and the Governor of the Bank had only the dimmest idea of what we had given away and what we had not. The Chancellor had been worked up into a great state of indignation about the sterling area which was based (in my opinion) on entire misapprehension of what we had been doing. The Governor of the Bank told me frankly that it was from my speech in the House of Lords he learnt for the first time that the loan was *not* tied to purchases in the U.S. and that about half of it was specifically for the purpose of providing us with funds to liberate the sterling area along the lines we were undertaking. Of course, if this had not been so, we should have been committing ourselves to what would be virtually impossible, and any amount of indignation would have been more than justified!

However, the ignorance was not the real trouble—I suppose that is normal among the great, and inevitable and indeed quite proper among the public. Both political parties were split on issues which had nothing to do with the technical details; and both sets of party leaders decided that a complete abdication of leadership would be the happiest way out. A section of the Socialists thought they detected too definite a smell of *laissez-faire*, at any rate of anti-planning, in the American conception of international affairs. This is only half-true; but the doctrine of non-discrimination does commit us to abjure Schachtian methods, which their Jewish economic advisers (who, like so many Jews, are either Nazi or Communist at heart and have no notion how the British Commonwealth was founded or is sustained) were hankering after. At any rate, it was easy to argue in a broad way that, as extreme versions of foreign trade planning through barter agreements were ruled out, our policy was no better than a specious revival of nineteenth century liberalism.

A section of the Conservatives, led by Max [Beaverbrook] and supported by others too near Winston [Churchill], were convinced, with some reason, that the proposed commercial policy ruled out Preference as a serious, substantial policy for the future; and that this, taken in conjunction with the opening of the sterling area, doomed the idea of an Empire economic bloc. It annoyed them, of course, to have me pointing out that the Empire in question would not include Canada (or probably South Africa) and would have to be built on the British loyalty and goodwill of India, Palestine, Egypt and Eire.

In fact both sides of the old Coalition (the Conservatives more shamelessly than the Socialists) were running out on the fundamental concepts which had been settled long ago and without which our negotiations could never have been fruitfully started. All the rest was smoke screen.

Nevertheless, it soon became obvious that both the above sections were minorities in their own parties and cut no ice whatever with the general public. The general public was upset solely because they were being told by those who ought to know, that, after all their past *and present* sufferings, they were being given a raw deal by their old comrades in U.S. As usual, there was not the smallest necessity for the party leaders to run away.

My strong belief is (though you may all be justified, as usual, in saying I am too optimistic) that the line I took in my speech met with an immediate response from genuine public opinion —more than was immediately obvious—and a lot of people quickly became rather ashamed of the way they had been talking. This was certainly so in the House of Lords. There cannot have been for many years such a crowded and excited sitting. Mingling in the division lobby and as the House broke up, it seemed to me clear that practically everyone was voting

Aye out of conviction, and not merely to avoid a constitutional crisis, and that, if there had been a free vote with no one abstaining, the majority would have been larger.

Cranborne, by the way, made a most masterly speech by way of getting out of a silly situation. A pure Cecilian utterance, which A.J.B[alfour] (whose shade one could feel hovering near) could not have done so well. He helped to give Max, who was sitting next him on the front bench, one of the most humiliating days of his life—and Max seemed painfully conscious that this was so. Cranborne, in my opinion, is worth ten times Anthony [Eden]. The combination of his diffidence and unimpressive appearance with some inherent quality of dignity and authority, which few today can reach, produces a remarkable effect. Old Lord Salisbury, as beautiful and pure a picture as ever, was there to hear him. However, I am prejudiced. I have never in my life been able to resist a Cecil.

One final conclusion. My impression is that the *fait accompli* is now being accepted, at any rate in official circles and in the Bank of England, as something which must be loyally and sincerely carried out. I think you can reassure the Americans on this, if the public reception of the programme here leads them to doubt it. Political trouble there will certain be, for the Cabinet is a poor, weak thing. But I am hopeful that the technicians will now turn their technique in the agreed direction.

For me, I think the time has come for me to slip out of the Treasury, if not suddenly, at least steadily. When I return to London from the country, I shall have to reach a clear notion what happens next. Being of a resigning temperament, I shall not last long in this galère in any case; so I had better go when I go quiet and friendly.

Yours ever,
[copy initialled] M.K.

P.S. Will you show this letter to Bob Brand?—though I infer from a telegram I have seen that he is not well.

APPENDICES

Appendix I

THE AMERICAN PROPOSALS OF 18 NOVEMBER

From NABOB 372, 21 November 1945

Following is text of U.S. draft memorandum of understanding on financial matters dated 18 November 1945.

1. *Amount of the line of credit*

(I) The Government of the United States will extend to the Government of the United Kingdom a line of credit of...billion.

(II) This line of credit will be available until December 31, 1951.

2. *Purpose of the credit*

(I) The purpose of the credit shall be to facilitate purchases by the United Kingdom of goods and services from the United States, to assist the United Kingdom to meet transitional post-war deficits in her current balance of payments, to help the United Kingdom to maintain adequate reserves of gold and dollars and to assist the United Kingdom to assume the obligations of multilateral trade, as defined in this and other agreements.

(II) It is understood that any amounts required to discharge obligations of the United Kingdom to third countries outstanding on the date of this contract will be found from resources other than this line of credit.

3. *Amortisation and interest*

(I) The amount of the credit outstanding on December 31, 1951 shall be repaid in 50 annual instalments, beginning on December 31, 1951, until 50 instalments have been paid, subject to the provisions of (4) below.

(II) The rate of interest shall be 2 per cent per annum, computed annually beginning with January 1, 1951, on the amount outstanding each year, and payable in 50 annual instalments, beginning on December 31, 1951, subject to the provisions of (4) below.

629

(III) The 50 annual instalments of principal repayments and interest shall be equal, amounting to 31·8 million dollars for each 1 billion dollars outstanding on December 31, 1951. Each instalment shall consist of the full amount of the interest due and the remainder of the instalment shall be the principal to be repaid in that year.

4. Waiver of interest payment

(I) The Government of the United States, at the request of the Government of the United Kingdom, will agree to waive in any year the amount of the interest due in that year if:

(a) as certified by the International Monetary Fund, the income of the U.K. from home-produced exports plus its net income from invisible current transactions in its balance of payments (as defined in Article XIX (I) of the Final Act of Bretton Woods) was on the average over the five preceding calendar years less than the amount of U.K. imports during 1936–8, fixed at 866 million pounds, as such figure may be adjusted for changes in the price level of these imports. If waiver is requested for an interest payment prior to that due in 1955, the average income shall be computed for the calendar years from 1950 through the year preceding the given year; and

(b) as certified by the International Monetary Fund, the U.K.'s official holdings (gross) of gold and convertible foreign exchange were at the end of the preceding calendar year less than the sum of (1) 15 percent of the average value of the U.K.'s commodity imports over the preceding five calendar years and (2) 25 percent of the current demand and short term liabilities against the U.K.'s official holdings of gold and convertible foreign exchange in favour of other governments and central banks, as of the end of the preceding calendar year. If waiver is requested for an interest payment prior to that due in 1955, the average value of imports shall be computed for the calendar years from 1950 through the year preceding the given year.

(II) Waiver of interest will not be requested or allowed in any year unless, the aggregate of the agreed releases or annual payments in respect of the following is reduced, through waivers or deferments during the life of this credit, by an amount proportionate to the reduction in the annual instalment of this credit:

(a) new loans to the U.K. Government arranged after January 1, 1945,

(b) sterling balances for release subsequent to 1950.

(III) Either Government shall be entitled to approach the other Government for reconsideration of the manner and time of payment, if in its opinion the prevailing conditions of international exchange justify such reconsideration.

5. *Accelerated repayment*

(I) The Government of the U.K. may accelerate repayment of the line of credit.

(II) If the Government of the U.K. accelerates releases or annual payments as described in 4(II) above in advance of the rate originally agreed, it will make an accelerated payment of an equal amount of the principal repayments in the next instalment due on this line of credit releases and annual payments of more than 175 million dollars per year under 4(II) (b) above shall be considered an accelerated payment.

6. *Sterling area exchange arrangements*

The Government of the United Kingdom will complete arrangements as early as practicable and in any case not later than the end of 1946 under which, immediately after the completion of such arrangements the sterling receipts from current transactions of all sterling area countries, apart from any receipts arising out of military expenditure by the United Kingdom prior to December 31, 1948 which it may be agreed to treat on the same basis as the balances accumulated during the war, will be freely available for current transactions in any currency area without discrimination with the result that any discrimination arising from the so-called dollar sterling pool will be entirely removed and that each member of the sterling area will have its current sterling and dollar receipts at its free disposition for current transactions anywhere.

7. *Other exchange arrangements*

The Governments of the United States and the United Kingdom agree that after December 31, 1946 or earlier if practicable they will impose no restrictions on payments and transfers for current international transactions, (as defined in the Articles of Agreement of the International Monetary Fund); but this obligation shall not apply to foreign owned balances accumulated prior to December 31, 1946 or to foreign owned balances arising from military expenditure prior to December 31, 1948.

8. *Exchange restrictions and import controls*

The Governments of the U.K. and the U.S. will impose no exchange restrictions on transactions permitted by the authorities controlling imports. If the government of either country imposes quantitative import restrictions as an aid to the restoration of equilibrium in the balances of payments, such restrictions shall be administered on a basis which does not discriminate against imports from the other country in respect of any produce; provided that this undertaking shall not apply (a) in cases in which its application would have the effect of preventing the country imposing such restrictions from utilising, for the purchase of needed imports, inconvertible currencies accumulated up to December 31 1946, or (b) in cases in which there may be special necessity for the country imposing such restrictions to assist, by measures not involving a substantial departure from the general rule of non-discrimination, a country whose economy has been disrupted by war. The provisions of this paragraph shall become effective as soon as practicable and in any case not later than the end of 1946.

9. *The accumulated sterling balances*

The Government of the U.K. has communicated its intentions to the Government of the U.S. as follows:

The Government of the United Kingdom intends to make an early settlement, varying according to the circumstances of each case, of the sterling balances accumulated by sterling area and other countries prior to such settlement (together with any future receipts arising out of military expenditure by the U.K. which it may be agreed to treat on the same basis). The settlements with the sterling area countries will be on the basis of dividing these accumulated balances into three categories, (a) balances to be released at once and convertible into any currency for current transactions, (b) balances to be similarly released by instalments over a period of years beginning in 1951, and (c) balances to be written off as a contribution to settlement of war and post-war indebtedness and in recognition of the benefits which the countries concerned might be expected to gain from such a settlement.

Appendix II

COMMENTS HANDED TO THE AMERICANS BY KEYNES AND LORD HALIFAX ON 25 NOVEMBER

From NABOB 396, 25 November 1945

Comments of the U.K. Government on the provisional American draft

1. Certain of the clauses in the draft (which is, they appreciate, of a provisional and tentative character) lately remitted to the Government of the U.K. are, in their view unacceptable, not because they are not pointing in the right direction, but because they attempt to go into more precise details in respect of the time and manner of application of agreed principles, than is either practicable or advisable.

2. The Government of the U.K. desire, therefore, to recall the discussions to their central objects and to emphasise how large a measure of agreement can be accomplished, if unnecessary points of difference can be avoided on matters of detail not essential to the main purpose.

3. On the assumption that agreement is reached on the measure and terms of the financial aid required to enable the U.K. to surmount the balance of trade difficulties of the transition, and subject always to the views of Parliament on matters which have not yet been submitted, the Government of the U.K. are ready to proceed as follows:–

(i) To modify the exchange arrangements of the sterling area as set forth in paragraph 6 of the American draft;

(ii) To recommend to Parliament the ratification of the Final Act of Bretton Woods as soon as a financial agreement has been reached with the U.S. administration;

(iii) To associate the Government of the U.K. with the proposals on commercial policy as in the documents recently drafted;

(iv) To modify progressively and at as early dates as circumstances permit any remaining exchange restrictions and import controls of the character referred to in paragraphs 7 and 8 of the American draft, and to shape their policy to this end; and

(v) To seek by voluntary agreement with the countries of the sterling area an early settlement of the accumulated sterling balances on terms varying according to the circumstances of each case, on the lines already indicated to the U.S. group.

4. To reach so comprehensive a measure of agreement over so wide and

so difficult a field would seem to them to represent enormous progress and to show how close together the American and the British positions are on essentials.

5. They are, therefore, all the more dismayed that the financial negotiations should drag on and be cumbered with over-precise and inevitably controversial conditions which are not necessary to the common purpose of the negotiations on the two sides. Such a situation cannot but have a bad effect on the relations between the two countries, and that, at a time when there is so much other important international business on which a common policy has to be worked out.

6. On the contrary, in a position of great complexity, the Government of the U.K. feel that they ought not to be asked to risk success in so difficult an endeavour as that which they are facing, by attempting to move more rapidly than circumstances can safely allow or with less liberty of manoeuvre than is both reasonable and desirable in negotiations in prospect with the many other countries concerned. They would remind the U.S. group that the policy of other countries and the results of the Commercial Conferences planned for 1946 are not yet known.

7. In particular, they cannot accept a time limit for completing the negotiations on the accumulated sterling area balances, for this would put them at a serious disadvantage in negotiating. The other party would know that the U.K. must meet them in order to fulfil its contract with the U.S. The Government of the U.K. intend, however, to begin negotiations early in 1946 and to carry them on as rapidly as possible. The policy is in their interest and they stand by it.

8. Nor, except to the extent indicated above, can they forgo prematurely the safeguards of the transitional arrangements provided for in the Bretton Woods plan and in the agreed paper on commercial policy, regardless of the course of events in the precarious period ahead and irrespective of reciprocal action by the other countries affected. The U.K. Government would, however, consider themselves pledged as already stated to shape their policy so as to terminate these arrangements as soon as practicable.

9. Turning to the terms of the proposed line of credit, the Government of the U.K. greatly regret that there should be a departure from the simplicity and certainty of the waiver clause based on the volume of the external income of the U.K., as it was originally communicated to them. They see the greatest difficulty in arriving at a suitable and indisputable definition of 'reserves'. They think it is impossible to define the adequacy of reserves at any given figure in a contract for forty-five years when so much may happen, which cannot now be foreseen in the methods and technique of conducting international financial relations. Moreover, any

such provision might give rise to the misconception that the U.S. wishes to keep the U.K. reserves in as weak a position as possible. Indeed a clause based on examining the statistical state of reserves must be rejected as quite wrong in principle and against the interest of both countries. The Bretton Woods Final Act, the projected provisions of the I.T.C. and the lasting liberalisation of the sterling area will be far more likely to endure over a long period of years if the U.K. hold substantial reserves than if they are in anxiety on this score and are liable to be reduced in any temporary adverse circumstances too near to bed-rock.

10. There is a far better solution of the issue which this objectionable provision seeks to solve. The object appears to be to prevent advantage being taken of the waiver rights under the criterion of external income in circumstances when the reserves were strong viewed in the light of the circumstances existing when the occasion arises. But in such circumstances the U.K. would not wish to take advantage of the waiver clause. To do so will always be, in the view of the U.K. Government, a grave matter, never to be acted upon if it is avoidable. Whenever this right is invoked the credit of the U.K. is bound to suffer. To invoke it, except in a case of clear necessity, must necessarily impair the good relations between the U.K. and the U.S. There will be no intention on the part of the U.K. to exercise their rights of waiver in any circumstances in which they see their way to avoid it. A readiness to accept the *bona fides* and honourable intention of the U.K. not to take advantage of the waiver clause to escape a liability which they are well able to meet, would be worth more than any amount of drafting ingenuity. Nor without such mutual confidence can there be good prospect of an enduring common policy in the wider field and larger hopes which it is the purpose of these discussions to keep in view.

11. The Government of the U.K. are also much disappointed that the U.S. Group have found no means of providing against difficulties arising, not out of the inability of the U.K. to earn an external income, but out of an inability or a reluctance on the part of the U.S. to receive sufficient goods and services from the rest of the world to discharge what the rest of the world owes to them in the balance of payments. They hope that a search for a suitable provision can be resumed. In any case they would suggest the inclusion of a clause to the following effect:–

Either Government shall be entitled to approach the other for a review and modification by mutual consent of this agreement if its working has become such as to burden international commerce within the meaning of Article VII of the Mutual Aid Agreement of February 23rd 1942 or is otherwise contrary to the intention of the two Governments in entering on this agreement.

635

12. Finally, the Government of the U.K. regret their inability to accept paragraphs 4(11) and 5(11) of the American draft inasmuch as they limit in advance the freedom of negotiation of the U.K. with sterling area creditors, a limitation which would be bound to carry with it political complications of the gravest nature within the British Commonwealth.

Appendix III

THE AMERICAN PROPOSALS HANDED TO THE BRITISH ON 2 DECEMBER

From Foreign Relations of the United States, 1945, *Vol. VI, pp. 173–7.*

United States draft memorandum of understanding on financial matters

(This is designed to serve as the basis for the more detailed contract, financial agreement and other documents which may be agreed.)

1. *Amount of the line of credit*

(i) The Government of the United States will extend to the Government of the United Kingdom a line of credit of...billion.

(ii) This line of credit will be available until December 31, 1951.

2. *Purpose of the credit*

The purpose of the credit shall be to facilitate purchases by the United Kingdom of goods and services from the United States, to assist the United Kingdom to meet transitional postwar deficits in her current balance of payments, to help the United Kingdom to maintain adequate reserves of gold and dollars and to assist the United Kingdom to assume the obligations of multilateral trade, as defined in this and other agreements.

3. *Amortization and interest*

(i) The amount of the credit outstanding on December 31, 1951 shall be repaid with interest in 50 annual installments, beginning on December 31, 1951, subject to the provisions of (4) below.

(ii) The rate of interest shall be 2 percent per annum. For the year 1951 interest shall be computed on the amount outstanding on December 31,

1951, and for each year thereafter, interest shall be computed on the amount outstanding on January 1, subject to the provisions of (4) below.

(iii) The 50 annual installments of principal repayments and interest shall be equal, amounting to $31·8 million for each $1 billion outstanding on December 31, 1951. Each installment shall consist of the full amount of the interest due and the remainder of the installment shall be the principal to be repaid in that year.

4. *Waiver of interest payments*

In any year in which the Government of the United Kingdom requests the Government of the United States to waive the amount of the interest due in that year, the Government of the United States will grant the waiver if:

(*a*) The Government of the U.K. finds that a waiver is necessary in view of the present and prospective conditions of international exchange and the level of its gold and foreign exchange reserves *and*

(*b*) As certified by the International Monetary Fund, the income of the U.K. from home-produced exports plus its net income from invisible current transactions in its balance of payments (as defined in Article XIV (i) of the Articles of Agreement of the International Monetary Fund) was on the average over the five preceding calendar years less than the amount of U.K. imports during 1936–8, fixed at £866 million, as such figures may be adjusted for changes in the price level of these imports. Any amount in excess of $175 million released or paid or used in any year on account of sterling balances accumulated in the hands of overseas governments, monetary authorities and banks before the date of this Agreement, shall be regarded as a capital transaction and therefore shall not be included in the above calculation of the net income from invisible current transactions for that year. If waiver is requested for an interest payment prior to that due in 1955, the average income shall be computed for the calendar years from 1950 through the year preceding the given year.

5. *Position of this credit in relation to other obligations*

(i) It is understood that any amounts required to discharge obligations of the United Kingdom to third countries outstanding on the date of this Agreement will be found from resources other than this line of credit.

(ii) The Government of the United Kingdom will not arrange any long-term loans from governments within the British Commonwealth after the date of this Agreement and before the end of 1951 on terms more favorable to the lender than the terms of this line of credit.

(iii) Waiver of interest will not be requested or allowed under 4 above in any year unless the aggregate of the releases, payments or other uses in that year of sterling balances accumulated in the hands of overseas governments, monetary authorities and banks before the date of this Agreement, are reduced proportionately, and unless interest payments on loans referred to in (ii) above are waived. The proportionate reduction of the releases, payments or other uses of sterling balances shall be calculated on the basis of the aggregate released in the most recent year in which waiver of interest was not requested.

(iv) The application of the principles set forth in this section shall be subject of full consultation between the two Governments as occasion may arise.

6. *Sterling area exchange arrangements*

The Government of the United Kingdom will complete arrangements as early as practicable and in any case not later than the end of 1946 under which, immediately after the completion of such arrangements, the sterling receipts from current transactions of all sterling area countries, apart from any receipts arising out of military expenditure by the United Kingdom prior to December 31, 1948, which it may be agreed to treat on the same basis as the balances accumulated during the war will be freely available for current transactions in any currency area without discrimination; with the result that any discrimination arising from the so-called sterling area dollar pool will be entirely removed and that each member of the sterling area will have its current sterling and dollar receipts at its free disposition for current transactions anywhere.

7. *Other exchange arrangements*

(i) The Government of the U.K. agrees that after the date of this Agreement it will apply no exchange restrictions, except in accordance with the Articles of Agreement of the International Monetary Fund, which will restrict payments or transfers in respect of products permitted to be imported into the U.K. from the U.S., or of other current transactions between the two countries as defined in Article XIX (i) of the said Articles or on the use of sterling balances in the hands of U.S. residents arising out of current transactions; and in pursuance of the policy of reducing restrictions on trade between the two countries at the earliest possible date it agrees not to avail itself, in respect of the transactions referred to above, of Article XIV of the Articles of Agreement of the International Monetary Fund.

(ii) The Governments of the U.S. and the U.K. agree that not later than one year after the effective date of this agreement, unless a later date is agreed upon after consultation, they will impose no restrictions on payments and transfers for current international transactions as defined in the Articles of Agreement of the International Monetary Fund. The obligations of this paragraph shall not apply:

(*a*) to balances of third countries and their nationals accumulated before this paragraph becomes effective;

(*b*) to restrictions imposed with the approval of the International Monetary Fund (but the U.K. and the U.S. agree that they will not continue to invoke the provisions of Article XIV, Section 2 of the Articles of Agreement of the International Monetary Fund after this paragraph becomes effective); or

(*c*) to restrictions imposed in connection with measures designed to uncover and dispose of assets of Germany and Japan.

(iii) The obligations assumed by the Governments of the U.S. and the U.K. under this section and section 8 are also assumed by all of their respective colonies, overseas territories, all territories under their protection, suzerainty, or authority and all territories in respect of which they exercise a mandate.

8. *Import arrangements*

If the Government of either country imposes or maintains quantitative import restrictions, such restrictions shall be administered on a basis which does not discriminate against imports from the other country in respect of any product; provided that this undertaking shall not apply (*a*) in cases in which its application would have the effect of preventing the country imposing such restrictions from utilizing, for the purchase of needed imports, inconvertible currencies accumulated up to December 31, 1946, or (*b*) in cases in which there may be special necessity for the country imposing such restrictions to assist, by measures not involving a substantial departure from the general rule of non-discrimination, a country whose economy has been disrupted by war. The provisions of this paragraph shall become effective not later than one year after the effective date of this Agreement unless a later date is agreed upon after consultation.

9. *Accumulated sterling balances*

(i) The Government of the U.K. has communicated its intentions to the Government of the U.S. as follows:

The Government of the United Kingdom intends to make an early settlement, varying according to the circumstances of each case, of the sterling balances accumulated by sterling area and other countries prior to such settlement (together with any future receipts arising out of military expenditure by the U.K. which it may be agreed to treat on the same basis). The settlements with the sterling area countries will be on the basis of dividing these accumulated balances into three categories, (*a*) balances to be released at once and convertible into any currency for current transactions, (*b*) balances to be similarly released by installments over a period of years beginning in 1951, and (*c*) balances to be written off as a contribution to the settlement of war and postwar indebtedness and in recognition of the benefits which the countries concerned might be expected to gain from such a settlement.

(ii) In view of the importance of the interest of the United States in the method of dealing with sterling balances from the standpoint of their relation to non-discriminatory trade policies, and in consideration of the fact that an important purpose of the present credit is to promote the development of multilateral trade and facilitate its early resumption on a non-discriminatory basis, the Government of the United Kingdom agrees that, not later than one year after the effective date of this Agreement unless a later date is agreed upon after consultation, any sterling balances available for payments, whether pursuant to settlement of [*or*] otherwise, will be available for use in any currency area without discrimination.

10. *Consultation on agreement*

Either Government shall be entitled to approach the other for a reconsideration of any of the provisions of this Agreement, if in its opinion the prevailing conditions of international exchange justify such reconsideration, with a view to agreeing upon modifications for presentation to their respective legislatures.

DOCUMENTS REPRODUCED IN
THIS VOLUME

DEBATES, MINUTES OF MEETINGS, PRESS STATEMENTS

* Since the Editor examined these documents, the Treasury has reported that the
relevant files of OF110/39/13/1, OF110/39/13/3 and OF110/59/6 have been
inadvertently destroyed. A Public Record Office search for the papers in the
Departmental files has so far been unsuccessful.

DOCUMENTS REPRODUCED IN THIS VOLUME

* Since the Editor examined these documents, the Treasury has reported that the relevant files of OF110/39/13/1, OF110/39/13/3 and OF110/59/6 have been inadvertently destroyed. A Public Record Office search for the papers in the Departmental files has so far been unsuccessful.

UNPUBLISHED LETTERS

DOCUMENTS REPRODUCED IN THIS VOLUME

* Since the Editor examined these documents, the Treasury has reported that the relevant files of OF110/39/13/1, OF110/39/13/3 and OF110/59/6 have been inadvertently destroyed. A Public Record Office search for the papers in the Departmental files has so far been unsuccessful.

ACKNOWLEDGEMENTS

The Royal Economic Society is grateful to the Controller of Her Majesty's Stationery Office for permission to reproduce Crown Copyright materials.

The Editors would also like to record their thanks to Professors L. S. Pressnell and R. S. Sayers and to Mr R. B. Bryce for advice; and to the Canada Council for financial assistance.

INDEX

Acheson, Dean, Assistant Under-Secretary in U.S. State Department, 70, 157, 163, 186, 190, 363; member, Morgenthau's technical sub-committee, 194; help behind the scenes, 214; relations with Crowley, 217, 512; influence with Truman, 513

Admiralty
delegation to Washington, 189
expenditure, 171, 265, 296, 468, 532; and refund of Canadian dollars, 234, 239
requirements, 193, 197

Africa
war expenditure in, 398, 451, post-war, 263, 407; justified by German defeat in, 264, 451
see also Central Africa; East African Colonies; North Africa; South Africa; West African Colonies

Agriculture, 328, 329
agricultural and forestry products from Canada, 149, 225–6

Air Agreement, 199

Air Chiefs, 210
see also Courtney, Air Chief Marshall

Aircraft: under lend lease, 173, 210; issues of American-type and other aircraft, 238–40, 242, 243; transport aircraft, 518

Aircraft industry: American, 143; British, 262

Air mail, 528

Air Ministry
delegates in Washington, 194–5, 196–7
expenditure, 171, 265; and refund of Canadian dollars, 234, 238–9, 242
Reserve Stores, 355
also mentioned, 89

Air programme, 331

Air traffic routes, 226

Air Training Schemes, for Canadian Air Force in U.K.: 1st scheme, 97–8, 101,

106–7, 237; 2nd scheme, 98, 101, 147–8, 237; cost of, 288, 354, 355–6, 357, 358

Aldrich, Winthrop William, American banker, 412–13, 540

Allied Forces, 120

Allies
British war debt to, 64, 92, 95, 175, 280, 281, 289, 387, 389, 441, 450, 521; 'financial appeasement', 55, 99; inter-allied debt, 48
loans to, 407, 469; from U.S., 609–10, 615–16, 617–18
man-power in Stage II, 111
military expenditure in, 122
post-war help for, 56–7; 'reparations', 291; reconstruction needs, 485
receipts from, 404
sterling balances held by, 477, 494–5, by European Allies, 283, 496–7, by 'Resident Allied Governments', 282
Treasury advances to Allied Governments, 264–5
U.K. exports and Allied war effort, 399, 461–2
and U.S.–U.K. settlement, 292
also mentioned, 178, 222, 463

Allocation of resources, 17; of dollar quota, 385, 438, 487, 582; of man-power and labour, 156, 471, 482; of raw material, 471; of shipping, 43, 201

'Alternatives I and II', see sterling balances: Stage III

America, see Canada; North America; South America; United States of America

American Air Force, 143, 262

American films, 526

'American Proposals of 18 November on financial matters, The' (1945), 629–32; comments on, handed to the Americans by Keynes and Lord

647